Foreword by
DARREN STEVENS

Editor
BENJ MOOREHEAD

Design
ROB WHITEHOUSE

This edition first published in the UK by TriNorth Ltd

ISBN: 978-1-909811-58-4

 A CIP Catalogue record for this book is available from the British Library.

Published by Jellyfish Publishing
www.jellyfishsolutions.co.uk

Editor: *Benj Moorehead;* Research and editorial: *Jo Harman, Phil Walker*
Design: *Rob Whitehouse;* Images: *Getty Images unless stated;*
Print: *Jellyfish Print Solutions*

Acknowledgements
The publishers would like to thank the county clubs and the players for their assistance in helping to put together this book. Additional information has been gathered from espncricinfo.com and cricketarchive.com.

CONTENTS

The
Cricketers'
Who's Who
2021

Openers

FOREWORD

By Darren Stevens

I think I've got every edition of *The Cricketers' Who's Who* since I became a pro cricketer in 1997. My dream has always been to appear on the front cover – just look at all the greats that have been on there. So I'm delighted to write the foreword to the 2021 edition.

Coping with the pandemic over the last year has been horrible for everyone. That we were able to play any cricket in 2020 was a great credit to those involved. But it was a funny old season. For Kent, our first match was at Chelmsford, which is always a tough place to play because Essex are well supported and a very strong team. But without spectators, the first couple of days felt like pre-season. You just didn't feel the intensity. It was only when I got the first one around my earholes that I realised we were in a proper competition.

It was a strange environment all summer. We couldn't change next to each other in the dressing rooms, showers weren't allowed, and for away games you were stuck in your hotel the whole time. Even just having lunch was quite complicated.

It was great to see the buzz on social media though, because of the amount of people who were able to watch domestic cricket online for the first time. Hopefully it provided some relief for everyone who was stuck at home.

One of the bright spots of last season was the emergence of young players. In fact there were quite a few lads out there who I'd never even heard of – although it's been like that for some time now! At Kent we've got 20-year-old Jordan Cox, who scored his maiden first-class hundred which he then turned into a double.

Youngsters like Jordan had more of a chance in 2020 because Kolpak and overseas players weren't able to come to the UK. With Kolpaks no longer available after Brexit, there should be more opportunities for young English talent to shine (even though the ECB has permitted two overseas players in the Championship this summer). After all, the main job of the counties is to make the England team as strong as possible. But most Kolpaks had played international cricket, so the standard of cricket may slightly drop off without them.

I thought the Bob Willis Trophy worked really well, so it's good to see a similar three-group structure being used again this summer, with a red-ball final at Lord's. I'm not a fan of two divisions because in the second division you'd end up preparing poor pitches to get results and win promotion. Whereas in the first division you'd play on featherbeds because you didn't want to lose games and be relegated. It became an on-side game in Division Two (where you'd bowl straighter on green pitches) and an off-side game in Division One (where you'd bowl wider on flat pitches).

I do worry about what's happening with 50-over cricket. The Royal London One-Day Cup will run at the same time as The Hundred this season, so the counties will lose a lot of quality players for that competition. I'm sure something will be sorted out the closer we get to the 2023 World Cup. Personally, I think 40-over cricket is most entertaining format, largely because it gets rid of those knockabout overs in the middle of an innings.

There's a big chunk of white-ball cricket in the middle of this summer and I'm hoping to push my case for selection in Kent's limited-overs sides. The physio tells me I should ease off a little, but I feel I need to keep ticking.

When I moved to Kent 15 years ago, I said to myself that if I'm playing when I'm 36 then I'll be a happy man. And now I'm about to turn 45. For the last few years I've been signing one-year contracts and perhaps that has helped me – it puts you under pressure to perform.

I was more of a batsman in my younger days at Leicester, but I've always loved my bowling. The trouble was that I could never get the ball in those Leicestershire teams – they were so strong in the bowling department. It was only when I went to Kent that I started bowling a bit more. A lot of credit must go to my old Kent captain Rob Key for first giving me an opportunity with the new ball – but don't tell him! We fell upon the idea in a game against Lancashire at Old Trafford in 2010 when we were struggling to dismiss the opposition. He gave me the new ball and I got three wickets in eight balls. And I've never looked back since!

Let me finish by wishing you all a very enjoyable summer of cricket, whether watching or playing. And here's hoping that we'll return to some degree of normality over the next few months.

Darren Stevens
March 2021

EDITOR'S NOTES

By Benj Moorehead

Welcome to the 42nd edition of *The Cricketers' Who's Who*.

Well, here we are a year on, crossing our fingers once again on the eve of the cricket season. But where last year we appeared to be staring into a black hole, there is now good reason for hope. Hope that we will get a full season of cricket, April to September. Hope even that spectators will fill cricket grounds across the country for the first time in 18 months. A packed house for England's final Test against India at Old Trafford in balmy late summer? It's not impossible.

The full impact of the pandemic on English cricket will not be known for a while yet. But our interview with the bigwigs of the Professional Cricketers' Association (see page 10) reveals the damage already done – namely a money-drain – and the intense work that has gone on behind the scenes to adapt to the new reality. Most of the 474 professional cricketers that fill these pages have accepted pay cuts of some kind. It is a delicate balance "between fighting for the players and at the same time being a responsible stakeholder," says Daryl Mitchell, the PCA's new director of operations.

And yet in other ways the summer game seems to have weathered the pandemic relatively well. Despite the empty seats, cricket has been very watchable on the telly, more so than other sports. Something to do with the focus on those 22 yards, perhaps, and the fact that cricket is essentially a game of set-pieces. Certainly last summer's Test matches left some indelible memories – the West Indies team on one knee, Broad's 500th Test wicket, Anderson's 600th, Buttler and Woakes at Manchester, the brilliance of Mohammad Rizwan, Zak Crawley's 267.

Even more improbably, county cricket served up something very special with the inspired creation of the Bob Willis Trophy. It was an awkward environment for the players, as Darren Stevens attests in his foreword to this edition, but weren't we grateful they were out there playing cricket. Millions watched on the counties' vastly improved live video streaming; for others it was enough to gaze at the scorecards. This was a triumph against the odds. And county cricket had its storylines too, not least the emergence of so many bright talents who dazzled in the absence of the overseas contingent. Scyld Berry captures last season's surreal splendour in his eulogy to what he calls "my most memorable cricket summer" (page 17) – and he's written on every one since 1976.

With all that's happened, it's worth pausing to unravel the domestic programme for this summer. It takes a little unravelling. The County Championship is back – but in two parts, a group phase leading to a three-division structure at the end of the summer (see page 29 for a full explanation). The Bob Willis Trophy is retained, with a five-day final at Lord's between the top two teams in Division One. The 50-over One-Day Cup returns, but it will run in the shadows of the first edition of The Hundred. Meanwhile T20 rumbles on, though we'll see if the 100-ball show steals some of its Blast.

This will also be the first summer since 2003 without Kolpaks who, as Daniel Gallan reflects on page 22, we may miss more than we thought we would. To soften the impact, the ECB have permitted two overseas players for each county in this year's Championship. Good luck to batsmen facing up to Hampshire's new-ball pair of Mohammad Abbas and Kyle Abbott in April and May.

English women's cricket underwent a reshuffle last year, producing eight new regional teams which contested last year's inaugural Rachael Heyhoe Flint Trophy. But the more significant development came last December, with the ECB awarding the first 41 full-time domestic contracts in the women's game. No longer is international cricket the only way for a woman to forge a career in the sport. We warmly welcome the 41 new professional cricketers into the *Who's Who* alongside the 17 centrally contracted England players, making our women's section bigger than ever before.

Full squads for the women's Hundred competition will not be confirmed before June, and this is the main reason that it has not been possible to provide proper coverage of the 100-ball tournament in these pages. But we are open to including The Hundred in next year's edition – if we can get our heads around a whole new army of stats!

To the important stuff: our legendary questionnaire which the players faithfully fill out every year (though it often requires the whip of the county media managers, to whom we are, as ever, very grateful). We asked them about the people who have had the greatest influence on their careers, with a ban on mums and dads. Taken together, the list of names is a tribute to the unsung heroes – teachers, coaches and all-round gurus – who persuade their pupils to follow their dreams: Dave Beal, Dave Cowper, the late Rick Kellaway, Fred Hemmingway, Sean Hooper, Colin de Lucchi, Dick Roberts, "Mr G", Phil Makinson, Bongani Ndaba, Lenny Cooper, Sue Day, Salliann Briggs… The players have also been telling us about odd things they've done during lockdown, which include a toilet-roll kick-up challenge – hence all those empty shelves – and, in more than one case, reading a book.

I hope you enjoy this one. Have a lovely summer.

Benj Moorehead
March 2021

"IT SURVIVED TWO WORLD WARS, IT WILL SURVIVE THIS"

In 2020 the Professional Cricketers' Association had to navigate one of the most challenging periods in its 54-year history. Phil Walker, editor-in-chief of Wisden Cricket Monthly, spoke to its outgoing chairman and current chief executive about the state of play and what's to come

Daryl Mitchell has been a member of the Professional Cricketers' Association (PCA) for the better part of two decades. They supported him in negotiations with Worcestershire over his first contract – a service they continue to provide for their members – helped to fund subsequent educational courses, paid for his coaching badges, and covered the costs of various work placements. He became a county rep, and for the past four years he sat as its chairman.

"It's a wonderful organisation that will always be close to my heart," says Mitchell, who in February became the PCA's first director of cricket operations after being succeeded as chairman by Middlesex's James Harris. For Mitchell, the PCA's most important work relates to those who need it most: the many professional cricketers, past and present, who have fallen on hard times. "The Professional Cricketers' Trust is in some ways probably the most difficult part of [the job], but it's also one of the most rewarding. You see the other side of the game – the dark side. The mental-health issues, the addictions, the challenges of transitioning away from the game, the pitfalls that people can walk into. The cases really open your eyes. It's possibly the most important and vital part of the PCA."

But like every wing of the organisation, the Trust took a hammering in 2020, with a shortfall of some £250k against expected funding. The knock-on effects are obvious. This is the new reality. One of squeezed cash, salary cuts and reduced squads. "The maths don't lie," says Rob Lynch, the PCA's chief executive.

The creation of the County Partnership Agreement (CPA), rolled out in January 2020 following a series of negotiations with the game's stakeholders, was meant to herald a new dawn of promise and security for the game's professional workforce. Then the virus struck. "It's just a massive shame that we are where we are," says Lynch. "Because the developments that were made with the CPA, and everything that was put in place for the next four- or five-year cycle, were a brilliant step forward for professional cricketers."

Since the virus took hold, the game has been firefighting, facing down challenges that carry echoes of society at large. "How can we get our players to understand the bigger picture as opposed to what's directly in front of them now?" asks Lynch. "Going forward, that's the most significant challenge we face."

Daryl Mitchell, the PCA's director of cricket operations
Photo by Jordan Mansfield

Both Lynch and Mitchell were willing to engage on a number of the big issues facing domestic cricket, starting with the most pressing of them…

How effectively has the organisation weathered the chaos of the last year?

Mitchell: Pretty well, I think. It hasn't been good for anybody, has it? It's been very collaborative between the PCA, ECB, and the counties. It was vitally important we got international cricket played last summer, in terms of the broadcast revenue, which obviously benefits the players and counties, and has a knock-on effect. As an organisation the players are obviously our priority, and I feel that they took a very mature response to everything, and hopefully we're going to come out the other side in relatively good shape.

Lynch: One thing that has really struck me is the role the PCA plays: to fight tooth and nail for its members – which is ultimately our remit – and balancing that with playing a responsible role in the game's recovery. Because you can't ignore the fact that the game's going to be losing pretty significant revenues. And we need to recognise that as a group. To date we've managed to work collectively with all the players across the game, and they have come together and made a really big contribution so far, through the cuts that have been agreed and the measures that were put in place, as well as even just a simple thing like agreeing to furlough.

Mitchell: It's been a mantra of ours to find that balance between fighting for the players and at the same time trying to be a responsible stakeholder. Ultimately if cricket and the counties suffer massive financial losses – well, they have suffered financial losses already – but if it were to cause unemployment or clubs were to go bust, then that's no good for anybody.

Was the buy-in from the players regarding pay cuts and furloughing as much as you'd hoped?

Mitchell: Yeah, absolutely. All of us have aimed to be transparent with regards to finances, and ultimately all the player representatives [one from each county] want to do the right thing by the game and the players they represent. And we have fought hard to protect the most vulnerable players, those who are out of contract. But ultimately it's about doing the right thing, trying to help the clubs and supporting the game as best as we possibly can.

Lynch: We went through three rounds of two-month agreements. So Covid hits, the season gets delayed. Everyone goes: "S**t, we've got to look at the numbers here. Right, guys, we need to talk to you about cuts and furlough." So the first agreement was for April and May. It was a 17-per-cent cut on salary and agreement to furlough for that two-month period. Then in June and July, we came together again.

Mitchell: The first renegotiation managed to get all players onto a new standard contract, which gave those players who are out of contract a guaranteed two-months' salary after the end of it. And then the second deal ensured that those players who are out of contract either weren't taking a pay cut or were going to be fully reimbursed if they found themselves out of a job come October. This is at the forefront of our thinking. We're trying to ensure that we don't have mass redundancies, and [we're] putting protections in place for a fair transition for those who are out of contract.

How was collaborating with the ECB and the first-class counties?

Lynch: One healthy thing that's come out of it is we've all decided that it's quite a good forum for the ECB, the PCA and the counties to come together and talk about issues in the game. It's really constructive dialogue. It goes without saying that a close relationship between the ECB and the PCA will be crucial for the long-term health of the game.

Rob Lynch, the PCA's chief executive
Photo by the PCA

Which hasn't always been the case?

Mitchell: In my time as chairman I think it [was] generally collaborative. The governing body and the players' union are always going to clash. There will always be disagreements over certain things. That is part of the role that both organisations play. But I think the approach taken is to try to be collaborative, and certainly in this situation I think we have worked together well. It's not just the PCA-ECB thing, you have to factor in the 18 counties as well. It can be complex, and you are going to have disagreements.

Lynch: There probably have been times in the past when it's been slightly fractious or challenging, and I suppose that's how it should be. Our agreement is pretty simple. We are governed by the views of 18 county dressing rooms. Our job is to represent and fight for those views. So, to a degree, our mandate is already set and we represent it. I mean, clearly, we play a role in helping dictate which directions those views go.

Does the sustainability of Test cricket globally impact on the sustainability of the 18-club county model?

Mitchell: They are very much linked. After all, one of the primary roles of the first-class counties is to produce England Test cricketers. But I'm very much a fan of the 18 clubs. These clubs have got 150-plus years of history, and I think maintaining that is of paramount importance. We have shown through this crisis that we are capable of coming out the other side. It survived two world wars, it will survive this.

But if Test cricket becomes increasingly marginalised and played by only a handful of countries, will that in turn potentially threaten our own model?

Mitchell: It's a difficult one. One thing I would say is that Test cricket is alive and well in this country. You can be sure there will be a clamour for tickets for the India series in particular this year and the grounds will be sold out. The broadcast revenue that Test cricket generates is huge for the game in this country. So it's certainly washing its face here. You could even argue there is an over-reliance on the England Test side in terms of the financial models of the ECB.

Lynch: My personal opinion is we need to strike a balance between being progressive and respecting tradition. Finding that balance is going to be tricky. We know that there's two or three countries that are heavily interested in Test cricket. But that's simply not the case around the world.

Mitchell: It's a concern. The ICC [International Cricket Council] has to manage it, and come up with ways to monetise it. I think, for example, the World Test Championship is a good thing but the format at the moment is a bit of a mess. The idea of the Test game having a world champion is a good one. How it actually works needs a rethink.

Young English players are more interested in playing in franchise leagues than Test cricket – myth or reality?

Mitchell: Looking back to my development, you learnt the forward defence, and then you developed your game from there. The way players learn the game now, it's completely different. I actually think it's added something to Test cricket – Ben Stokes would not have played that innings at Headingley without the skills that he developed in white-ball cricket. I think if you ask the players, the pinnacle is certainly Test cricket, and every young player in the Worcestershire dressing room says the same. Everyone wants to get to play an Ashes

Test match. But the reality is that is a very difficult thing to achieve. There's only 11 blokes playing any given Test match. From a career-development and financial perspective, we are probably looking at 40 to 50 English players going away in the winter to play in these tournaments and adding to their income, and then with the advent of The Hundred as well, that can be another revenue stream on top of their county contracts. It is a much easier task to be a white-ball specialist than it is to become a Test player.

Lynch: What happens if in 20 years' time Test cricket is played between Australia and England only? We're gradually seeing more and more players being interested in floating around the world. We've got to understand how a young kid coming into the game is still interested in batting for 100 overs, versus getting 21 off seven balls. So, you know, it's not a simple question for any of us. From the PCA's perspective, the 18-county model is currently the best way to maximise how many people can be employed. So from where we sit today, with the challenges we're going to face securing as many jobs and people's futures as we can, this is the immediate key.

How much was the PCA part of the conversation regarding the three-tiered conference system for first-class cricket in 2021, having been trialled last year?

Mitchell: We [were] involved quite heavily. All the feedback I had from players [was] really positive. I think everyone enjoyed their little leagues with the chance to progress, and this year's structure has been met with excitement. [It] offers all teams the chance to get through to that "Super September" top six, with those final games to determine the champion. The opportunity to have a final like the Sheffield Shield has in Australia – and for it to be played at Lord's – is something that every county cricketer would love to be a part of. For as long as I've been in the game, I definitely think this is the best format that I've seen.

The PCA is in favour of The Hundred, which is due to launch this summer. Are you personally confident of its success?

Mitchell: We'll have to wait and see until it kicks off, but my belief is it's an aspirational competition – I think people will want to play in it. I believe that every one of our members entered the draft and wanted to be a part of the competition, of which only 90-odd got picked. Getting it on free-to-air television is massive, and I think we've got to give it a go. It's already brought in a huge amount of broadcasting revenue, and it's potentially a massive tournament with great overseas players playing in it.

Any reservations?

Mitchell: It's a new thing and there are no guarantees. But I am not sure it is as big a gamble as some people make out, because it is bankrolled by the broadcasters to a degree already. Obviously county members are upset that it is not their counties they are supporting, but hopefully we can fill stadiums and get bums on seats.

Does it have the potential to increase the intensity and standard of the T20 Blast?

Mitchell: Absolutely. The wildcard selections for The Hundred [whereby each team picks one final player during this year's T20 Blast] is a really positive thing. It will be a narrative throughout the T20 Blast, with those extra slots up for grabs, especially with replacements needed for injuries and international call-ups. The Blast is a fantastic competition. Even last year without crowds there was still some really high-quality cricket, and I think that will continue to be strong.

The news that 41 new female players have joined up as members, widening the professionalisation of the game, is welcome...

Mitchell: It's great to be able to welcome these new members and we sincerely hope that number grows over the next couple of years. But also for the game as a whole, having professional women's cricket is a huge step forward in terms of developing a successful England team. Heather Knight is a vice-chair on the board, and we've got Isa Guha too, so they have had a lot of input on the direction of travel for the PCA over the last couple of years. It's a massive growth area for the game and it's a massive growth area for the PCA.

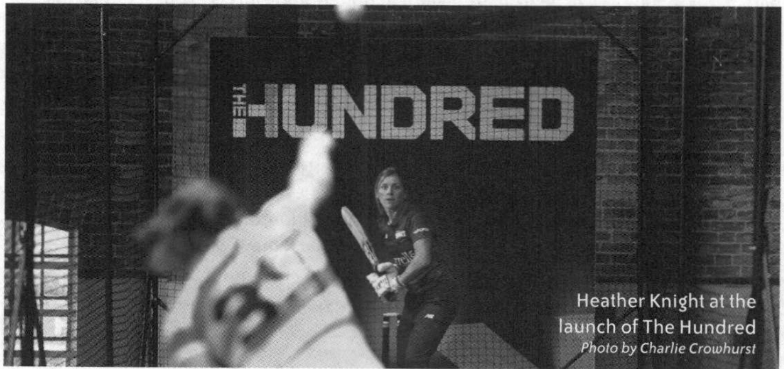

Heather Knight at the launch of The Hundred
Photo by Charlie Crowhurst

THE SEASON LIKE NO OTHER

Scyld Berry, cricket writer for the Telegraph and former editor of Wisden, reflects upon the strange delights of doing the county rounds during a pandemic

As sunset approached at Old Trafford and the floodlights took effect, while Australia's batting collapsed in the third and decisive ODI, normally you would have expected 25,000 spectators – many well-lubricated – to have raised the roof with raucous songs about David Warner and Steve Smith. The sole sound, instead, came from the floodlights: nothing electrical amiss but the tweeting of hundreds of birds – swifts, martlets, house martins? – gathering to migrate and keeping themselves warm meanwhile by nestling on top of the lightbulbs.

Last season was my most memorable cricket summer. I have never felt so privileged to be covering the professional game, because almost nobody else could watch, and because I saw or sensed so much afresh. Normally I would never have sat on the top floor of the Old Trafford pavilion in a hospitality suite, but social distancing demanded that I should look across to the Pennines and listen to birdsong, such as many of us heard for the first time.

Never has it been so important to have a human activity which lasts all day for several days and which has no relevance whatever to the material world; to have a niche or nest we can inhabit, free of anxiety, for respite. Cricket can be derided as a complete waste of time; but precisely because it consumes so much time, this summer has been invaluable.

The Bob Willis Trophy made my season: I only watched the Tests on television as the ECB admitted one correspondent per newspaper to the bio-bubbles at Old Trafford and Southampton, and my colleague Nick Hoult had taken over as the *Telegraph* cricket correspondent. I managed to see all five rounds of the BWT in part and the final at Lord's. I visited nine grounds in all, from The Oval when a crowd of 2,500 was admitted for Surrey's T20 against Hampshire, as a trial, to Grace Road when the whole of Leicester was locked down and bio-security was so strict that not even water was available, hot or cold. Overall I averaged 35.8, which would have been my highest batting average for many a season, except that it was my mean temperature when tested with a thermometer at the entrances.

It was weird going to the opening day of the BWT at Edgbaston on August 1, exactly one year after Stuart Broad had been roared on in the opening Ashes Test. Nobody in the stands, nobody in the press box half an hour before the start, no sustenance, or so we had been warned, and this at Edgbaston, hitherto the capital of catering in British cricket. Slowly, being a cricket match, and Edgbaston, things warmed up: the game between Warwickshire and Northants started, with sanitisation breaks every six overs; a handful of people trickled into the box; talk and humour could not be banned; and at lunchtime a cardboard box with a hot meal was served that would have shamed many an airline.

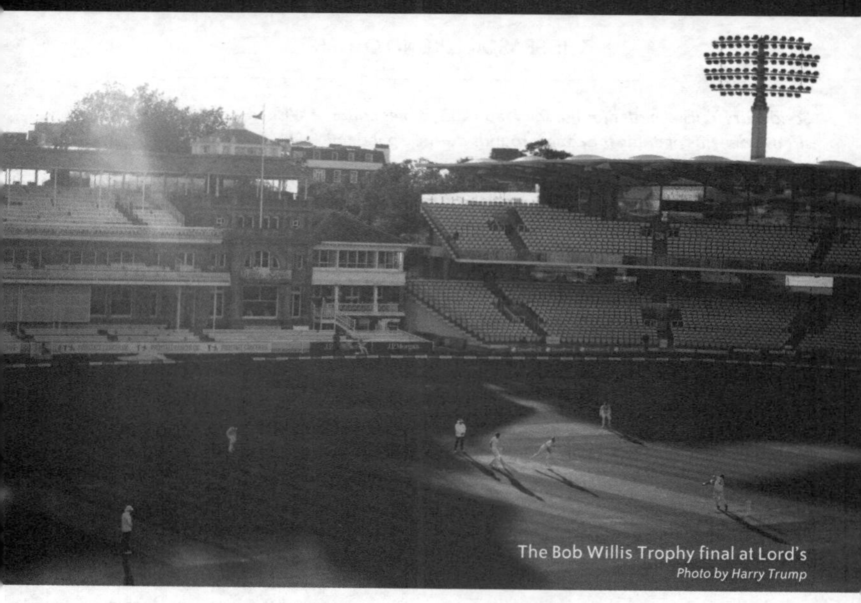
The Bob Willis Trophy final at Lord's
Photo by Harry Trump

For this opening day of the county season, 2,500 spectators were going to be admitted to both Edgbaston and The Oval, until the government said no, two days before. I still do not fully understand. Spectators could have been instructed to sit in separate households, in the open air, on alternate rows, and to make extra-long queues for loos. Surely the virus would have spread more slowly among a couple of thousand in a cricket ground than in pubs and jam-packed planes. Live-streaming of county games escalated, as one beneficial consequence of Covid, but there is nothing like meeting and talking to people – two metres apart.

This privilege added piquancy. As in wartime, you appreciate pleasures more when others can't. It was not only my job but social responsibility to convey to readers the happiness to be had at these cricket matches, and I did not have to feign it. In atmosphere these BWT matches were like club or village games played by professional cricketers who had to supply their own applause. There was a zone or inner ring for players and coaching staff, but at grounds other than Leicester (where a player who left the ground could not return on the same day to collect his kit), the parameters could be relaxed. I have never learnt so much about wobble-seam than when listening to Worcestershire's bowling coach Alan Richardson on the boundary edge at New Road.

My favourite day? Arundel, I suppose, except it was not even half a day, just a morning session, before it rained and the Castle ground's old-time drainage could not cope. Sir Alastair Cook resumed on his overnight 75, with a nightwatchman, before Dan Lawrence played strokes that had gone down well in Australia on the Lions tour the previous winter. I took a chair and sat beside the sightscreen, on the grassy bank at one end, and heard the rare acoustics of that amphitheatre. Again, it was like birdsong one had never heard before – larks ascending in place of planes descending – as the ball hitting Cook's bat made a far deeper sound.

Although it was Arundel, Sussex were not involved. It was Hampshire's base for the summer while England used their Ageas Bowl. And gradually I understood what it must have been like to have watched or played cricket on this same ground in August 1914 – a

Tim Bresnan and Craig Miles of Warwickshire
Photo by Michael Steele

game, say, between the Duke of Norfolk's XI and Free Foresters. Players had forenames like Tom and Felix, or Alastair, who proceeded immaculately to his century. Hampshire's captain started the day's play with a leg-spinner (Mason Crane). Nothing so rowdy as shouts and cheers from teammates if a batsman hit a boundary: most county sides cheered, but only polite applause at Arundel. Several marquees; the rich green vista over the Arun and across the Weald; no crowd, because the world was intent on more important things; and yet the game went on, a tiny bubble of its own, soon to be burst.

When I attended Lord's for the BWT final, the Indian summer ended on the eve of the game, replaced by a biting wind from the north. The silent, empty Underground. A city more unreal than Eliot could have known. Even Lord's was unfamiliar. Everything was in place around the pavilion – the lawns in the Harris and Warner gardens mown and manicured, flower boxes behind the pavilion, piles of hats with ribboned bands stacked neatly in the closed MCC and Middlesex shop – but nobody around, and the whole Nursery End sealed, keeping cricketers out. Girders clanged behind the new Compton and Edrich, reversing vehicles beeped. Nothing disturbed Cook while he batted all day, until the sun set in the gap between the pavilion and Warner Stand.

I will treasure Cook's 172 because he was more rounded – less angular, less tense with patriotism, I suppose – than in any Test innings, and he cover-drove with a flourish of his wrists to sign off the stroke. He ran – sprinted a couple of times – between the wickets as if chasing his spring lambs. His low-burn intensity and stubbornness were something unchanging in a world that had completely changed.

The media centre being out of bounds, we were quartered in the Tavern Stand, looking out on the autumnal field in the face of that north wind.

For the field is full of shades as I near a shadowy coast

Some of the figures were more ghostly than Francis Thompson's shades: faceless figures in masks, anoraks, bobble-hats and gloves, who ran on every over with caps and sanitising fluids, or to collect the sweater of the man about to bowl, as umpires were not allowed to do what they have always done.

An air of impermanence was heightened by the red advertisement in front of the Grandstand promoting the Ruth Strauss Foundation, bless her. Around the ground were signs supporting Prostate Cancer UK, the charity chosen to commemorate the late Bob Willis.

Alastair Cook bats at Arundel
Photo by Charlie Crowhurst

And a ghostly batsman plays to the bowling of a ghost

… who might have been old Bob, "Goose" himself, running in from the Nursery End, bouncing hair and batsmen, pumping knees and elbows.

Lord's used to be called Dark's, after James Dark, who bought the lease, developed the ground then sold it to MCC. Strange to think that in the course of the following two centuries, even in wartime, this ground had never before seen so little cricket and so few cricketers as it did last summer.

Let us hope the new Dark Age does not endure.

A FINAL WORD ON KOLPAK

With Britain's exit from the EU closing the Kolpak loophole, Daniel Gallan spoke to three South Africans about their experience of playing under a controversial title which led to tension both at home and in the shires

Perhaps it's the way the word attacks the ear that is upsetting to so many people. Or maybe it's because it's so unmistakably foreign. South Africa has 11 official languages, but this word has come from another universe.

Kolpak. Just uttering it in the vicinity of a South African cricket fan is enough to trigger a rant about nationalism and patriotic duty. On the subject of wearing the Protea and representing the country, there is rarely room for nuance.

Not that it matters now. When the clocks struck midnight on January 1 2021, sounding the United Kingdom's divorce from the European Union, among the casualties was the strange loophole that has caused so much friction in the world of cricket.

This story begins in 2003, when the Slovakian handball player Maros Kolpak won a legal dispute against his German club at the European Court of Justice. The ruling allowed Kolpak to renew his contract with TSV Östringen, despite the team already possessing two non-EU players, because he was a German resident and Slovakia were part of the EU Association Agreement.

A precedent was set. Thanks to a free-trade deal between the EU and various African, Caribbean and Pacific nations, cricketers from these regions could now circumnavigate the ECB's limit on overseas players per county. The only catch was that they had to revoke their status as an international cricketer.

Many of the South Africans who went on to do so were labelled as traitors and sell-outs, but it was not always so. In fact, few Proteas supporters even noticed when the deluge was merely a trickle.

"I left without much fanfare," says Claude Henderson, the left-arm spinner who became the first Kolpak cricketer when he signed with Leicestershire in March 2004. "Those who did pay attention were curious to see what would happen. I suppose you could say I was a guinea pig."

Henderson was 31 when he arrived at Grace Road. He had played his seventh and final Test match in 2002 and the last of his four one-day internationals a year earlier. He knew his

Ashwell Prince and Andrew Gale at Old Trafford, 2014
Photo by Jan Kruger

time on the international stage was over. Looking ahead, he saw nothing but mundane toil on South Africa's domestic circuit, playing at familiar grounds against familiar opponents. When the opportunity for a new challenge arose, he didn't need much convincing.

"I made my decision within a week," he says. "I had always wanted to play county cricket but I wasn't a big-enough name. Back then, guys who played as overseas professionals had impressive track records at Test level. Leicestershire were the only club who were happy to take a punt. Once I found out that it was all legal, I went for it."

During his 10 years with the club, Henderson repaid that faith by collecting 343 first-class wickets and helping the Foxes to three Twenty20 titles. However, not everyone was pleased with his success.

"The ECB weren't happy as I was another foreigner who couldn't play for England occupying a spot that could have gone to a local," Henderson explains. "I would also get the odd comment from opposition players. They'd say the word 'Kolpak' as if it was a swearword. I didn't take it personally. That's the nature of the game. I know I performed and gave back to English cricket."

By 2010 a Kolpak contract was an increasingly desirable option for South African cricketers whose international hopes had faded, such as Lance Klusener and Zander de Bruyn, but also for aspiring talents like Paul Harris and Faf du Plessis, who treated county cricket as a finishing school and duly returned home when the national selectors came calling.

"Not one South African who has come here hasn't improved his game," says Henderson. "Every week you're playing against a new team on a new pitch and you have to be on it all the time. There really is no hiding over here."

And this was clearly a mutually beneficial arrangement. Most Kolpaks arrived with some sort of pedigree and, whether they had lit up the international arena or not, in nearly all cases they improved the teams they played in.

"There are a lot of quality cricketers on the English circuit, but let's be honest: there are also a lot of average cricketers as well," says Ashwell Prince, the left-handed strokemaker who made 119 appearances for South Africa before signing as a Kolpak with Lancashire in 2013. "But it's their country and their system, so you can understand why some people got upset."

Apart from scoring 261 against Glamorgan in a third-wicket stand of 501 with his countryman Alviro Petersen, Prince's time as a Kolpak is perhaps best remembered for an altercation with then Yorkshire skipper Andrew Gale during the Roses match at Old Trafford in 2014. Gale insulted Prince for being a Kolpak and instructed him to go back to his own country (in slightly less flattering terms) as the two exchanged verbal volleys. Gale was banned for two matches and agreed to attend an anger-management course.

The Kolpak debate picks at old wounds. Of the 42 South Africans to have played county cricket as a Kolpak, 36 are white. Most of them are the products of elite schools that remain oases of privilege in a country which in 2019 the World Bank described as the world's most unequal society. For many critics, these players were the embodiment of a wider migration of disgruntled and disaffected whites who turned their back on their homeland.

Indeed, shortly after Rilee Rossouw told South Africa's then coach Russell Domingo by email that he had signed a Kolpak deal with Hampshire in 2017 – spelling Domingo's name wrong in the process – the conversation soon focused on the colour of Rossouw's skin.

"If that had been a player of colour, everyone would have said 'transformation'," Domingo said in a fiery press conference, referring to the fact that the selectors had stuck with Rossouw despite the fact he had registered four ducks in his first six ODI innings.

South Africa's first-class players are squeezed into six franchises that must adhere to the national board's selection targets of fielding six "players of colour" in each starting XI, including three "black Africans". As a result, on any given matchday there are 30 places available across the country for white cricketers.

"I think there have been a lot of soft options taken," says Prince when asked if this is a factor behind the Kolpak exodus. "Nobody has a right to play for the Proteas, and players should fight until the bitter end for a place. If a player is over 30 years old and has given himself every chance to play for the Proteas and it hasn't materialised, then fair enough. The vast majority of players who took the Kolpak option when in the prime of their careers were non-starters for the Proteas, when all Proteas players were fit. It's easier to tell the world that you're leaving because of political reasons."

* * *

When the result of the Brexit referendum was announced in June 2016, the time of the Kolpak was slipping away. That November, Hardus Viljoen, Simon Harmer and Stiaan van Zyl all signed Kolpak deals before their 30th birthdays. A year later, Kyle Abbott and Rilee Rossouw, aged 29 and 27 respectively, joined them.

"We got a lot of heat when we left, but I know I did what was best for me," says Abbott, who joined Hampshire two months after taking nine wickets in a series-clinching Test win at Hobart against Australia. "I knew full well that when I signed there would be an end to Kolpaks. But I didn't sign because of Brexit. It was purely a cricket decision that was best suited to me."

With the exception of Harmer, whose off-spin has inspired Essex to four trophies in four seasons, Abbott has arguably had the greatest impact among Kolpaks in recent years. His disciplined seam bowling is tailor-made for English conditions and, since quitting international cricket, he has claimed 183 first-class wickets at 18.78 – including Hampshire's best-ever figures of 17 for 86 against Somerset in 2019.

"It hasn't been easy though," Abbott says. "I was on the boundary at Gloucestershire and was told to 'f**k off back to where you came from'. There were also some bitter players, especially when a few Kolpak guys got contracts in The Hundred ahead of them. And then of course there's the backlash back home. But I believe the people who understand cricket know the real story. The super passionate fans who are South African through and through will never get it. They see me as a coward. I knew I would cause upset when I left."

Abbott has not ruled out a return to the Proteas – "I'd love to wear that shirt again" – but accepts it is unlikely. This season he will turn out for Hampshire as an overseas player – the ECB have extended the limit to two per county in Championship cricket following the termination of Kolpak contracts – but others will be forced to return to South Africa. With just two years left on his Hampshire contract, Abbott may have to follow.

He is unsure how he will be welcomed back into the system, if at all. A lot has changed since Claude Henderson took a leap into the unknown in 2004. Emotions have flooded the discourse and the picture is often seen through a jingoistic lens. And, no matter how one spins it, in several cases those who have decided to leave have weakened the South African national team.

One day the Kolpak will be a mere footnote in cricket's great narrative. But for a generation of fans, and those players branded with the scarlet K, this harsh-sounding word will forever carry its sting.

This article appeared in the March 2021 issue of Wisden Cricket Monthly.

Hampshire's Kyle Abbott
Photo by Alex Davidson

CAPTAIN: Joe Root (Test), Eoin Morgan (ODI/T20I)
COACH: Chris Silverwood

ENGLAND MEN'S SUMMER FIXTURES IN 2021

June 2
England vs New Zealand
1st Test, Lord's

June 10
England vs New Zealand
2nd Test, Edgbaston

June 23
England vs Sri Lanka
1st T20I, Cardiff

June 24
England vs Sri Lanka
2nd T20I, Cardiff

June 26
England vs Sri Lanka
3rd T20I, Southampton

June 29
England vs Sri Lanka
1st ODI, Chester-le-Street

July 1
England vs Sri Lanka
2nd ODI, The Oval

July 4
England vs Sri Lanka
3rd ODI, Bristol

July 8
England vs Pakistan
1st ODI, Cardiff

July 10
England vs Pakistan
2nd ODI, Lord's

July 13
England vs Pakistan
3rd ODI, Edgbaston

July 16
England vs Pakistan
1st T20I, Trent Bridge

July 18
England vs Pakistan
2nd T20I, Headingley

July 20
England vs Pakistan
3rd T20I, Old Trafford

August 4
England vs India
1st Test, Trent Bridge

August 12
England vs India
2nd Test, Lord's

August 25
England vs India
3rd Test, Headingley

September 2
England vs India
4th Test, The Oval

September 10
England vs India
5th Test, Old Trafford

2021 KEY DATES – MEN

To mitigate against the effect of the pandemic, the counties have agreed on a new structure for the 2021 County Championship. The teams have been put into three seeded groups of six and will play each other home and away. The top two in each group go into Division One, with the rest making up Divisions Two and Three. Each team will play four further matches in the divisional stage, with the winner of Division One being crowned Championship winners. The top two in Division One will then contest the Bob Willis Trophy in a five-day final at Lord's.

April 8-June 3	First group phase of County Championship
June 9-July 18	T20 Blast group stage
July 4-July 11	Second group phase of County Championship
July 21-August 21	The Hundred (final at Lord's on August 21)
July 22-August 19	One-Day Cup (final at Trent Bridge on August 19)
August 24-27	T20 Blast quarter-finals
August 30-September 24	Divisional phase of County Championship
September 18	T20 Blast Finals Day, Edgbaston
September 27	Bob Willis Trophy final, Lord's

2021 KEY DATES – WOMEN

The ECB had not released England Women's summer fixtures at the time of going to press, with India, South Africa and New Zealand all in line to tour this summer. The BCCI announced in March that India will play a Test match against England "later this year". It would be the first Test between the teams since 2014. In domestic cricket, the eight regional teams created last year will contest the 50-over Rachael Heyhoe Flint Trophy and a new Regional T20 competition. Eight city-based teams will compete in The Hundred, which mirrors the men's tournament.

May 29-June 12	First phase of Rachael Heyhoe Flint Trophy (50-over)
June 26-July 10	First phase of Regional T20
July 21-August 21	The Hundred (final at Lord's on August 21)
August 25-30	Second phase of Regional T20
September 5	Regional T20 final (venue TBC)
September 10-22	Second phase of Rachael Heyhoe Flint Trophy
September 25	Rachael Heyhoe Flint Trophy final (venue TBC)

KEY

THE PLAYERS

LHB – Left-hand batsman
LB – Leg-break bowler
LF – Left-arm fast bowler
LFM – Left-arm fast-medium bowler
LM – Left-arm medium bowler
LMF – Left-arm medium-fast bowler
MCCU – Marylebone Cricket Club University
MVP – Denotes a player's presence in the top 100 places of the 2020 PCA County and Domestic Women's MVP Rankings (the number next to 'MVP' denotes the player's specific placing)
OB – Off-break bowler
R – 1,000 or more first-class runs in an English season (the number next to 'R' denotes how many times the player has achieved this feat)
RF – Right-arm fast bowler
RFM – Right-arm fast-medium bowler
RHB – Right-hand batsman
RM – Right-arm medium bowler
RMF – Right-arm medium-fast bowler
SLA – Slow left-arm orthodox bowler
SLW – Slow left-arm wrist-spin bowler
UCCE – University Centre of Cricketing Excellence
W – 50 or more first-class wickets in an English season (the number next to 'W' denotes how many times the player has achieved this feat)
WK – Wicketkeeper
* – Not-out innings (e.g. 137*)

THE TEAMS

(s) – A competition has been shared between two or more winners
BWT – Bob Willis Trophy (English domestic first-class competition, 2020-2021)
C&G – Cheltenham & Gloucester Trophy (English domestic 50-over competition, 2001-2006)
CB40 – Clydesdale Bank 40 (English domestic 40-over competition, 2010-2012)
CC1/CC2 – County Championship Division One/Division Two
FP Trophy – Friends Provident Trophy (English domestic 50-over competition, 2007-2009)
Gillette – Gillette Cup (English domestic limited-overs competition, 1963-1980)
NatWest – NatWest Trophy (English domestic limited-overs competition, 1981-2000)
Pro40 – NatWest Pro40 (English domestic 40-over competition, 2005-2009)
REL – A player has been released by the relevant county
RET – A player has retired
RL50 – Royal London One-Day Cup (English domestic 50-over competition, 2014-2021)
T20 Cup – English domestic T20 competition (2003-2021)
YB40 – Yorkshire Bank 40 (English domestic 40-over competition, 2013)

NOTES: In the men's section, the statistics given for a player's best batting and best bowling performance are for first-class cricket, except where indicated. In the women's section, these statistics are for List-A cricket, except where indicated. A field within a player's career statistics which is marked with an '-' indicates that a particular statistic is inapplicable – such as a player who has never bowled a ball in first-class cricket – or unavailable. All stats correct as of March 11, 2021.

The Teams

DERBYSHIRE

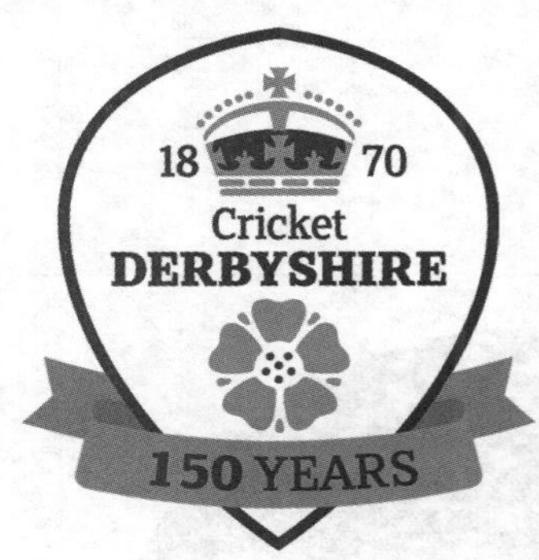

FORMED: 1870
HOME GROUND: The Incora County Ground, Derby
ONE-DAY NAME: Derbyshire Falcons
CAPTAIN: Billy Godleman
2020 RESULTS: BWT: 2/6 North Group; T20: 6/6 North Group
HONOURS: Championship: 1936; Gillette/NatWest/C&G/FP Trophy: 1981; Benson & Hedges Cup: 1993; Sunday League: 1990

THE LOWDOWN

Derbyshire's strong showing in last summer's Bob Willis Trophy – they might even have made the final were it not for the weather – was credit to an inexperienced attack which contained only one bowler aged over 26. With Tony Palladino released after 10 years of loyal service and Ravi Rampaul no longer covered by Kolpak, the arrival of towering Australian quick Billy Stanlake to take the new ball with the influential Luis Reece is most welcome. They will be supported by a youthful crop of seamers including left-armer Michael Cohen (22), Lancashire-born Ben Aitchison (21) and former England U19 paceman Sam Conners (22). South African quick Dustin Melton, who played as a Kolpak last summer, returns on an overseas contract but will qualify as a local player later this year. Derbyshire are blessed with allrounders, among them leg-spinner Matt Critchley, who took 17 wickets at 26 last summer and appears to be relishing batting in the top six. Derbyshire managed a solitary T20 victory last summer and will look to rekindle the form which took them to Finals Day in 2019.

IN: Brooke Guest (Lan), George Scrimshaw (unattached), Billy Stanlake (Aus), Ben McDermott (Aus, RL50/T20)
OUT: Tony Palladino, Ravi Rampaul (both REL)

HEAD OF CRICKET: DAVE HOUGHTON

A former Zimbabwe captain, Houghton averaged 43 from 22 Tests after his country acquired Test status in 1992. He has served as batting coach for Derbyshire, Somerset and Middlesex and was head coach at Derbyshire between 2004 and 2007, returning to the club in October 2018 as head of cricket. Former England paceman Ajmal Shahzad was appointed assistant/bowling coach to replace Steve Kirby, who left to join Somerset in December. Dominic Cork looks after the T20 side.

BOB WILLIS TROPHY AVERAGES 2020

Batting

	Mat	Inns	NO	Runs	HS	Ave	SR	100	50	4s	6s
FJ Hudson-Prentice	3	5	2	145	91*	48.33	52.34	0	1	20	0
LM Reece	4	7	1	277	122	46.16	53.47	1	2	34	3
MA Cohen	2	3	2	43	30*	43.00	43.87	0	0	4	0
JL du Plooy	5	7	0	296	130	42.28	56.48	1	1	40	3
MJJ Critchley	5	7	1	234	63	39.00	49.78	0	1	25	0
AK Dal	4	4	1	108	78*	36.00	66.25	0	1	18	0
HR Hosein	4	6	1	167	84	33.40	45.50	0	2	20	1
WL Madsen	5	8	1	213	103	30.42	41.60	1	1	31	0
BA Godleman	5	8	0	226	86	28.25	51.24	0	3	33	1
TA Wood	1	1	0	26	26	26.00	45.61	0	0	3	0
MH McKiernan	2	4	0	103	52	25.75	28.69	0	1	11	0
S Conners	4	4	2	45	21	22.50	20.45	0	0	4	0
AL Hughes	2	2	0	40	27	20.00	35.08	0	0	6	0
BW Aitchison	3	1	0	8	8	8.00	100.00	0	0	1	0
DR Melton	3	3	1	11	11	5.50	35.48	0	0	0	1
E Barnes	2	1	0	4	4	4.00	26.66	0	0	1	0
BD Guest	1	-	-	-	-	-	-	-	-	-	-

Bowling

	Overs	Mdns	Runs	Wkts	BBI	BBM	Ave	Econ	SR	5w	10w
JL du Plooy	9.0	1	41	2	1/16	1/16	20.50	4.55	27.0	0	0
MH McKiernan	10.2	2	48	2	2/3	2/16	24.00	4.64	31.0	0	0
LM Reece	132.3	40	340	13	3/51	5/103	26.15	2.56	61.1	0	0
MJJ Critchley	128.4	14	457	17	6/73	6/88	26.88	3.55	45.4	1	0
MA Cohen	44.2	7	191	7	3/47	5/98	27.28	4.30	38.0	0	0
DR Melton	70.0	13	233	8	4/22	5/47	29.12	3.32	52.5	0	0
BW Aitchison	78.0	20	211	6	3/55	4/112	35.16	2.70	78.0	0	0
E Barnes	32.0	6	107	3	2/24	2/64	35.66	3.34	64.0	0	0
S Conners	94.2	23	328	9	3/63	4/132	36.44	3.47	62.8	0	0
AK Dal	43.0	10	95	2	1/8	1/30	47.50	2.20	129.0	0	0
AL Hughes	21.0	2	79	1	1/16	1/51	79.00	3.76	126.0	0	0
FJ Hudson-Prentice	34.0	8	105	1	1/44	1/44	105.00	3.08	204.0	0	0
WL Madsen	1.0	0	4	0	-	-	-	4.00	-	0	0

Catches/Stumpings:
14 Hosein (inc 1st), 10 Madsen, 5 du Plooy, 4 Critchley, Reece, 3 McKiernan, 2 Aitchison, Dal, Godleman, 1 Guest, Hudson-Prentice

VITALITY BLAST AVERAGES 2020

Batting

	Mat	Inns	NO	Runs	HS	Ave	SR	100	50	4s	6s
TA Wood	2	1	0	67	67	67.00	139.58	0	1	6	2
WL Madsen	8	8	0	192	68	24.00	138.12	0	1	20	5
AK Dal	8	7	4	65	25	21.66	122.64	0	0	5	1
BA Godleman	9	8	0	166	49	20.75	101.21	0	0	17	1
JL du Plooy	9	8	1	138	53*	19.71	139.39	0	1	12	4
AL Hughes	8	7	1	116	36*	19.33	130.33	0	0	10	3
MJJ Critchley	9	8	0	154	44	19.25	111.59	0	0	12	4
FJ Hudson-Prentice	1	1	0	16	16	16.00	106.66	0	0	1	1
LM Reece	9	8	1	110	42	15.71	103.77	0	0	11	2
MA Cohen	5	2	1	14	7*	14.00	93.33	0	0	1	0
MH McKiernan	8	7	1	71	25	11.83	126.78	0	0	6	2
BD Guest	4	3	3	36	22*	-	133.33	0	0	3	0
HR Hosein	5	2	2	11	10*	-	100.00	0	0	0	0
S Conners	6	1	1	2	2*	-	100.00	0	0	0	0
E Barnes	4	-	-	-	-	-	-	-	-	-	-
DR Melton	4	-	-	-	-	-	-	-	-	-	-

Bowling

	Overs	Mdns	Runs	Wkts	BBI	Ave	Econ	SR	4w	5w
MH McKiernan	18.0	0	131	2	2/22	65.50	7.27	54.0	0	0
WL Madsen	15.0	0	113	2	1/25	56.50	7.53	45.0	0	0
MJJ Critchley	30.1	0	235	4	1/21	58.75	7.79	45.2	0	0
AL Hughes	21.0	0	164	4	2/34	41.00	7.80	31.5	0	0
AK Dal	1.0	0	8	0	-	-	8.00	-	0	0
DR Melton	13.0	0	124	4	2/37	31.00	9.53	19.5	0	0
S Conners	12.0	0	120	3	2/38	40.00	10.00	24.0	0	0
LM Reece	15.0	0	151	3	2/31	50.33	10.06	30.0	0	0
MA Cohen	13.0	0	136	3	2/23	45.33	10.46	26.0	0	0
E Barnes	7.0	0	81	2	2/27	40.50	11.57	21.0	0	0
FJ Hudson-Prentice	4.0	0	52	1	1/52	52.00	13.00	24.0	0	0
JL du Plooy	2.2	0	32	1	1/17	32.00	13.71	14.0	0	0

Catches/Stumpings:
4 du Plooy, Melton, 3 Guest, 2 Dal, Godleman, McKiernan, Reece, 1 Critchley, Hosein, Hudson-Prentice, Hughes, Wood

DURHAM

FORMED: 1882
HOME GROUND: Emirates Riverside, Chester-le-Street
CAPTAIN: Scott Borthwick, TBC (RL50 & T20)
2020 RESULTS: BWT: 6/6 North Group; T20: 4/6 North Group
HONOURS: Championship: (3) 2008, 2009, 2013; Gillette/NatWest/C&G/FP Trophy: 2007; Pro40/National League/CB40/YB40/RL50: 2014

THE LOWDOWN

Well into September last year Durham were still without a win, having lost two of five red-ball matches and four of five in the Blast. Then, hey presto: four thumping T20 victories to give themselves a shot at making the quarter-finals against Notts, a match they very nearly won. But there was one familiar theme throughout: bowling strong, batting not so much. Alex Lees put in some blistering displays in both formats but couldn't conceal the shortcomings of the other batsmen. Ned Eckersley, who stood in for Cameron Bancroft as four-day captain, made just one fifty, Cameron Steel scratched 22 runs in five innings while Sean Dickson, signed from Kent last summer, managed only 41 runs in his opening seven first-class knocks for his new county. Help arrives with the return of Scott Borthwick as red-ball skipper after four years at Surrey, while Bancroft has been re-signed for the Championship campaign. The seam attack is led as ever by Chris Rushworth. A new T20 captain is needed to replace Nathan Rimmington. The club have lost Academy graduate Scott Steel to Leicestershire despite offering the batsman a new contract.

IN: Scott Borthwick (Sur), Cameron Bancroft (Aus, CC)
OUT: Scott Steel (Lei), Sol Bell, Josh Coughlin, Gareth Harte, Nathan Rimmington, James Weighell, Ben Whitehead (all REL)

FIRST-TEAM COACH: JAMES FRANKLIN

Franklin was appointed to succeed Jon Lewis in January 2019 as part of a structural overhaul which saw Marcus North become the director of cricket. A former New Zealand allrounder who played in 31 Tests and 110 ODIs, Franklin had four seasons at Middlesex and captained the club to the Championship title in 2016. He also had brief spells with Notts and Essex. North played 21 Tests for Australia as well as scoring over 4,000 first-class runs for six different counties, including a successful season for Durham in 2004.

BOB WILLIS TROPHY AVERAGES 2020

Batting

	Mat	Inns	NO	Runs	HS	Ave	SR	100	50	4s	6s
AZ Lees	5	8	0	386	106	48.25	38.21	1	3	39	0
GJ Harte	5	8	2	250	72	41.66	40.78	0	1	30	0
BA Raine	4	7	4	124	31	41.33	43.81	0	0	15	0
DG Bedingham	5	8	0	253	96	31.62	55.84	0	2	31	2
MA Jones	2	3	0	84	82	28.00	32.81	0	1	8	0
EJH Eckersley	5	8	2	152	78*	25.33	36.36	0	1	10	0
BA Carse	3	5	0	100	41	20.00	52.63	0	0	14	1
SW Poynter	2	3	0	58	50	19.33	40.27	0	1	9	0
P Coughlin	4	6	0	114	90	19.00	51.12	0	1	13	0
JTA Burnham	3	5	0	72	31	14.40	41.86	0	0	12	0
SR Dickson	5	8	0	97	56	12.12	27.32	0	1	11	0
C Rushworth	4	7	2	54	25	10.80	43.20	0	0	7	0
CT Steel	3	5	0	22	11	4.40	21.78	0	0	2	0
MJ Potts	2	3	0	10	10	3.33	26.31	0	0	1	0
MET Salisbury	3	3	0	5	4	1.66	10.41	0	0	0	0

Bowling

	Overs	Mdns	Runs	Wkts	BBI	BBM	Ave	Econ	SR	5w	10w
CT Steel	2.0	0	8	1	1/8	1/8	8.00	4.00	12.0	0	0
AZ Lees	2.0	0	19	1	1/12	1/12	19.00	9.50	12.0	0	0
C Rushworth	104.0	14	358	16	7/108	7/137	22.37	3.44	39.0	1	0
MET Salisbury	53.1	14	148	5	4/57	4/57	29.60	2.78	63.8	0	0
BA Raine	105.1	25	308	9	3/53	3/62	34.22	2.92	70.1	0	0
MJ Potts	36.0	9	94	2	1/19	1/44	47.00	2.61	108.0	0	0
BA Carse	49.0	4	245	3	2/110	2/118	81.66	5.00	98.0	0	0
P Coughlin	78.4	9	304	3	3/46	3/77	101.33	3.86	157.3	0	0
GJ Harte	50.4	5	206	2	1/41	1/41	103.00	4.06	152.0	0	0
SW Poynter	4.0	0	21	0	-	-	-	5.25	-	0	0

Catches/Stumpings:

4 Dickson, Lees, 3 Bedingham, Eckersley, 2 Coughlin, Jones, 1 Burnham, Potts

VITALITY BLAST AVERAGES 2020

Batting

	Mat	Inns	NO	Runs	HS	Ave	SR	100	50	4s	6s
AZ Lees	10	9	2	365	77*	52.14	125.86	0	4	32	6
BA Raine	7	6	1	167	71	33.40	146.49	0	2	7	13
G Clark	10	9	0	261	68	29.00	171.71	0	2	29	10
BA Carse	10	9	3	172	35	28.66	154.95	0	0	12	8
L Trevaskis	10	5	3	47	31*	23.50	114.63	0	0	1	3
P Coughlin	10	7	2	78	22*	15.60	132.20	0	0	6	3
SW Poynter	3	2	0	31	23	15.50	114.81	0	0	0	0
F Behardien	7	5	0	71	26	14.20	87.65	0	0	5	0
DG Bedingham	10	7	0	97	33	13.85	108.98	0	0	4	4
MJ Potts	10	4	2	20	12	10.00	100.00	0	0	2	0
S Steel	10	6	0	40	19	6.66	102.56	0	0	2	1
SR Dickson	2	1	0	5	5	5.00	71.42	0	0	0	0
NJ Rimmington	10	3	1	8	5	4.00	88.88	0	0	0	0
MA Wood	1	1	1	6	6*	-	200.00	0	0	1	0

Bowling

	Overs	Mdns	Runs	Wkts	BBI	Ave	Econ	SR	4w	5w
MA Wood	4.0	0	24	1	1/24	24.00	6.00	24.0	0	0
S Steel	24.0	0	175	6	3/20	29.16	7.29	24.0	0	0
MJ Potts	32.0	1	235	13	3/8	18.07	7.34	14.7	0	0
L Trevaskis	33.0	1	254	10	2/17	25.40	7.69	19.8	0	0
BA Carse	25.0	0	199	3	1/18	66.33	7.96	50.0	0	0
NJ Rimmington	30.0	0	263	9	2/31	29.22	8.76	20.0	0	0
P Coughlin	20.0	0	211	13	3/22	16.23	10.55	9.2	0	0

Catches/Stumpings:
8 Bedingham (inc 1st), 7 Trevaskis, 5 Clark, 4 Lees, 3 Rimmington, 2 Carse, Coughlin, 1 Behardien, Dickson, Potts, Poynter, Raine, Steel

ESSEX

FORMED: 1876
HOME GROUND: The Cloudfm County Ground, Chelmsford
ONE-DAY NAME: Essex Eagles
CAPTAIN: Tom Westley, Simon Harmer (T20)
2020 RESULTS: BWT: Winners; T20: 5/6 South Group
HONOURS: Championship: (8) 1979, 1983, 1984, 1986, 1991, 1992, 2017, 2019; Bob Willis Trophy: 2020; Gillette/NatWest/C&G/FP Trophy: (3) 1985, 1997, 2008; B&H Cup: (2) 1979, 1998; Pro40/National League/CB40/YB40/RL50: (2) 2005, 2006; Sunday League: (3) 1981, 1984, 1985; T20 Cup: 2019

THE LOWDOWN

After five trophies in five years, are these Eagles still hungry? You bet. Indeed, Tom Westley's men can emulate the class of '91 and '92 by defending the Championship crown this summer. (And, for bragging rights, they can claim the Bob Willis Trophy in between.) No one has an answer to Essex's bowling attack, which dismissed the opposition for less than 200 on seven out of eight occasions on the way to last year's Lord's final. Simon Harmer, who now qualifies as overseas, has 255 first-class wickets at 19.55 since joining in 2017; Jamie Porter, perennially ignored by England, has 226 at 21.50 in that period. The unsung hero is 23-year-old paceman Sam Cook (95 at 21.42). And now Peter Siddle is set to rejoin the fold to complete his two-year contract. The batting is not quite as fearsome, despite the mighty presence of Alastair Cook. Tom Westley has one hundred in his last 36 innings, Dan Lawrence may be tied up with England, and Ryan ten Doeschate turns 41 in June. Doubts surround the future of T20 star Cameron Delport after the ECB ruled that an ancestral visa does not allow him to play as a local player in the post-Kolpak era.

IN: (none)
OUT: Rishi Patel (Lei)

HEAD COACH: ANTHONY MCGRATH

McGrath scored more than 23,000 runs and took 240 wickets in an 18-year career for Yorkshire, appearing in four Tests and 14 ODIs. He was assistant coach to Chris Silverwood when Essex won the Championship in 2017 and has since won three trophies in two seasons as head coach: a Championship-T20 double in 2019 followed by the Bob Willis Trophy last summer. Derek Bowden has stepped down as CEO, with chairman John Faragher taking on the role temporarily.

BOB WILLIS TROPHY AVERAGES 2020

Batting

	Mat	Inns	NO	Runs	HS	Ave	SR	100	50	4s	6s
AJA Wheater	6	9	4	291	83*	58.20	47.39	0	2	34	0
AN Cook	6	11	1	563	172	56.30	55.14	2	1	77	0
PI Walter	5	9	2	266	46	38.00	44.48	0	0	38	0
RN ten Doeschate	5	7	0	218	78	31.14	41.20	0	1	22	1
DW Lawrence	4	6	1	144	60	28.80	53.53	0	1	17	1
FIN Khushi	4	5	0	125	66	25.00	54.34	0	1	16	0
V Chopra	2	4	0	89	41	22.25	47.59	0	0	9	0
NLJ Browne	4	8	0	142	61	17.75	34.63	0	1	19	0
T Westley	6	11	1	172	51	17.20	40.37	0	1	21	0
SR Harmer	6	9	1	111	32	13.87	40.07	0	0	13	0
AP Beard	5	6	2	43	17	10.75	32.82	0	0	5	0
JA Porter	6	8	4	30	13	7.50	18.86	0	0	2	0
SJ Cook	5	5	1	26	15*	6.50	35.61	0	0	2	1
MR Quinn	2	2	0	13	13	6.50	72.22	0	0	1	0

Bowling

	Overs	Mdns	Runs	Wkts	BBI	BBM	Ave	Econ	SR	5w	10w
RN ten Doeschate	6.0	0	14	1	1/14	1/14	14.00	2.33	36.0	0	0
SR Harmer	257.1	81	603	38	8/64	14/131	15.86	2.34	40.6	3	1
SJ Cook	140.0	39	318	17	5/76	7/55	18.70	2.27	49.4	1	0
JA Porter	185.5	48	553	27	5/60	8/88	20.48	2.97	41.2	1	0
AP Beard	78.1	17	265	11	4/21	4/30	24.09	3.39	42.6	0	0
MR Quinn	55.3	10	156	3	1/19	2/95	52.00	2.81	111.0	0	0
DW Lawrence	2.0	1	2	0	- -	-	-	1.00	-	0	0
PI Walter	15.0	1	53	0	-	-	-	3.53	-	0	0

Catches/Stumpings:
20 Wheater (inc 3st), 10 A Cook, Harmer, 5 Khushi, 4 Browne, Chopra, 3 Porter, Westley, 2 Walter, 1 Beard

VITALITY BLAST AVERAGES 2020

Batting

	Mat	Inns	NO	Runs	HS	Ave	SR	100	50	4s	6s
RN ten Doeschate	9	8	3	255	52	51.00	137.09	0	1	15	9
AJA Wheater	6	5	1	135	63	33.75	118.42	0	1	8	3
T Westley	8	7	0	191	51	27.28	137.41	0	1	22	4
DW Lawrence	9	8	1	190	81	27.14	136.69	0	1	15	8
CS Delport	10	10	1	222	64	24.66	133.73	0	1	28	8
PI Walter	10	8	1	147	76	21.00	144.11	0	1	14	6
V Chopra	6	6	1	84	41	16.80	107.69	0	0	6	3
SR Harmer	10	6	1	73	23	14.60	121.66	0	0	6	3
MS Pepper	5	5	1	49	34*	12.25	98.00	0	0	5	0
AP Beard	2	1	0	9	9	9.00	180.00	0	0	2	0
RJ Das	1	1	0	7	7	7.00	87.50	0	0	1	0
ASS Nijjar	9	4	2	9	5	4.50	75.00	0	0	0	0
JH Plom	5	3	1	7	5	3.50	77.77	0	0	1	0
SJ Cook	4	1	0	0	0	0.00	0.00	0	0	0	0
FIN Khushi	1	1	0	0	0	0.00	0.00	0	0	0	0
S Snater	6	3	3	28	16*	-	155.55	0	0	5	0
BMJ Allison	1	1	1	1	1*	-	100.00	0	0	0	0
MR Quinn	8	1	1	0	0*	-	0.00	0	0	0	0

Bowling

	Overs	Mdns	Runs	Wkts	BBI	Ave	Econ	SR	4w	5w
PI Walter	17.0	1	113	7	2/13	16.14	6.64	14.5	0	0
SR Harmer	39.0	0	281	10	2/21	28.10	7.20	23.4	0	0
JH Plom	16.4	0	129	7	3/32	18.42	7.74	14.2	0	0
ASS Nijjar	32.0	0	251	8	3/22	31.37	7.84	24.0	0	0
MR Quinn	26.5	1	213	10	2/24	21.30	7.93	16.1	0	0
DW Lawrence	14.0	0	112	4	2/3	28.00	8.00	21.0	0	0
CS Delport	14.2	0	117	4	2/22	29.25	8.16	21.5	0	0
S Snater	15.0	0	128	4	2/22	32.00	8.53	22.5	0	0
SJ Cook	13.0	0	120	4	2/25	30.00	9.23	19.5	0	0
BMJ Allison	3.0	0	32	1	1/32	32.00	10.66	18.0	0	0
AP Beard	7.0	0	95	4	3/41	23.75	13.57	10.5	0	0

Catches/Stumpings:

9 Harmer, 7 Walter, 4 Nijjar, Snater, Westley, 3 Lawrence, Pepper, ten Doeschate, 2 Allison, Chopra, Delport, Plom, Quinn, 1 S Cook

GLAMORGAN

FORMED: 1888
HOME GROUND: Sophia Gardens, Cardiff
CAPTAIN: Chris Cooke, David Lloyd (RL50)
2020 RESULTS: BWT: 6/6 Central Group; T20: 5/6 Central Group
HONOURS: Championship: (3) 1948, 1969, 1997; Pro40/National League/CB40/YB40/RL50: (2) 2002, 2004; Sunday League: 1993

THE LOWDOWN

Glamorgan struggled without their foreign imports last year, off the pace in T20 and winless in the Bob Willis Trophy. Marchant de Lange has joined Somerset but – all being well – Colin Ingram and Marnus Labuschagne return this summer, both having signed two-year contracts. With two overseas slots now available in Championship cricket, experienced Australian seamer Michael Neser has also been brought in and is likely to share the new ball with compatriot Michael Hogan, a British passport-holder who turns 40 this summer. Along with Labuschagne, Glamorgan will hope the return of vice-captain David Lloyd – who missed all red-ball cricket last year with a broken foot – will shore up a fragile top-order. Callum Taylor showed his potential with a hundred on first-class debut but the future of opener Charlie Hemphrey is uncertain after he was told he cannot qualify as a local player in both England and Australia. With money tight, the club have let go of a clutch of players, including 37-year-old allrounder Graham Wagg, who was released after 10 years despite little sign of diminishing returns. Ireland captain Andrew Balbirnie will deputise for Labuschagne until his arrival in May.

IN: Andrew Balbirnie (Ire, CC), Marnus Labuschagne, Michael Neser (both Aus)
OUT: Marchant de Lange (Som), Kieran Bull, Connor Brown, Owen Morgan, Graham Wagg (all REL)

HEAD COACH: MATTHEW MAYNARD

Maynard replaced Robert Croft ahead of the 2019 season, having previously coached Glamorgan between 2008 and 2010. He has also served as Somerset's director of cricket. A dashing batsman for Glamorgan for 20 years, Maynard made a club-record 54 centuries and helped the county win the Championship in 1997. Former Cardiff City goalkeeper Mark Walton has been appointed junior Academy coach and also takes on a mentoring role for the senior players.

BOB WILLIS TROPHY AVERAGES 2020

Batting

	Mat	Inns	NO	Runs	HS	Ave	SR	100	50	4s	6s
CZ Taylor	2	4	0	153	106	38.25	67.10	1	0	19	6
M de Lange	3	5	1	131	113	32.75	121.29	1	0	8	10
CB Cooke	5	10	1	294	82	32.66	48.19	0	3	37	0
WT Root	5	10	1	286	118	31.77	40.45	1	1	39	1
MG Hogan	4	7	4	78	33*	26.00	93.97	0	0	10	3
T van der Gugten	4	7	3	98	30*	24.50	40.66	0	0	14	0
NJ Selman	5	10	0	215	73	21.50	35.53	0	2	27	0
GG Wagg	3	6	1	100	54	20.00	50.00	0	1	13	0
DA Douthwaite	5	10	1	160	86	17.77	52.45	0	1	19	4
LJ Carey	1	2	0	34	23	17.00	60.71	0	0	5	0
AO Morgan	1	2	0	28	28	14.00	41.17	0	0	3	0
KS Carlson	4	8	0	109	79	13.62	36.57	0	1	14	0
TN Cullen	3	6	0	80	26	13.33	52.28	0	0	14	0
RAJ Smith	1	2	0	26	23	13.00	66.66	0	0	4	1
JM Cooke	2	4	0	48	23	12.00	29.44	0	0	5	0
CR Hemphrey	3	6	0	62	20	10.33	27.55	0	0	7	0
KA Bull	4	8	1	50	23	7.14	24.39	0	0	6	0

Bowling

	Overs	Mdns	Runs	Wkts	BBI	BBM	Ave	Econ	SR	5w	10w
RAJ Smith	14.0	4	41	3	3/41	3/41	13.66	2.92	28.0	0	0
M de Lange	81.2	17	218	9	4/84	4/115	24.22	2.68	54.2	0	0
GG Wagg	73.0	14	272	11	3/38	5/139	24.72	3.72	39.8	0	0
LJ Carey	24.5	4	82	3	3/54	3/82	27.33	3.30	49.6	0	0
T van der Gugten	119.0	31	362	12	3/45	5/115	30.16	3.04	59.5	0	0
DA Douthwaite	121.1	16	473	14	3/42	5/103	33.78	3.90	51.9	0	0
CZ Taylor	26.0	2	81	2	1/20	1/20	40.50	3.11	78.0	0	0
AO Morgan	11.5	0	43	1	1/43	1/43	43.00	3.63	71.0	0	0
MG Hogan	139.0	32	397	8	3/59	3/90	49.62	2.85	104.2	0	0
KA Bull	102.3	4	462	9	3/112	4/221	51.33	4.50	68.3	0	0
KS Carlson	1.0	0	2	0	-	-	-	2.00	-	0	0
CR Hemphrey	9.0	0	37	0	-	-	-	4.11	-	0	0

Catches/Stumpings:

18 C Cooke (inc 2st), 10 Selman, 6 Cullen, 3 Douthwaite, Hemphrey, van der Gugten, Wagg, 2 Carlson, de Lange, 1 Bull, Carey, J Cooke, Hogan, Root

VITALITY BLAST AVERAGES 2020

Batting

	Mat	Inns	NO	Runs	HS	Ave	SR	100	50	4s	6s
A Balbirnie	9	9	2	255	99*	36.42	144.88	0	2	25	7
DL Lloyd	5	5	0	160	56	32.00	139.13	0	1	15	5
CB Cooke	9	9	2	221	72	31.57	123.46	0	2	12	9
NJ Selman	6	6	0	176	78	29.33	123.94	0	1	20	4
T van der Gugten	8	4	2	49	34*	24.50	140.00	0	0	3	2
AG Salter	9	5	3	45	14	22.50	115.38	0	0	3	2
DA Douthwaite	6	6	2	75	23*	18.75	178.57	0	0	6	6
M de Lange	7	6	2	68	28*	17.00	128.30	0	0	7	2
AO Morgan	4	3	0	44	24	14.66	112.82	0	0	4	2
CZ Taylor	7	7	1	76	23	12.66	84.44	0	0	6	1
WT Root	3	3	0	35	29	11.66	72.91	0	0	3	0
GG Wagg	6	4	0	30	13	7.50	90.90	0	0	2	0
KS Carlson	5	5	0	23	7	4.60	67.64	0	0	2	0
RAJ Smith	6	2	0	2	1	1.00	33.33	0	0	0	0
P Sisodiya	9	2	2	4	4*	-	400.00	0	0	1	0

Bowling

	Overs	Mdns	Runs	Wkts	BBI	Ave	Econ	SR	4w	5w
P Sisodiya	36.0	1	232	10	3/26	23.20	6.44	21.6	0	0
T van der Gugten	28.0	0	209	14	3/17	14.92	7.46	12.0	0	0
CZ Taylor	5.0	0	38	3	2/9	12.66	7.60	10.0	0	0
M de Lange	21.4	0	168	5	2/23	33.60	7.75	26.0	0	0
RAJ Smith	22.0	0	178	5	2/13	35.60	8.09	26.4	0	0
AG Salter	36.0	0	293	10	4/20	29.30	8.13	21.6	1	0
GG Wagg	16.0	0	143	3	3/34	47.66	8.93	32.0	0	0
DA Douthwaite	7.0	0	64	1	1/29	64.00	9.14	42.0	0	0

Catches/Stumpings:
9 C Cooke (inc 3st), 4 Taylor, 3 Balbirnie, Wagg, 2 Carlson, de Lange, Douthwaite, Root, Salter, Sisodiya, 1 Lloyd, Morgan, Smith

GLOUCESTERSHIRE

FORMED: 1871
HOME GROUND: The Bristol County Ground, Bristol
CAPTAIN: Chris Dent, Jack Taylor (T20)
2020 RESULTS: BWT: 5/6 Central Group; T20: Semi-finalists
HONOURS: Gillette/NatWest/C&G/FP Trophy: (5) 1973, 1999, 2000, 2003, 2004; Benson & Hedges Cup: (3) 1977, 1999, 2000; Pro40/National League/CB40/YB40/RL50: (2) 2000, 2015

THE LOWDOWN

It is tough on Gloucestershire – and on Lancashire and Northants – that their promotion from Division Two in 2019 seems to have counted for little: last year we had the Bob Willis Trophy, this year a revamped County Championship. Then in March they lost their prized head coach, Richard Dawson, to the ECB. Nevertheless, a positive spirit prevails after the club reached T20 Finals Day for the first time in 13 years. Veteran Ian Cockbain warmed to his new role as a T20 specialist last summer, smiting 399 runs in 11 matches, while spinner Tom Smith was the only bowler in the country to go at less than six an over. Their red-ball cricket was less impressive, as was plainly demonstrated when they were dismissed for 76 and 70 at Taunton. No one made a century and James Bracey, detained in England's Test bubble, was badly missed at the top of the order. The pace attack looks strong, with David Payne and Ryan Higgins, who were outstanding last summer, supported by the re-signed Australian seamer Dan Worrall. Only a frontline spinner seems to be lacking. Fast bowler Stuart Whittingham was forced to retire aged 26 because of a back injury.

IN: Jared Warner (Yor), Dan Worrall (Aus)
OUT: Gareth Roderick (Wor), George Drissell (REL), Stuart Whittingham (RET)

HEAD COACH: IAN HARVEY

Harvey was promoted from assistant coach on an interim basis after Richard Dawson took on a full-time ECB role in March. The former Australian allrounder, who played 168 times for Gloucestershire between 1999 and 2006, has worked alongside Dawson since the latter became head coach ahead of the 2015 season. They won the One-Day Cup in their first season in charge and secured Championship promotion in 2019. The club intend to appoint a long-term replacement for Dawson later this year.

BOB WILLIS TROPHY AVERAGES 2020

Batting

	Mat	Inns	NO	Runs	HS	Ave	SR	100	50	4s	6s
GL van Buuren	5	8	0	244	72	30.50	45.01	0	2	33	0
TMJ Smith	2	2	1	30	24*	30.00	24.00	0	0	2	0
RF Higgins	5	8	1	173	51	24.71	47.65	0	1	20	1
CDJ Dent	4	7	0	170	92	24.28	47.09	0	2	19	0
GFB Scott	4	6	2	87	44*	21.75	32.95	0	0	7	0
TC Lace	3	4	0	73	42	18.25	39.03	0	0	12	0
JMR Taylor	2	4	0	71	34	17.75	23.43	0	0	11	0
GH Roderick	4	7	1	101	39	16.83	40.56	0	0	11	0
GT Hankins	5	8	0	130	69	16.25	34.85	0	1	11	1
BG Charlesworth	4	6	0	78	51	13.00	30.46	0	1	9	0
MAH Hammond	1	2	0	23	14	11.50	37.70	0	0	3	0
MD Taylor	5	7	2	43	19*	8.60	53.75	0	0	5	1
J Shaw	5	7	0	50	21	7.14	39.37	0	0	8	0
DA Payne	4	5	1	24	14	6.00	38.70	0	0	2	0
JR Bracey	1	1	0	4	4	4.00	17.39	0	0	1	0
TJ Price	1	2	0	0	0	0.00	0.00	0	0	0	0

Bowling

	Overs	Mdns	Runs	Wkts	BBI	BBM	Ave	Econ	SR	5w	10w
DA Payne	95.0	29	199	14	5/31	8/61	14.21	2.09	40.7	1	0
RF Higgins	148.4	41	391	17	7/42	11/96	23.00	2.63	52.4	1	1
MD Taylor	115.0	22	330	11	3/43	5/80	30.00	2.86	62.7	0	0
J Shaw	99.5	17	328	8	3/13	3/62	41.00	3.28	74.8	0	0
GFB Scott	44.0	9	129	3	2/34	2/60	43.00	2.93	88.0	0	0
GL van Buuren	21.0	5	60	1	1/7	1/7	60.00	2.85	126.0	0	0
TJ Price	18.0	1	80	1	1/69	1/80	80.00	4.44	108.0	0	0
BG Charlesworth	27.0	6	103	1	1/40	1/55	103.00	3.81	162.0	0	0
JMR Taylor	0.1	0	4	0	-	-	-	24.00	-	0	0
TMJ Smith	5.0	0	10	0	-	-	-	2.00	-	0	0

Catches/Stumpings:
12 Roderick, 7 Hankins, 4 Dent, 3 van Buuren, 2 Higgins, 1 Hammond, Lace, J Taylor

VITALITY BLAST AVERAGES 2020

Batting

	Mat	Inns	NO	Runs	HS	Ave	SR	100	50	4s	6s
BAC Howell	5	4	2	96	49*	48.00	213.33	0	0	7	8
IA Cockbain	11	11	2	399	89	44.33	169.78	0	3	31	22
CDJ Dent	11	11	0	371	87	33.72	153.30	0	4	48	9
RF Higgins	11	11	4	200	30*	28.57	130.71	0	0	20	2
GL van Buuren	11	6	3	79	53	26.33	161.22	0	1	4	4
JMR Taylor	11	10	4	133	31*	22.16	117.69	0	0	5	5
MAH Hammond	10	10	0	210	49	21.00	116.66	0	0	24	4
JR Bracey	11	9	2	125	39*	17.85	134.40	0	0	8	4
GFB Scott	7	4	0	63	33	15.75	131.25	0	0	4	2
GT Hankins	1	1	0	7	7	7.00	63.63	0	0	1	0
DA Payne	11	2	1	0	0*	0.00	0.00	0	0	0	0
MD Taylor	7	1	0	0	0	0.00	0.00	0	0	0	0
TMJ Smith	11	2	2	5	4*	-	125.00	0	0	1	0
J Shaw	3	-	-	-	-	-	-	-	-	-	-

Bowling

	Overs	Mdns	Runs	Wkts	BBI	Ave	Econ	SR	4w	5w
TMJ Smith	41.0	0	243	14	5/16	17.35	5.92	17.5	0	1
J Shaw	5.0	0	33	1	1/13	33.00	6.60	30.0	0	0
GL van Buuren	33.0	0	224	12	3/15	18.66	6.78	16.5	0	0
DA Payne	37.5	0	299	16	3/18	18.68	7.90	14.1	0	0
BAC Howell	18.0	0	146	7	3/16	20.85	8.11	15.4	0	0
GFB Scott	4.0	0	36	1	1/24	36.00	9.00	24.0	0	0
RF Higgins	34.4	0	329	16	4/34	20.56	9.49	13.0	1	0
MD Taylor	24.1	0	237	8	3/29	29.62	9.80	18.1	0	0

Catches/Stumpings:
6 Bracey (inc 5st), Cockbain, 5 Howell, Scott, Dent, Smith, J Taylor, 3 Hammond, Higgins, 2 Payne, 1 Shaw, M Taylor, van Buuren

HAMPSHIRE

FORMED: 1863
HOME GROUND: The Ageas Bowl, Southampton
CAPTAIN: James Vince
2020 RESULTS: BWT: 4/6 South Group; T20: 6/6 South Group
HONOURS: Championship: (2) 1961, 1973; Gillette/NatWest/C&G/FP Trophy: (3) 1991, 2005, 2009; Benson & Hedges Cup: (2) 1988, 1992; Pro40/National League/CB40/YB40/RL50: (2) 2012, 2018; Sunday League: (3) 1975, 1978, 1986; T20 Cup: (2) 2010, 2012

THE LOWDOWN

No county had it easy last year, but Hampshire had it harder than most. The travel bans decimated their star-studded bowling attack, with Kyle Abbott, Fidel Edwards, Nathan Lyon all absent. The captain, James Vince, was tied up with England for all but six T20 matches. Liam Dawson, their senior allrounder, ruptured his achilles in his first game and missed the rest of the campaign. Keith Barker missed the whole of September after undergoing a knee operation. So Hampshire did well to win two of five matches in the Bob Willis Trophy, even if their T20 cricket was largely indifferent. Among the standouts were 24-year-old Joe Weatherley, the club's leading run-scorer in the Bob Willis Trophy, and leg-spinner Mason Crane, who proved his red-ball threat with 14 wickets at 13.57. Ian Holland was very effective with the new ball in the absence of the overseas heavyweights. Edwards has left post-Kolpak era but Abbott returns as an overseas and is joined by Pakistan's Mohammad Abbas until the end of May in what should be a formidable new-ball pairing. Vince should be a regular in 2021, while Barker, Dawson and long-term absentee Aneurin Donald are all expected to be fit come April.

IN: Mohammad Abbas (Pak, CC)
OUT: Harry Came, Fidel Edwards, Oli Soames (all REL)

FIRST-TEAM MANAGER: ADRIAN BIRRELL

The vastly experienced Birrell took over from Craig White in December 2018 and led Hampshire to the 50-over final in his first season. A former Eastern Province allrounder, Birrell made his name as coach of Ireland, guiding the team to a famous victory over Pakistan in the 2007 World Cup. In 2010 he was put in charge of England U19 before beginning a four-year stint as South Africa's assistant coach. Birrell works alongside director of cricket Giles White, with Jimmy Adams and Alfonso Thomas acting as assistant coaches.

BOB WILLIS TROPHY AVERAGES 2020

Batting

	Mat	Inns	NO	Runs	HS	Ave	SR	100	50	4s	6s
JJ Weatherley	5	7	1	263	98	43.83	40.77	0	2	38	0
KHD Barker	2	4	2	63	28*	31.50	55.26	0	0	10	0
TAR Scriven	2	3	0	84	68	28.00	45.40	0	1	11	0
SA Northeast	5	7	0	181	81	25.85	46.77	0	2	21	0
BTJ Wheal	3	3	2	24	14*	24.00	20.00	0	0	3	0
TP Alsop	5	7	0	164	87	23.42	47.26	0	1	19	0
LD McManus	5	7	0	142	50	20.28	53.18	0	1	19	1
SW Currie	1	2	0	38	38	19.00	44.18	0	0	7	0
IG Holland	5	7	0	115	42	16.42	47.52	0	0	17	0
JK Fuller	4	5	1	61	30	15.25	81.33	0	0	9	0
HRC Came	4	5	0	49	25	9.80	28.16	0	0	6	0
FS Organ	5	7	0	60	16	8.57	38.46	0	0	10	0
MS Crane	4	5	1	33	25*	8.25	55.93	0	0	6	0
AS Dale	2	4	1	7	6	2.33	13.46	0	0	0	0
RA Stevenson	2	1	0	0	0	0.00	0.00	0	0	0	0
LA Dawson	1	1	1	43	43*	-	58.10	0	0	8	0

Bowling

	Overs	Mdns	Runs	Wkts	BBI	BBM	Ave	Econ	SR	5w	10w
FS Organ	27.0	3	90	7	4/42	4/42	12.85	3.33	23.1	0	0
MS Crane	60.4	8	190	14	3/19	6/69	13.57	3.13	26.0	0	0
IG Holland	129.0	41	297	17	6/60	7/77	17.47	2.30	45.5	1	0
AS Dale	21.0	4	73	4	3/20	3/35	18.25	3.47	31.5	0	0
SW Currie	17.0	4	58	3	3/42	3/58	19.33	3.41	34.0	0	0
LA Dawson	16.5	5	39	2	2/39	2/39	19.50	2.31	50.5	0	0
RA Stevenson	32.0	8	103	5	4/70	4/70	20.60	3.21	38.4	0	0
TAR Scriven	21.0	3	79	3	2/24	2/59	26.33	3.76	42.0	0	0
KHD Barker	66.0	13	201	7	2/44	4/97	28.71	3.04	56.5	0	0
JK Fuller	70.0	12	293	9	4/17	4/34	32.55	4.18	46.6	0	0
BTJ Wheal	61.0	21	203	5	2/11	3/71	40.60	3.32	73.2	0	0

Catches/Stumpings:
13 McManus (inc 2st), 5 Alsop, 4 Holland, 3 Dawson, 2 Currie, Fuller, Weatherley, 1 Barker, Came, Organ, Scriven

VITALITY BLAST AVERAGES 2020

Batting

	Mat	Inns	NO	Runs	HS	Ave	SR	100	50	4s	6s
JK Fuller	10	10	4	205	53*	34.16	131.41	0	2	9	10
IG Holland	10	10	5	161	65	32.20	130.89	0	1	8	6
TP Alsop	8	8	0	197	51	24.62	110.05	0	1	21	2
MS Crane	9	3	2	24	12*	24.00	85.71	0	0	1	0
JJ Weatherley	9	9	0	185	68	20.55	121.71	0	1	14	4
RA Stevenson	9	4	2	39	17	19.50	139.28	0	0	6	0
SA Northeast	9	9	0	149	37	16.55	98.67	0	0	14	2
JM Vince	6	6	0	93	48	15.50	98.93	0	0	12	0
CP Wood	10	5	2	36	18	12.00	76.59	0	0	3	1
HG Munsey	5	5	0	55	32	11.00	91.66	0	0	6	2
LD McManus	8	8	0	79	26	9.87	95.18	0	0	3	3
Shaheen Shah Afridi	7	3	2	9	9*	9.00	60.00	0	0	1	0
FS Organ	3	3	0	21	9	7.00	91.30	0	0	2	0
SW Currie	4	2	1	2	2	2.00	50.00	0	0	0	0
CG Harrison	2	2	1	2	2*	2.00	100.00	0	0	0	0
TAR Scriven	1	1	0	2	2	2.00	28.57	0	0	0	0

Bowling

	Overs	Mdns	Runs	Wkts	BBI	Ave	Econ	SR	4w	5w
JM Vince	1.0	0	6	0	-	-	6.00	-	0	0
MS Crane	30.0	0	198	9	3/18	22.00	6.60	20.0	0	0
FS Organ	8.0	0	54	3	2/21	18.00	6.75	16.0	0	0
IG Holland	22.1	0	162	3	1/25	54.00	7.30	44.3	0	0
Shaheen Shah Afridi	26.0	0	210	7	6/19	30.00	8.07	22.2	0	1
CP Wood	33.0	0	268	6	2/29	44.66	8.12	33.0	0	0
RA Stevenson	24.4	0	232	3	1/25	77.33	9.40	49.3	0	0
SW Currie	6.0	0	58	1	1/28	58.00	9.66	36.0	0	0
CG Harrison	6.2	0	64	1	1/39	64.00	10.10	38.0	0	0
JK Fuller	8.0	0	95	1	1/54	95.00	11.87	48.0	0	0

Catches/Stumpings:
3 Alsop (inc 1st), McManus (inc 1st), Wood, 2 Crane, Fuller, Northeast, Stevenson, Vince, Weatherley, 1 Harrison, Munsey

KENT

FORMED: 1870
HOME GROUND: The Spitfire Ground, St Lawrence, Canterbury
ONE-DAY NAME: Kent Spitfires
CAPTAIN: Sam Billings
2020 RESULTS: BWT: 2/6 South Group; T20: Quarter-finalists
HONOURS: Championship: (7) 1906, 1909, 1910, 1913, 1970, 1977(s), 1978; Gillette/NatWest/C&G/FP Trophy: (2) 1967, 1974; Pro40/National League/CB40/RL50: 2001; Benson & Hedges Cup: (3) 1973, 1976, 1978; Sunday League: (4) 1972, 1973, 1976, 1995; T20 Cup: 2007

THE LOWDOWN

Kent pushed Essex all the way in the group stages of the Bob Willis Trophy last summer and would have made the Lord's final but for the narrow defeat at Chelmsford in the first game of the season, when they were dismissed for 112 in their second innings. The club won three of their remaining four fixtures, with 20-year-old Jordan Cox and new signing Jack Leaning both making double-hundreds in an innings victory against Sussex at Canterbury. But it was inevitably Darren Stevens who, at the age of 44, stole the show yet again. Only Simon Harmer and Craig Overton managed more than his 29 wickets, and each of them played a game more; only Harmer bowled more than his 209 overs. It was easy to overlook the fine efforts of his fellow seamers Harry Podmore (19 wickets at 16.15) and Matt Milnes (15 at 23.66). It's an impressive attack, further boosted by the arrival of West Indies quick Miguel Cummins for the first eight red-ball matches. Kent also had a strong T20 campaign, inspired by the runs of Zak Crawley and Daniel Bell-Drummond who, with Sam Billings often on England duty, proved a capable stand-in skipper and has been appointed the club's vice-captain.

IN: Nathan Gilchrist (Som), Miguel Cummins (Mid, WI, CC)
OUT: Sean Dickson (Dur), Calum Haggett, Ivan Thomas (both REL)

HEAD COACH: MATT WALKER

Walker scored nearly 20,000 runs for Kent and Essex between 1992 and 2011. He was assistant to Jimmy Adams before his promotion to head coach ahead of the 2017 season, having previously worked with Essex and England Lions. In 2018 Walker led Kent to Championship promotion and a Lord's one-day final. He signed a new two-year contract at the end of last summer. Former England wicketkeeper Paul Downton has been director of cricket since 2018.

BOB WILLIS TROPHY AVERAGES 2020

Batting

	Mat	Inns	NO	Runs	HS	Ave	SR	100	50	4s	6s
JL Denly	1	1	0	89	89	89.00	57.79	0	1	14	0
HG Kuhn	2	4	1	202	140	67.33	57.71	1	0	25	2
JM Cox	4	6	1	324	238*	64.80	53.02	1	0	39	4
Z Crawley	1	2	0	105	105	52.50	97.22	1	0	18	0
MK O'Riordan	5	8	3	216	52*	43.20	45.00	0	1	32	0
JA Leaning	5	8	1	279	220*	39.85	52.14	1	0	36	0
HW Podmore	3	3	1	79	47	39.50	91.86	0	0	12	1
DJ Bell-Drummond	5	9	1	185	45	23.12	54.89	0	0	25	0
OG Robinson	5	6	0	138	78	23.00	57.02	0	1	21	1
G Stewart	4	6	0	129	58	21.50	61.72	0	1	15	2
SW Billings	2	1	0	20	20	20.00	50.00	0	0	4	0
NN Gilchrist	1	2	0	38	25	19.00	48.10	0	0	7	0
ME Milnes	4	6	0	96	43	16.00	43.83	0	0	14	0
DI Stevens	5	6	0	77	36	12.83	56.20	0	0	11	1
Hamidullah Qadri	4	5	2	11	5	3.66	26.19	0	0	1	0
IAA Thomas	2	2	1	3	3*	3.00	20.00	0	0	0	0
FJ Klaassen	1	1	1	0	0*	-	0.00	0	0	0	0
TD Groenewald	1	-	-	-	-	-	-	-	-	-	-

Bowling

	Overs	Mdns	Runs	Wkts	BBI	BBM	Ave	Econ	SR	5w	10w
DI Stevens	209.0	64	452	29	5/37	9/72	15.58	2.16	43.2	3	0
HW Podmore	117.3	30	307	19	5/43	7/92	16.15	2.61	37.1	1	0
FJ Klaassen	27.0	6	80	4	4/44	4/80	20.00	2.96	40.5	0	0
ME Milnes	119.3	29	355	15	4/46	7/112	23.66	2.97	47.8	0	0
MK O'Riordan	62.1	5	255	8	3/50	4/72	31.87	4.10	46.6	0	0
IAA Thomas	30.0	3	136	4	4/32	4/74	34.00	4.53	45.0	0	0
TD Groenewald	28.0	5	119	2	1/53	2/119	59.50	4.25	84.0	0	0
G Stewart	95.5	19	299	5	3/48	3/87	59.80	3.12	115.0	0	0
Hamidullah Qadri	38.4	7	104	1	1/24	1/58	104.00	2.68	232.0	0	0
JA Leaning	2.0	1	2	0	-	-	-	1.00	-	0	0
JL Denly	2.0	0	12	0	-	-	-	6.00	-	0	0
DJ Bell-Drummond	5.0	0	22	0	-	-	-	4.40	-	0	0
NN Gilchrist	9.0	1	52	0	-	-	-	5.77	-	0	0

Catches/Stumpings:
22 Robinson, 9 Leaning, 6 Cox, 5 Kuhn, 3 Bell-Drummond, Stevens, 2 Billings, Podmore, 1 Crawley, Denly, Klaassen, Milnes, O'Riordan

VITALITY BLAST AVERAGES 2020

Batting

	Mat	Inns	NO	Runs	HS	Ave	SR	100	50	4s	6s
DJ Bell-Drummond	11	11	1	423	89	42.30	154.94	0	3	53	12
Z Crawley	11	11	2	342	108*	38.00	156.88	1	1	43	7
JA Leaning	11	9	3	201	55*	33.50	138.62	0	1	18	6
SW Billings	3	3	0	86	50	28.66	132.30	0	1	8	2
JL Denly	6	6	0	152	38	25.33	142.05	0	0	11	6
AJ Blake	11	9	1	171	52*	21.37	134.64	0	1	11	8
JM Cox	8	6	2	75	39*	18.75	122.95	0	0	6	2
HG Kuhn	8	8	2	104	42*	17.33	118.18	0	0	11	0
G Stewart	11	9	3	79	21*	13.16	98.75	0	0	3	3
ME Milnes	10	3	2	6	3	6.00	85.71	0	0	0	0
CJ Haggett	3	1	1	15	15*	-	107.14	0	0	1	0
Imran Qayyum	11	1	1	8	8*	-	88.88	0	0	0	0
TD Groenewald	4	2	2	7	6*	-	87.50	0	0	1	0
OG Robinson	2	1	1	1	1*	-	33.33	0	0	0	0
FJ Klaassen	11	-	-	-	-	-	-	-	-	-	-

Bowling

	Overs	Mdns	Runs	Wkts	BBI	Ave	Econ	SR	4w	5w
JA Leaning	6.0	0	43	0	-	-	7.16	-	0	0
JL Denly	21.0	0	166	3	1/19	55.33	7.90	42.0	0	0
TD Groenewald	15.0	0	119	4	2/31	29.75	7.93	22.5	0	0
Imran Qayyum	41.0	0	329	11	3/25	29.90	8.02	22.3	0	0
AJ Blake	7.0	0	60	0	-	-	8.57	-	0	0
G Stewart	37.4	0	329	6	2/28	54.83	8.73	37.6	0	0
ME Milnes	37.0	0	338	7	3/19	48.28	9.13	31.7	0	0
FJ Klaassen	40.4	0	374	13	3/36	28.76	9.19	18.7	0	0
CJ Haggett	9.0	0	93	2	1/28	46.50	10.33	27.0	0	0

Catches/Stumpings:

7 Blake, Cox (inc 2st), 5 Bell-Drummond, 3 Billings, Crawley, 2 Kuhn, Leaning, Qayyum, Robinson, 1 Denly, Klaassen, Milnes, Stewart

LANCASHIRE

FORMED: 1864
HOME GROUND: Emirates Old Trafford, Manchester
ONE-DAY NAME: Lancashire Lightning
CAPTAIN: Dane Vilas
2020 RESULTS: BWT: 3/6 North Group; T20: Semi-finalists
HONOURS: Championship: (9) 1897, 1904, 1926, 1927, 1928, 1930, 1934, 1950(s), 2011; Gillette/NatWest/C&G/FP Trophy: (7) 1970, 1971, 1972, 1985, 1990, 1996, 1998; Benson & Hedges Cup: (4) 1984, 1990, 1995, 1996; Pro40/National League/CB40/YB40/RL50: 1999; Sunday League: (4) 1969, 1970, 1989, 1998; T20 Cup: 2015

THE LOWDOWN

Burgeoning youth was a theme of county cricket in 2020, and nowhere was it plainer to see than at Lancashire. A combination of injuries and England call-ups meant that six players made their first-class debut. Tom Bailey aside, the bowling attack was made up of novices, all of whom did themselves proud. Slow left-armer Jack Morley took debut match figures of 40-15-71-5 at Liverpool while Tom Hartley, who also bowls left-arm spin, was an ever-present in the T20 side. Among the debutants were four seamers, and with the additions of Australian Test seamer Jackson Bird for six red-ball matches and Jack Blatherwick from Notts, plus Saqib Mahmood and Richard Gleeson to come back into the fold, Lancashire have softened the blow of Graham Onions' retirement. Luke Wells has arrived from Sussex to bolster a batting line-up which failed to produce a single hundred last year, although Alex Davies was a solid presence at the top of the order. But the best news over the winter was confirmation that club captain Dane Vilas will stay at Old Trafford after making the switch from Kolpak to overseas. The signing of Finn Allen, the exciting 21-year-old Kiwi, for the duration of the Blast campaign will add firepower to the batting unit.

IN: Jack Blatherwick (Not), Luke Wells (Sus), Jackson Bird (Aus, CC), Finn Allen (NZ, T20)
OUT: Brooke Guest (Der), Toby Lester, Stephen Parry (both REL), Graham Onions (RET)

HEAD COACH: GLEN CHAPPLE

Chapple took 1,373 wickets in 664 appearances during a 23-year career at Old Trafford and captained the side to the Championship title in 2011. He took over as coach from Ashley Giles in January 2017, since when Lancashire's Championship form has been up and down: runners-up in 2017, relegated in 2018, promoted in 2019. The freshly retired Graham Onions is the club's new bowling coach. Former Manchester United commercial director Andy Anson was appointed chairman in September.

BOB WILLIS TROPHY AVERAGES 2020

Batting

	Mat	Inns	NO	Runs	HS	Ave	SR	100	50	4s	6s
SJ Croft	4	5	2	199	63	66.33	39.25	0	3	25	0
AL Davies	5	8	1	337	86	48.14	61.49	0	4	54	1
JJ Bohannon	5	7	0	257	94	36.71	40.66	0	2	23	1
DJ Vilas	5	7	0	247	90	35.28	55.38	0	1	37	0
TW Hartley	4	4	3	35	13*	35.00	21.21	0	0	2	0
DJ Lamb	3	4	1	104	50*	34.66	50.00	0	1	12	1
GP Balderson	5	7	2	156	61*	31.20	39.69	0	1	18	2
KK Jennings	5	8	1	182	81	26.00	38.64	0	1	23	2
L Wood	2	2	0	52	46	26.00	52.00	0	0	6	0
LS Livingstone	2	2	0	37	23	18.50	59.67	0	0	5	0
TE Bailey	4	4	1	47	38*	15.66	51.08	0	0	4	2
RP Jones	3	5	0	77	23	15.40	31.04	0	0	9	0
GID Lavelle	1	2	0	20	13	10.00	34.48	0	0	1	0
RJ Gleeson	1	1	0	6	6	6.00	20.68	0	0	0	0
JP Morley	1	1	0	3	3	3.00	6.52	0	0	0	0
LJ Hurt	2	2	0	3	2	1.50	16.66	0	0	0	0
GD Burrows	2	1	0	1	1	1.00	11.11	0	0	0	0
EHT Moulton	1	2	0	0	0	0.00	0.00	0	0	0	0

Bowling

	Overs	Mdns	Runs	Wkts	BBI	BBM	Ave	Econ	SR	5w	10w
JP Morley	40.0	15	71	5	4/62	5/71	14.20	1.77	48.0	0	0
DJ Lamb	68.1	13	203	12	4/55	7/72	16.91	2.97	34.0	0	0
RJ Gleeson	18.0	4	52	3	3/32	3/52	17.33	2.88	36.0	0	0
LS Livingstone	21.3	2	92	5	3/79	3/79	18.40	4.27	25.8	0	0
TE Bailey	111.4	44	282	13	3/11	4/25	21.69	2.52	51.5	0	0
LJ Hurt	48.0	6	182	7	4/27	5/71	26.00	3.79	41.1	0	0
KK Jennings	15.0	3	28	1	1/14	1/14	28.00	1.86	90.0	0	0
GD Burrows	40.0	8	127	4	2/20	2/38	31.75	3.17	60.0	0	0
GP Balderson	104.0	23	296	9	3/63	3/82	32.88	2.84	69.3	0	0
L Wood	44.0	8	118	3	2/31	3/71	39.33	2.68	88.0	0	0
TW Hartley	111.0	28	324	6	3/79	3/117	54.00	2.91	111.0	0	0
RP Jones	3.0	2	4	0	-	-	-	1.33	-	0	0
SJ Croft	1.0	0	6	0	-	-	-	6.00	-	0	0
EHT Moulton	27.0	4	110	0	-	-	-	4.07	-	0	0

Catches/Stumpings:
8 Jennings, 7 Davies, 6 Croft, 5 Vilas, 4 Bohannon, 3 Jones, 2 Hartley, Lavelle, 1 Lamb, Livingstone

VITALITY BLAST AVERAGES 2020

Batting

	Mat	Inns	NO	Runs	HS	Ave	SR	100	50	4s	6s
DJ Lamb	11	6	5	69	29*	69.00	104.54	0	0	6	0
KK Jennings	7	6	2	233	108	58.25	134.68	1	0	22	3
SJ Croft	10	9	0	272	58	30.22	125.92	0	1	12	16
AL Davies	11	10	0	299	82	29.90	121.54	0	3	32	6
LS Livingstone	7	7	0	192	69	27.42	156.09	0	1	13	14
RP Jones	10	7	4	77	38*	25.66	105.47	0	0	5	1
DJ Vilas	11	10	3	144	44*	20.57	122.03	0	0	9	4
S Mahmood	5	2	1	10	6	10.00	71.42	0	0	0	0
GID Lavelle	2	2	0	18	12	9.00	90.00	0	0	2	0
TW Hartley	11	2	1	4	4	4.00	57.14	0	0	1	0
MW Parkinson	11	1	0	3	3	3.00	42.85	0	0	0	0
JJ Bohannon	7	6	2	10	4	2.50	40.00	0	0	0	0
L Wood	8	3	1	3	2*	1.50	60.00	0	0	0	0
TE Bailey	6	-	-	-	-	-	-	-	-	-	-
LJ Hurt	3	-	-	-	-	-	-	-	-	-	-
SD Parry	1	-	-	-	-	-	-	-	-	-	-

Bowling

	Overs	Mdns	Runs	Wkts	BBI	Ave	Econ	SR	4w	5w
SD Parry	4.0	0	17	1	1/17	17.00	4.25	24.0	0	0
TE Bailey	16.0	0	111	10	5/17	11.10	6.93	9.6	0	1
SJ Croft	11.0	0	77	4	2/29	19.25	7.00	16.5	0	0
TW Hartley	36.0	0	256	6	2/21	42.66	7.11	36.0	0	0
L Wood	19.0	0	143	7	3/21	20.42	7.52	16.2	0	0
LS Livingstone	25.2	0	191	9	4/23	21.22	7.53	16.8	1	0
MW Parkinson	40.2	0	310	15	3/9	20.66	7.68	16.1	0	0
S Mahmood	15.0	0	116	4	1/14	29.00	7.73	22.5	0	0
DJ Lamb	28.0	1	226	7	1/14	32.28	8.07	24.0	0	0
LJ Hurt	8.0	0	85	2	2/29	42.50	10.62	24.0	0	0

Catches/Stumpings:

12 Davies (inc 6st), 9 Vilas, 7 Jones, 6 Bohannon, 3 Croft, Hurt, Wood, 2 Bailey, Livingstone, 1 Hartley

LEICESTERSHIRE

FORMED: 1879
HOME GROUND: Uptonsteel County Ground, Leicester
ONE-DAY NAME: Leicestershire Foxes
CAPTAIN: Colin Ackermann
2020 RESULTS: BWT: 5/6 North Group; T20: Quarter-finalists
HONOURS: Championship: (3) 1975, 1996, 1998; Benson & Hedges Cup: (3) 1972, 1975, 1985; Sunday League: (2) 1974, 1977; T20 Cup: (3) 2004, 2006, 2011

THE LOWDOWN

Following a dismal return in 2019 (bottom in all formats), Leicestershire will have been heartened by some spirited performances in last year's truncated season. It began in August with a dramatic win against Lancashire in the Bob Willis Trophy, when they chased 150 in 16 overs, and ended in October with a thrilling tie against Nottinghamshire in the T20 quarter-finals (Notts prevailed by virtue of making more runs during the Powerplay overs). For Colin Ackermann it was an encouraging first summer as club captain. With Paul Horton retired and Mark Cosgrove released, Leicestershire are more dependent than ever on Ackermann's leadership and runs, although reinforcements landed over the winter. The biggest coup was 21-year-old Scott Steel, an attacking opener prised from Durham despite the county's attempts to keep him. Promising allrounder Tom Taylor has departed after turning down a new deal and joining Northamptonshire, but Australian Test opener Marcus Harris has signed up for red-ball and 50-over cricket. Arron Lilley penned a new white-ball contract after finishing as the club's leading run-scorer in last year's T20 Blast. Afghan fast bowler Naveen-ul-Haq, 21, has been signed for the Blast.

IN: Ed Barnes (Yor), Rishi Patel (Ess), Scott Steel (Dur), Marcus Harris (Aus, CC/RL50), Naveen-ul-Haq (Afg, T20)
OUT: Tom Taylor (Nor), Mark Cosgrove (REL), Paul Horton (RET)

HEAD COACH: PAUL NIXON

Nixon was appointed in early 2018 to replace Pierre de Bruyn, who had resigned the previous year after less than a season as head coach. A former England wicketkeeper who won two Championship titles with the club, Nixon retired in 2011 after inspiring Leicestershire to a stunning T20 triumph at the age of 40. He won the Caribbean Premier League twice as coach of Jamaica Tallawahs and has also worked in the Bangladesh Premier League.

BOB WILLIS TROPHY AVERAGES 2020

Batting

	Mat	Inns	NO	Runs	HS	Ave	SR	100	50	4s	6s
CN Ackermann	5	9	2	379	94	54.14	60.93	0	4	52	1
BT Slater	2	4	0	197	172	49.25	52.53	1	0	21	3
TAI Taylor	3	3	1	78	57	39.00	79.59	0	1	7	2
HJ Swindells	5	7	2	188	52*	37.60	48.20	0	1	23	0
CJC Wright	2	2	1	33	23	33.00	38.82	0	0	6	0
ST Evans	3	5	0	148	85	29.60	37.46	0	1	17	0
HE Dearden	5	9	0	234	70	26.00	60.00	0	1	35	3
GT Griffiths	3	3	2	23	11*	23.00	43.39	0	0	3	0
WJ Weighell	1	1	0	23	23	23.00	48.93	0	0	4	0
CF Parkinson	3	3	1	42	21	21.00	36.52	0	0	3	1
BWM Mike	4	6	1	99	51*	19.80	72.79	0	1	11	2
Hassan Azad	5	8	0	144	58	18.00	32.07	0	1	18	0
GH Rhodes	4	7	2	83	22*	16.60	35.47	0	0	11	0
WS Davis	2	2	0	28	20	14.00	34.14	0	0	2	0
D Klein	4	5	1	53	27	13.25	67.08	0	0	7	0
RK Patel	1	2	0	24	19	12.00	30.76	0	0	4	0
AM Lilley	1	2	0	18	13	9.00	36.00	0	0	2	0
HA Evans	2	3	0	16	15	5.33	114.28	0	0	3	0

Bowling

	Overs	Mdns	Runs	Wkts	BBI	BBM	Ave	Econ	SR	5w	10w
AM Lilley	6.0	1	21	3	3/21	3/21	7.00	3.50	12.0	0	0
Hassan Azad	2.1	0	15	1	1/15	1/15	15.00	6.92	13.0	0	0
CN Ackermann	35.0	12	92	4	2/24	2/27	23.00	2.62	52.5	0	0
CF Parkinson	79.3	22	192	8	3/30	5/62	24.00	2.41	59.6	0	0
CJC Wright	57.0	21	141	5	2/39	4/91	28.20	2.47	68.4	0	0
BWM Mike	88.1	13	279	9	4/39	4/94	31.00	3.16	58.7	0	0
WS Davis	30.0	6	106	3	2/75	2/75	35.33	3.53	60.0	0	0
GT Griffiths	61.5	13	181	5	3/52	3/52	36.20	2.92	74.2	0	0
D Klein	95.0	10	332	9	3/44	3/61	36.88	3.49	63.3	0	0
TAI Taylor	93.0	25	247	6	2/49	2/49	41.16	2.65	93.0	0	0
HA Evans	35.2	7	140	3	2/59	2/67	46.66	3.96	70.6	0	0
ST Evans	3.0	0	22	0	-	-	-	7.33	-	0	0
WJ Weighell	6.0	0	29	0	-	-	-	4.83	-	0	0

Catches/Stumpings:
11 Swindells, 6 Ackermann, 4 Rhodes, 3 Azad, S Evans, 2 Mike, 1 Dearden, H Evans, Griffiths, Lilley, Taylor

VITALITY BLAST AVERAGES 2020

Batting

	Mat	Inns	NO	Runs	HS	Ave	SR	100	50	4s	6s
CF Parkinson	9	6	5	46	13*	46.00	117.94	0	0	3	0
HJ Swindells	3	3	1	68	58	34.00	123.63	0	1	9	0
AM Lilley	9	9	0	278	69	30.88	139.00	0	1	19	14
CN Ackermann	9	9	1	246	67*	30.75	122.38	0	2	17	8
GJ Delany	9	9	0	193	68	21.44	138.84	0	2	20	9
NR Welch	5	5	0	101	43	20.20	103.06	0	0	7	5
BWM Mike	7	6	2	70	22*	17.50	179.48	0	0	6	4
HE Dearden	8	8	1	120	36*	17.14	88.88	0	0	9	1
GH Rhodes	5	5	2	41	30*	13.66	97.61	0	0	2	0
LJ Hill	9	8	1	83	22	11.85	102.46	0	0	6	0
TAI Taylor	5	5	0	43	19	8.60	102.38	0	0	2	1
WS Davis	9	3	2	4	4*	4.00	33.33	0	0	0	0
GT Griffiths	9	1	1	1	1*	-	100.00	0	0	0	0
D Klein	3	1	1	0	0*	-	-	0	0	0	0

Bowling

	Overs	Mdns	Runs	Wkts	BBI	Ave	Econ	SR	4w	5w
CF Parkinson	32.0	0	210	10	3/21	21.00	6.56	19.2	0	0
D Klein	10.0	0	66	2	1/22	33.00	6.60	30.0	0	0
BWM Mike	8.0	0	55	3	2/19	18.33	6.87	16.0	0	0
CN Ackermann	21.0	0	150	8	3/18	18.75	7.14	15.7	0	0
TAI Taylor	11.0	0	86	2	1/7	43.00	7.81	33.0	0	0
GT Griffiths	23.0	0	180	10	4/35	18.00	7.82	13.8	1	0
AM Lilley	7.0	0	60	0	-	-	8.57	-	0	0
GJ Delany	17.0	0	148	6	2/26	24.66	8.70	17.0	0	0
WS Davis	21.2	0	186	7	3/38	26.57	8.71	18.2	0	0

Catches/Stumpings:
5 Ackermann, Davis, 4 Hill (inc 2st), 3 Lilley, Mike, Parkinson, Taylor, 2 Klein, 1 Dearden, Delany, Griffiths, Rhodes, Swindells, Welch

MIDDLESEX

FORMED: 1864
HOME GROUND: Lord's Cricket Ground, London
CAPTAIN: Peter Handscomb, Eoin Morgan (T20)
2020 RESULTS: BWT: 3/6 South Group; T20: 4/6 South Group
HONOURS: Championship: (13) 1903, 1920, 1921, 1947, 1949(s), 1976, 1977(s), 1980, 1982, 1985, 1990, 1993, 2016; Gillette/NatWest/C&G/FP Trophy: (4) 1977, 1980, 1984, 1998; Benson & Hedges Cup: (2) 1983, 1986; Sunday League: 1992; T20 Cup: 2008

THE LOWDOWN

Consistency eludes Middlesex, in terms of results but also team selection. Covid deferred the arrival of Australian batsman Peter Handscomb as club captain, but he will take up the role this summer. Eoin Morgan, the T20 skipper, did not play at all in the Blast (Steven Finn deputised). Injuries continue to plague the seam attack. Toby Roland-Jones missed all of 2020 with thigh and shoulder injuries, Tom Helm appeared just once in the Bob Willis Trophy, and Finn wasn't risked at all given his suspect knees. The exception to the rule was naturally Tim Murtagh, who took 25 wickets at 12.72. The batting is weaker without Dawid Malan, which made the decision to allow Tom Lace to join Gloucestershire last August seem strange. Stevie Eskinazi was the second-highest run-scorer in the T20 Blast but could hardly muster a run as stand-in captain in first-class cricket, although Nick Gubbins returned to form with a brilliant 192 at The Oval. Thilan Walallawita, a 22-year-old left-arm spinner born in Sri Lanka, played in all five Bob Willis Trophy games and took 3-19 on T20 debut, while allrounder Luke Hollman also impressed in his first year as a professional.

IN: Peter Handscomb (Aus), Mitchell Marsh (Aus, T20), Mujeeb Ur Rahman (Afg, T20)
OUT: Miguel Cummins (Ken), Dan Lincoln (REL)

HEAD COACH: STUART LAW

The former Australian batsman was appointed after the 2018 season as part of sweeping changes which saw the departure of Richard Scott after nearly a decade as head coach. Law had a two-year stint as West Indies coach prior to joining Middlesex and performed similar roles with Sri Lanka and Bangladesh. He has also coached his native Queensland and Brisbane Heat in domestic cricket. As a player, Law scored 65 hundreds for Essex and Lancashire between 1996 and 2008. Dimitri Mascarenhas, the former England and Hampshire allrounder, continues as the club's T20 bowling coach.

BOB WILLIS TROPHY AVERAGES 2020

Batting

	Mat	Inns	NO	Runs	HS	Ave	SR	100	50	4s	6s
NRT Gubbins	4	8	0	350	192	43.75	58.33	1	1	40	1
JA Simpson	5	9	2	250	53	35.71	46.64	0	1	31	1
RG White	3	5	0	176	99	35.20	41.50	0	1	25	1
MDE Holden	5	10	0	299	72	29.90	48.46	0	1	42	2
MK Andersson	5	9	1	227	92	28.37	63.94	0	2	36	0
JAR Harris	4	7	2	128	41	25.60	40.25	0	0	18	0
SD Robson	5	10	1	215	82*	23.88	44.05	0	1	27	0
SS Eskinazi	5	10	1	151	29	16.77	45.61	0	0	21	0
BC Cullen	2	3	0	49	34	16.33	26.92	0	0	2	1
TG Helm	1	2	0	29	28	14.50	54.71	0	0	4	1
ML Cummins	3	2	0	26	25	13.00	37.14	0	0	3	0
JLB Davies	1	1	0	13	13	13.00	20.31	0	0	1	0
NA Sowter	2	4	2	25	20	12.50	40.32	0	0	4	0
TJ Murtagh	4	5	2	26	11*	8.66	72.22	0	0	4	0
TN Walallawita	5	6	2	22	11	5.50	42.30	0	0	4	0
ER Bamber	1	1	1	24	24*	-	48.97	0	0	3	0

Bowling

	Overs	Mdns	Runs	Wkts	BBI	BBM	Ave	Econ	SR	5w	10w
SD Robson	4.0	3	6	2	2/0	2/0	3.00	1.50	12.0	0	0
TJ Murtagh	145.5	48	318	25	5/34	7/74	12.72	2.18	35.0	2	0
MK Andersson	75.5	15	250	14	4/38	7/98	17.85	3.29	32.5	0	0
ML Cummins	92.1	28	269	13	5/62	5/74	20.69	2.91	42.5	1	0
JAR Harris	89.0	19	284	9	2/46	3/93	31.55	3.19	59.3	0	0
BC Cullen	30.0	5	110	3	2/51	2/51	36.66	3.66	60.0	0	0
NA Sowter	52.5	16	120	3	1/4	2/34	40.00	2.27	105.6	0	0
TN Walallawita	88.2	28	245	6	3/28	4/51	40.83	2.77	88.3	0	0
TG Helm	24.3	7	66	1	1/41	1/66	66.00	2.69	147.0	0	0
ER Bamber	21.0	6	79	1	1/56	1/79	79.00	3.76	126.0	0	0
NRT Gubbins	1.3	0	2	0	-	-	-	1.33	-	0	0

Catches/Stumpings:
20 Simpson (inc 1st), 8 Robson, 7 Eskinazi, 5 Sowter, 4 Holden, 3 Andersson, 1 Cullen, Gubbins, Murtagh, White

VITALITY BLAST AVERAGES 2020

Batting

	Mat	Inns	NO	Runs	HS	Ave	SR	100	50	4s	6s
SS Eskinazi	10	10	0	413	84	41.30	148.02	0	4	31	17
JA Simpson	10	10	2	288	48	36.00	132.71	0	0	13	14
LBK Hollman	7	7	3	139	46	34.75	139.00	0	0	10	4
JB Cracknell	4	4	0	123	50	30.75	148.19	0	1	19	2
MDE Holden	9	9	1	220	102*	27.50	134.96	1	0	19	8
NRT Gubbins	4	4	0	87	53	21.75	117.56	0	1	9	0
DJ Lincoln	6	6	2	67	24*	16.75	103.07	0	0	4	1
TG Helm	10	6	4	32	12*	16.00	100.00	0	0	1	0
JLB Davies	4	4	0	48	23	12.00	106.66	0	0	2	0
MK Andersson	10	10	1	94	24	10.44	103.29	0	0	9	0
JAR Harris	5	3	1	14	7*	7.00	70.00	0	0	1	0
NA Sowter	10	4	1	16	8	5.33	76.19	0	0	1	0
ST Finn	10	3	2	2	1*	2.00	66.66	0	0	0	0
TJ Murtagh	5	1	0	0	0	0.00	0.00	0	0	0	0
TN Walallawita	1	1	0	0	0	0.00	0.00	0	0	0	0
ML Cummins	5	-	-	-	-	-	-	-	-	-	-

Bowling

	Overs	Mdns	Runs	Wkts	BBI	Ave	Econ	SR	4w	5w
TN Walallawita	4.0	0	19	3	3/19	6.33	4.75	8.0	0	0
TJ Murtagh	18.0	0	119	7	2/20	17.00	6.61	15.4	0	0
LBK Hollman	24.0	0	163	9	3/18	18.11	6.79	16.0	0	0
NA Sowter	36.0	0	262	10	3/30	26.20	7.27	21.6	0	0
NRT Gubbins	1.0	0	8	0	-	-	8.00	-	0	0
ST Finn	33.0	0	266	14	3/18	19.00	8.06	14.1	0	0
TG Helm	32.2	0	273	12	2/12	22.75	8.44	16.1	0	0
ML Cummins	15.5	0	153	3	1/26	51.00	9.66	31.6	0	0
JAR Harris	10.0	0	131	1	1/46	131.00	13.10	60.0	0	0
MK Andersson	3.0	0	48	0	-	-	16.00	-	0	0

Catches/Stumpings:
7 Andersson, 6 Eskinazi, Simpson (inc 1st), 5 Sowter, 4 Lincoln, 3 Finn, Harris, Holden, 2 Hollman, 1 Cummins, Gubbins, Murtagh

NORTHAMPTONSHIRE

FORMED: 1878
HOME GROUND: County Ground, Northampton
ONE-DAY NAME: Northamptonshire Steelbacks
CAPTAIN: Adam Rossington, Josh Cobb (RL50 & T20)
2020 RESULTS: BWT: 4/6 Central Group; T20: Quarter-finalists
HONOURS: Gillette/NatWest/C&G/FP Trophy: (2) 1976, 1992; Benson & Hedges Cup: 1980; T20 Cup: (2) 2013, 2016

THE LOWDOWN

It was hard to know what to make of Northants last summer. They were bowled out for 142, 67 and 154 in three of their first four innings in the Bob Willis Trophy, with a score of 507-6 sandwiched in the middle. Later, in a crunch T20 at Edgbaston, the Steelbacks chased down 192 after being 71-6, only to then be shot out for 113 in the quarter-final against Gloucestershire. Adam Rossington and Luke Procter both made red-ball hundreds but only 24-year-old Charlie Thurston (357 runs in eight innings) offered consistency with the bat in first-class cricket. Of the seamers, Ben Sanderson was on the money as always and Jack White looked comfortable at this level a year after being plucked from Australian Grade cricket, but both need better support from the other bowlers. Blessing Muzarabani was released after his Kolpak status expired but South African opener Richard Levi qualifies as a local player. Simon Kerrigan will challenge Saif Zaib for the spinner's berth after joining last summer. The chances of a third T20 trophy are boosted by the arrival of Mohammad Nabi, the world's No.1 T20 allrounder when the club signed him in December.

IN: Tom Taylor (Lei), Wayne Parnell (SA), Mohammad Nabi (Afg, T20)
OUT: Brett Hutton (Not), Blessing Muzarabani, Rob Newton, Tom Sole (all REL)

HEAD COACH: DAVID RIPLEY

Ripley hasn't left the club since making his Second XI debut in 1982. As a keeper-batsman, he scored over 10,000 runs and claimed more than 1,000 dismissals for the county before retiring in 2001 and joining the backroom staff. He was promoted from Second XI coach in 2012 and led the club to their maiden T20 title the following year, repeating the trick in 2016. More success followed in 2019 with Championship promotion, only for the pandemic to scupper Northants' return to the top flight.

www.nccc.co.uk / tel: 01604 514455

BOB WILLIS TROPHY AVERAGES 2020

	Mat	Inns	NO	Runs	HS	Ave	SR	100	50	4s	6s
LA Procter	4	6	2	200	112*	50.00	53.47	1	0	32	1
CO Thurston	5	8	0	357	115	44.62	63.18	1	2	44	3
AM Rossington	3	6	1	196	135*	39.20	40.57	1	0	26	0
R Vasconcelos	5	8	1	222	58	31.71	52.11	0	2	37	0
NL Buck	2	3	1	61	32	30.50	83.56	0	0	5	4
BJ Curran	4	8	0	238	82	29.75	54.71	0	2	37	0
EN Gay	4	6	1	121	77*	24.20	44.98	0	1	15	0
GK Berg	2	4	0	63	45	15.75	48.09	0	0	6	0
RI Keogh	4	6	0	80	31	13.33	41.23	0	0	12	0
RE Levi	1	2	0	19	11	9.50	51.35	0	0	3	0
B Muzarabani	4	5	2	27	15	9.00	36.00	0	0	4	0
BA Hutton	2	1	0	9	9	9.00	24.32	0	0	0	0
BW Sanderson	2	3	0	23	23	7.66	52.27	0	0	3	0
SA Zaib	4	5	0	36	23	7.20	34.95	0	0	5	1
AG Wakely	1	2	0	11	9	5.50	19.64	0	0	1	0
CJ White	4	4	2	9	7*	4.50	36.00	0	0	0	1
SC Kerrigan	2	1	0	1	1	1.00	20.00	0	0	0	0
BD Glover	1	2	0	0	0	0.00	0.00	0	0	0	0
HOM Gouldstone	1	-	-	-	-	-	-	-	-	-	-

Batting

	Overs	Mdns	Runs	Wkts	BBI	BBM	Ave	Econ	SR	5w	10w
BW Sanderson	55.1	14	166	11	5/28	9/89	15.09	3.00	30.0	1	0
NL Buck	64.0	21	173	9	3/42	6/109	19.22	2.70	42.6	0	0
CJ White	88.0	20	260	13	4/35	8/83	20.00	2.95	40.6	0	0
SA Zaib	28.0	5	84	4	2/11	4/68	21.00	3.00	42.0	0	0
BA Hutton	39.0	8	136	6	4/77	5/114	22.66	3.48	39.0	0	0
BD Glover	24.0	5	94	4	2/45	4/94	23.50	3.91	36.0	0	0
B Muzarabani	70.5	17	278	11	4/29	5/130	25.27	3.92	38.6	0	0
SC Kerrigan	23.3	4	89	3	2/54	2/88	29.66	3.78	47.0	0	0
GK Berg	47.0	9	203	6	4/64	5/100	33.83	4.31	47.0	0	0
LA Procter	30.0	5	130	2	1/9	1/15	65.00	4.33	90.0	0	0
RI Keogh	38.0	10	112	1	1/96	1/96	112.00	2.94	228.0	0	0

Bowling

Catches/Stumpings:
14 Vasconcelos (inc 1st), 8 Rossington, 5 Curran, 4 Gay, 3 Berg, 2 Thurston, Zaib, 1 Gouldstone, Hutton, Keogh, Kerrigan, Levi, Muzarabani, Procter, Wakely

VITALITY BLAST AVERAGES 2020

Batting

	Mat	Inns	NO	Runs	HS	Ave	SR	100	50	4s	6s
TAI Taylor	2	2	1	77	50*	77.00	183.33	0	1	8	4
GG White	10	9	6	96	37*	32.00	171.42	0	0	9	5
PR Stirling	10	10	1	232	80*	25.77	152.63	0	1	26	11
RI Keogh	2	2	0	49	37	24.50	116.66	0	0	4	1
R Vasconcelos	3	3	0	67	34	22.33	109.83	0	0	8	0
AM Rossington	8	7	0	156	51	22.28	118.18	0	1	15	2
RE Levi	10	10	0	196	50	19.60	130.66	0	1	19	9
SA Zaib	8	7	1	116	30	19.33	131.81	0	0	15	2
JJ Cobb	10	10	1	156	49	17.33	94.54	0	0	14	5
LA Procter	5	5	1	69	20*	17.25	113.11	0	0	6	0
TB Sole	3	2	0	33	25	16.50	82.50	0	0	4	0
AG Wakely	8	7	1	91	36*	15.16	84.25	0	0	2	1
NL Buck	10	5	3	28	16*	14.00	112.00	0	0	1	2
GK Berg	5	4	0	20	11	5.00	95.23	0	0	3	0
BW Sanderson	10	3	2	3	2	3.00	60.00	0	0	0	0
BD Glover	6	1	1	0	0*	-	0.00	0	0	0	0

Bowling

	Overs	Mdns	Runs	Wkts	BBI	Ave	Econ	SR	4w	5w
JJ Cobb	26.0	0	159	3	1/17	53.00	6.11	52.0	0	0
LA Procter	10.0	0	64	2	1/11	32.00	6.40	30.0	0	0
SA Zaib	8.0	0	54	2	1/20	27.00	6.75	24.0	0	0
PR Stirling	8.0	0	57	3	2/26	19.00	7.12	16.0	0	0
GG White	39.5	0	299	12	3/28	24.91	7.50	19.9	0	0
GK Berg	12.0	0	96	4	2/31	24.00	8.00	18.0	0	0
BW Sanderson	31.5	0	267	12	3/11	22.25	8.38	15.9	0	0
NL Buck	28.0	1	250	10	4/29	25.00	8.92	16.8	1	0
BD Glover	17.0	0	155	7	2/32	22.14	9.11	14.5	0	0
TAI Taylor	5.0	0	51	2	2/38	25.50	10.20	15.0	0	0

Catches/Stumpings:
6 Sanderson, Zaib, 5 Levi, Sole, 4 Stirling, 3 Buck, Cobb, Glover, 2 Berg, Rossington (inc 1st), White, 1 Vasconcelos, Wakely

NOTTINGHAMSHIRE

FORMED: 1841
HOME GROUND: Trent Bridge, Nottingham
ONE-DAY NAME: Notts Outlaws
CAPTAIN: Steven Mullaney, Haseeb Hameed (RL50), Dan Christian (T20)
2020 RESULTS: BWT: 4/6 North Group; T20: Winners
HONOURS: County Championship: (6) 1907, 1929, 1981, 1987, 2005, 2010; Gillette/NatWest/C&G/FP Trophy: 1987; Pro40/National League/CB40/YB40/RL50: (2) 2013, 2017; Benson & Hedges Cup: 1989; Sunday League: 1991; T20 Cup: (2) 2017, 2020

THE LOWDOWN

Nottinghamshire confirmed themselves as T20 kings after winning the Blast for the second time in four years, losing only once in the group stages. Captain fantastic Dan Christian returns this summer, and the power of the batting line-up makes Notts favourites again, with Joe Clarke and Ben Duckett running riot last year. By contrast Notts failed to win once in the Bob Willis Trophy, and their last red-ball victory was back in June 2018. Yet that does not tell the whole story. They should have won the two matches they lost last year (failing to defend 365 and then to chase down 188) and were the dominant team in all three weather-affected draws. The seam attack was excellent even in the absence of the injured Luke Fletcher, and there were runs all the way down from the outstanding Duckett (394 at 56) to Samit Patel in his new role as a No.8. Haseeb Hameed made three fifties in seven innings in his first season at Trent Bridge. There were two intriguing arrivals over the winter: 22-year-old Toby Pettman, a 6ft 7in fast bowler from Oxford MCCU, and former Zimbabwe U19 keeper-batsman Dane Schadendorf, who qualifies as a local player through his British passport.

IN: Brett Hutton (Nor), Toby Pettman (Oxf MCCU), Dane Schadendorf (Zim, UK passport)
OUT: Jack Blatherwick (Lan), Chris Nash (REL)

HEAD COACH: PETER MOORES

Moores scored 7,000 first-class runs and claimed 517 dismissals for Sussex between 1985 and 1998. He had two spells as England head coach and won the Championship with Sussex in 2003 and Lancashire in 2011. Moores replaced Mick Newell (now the director of cricket) in 2016 and immediately led the club to the cup double as well as Championship promotion. Notts finished bottom of Division One in 2019 but added a third white-ball trophy last summer. Moores' assistant is Kevin Shine, the former ECB lead fast-bowling coach.

BOB WILLIS TROPHY AVERAGES 2020

Batting

	Mat	Inns	NO	Runs	HS	Ave	SR	100	50	4s	6s
BT Slater	3	3	0	228	142	76.00	44.35	1	1	28	0
BM Duckett	5	8	1	394	150	56.28	68.88	2	0	56	0
H Hameed	5	7	0	272	87	38.85	40.84	0	3	43	0
JM Clarke	5	8	1	263	133	37.57	58.70	1	1	35	0
JDM Evison	1	2	0	69	38	34.50	62.72	0	0	8	2
SJ Mullaney	5	7	0	235	67	33.57	70.99	0	2	35	3
SR Patel	5	7	0	210	80	30.00	71.67	0	2	29	1
TJ Moores	5	7	0	207	106	29.57	67.64	1	0	30	3
CD Nash	2	4	0	78	59	19.50	61.41	0	1	11	1
M Carter	3	4	1	50	22	16.66	104.16	0	0	5	3
PD Trego	5	8	0	116	39	14.50	73.41	0	0	12	3
JT Ball	3	5	1	56	34	14.00	67.46	0	0	8	2
ZJ Chappell	4	4	1	1	1	0.33	3.84	0	0	0	0
LW James	1	1	1	36	36*	-	112.50	0	0	3	1
TE Barber	3	3	3	2	2*	-	15.38	0	0	0	0

Bowling

	Overs	Mdns	Runs	Wkts	BBI	BBM	Ave	Econ	SR	5w	10w
CD Nash	11.2	1	38	3	3/20	3/38	12.66	3.35	22.6	0	0
JDM Evison	22.5	4	74	4	3/38	4/74	18.50	3.24	34.2	0	0
M Carter	149.2	54	263	11	4/76	6/120	23.90	1.76	81.4	0	0
PD Trego	134.3	44	342	12	3/33	5/109	28.50	2.54	67.2	0	0
ZJ Chappell	131.2	30	431	15	4/59	6/123	28.73	3.28	52.5	0	0
SR Patel	156.2	36	388	13	4/80	4/114	29.84	2.48	72.1	0	0
JT Ball	112.5	30	336	10	3/71	6/169	33.60	2.97	67.7	0	0
TE Barber	79.0	9	289	7	3/42	3/74	41.28	3.65	67.7	0	0
SJ Mullaney	80.0	22	183	4	1/23	1/35	45.75	2.28	120.0	0	0
LW James	16.0	2	55	1	1/43	1/55	55.00	3.43	96.0	0	0
BM Duckett	1.0	0	2	0	-	-	-	2.00	-	0	0

Catches/Stumpings:
15 Moores (inc 1st), 10 Mullaney, 8 Hameed, 4 Duckett, 3 Ball, Carter, Chappell, 2 Patel, Slater, 1 Evison, James, Nash, Trego

VITALITY BLAST AVERAGES 2020

Batting

	Mat	Inns	NO	Runs	HS	Ave	SR	100	50	4s	6s
SR Patel	11	5	4	44	28*	44.00	146.66	0	0	4	1
BM Duckett	11	11	3	340	86*	42.50	137.65	0	4	41	4
JM Clarke	11	11	1	371	100*	37.10	175.00	1	2	35	22
PD Trego	1	1	0	31	31	31.00	147.61	0	0	5	1
DT Christian	11	10	4	173	33*	28.83	144.16	0	0	15	10
TJ Moores	11	9	2	188	51	26.85	135.25	0	1	19	7
SJ Mullaney	11	5	3	53	16*	26.50	143.24	0	0	2	3
CD Nash	10	9	1	185	55	23.12	122.51	0	2	21	5
AD Hales	11	11	0	202	49	18.36	164.22	0	0	27	8
Imad Wasim	9	4	4	33	26*	-	122.22	0	0	1	2
JT Ball	10	-	-	-	-	-	-	-	-	-	-
M Carter	9	-	-	-	-	-	-	-	-	-	-
ZJ Chappell	1	-	-	-	-	-	-	-	-	-	-
LJ Fletcher	4	-	-	-	-	-	-	-	-	-	-

Bowling

	Overs	Mdns	Runs	Wkts	BBI	Ave	Econ	SR	4w	5w
SJ Mullaney	27.0	1	193	9	2/17	21.44	7.14	18.0	0	0
Imad Wasim	32.0	0	231	8	2/24	28.87	7.21	24.0	0	0
SR Patel	38.0	0	286	11	2/19	26.00	7.52	20.7	0	0
JT Ball	34.1	1	259	19	3/28	13.63	7.58	10.7	0	0
DT Christian	35.0	0	278	9	4/23	30.88	7.94	23.3	1	0
M Carter	22.0	0	191	7	2/16	27.28	8.68	18.8	0	0
ZJ Chappell	2.5	0	27	0	-	-	9.52	-	0	0
LJ Fletcher	15.0	0	148	8	5/43	18.50	9.86	11.2	0	1

Catches/Stumpings:
11 Hales, 6 Duckett, Moores (inc 2st), 5 Ball, Mullaney, 4 Nash, Wasim, 3 Carter, Christian, 2 Clarke, Patel

SOMERSET

FORMED: 1875
HOME GROUND: The Cooper Associates County Ground, Taunton
CAPTAIN: Tom Abell, Lewis Gregory (T20)
2020 RESULTS: BWT: Runners-up; T20: 4/6 Central Group
HONOURS: Gillette/NatWest/C&G/FP Trophy: (3) 1979, 1983, 2001; Pro40/National League/CB40/YB40/RL50: 2019; Benson & Hedges Cup: (2) 1981, 1982; Sunday League: 1979; T20 Cup: 2005

THE LOWDOWN

Amid the peculiarity of last season there was something very normal: Somerset finished runners-up. But they did it differently this time, with 100 out of 109 wickets falling to the seamers, thus dismissing the myth of Ciderabad which says that Somerset only win with spin (they begin the new season with an eight-point penalty for preparing a "poor" pitch in the 2019 decider against Essex). Craig Overton and the unsung Josh Davey took 54 wickets at 13.59 between them, leading a rampant pace attack which dismissed the opposition for double-figure scores on three occasions before the Lord's final, never conceding more than 200. Only rain at Edgbaston denied Somerset a clean sweep of their group matches. The standout player, however, was debutant batsman Tom Lammonby, whose three centuries included a match-winning 107 not out in the crunch game against Worcestershire. Six players made hundreds, including a maiden first-class century for Jamie Overton batting at No.10. Jamie has since left for Surrey but Somerset still have plenty of fast-bowling options, especially with the arrival of Marchant de Lange. Losing Dom Bess to Yorkshire may be more of a blow, with Jack Leach seeming to be England's first-choice spinner.

IN: Marchant de Lange (Gla, SA)
OUT: Dom Bess (Yor), Nathan Gilchrist (Ken), Jamie Overton (Sur)

HEAD COACH: JASON KERR

A former Somerset allrounder, Kerr has been part of the coaching staff since 2005. He was promoted from bowling coach to head coach in 2017 and works alongside director of cricket Andy Hurry. Somerset have been runners-up in red-ball cricket in each of Kerr's three seasons in charge and won the One-Day Cup in 2019. Ex-Somerset seamer Steve Kirby was appointed bowling coach in December after two years at Derbyshire, replacing the Ireland-bound Stuart Barnes. Marcus Trescothick left after a year as assistant coach to become England's batting coach.

BOB WILLIS TROPHY AVERAGES 2020

Batting

	Mat	Inns	NO	Runs	HS	Ave	SR	100	50	4s	6s
TA Lammonby	6	11	2	459	116	51.00	51.68	3	0	52	5
SM Davies	6	10	2	320	123*	40.00	62.13	1	1	44	0
TB Abell	6	11	1	386	119	38.60	58.22	2	1	58	2
J Overton	4	6	0	206	120	34.33	126.38	1	1	26	10
GA Bartlett	4	6	1	160	100*	32.00	44.69	1	0	25	0
C Overton	6	10	2	248	66	31.00	66.48	0	2	33	4
JA Brooks	5	7	2	139	72	27.80	97.20	0	1	19	2
BGF Green	3	5	0	127	54	25.40	37.57	0	1	15	1
EJ Byrom	6	11	0	271	117	24.63	48.13	1	0	44	0
JC Hildreth	4	6	0	124	45	20.66	55.60	0	0	18	0
JH Davey	6	9	3	113	28	18.83	45.56	0	0	18	1
L Gregory	3	5	0	78	37	15.60	60.46	0	0	6	6
RE van der Merwe	4	6	1	57	30	11.40	52.77	0	0	6	1
T Banton	2	3	0	33	18	11.00	52.38	0	0	5	0
MJ Leach	2	3	0	29	21	9.66	40.84	0	0	4	0

Bowling

	Overs	Mdns	Runs	Wkts	BBI	BBM	Ave	Econ	SR	5w	10w
RE van der Merwe	6.0	2	8	1	1/8	1/8	8.00	1.33	36.0	0	0
J Overton	68.1	24	186	15	5/48	7/64	12.40	2.72	27.2	1	0
C Overton	196.2	66	403	30	5/26	9/51	13.43	2.05	39.2	2	0
JH Davey	150.2	55	331	24	4/25	7/46	13.79	2.20	37.5	0	0
TB Abell	16.2	5	50	3	3/4	3/4	16.66	3.06	32.6	0	0
L Gregory	102.3	22	318	18	6/72	8/124	17.66	3.10	34.1	1	0
TA Lammonby	12.0	3	38	2	1/4	1/4	19.00	3.16	36.0	0	0
JA Brooks	89.5	23	254	13	4/40	5/56	19.53	2.82	41.4	0	0
MJ Leach	52.0	17	112	3	3/38	3/90	37.33	2.15	104.0	0	0
EJ Byrom	1.0	0	4	0	-	-	-	4.00	-	0	0

Catches/Stumpings:
19 Davies, 10 Hildreth, 7 C Overton, J Overton, 5 Abell, 4 Lammonby, van der Merwe, 3 Byrom, 2 Bartlett, 1 Brooks, Davey, Gregory, Leach

VITALITY BLAST AVERAGES 2020

Batting

	Mat	Inns	NO	Runs	HS	Ave	SR	100	50	4s	6s
RE van der Merwe	9	6	3	127	41*	42.33	176.38	0	0	10	5
TA Lammonby	6	5	2	121	43*	40.33	177.94	0	0	7	9
JC Hildreth	4	4	1	119	34*	39.66	141.66	0	0	12	3
Babar Azam	7	7	1	218	114*	36.33	137.97	1	0	19	7
TB Abell	9	9	2	227	74*	32.42	136.74	0	2	23	3
C Overton	5	2	1	26	17*	26.00	118.18	0	0	3	1
L Gregory	7	5	0	118	50	23.60	157.33	0	1	10	5
SM Davies	9	9	0	182	60	20.22	131.88	0	1	23	2
ORT Sale	9	4	3	19	14*	19.00	118.75	0	0	0	1
WCF Smeed	5	5	0	94	82	18.80	117.50	0	1	7	5
GA Bartlett	3	3	0	41	24	13.66	128.12	0	0	5	1
BGF Green	3	2	0	24	14	12.00	141.17	0	0	1	2
EJ Byrom	5	4	0	41	18	10.25	110.81	0	0	3	1
JH Davey	5	3	2	9	6*	9.00	112.50	0	0	1	0
J Overton	1	1	0	1	1	1.00	50.00	0	0	0	0
LP Goldsworthy	3	1	1	38	38*	-	131.03	0	0	4	0
MTC Waller	9	-	-	-	-	-	-	-	-	-	-

Bowling

	Overs	Mdns	Runs	Wkts	BBI	Ave	Econ	SR	4w	5w
MTC Waller	34.0	0	212	8	3/18	26.50	6.23	25.5	0	0
J Overton	3.0	0	21	0	-	-	7.00	-	0	0
RE van der Merwe	29.0	1	209	3	2/15	69.66	7.20	58.0	0	0
LP Goldsworthy	11.0	0	86	5	2/21	17.20	7.81	13.2	0	0
JH Davey	15.0	0	123	11	4/41	11.18	8.20	8.1	1	0
TA Lammonby	5.0	0	45	1	1/14	45.00	9.00	30.0	0	0
C Overton	14.5	0	137	6	3/36	22.83	9.23	14.8	0	0
L Gregory	19.0	0	176	9	2/18	19.55	9.26	12.6	0	0
ORT Sale	29.4	0	301	13	3/32	23.15	10.14	13.6	0	0
BGF Green	7.0	0	77	4	4/26	19.25	11.00	10.5	1	0
TB Abell	0.2	0	11	0	-	-	33.00	-	0	0

Catches/Stumpings:
9 Gregory, 6 Abell, Azam, 4 Davies, van der Merwe, Waller, 3 Davey, Sale, 2 Bartlett, Green, Hildreth, C Overton, Smeed, 1 Goldsworthy

SURREY

FORMED: 1845
GROUND: The Kia Oval, London
CAPTAIN: Rory Burns, Jade Dernbach (T20)
2020 RESULTS: BWT: 5/6 South Group; T20: Runners-up
HONOURS: Championship: (20) 1890, 1891, 1892, 1894, 1895, 1899, 1914, 1950, 1952, 1953, 1954, 1955, 1956, 1957, 1958, 1971, 1999, 2000, 2002, 2018; Gillette/NatWest/C&G/FP Trophy: 1982; Benson & Hedges Cup: (3) 1974, 1997, 2001; Pro40/National League/CB40/YB40/RL50: (2) 2003, 2011; Sunday League: 1996; T20 Cup: 2003

THE LOWDOWN

Events conspired against Surrey last season. Head coach Michael Di Venuto was marooned in Australia on account of the virus and left the club in May. Club captain Rory Burns was bubbled up with England, while T20 skipper Jade Dernbach did not play all season due to injury. So many players were injured or missing that the club had to arrange emergency loan deals with other counties. And yet the summer nearly ended in glory, with the T20 side galloping to the Blast final on the back of nine straight wins, inspired by their unremitting 42-year-old stand-in captain, Gareth Batty. Laurie Evans led the T20 scoring charts after joining from Sussex last August. Elsewhere the story was of blossoming youth. Left-arm spinner Daniel Moriarty, a former South Africa U19 bowler, took 17 wickets in two first-class matches and only Jake Ball took more wickets in the T20 Blast. Will Jacks, 22, continued to impress while 20-year-old keeper Jamie Smith played in 14 of Surrey's 18 matches. Morné Morkel has gone back to South Africa but Hashim Amla returns this summer as an overseas player. Jamie Overton will add some serious nip to the pace attack, with West Indian seamer Kemar Roach signing for the first seven Championship matches.

IN: Laurie Evans (Sus), Jamie Overton (Som), Kemar Roach (WI, CC)
OUT: Scott Borthwick (Dur), Morné Morkel (REL)

HEAD COACH: VIKRAM SOLANKI

Solanki was promoted from assistant to head coach in June 2020 to replace Michael Di Venuto, whose four-year tenure ended when travel restrictions prevented the Australian's arrival last season. Solanki was appointed as Surrey's assistant in January 2018, helping the club to their first Championship title in 16 years that summer. He played 51 ODIs for England and scored more than 15,000 first-class runs for Worcestershire between 1995 and 2012 before finishing his playing days at The Oval.

BOB WILLIS TROPHY AVERAGES 2020

Batting

	Mat	Inns	NO	Runs	HS	Ave	SR	100	50	4s	6s
RJ Burns	1	2	0	155	103	77.50	80.72	1	1	23	0
BT Foakes	2	4	1	227	118	75.66	45.03	1	1	26	1
J Overton	1	1	0	55	55	55.00	70.51	0	1	8	1
WG Jacks	5	10	2	248	84*	31.00	46.96	0	2	35	1
JL Smith	5	10	1	274	80	30.44	45.81	0	1	46	4
LJ Evans	3	6	0	172	65	28.66	63.23	0	1	29	1
HM Amla	1	2	0	44	26	22.00	53.01	0	0	4	2
SG Borthwick	5	10	0	192	92	19.20	37.13	0	2	23	1
SM Curran	1	2	0	35	21	17.50	72.91	0	0	5	0
M Morkel	1	2	0	33	33	16.50	126.92	0	0	7	0
R Clarke	3	6	0	91	30	15.16	43.12	0	0	17	0
MD Stoneman	4	8	0	106	45	13.25	35.69	0	0	20	0
RS Patel	3	6	0	78	44	13.00	37.86	0	0	10	0
JJ Roy	1	2	0	18	14	9.00	58.06	0	0	2	0
JPA Taylor	3	5	1	34	22	8.50	32.69	0	0	5	0
AW Finch	3	5	1	29	10	7.25	22.48	0	0	2	0
MP Dunn	3	6	1	28	12	5.60	18.91	0	0	4	0
AAP Atkinson	2	4	0	21	15	5.25	50.00	0	0	2	1
A Virdi	5	9	4	26	12	5.20	35.13	0	0	4	0
J Clark	1	2	0	8	7	4.00	10.25	0	0	0	0
D Moriarty	2	3	0	1	1	0.33	4.34	0	0	0	0

Bowling

	Overs	Mdns	Runs	Wkts	BBI	BBM	Ave	Econ	SR	5w	10w
R Clarke	88.0	23	190	13	5/20	6/75	14.61	2.15	40.6	1	0
SM Curran	39.5	7	124	7	4/39	7/124	17.71	3.11	34.1	0	0
D Moriarty	98.2	15	342	17	6/70	11/224	20.11	3.47	34.7	3	1
A Virdi	179.0	26	570	22	6/101	7/120	25.90	3.18	48.8	1	0
AW Finch	74.1	9	215	8	4/38	4/80	26.87	2.89	55.6	0	0
AAP Atkinson	35.4	5	128	4	2/57	3/102	32.00	3.58	53.5	0	0
JPA Taylor	46.0	6	171	4	2/31	2/37	42.75	3.71	69.0	0	0
MP Dunn	70.4	16	239	5	3/53	3/53	47.80	3.38	84.8	0	0
SG Borthwick	43.0	3	161	2	1/16	1/28	80.50	3.74	129.0	0	0
WG Jacks	6.0	0	17	0	-	-	-	2.83	-	0	0
M Morkel	14.0	7	28	0	-	-	-	2.00	-	0	0
J Clark	11.0	3	30	0	-	-	-	2.72	-	0	0
J Overton	21.0	3	70	0	-	-	-	3.33	-	0	0
RS Patel	14.0	1	72	0	-	-	-	5.14	-	0	0

Catches/Stumpings:
8 Smith, 6 Jacks, 5 Borthwick, Foakes (inc 1st), Patel, 4 Clarke, 2 Burns, Dunn, Overton, 1 Amla, Evans, Finch, Roy, Stoneman, Taylor, Virdi

VITALITY BLAST AVERAGES 2020

Batting

	Mat	Inns	NO	Runs	HS	Ave	SR	100	50	4s	6s
LJ Evans	11	11	3	363	88*	45.37	153.16	0	3	28	15
JJ Roy	5	5	0	206	72	41.20	131.21	0	3	27	2
HM Amla	8	8	1	271	75	38.71	124.88	0	3	27	5
WG Jacks	13	12	3	309	65	34.33	149.27	0	3	33	9
J Overton	10	5	2	103	40*	34.33	194.33	0	0	9	6
AAP Atkinson	9	3	2	30	14	30.00	176.47	0	0	2	2
JL Smith	9	5	2	89	38*	29.66	97.80	0	0	6	0
RJ Burns	13	9	3	141	56*	23.50	127.02	0	1	14	2
BT Foakes	12	8	2	141	60*	23.50	110.15	0	1	14	1
SG Borthwick	3	1	0	13	13	13.00	92.85	0	0	1	0
R Clarke	2	2	1	13	7	13.00	118.18	0	0	1	0
LE Plunkett	6	2	1	4	4	4.00	133.33	0	0	0	0
JPA Taylor	2	1	0	3	3	3.00	50.00	0	0	0	0
MP Dunn	4	1	1	0	0*	-	-	0	0	0	0
GJ Batty	10	-	-	-	-	-	-	-	-	-	-
J Clark	1	-	-	-	-	-	-	-	-	-	-
D Moriarty	13	-	-	-	-	-	-	-	-	-	-
MD Stoneman	1	-	-	-	-	-	-	-	-	-	-
RJW Topley	11	-	-	-	-	-	-	-	-	-	-

Bowling

	Overs	Mdns	Runs	Wkts	BBI	Ave	Econ	SR	4w	5w
GJ Batty	30.2	0	196	10	3/18	19.60	6.46	18.2	0	0
WG Jacks	32.2	0	209	13	4/15	16.07	6.46	14.9	1	0
SG Borthwick	9.0	0	60	3	2/34	20.00	6.66	18.0	0	0
D Moriarty	45.0	0	311	17	3/25	18.29	6.91	15.8	0	0
LE Plunkett	16.0	0	114	7	3/12	16.28	7.12	13.7	0	0
RJW Topley	40.0	0	291	15	4/20	19.40	7.27	16.0	1	0
R Clarke	4.0	0	30	1	1/17	30.00	7.50	24.0	0	0
MP Dunn	12.3	0	100	4	2/24	25.00	8.00	18.7	0	0
AAP Atkinson	21.0	0	200	7	2/18	28.57	9.52	18.0	0	0
J Overton	17.0	0	173	1	1/29	173.00	10.17	102.0	0	0
JPA Taylor	2.0	0	34	1	1/6	34.00	17.00	12.0	0	0

Catches/Stumpings:
10 Overton, 9 Foakes (inc 4st), 8 Burns, 7 Jacks, 4 Smith, 3 Atkinson, Clarke, Topley, 2 Borthwick, Evans, Plunkett, Roy, 1 Amla, Batty, Moriarty

SUSSEX

FORMED: 1839
HOME GROUND: The 1st Central County Ground, Hove
ONE-DAY NAME: Sussex Sharks
CAPTAIN: Ben Brown, Luke Wright (T20)
2020 RESULTS: BWT: 6/6 South Group; T20: Quarter-finalists
HONOURS: Championship: (3) 2003, 2006, 2007; Gillette/NatWest/C&G/FP Trophy: (5) 1963, 1964, 1978, 1986, 2006; Pro40/ National League/CB40/YB40/RL50: (2) 2008, 2009; Sunday League: 1982; T20 Cup: 2009

THE LOWDOWN

After three seasons at Hove, Jason Gillespie cut short his reign as coach at the end of last summer to take charge of South Australia. Ian Salisbury is tasked with revitalising the club's red-ball form, with James Kirtley looking after the T20 side. The short format still looks Sussex's best bet. Rashid Khan is due to return this summer – and Sussex will need him with left-arm spinner Danny Briggs joining Warwickshire – while ex-Kolpak David Wiese has agreed a T20 deal as an overseas player. Captain Luke Wright was in vintage form in 2020 and has signed on for another three years, although Ravi Bopara flopped badly in his first season at Hove. The Championship campaign should be boosted by the return of Stiaan van Zyl – absent last summer and now qualified as an overseas – and the belated arrival of Australian batsman Travis Head to play in all formats. The bowling stocks are healthy, with left-arm quick George Garton looking the real deal and off-spinner Jack Carson making a big impression in his debut season. Mitchell Claydon will miss the first two matches of the season after he was found guilty of using hand-sanitiser to tamper with the ball.

IN: Sean Hunt (unattached), Travis Head (Aus), Rashid Khan (Afg, T20)
OUT: Danny Briggs (War), Luke Wells (Lan), Harry Finch, Will Sheffield (both REL)

HEAD COACH: IAN SALISBURY

Salisbury was appointed spin-bowling coach in March 2020 and now takes charge of the Championship and 50-over sides. A former leg-spinner who played 15 Tests, Salisbury took 749 first-class wickets for Sussex and Surrey between 1989 and 2007. He became Surrey coach in 2012 but was sacked the following year, later becoming the first full-time head coach of the England Physical Disability team. Former Sussex and England paceman James Kirtley is the new T20 coach, while Sarah Taylor has joined the staff to oversee the wicketkeepers.

www.sussexcricket.co.uk / tel: 0844 264 0202

BOB WILLIS TROPHY AVERAGES 2020

Batting

	Mat	Inns	NO	Runs	HS	Ave	SR	100	50	4s	6s
PD Salt	4	8	0	290	80	36.25	64.87	0	3	38	3
D Wiese	1	2	0	61	57	30.50	89.70	0	1	6	3
TJ Haines	5	10	1	249	117	27.66	40.09	1	0	35	1
BC Brown	5	10	0	270	98	27.00	48.38	0	2	35	0
HZ Finch	5	10	0	259	69	25.90	49.61	0	2	47	0
DMW Rawlins	5	10	0	252	65	25.20	82.62	0	1	33	8
SC Meaker	3	6	1	106	42	21.20	64.24	0	0	17	0
AD Thomason	3	6	0	111	49	18.50	32.45	0	0	13	0
GHS Garton	4	8	1	109	54*	15.57	45.99	0	1	11	2
ME Claydon	4	8	3	77	24	15.40	66.37	0	0	13	0
OE Robinson	2	4	0	56	23	14.00	80.00	0	0	9	0
TGR Clark	4	8	0	110	65	13.75	40.74	0	1	19	0
HT Crocombe	4	8	4	45	15	11.25	26.16	0	0	6	0
J Coles	1	2	0	21	11	10.50	38.88	0	0	2	0
JJ Carson	4	8	0	57	21	7.12	35.62	0	0	5	2
WA Sheffield	1	2	0	7	6	3.50	21.21	0	0	1	0

Bowling

	Overs	Mdns	Runs	Wkts	BBI	BBM	Ave	Econ	SR	5w	10w
J Coles	13.0	0	35	3	2/32	3/35	11.66	2.69	26.0	0	0
OE Robinson	73.1	22	175	14	5/29	8/65	12.50	2.39	31.3	1	0
JJ Carson	108.1	17	340	15	5/93	6/139	22.66	3.14	43.2	1	0
GHS Garton	70.3	13	282	12	5/26	9/76	23.50	4.00	35.2	1	0
ME Claydon	102.0	25	294	11	3/23	4/82	26.72	2.88	55.6	0	0
D Wiese	13.0	3	32	1	1/32	1/32	32.00	2.46	78.0	0	0
TJ Haines	25.0	3	72	2	1/18	1/24	36.00	2.88	75.0	0	0
WA Sheffield	15.0	0	54	1	1/45	1/54	54.00	3.60	90.0	0	0
HT Crocombe	71.0	13	245	3	2/36	2/47	81.66	3.45	142.0	0	0
DMW Rawlins	69.5	8	261	3	1/14	2/138	87.00	3.73	139.6	0	0
SC Meaker	46.5	5	225	2	1/17	2/56	112.50	4.80	140.5	0	0

Catches/Stumpings:
11 Brown (inc 1st), 6 Finch, Salt, 4 Garton, 2 Clark, 1 Carson, Crocombe, Haines, Thomason, Wiese

VITALITY BLAST AVERAGES 2020

Batting

	Mat	Inns	NO	Runs	HS	Ave	SR	100	50	4s	6s
D Wiese	10	9	2	281	79*	40.14	145.59	0	1	20	13
LJ Wright	11	11	0	411	83	37.36	137.00	0	2	53	7
AD Thomason	4	4	2	73	47	36.50	125.86	0	0	5	2
PD Salt	8	8	0	211	56	26.37	167.46	0	1	23	9
GHS Garton	11	8	4	101	34*	25.25	116.09	0	0	9	3
DMW Rawlins	11	11	1	208	62*	20.80	132.48	0	1	17	12
CS MacLeod	7	7	0	102	40	14.57	95.32	0	0	12	0
HZ Finch	4	4	1	37	14	12.33	97.36	0	0	2	1
RS Bopara	11	11	1	122	24	12.20	93.84	0	0	7	3
TS Mills	9	1	0	10	10	10.00	100.00	0	0	0	1
DR Briggs	11	2	1	3	2*	3.00	60.00	0	0	0	0
OE Robinson	10	7	3	5	3	1.25	62.50	0	0	0	0
BC Brown	3	1	1	15	15*	-	214.28	0	0	2	0
WAT Beer	7	2	2	13	7*	-	130.00	0	0	1	0
CJ Jordan	2	1	1	3	3*	-	100.00	0	0	0	0
ME Claydon	2	-	-	-	-	-	-	-	-	-	-

Bowling

	Overs	Mdns	Runs	Wkts	BBI	Ave	Econ	SR	4w	5w
DR Briggs	38.0	0	249	12	3/17	20.75	6.55	19.0	0	0
CJ Jordan	7.0	0	47	2	1/19	23.50	6.71	21.0	0	0
DMW Rawlins	15.0	0	106	8	3/21	13.25	7.06	11.2	0	0
ME Claydon	8.0	0	61	3	2/25	20.33	7.62	16.0	0	0
GHS Garton	30.0	1	231	14	4/21	16.50	7.70	12.8	2	0
TS Mills	31.0	0	248	11	2/23	22.54	8.00	16.9	0	0
RS Bopara	11.0	0	92	0	-	-	8.36	-	0	0
WAT Beer	15.0	0	132	4	3/34	33.00	8.80	22.5	0	0
OE Robinson	33.0	1	301	9	2/25	33.44	9.12	22.0	0	0
D Wiese	11.1	0	113	1	1/7	113.00	10.11	67.0	0	0

Catches/Stumpings:
6 MacLeod, 5 Garton, Robinson, 4 Wiese, 3 Briggs, Rawlins, 2 Bopara, Brown, Salt, Wright, 1 Beer, Claydon, Finch, Mills

WARWICKSHIRE

FORMED: 1882
HOME GROUND: Edgbaston Stadium, Birmingham
T20 BLAST NAME: Birmingham Bears
CAPTAIN: Will Rhodes
2020 RESULTS: BWT: 3/6 Central Group; T20: 3/6 Central Group
HONOURS: Championship: (7) 1911, 1951, 1972, 1994, 1995, 2004, 2012; Gillette/NatWest/C&G/FP Trophy: (5) 1966, 1968, 1989, 1993, 1995; Benson & Hedges Cup: (2) 1994, 2002; Pro40/National League/CB40/YB40/RL50: (2) 2010, 2016; Sunday League: (3) 1980, 1994, 1997; T20 Cup: 2014

THE LOWDOWN

Warwickshire are heading into a new era, having now lost all the big-hitters who formed the bedrock of the side over the last decade and more. Rikki Clarke left in 2017, Keith Barker and Jonathan Trott the following year, and last summer the mighty trio of Ian Bell, Jeetan Patel and Tim Ambrose all retired. Furthermore, there is a new coach in Mark Robinson, appointed in January after the board cut ties with Jim Troughton, another Warwickshire old boy. It is, then, a delicate time in the club's transition. But club captain Will Rhodes appears to be warming to the task. His 207 at New Road in last year's Bob Willis Trophy was the highlight of Warwickshire's summer. The rest of the batting looks a little shaky, athough the arrival of Pieter Malan, the experienced South African opener, should help shore things up. The additions of Danny Briggs from Sussex and Tim Bresnan, signed from Yorkshire last July, bring much-needed experience as well as support for Oliver Hannon-Dalby, outstanding with the ball again last summer. The club have handed a first pro contract to 27-year-old Jake Lintott, a left-arm wrist-spinner who impressed on a short-term T20 deal.

IN: Tim Bresnan (Yor), Danny Briggs (Sus), Jake Lintott (unattached), Pieter Malan (SA, CC), Carlos Brathwaite (WI, T20)
OUT: Liam Banks (REL), Tim Ambrose, Ian Bell, Jeetan Patel (all RET)

FIRST-TEAM COACH: MARK ROBINSON

Warwickshire appointed Robinson in January after parting ways with Jim Troughton at the end of last summer. He won six trophies as Sussex coach between 2005 and 2015, including two Championship titles, before taking charge of England Women for a four-year stint which included the 2017 World Cup triumph. Born in Hull, Robinson took 584 first-class wickets as a seamer for Northants, Yorkshire and Sussex between 1987 and 2002. Paul Farbrace, the former England assistant coach, is the club's director of cricket.

BOB WILLIS TROPHY AVERAGES 2020

Batting

	Mat	Inns	NO	Runs	HS	Ave	SR	100	50	4s	6s
TT Bresnan	4	6	2	214	105	53.50	45.53	1	0	27	2
WMH Rhodes	5	9	1	423	207	52.87	51.83	1	0	51	0
DR Mousley	2	3	0	149	71	49.66	51.73	0	1	18	0
MJ Lamb	3	4	0	101	65	25.25	42.08	0	1	19	0
IR Bell	5	8	0	184	90	23.00	50.68	0	2	29	0
EA Brookes	1	2	1	21	15*	21.00	63.63	0	0	2	0
LC Norwell	1	2	1	19	12	19.00	118.75	0	0	3	1
SR Hain	5	8	0	146	65	18.25	35.26	0	2	20	0
AT Thomson	5	8	0	146	46	18.25	38.42	0	0	18	3
RM Yates	5	9	1	137	88	17.12	31.42	0	1	18	0
MGK Burgess	5	8	0	135	39	16.87	49.63	0	0	20	1
OJ Hannon-Dalby	5	7	3	43	19	10.75	37.39	0	0	8	0
CN Miles	3	5	2	27	13*	9.00	41.53	0	0	4	0
HJH Brookes	2	4	0	23	12	5.75	35.38	0	0	3	0
OP Stone	1	1	1	36	36*	-	120.00	0	0	5	1
RN Sidebottom	3	2	2	13	13*	-	38.23	0	0	2	0

Bowling

	Overs	Mdns	Runs	Wkts	BBI	BBM	Ave	Econ	SR	5w	10w
OP Stone	17.0	3	49	4	4/39	4/49	12.25	2.88	25.5	0	0
OJ Hannon-Dalby	196.3	53	523	25	6/33	12/110	20.92	2.66	47.1	2	1
LC Norwell	44.0	10	95	4	4/43	4/95	23.75	2.15	66.0	0	0
WMH Rhodes	79.4	16	245	10	4/46	5/98	24.50	3.07	47.8	0	0
TT Bresnan	116.0	36	275	10	4/99	4/59	27.50	2.37	69.6	0	0
RN Sidebottom	88.0	12	331	8	3/37	5/85	41.37	3.76	66.0	0	0
CN Miles	74.0	17	265	4	1/51	2/102	66.25	3.58	111.0	0	0
AT Thomson	100.0	14	276	4	2/3	3/119	69.00	2.76	150.0	0	0
HJH Brookes	51.0	6	203	2	2/66	2/118	101.50	3.98	153.0	0	0
EA Brookes	3.0	1	13	0	-	-	-	4.33	-	0	0
DR Mousley	9.0	1	37	0	-	-	-	4.11	-	0	0
RM Yates	22.0	9	37	0	-	-	-	1.68	-	0	0

Catches/Stumpings:
16 Burgess (inc 1st), 5 Bell, Bresnan, Hain, 2 Rhodes, Yates, 1 H Brookes, Hannon-Dalby, Lamb, Mousley, Stone, Thomson

VITALITY BLAST AVERAGES 2020

Batting

	Mat	Inns	NO	Runs	HS	Ave	SR	100	50	4s	6s
SR Hain	9	9	4	284	73*	56.80	139.21	0	3	25	10
DR Mousley	3	3	1	101	58*	50.50	126.25	0	1	7	3
AJ Hose	9	9	0	268	119	29.77	154.02	1	0	27	13
HJH Brookes	9	5	2	72	31*	24.00	130.90	0	0	8	2
RM Yates	4	4	0	89	37	22.25	158.92	0	0	8	6
IR Bell	3	3	0	41	28	13.66	93.18	0	0	3	1
OP Stone	8	4	1	41	22*	13.66	120.58	0	0	1	2
WMH Rhodes	9	9	0	120	46	13.33	117.64	0	0	12	2
MGK Burgess	8	8	3	64	17*	12.80	108.47	0	0	3	3
EJ Pollock	5	5	0	61	21	12.20	115.09	0	0	4	5
TT Bresnan	9	5	1	46	28	11.50	117.94	0	0	4	1
JB Lintott	9	4	1	27	12	9.00	96.42	0	0	3	0
V Kelley	1	1	0	5	5	5.00	50.00	0	0	0	0
JS Patel	9	4	1	5	4*	1.66	50.00	0	0	0	0
DP Sibley	3	3	0	4	4	1.33	57.14	0	0	1	0
LC Norwell	1	-	-	-	-	-	-	-	-	-	-

Bowling

	Overs	Mdns	Runs	Wkts	BBI	Ave	Econ	SR	4w	5w
JB Lintott	30.0	0	189	10	3/11	18.90	6.30	18.0	0	0
JS Patel	33.0	0	281	6	2/27	46.83	8.51	33.0	0	0
OP Stone	28.0	0	245	14	3/45	17.50	8.75	12.0	0	0
WMH Rhodes	9.0	0	79	0	-	-	8.77	-	0	0
TT Bresnan	25.5	0	232	12	3/25	19.33	8.98	12.9	0	0
HJH Brookes	31.0	1	287	11	2/24	26.09	9.25	16.9	0	0
DR Mousley	2.0	0	22	1	1/9	22.00	11.00	12.0	0	0
LC Norwell	4.0	0	53	1	1/53	53.00	13.25	24.0	0	0

Catches/Stumpings:
7 Lintott, 5 Burgess, 4 Hose, Sibley, Stone, 3 Bresnan, Patel, 2 Kelley (inc 2st), 1 Bell, Hain, Mousley, Rhodes, Yates

WORCESTERSHIRE

FORMED: 1865
HOME GROUND: New Road, Worcester
ONE-DAY NAME: Worcestershire Rapids
CAPTAIN: Joe Leach, Moeen Ali (T20)
2020 RESULTS: BWT: 2/6 Central Group; T20: 6/6 Central Group
HONOURS: Championship: (5) 1964, 1965, 1974, 1988, 1989; Gillette/NatWest/C&G/FP Trophy: 1994; Benson & Hedges Cup: 1991; Pro40/National League/CB40/YB40/RL50: 2007; Sunday League: (3) 1971, 1987, 1988; T20 Cup: 2018

THE LOWDOWN

Worcestershire were only a whisker from reaching last summer's Bob Willis Trophy final, denied in the end by a brilliant Tom Lammonby hundred in the showdown against Somerset. After finishing ninth in Division Two in 2019, this was a welcome return to form in red-ball cricket. The big difference from 2019 was the batting, with four Worcestershire players among the top 15 run-scorers in the country. Opener Jake Libby, second on that list with 498 runs in nine innings, enjoyed a dream first season after joining from Notts, and Tom Fell scored his first hundred since returning from testicular cancer in 2016. The four-pronged seam attack of Leach, Barnard, Tongue and Morris looks settled, with 22-year-old Dillon Pennington pushing for first-team selection. The missing piece is a frontline spinner. Long-serving wicketkeeper Ben Cox signed a new three-year contract but may face stiff competition from keeper-batsman Gareth Roderick, who joined from Gloucestershire last July. After back-to-back T20 finals in 2018 and 2019, the Rapids will be keen to write off last summer's no-show as a blip. The arrival of Ben Dwarshuis, the Aussie left-arm quick who starred in the Sydney Sixers' recent Big Bash triumph, should help in that regard.

IN: Ben Dwarshuis (Aus, T20)
OUT: Wayne Parnell, George Scrimshaw, Ben Twohig, Olly Westbury (all REL)

FIRST-TEAM COACH: ALEX GIDMAN

Gidman was promoted from Second XI coach after playing a major role in the club's first T20 title in 2018, having joined the backroom staff earlier that year in the wake of Steve Rhodes' departure. A former Gloucestershire captain, Gidman turned to coaching in 2016 after spending one season as a player at New Road. Bowling coach Alan Richardson will take charge of the 50-over team while Gidman is with Birmingham Phoenix for The Hundred.

 www.wccc.co.uk / tel: 01905 748474

BOB WILLIS TROPHY AVERAGES 2020

Batting

	Mat	Inns	NO	Runs	HS	Ave	SR	100	50	4s	6s
JD Libby	5	9	0	498	184	55.33	47.83	1	3	56	2
BL D'Oliveira	5	8	1	367	174	52.42	68.21	1	1	48	2
TC Fell	5	9	2	336	110*	48.00	45.28	1	1	41	0
OB Cox	5	8	3	225	45*	45.00	65.02	0	0	27	2
DKH Mitchell	5	9	0	384	110	42.66	46.60	1	2	50	0
JA Haynes	5	9	2	285	51	40.71	53.37	0	2	37	0
EG Barnard	5	6	2	84	48*	21.00	51.53	0	0	5	1
MH Wessels	5	8	0	157	88	19.62	92.35	0	1	25	0
J Leach	5	6	1	47	17	9.40	65.27	0	0	5	1
DY Pennington	3	4	2	15	11*	7.50	51.72	0	0	3	0
JC Tongue	4	3	2	1	1*	1.00	11.11	0	0	0	0
CAJ Morris	3	-	-	-	-	-	-	-	-	-	-

Bowling

	Overs	Mdns	Runs	Wkts	BBI	BBM	Ave	Econ	SR	5w	10w
EG Barnard	148.5	40	390	18	4/25	7/78	21.66	2.62	49.6	0	0
CAJ Morris	99.3	21	315	14	5/80	6/104	22.50	3.16	42.6	1	0
DY Pennington	90.1	22	248	11	3/30	5/106	22.54	2.75	49.1	0	0
JD Libby	14.4	2	46	2	2/45	2/45	23.00	3.13	44.0	0	0
J Leach	169.3	44	490	19	4/67	6/79	25.78	2.89	53.5	0	0
JC Tongue	117.1	26	363	14	3/38	6/80	25.92	3.09	50.2	0	0
BL D'Oliveira	95.0	13	312	6	2/31	4/85	52.00	3.28	95.0	0	0
DKH Mitchell	31.0	7	63	1	1/7	1/7	63.00	2.03	186.0	0	0

Catches/Stumpings:
25 Cox, 7 Mitchell, 5 Barnard, 4 Wessels, 3 Fell, 2 D'Oliveira, Libby, 1 Haynes, Leach, Pennington

VITALITY BLAST AVERAGES 2020

Batting

	Mat	Inns	NO	Runs	HS	Ave	SR	100	50	4s	6s
JD Libby	9	9	1	318	75*	39.75	137.06	0	2	30	5
HD Rutherford	9	9	0	352	100	39.11	160.00	1	1	33	19
DKH Mitchell	8	5	3	67	45	33.50	152.27	0	0	3	4
OB Cox	9	9	3	176	56*	29.33	129.41	0	1	17	5
BL D'Oliveira	8	7	2	143	61	28.60	128.82	0	1	9	5
JA Haynes	7	7	0	149	41	21.28	137.96	0	0	18	4
RA Whiteley	9	9	2	118	25	16.85	131.11	0	0	9	4
MH Wessels	6	6	0	79	30	13.16	102.59	0	0	8	0
DY Pennington	6	3	2	12	10*	12.00	200.00	0	0	2	0
EG Barnard	9	6	1	53	16	10.60	132.50	0	0	5	2
PR Brown	8	2	2	14	7*	-	87.50	0	0	1	0
AW Finch	5	1	1	3	3*	-	60.00	0	0	0	0
CAJ Morris	6	1	1	1	1*	-	50.00	0	0	0	0

Bowling

	Overs	Mdns	Runs	Wkts	BBI	Ave	Econ	SR	4w	5w
JD Libby	6.0	0	43	0	-	-	7.16	-	0	0
DKH Mitchell	28.0	0	218	6	3/35	36.33	7.78	28.0	0	0
BL D'Oliveira	22.0	0	187	3	1/11	62.33	8.50	44.0	0	0
EG Barnard	30.0	0	260	10	3/44	26.00	8.66	18.0	0	0
AW Finch	16.0	0	147	4	1/22	36.75	9.18	24.0	0	0
CAJ Morris	19.2	0	193	6	2/44	32.16	9.98	19.3	0	0
DY Pennington	21.0	0	211	5	2/27	42.20	10.04	25.2	0	0
PR Brown	30.4	0	333	8	3/39	41.62	10.85	23.0	0	0
RA Whiteley	1.0	0	13	0	-	-	13.00	-	0	0

Catches/Stumpings:
6 Whiteley, 4 Barnard, Cox, Mitchell, 3 D'Oliveira, Wessels, 2 Haynes, Morris, Pennington, 1 Brown, Libby, Rutherford

YORKSHIRE

FORMED: 1863
HOME GROUND: Emerald Headingley Stadium, Leeds
ONE-DAY NAME: Yorkshire Vikings
CAPTAIN: Steven Patterson, David Willey (T20)
2020 RESULTS: BWT: 1/6 North Group; T20: 5/6 North Group
HONOURS: County Championship: (33) 1893, 1896, 1898, 1900, 1901, 1902, 1905, 1908, 1912, 1919, 1922, 1923, 1924, 1925, 1931, 1932, 1933, 1935, 1937, 1938, 1939, 1946, 1949, 1959, 1960, 1962, 1963, 1966, 1967, 1968, 2001, 2014, 2015; Gillette/NatWest/C&G/FP Trophy: (3) 1965, 1969, 2002; Benson & Hedges Cup: 1987; Sunday League: 1983

THE LOWDOWN

Buoyed by strong performances in the Bob Willis Trophy, CEO Mark Arthur believes this is the strongest Yorkshire squad since they won back-to-back Championship titles in 2014 and 2015. The club finished top of their group last summer and missed out on a Lord's final by just three points. Winning three out of five was good going, and it could have been even better if rain hadn't ruined their other two fixtures. Dawid Malan stole the limelight with a career-best 219 against Derbyshire but there were promising signs from young talents such as Harry Brook, who made three fifties in seven innings, and allrounder Jordan Thompson, who came within two runs of a maiden hundred and finished as Yorkshire's leading wicket-taker (15 at 16.40). All the seamers did well, although Duanne Olivier's tendency to leak runs might come under greater scrutiny now that he holds one of the overseas slots. Dom Bess may have been the signing of the summer, finally offering Yorkshire a top-class spin option in four-day cricket. But much of the optimism drained away after former allrounder Azeem Rafiq spoke out about racial discrimination during his time at Headingley. Rafiq filed a legal complaint against the club in February.

IN: Dom Bess (Som), Lockie Ferguson (NZ, T20)
OUT: Ed Barnes (Lei), Jared Warner (Glo), James Logan (REL)

HEAD COACH: ANDREW GALE

After a 14-year career at Yorkshire – eight of them as skipper – Gale made the transition from captain to coach following Jason Gillespie's departure in 2016. Under Gillespie, Yorkshire won the Championship in 2014 and 2015, but success has been elusive over the last few years. Gale works with director of cricket Martyn Moxon, while Paul Grayson, who took charge of Essex between 2007 and 2015, is the batting coach.

BOB WILLIS TROPHY AVERAGES 2020

THE YORKSHIRE
COUNTY CRICKET CLUB

Batting

	Mat	Inns	NO	Runs	HS	Ave	SR	100	50	4s	6s
DJ Malan	3	5	0	332	219	66.40	78.85	1	1	45	5
JA Thompson	5	6	1	234	98	46.80	60.62	0	2	31	5
JA Tattersall	5	7	1	265	71	44.16	36.15	0	3	32	0
HC Brook	5	7	1	258	66*	43.00	65.31	0	3	32	7
JM Bairstow	2	3	0	102	75	34.00	50.49	0	1	19	0
GCH Hill	2	2	1	33	29	33.00	49.25	0	0	6	0
A Lyth	5	8	1	220	103	31.42	40.59	1	1	26	4
T Kohler-Cadmore	5	8	1	127	41	18.14	65.46	0	0	21	0
BO Coad	2	2	0	32	28	16.00	76.19	0	0	5	0
D Olivier	4	4	1	33	20*	11.00	39.75	0	0	6	0
WAR Fraine	3	4	0	32	14	8.00	33.33	0	0	5	0
JW Shutt	3	4	3	7	7*	7.00	11.86	0	0	1	0
SA Patterson	4	4	0	23	11	5.75	43.39	0	0	3	0
TW Loten	2	2	0	11	11	5.50	18.96	0	0	1	0
JD Warner	1	1	0	4	4	4.00	22.22	0	0	0	0
MD Fisher	2	2	0	2	1	1.00	5.88	0	0	0	0
DJ Leech	2	2	1	1	1	1.00	4.16	0	0	0	0

Bowling

	Overs	Mdns	Runs	Wkts	BBI	BBM	Ave	Econ	SR	5w	10w
BO Coad	69.0	28	87	12	5/18	8/41	7.25	1.26	34.5	1	0
DJ Malan	6.0	1	24	2	2/24	2/24	12.00	4.00	18.0	0	0
JA Thompson	104.0	25	246	15	5/31	5/51	16.40	2.36	41.6	1	0
SA Patterson	106.3	37	197	11	3/27	4/82	17.90	1.84	58.0	0	0
MD Fisher	67.0	22	180	10	4/54	6/97	18.00	2.68	40.2	0	0
JD Warner	9.0	0	23	1	1/23	1/23	23.00	2.55	54.0	0	0
DJ Leech	34.0	5	134	4	2/72	2/62	33.50	3.94	51.0	0	0
D Olivier	91.0	18	364	10	3/29	5/117	36.40	4.00	54.6	0	0
A Lyth	23.0	3	75	2	1/12	1/12	37.50	3.26	69.0	0	0
JW Shutt	19.2	0	104	2	2/14	2/63	52.00	5.37	58.0	0	0
GCH Hill	25.0	8	54	1	1/27	1/27	54.00	2.16	150.0	0	0
HC Brook	14.1	1	49	0	-	-	-	3.45	-	0	0

Catches/Stumpings:
9 Tattersall, 5 Bairstow, Lyth, 4 Brook, 3 Olivier, 2 Fisher, Kohler-Cadmore, Malan, Shutt, Thompson, 1 Coad, Fraine

VITALITY BLAST AVERAGES 2020

Batting

	Mat	Inns	NO	Runs	HS	Ave	SR	100	50	4s	6s
JE Root	5	5	1	278	65	69.50	144.79	0	4	32	4
A Lyth	8	8	0	308	71	38.50	157.94	0	3	31	12
T Kohler-Cadmore	4	4	1	110	85*	36.66	137.50	0	1	4	6
JA Tattersall	7	5	3	63	22*	31.50	114.54	0	0	4	1
WAR Fraine	8	8	2	163	44*	27.16	187.35	0	0	11	12
HC Brook	8	8	1	189	50*	27.00	145.38	0	1	17	6
DJ Willey	2	1	0	27	27	27.00	158.82	0	0	3	0
JA Thompson	8	7	1	89	44	14.83	148.33	0	0	6	5
DJ Malan	4	4	0	36	27	9.00	83.72	0	0	5	0
D Olivier	3	1	0	8	8	8.00	100.00	0	0	0	1
GCH Hill	4	3	0	21	14	7.00	87.50	0	0	2	0
JH Wharton	2	2	0	12	8	6.00	63.15	0	0	1	0
BO Coad	4	2	0	11	7	5.50	55.00	0	0	0	0
MW Pillans	4	2	0	10	5	5.00	111.11	0	0	1	0
MD Fisher	4	2	0	0	0	0.00	0.00	0	0	0	0
JE Poysden	4	1	1	0	0*	-	-	0	0	0	0
ML Revis	2	1	1	0	0*	-	0.00	0	0	0	0
JW Shutt	4	2	2	0	0*	-	0.00	0	0	0	0
BD Birkhead	1	-	-	-	-	-	-	-	-	-	-
SA Wisniewski	2	-	-	-	-	-	-	-	-	-	-

Bowling

	Overs	Mdns	Runs	Wkts	BBI	Ave	Econ	SR	4w	5w
A Lyth	19.0	0	125	3	2/28	41.66	6.57	38.0	0	0
JE Root	17.0	0	112	7	2/7	16.00	6.58	14.5	0	0
D Olivier	11.0	0	73	5	2/16	14.60	6.63	13.2	0	0
DJ Willey	7.1	0	49	5	3/26	9.80	6.83	8.6	0	0
GCH Hill	6.3	0	50	1	1/9	50.00	7.69	39.0	0	0
SA Wisniewski	4.0	0	32	0	-	-	8.00	-	0	0
DJ Malan	2.0	0	16	0	-	-	8.00	-	0	0
MD Fisher	15.0	0	122	8	3/21	15.25	8.13	11.2	0	0
BO Coad	15.0	0	129	6	3/40	21.50	8.60	15.0	0	0
JE Poysden	13.0	0	114	5	3/32	22.80	8.76	15.6	0	0
JW Shutt	12.0	0	107	2	1/24	53.50	8.91	36.0	0	0
JA Thompson	22.0	0	204	8	2/25	25.50	9.27	16.5	0	0
MW Pillans	11.1	0	128	2	1/22	64.00	11.46	33.5	0	0
HC Brook	1.0	0	13	1	1/13	13.00	13.00	6.0	0	0

Catches/Stumpings:
8 Tattersall (inc 2st), 7 Brook, 4 Fraine, Lyth, Thompson, 3 Kohler-Cadmore, 2 Fisher, Hill, Root, Willey, 1 Birkhead, Coad, Olivier, Pillans, Poysden, Shutt

Men's Players

MOHAMMAD ABBAS

RHB / RMF / R0 / W1

FULL NAME: Mohammad Abbas
BORN: March 10, 1990, Sialkot, Punjab
SQUAD NO: 38
TEAMS: Pakistan, Hampshire, Khan Research Laboratories, Islamabad, Leicestershire, Multan Sultans, Pakistan Television, Rawalpindi, Sialkot, Southern Punjab, Sui Northern Gas Pipelines Limited
ROLE: Bowler
DEBUT: Test: 2017; ODI: 2019; First-class: 2009; List A: 2009; T20: 2013

BEST BATTING: 40 Khan Research Laboratories vs Karachi Whites, Karachi, 2016
BEST BOWLING: 8-46 Khan Research Laboratories vs Karachi Whites, Karachi, 2016
COUNTY CAP: 2018 (Leicestershire)

TWITTER: @Mohmmadabbas11
NOTES: Hampshire have signed the Pakistan seamer to play Championship cricket for the first two months of the season, hoping he will form a potent new-ball pair with fellow overseas paceman Kyle Abbott. Abbas had a hugely successful spell at Leicestershire in 2018 and 2019, taking 50 Championship wickets at 17.72 in his debut season in county cricket and following it up with 29 at 25.75 the next summer. He was due to play for Nottinghamshire last year but the deal was cancelled in the wake of the pandemic. A late bloomer, the 30-year-old has emerged as one of the most skilful seamers in the world, becoming the joint-second-fastest to take 50 Test wickets for Pakistan (10 matches), behind only Yasir Shah (9)

Batting	Mat	Inns	NO	Runs	HS	Ave	SR	100	50	Ct	St
Tests	23	33	14	109	29	5.73	17.19	0	0	6	0
ODIs	3	-	-	-	-	-	-	-	-	0	0
First-class	116	164	60	715	40	6.87	27.55	0	0	32	0
List A	55	31	13	137	15*	7.61	53.10	0	0	13	0
T20s	32	10	7	32	15*	10.66	152.38	0	0	7	0
Bowling	**Mat**	**Balls**	**Runs**	**Wkts**	**BBI**	**BBM**	**Ave**	**Econ**	**SR**	**5w**	**10**
Tests	23	4738	1916	84	5/33	10/95	22.80	2.42	56.4	4	1
ODIs	3	162	153	1	1/44	1/44	153.00	5.66	162.0	0	0
First-class	116	22738	10191	485	8/46	14/93	21.01	2.68	46.8	35	11
List A	55	2693	2191	75	4/31	4/31	29.21	4.88	35.9	0	0
T20s	32	678	971	26	3/22	3/22	37.34	8.59	26.0	0	0

KYLE ABBOTT

RHB / RFM / R0 / W3

FULL NAME: Kyle John Abbott
BORN: June 18, 1987, Empangeni, KwaZulu-Natal, South Africa
SQUAD NO: 11
NICKNAME: Jimmy
TEAMS: South Africa, Hampshire, Dolphins, Jafna Stallions, Kings XI Punjab, KwaZulu-Natal, Middlesex, Titans, Worcestershire
ROLE: Bowler
DEBUT: Test: 2013; ODI: 2013; T20I: 2013; First-class: 2009; List A: 2009; T20: 2011

BEST BATTING: 97* Hampshire vs Lancashire, Old Trafford, 2017
BEST BOWLING: 9-40 Hampshire vs Somerset, Southampton, 2019
COUNTY CAP: 2017 (Hampshire)

MOST EXCITING DAY AS A CRICKETER? Playing in the 2015 World Cup
CHILDHOOD SPORTING HERO? Lance Klusener
IF YOU COULD TAKE ONE COUNTY CRICKETER'S BEST SHOT AND ADD IT TO YOUR OWN GAME? James Vince's cover-drive
TOUGHEST OPPONENT IN COUNTY CRICKET? Alastair Cook
MOST ECCENTRIC TEAMMATE? Aneurin Donald – he's Welsh
WHAT WOULD YOU DO IF YOU WERE IN CHARGE OF COUNTY CRICKET? Go back to a two-division Championship, be more lenient on over-rates
FAVOURITE SMELL? A fire in the African bush
TWITTER: @Kyle_Abbott87

Batting	Mat	Inns	NO	Runs	HS	Ave	SR	100	50	Ct	St
Tests	11	14	0	95	17	6.78	28.10	0	0	4	0
ODIs	28	13	4	76	23	8.44	60.31	0	0	7	0
T20Is	21	6	4	23	9*	11.50	115.00	0	0	7	0
First-class	114	157	30	2427	97*	19.11	47.65	0	9	18	0
List A	105	51	20	507	56	16.35	84.50	0	1	28	0
T20s	155	54	30	324	30	13.50	117.81	0	0	33	0
Bowling	**Mat**	**Balls**	**Runs**	**Wkts**	**BBI**	**BBM**	**Ave**	**Econ**	**SR**	**5w**	**10**
Tests	11	2081	886	39	7/29	9/68	22.71	2.55	53.3	3	0
ODIs	28	1303	1051	34	4/21	4/21	30.91	4.83	38.3	0	0
T20Is	21	436	579	26	3/20	3/20	22.26	7.96	16.7	0	0
First-class	114	19663	9256	442	9/40	17/86	20.94	2.82	44.4	30	4
List A	105	4762	4153	142	4/21	4/21	29.24	5.23	33.5	0	0
T20s	155	3228	4457	155	5/14	5/14	28.75	8.28	20.8	1	0

TOM ABELL RHB / RM / R0 / W0 / MVP18

FULL NAME: Thomas Benjamin Abell
BORN: March 5, 1994, Taunton
SQUAD NO: 28
HEIGHT: 5ft 11in
NICKNAME: Siddy
EDUCATION: Taunton School; University of Exeter
TEAMS: Somerset, England Lions, Rangpur Rangers
ROLE: Batsman
DEBUT: First-class: 2014; List A: 2015; T20: 2016

BEST BATTING: 135 Somerset vs Lancashire, Old Trafford, 2016
BEST BOWLING: 4-39 Somerset vs Warwickshire, Edgbaston, 2019
COUNTY CAP: 2018

MOST EXCITING DAY AS A CRICKETER? Winning the One-Day Cup in 2019
CHILDHOOD SPORTING HERO? Jonny Wilkinson
FIRST CRICKET CLUB? Taunton CC, Somerset
IF YOU COULD TAKE ONE COUNTY CRICKETER'S BEST SHOT AND ADD IT TO YOUR OWN GAME? James Hildreth's cover-drive
TOUGHEST OPPONENT IN COUNTY CRICKET? Morné Morkel
MOST ECCENTRIC TEAMMATE? Eddie Byrom – he's the nicest guy in the world but just lives in his own world!
WHAT WOULD YOU DO IF YOU WERE IN CHARGE OF COUNTY CRICKET? Stick with a two-division Championship and make sure that everyone plays each other twice, reinstate the Lord's final for 50-over cricket
STRANGEST THING YOU'VE DONE DURING LOCKDOWN? Trying to learn the ukelele
FAVOURITE SMELL? Petrol
TWITTER: @tomabell1

Batting	Mat	Inns	NO	Runs	HS	Ave	SR	100	50	Ct	St
First-class	81	146	14	4241	135	32.12	48.96	7	24	55	0
List A	25	21	1	636	106	31.80	79.30	1	1	7	0
T20s	46	41	9	974	101*	30.43	140.95	1	4	31	0
Bowling	**Mat**	**Balls**	**Runs**	**Wkts**	**BBI**	**BBM**	**Ave**	**Econ**	**SR**	**5w**	**10**
First-class	81	1710	1008	40	4/39	6/70	25.20	3.53	42.7	0	0
List A	25	36	26	2	2/19	2/19	13.00	4.33	18.0	0	0
T20s	46	60	100	2	1/11	1/11	50.00	10.00	30.0	0	0

COLIN ACKERMANN RHB / OB / R0 / W0 / MVP5

FULL NAME: Colin Niel Ackermann
BORN: April 4, 1991, George, Cape Province, South Africa
SQUAD NO: 48
HEIGHT: 6ft 1in
NICKNAME: Ackers
EDUCATION: Grey High School, Port Elizabeth; University of South Africa
TEAMS: Netherlands, Leicestershire, Eastern Province, South Africa U19, Warriors
ROLE: Allrounder
DEBUT: T20I: 2019; First-class: 2010; List A: 2010; T20: 2011

BEST BATTING: 196* Leicestershire vs Middlesex, Leicester, 2018
BEST BOWLING: 5-69 Leicestershire vs Sussex, Hove, 2019

MOST EXCITING DAY AS A CRICKETER? Making my professional debut in 2010
FAMILY TIES? My younger brother Travis Ackermann plays for South Western Districts in South Africa
CHILDHOOD SPORTING HERO? Jacques Kallis
BIGGEST INFLUENCE ON YOUR DEVELOPMENT AS A CRICKETER (EXCLUDING PARENTS)? Attending Grey High School, Port Elizabeth
FIRST CRICKET CLUB? Kibworth CC, Leicestershire
IF YOU COULD TAKE ONE COUNTY CRICKETER'S BEST SHOT AND ADD IT TO YOUR OWN GAME? Dieter Klein's pull
STRANGEST THING YOU'VE DONE DURING LOCKDOWN? Shaving my hair with a beard trimmer
FAVOURITE SMELL? Lamb chops on the braai
TWITTER: @ackers38

Batting	Mat	Inns	NO	Runs	HS	Ave	SR	100	50	Ct	St
T20Is	11	11	3	243	43*	30.37	123.97	0	0	4	0
First-class	130	228	27	8243	196*	41.00	49.61	17	52	118	0
List A	83	76	14	2260	152*	36.45	78.74	2	15	55	0
T20s	116	111	17	2700	79*	28.72	120.10	0	15	57	0
Bowling	**Mat**	**Balls**	**Runs**	**Wkts**	**BBI**	**BBM**	**Ave**	**Econ**	**SR**	**5w**	**10**
T20Is	11	150	147	5	1/6	1/6	29.40	5.88	30.0	0	0
First-class	130	5003	2699	64	5/69	5/69	42.17	3.23	78.1	1	0
List A	83	2065	1663	42	4/48	4/48	39.59	4.83	49.1	0	0
T20s	116	1256	1452	55	7/18	7/18	26.40	6.93	22.8	1	0

BEN AITCHISON RHB / RFM / R0 / W0

FULL NAME: Benjamin William Aitchison
BORN: July 6, 1999, Southport, Lancashire
SQUAD NO: 11
HEIGHT: 6ft 4in
NICKNAME: Biggen
EDUCATION: Merchant Taylors' School, Crosby, Merseyside
TEAMS: Derbyshire
ROLE: Bowler
DEBUT: First-class: 2020

BEST BATTING: 8 Derbyshire vs Nottinghamshire, Trent Bridge, 2020
BEST BOWLING: 3-55 Derbyshire vs Nottinghamshire, Trent Bridge, 2020

MOST EXCITING DAY AS A CRICKETER? Chasing down 365 to win at Trent Bridge on the fourth day of my first-class debut
CHILDHOOD SPORTING HERO? Steven Gerrard
BIGGEST INFLUENCE ON YOUR DEVELOPMENT AS A CRICKETER (EXCLUDING PARENTS)? Jason Coleman, current head coach of Parramatta District CC in Sydney
IF YOU COULD TAKE ONE COUNTY CRICKETER'S BEST SHOT AND ADD IT TO YOUR OWN GAME? Wayne Madsen's upper-cut
TOUGHEST OPPONENT IN COUNTY CRICKET? Dawid Malan
WHAT WOULD YOU DO IF YOU WERE IN CHARGE OF COUNTY CRICKET? Offer the second new ball earlier, have shorter hours of play
STRANGEST THING YOU'VE DONE DURING LOCKDOWN? Running in a cricket jumper
FAVOURITE SMELL? Crispy bacon
GUILTY PLEASURE? Rom-coms
TWITTER: @Benaitchison123

Batting	Mat	Inns	NO	Runs	HS	Ave	SR	100	50	Ct	St
First-class	3	1	0	8	8	8.00	100.00	0	0	2	0
Bowling	**Mat**	**Balls**	**Runs**	**Wkts**	**BBI**	**BBM**	**Ave**	**Econ**	**SR**	**5w**	**10**
First-class	3	468	211	6	3/55	4/112	35.16	2.70	78.0	0	0

KASEY ALDRIDGE

RHB / RFM / R0 / W0

FULL NAME: Kasey Luke Aldridge
BORN: December 24, 2000, Bristol
SQUAD NO: 5
HEIGHT: 6ft 4in
NICKNAME: Fred
EDUCATION: Millfield School, Somerset
TEAMS: Somerset, England U19
ROLE: Allrounder

MOST EXCITING DAY AS A CRICKETER? Playing for England in last year's U19 World Cup
CHILDHOOD SPORTING HERO? Andrew Flintoff
BIGGEST INFLUENCE ON YOUR DEVELOPMENT AS A CRICKETER (EXCLUDING PARENTS)? My prep-school coach Dave Beal
FIRST CRICKET CLUB? Glastonbury CC, Somerset
IF YOU COULD TAKE ONE COUNTY CRICKETER'S BEST SHOT AND ADD IT TO YOUR OWN GAME? Steven Davies's cover-drive
MOST ECCENTRIC TEAMMATE? Ollie Sale – for his haircuts
FAVOURITE SMELL? Dry milk powder
IF YOU WERE AN ANIMAL, WHICH WOULD IT BE? An eagle
GUILTY PLEASURE? Domino's Pizza
TWITTER: @KaseyAldridge1
NOTES: The England U19 fast bowler has come through the Somerset Academy and signed a new two-year contract in February. Aldridge made his England U19 debut in 2019 and took 5-18 against West Indies at North Sound later that year before heading to South Africa with the World Cup squad. A capable batsman down the order, Aldridge has the potential to develop into a genuine allrounder. "In addition to Kasey's qualities with the bat, his key attributes as a bowler are that he possesses pace and bounce, and it has been pleasing to see him bowl a threatening line and length more often," said Steve Snell, Somerset's Academy director

MOEEN ALI

LHB / OB / R2 / W0

WORCESTERSHIRE

FULL NAME: Moeen Munir Ali
BORN: June 18, 1987, Birmingham
SQUAD NO: 8
HEIGHT: 6ft
NICKNAME: Brother Mo
EDUCATION: Moseley School, Birmingham
TEAMS: England, Worcestershire, Cape Town Blitz, Chennai Super Kings, Matabeleland Tuskers, Multan Sultans, Royal Challengers Bangalore, Warwickshire
ROLE: Allrounder
DEBUT: Test: 2014; ODI: 2014; T20I: 2014; First-class: 2005; List A: 2006; T20: 2007

BEST BATTING: 250 Worcestershire vs Glamorgan, Worcester, 2013
BEST BOWLING: 6-29 Worcestershire vs Lancashire, Old Trafford, 2012
COUNTY CAP: 2007 (Worcestershire)

FAMILY TIES? My cousin Kabir played for England and my brother Kadeer played for Worcestershire, Gloucestershire and Leicestershire
CHILDHOOD SPORTING HERO? Saeed Anwar
FIRST CRICKET CLUB? Moseley Ashfield CC, Birmingham
NOTES: After three seasons at Royal Challengers Bangalore, Moeen was bought by Chennai Super Kings for the 2021 edition of the tournament, scheduled to take place in April and May

Batting	Mat	Inns	NO	Runs	HS	Ave	SR	100	50	Ct	St
Tests	61	106	8	2831	155*	28.88	51.56	5	14	33	0
ODIs	106	86	14	1790	128	24.86	103.22	3	5	32	0
T20Is	34	31	8	392	72*	17.04	134.70	0	2	8	0
First-class	195	334	27	11251	250	36.64	55.19	20	69	113	0
List A	223	197	16	5085	158	28.09	102.35	11	20	65	0
T20s	167	158	16	3513	121*	24.73	140.18	2	19	54	0
Bowling	**Mat**	**Balls**	**Runs**	**Wkts**	**BBI**	**BBM**	**Ave**	**Econ**	**SR**	**5w**	**10**
Tests	61	11338	6850	189	6/53	10/112	36.24	3.62	59.9	5	1
ODIs	106	4924	4305	85	4/46	4/46	50.64	5.24	57.9	0	0
T20Is	34	440	630	17	2/21	2/21	37.05	8.59	25.8	0	0
First-class	195	24068	14191	376	6/29	12/96	37.74	3.53	64.0	12	2
List A	223	8035	7188	160	4/33	4/33	44.92	5.36	50.2	0	0
T20s	167	2315	2966	110	5/34	5/34	26.96	7.68	21.0	1	0

FINN ALLEN

RHB / WK

FULL NAME: Finnley Hugh Allen
BORN: April 22, 1999, Auckland, New Zealand
SQUAD NO: TBC
EDUCATION: Saint Kentigern College, Auckland
TEAMS: Lancashire, Auckland, New Zealand U19, Wellington
ROLE: Batsman
DEBUT: First-class: 2018; List A: 2018; T20: 2017

BEST BATTING: 92* Wellington Firebirds vs Otago Volts, Dunedin, 2021 (T20)

NOTES: The New Zealand batsman shot to prominence over the winter after a series of blistering displays at the top of the order in his country's domestic T20 competition. Allen was the standout performer of a Wellington Firebirds team which defended their Super Smash title in February, top-scoring with 512 runs in just 11 innings at the astonishing strike rate of 193.93. The highlight was a 16-ball half-century against Central Stags, the third-fastest in New Zealand domestic T20 cricket, and his 25 sixes were more than anyone else managed in the tournament. Allen, who turns 22 in April and can keep wicket, was immediately called up to the Kiwis' T20I squad for the home series against Australia and a month later was drafted in by Royal Challengers Bangalore as a late replacement for the 2021 edition of the IPL. Lancashire have signed Allen for the duration of this summer's T20 Blast. "I believe that this is a signing which will excite supporters and improve what is already a very strong T20 outfit, as shown in last year's campaign," said Paul Allott, Lancashire's director of cricket

Batting	Mat	Inns	NO	Runs	HS	Ave	SR	100	50	Ct	St
First-class	12	20	2	343	66	19.05	45.73	0	3	12	0
List A	20	20	0	501	128	25.05	103.94	1	1	9	0
T20s	13	13	2	537	92*	48.81	183.27	0	6	3	0
Bowling	**Mat**	**Balls**	**Runs**	**Wkts**	**BBI**	**BBM**	**Ave**	**Econ**	**SR**	**5w**	**10**
First-class	12	18	15	1	1/15	1/15	15.00	5.00	18.0	0	0
List A	20	162	157	1	1/32	1/32	157.00	5.81	162.0	0	0
T20s	13	6	8	0	-	-	-	8.00	-	0	0

BEN ALLISON

RHB / RFM / R0 / W0

FULL NAME: Benjamin Michael John Allison
BORN: December 18, 1999, Colchester, Essex
SQUAD NO: 65
HEIGHT: 6ft 6in
NICKNAME: Pooey
EDUCATION: New Hall School, Chelmsford; Chelmsford College
TEAMS: Essex, England U19, Gloucestershire
ROLE: Bowler
DEBUT: First-class: 2019; T20: 2020

BEST BOWLING: 3-109 Gloucestershire vs Derbyshire, Derby 2019

MOST EXCITING DAY AS A CRICKETER? Winning the T20 Blast in 2019, even though I wasn't playing
CHILDHOOD SPORTING HERO? Stuart Broad
IF YOU COULD TAKE ONE COUNTY CRICKETER'S BEST SHOT AND ADD IT TO YOUR OWN GAME? Varun Chopra's pull
MOST ECCENTRIC TEAMMATE? Will Buttleman – you just cannot take him seriously, he always comes out with something outrageous
STRANGEST THING YOU'VE DONE DURING LOCKDOWN? My own washing
FAVOURITE SMELL? Petrol
GUILTY PLEASURE? Fizzy strawberry pencils

Batting	Mat	Inns	NO	Runs	HS	Ave	SR	100	50	Ct	St
First-class	1	1	0	0	0	0.00	0.00	0	0	0	0
T20s	1	1	1	1	1*	-	100.00	0	0	2	0
Bowling	**Mat**	**Balls**	**Runs**	**Wkts**	**BBI**	**BBM**	**Ave**	**Econ**	**SR**	**5w**	**10**
First-class	1	246	139	4	3/109	4/139	34.75	3.39	61.5	0	0
T20s	1	18	32	1	1/32	1/32	32.00	10.66	18.0	0	0

TOM ALSOP LHB / SLA / WK / R0 / W0

FULL NAME: Thomas Philip Alsop
BORN: November 27, 1995, High Wycombe, Buckinghamshire
SQUAD NO: 9
HEIGHT: 5ft 11in
NICKNAME: Lance
EDUCATION: Lavington School; The John Bentley School, Wiltshire
TEAMS: Hampshire, England Lions
ROLE: Batsman/wicketkeeper
DEBUT: First-class: 2014; List A: 2014; T20: 2016

BEST BATTING: 150 Hampshire vs Warwickshire, Edgbaston, 2019
BEST BOWLING: 2-59 Hampshire vs Yorkshire, Headingley, 2016

MOST EXCITING DAY AS A CRICKETER? Winning the Lord's one-day final in 2018
CHILDHOOD SPORTING HERO? Michael Clarke
FIRST CRICKET CLUB? Bishop Canning CC, Wiltshire
IF YOU COULD TAKE ONE COUNTY CRICKETER'S BEST SHOT AND ADD IT TO YOUR OWN GAME? James Vince's cover-drive
TOUGHEST OPPONENT IN COUNTY CRICKET? Rikki Clarke
WHAT WOULD YOU DO IF YOU WERE IN CHARGE OF COUNTY CRICKET? Schedule an opening round of Championship matches abroad to avoid the cold and rain (and find an investor to fund it!)
WHAT WOULD YOU DO IF YOU WERE PRIME MINISTER? Rejoin the EU
STRANGEST THING YOU'VE DONE DURING LOCKDOWN? Becoming nocturnal for a while
FAVOURITE SMELL? Lavender
GUILTY PLEASURE? Cadbury Fruit and Nut (big bar) with a cold glass of milk

Batting	Mat	Inns	NO	Runs	HS	Ave	SR	100	50	Ct	St
First-class	49	81	4	1999	150	25.96	46.95	2	14	65	0
List A	48	48	3	1465	130*	32.55	77.80	4	6	33	5
T20s	39	37	4	772	85	23.39	113.52	0	3	15	3
Bowling	**Mat**	**Balls**	**Runs**	**Wkts**	**BBI**	**BBM**	**Ave**	**Econ**	**SR**	**5w**	**10**
First-class	49	84	81	3	2/59	2/59	27.00	5.78	28.0	0	0
List A	48	-	-	-	-	-	-	-	-	-	-
T20s	39	-	-	-	-	-	-	-	-	-	-

HASHIM AMLA RHB / OB / R0 / W0

FULL NAME: Hashim Mahomed Amla
BORN: March 31, 1983, Durban, South Africa
SQUAD NO: 1
HEIGHT: 6ft
TEAMS: South Africa, Surrey, Barbados Tridents, Cape Cobras, Derbyshire, Dolphins, Durban Heat, Essex, Hampshire, Khulna Tigers, Kings XI Punjab, KwaZulu-Natal, Nottinghamshire, Trinbago Knight Riders
ROLE: Batsman
DEBUT: Test: 2004; ODI: 2008; T20I: 2009; First-class: 1999; List A: 2002; T20: 2004

BEST BATTING: 311* South Africa vs England, The Oval, 2012
BEST BOWLING: 1-10 South Africa A vs India A, Kimbereley, 2002
COUNTY CAP: 2010 (Nottinghamshire)

TWITTER: @amlahash
NOTES: After calling time on his illustrious international career in August 2019, Amla signed a two-year Kolpak contract with Surrey to play across all formats. He only played T20 cricket last year after his arrival was delayed by travel restrictions, but he made up for lost time by cracking three fifties to help Surrey reach Finals Day. Amla will fill one of the overseas slots this summer following Britain's withdrawal from the EU. The 38-year-old previously represented the county in 2013 and 2014, scoring 663 first-class runs at 47.35, and has a wealth of experience in the English domestic game, having also had spells at Derbyshire, Essex, Hampshire and Nottinghamshire. He is still the only South African to have scored a Test triple-century – 311* against England at The Oval in 2012 – and is the fastest batsman to reach 7,000 ODI runs (150 innings)

Batting	Mat	Inns	NO	Runs	HS	Ave	SR	100	50	Ct	St
Tests	124	215	16	9282	311*	46.64	49.97	28	41	108	0
ODIs	181	178	14	8113	159	49.46	88.39	27	39	87	0
T20Is	44	44	6	1277	97*	33.60	132.05	0	8	19	0
First-class	238	398	31	17809	311*	48.52	-	52	88	186	0
List A	243	237	16	9973	159	45.12	-	30	52	108	0
T20s	163	162	15	4563	104*	31.04	126.08	2	30	39	0
Bowling	**Mat**	**Balls**	**Runs**	**Wkts**	**BBI**	**BBM**	**Ave**	**Econ**	**SR**	**5w**	**10**
Tests	124	54	37	0	-	-	-	4.11	-	0	0
ODIs	181	-	-	-	-	-	-	-	-	-	-
T20Is	44	-	-	-	-	-	-	-	-	-	-
First-class	238	393	277	1	1/10	-	277.00	4.22	393.0	0	0
List A	243	16	28	0	-	-	-	10.50	-	0	0
T20s	163	2	5	0	-	-	-	15.00	-	0	0

JAMES ANDERSON

LHB / RFM / R0 / W3

FULL NAME: James Michael Anderson
BORN: July 30, 1982, Burnley, Lancashire
SQUAD NO: 9
HEIGHT: 6ft 2in
NICKNAME: Jimmy
EDUCATION: St Theodore's Roman Catholic High School, Burnley
TEAMS: England, Lancashire, Auckland
ROLE: Bowler
DEBUT: Test: 2003; ODI: 2002; T20I: 2007; First-class: 2002; List A: 2000; T20: 2004

BEST BATTING: 81 England vs India, Trent Bridge, 2014
BEST BOWLING: 7-42 England vs West Indies, Lord's, 2017
COUNTY CAP: 2003; BENEFIT: 2012

FAMILY TIES? My dad played for Burnley CC
CHILDHOOD SPORTING HERO? Peter Martin
SURPRISING FACT ABOUT YOU? I'm allergic to mushrooms
TWITTER: @jimmy9

Batting	Mat	Inns	NO	Runs	HS	Ave	SR	100	50	Ct	St
Tests	160	223	94	1233	81	9.55	39.99	0	1	97	0
ODIs	194	79	43	273	28	7.58	48.66	0	0	53	0
T20Is	19	4	3	1	1*	1.00	50.00	0	0	3	0
First-class	257	330	134	1874	81	9.56	-	0	1	150	0
List A	261	105	63	376	28	8.95	-	0	0	68	0
T20s	44	10	6	23	16	5.75	88.46	0	0	8	0
Bowling	**Mat**	**Balls**	**Runs**	**Wkts**	**BBI**	**BBM**	**Ave**	**Econ**	**SR**	**5w**	**10**
Tests	160	34326	16251	614	7/42	11/71	26.46	2.84	55.9	30	3
ODIs	194	9584	7861	269	5/23	5/23	29.22	4.92	35.6	2	0
T20Is	19	422	552	18	3/23	3/23	30.66	7.84	23.4	0	0
First-class	257	51452	24488	989	7/42	-	24.76	2.85	52.0	50	6
List A	261	12730	10230	358	5/23	5/23	28.57	4.82	35.5	2	0
T20s	44	933	1318	41	3/23	3/23	32.14	8.47	22.7	0	0

MARTIN ANDERSSON RHB / RM / R0 / W0 / MVP64

FULL NAME: Martin Kristoffer Andersson
BORN: September 6, 1996, Reading
SQUAD NO: 24
HEIGHT: 6ft 2in
NICKNAME: Pasty
EDUCATION: Reading Blue Coat School; University of Leeds
TEAMS: Middlesex, Derbyshire
ROLE: Allrounder
DEBUT: First-class: 2017; T20: 2018

BEST BATTING: 92 Middlesex vs Hampshire, Radlett, 2020
BEST BOWLING: 4-25 Derbyshire vs Glamorgan, Derby, 2018

CHILDHOOD SPORTING HERO? Andrew Flintoff
FIRST CRICKET CLUB? Reading CC, Berkshire
IF YOU COULD TAKE ONE COUNTY CRICKETER'S BEST SHOT AND ADD IT TO YOUR OWN GAME? Nathan Sowter's cut
TOUGHEST OPPONENT IN COUNTY CRICKET? Graham Onions – an absolute wizard with the ball
WHAT WOULD YOU DO IF YOU WERE IN CHARGE OF COUNTY CRICKET? A no-ball should only cost a maximum of one run
WHAT WOULD YOU DO IF YOU WERE PRIME MINISTER? Launch an ambitious policy to tackle climate change
FAVOURITE SMELL? The smell of home in Sweden
SURPRISING FACT ABOUT YOU? My karaoke song of choice is Basshunter's "Now You're Gone" in Swedish. I have 90 per cent of my middle finger left – the other 10 per cent was left in a door frame in a building at school
GUILTY PLEASURE? Eating Nutella straight from the jar
TWITTER: @MartinAnderss11

Batting	Mat	Inns	NO	Runs	HS	Ave	SR	100	50	Ct	St
First-class	13	24	3	421	92	20.04	51.34	0	3	9	0
T20s	11	11	1	95	24	9.50	101.06	0	0	8	0
Bowling	**Mat**	**Balls**	**Runs**	**Wkts**	**BBI**	**BBM**	**Ave**	**Econ**	**SR**	**5w**	**10**
First-class	13	875	489	26	4/25	7/98	18.80	3.35	33.6	0	0
T20s	11	24	55	0	-	-	-	13.75	-	0	0

JOFRA ARCHER RHB / RFM / R0 / W1

FULL NAME: Jofra Chioke Archer
BORN: April 1, 1995, Bridgetown, Barbados
SQUAD NO: 22
HEIGHT: 6ft 2in
NICKNAME: Jof
EDUCATION: Christ Church Foundation School, Bridgetown, Barbados
TEAMS: England, Sussex, Hobart Hurricanes, Khulna Titans, Quetta Gladiators, Rajasthan Royals, West Indies U19
ROLE: Bowler
DEBUT: Test: 2019; ODI: 2019; T20I: 2019; First-class: 2016; List A: 2016; T20: 2016

BEST BATTING: 81* Sussex vs Northamptonshire, Northampton, 2017
BEST BOWLING: 7-67 Sussex vs Kent, Hove, 2017
COUNTY CAP: 2017

FIRST CRICKET CLUB? Pickwick CC, Bridgetown, Barbados
MOST INTERESTING TEAMMATE? Adil Rashid – he's just hilarious
SURPRISING FACT ABOUT YOU? I'm ambidextrous
IF YOU WERE AN ANIMAL, WHICH WOULD IT BE? An eagle
TWITTER: @craig_arch
NOTES: Archer was retained by Rajasthan Royals for the 2021 IPL so will not be available for Sussex in the early part of the season

Batting	Mat	Inns	NO	Runs	HS	Ave	SR	100	50	Ct	St
Tests	13	20	0	155	30	7.75	50.65	0	0	2	0
ODIs	17	9	5	27	8*	6.75	79.41	0	0	5	0
T20Is	7	-	-	-	-	-	-	-	-	0	0
First-class	42	62	10	1199	81*	23.05	67.13	0	6	21	0
List A	31	20	8	219	45	18.25	114.06	0	0	9	0
T20s	115	59	28	532	36	17.16	146.55	0	0	31	0
Bowling	**Mat**	**Balls**	**Runs**	**Wkts**	**BBI**	**BBM**	**Ave**	**Econ**	**SR**	**5w**	**10**
Tests	13	2609	1304	42	6/45	8/85	31.04	2.99	62.1	3	0
ODIs	17	911	720	30	3/27	3/27	24.00	4.74	30.3	0	0
T20Is	7	162	216	7	2/29	2/29	30.85	8.00	23.1	0	0
First-class	42	8748	4467	178	7/67	11/137	25.09	3.06	49.1	8	1
List A	31	1642	1365	51	5/42	5/42	26.76	4.98	32.1	1	0
T20s	115	2562	3271	146	4/18	4/18	22.40	7.66	17.5	0	0

JAMIE ATKINS

RHB / RFM / R0 / W0

SUSSEX

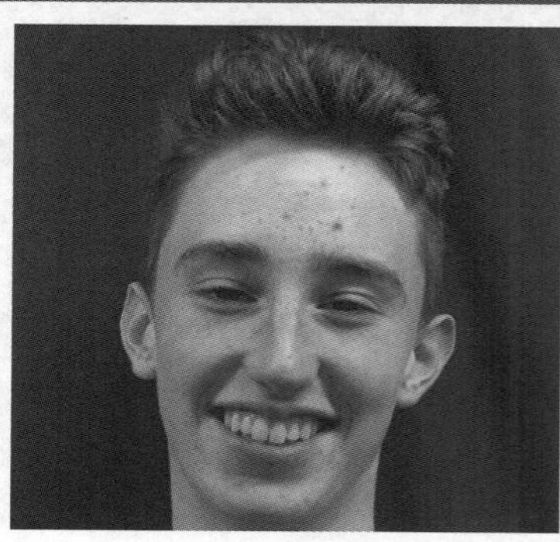

FULL NAME: Jamie Atkins
BORN: May 20, 2002
SQUAD NO: 32
HEIGHT: 6ft 6in
NICKNAME: J
EDUCATION: Eastbourne College
TEAMS: Sussex
ROLE: Bowler

MOST EXCITING DAY AS A CRICKETER? Playing in the U18 North vs South game last year
CHILDHOOD SPORTING HERO? Steven Gerrard
BIGGEST INFLUENCE ON YOUR DEVELOPMENT AS A CRICKETER (EXCLUDING PARENTS)? James Kirtley at Sussex – he has trusted my bowling action
FIRST CRICKET CLUB? Roffey CC, Horsham
IF YOU COULD TAKE ONE COUNTY CRICKETER'S BEST SHOT AND ADD IT TO YOUR OWN GAME? Jos Buttler's ramp
MOST ECCENTRIC TEAMMATE? Phil Salt – you always have to keep your wits about you when he's around
WHAT WOULD YOU DO IF YOU WERE IN CHARGE OF COUNTY CRICKET? Introduce a four-over Powerplay, allow substitutes
WHAT WOULD YOU DO IF YOU WERE PRIME MINISTER? Lower taxes, offer free school meals, reverse Brexit
STRANGEST THING YOU'VE DONE DURING LOCKDOWN? Growing a mullet
GUILTY PLEASURE? "Careless Whisper" by George Michael
TWITTER: @JamieAtkins2005
NOTES: The 18-year-old fast bowler signed his first professional contract last October alongside fellow Sussex Academy graduates Jack Carson and Henry Crocombe. At 6ft 6in tall, Atkins generates plenty of bounce and is not short of pace – last September he was clocked at 88mph while taking a five-wicket haul during a North vs South U18 match

GUS ATKINSON RHB / RMF / R0 / W0

FULL NAME: Angus Alexander Patrick Atkinson
BORN: January 19, 1998, Chelsea, Middlesex
SQUAD NO: 37
HEIGHT: 6ft 2in
NICKNAME: G-bus
EDUCATION: Northcote Lodge, London; Bradfield College, Berkshire
TEAMS: Surrey
ROLE: Bowler
DEBUT: First-class: 2020; T20: 2020

BEST BATTING: 15 Surrey vs Essex, Chelmsford, 2020
BEST BOWLING: 2-57 Surrey vs Essex, Chelmsford, 2020

CHILDHOOD SPORTING HERO? Andrew Flintoff
BIGGEST INFLUENCE ON YOUR DEVELOPMENT AS A CRICKETER (EXCLUDING PARENTS)? Julian Wood, my school coach who believed in my ability before I did
FIRST CRICKET CLUB? Spencer CC, London
BEST INNINGS YOU'VE SEEN? Aaron Finch's 117 not out from 52 balls against Middlesex at The Oval in the 2018 T20 Blast. Never seen anything like it
IF YOU COULD TAKE ONE COUNTY CRICKETER'S BEST SHOT AND ADD IT TO YOUR OWN GAME? Ollie Pope's cut
TOUGHEST OPPONENT IN COUNTY CRICKET? Alastair Cook
MOST ECCENTRIC TEAMMATE? Gareth Batty – for his enthusiasm and comedy
SURPRISING FACT ABOUT YOU? I had a rugby trial for Harlequins aged 13
TWITTER: @gus_atkinson1

Batting	Mat	Inns	NO	Runs	HS	Ave	SR	100	50	Ct	St
First-class	2	4	0	21	15	5.25	50.00	0	0	0	0
T20s	9	3	2	30	14	30.00	176.47	0	0	3	0
Bowling	**Mat**	**Balls**	**Runs**	**Wkts**	**BBI**	**BBM**	**Ave**	**Econ**	**SR**	**5w**	**10**
First-class	2	214	128	4	2/57	3/102	32.00	3.58	53.5	0	0
T20s	9	126	200	7	2/18	2/18	28.57	9.52	18.0	0	0

HASSAN AZAD

LHB / OB / R1 / W0

FULL NAME: Mohammad Hassan Azad
BORN: January 7, 1994, Quetta, Balochistan, Pakistan
SQUAD NO: 42
EDUCATION: Bilborough Sixth Form College, Nottingham; Loughborough University
TEAMS: Leicestershire
ROLE: Batsman
DEBUT: First-class: 2015

BEST BATTING: 139 Leicestershire vs Loughborough MCCU, Leicester, 2019
BEST BOWLING: 1-15 Leicestershire vs Durham, Leicester, 2020

TWITTER: @Bat_Pad_Man
NOTES: The Pakistan-born left-hander was a revelation for struggling Leicestershire in 2019, scoring 1,189 Championship runs at 54.05 including three hundreds. He was less effective across five matches in the Bob Willis Trophy last year, making just 144 runs from eight innings. A gritty opener who is yet to play white-ball cricket, Azad was captained by Babar Azam when representing Pakistan U15 in 2008 but moved to England aged 15 and now qualifies as a local player. He was briefly on Nottinghamshire's books only to be released by the club in 2014. But his game improved while at Loughborough University, where he studied Chemical Engineering, and he was picked up by Leicestershire in 2019 after a number of impressive performances for the MCCU side. Last summer the 27-year-old signed a new contract that keeps him at the club until the end of next season

Batting	Mat	Inns	NO	Runs	HS	Ave	SR	100	50	Ct	St
First-class	29	46	5	1803	139	43.97	40.38	4	11	14	0
Bowling	**Mat**	**Balls**	**Runs**	**Wkts**	**BBI**	**BBM**	**Ave**	**Econ**	**SR**	**5w**	**10**
First-class	29	19	17	1	1/15	1/15	17.00	5.36	19.0	0	0

TOM BAILEY

RHB / RFM / R0 / W1 / MVP47

FULL NAME: Thomas Ernest Bailey
BORN: April 21, 1991, Preston, Lancashire
SQUAD NO: 8
HEIGHT: 6ft 4in
NICKNAME: Jebby
EDUCATION: Myerscough College, Lancashire
TEAMS: Lancashire, England Lions
ROLE: Bowler
DEBUT: First-class: 2012; List A: 2014; T20: 2015

BEST BATTING: 68 Lancashire vs Northamptonshire, Old Trafford, 2019
BEST BOWLING: 5-12 Lancashire vs Leicestershire, Leicester, 2015
COUNTY CAP: 2018

MOST EXCITING DAY AS A CRICKETER? Receiving my county cap in 2018
CHILDHOOD SPORTING HERO? I didn't really have one but I always wanted to bowl like Steve Harmison
FIRST CRICKET CLUB? Vernon Carus CC, Lancashire
IF YOU COULD TAKE ONE COUNTY CRICKETER'S BEST SHOT AND ADD IT TO YOUR OWN GAME? Alastair Cook's pull
TOUGHEST OPPONENT IN COUNTY CRICKET? Adam Lyth – the ball ends up in the stands most times I bowl at him
MOST ECCENTRIC TEAMMATE? Rob Jones – go and watch his hundred celebration against Middlesex in 2019
WHAT WOULD YOU DO IF YOU WERE IN CHARGE OF COUNTY CRICKET? Make sure that white-ball cricket is played with a Dukes ball, outlaw flat pitches, make all boundaries no shorter than 80m
WHAT WOULD YOU DO IF YOU WERE PRIME MINISTER? Dig up Yorkshire and start afresh
STRANGEST THING YOU'VE DONE DURING LOCKDOWN? Reading a book
TWITTER: @TomBaildog

Batting	Mat	Inns	NO	Runs	HS	Ave	SR	100	50	Ct	St
First-class	60	80	13	1175	68	17.53	50.38	0	5	14	0
List A	15	11	6	81	33	16.20	89.01	0	0	2	0
T20s	19	4	1	18	10	6.00	112.50	0	0	8	0
Bowling	**Mat**	**Balls**	**Runs**	**Wkts**	**BBI**	**BBM**	**Ave**	**Econ**	**SR**	**5w**	**10**
First-class	60	10627	5155	206	5/12	10/98	25.02	2.91	51.5	9	2
List A	15	679	660	20	3/31	3/31	33.00	5.83	33.9	0	0
T20s	19	312	462	21	5/17	5/17	22.00	8.88	14.8	1	0

JONNY BAIRSTOW RHB / WK / R3 / W0

FULL NAME: Jonathan Marc Bairstow
BORN: September 26, 1989, Bradford
SQUAD NO: 21
NICKNAME: Bluey
EDUCATION: St Peter's School, York; Leeds Metropolitan University
TEAMS: England, Yorkshire, Peshawar Zalmi, Sunrisers Hyderabad
ROLE: Batsman/wicketkeeper
DEBUT: Test: 2012; ODI: 2011; T20I: 2011; First-class: 2009; List A: 2009; T20: 2010

BEST BATTING: 246 Yorkshire vs Hampshire, Headingley, 2016

COUNTY CAP: 2011

FAMILY TIES? My father David played for Yorkshire and England
CHILDHOOD SPORTING HERO? Sachin Tendulkar
SURPRISING FACT ABOUT YOU? I played football for the Leeds United Academy for seven years
TWITTER: @jbairstow21
NOTES: Bairstow was retained by Sunrisers Hyderabad for the 2021 IPL

Batting	Mat	Inns	NO	Runs	HS	Ave	SR	100	50	Ct	St
Tests	74	131	8	4197	167*	34.12	54.82	6	21	186	13
ODIs	83	76	8	3207	141*	47.16	103.71	10	13	39	2
T20Is	46	40	7	932	86*	28.24	139.52	0	6	33	0
First-class	187	310	34	11845	246	42.91		24	63	477	24
List A	151	138	14	5129	174	41.36	103.07	13	23	90	8
T20s	136	123	20	2975	114	28.88	134.49	2	15	82	13

Bowling	Mat	Balls	Runs	Wkts	BBI	BBM	Ave	Econ	SR	5w	10
Tests	74	-	-	-	-	-	-	-	-	-	-
ODIs	83	-	-	-	-	-	-	-	-	-	-
T20Is	46	-	-	-	-	-	-	-	-	-	-
First-class	187	6	1	0	-	-	-	1.00	-	0	0
List A	151	-	-	-	-	-	-	-	-	-	-
T20s	136	-	-	-	-	-	-	-	-	-	-

ANDREW BALBIRNIE

RHB / OB / R0 / W0

FULL NAME: Andrew Balbirnie
BORN: December 28, 1990, Dublin, Ireland
SQUAD NO: 63
EDUCATION: St Andrew's College, Dublin
TEAMS: Ireland, Glamorgan, Leinster Lightning, Middlesex
ROLE: Batsman
DEBUT: Test: 2018; ODI: 2010; T20I: 2015; First-class: 2012; List A: 2010; T20: 2014

BEST BATTING: 205* Ireland vs Netherlands, Malahide, 2017
BEST BOWLING: 4-23 Leinster Lightning vs North West Warriors, Bready, 2017

TWITTER: @balbo90
NOTES: The Ireland captain has joined Glamorgan on a short-term deal for the first month of the season, with Marnus Labuschagne not expected to arrive at the club until the end of the Australian domestic season in early May. Balbirnie was Glamorgan's leading run-scorer in last season's T20 Blast, making 255 runs with a highest score of 99 against Gloucestershire at Cardiff. The 30-year-old had three seasons at Middlesex between 2014 and 2016 and has played in all formats for Ireland, leading his country to a famous ODI win over England last year. He has not played red-ball cricket since 2019. "I'm really excited to be playing first-class cricket, it's the biggest test and my favourite format of the game," said Balbirnie. "To come in for a short space of time and fill Marnus Labuschagne's boots will be very hard after his brilliant season in 2019, but I'm looking to score runs, contribute to wins and enjoy my cricket with a really great bunch of people"

Batting	Mat	Inns	NO	Runs	HS	Ave	SR	100	50	Ct	St
Tests	3	6	0	146	82	24.33	59.10	0	2	3	0
ODIs	75	72	4	2122	145*	31.20	76.13	6	10	24	0
T20Is	43	39	2	945	83	25.54	129.80	0	4	16	0
First-class	30	42	3	1296	205*	33.23	55.26	2	8	28	0
List A	104	98	6	3366	160*	36.58	80.35	10	15	32	0
T20s	80	74	7	1841	99*	27.47	133.02	0	10	31	0
Bowling	**Mat**	**Balls**	**Runs**	**Wkts**	**BBI**	**BBM**	**Ave**	**Econ**	**SR**	**5w**	**10**
Tests	3	6	8	0	-	-	-	8.00	-	0	0
ODIs	75	60	68	2	1/26	1/26	34.00	6.80	30.0	0	0
T20Is	43	-	-	-	-	-	-	-	-	-	-
First-class	30	609	245	13	4/23	5/23	18.84	2.41	46.8	0	0
List A	104	96	112	2	1/26	1/26	56.00	7.00	48.0	0	0
T20s	80	-	-	-	-	-	-	-	-	-	-

GEORGE BALDERSON LHB / RM / R0 / W0

FULL NAME: George Philip Balderson
BORN: October 11, 2000, Manchester
SQUAD NO: 10
HEIGHT: 5ft 10in
NICKNAME: Baldy
EDUCATION: Cheadle Hulme High School, Greater Manchester
TEAMS: Lancashire, England U19
ROLE: Allrounder
DEBUT: First-class: 2020

BEST BATTING: 61* Lancashire vs Derbyshire, Liverpool, 2020
BEST BOWLING: 3-63 Lancashire vs Derbyshire, Liverpool, 2020

MOST EXCITING DAY AS A CRICKETER? Beating Derbyshire on the final day at Liverpool last season
CHILDHOOD SPORTING HERO? Jimmy Anderson
FIRST CRICKET CLUB? Cheadle Hulme CC, Greater Manchester. I'd watch my dad play there every Saturday
IF YOU COULD TAKE ONE COUNTY CRICKETER'S BEST SHOT AND ADD IT TO YOUR OWN GAME? Keaton Jennings's reverse-sweep
BIGGEST CRICKETING REGRET? Bowling leg-spin until I was 14
IF YOU WERE AN ANIMAL, WHICH WOULD IT BE? An elephant
GUILTY PLEASURE? Taylor Swift
TWITTER: @BaldersonGeorge

Batting	Mat	Inns	NO	Runs	HS	Ave	SR	100	50	Ct	St
First-class	5	7	2	156	61*	31.20	39.69	0	1	0	0
Bowling	**Mat**	**Balls**	**Runs**	**Wkts**	**BBI**	**BBM**	**Ave**	**Econ**	**SR**	**5w**	**10**
First-class	5	624	296	9	3/63	3/82	32.88	2.84	69.3	0	0

JAKE BALL RHB / RFM / R0 / W1 / MVP30

FULL NAME: Jacob Timothy Ball
BORN: March 14, 1991, Mansfield, Nottinghamshire
SQUAD NO: 28
HEIGHT: 6ft 3in
NICKNAME: Yak
EDUCATION: Meden School, Mansfield
TEAMS: England, Nottinghamshire, Sydney Sixers
ROLE: Bowler
DEBUT: Test: 2016; ODI: 2016; T20I: 2018; First-class: 2011; List A: 2009; T20: 2011

BEST BATTING: 49* Nottinghamshire vs Warwickshire, Trent Bridge, 2015
BEST BOWLING: 6-49 Nottinghamshire vs Sussex, Trent Bridge, 2015
COUNTY CAP: 2016

FAMILY TIES? My uncle Bruce French played for England
FIRST CRICKET CLUB? Welbeck Colliery CC, Nottinghamshire
BEST INNINGS YOU'VE SEEN? Alastair Cook's double century at the MCG in the 2017/18 Ashes. As a member of the squad I got to see how hard he worked for that innings over the whole tour
SURPRISING FACT ABOUT YOU? I was a batter till the age of 15
TWITTER: @Jakeball30

Batting	Mat	Inns	NO	Runs	HS	Ave	SR	100	50	Ct	St
Tests	4	8	0	67	31	8.37	53.60	0	0	1	0
ODIs	18	6	2	38	28	9.50	77.55	0	0	5	0
T20Is	2	-	-	-	-	-	-	-	-	1	0
First-class	66	101	24	1020	49*	13.24	74.12	0	0	13	0
List A	96	38	15	198	28	8.60	99.00	0	0	19	0
T20s	82	16	10	39	8*	6.50	81.25	0	0	23	0
Bowling	**Mat**	**Balls**	**Runs**	**Wkts**	**BBI**	**BBM**	**Ave**	**Econ**	**SR**	**5w**	**10**
Tests	4	612	343	3	1/47	1/47	114.33	3.36	204.0	0	0
ODIs	18	947	980	21	5/51	5/51	46.66	6.20	45.0	1	0
T20Is	2	42	83	2	1/39	1/39	41.50	11.85	21.0	0	0
First-class	66	10086	5770	201	6/49	9/57	28.70	3.43	50.1	6	0
List A	96	4060	3984	118	5/51	5/51	33.76	5.88	34.4	1	0
T20s	82	1629	2391	98	3/25	3/25	24.39	8.80	16.6	0	0

GARY BALLANCE

LHB / LB / R4 / W0

FULL NAME: Gary Simon Ballance
BORN: November 22, 1989, Zimbabwe
SQUAD NO: 19
NICKNAME: Gazza
EDUCATION: Peterhouse School, Marondera, Zimbabwe; Harrow School, London
TEAMS: England, Yorkshire, Derbyshire, Mid West Rhinos, Zimbabwe U19
ROLE: Batsman
DEBUT: Test: 2014; ODI: 2013; First-class: 2008; List A: 2006; T20: 2010

BEST BATTING: 210 Mid West Rhinos vs Southern Rocks, Masvingo, 2011

COUNTY CAP: 2012 (Yorkshire)

NOTES: A close family friend of former Zimbabwe skipper David Houghton, Ballance signed for Derbyshire aged 16 before joining the Yorkshire Academy in 2008. He played for Zimbabwe at the 2006 U19 World Cup before qualifying to play for England. He made his Test debut at Sydney in the 2013/14 Ashes and hit three centuries the following summer to cement the No.3 spot but lost his place during the 2015 Ashes. His most recent Test was in 2017. The 31-year-old captained Yorkshire for one season but stood down in 2018 to take a break from cricket for personal reasons. He soon returned to action and went on to score 975 runs in 2019 to finish as the club's leading Championship run-scorer for the third season in a row. But Ballance didn't play at all for Yorkshire last year, with the club announcing that he was suffering "heightened feelings of anxiety and stress following a long period of isolation due to the Covid-19 lockdown, his own recent viral illness and other personal factors"

Batting	Mat	Inns	NO	Runs	HS	Ave	SR	100	50	Ct	St
Tests	23	42	2	1498	156	37.45	47.16	4	7	22	0
ODIs	16	15	1	297	79	21.21	67.04	0	2	8	0
First-class	160	262	24	11282	210	47.40	51.86	40	51	120	0
List A	110	102	14	4360	156	49.54	90.06	8	26	43	0
T20s	91	80	9	1648	79	23.21	122.16	0	6	46	0
Bowling	**Mat**	**Balls**	**Runs**	**Wkts**	**BBI**	**BBM**	**Ave**	**Econ**	**SR**	**5w**	**10**
Tests	23	12	5	0	-	-	-	2.50	-	0	0
ODIs	16	-	-	-	-	-	-	-	-	-	-
First-class	160	162	154	0	-	-	-	5.70	-	0	0
List A	110	-	-	-	-	-	-	-	-	-	-
T20s	91	-	-	-	-	-	-	-	-	-	-

ETHAN BAMBER

RHB / RFM / R0 / W0

FULL NAME: Ethan Read Bamber
BORN: December 17, 1998, Westminster
SQUAD NO: 54
HEIGHT: 5ft 11in
NICKNAME: Eth
EDUCATION: Mill Hill School, London; University of Exeter
TEAMS: Middlesex, England U19, Gloucestershire
ROLE: Bowler
DEBUT: First-class: 2018; T20: 2019

BEST BATTING: 27* Middlesex vs Gloucestershire, Bristol, 2018
BEST BOWLING: 5-93 Middlesex vs Derbyshire, Lord's, 2019

MOST EXCITING DAY AS A CRICKETER? Day four of Middlesex's Championship game against Sussex at Lord's in 2018, when I helped bowl out our opponents to win the match
CHILDHOOD SPORTING HERO? Ronan O'Gara
FIRST CRICKET CLUB? North Middlesex CC, London
IF YOU COULD TAKE ONE COUNTY CRICKETER'S BEST SHOT AND ADD IT TO YOUR OWN GAME? Joe Cracknell's "no-look" guide to third man
BIGGEST CRICKETING REGRET? Getting out with a shocking shot when the other batter was on 98
WHAT WOULD YOU DO IF YOU WERE PRIME MINISTER? Make sure that everyone learns something about how to cook by the age of 15
STRANGEST THING YOU'VE DONE DURING LOCKDOWN? Playing with Lego
GUILTY PLEASURE? Cereal
TWITTER: @etbamber

Batting	Mat	Inns	NO	Runs	HS	Ave	SR	100	50	Ct	St
First-class	14	22	7	160	27*	10.66	31.18	0	0	2	0
T20s	1	1	1	0	0*	-	0.00	0	0	0	0
Bowling	**Mat**	**Balls**	**Runs**	**Wkts**	**BBI**	**BBM**	**Ave**	**Econ**	**SR**	**5w**	**10**
First-class	14	2612	1233	48	5/93	6/70	25.68	2.83	54.4	1	0
T20s	1	24	38	1	1/38	1/38	38.00	9.50	24.0	0	0

CAMERON BANCROFT

RHB / WK / R0 / W0

FULL NAME: Cameron Timothy Bancroft
BORN: November 19, 1992, Perth, Australia
SQUAD NO: 4
HEIGHT: 6ft 1in
NICKNAME: Bangers
EDUCATION: Aquinas College, Perth
TEAMS: Australia, Durham, Gloucestershire, Perth Scorchers, Western Australia
ROLE: Batsman/wicketkeeper
DEBUT: Test: 2017; T20I: 2016; First-class: 2013; List A: 2011; T20: 2014

BEST BATTING: 228* Western Australia vs South Australia, Perth, 2017
BEST BOWLING: 1-10 Western Australia vs Queensland, Brisbane, 2019
COUNTY CAP: 2016 (Gloucestershire)

TWITTER: @cbancroft4
NOTES: Durham have re-signed the Australian opener to play in the County Championship following the conclusion of the Australian domestic season. Bancroft, who can also keep wicket, scored 726 first-class runs in his first season at Chester-le-Street in 2019, when he also captained the club. He wasn't able to return last summer on account of the pandemic but penned a new one-year deal in March. Bancroft's previous county experience was with Gloucestershire in 2016 and 2017. He was due to play for Somerset in 2019 only to have his contract terminated following the ball-tampering scandal in Cape Town which led to him being suspended for nine months by Cricket Australia. Bancroft returned to the Test side for the 2019 Ashes but hasn't appeared for Australia since then and was dropped by Western Australia at the end of the 2019/20 season after a dire run of scores. He returned to form over the winter, having scored two hundreds for his state side up until March 11

Batting	Mat	Inns	NO	Runs	HS	Ave	SR	100	50	Ct	St
Tests	10	18	1	446	82*	26.23	42.80	0	3	16	0
T20Is	1	1	1	0	0*	-	-	0	0	1	0
First-class	107	195	15	6785	228*	37.69	42.88	16	27	139	1
List A	58	55	8	1900	176	40.42	83.07	3	12	48	1
T20s	58	51	13	1246	87*	32.78	123.85	0	9	22	5
Bowling	**Mat**	**Balls**	**Runs**	**Wkts**	**BBI**	**BBM**	**Ave**	**Econ**	**SR**	**5w**	**10**
Tests	10	-	-	-	-	-	-	-	-	-	-
T20Is	1	-	-	-	-	-	-	-	-	-	-
First-class	107	66	77	2	1/10	1/10	38.50	7.00	33.0	0	0
List A	58	-	-	-	-	-	-	-	-	-	-
T20s	58	-	-	-	-	-	-	-	-	-	-

TOM BANTON

RHB / WK / R0 / W0

FULL NAME: Thomas Banton
BORN: November 11, 1998, Chiltern, Buckinghamshire
SQUAD NO: 18
HEIGHT: 6ft 2in
EDUCATION: Bromsgrove School, Worcestershire; King's College, Taunton
TEAMS: England, Somerset, Brisbane Heat, Kolkata Knight Riders, Peshawar Zalmi, Quetta Gladiators
ROLE: Batsman/wicketkeeper
DEBUT: ODI: 2020; T20I: 2019; First-class: 2018; List A: 2018; T20: 2017

BEST BATTING: 79 Somerset vs Hampshire, Taunton, 2019

FIRST CRICKET CLUB? Sutton CC, London
BEST INNINGS YOU'VE SEEN? Johann Myburgh smashing 103 off 44 balls against Essex in the 2018 T20 Blast. I was batting at the other end as we chased down 136 without losing a wicket
BIGGEST CRICKETING REGRET? Not playing for Somerset at the age of 10
SURPRISING FACT ABOUT YOU? I love playing hockey
TWITTER: @tombanton18

Batting	Mat	Inns	NO	Runs	HS	Ave	SR	100	50	Ct	St
ODIs	6	5	0	134	58	26.80	92.41	0	1	2	0
T20Is	9	9	0	205	71	22.77	143.35	0	1	6	0
First-class	14	24	0	603	79	25.12	57.86	0	5	7	0
List A	24	22	0	658	112	29.90	87.50	2	4	16	1
T20s	44	43	2	1120	100	27.31	151.35	1	8	20	3
Bowling	**Mat**	**Balls**	**Runs**	**Wkts**	**BBI**	**BBM**	**Ave**	**Econ**	**SR**	**5w**	**10**
ODIs	6	-	-	-	-	-	-	-	-	-	-
T20Is	9	-	-	-	-	-	-	-	-	-	-
First-class	14	-	-	-	-	-	-	-	-	-	-
List A	24	-	-	-	-	-	-	-	-	-	-
T20s	44	-	-	-	-	-	-	-	-	-	-

TOM BARBER

RHB / LF / R0 / W0

FULL NAME: Thomas Edward Barber
BORN: August 8, 1995, Poole, Dorset
SQUAD NO: 18
HEIGHT: 6ft 3in
NICKNAME: Barbs
EDUCATION: Bournemouth Grammar School
TEAMS: Nottinghamshire, England U19, Hampshire, Middlesex
ROLE: Bowler
DEBUT: First-class: 2018; List A: 2014; T20: 2017

BEST BATTING: 3 Middlesex vs Sussex, Hove, 2018
BEST BOWLING: 3-42 Nottinghamshire vs Lancashire, Trent Bridge, 2020

MOST EXCITING DAY AS A CRICKETER? Making my T20 debut in front of a packed house at Lord's in 2017 – and it was on the TV!
CHILDHOOD SPORTING HERO? Andrew Flintoff
FIRST CRICKET CLUB? Parley CC, Dorset
IF YOU COULD TAKE ONE COUNTY CRICKETER'S BEST SHOT AND ADD IT TO YOUR OWN GAME? Tim Murtagh's back-away-and-slash through the off-side
BEST INNINGS YOU'VE SEEN? Paul Stirling's 66 off 36 balls for my old club Middlesex against Surrey in the 2018 T20 Blast. Sixes all over the place
MOST INTERESTING TEAMMATE? AB de Villiers at Middlesex in 2019 – one of the greatest cricketers ever and he has time for everyone
FAVOURITE SMELL? The seaside
TWITTER: @Tom_Barber20

Batting	Mat	Inns	NO	Runs	HS	Ave	SR	100	50	Ct	St
First-class	5	6	4	5	3	2.50	18.51	0	0	0	0
List A	7	6	0	1	1	0.16	5.88	0	0	0	0
T20s	11	5	0	3	2	0.60	37.50	0	0	1	0
Bowling	**Mat**	**Balls**	**Runs**	**Wkts**	**BBI**	**BBM**	**Ave**	**Econ**	**SR**	**5w**	**10**
First-class	5	678	420	7	3/42	3/74	60.00	3.71	96.8	0	0
List A	7	300	322	9	3/62	3/62	35.77	6.44	33.3	0	0
T20s	11	209	392	12	4/28	4/28	32.66	11.25	17.4	0	0

KEITH BARKER

LHB / LFM / RO / W3

FULL NAME: Keith Hubert Douglas Barker
BORN: October 21, 1986, Manchester
SQUAD NO: 10
HEIGHT: 6ft 3in
NICKNAME: Barks
EDUCATION: Moorhead High School, Accrington; Preston College
TEAMS: Hampshire, Warwickshire
ROLE: Allrounder
DEBUT: First-class: 2009; List A: 2009; T20: 2009

BEST BATTING: 125 Warwickshire vs Surrey, Guildford, 2013
BEST BOWLING: 6-40 Warwickshire vs Somerset, Taunton, 2012
COUNTY CAP: 2013 (Warwickshire)

MOST EXCITING DAY AS A CRICKETER? Winning the 2012 County Championship with Warwickshire
FAMILY TIES? My father, godfather and brothers all played various levels of cricket
CHILDHOOD SPORTING HERO? Brian Lara
BIGGEST INFLUENCE ON YOUR DEVELOPMENT AS A CRICKETER (EXCLUDING PARENTS)? Dean Barker (brother) – we always played cricket as kids and I was determined to beat him every time. Never did though
FIRST CRICKET CLUB? Enfield CC, Lancashire
IF YOU COULD TAKE ONE COUNTY CRICKETER'S BEST SHOT AND ADD IT TO YOUR OWN GAME? Varun Chopra's pull
IF YOU WERE AN ANIMAL, WHICH WOULD IT BE? A silverback gorilla
SURPRISING FACT ABOUT YOU? I never scored a hundred for the Enfield first team

Batting	Mat	Inns	NO	Runs	HS	Ave	SR	100	50	Ct	St
First-class	129	173	31	4018	125	28.29	57.50	6	17	36	0
List A	62	39	11	560	56	20.00	94.59	0	1	14	0
T20s	65	35	7	383	46	13.67	111.01	0	0	17	0
Bowling	**Mat**	**Balls**	**Runs**	**Wkts**	**BBI**	**BBM**	**Ave**	**Econ**	**SR**	**5w**	**10**
First-class	129	21004	10324	404	6/40	10/70	25.55	2.94	51.9	15	1
List A	62	2342	2263	69	4/33	4/33	32.79	5.79	33.9	0	0
T20s	65	1206	1588	69	4/19	4/19	23.01	7.90	17.4	0	0

ED BARNARD

RHB / RFM / R0 / W0 / MVP31

FULL NAME: Edward George Barnard
BORN: November 20, 1995, Shrewsbury
SQUAD NO: 30
HEIGHT: 6ft
NICKNAME: Barndoor
EDUCATION: Meole Brace School, Shrewsbury; Shrewsbury School
TEAMS: Worcestershire, England Lions
ROLE: Bowler
DEBUT: First-class: 2015; List A: 2015; T20: 2015

BEST BATTING: 75 Worcestershire vs Durham, Worcester, 2017
BEST BOWLING: 6-37 Worcestershire vs Somerset, Taunton, 2018

MOST EXCITING DAY AS A CRICKETER? Winning the T20 Blast in 2018
FAMILY TIES? Dad (Andy) played for Shropshire; brother (Mike) played for Shropshire and first-class cricket for Oxford MCCU; brother (Steve) played for Shropshire
CHILDHOOD SPORTING HERO? Alan Shearer
FIRST CRICKET CLUB? Shrewsbury CC, Shropshire. We were the National Knockout champions in 1983 and 2011
IF YOU COULD TAKE ONE COUNTY CRICKETER'S BEST SHOT AND ADD IT TO YOUR OWN GAME? Riki Wessels's sweep
BEST INNINGS YOU'VE SEEN? Ben Cox's 46 not out to beat Sussex in the 2018 T20 final
TOUGHEST OPPONENT IN COUNTY CRICKET? Sam Hain – I don't think I've seen him fail against us
STRANGEST THING YOU'VE DONE DURING LOCKDOWN? A couple of Zumba fitness classes
FAVOURITE SMELL? Can't decide between chocolate or petrol
TWITTER: @EdBarn95

Batting	Mat	Inns	NO	Runs	HS	Ave	SR	100	50	Ct	St
First-class	65	96	16	2112	75	26.40	53.72	0	12	40	0
List A	44	32	13	554	61	29.15	100.36	0	3	19	0
T20s	75	47	19	463	42*	16.53	133.42	0	0	43	0
Bowling	**Mat**	**Balls**	**Runs**	**Wkts**	**BBI**	**BBM**	**Ave**	**Econ**	**SR**	**5w**	**10**
First-class	65	10154	5476	205	6/37	11/89	26.71	3.23	49.5	5	1
List A	44	1908	1867	53	3/26	3/26	35.22	5.87	36.0	0	0
T20s	75	1208	1796	48	3/29	3/29	37.41	8.92	25.1	0	0

ED BARNES

RHB / RFM / R0 / W0

FULL NAME: Edward Barnes
BORN: November 26, 1997, York
SQUAD NO: 62
HEIGHT: 6ft
NICKNAME: Barnsey
EDUCATION: King James School, Knaresborough, North Yorkshire
TEAMS: Leicestershire, England U19, Yorkshire
ROLE: Bowler
DEBUT: First-class: 2020; T20: 2020

BEST BATTING: 4 Leicestershire vs Derbyshire, Leicester, 2020
BEST BOWLING: 2-24 Leicestershire vs Derbyshire, Leicester, 2020

MOST EXCITING DAY AS A CRICKETER? My first-class debut at Grace Road last summer
CHILDHOOD SPORTING HERO? Tim Bresnan
BIGGEST INFLUENCE ON YOUR DEVELOPMENT AS A CRICKETER (EXCLUDING PARENTS)? Michael Vaughan. My first-ever cricket session was during a summer camp and Vaughan was there on the one day that I was there. That inspired me going forward
IF YOU COULD TAKE ONE COUNTY CRICKETER'S BEST SHOT AND ADD IT TO YOUR OWN GAME? The Jos Buttler scoop
TOUGHEST OPPONENT IN COUNTY CRICKET? Alex Davies – so hard to bowl to, such a small margin of error. And he's a 360-degree batsman
WHAT WOULD YOU DO IF YOU WERE IN CHARGE OF COUNTY CRICKET? Change to a three-tiered Championship, push for more cricket on free-to-air TV and for a Championship and T20 highlights show
WHAT WOULD YOU DO IF YOU WERE PRIME MINISTER? Shave, redecorate No.10 and employ someone who knows more than me
STRANGEST THING YOU'VE DONE DURING LOCKDOWN? Writing a song
FAVOURITE SMELL? Garlic
GUILTY PLEASURE? Emmerdale

Batting	Mat	Inns	NO	Runs	HS	Ave	SR	100	50	Ct	St
First-class	2	1	0	4	4	4.00	26.66	0	0	0	0
T20s	4	-	-	-	-	-	-	-	-	0	0
Bowling	**Mat**	**Balls**	**Runs**	**Wkts**	**BBI**	**BBM**	**Ave**	**Econ**	**SR**	**5w**	**10**
First-class	2	192	107	3	2/24	2/64	35.66	3.34	64.0	0	0
T20s	4	42	81	2	2/27	2/27	40.50	11.57	21.0	0	0

GEORGE BARTLETT RHB / OB / R0 / W0

FULL NAME: George Anthony Bartlett
BORN: March 14, 1998, Frimley, Surrey
SQUAD NO: 14
HEIGHT: 6ft 1in
NICKNAME: GB
EDUCATION: Millfield School, Somerset
TEAMS: Somerset, England U19
ROLE: Batsman
DEBUT: First-class: 2017; List A: 2019; T20: 2020

BEST BATTING: 137 Somerset vs Surrey, Guildford, 2019

MOST EXCITING DAY AS A CRICKETER? Winning the One-Day Cup at Lord's in 2019
CHILDHOOD SPORTING HERO? Marcus Trescothick
BIGGEST INFLUENCE ON YOUR DEVELOPMENT AS A CRICKETER (EXCLUDING PARENTS)? My school coaches
FIRST CRICKET CLUB? Westlands CC, Yeovil, Somerset
IF YOU COULD TAKE ONE COUNTY CRICKETER'S BEST SHOT AND ADD IT TO YOUR OWN GAME? Jack Brooks's cut over the slips
MOST ECCENTRIC TEAMMATE? Eddie Byrom
WHAT WOULD YOU DO IF YOU WERE IN CHARGE OF COUNTY CRICKET? Use Kookaburra balls in the County Championship and ban the shining of the cricket ball
STRANGEST THING YOU'VE DONE DURING LOCKDOWN? Shaving my head
FAVOURITE SMELL? Freshly cut grass
IF YOU WERE AN ANIMAL, WHICH WOULD IT BE? A bald eagle
TWITTER: @georgebartlett9

Batting	Mat	Inns	NO	Runs	HS	Ave	SR	100	50	Ct	St
First-class	29	51	3	1338	137	27.87	55.17	4	3	8	0
List A	9	9	3	207	57*	34.50	99.51	0	1	4	0
T20s	3	3	0	41	24	13.66	128.12	0	0	2	0
Bowling	**Mat**	**Balls**	**Runs**	**Wkts**	**BBI**	**BBM**	**Ave**	**Econ**	**SR**	**5w**	**10**
First-class	29	20	27	0	-	-	-	8.10	-	0	0
List A	9	-	-	-	-	-	-	-	-	-	-
T20s	3	-	-	-	-	-	-	-	-	-	-

SAM BATES LHB / WK / R0 / W0

FULL NAME: Samuel David Bates
BORN: September 14, 1999, Leicester
SQUAD NO: 14
HEIGHT: 6ft 3in
NICKNAME: Bato
EDUCATION: Brookvale Groby, Leicestershire; Gateway College, Leicester
TEAMS: Leicestershire
ROLE: Wicketkeeper

MOST EXCITING DAY AS A CRICKETER? Signing my first professional contract last year with Leicestershire, my home-town club
CHILDHOOD SPORTING HERO? James Taylor
BIGGEST INFLUENCE ON YOUR DEVELOPMENT AS A CRICKETER (EXCLUDING PARENTS)? Dips Patel, currently the Leicestershire Second XI coach. He has spent countless hours coaching me, and he never said no to a session whether it was 6am or 11pm
IF YOU COULD TAKE ONE COUNTY CRICKETER'S BEST SHOT AND ADD IT TO YOUR OWN GAME? Alastair Cook's clip off the hip
MOST ECCENTRIC TEAMMATE? Dieter Klein – a very funny and confident man!
WHAT WOULD YOU DO IF YOU WERE PRIME MINISTER? Re-enact the Hugh Grant dance scene in Love Actually. On a more serious note, give NHS staff free parking
STRANGEST THING YOU'VE DONE DURING LOCKDOWN? Growing a mullet
FAVOURITE SMELL? Freshy cut grass on game day
GUILTY PLEASURE? Listening to James Blunt
TWITTER: @Batsey101

GARETH BATTY

RHB / OB / R0 / W2

FULL NAME: Gareth Jon Batty
BORN: October 13, 1977, Bradford
SQUAD NO: 13
HEIGHT: 5ft 11in
NICKNAME: Bats
EDUCATION: Bingley Grammar School, West Yorkshire
TEAMS: England, Surrey, Worcestershire, Yorkshire
ROLE: Bowler
DEBUT: Test: 2003; ODI: 2002; T20I: 2009; First-class: 1997; List A: 1998; T20: 2003

BEST BATTING: 133 Worcestershire vs Surrey, The Oval, 2004
BEST BOWLING: 8-64 Surrey vs Warwickshire, Edgbaston, 2019
COUNTY CAP: 2011 (Surrey); BENEFIT: 2017 (Surrey)

CHILDHOOD SPORTING HERO? Joel Garner
FAMILY TIES? Dad played for Yorkshire Second XI and my brother Jeremy played for Yorkshire and Somerset
FIRST CRICKET CLUB? Bradford & Bingley CC, West Yorkshire
MOST INTERESTING TEAMMATE? Kumar Sangakkara
SURPRISING FACT ABOUT YOU? This is my 25th year as a pro
IF YOU WERE AN ANIMAL, WHICH WOULD IT BE? Bagpuss

Batting	Mat	Inns	NO	Runs	HS	Ave	SR	100	50	Ct	St
Tests	9	12	2	149	38	14.90	25.68	0	0	3	0
ODIs	10	8	2	30	17	5.00	41.09	0	0	4	0
T20Is	1	1	0	4	4	4.00	57.14	0	0	0	0
First-class	261	389	68	7399	133	23.04	-	3	30	163	0
List A	271	200	44	2374	83*	15.21	-	0	5	84	0
T20s	181	93	33	623	87	10.38	101.30	0	1	49	0
Bowling	**Mat**	**Balls**	**Runs**	**Wkts**	**BBI**	**BBM**	**Ave**	**Econ**	**SR**	**5w**	**10**
Tests	9	1714	914	15	3/55	5/153	60.93	3.19	114.2	0	0
ODIs	10	440	366	5	2/40	2/40	73.20	4.99	88.0	0	0
T20Is	1	18	17	0	-	-	-	5.66	-	0	0
First-class	261	46183	22356	682	8/64	-	32.78	2.90	67.7	27	4
List A	271	10713	8283	255	5/35	5/35	32.48	4.63	42.0	3	0
T20s	181	3230	3932	147	4/13	4/13	26.74	7.30	21.9	0	0

AARON BEARD LHB / RMF / R0 / W0

FULL NAME: Aaron Paul Beard
BORN: October 15, 1997, Chelmsford
SQUAD NO: 14
HEIGHT: 5ft 11in
NICKNAME: Beardo
EDUCATION: The Boswells School, Chelmsford; Great Baddow High School, Chelmsford
TEAMS: Essex, England U19
ROLE: Bowler
DEBUT: First-class: 2016; List A: 2019; T20: 2019

BEST BATTING: 58* Essex vs Durham MCCU, Chelmsford, 2017
BEST BOWLING: 4-21 Essex vs Middlesex, Chelmsford, 2020

MOST EXCITING DAY AS A CRICKETER? Taking 4-62 against Sri Lanka on my first-class debut in 2016
CHILDHOOD SPORTING HERO? David Beckham
FIRST CRICKET CLUB? Writtle CC, Essex
MOST INTERESTING TEAMMATE? Simon Harmer – he has in-depth knowledge of nearly everything
BEST INNINGS YOU'VE SEEN? Dan Lawrence hitting 141 against Lancashire at Chelmsford in 2017. He batted out the final day to get Essex a draw after we had lost some early wickets
WHAT WOULD YOU DO IF YOU WERE IN CHARGE OF COUNTY CRICKET? Change the lbw rule: if it's hitting the stumps, it is out
IF YOU WERE AN ANIMAL, WHICH WOULD IT BE? A bearded dragon
TWITTER: @aaronbeard_14

Batting	Mat	Inns	NO	Runs	HS	Ave	SR	100	50	Ct	St
First-class	22	24	11	234	58*	18.00	44.23	0	1	5	0
List A	2	2	1	24	22*	24.00	120.00	0	0	0	0
T20s	10	3	1	26	13	13.00	152.94	0	0	1	0
Bowling	**Mat**	**Balls**	**Runs**	**Wkts**	**BBI**	**BBM**	**Ave**	**Econ**	**SR**	**5w**	**10**
First-class	22	2499	1498	49	4/21	7/45	30.57	3.59	51.0	0	0
List A	2	114	97	3	3/51	3/51	32.33	5.10	38.0	0	0
T20s	10	162	288	10	3/41	3/41	28.80	10.66	16.2	0	0

DAVID BEDINGHAM RHB / OB / R0 / W0

FULL NAME: David Guy Bedingham
BORN: April 22, 1994, George, Western Cape, South Africa
SQUAD NO: 5
HEIGHT: 6ft
NICKNAME: Bedders
EDUCATION: Wynberg Boys' High School, Cape Town; Stellenbosch University, Western Province
TEAMS: Durham, Boland, Cape Cobras, South Africa U19, Western Province
ROLE: Batsman
DEBUT: First-class: 2013; List A: 2013; T20: 2015

BEST BATTING: 147 Boland vs Easterns, Paarl, 2018

MOST EXCITING DAY AS A CRICKETER? Playing against most of my heroes in the Mzansi Super League (South Africa's T20 franchise competition)
CHILDHOOD SPORTING HERO? Roger Federer
BIGGEST INFLUENCE ON YOUR DEVELOPMENT AS A CRICKETER (EXCLUDING PARENTS)? Ashwell Prince – he really understood me and gave me the confidence to play my way
IF YOU COULD TAKE ONE COUNTY CRICKETER'S BEST SHOT AND ADD IT TO YOUR OWN GAME? Ben Duckett's reverse-sweep
TOUGHEST OPPONENT IN COUNTY CRICKET? Ben Coad – he doesn't offer many bad balls
WHAT WOULD YOU DO IF YOU WERE IN CHARGE OF COUNTY CRICKET? Allow a free hit for a front-foot no-ball
STRANGEST THING YOU'VE DONE DURING LOCKDOWN? Walking around in the snow to take exercise
FAVOURITE SMELL? A Sunday roast
GUILTY PLEASURE? A slab of chocolate

Batting	Mat	Inns	NO	Runs	HS	Ave	SR	100	50	Ct	St
First-class	37	63	6	2495	147	43.77	60.23	7	9	35	0
List A	20	20	3	504	104*	29.64	76.94	2	2	6	0
T20s	32	28	1	597	73	22.11	122.58	0	3	9	1
Bowling	**Mat**	**Balls**	**Runs**	**Wkts**	**BBI**	**BBM**	**Ave**	**Econ**	**SR**	**5w**	**10**
First-class	37	18	18	0	-	-	-	6.00	-	0	0
List A	20	39	25	0	-	-	-	3.84	-	0	0
T20s	32	-	-	-	-	-	-	-	-	-	-

WILL BEER

RHB / LB / R0 / W0

FULL NAME: William Andrew Thomas Beer
BORN: October 8, 1988, Crawley, Sussex
SQUAD NO: 18
HEIGHT: 5ft 10in
NICKNAME: Beery
EDUCATION: Reigate Grammar School; Collyer's Sixth Form College, Horsham
TEAMS: Sussex, England U19
ROLE: Bowler
DEBUT: First-class: 2008; List A: 2009; T20: 2008

BEST BATTING: 97 Sussex vs Gloucestershire, Arundel, 2019
BEST BOWLING: 6-29 Sussex vs South Africa A, Arundel, 2017

CHILDHOOD SPORTING HERO? David Beckham
BIGGEST INFLUENCE ON YOUR DEVELOPMENT AS A CRICKETER (EXCLUDING PARENTS)? Shane Warne – purely because I wanted so much to bowl like him
FIRST CRICKET CLUB? Horsham CC, West Sussex
TOUGHEST OPPONENT IN COUNTY CRICKET? Neil McKenzie – he always got Hampshire over the line against Sussex
WHAT WOULD YOU DO IF YOU WERE IN CHARGE OF COUNTY CRICKET? Bring back 40-over cricket, increase time allowance in T20, get domestic cricket on TV
WHAT WOULD YOU DO IF YOU WERE PRIME MINISTER? Make a law that golf courses cannot close
STRANGEST THING YOU'VE DONE DURING LOCKDOWN? Moving house, twice
IF YOU WERE AN ANIMAL, WHICH WOULD IT BE? A horse – it's my dream to run the cross country at the Cheltenham Festival
GUILTY PLEASURE? Dairy Milk Giant Buttons
TWITTER: @willbeer18

Batting	Mat	Inns	NO	Runs	HS	Ave	SR	100	50	Ct	St
First-class	27	34	7	755	97	27.96	36.31	0	4	6	0
List A	60	37	9	444	75	15.85	82.07	0	1	15	0
T20s	118	58	21	350	37	9.45	124.11	0	0	23	0
Bowling	**Mat**	**Balls**	**Runs**	**Wkts**	**BBI**	**BBM**	**Ave**	**Econ**	**SR**	**5w**	**10**
First-class	27	2754	1480	40	6/29	11/91	37.00	3.22	68.8	2	1
List A	60	2598	2246	54	3/27	3/27	41.59	5.18	48.1	0	0
T20s	118	2082	2587	97	3/14	3/14	26.67	7.45	21.4	0	0

DANIEL BELL-DRUMMOND RHB / RM / R1 / W0 / MVP29

KENT

FULL NAME: Daniel James Bell-Drummond
BORN: August 4, 1993, Lewisham, London
SQUAD NO: 23
HEIGHT: 5ft 11in
NICKNAME: DBD
EDUCATION: Millfield School, Somerset; Anglia Ruskin University
TEAMS: Kent, Auckland, Colombo Kings, England Lions, Rajshahi Kings
ROLE: Batsman
DEBUT: First-class: 2011; List A: 2011; T20: 2011

BEST BATTING: 206* Kent vs Loughborough MCCU, Canterbury, 2016
BEST BOWLING: 2-6 Kent vs Loughborough MCCU, Canterbury, 2019
COUNTY CAP: 2015

FAMILY TIES? My father got me into cricket. I've always really enjoyed spending time at my local club Catford Wanderers CC
CHILDHOOD SPORTING HERO? Thierry Henry
TWITTER: @deebzz23
NOTES: A stylish strokeplayer, Bell-Drummond had been tipped to open the batting for England since he was a teenager but hasn't been able to establish the sort of four-day consistency to attract the England selectors. The 27-year-old reminded everyone of his long-format talent in 2019, scoring 987 first-class runs which included a hundred against Warwickshire at Canterbury – his first in the Championship in more than three years. A key member of the Kent side in the short formats, Bell-Drummond was the leading run-scorer in last year's T20 Blast, with 423 runs from just 11 innings. Last summer he captained the club in the absence of Sam Billings and Joe Denly, winning two of three matches as skipper in the Bob Willis Trophy and five of eight in the T20 Blast. He signed a new three-year deal last December and has replaced Denly as Kent's vice-captain

Batting	Mat	Inns	NO	Runs	HS	Ave	SR	100	50	Ct	St
First-class	117	201	17	5997	206*	32.59	50.00	10	30	47	0
List A	89	88	8	3381	171*	42.26	81.50	6	22	32	0
T20s	108	106	7	3043	112*	30.73	133.75	1	23	34	0
Bowling	**Mat**	**Balls**	**Runs**	**Wkts**	**BBI**	**BBM**	**Ave**	**Econ**	**SR**	**5w**	**10**
First-class	117	523	263	10	2/6	3/44	26.30	3.01	52.3	0	0
List A	89	155	121	5	2/22	2/22	24.20	4.68	31.0	0	0
T20s	108	105	179	5	2/19	2/19	35.80	10.22	21.0	0	0

GARETH BERG

RHB / RMF / R0 / W0

FULL NAME: Gareth Kyle Berg
BORN: January 18, 1981, Cape Town, South Africa
SQUAD NO: 13
HEIGHT: 6ft
NICKNAME: Batman
EDUCATION: South African College School, Cape Town
TEAMS: Italy, Northamptonshire, Hampshire, Middlesex
ROLE: Allrounder
DEBUT: First-class: 2008; List A: 2008; T20: 2009

BEST BATTING: 130* Middlesex vs Leicestershire, Leicester, 2011
BEST BOWLING: 6-56 Hampshire vs Yorkshire, Southampton, 2016
COUNTY CAP: 2010 (Middlesex); 2016 (Hampshire)

MOST EXCITING DAY AS A CRICKETER? Winning the Lord's one-day final with Hampshire in 2018
BIGGEST INFLUENCE ON YOUR DEVELOPMENT AS A CRICKETER (EXCLUDING PARENTS)? My uncle Colin de Lucchi who taught me from the age of three
FIRST CRICKET CLUB? My first English club was Southgate CC, London
IF YOU COULD TAKE ONE COUNTY CRICKETER'S BEST SHOT AND ADD IT TO YOUR OWN GAME? Adam Rossington's slog-sweep off the fast bowlers
TOUGHEST OPPONENT IN COUNTY CRICKET? Chris Rushworth – consistent probing
STRANGEST THING YOU'VE DONE DURING LOCKDOWN? Getting a walk-through pint from my local pub
GUILTY PLEASURE? Chocolate and Netflix before bed
TWITTER: @Bergy646

Batting	Mat	Inns	NO	Runs	HS	Ave	SR	100	50	Ct	St
First-class	133	201	23	5011	130*	28.15	64.13	2	27	68	0
List A	103	77	13	1474	75	23.03	93.05	0	7	39	0
T20s	94	72	22	1083	90	21.66	126.22	0	3	24	0
Bowling	**Mat**	**Balls**	**Runs**	**Wkts**	**BBI**	**BBM**	**Ave**	**Econ**	**SR**	**5w**	**10**
First-class	133	17432	8778	279	6/56	7/45	31.46	3.02	62.4	5	0
List A	103	3634	3184	97	5/26	5/26	32.82	5.25	37.4	1	0
T20s	94	1621	2163	74	4/20	4/20	29.22	8.00	21.9	0	0

DOM BESS

RHB / OB / R0 / W0

FULL NAME: Dominic Mark Bess
BORN: July 22, 1997, Exeter, Devon
SQUAD NO: 22
HEIGHT: 5ft 11in
NICKNAME: Moonhead
EDUCATION: Blundell's School, Tiverton, Devon
TEAMS: England, Yorkshire, Somerset
ROLE: Bowler
DEBUT: Test: 2018; First-class: 2016; List A: 2018; T20: 2016

BEST BATTING: 107 MCC vs Essex, Barbados, 2018
BEST BOWLING: 7-117 Somerset vs Hampshire, Taunton, 2017

FIRST CRICKET CLUB? Sidmouth CC, Devon. A beautiful coastal cricket club with a thatched roof
CHILDHOOD SPORTING HERO? Graeme Swann
BEST INNINGS YOU'VE SEEN? James Hildreth scoring a hundred on one leg against Nottinghamshire in 2016
MOST INTERESTING TEAMMATE? Eddie Byrom. That bloke is on a different planet. Very funny to sit next to and watch the game with
IF YOU WERE AN ANIMAL, WHICH WOULD IT BE? A panda – just because they like eating
TWITTER: @DomBess99

Batting	Mat	Inns	NO	Runs	HS	Ave	SR	100	50	Ct	St
Tests	14	19	5	319	57	22.78	44.92	0	1	3	0
First-class	51	77	14	1475	107	23.41	51.19	1	6	22	0
List A	15	12	1	100	24*	9.09	66.66	0	0	5	0
T20s	8	4	1	9	5*	3.00	75.00	0	0	0	0
Bowling	**Mat**	**Balls**	**Runs**	**Wkts**	**BBI**	**BBM**	**Ave**	**Econ**	**SR**	**5w**	**10**
Tests	14	2502	1223	36	5/30	8/130	33.97	2.93	69.5	2	0
First-class	51	8667	4352	146	7/117	10/162	29.80	3.01	59.3	10	1
List A	15	648	616	11	3/35	3/35	56.00	5.70	58.9	0	0
T20s	8	156	216	5	2/30	2/30	43.20	8.30	31.2	0	0

JACOB BETHELL LHB / SLA / R0 / W0

FULL NAME: Jacob Graham Bethell
BORN: October 23, 2003, Barbados
SQUAD NO: 2
HEIGHT: 5ft 10in
NICKNAME: Beth
EDUCATION: Harrison College, Barbados; Rugby School, Warwickshire
TEAMS: Warwickshire
ROLE: Allrounder

MOST EXCITING DAY AS A CRICKETER? The final day of the Bunbury Festival in 2018
CHILDHOOD SPORTING HERO? Sir Garry Sobers
BIGGEST INFLUENCE ON YOUR DEVELOPMENT AS A CRICKETER (EXCLUDING PARENTS)? Michael Powell (former Warwickshire captain and director of cricket at Rugby School)
WHAT WOULD YOU DO IF YOU WERE IN CHARGE OF COUNTY CRICKET? Play more red-ball matches, play more at outgrounds, and try to incentivise crowds for Championship games
WHAT WOULD YOU DO IF YOU WERE PRIME MINISTER? Create more opportunities for ethnic minorities
STRANGEST THING YOU'VE DONE DURING LOCKDOWN? Making a golf net out of my mum's bedsheets
FAVOURITE SMELL? New batting gloves
NOTES: The 17-year-old allrounder signed his first professional contract at Warwickshire earlier this year. Born and raised in Barbados, Bethell was named Player of the Tournament in the West Indies U15 competition in 2015 and his talent was enough to earn him a scholarship at Rugby School aged 12. He was recommended to Warwickshire by the club's former captain Michael Powell, now director of cricket at Rugby School, and made his Second XI debut in 2019. Bethell is seen as one of the most exciting prospects in recent years. "Jacob has the potential to achieve a huge amount in his professional career at Warwickshire," said Paul Greetham, the club's high performance manager. "He can bat anywhere in the top order, he presents a very attractive slow left-arm spin option and he is a natural athlete who is excellent in the field"

SAM BILLINGS

RHB / WK / R0 / W0

FULL NAME: Samuel William Billings
BORN: June 15, 1991, Pembury, Kent
SQUAD NO: 7
HEIGHT: 6ft
NICKNAME: Bilbo
EDUCATION: Haileybury & Imperial College, Herts; Loughborough University
TEAMS: England, Kent, Chennai Super Kings, Delhi Capitals, Islamabad United, Sydney Sixers, Sydney Thunder
ROLE: Batsman/wicketkeeper
DEBUT: ODI: 2015; T20I: 2015; First-class: 2011; List A: 2011; T20: 2011

BEST BATTING: 171 Kent vs Gloucestershire, Bristol, 2016

COUNTY CAP: 2015

MOST EXCITING DAY AS A CRICKETER? Making my England debut
CHILDHOOD SPORTING HERO? Lewis Hamilton
FIRST CRICKET CLUB? Hartley Country Club, Dartford, Kent
MOST INTERESTING TEAMMATE? Mohammad Nabi – he's an amazing guy who had an incredible journey to become the best T20 allrounder in the world
TWITTER: @sambillings
NOTES: England's batsman/wicketkeeper returns to the IPL this year for the first time since 2018 after he was re-signed by Delhi Capitals. Though he is formally Kent's club captain, the 29-year-old's appearances for his county have been limited for a number of seasons due to his international and T20 commitments

Batting	Mat	Inns	NO	Runs	HS	Ave	SR	100	50	Ct	St
ODIs	21	18	2	586	118	36.62	93.46	1	4	16	0
T20Is	30	27	4	391	87	17.00	133.44	0	2	16	1
First-class	70	103	11	3178	171	34.54	60.17	6	14	167	11
List A	97	86	15	3023	175	42.57	104.31	7	20	85	8
T20s	187	175	26	3527	95*	23.67	131.01	0	21	107	17
Bowling	**Mat**	**Balls**	**Runs**	**Wkts**	**BBI**	**BBM**	**Ave**	**Econ**	**SR**	**5w**	**10**
ODIs	21	-	-	-	-	-	-	-	-	-	-
T20Is	30	-	-	-	-	-	-	-	-	-	-
First-class	70	1	4	0	-	-	-	24.00	-	0	0
List A	97	-	-	-	-	-	-	-	-	-	-
T20s	187	-	-	-	-	-	-	-	-	-	-

JACKSON BIRD

RHB / RFM / R0 / W0

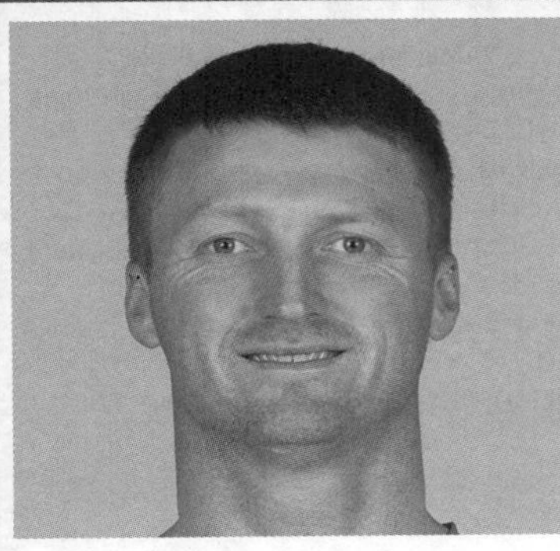

FULL NAME: Jackson Munro Bird
BORN: December 11, 1986, Sydney, Australia
SQUAD NO: TBC
EDUCATION: St Pius X College, Chatswood, Sydney; Saint Ignatius' College Riverview, Sydney
TEAMS: Australia, Lancashire, Hampshire, Melbourne Stars, Nottinghamshire, Sydney Sixers, Tasmania
ROLE: Bowler
DEBUT: Test: 2012; First-class: 2011; List A: 2011; T20: 2012

BEST BATTING: 54 Tasmania vs New South Wales, Hobart, 2021
BEST BOWLING: 7-18 Tasmania vs New South Wales, Hobart, 2021
COUNTY CAP: 2016 (Nottinghamshire)

NOTES: The veteran Australian seamer has joined Lancashire for six Championship matches starting from the third game of the season on April 22. "Jackson's skills bowling with the new ball and his vast experience will complement our current pace attack nicely," said Paul Allott, Lancashire's director of cricket. "Following Graham Onions's retirement at the end of last season, it was important that we were able to add depth to our quick-bowling ranks and help to replace his on-field leadership of the attack. Richard Gleeson will be unavailable due to a back injury for the first part of the season, so Jackson will give us another option for those six four-day fixtures." Bird played the most recent of his nine Tests against England during the 2017/18 Ashes and has had previous stints with Hampshire and Nottinghamshire in county cricket. The 34-year-old was in fine form for Tasmania in the 2020/21 Sheffield Shield, taking 30 wickets at 22.10 in seven matches up until March 22

Batting	Mat	Inns	NO	Runs	HS	Ave	SR	100	50	Ct	St
Tests	9	9	6	43	19*	14.33	30.49	0	0	2	0
First-class	98	135	35	1193	54	11.93	58.59	0	2	48	0
List A	38	19	8	163	28*	14.81	100.61	0	0	16	0
T20s	72	21	12	75	14*	8.33	82.41	0	0	32	0
Bowling	**Mat**	**Balls**	**Runs**	**Wkts**	**BBI**	**BBM**	**Ave**	**Econ**	**SR**	**5w**	**10**
Tests	9	1934	1042	34	5/59	7/117	30.64	3.23	56.8	1	0
First-class	98	20092	9954	409	7/18	11/95	24.33	2.97	49.1	18	5
List A	38	2047	1601	48	6/25	6/25	33.35	4.69	42.6	1	0
T20s	72	1437	1831	61	4/31	4/31	30.01	7.64	23.5	0	0

ALEX BLAKE

LHB / RM

FULL NAME: Alexander James Blake
BORN: January 25, 1989, Farnborough, Kent
SQUAD NO: 10
HEIGHT: 6ft 2in
NICKNAME: TS
EDUCATION: Hayes Secondary School, Kent; Leeds Metropolitan University
TEAMS: Kent, England U19
ROLE: Batsman
DEBUT: First-class: 2008; List A: 2007; T20: 2010

BEST BATTING: 71* Kent vs Hampshire, Southampton, 2015 (T20)
BEST BOWLING: 1-17 Kent vs Gloucestershire, Canterbury, 2019 (T20)
COUNTY CAP: 2017

MOST EXCITING DAY AS A CRICKETER? Receiving my county cap in 2017
CHILDHOOD SPORTING HERO? Ryan Giggs
FIRST CRICKET CLUB? Bromley Town CC, London
IF YOU COULD TAKE ONE COUNTY CRICKETER'S BEST SHOT AND ADD IT TO YOUR OWN GAME? Jos Buttler's paddle-scoop
TOUGHEST OPPONENT IN COUNTY CRICKET? Mohammad Amir – he always seems to uproot my stumps with a filthy in-swinging toe-crusher
WHAT WOULD YOU DO IF YOU WERE IN CHARGE OF COUNTY CRICKET? Introduce home and away kits for white-ball cricket, put roofs on grounds to stop games being rained off
STRANGEST THING YOU'VE DONE DURING LOCKDOWN? Making videos which involve toilet rolls
GUILTY PLEASURE? Listening to Little Mix
TWITTER: @aj_blake10
NOTES: The Kent batsman has signed a white-ball contract which runs until the end of the 2022 season

Batting	Mat	Inns	NO	Runs	HS	Ave	SR	100	50	Ct	St
First-class	46	72	6	1511	105*	22.89	55.61	1	6	25	0
List A	106	88	18	2125	116	30.35	100.14	1	12	53	0
T20s	128	110	26	1772	71*	21.09	135.26	0	9	66	0
Bowling	**Mat**	**Balls**	**Runs**	**Wkts**	**BBI**	**BBM**	**Ave**	**Econ**	**SR**	**5w**	**10**
First-class	46	210	138	3	2/9	2/9	46.00	3.94	70.0	0	0
List A	106	204	223	4	2/13	2/13	55.75	6.55	51.0	0	0
T20s	128	72	89	1	1/17	1/17	89.00	7.41	72.0	0	0

JACK BLATHERWICK

RHB / RFM / R0 / W0

FULL NAME: Jack Morgan Blatherwick
BORN: June 4, 1998, Nottingham
SQUAD NO: 4
HEIGHT: 6ft 2in
NICKNAME: The Milkman
EDUCATION: Holgate Academy, Hucknall; Central College, Nottingham
TEAMS: Lancashire, England U19, Nottinghamshire
ROLE: Bowler
DEBUT: First-class: 2019; List A: 2018

BEST BATTING: 4* Nottinghamshire vs Warwickshire, Trent Bridge, 2019
BEST BOWLING: 1-82 Nottinghamshire vs Surrey, The Oval, 2019

MOST EXCITING DAY AS A CRICKETER? Making my List A debut for Nottinghamshire at Trent Bridge on a "family fun day" in front of a full house
FAMILY TIES? My uncle is the former Nottingham Forest defender Steve Blatherwick
CHILDHOOD SPORTING HERO? Andrew Flintoff
BIGGEST INFLUENCE ON YOUR DEVELOPMENT AS A CRICKETER (EXCLUDING PARENTS)? Mike Hendrick at Notts – old-school but really knowledgeable
FIRST CRICKET CLUB? Kimberley Institute CC, Nottingham
IF YOU COULD TAKE ONE COUNTY CRICKETER'S BEST SHOT AND ADD IT TO YOUR OWN GAME? Joe Clarke's cover-drive
MOST ECCENTRIC TEAMMATE? Luke Wood – he wakes up before his alarm goes off
FAVOURITE SMELL? A Sunday roast
GUILTY PLEASURE? Music from the 1970s and '80s
TWITTER: @BlatherwickJM

Batting	Mat	Inns	NO	Runs	HS	Ave	SR	100	50	Ct	St
First-class	2	2	2	6	4*	-	50.00	0	0	0	0
List A	3	3	2	6	3*	6.00	28.57	0	0	1	0
Bowling	**Mat**	**Balls**	**Runs**	**Wkts**	**BBI**	**BBM**	**Ave**	**Econ**	**SR**	**5w**	**10**
First-class	2	208	192	2	1/82	1/82	96.00	5.53	104.0	0	0
List A	3	48	72	1	1/55	1/55	72.00	9.00	48.0	0	0

JOSH BOHANNON

RHB / RMF / R0 / W0

FULL NAME: Joshua James Bohannon
BORN: April 9, 1997, Bolton, Lancashire
SQUAD NO: 20
HEIGHT: 5ft 9in
NICKNAME: Bosh
EDUCATION: Harper Green High School, Bolton
TEAMS: Lancashire
ROLE: Allrounder
DEBUT: First-class: 2018; List A: 2018; T20: 2018

BEST BATTING: 174 Lancashire vs Derbyshire, Old Trafford, 2019
BEST BOWLING: 3-46 Lancashire vs Hampshire, Southampton, 2018

MOST EXCITING DAY AS A CRICKETER? Making my first-class debut at The Oval in 2018
CHILDHOOD SPORTING HERO? Andrew Flintoff
BIGGEST INFLUENCE ON YOUR DEVELOPMENT AS A CRICKETER (EXCLUDING PARENTS)? My girlfriend Lucy and her dad Ian
FIRST CRICKET CLUB? Farnworth CC, Greater Manchester
TOUGHEST OPPONENT IN COUNTY CRICKET? Morné Morkel
WHAT WOULD YOU DO IF YOU WERE IN CHARGE OF COUNTY CRICKET? Play more often at outgrounds, increase the number of pink-ball games
STRANGEST THING YOU'VE DONE DURING LOCKDOWN? Buying a house
SURPRISING FACT ABOUT YOU? I played junior cricket alongside Haseeb Hameed at Farnworth Social Circle CC (Bolton league)
GUILTY PLEASURE? Gogglebox on TV
TWITTER: @joshbo97

Batting	Mat	Inns	NO	Runs	HS	Ave	SR	100	50	Ct	St
First-class	21	28	4	984	174	41.00	47.51	1	6	10	0
List A	15	10	2	210	55*	26.25	93.75	0	1	3	0
T20s	21	13	5	77	23	9.62	84.61	0	0	11	0
Bowling	**Mat**	**Balls**	**Runs**	**Wkts**	**BBI**	**BBM**	**Ave**	**Econ**	**SR**	**5w**	**10**
First-class	21	820	468	10	3/46	4/82	46.80	3.42	82.0	0	0
List A	15	150	208	1	1/33	1/33	208.00	8.32	150.0	0	0
T20s	21	-	-	-	-	-	-	-	-	-	-

RAVI BOPARA RHB / RM / R1 / W0

FULL NAME: Ravinder Singh Bopara
BORN: May 4, 1985, Forest Gate, London
SQUAD NO: 23
HEIGHT: 5ft 10in
NICKNAME: Puppy
EDUCATION: Brampton Manor, London
TEAMS: England, Sussex, Auckland, Essex, Gloucestershire, Karachi Kings, Kings XI Punjab, Multan Sultans, Peshawar Zalmi, Sunrisers Hyderabad, Sydney Sixers
ROLE: Allrounder
DEBUT: Test: 2007; ODI: 2007; T20I: 2008; First-class: 2002; List A: 2002; T20: 2003

BEST BATTING: 229 Essex vs Northamptonshire, Chelmsford, 2007
BEST BOWLING: 5-49 Essex vs Derbyshire, Chelmsford, 2016
COUNTY CAP: 2005 (Essex); BENEFIT: 2015 (Essex)

MOST EXCITING DAY AS A CRICKETER? Playing against Sachin Tendulkar
CHILDHOOD SPORTING HERO? Sachin Tendulkar
BIGGEST INFLUENCE ON YOUR DEVELOPMENT AS A CRICKETER (EXCLUDING PARENTS)? Graham Gooch and Sachin Tendulkar
TOUGHEST OPPONENT IN COUNTY CRICKET? Saeed Ajmal – he was tough to pick
WHAT WOULD YOU DO IF YOU WERE IN CHARGE OF COUNTY CRICKET? Introduce a 10-over competition
FAVOURITE SMELL? Dog ears
SURPRISING FACT ABOUT YOU? I have a fast-food business
TWITTER: @ravibopara

Batting	Mat	Inns	NO	Runs	HS	Ave	SR	100	50	Ct	St
Tests	13	19	1	575	143	31.94	52.89	3	0	6	0
ODIs	120	109	21	2695	101*	30.62	77.84	1	14	35	0
T20Is	38	35	10	711	65*	28.44	118.69	0	3	7	0
First-class	221	357	40	12821	229	40.44	51.54	31	55	118	0
List A	323	301	56	9845	201*	40.18	-	15	60	103	0
T20s	372	339	74	7384	105*	27.86	121.40	1	37	125	0
Bowling	**Mat**	**Balls**	**Runs**	**Wkts**	**BBI**	**BBM**	**Ave**	**Econ**	**SR**	**5w**	**10**
Tests	13	434	290	1	1/39	1/39	290.00	4.00	434.0	0	0
ODIs	120	1860	1523	40	4/38	4/38	38.07	4.91	46.5	0	0
T20Is	38	322	387	16	4/10	4/10	24.18	7.21	20.1	0	0
First-class	221	15462	9381	257	5/49	-	36.50	3.64	60.1	3	0
List A	323	8097	7197	248	5/63	5/63	29.02	5.33	32.6	1	0
T20s	372	4767	5967	234	6/16	6/16	25.50	7.51	20.3	1	0

SCOTT BORTHWICK

LHB / LB / R3 / W0

FULL NAME: Scott George Borthwick
BORN: April 19, 1990, Sunderland, County Durham
SQUAD NO: 16
HEIGHT: 5ft 10in
NICKNAME: Badger
EDUCATION: Farringdon Community Sports College, Sunderland
TEAMS: England, Durham, Chilaw Marians, Surrey, Wellington
ROLE: Allrounder
DEBUT: Test: 2014; ODI: 2011; T20I: 2011; First-class 2009; List A: 2009; T20: 2008

BEST BATTING: 216 Durham vs Middlesex, Chester-le-Street, 2014
BEST BOWLING: 6-70 Durham vs Surrey, The Oval, 2013
COUNTY CAP: 2018 (Surrey)

MOST EXCITING DAY AS A CRICKETER? Making my England debut
CHILDHOOD SPORTING HERO? Shane Warne
BIGGEST INFLUENCE ON YOUR DEVELOPMENT AS A CRICKETER (EXCLUDING PARENTS)? Geoff Cook – he was Academy director when I joined the Durham Academy, and he was head coach when I made my first-team debut
FIRST CRICKET CLUB? Eppleton CC, Sunderland. I made my first-team debut aged 13 and got a 44-ball duck (on a poor pitch)
STRANGEST THING YOU'VE DONE DURING LOCKDOWN? Getting married with no guests
GUILTY PLEASURE? Eating Galaxy chocolate while playing Football Manager
TWITTER: @Borthwick16

Batting	Mat	Inns	NO	Runs	HS	Ave	SR	100	50	Ct	St
Tests	1	2	0	5	4	2.50	26.31	0	0	2	0
ODIs	2	2	0	18	15	9.00	112.50	0	0	0	0
T20Is	1	1	0	14	14	14.00	87.50	0	0	1	0
First-class	169	285	25	9288	216	35.72	52.72	19	50	221	0
List A	99	72	11	1350	87	22.13	78.67	0	7	32	0
T20s	94	50	18	561	62	17.53	95.40	0	1	44	0
Bowling	**Mat**	**Balls**	**Runs**	**Wkts**	**BBI**	**BBM**	**Ave**	**Econ**	**SR**	**5w**	**10**
Tests	1	78	82	4	3/33	4/82	20.50	6.30	19.5	0	0
ODIs	2	54	72	0	-	-	-	8.00	-	0	0
T20Is	1	24	15	1	1/15	1/15	15.00	3.75	24.0	0	0
First-class	169	12241	8101	208	6/70	8/84	38.94	3.97	58.8	3	0
List A	99	2750	2773	69	5/38	5/38	40.18	6.05	39.8	1	0
T20s	94	1160	1566	67	4/18	4/18	23.37	8.10	17.3	0	0

NAT BOWLEY

LHB / OB / R0 / W0

FULL NAME: Nathan John Bowley
BORN: August 3, 2001, Nottingham
SQUAD NO: 33
HEIGHT: 6ft 3in
EDUCATION: Woodbrook Vale School, Loughborough; Loughborough College
TEAMS: Leicestershire
ROLE: Bowler

MOST EXCITING DAY AS A CRICKETER? Qualifying for the T20 Blast quarter-finals on the final day of the group stages last season
CHILDHOOD SPORTING HERO? Graeme Swann
BIGGEST INFLUENCE ON YOUR DEVELOPMENT AS A CRICKETER (EXCLUDING PARENTS)? Dips Patel (Leicestershire Second XI coach) and Jigar Naik (spin-bowling coach) – I have worked with both of them since I was 13
FIRST CRICKET CLUB? Loughborough Outwoods CC, Leicestershire
IF YOU COULD TAKE ONE COUNTY CRICKETER'S BEST SHOT AND ADD IT TO YOUR OWN GAME? Tom Banton's reverse-sweep
TOUGHEST OPPONENT IN COUNTY CRICKET? Haseeb Hameed – he didn't look like getting out all day when he made a hundred for Lancashire against us in a Second XI game in 2019
MOST ECCENTRIC TEAMMATE? Dieter Klein – he's always doing something to make someone laugh
WHAT WOULD YOU DO IF YOU WERE IN CHARGE OF COUNTY CRICKET? Increase the amount of red-ball cricket, make more spin-friendly pitches
STRANGEST THING YOU'VE DONE DURING LOCKDOWN? Putting on my Leicester City shirt for a cup final on Football Manager (video game)
FAVOURITE SMELL? A roast dinner
GUILTY PLEASURE? One Direction
TWITTER: @nat_bowley

JAMES BRACEY

LHB / WK / R0 / W0

FULL NAME: James Robert Bracey
BORN: May 3, 1997, Bristol
SQUAD NO: 25
HEIGHT: 6ft 1in
NICKNAME: Bob
EDUCATION: The Ridings High School, Bristol; SGS Filton College; Loughborough University
TEAMS: Gloucestershire, England Lions
ROLE: Batsman/wicketkeeper
DEBUT: First-class: 2016; List A: 2019; T20: 2019

BEST BATTING: 156 Gloucestershire vs Glamorgan, Cardiff, 2017

COUNTY CAP: 2016

FAMILY TIES? My older brother Sam has played first-class cricket for Cardiff MCCU
CHILDHOOD SPORTING HERO? Rickie Lambert – Bristol Rovers legend
FIRST CRICKET CLUB? Winterbourne CC, Bristol
MOST INTERESTING TEAMMATE? Benny Howell – he's always coming up with new theories
SURPRISING FACT ABOUT YOU? I was probably the only child ever who did not like Ketchup or baked beans
IF YOU WERE AN ANIMAL, WHICH WOULD IT BE? A badger
TWITTER: @bobbybracey114

Batting	Mat	Inns	NO	Runs	HS	Ave	SR	100	50	Ct	St
First-class	39	66	6	2096	156	34.93	46.87	5	8	49	0
List A	9	9	1	487	113*	60.87	108.94	1	4	5	0
T20s	24	21	2	370	64	19.47	123.33	0	1	8	8
Bowling	**Mat**	**Balls**	**Runs**	**Wkts**	**BBI**	**BBM**	**Ave**	**Econ**	**SR**	**5w**	**10**
First-class	39	60	35	0	-	-	-	3.50	-	0	0
List A	9	18	23	1	1/23	1/23	23.00	7.66	18.0	0	0
T20s	24	-	-	-	-	-	-	-	-	-	-

CARLOS BRATHWAITE RHB / RMF

FULL NAME: Carlos Ricardo Brathwaite
BORN: July 18, 1988, Christ Church, Barbados
SQUAD NO: 26
TEAMS: West Indies, Warwickshire, Antigua Hawksbills, Barbados, Barisal Bulls, Combined Campuses & Colleges, Delhi Daredevils, Jamaica Tallawahs, Kent, Khulna Titans, Kolkata Knight Riders, Multan Sultans, St Kitts & Nevis Patriots, Sunrisers Hyderabad, Sydney Sixers
ROLE: Allrounder
DEBUT: Test: 2015; ODI: 2011; T20I: 2011; First-class: 2011; List A: 2011; T20: 2011

BEST BATTING: 64* Khulna Titans vs Dhaka Dynamites, Mirpur, 2017 (T20)
BEST BOWLING: 4-15 St Kitts & Nevis Patriots vs Barbados Tridents, Bridgetown, 2017 (T20)

TWITTER: @TridentSportsX
NOTES: Brathwaite's extraordinary innings in the 2016 World T20 final, when he belted Ben Stokes for four consecutive sixes to seal the trophy for West Indies at Eden Gardens, has gone down in legend, and the Edgbaston faithful will hope to be treated to similar pyrotechnics from the big-hitting Bajan this summer. Brathwaite is set to join the Birmingham Bears for their T20 Blast campaign, his second appearance in the competition following a five-match spell with Kent in 2018. The former Windies T20 skipper has played for three franchises at the IPL and helped Sydney Sixers defend their Big Bash crown in February. "He's a game-changer who will add vital firepower to our middle order, but his variation with the ball gives us another strong seam-bowling option," said Paul Farbrace, Warwickshire's director of cricket

Batting	Mat	Inns	NO	Runs	HS	Ave	SR	100	50	Ct	St
Tests	3	5	1	181	69	45.25	63.73	0	3	0	0
ODIs	44	37	3	559	101	16.44	91.04	1	1	11	0
T20Is	41	27	6	310	37*	14.76	113.13	0	0	19	0
First-class	39	64	9	1522	109	27.67	-	1	9	20	0
List A	92	78	11	1350	113	20.14	-	2	4	31	0
T20s	195	147	35	1698	64*	15.16	135.08	0	2	78	0
Bowling	**Mat**	**Balls**	**Runs**	**Wkts**	**BBI**	**BBM**	**Ave**	**Econ**	**SR**	**5w**	**10**
Tests	3	408	242	1	1/30	1/139	242.00	3.55	408.0	0	0
ODIs	44	1825	1766	43	5/27	5/27	41.06	5.80	42.4	1	0
T20Is	41	709	1013	31	3/20	3/20	32.67	8.57	22.8	0	0
First-class	39	4472	2098	88	7/90	9/61	23.84	2.81	50.8	2	0
List A	92	3500	3018	105	5/27	5/27	28.74	5.17	33.3	1	0
T20s	195	3536	4789	174	4/15	4/15	27.52	8.12	20.3	0	0

TIM BRESNAN

RHB / RFM / R0 / W0 / MVP26

FULL NAME: Timothy Thomas Bresnan
BORN: February 28, 1985, Pontefract, Yorkshire
SQUAD NO: 3
HEIGHT: 6ft
NICKNAME: Brezzylad
EDUCATION: Castleford High School, West Yorkshire; New College Pontefract
TEAMS: England, Warwickshire, Hobart Hurricanes, Perth Scorchers, Yorkshire
ROLE: Allrounder
DEBUT: Test: 2009; ODI: 2006; T20I: 2006; First-class: 2003; List A: 2001; T20: 2003

BEST BATTING: 169* Yorkshire vs Durham, Chester-le-Street, 2015
BEST BOWLING: 5-28 Yorkshire vs Hampshire, Headingley, 2018
COUNTY CAP: 2006 (Yorkshire); BENEFIT: 2014 (Yorkshire)

MOST EXCITING DAY AS A CRICKETER? Boxing Day of the 2010/11 Ashes at the MCG
CHILDHOOD SPORTING HERO? Shaun Pollock
BIGGEST INFLUENCE ON YOUR DEVELOPMENT AS A CRICKETER (EXCLUDING PARENTS)? The senior pros – they showed me how to play the game the right way
FIRST CRICKET CLUB? Townville CC, Castleford, West Yorkshire
IF YOU COULD TAKE ONE COUNTY CRICKETER'S BEST SHOT AND ADD IT TO YOUR OWN GAME? Steven Davies's cover-drive
TOUGHEST OPPONENT IN COUNTY CRICKET? Kumar Sangakkara
STRANGEST THING YOU'VE DONE DURING LOCKDOWN? Trying to school my kids
GUILTY PLEASURE? Gold Rush on the Discovery Channel
TWITTER: @timbresnan

Batting	Mat	Inns	NO	Runs	HS	Ave	SR	100	50	Ct	St
Tests	23	26	4	575	91	26.13	39.43	0	3	8	0
ODIs	85	64	20	871	80	19.79	90.25	0	1	20	0
T20Is	34	22	9	216	47*	16.61	127.05	0	0	10	0
First-class	202	278	43	6813	169*	28.99	47.15	7	34	107	0
List A	279	203	54	3221	95*	21.61	91.11	0	10	73	0
T20s	182	132	52	1639	51	20.48	131.96	0	1	61	0
Bowling	**Mat**	**Balls**	**Runs**	**Wkts**	**BBI**	**BBM**	**Ave**	**Econ**	**SR**	**5w**	**10**
Tests	23	4674	2357	72	5/48	8/141	32.73	3.02	64.9	1	0
ODIs	85	4221	3813	109	5/48	5/48	34.98	5.42	38.7	1	0
T20Is	34	663	887	24	3/10	3/10	36.95	8.02	27.6	0	0
First-class	202	33544	17367	562	5/28		30.90	3.10	59.6	9	0
List A	279	12338	10794	315	5/48	5/48	34.26	5.24	39.1	1	0
T20s	182	3427	4654	180	6/19	6/19	25.85	8.14	19.0	1	0

DANNY BRIGGS

RHB / SLA / R0 / W0

FULL NAME: Danny Richard Briggs
BORN: April 30, 1991, Newport, Isle of Wight
SQUAD NO: 14
HEIGHT: 6ft 2in
NICKNAME: Briggsy
EDUCATION: Carisbrooke High School, Isle of Wight
TEAMS: England, Warwickshire, Hampshire, Sussex
ROLE: Bowler
DEBUT: ODI: 2012; T20I: 2012; First-class: 2009; List A: 2009; T20: 2010

BEST BATTING: 120* Sussex vs South Africa A, Arundel, 2017
BEST BOWLING: 6-45 England Lions vs Windward Islands, Roseau, 2011
COUNTY CAP: 2012 (Hampshire)

MOST EXCITING DAY AS A CRICKETER? It's a toss-up between my England debut and playing in T20 Finals Day
CHILDHOOD SPORTING HERO? Shane Warne
BIGGEST INFLUENCE ON YOUR DEVELOPMENT AS A CRICKETER (EXCLUDING PARENTS)? Sam Garaway – my first coach who made me fall in love with the game
FIRST CRICKET CLUB? Ventnor CC, Isle of Wight
IF YOU COULD TAKE ONE COUNTY CRICKETER'S BEST SHOT AND ADD IT TO YOUR OWN GAME? Ian Bell's cover-drive
TOUGHEST OPPONENT IN COUNTY CRICKET? Shiv Chanderpaul – he was so hard to bowl at as a spinner
TWITTER: @DannyBriggs19

Batting	Mat	Inns	NO	Runs	HS	Ave	SR	100	50	Ct	St
ODIs	1	-	-	-	-	-	-	-	-	0	0
T20Is	7	1	1	0	0*	-	-	0	0	1	0
First-class	108	138	38	1769	120*	17.69	-	1	1	38	0
List A	107	56	24	402	37*	12.56	93.27	0	0	34	0
T20s	183	42	27	155	35*	10.33	112.31	0	0	31	0
Bowling	**Mat**	**Balls**	**Runs**	**Wkts**	**BBI**	**BBM**	**Ave**	**Econ**	**SR**	**5w**	**10**
ODIs	1	60	39	2	2/39	2/39	19.50	3.90	30.0	0	0
T20Is	7	108	199	5	2/25	2/25	39.80	11.05	21.6	0	0
First-class	108	18642	9390	270	6/45	9/96	34.77	3.02	69.0	8	0
List A	107	4916	4188	112	4/32	4/32	37.39	5.11	43.8	0	0
T20s	183	3678	4431	197	5/19	5/19	22.49	7.22	18.6	1	0

STUART BROAD

LHB / RFM / R0 / W0

FULL NAME: Stuart Christopher John Broad
BORN: June 24, 1986, Nottingham
SQUAD NO: 8
HEIGHT: 6ft 5in
NICKNAME: Broady
EDUCATION: Oakham School, Rutland
TEAMS: England, Nottinghamshire, Hobart Hurricanes, Kings XI Punjab, Leicestershire
ROLE: Bowler
DEBUT: Test: 2007; ODI: 2006; T20I: 2006; First-class: 2005; List A: 2005; T20: 2006

BEST BATTING: 169 England vs Pakistan, Lord's, 2010
BEST BOWLING: 8-15 England vs Australia, Trent Bridge, 2015
COUNTY CAP: 2007 (Leicestershire); 2008 (Notts); BENEFIT: 2019 (Notts)

FAMILY TIES? My father Chris played for England, Nottinghamshire and Gloucestershire and is now an ICC match official
CHILDHOOD SPORTING HERO? Shaun Pollock
TWITTER: @StuartBroad8

Batting	Mat	Inns	NO	Runs	HS	Ave	SR	100	50	Ct	St
Tests	146	213	36	3355	169	18.95	65.36	1	13	47	0
ODIs	121	68	25	529	45*	12.30	74.61	0	0	27	0
T20Is	56	26	10	118	18*	7.37	100.00	0	0	21	0
First-class	231	325	56	5325	169	19.79	63.17	1	25	83	0
List A	151	80	28	620	45*	11.92	75.88	0	0	32	0
T20s	85	32	12	152	18*	7.60	102.01	0	0	26	0
Bowling	**Mat**	**Balls**	**Runs**	**Wkts**	**BBI**	**BBM**	**Ave**	**Econ**	**SR**	**5w**	**10**
Tests	146	29316	14328	517	8/15	11/121	27.71	2.93	56.7	18	3
ODIs	121	6109	5364	178	5/23	5/23	30.13	5.26	34.3	1	0
T20Is	56	1173	1491	65	4/24	4/24	22.93	7.62	18.0	0	0
First-class	231	43343	21916	811	8/15	-	27.02	3.03	53.4	30	4
List A	151	7496	6591	216	5/23	5/23	30.51	5.27	34.7	1	0
T20s	85	1788	2144	100	4/24	4/24	21.44	7.19	17.8	0	0

HARRY BROOK

RHB / RMF / R0 / W0 / MVP81

FULL NAME: Harry Cherrington Brook
BORN: February 22, 1999, Keighley, Yorkshire
SQUAD NO: 88
HEIGHT: 6ft
EDUCATION: Sedbergh School, Cumbria
TEAMS: Yorkshire, England U19
ROLE: Batsman
DEBUT: First-class: 2016; List A: 2017; T20: 2018

BEST BATTING: 124 Yorkshire vs Essex, Chelmsford, 2018
BEST BOWLING: 1-54 Yorkshire vs Somerset, Scarborough, 2017

MOST EXCITING DAY AS A CRICKETER? My first-class debut for Yorkshire against Pakistan A at Headingley in 2016
CHILDHOOD SPORTING HERO? Jacques Kallis
SURPRISING FACT ABOUT YOU? I love Tinder
GUILTY PLEASURE? Peaky Blinders
TWITTER: @harry_brook88

Batting	Mat	Inns	NO	Runs	HS	Ave	SR	100	50	Ct	St
First-class	33	54	1	1285	124	24.24	60.44	2	6	19	0
List A	15	12	1	343	103	31.18	99.42	1	1	4	0
T20s	25	25	5	556	50*	27.80	145.93	0	1	14	0
Bowling	**Mat**	**Balls**	**Runs**	**Wkts**	**BBI**	**BBM**	**Ave**	**Econ**	**SR**	**5w**	**10**
First-class	33	332	181	1	1/54	1/65	181.00	3.27	332.0	0	0
List A	15	18	19	0	-	-	-	6.33	-	0	0
T20s	25	12	26	1	1/13	1/13	26.00	13.00	12.0	0	0

ETHAN BROOKES

RHB / RMF / R0 / W0

FULL NAME: Ethan Alexander Brookes
BORN: May 23, 2001, Solihull, Warwickshire
SQUAD NO: 77
HEIGHT: 6ft 2in
NICKNAME: Eth
EDUCATION: Solihull School
TEAMS: Warwickshire
ROLE: Bowler
DEBUT: First-class: 2019

BEST BATTING: 15* Warwickshire vs Glamorgan, Cardiff, 2020

MOST EXCITING DAY AS A CRICKETER? Playing at Lord's for the English Schools Cricket Association and making my first-team debut for Warwickshire in the County Championship in 2019
CHILDHOOD SPORTING HERO? Andrew Flintoff
BIGGEST INFLUENCE ON YOUR DEVELOPMENT AS A CRICKETER (EXCLUDING PARENTS)? Dave Cowper – my very first coach who helped me with the fundamentals
FIRST CRICKET CLUB? Olton & West Warwicks CC, Solihull
IF YOU COULD TAKE ONE COUNTY CRICKETER'S BEST SHOT AND ADD IT TO YOUR OWN GAME? Eoin Morgan's reverse-sweep
TOUGHEST OPPONENT IN COUNTY CRICKET? Simon Harmer
MOST ECCENTRIC TEAMMATE? Rob Yates – known as 'The President' by all
WHAT WOULD YOU DO IF YOU WERE IN CHARGE OF COUNTY CRICKET? Introduce the Decision Review System
STRANGEST THING YOU'VE DONE DURING LOCKDOWN? Growing a mullet
FAVOURITE SMELL? Fresh paint
GUILTY PLEASURE? Call of Duty (video game)
TWITTER: @ethanbrookes2

Batting	Mat	Inns	NO	Runs	HS	Ave	SR	100	50	Ct	St
First-class	2	3	1	21	15*	10.50	52.50	0	0	0	0
Bowling	**Mat**	**Balls**	**Runs**	**Wkts**	**BBI**	**BBM**	**Ave**	**Econ**	**SR**	**5w**	**10**
First-class	2	90	54	0	-	-	-	3.60	-	0	0

HENRY BROOKES

RHB / RMF / R0 / W0

FULL NAME: Henry James Hamilton Brookes
BORN: August 21, 1999, Solihull, Warwickshire
SQUAD NO: 10
HEIGHT: 6ft 4in
EDUCATION: Tudor Grange Academy, Solihull
TEAMS: Warwickshire, England Lions
ROLE: Bowler
DEBUT: First-class: 2017; List A: 2018; T20: 2018

BEST BATTING: 84 Warwickshire vs Kent, Edgbaston, 2019
BEST BOWLING: 4-54 Warwickshire vs Northamptonshire, Edgbaston, 2018

MOST EXCITING DAY AS A CRICKETER? Winning Division Two of the County Championship with Warwickshire in 2018
FAMILY TIES? My brother Ben has played age-group cricket for Warwickshire and my other brother Ethan plays with me at the club
CHILDHOOD SPORTING HERO? Andrew Flintoff
BIGGEST INFLUENCE ON YOUR DEVELOPMENT AS A CRICKETER (EXCLUDING PARENTS)? My grandad – what a hero
FIRST CRICKET CLUB? Olton & West Warwicks CC, Solihull
IF YOU COULD TAKE ONE COUNTY CRICKETER'S BEST SHOT AND ADD IT TO YOUR OWN GAME? Ben Stokes's hook
TOUGHEST OPPONENT IN COUNTY CRICKET? Alastair Cook
MOST ECCENTRIC TEAMMATE? Sam Hain – he gets dressed in the dark
TWITTER: @BrookesHenry

Batting	Mat	Inns	NO	Runs	HS	Ave	SR	100	50	Ct	St
First-class	19	29	3	488	84	18.76	50.88	0	3	8	0
List A	12	5	2	13	12*	4.33	108.33	0	0	1	0
T20s	24	11	2	94	31*	10.44	120.51	0	0	3	0
Bowling	**Mat**	**Balls**	**Runs**	**Wkts**	**BBI**	**BBM**	**Ave**	**Econ**	**SR**	**5w**	**10**
First-class	19	3117	2066	55	4/54	8/119	37.56	3.97	56.6	0	0
List A	12	551	601	17	3/50	3/50	35.35	6.54	32.4	0	0
T20s	24	526	778	31	3/26	3/26	25.09	8.87	16.9	0	0

JACK BROOKS

RHB / RFM / R0 / W4

FULL NAME: Jack Alexander Brooks
BORN: June 4, 1984, Oxford
SQUAD NO: 70
HEIGHT: 6ft 2in
NICKNAME: Headband Warrior
EDUCATION: Wheatley Park School, South Oxfordshire
TEAMS: Somerset, England Lions, Northamptonshire, Yorkshire
ROLE: Bowler
DEBUT: First-class: 2009; List A: 2009; T20: 2010

BEST BATTING: 109* Yorkshire vs Lancashire, Old Trafford, 2017
BEST BOWLING: 6-65 Yorkshire vs Middlesex, Lord's, 2016
COUNTY CAP: 2012 (Northamptonshire); 2013 (Yorkshire)

MOST EXCITING DAY AS A CRICKETER? Two days: my first-class debut for Northants against the Australians in 2009, and winning the Championship for the first time with Yorkshire at Trent Bridge in 2014
CHILDHOOD SPORTING HERO? Dennis Lillee
BIGGEST INFLUENCE ON YOUR DEVELOPMENT AS A CRICKETER (EXCLUDING PARENTS)? My brother Nathan – he was 10 years older than me and never let me win, so I really had to earn my victories
FIRST CRICKET CLUB? Tiddington CC, Oxfordshire
IF YOU COULD TAKE ONE COUNTY CRICKETER'S BEST SHOT AND ADD IT TO YOUR OWN GAME? Any of Tom Banton's variations on a leg-side swipe
TOUGHEST OPPONENT IN COUNTY CRICKET? Alastair Cook – he never plays a false shot and has such a tight defence. Too good for county bowlers
WHAT WOULD YOU DO IF YOU WERE IN CHARGE OF COUNTY CRICKET? Schedule Championship cricket for the summer holidays
GUILTY PLEASURE? A sausage roll
TWITTER: @brooksyferret

Batting	Mat	Inns	NO	Runs	HS	Ave	SR	100	50	Ct	St
First-class	133	165	58	1827	109*	17.07	58.91	1	5	32	0
List A	36	15	5	49	10	4.90	52.12	0	0	4	0
T20s	56	10	6	59	33*	14.75	134.09	0	0	16	0
Bowling	**Mat**	**Balls**	**Runs**	**Wkts**	**BBI**	**BBM**	**Ave**	**Econ**	**SR**	**5w**	**10**
First-class	133	21987	12885	475	6/65	9/84	27.12	3.51	46.2	20	0
List A	36	1584	1276	37	3/30	3/30	34.48	4.83	42.8	0	0
T20s	56	1029	1282	47	5/21	5/21	27.27	7.47	21.8	1	0

BEN BROWN

RHB / WK / R1 / W0

FULL NAME: Ben Christopher Brown
BORN: November 23, 1988, Crawley, Sussex
SQUAD NO: 26
HEIGHT: 5ft 8in
NICKNAME: Goblin
EDUCATION: Ardingly College, West Sussex; Manchester Metropolitan University
TEAMS: Sussex, England U19
ROLE: Wicketkeeper/batsman
DEBUT: First-class: 2007; List A: 2007; T20: 2008

BEST BATTING: 163 Sussex vs Durham, Hove, 2014
BEST BOWLING: 1-48 Sussex vs Essex, Colchester, 2016
COUNTY CAP: 2014

MOST EXCITING DAY AS A CRICKETER? Being capped at Sussex and becoming club captain
CHILDHOOD SPORTING HERO? Gianfranco Zola
FIRST CRICKET CLUB? Balcombe CC, West Sussex. My dad won the Sally Miller Trophy when he played for them and hasn't kept quiet about it ever since
IF YOU COULD TAKE ONE COUNTY CRICKETER'S BEST SHOT AND ADD IT TO YOUR OWN GAME? Andre Russell's long bombs!
MOST ECCENTRIC TEAMMATE? Phil Salt – he's always entertaining us on and off the field
STRANGEST THING YOU'VE DONE DURING LOCKDOWN? Doing a fake toss in my garden while wearing my whites and blazer on the first morning of the cancelled County Championship
FAVOURITE SMELL? Molton Brown shower gel
SURPRISING FACT ABOUT YOU? I don't like cheese
GUILTY PLEASURE? Cadbury Dairy Milk
TWITTER: @Ben_brown26

Batting	Mat	Inns	NO	Runs	HS	Ave	SR	100	50	Ct	St
First-class	145	229	34	7673	163	39.34	61.50	18	42	407	18
List A	74	58	13	1102	73*	24.48	88.65	0	8	67	12
T20s	82	65	9	840	68	15.00	112.00	0	1	41	7
Bowling	**Mat**	**Balls**	**Runs**	**Wkts**	**BBI**	**BBM**	**Ave**	**Econ**	**SR**	**5w**	**10**
First-class	145	120	109	1	1/48	1/48	109.00	5.45	120.0	0	0
List A	74	-	-	-	-	-	-	-	-	-	-
T20s	82	-	-	-	-	-	-	-	-	-	-

PAT BROWN

RHB / RM / R0 / W0

WORCESTERSHIRE

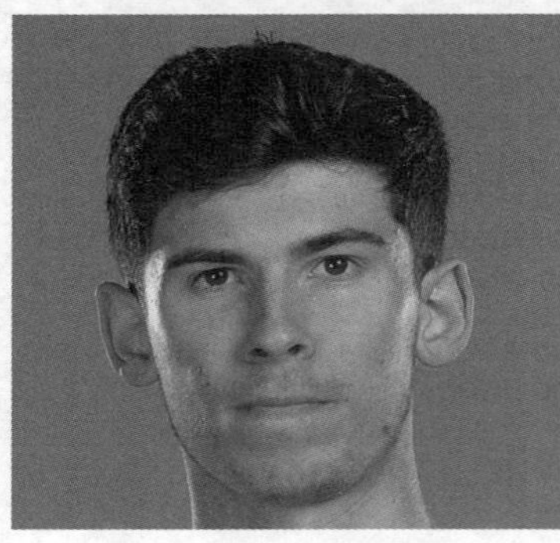

FULL NAME: Patrick Rhys Brown
BORN: August 23, 1998, Peterborough, Cambridgeshire
SQUAD NO: 36
HEIGHT: 6ft 2in
NICKNAME: Brownfish
EDUCATION: Bourne Grammar School, Lincolnshire; University of Worcester
TEAMS: England, Worcestershire
ROLE: Bowler
DEBUT: T20I: 2019; First-class: 2017; List A: 2018; T20: 2017

BEST BATTING: 5* Worcestershire vs Sussex, Worcester, 2017
BEST BOWLING: 2-15 Worcestershire vs Gloucestershire, Worcester, 2017

MOST EXCITING DAY AS A CRICKETER? Winning the T20 Blast in 2018
CHILDHOOD SPORTING HERO? Andrew Flintoff
BIGGEST INFLUENCE ON YOUR DEVELOPMENT AS A CRICKETER (EXCLUDING PARENTS)? Ross Dewar, my strength and conditioning coach at Worcestershire
FIRST CRICKET CLUB? Market Deeping CC, Lincolnshire
IF YOU COULD TAKE ONE COUNTY CRICKETER'S BEST SHOT AND ADD IT TO YOUR OWN GAME? Daryl Mitchell's guide to third man
WHAT WOULD YOU DO IF YOU WERE IN CHARGE OF COUNTY CRICKET? Make the lbw law simpler: if it's hitting the stumps, it's out, right?
SURPRISING FACT ABOUT YOU? I'm not as grumpy as I seem when I am bowling
TWITTER: @patbrowny6

Batting	Mat	Inns	NO	Runs	HS	Ave	SR	100	50	Ct	St
T20Is	4	1	1	4	4*	-	44.44	0	0	2	0
First-class	5	6	4	14	5*	7.00	25.00	0	0	2	0
List A	10	2	1	3	3	3.00	42.85	0	0	3	0
T20s	48	10	7	22	7*	7.33	57.89	0	0	11	0
Bowling	**Mat**	**Balls**	**Runs**	**Wkts**	**BBI**	**BBM**	**Ave**	**Econ**	**SR**	**5w**	**10**
T20Is	4	78	128	3	1/29	1/29	42.66	9.84	26.0	0	0
First-class	5	376	266	7	2/15	3/70	38.00	4.24	53.7	0	0
List A	10	418	438	12	3/53	3/53	36.50	6.28	34.8	0	0
T20s	48	970	1423	60	4/21	4/21	23.71	8.80	16.1	0	0

NICK BROWNE

LHB / LB / R3 / W0

FULL NAME: Nicholas Laurence Joseph Browne
BORN: March 24, 1991, Leytonstone, Essex
SQUAD NO: 10
HEIGHT: 6ft 3in
NICKNAME: Orse
EDUCATION: Trinity Catholic High School, London
TEAMS: Essex
ROLE: Batsman
DEBUT: First-class: 2013; List A: 2015; T20: 2015

BEST BATTING: 255 Essex vs Derbyshire, Chelmsford, 2016

COUNTY CAP: 2015

MOST EXCITING DAY AS A CRICKETER? Winning the County Championship on the last day at Taunton in 2019
CHILDHOOD SPORTING HERO? Marcus Trescothick
BIGGEST INFLUENCE ON YOUR DEVELOPMENT AS A CRICKETER (EXCLUDING PARENTS)? My two older brothers, both of whom I played club cricket with
FIRST CRICKET CLUB? South Woodford CC, London. My parents met each other at the club
IF YOU COULD TAKE ONE COUNTY CRICKETER'S BEST SHOT AND ADD IT TO YOUR OWN GAME? It's a hard one between Alastair Cook's pull and James Vince's cover-drive
TOUGHEST OPPONENT IN COUNTY CRICKET? In club cricket it was the Jamaican fast bowler Andrew Robertson, who played for Woodford Wells in the Essex Premier League. At county level it was Matthew Hoggard. I found them both very hard to face early in my career
WHAT WOULD YOU DO IF YOU WERE IN CHARGE OF COUNTY CRICKET? Keep with an elite first division with eight teams, with two overseas players per county like for this season
FAVOURITE SMELL? Fresh leather
TWITTER: @NickBrowne4

Batting	Mat	Inns	NO	Runs	HS	Ave	SR	100	50	Ct	St
First-class	95	157	10	5673	255	38.59	48.44	15	24	73	0
List A	21	18	0	557	99	30.94	89.83	0	3	7	0
T20s	14	12	2	165	38	16.50	114.58	0	0	6	0
Bowling	**Mat**	**Balls**	**Runs**	**Wkts**	**BBI**	**BBM**	**Ave**	**Econ**	**SR**	**5w**	**10**
First-class	95	268	175	0	-	-	-	3.91	-	0	0
List A	21	-	-	-	-	-	-	-	-	-	-
T20s	14	-	-	-	-	-	-	-	-	-	-

NATHAN BUCK RHB / RFM / R0 / W0 / MVP67

FULL NAME: Nathan Liam Buck
BORN: April 26, 1991, Leicester
SQUAD NO: 11
HEIGHT: 6ft 3in
EDUCATION: Ashby Grammar School, Ashby-de-la-Zouch
TEAMS: Northamptonshire, England Lions, Lancashire, Leicestershire
ROLE: Bowler
DEBUT: First-class: 2009; List A: 2009; T20: 2010

BEST BATTING: 53 Northamptonshire vs Glamorgan, Cardiff, 2019
BEST BOWLING: 6-34 Northamptonshire vs Durham, Chester-le-Street, 2017
COUNTY CAP: 2011 (Leicestershire)

MOST EXCITING DAY AS A CRICKETER? Every day of a Championship match when the clock strikes 1pm
FIRST CRICKET CLUB? Grace Dieu Park CC, Leicestershire. I got hit into the forest on many occasions
BIGGEST CRICKETING REGRET? Not getting "off 'em" on debut
WHAT WOULD YOU DO IF YOU WERE IN CHARGE OF COUNTY CRICKET? Allow each team to have 10 specialised fielders when bowling
WHAT WOULD YOU DO IF YOU WERE PRIME MINISTER? Ban cricket on bank holidays
FAVOURITE SMELL? Sun cream
SURPRISING FACT ABOUT YOU? I got seven A stars and three As in my GCSEs
GUILTY PLEASURE? Getting hit on the shin
TWITTER: @nathanbuck17

Batting	Mat	Inns	NO	Runs	HS	Ave	SR	100	50	Ct	St
First-class	96	134	37	1406	53	14.49	-	0	3	17	0
List A	61	29	11	141	21	7.83	72.30	0	0	13	0
T20s	63	19	11	70	16*	8.75	90.90	0	0	13	0
Bowling	**Mat**	**Balls**	**Runs**	**Wkts**	**BBI**	**BBM**	**Ave**	**Econ**	**SR**	**5w**	**10**
First-class	96	14640	8699	259	6/34	8/107	33.58	3.56	56.5	8	0
List A	61	2527	2632	69	4/39	4/39	38.14	6.24	36.6	0	0
T20s	63	1237	1808	71	4/26	4/26	25.46	8.76	17.4	0	0

SOL BUDINGER LHB / OB / WK / R0 / W0

FULL NAME: Soloman George Budinger
BORN: August 21, 1999, Colchester, Essex
SQUAD NO: 1
HEIGHT: 6ft
NICKNAME: Lord
EDUCATION: The Southport School, Queensland, Australia
TEAMS: Nottinghamshire
ROLE: Batsman

MOST EXCITING DAY AS A CRICKETER? Being a member of the Notts Outlaws squad which won the T20 Blast last summer
CHILDHOOD SPORTING HERO? David Gower
BIGGEST INFLUENCE ON YOUR DEVELOPMENT AS A CRICKETER (EXCLUDING PARENTS)? Ant Botha, Nottinghamshire assistant coach. He developed me from a club player to a pro cricketer, so I wouldn't be where I am now without him
FIRST CRICKET CLUB? Coomera Hope Island CC, Queensland, Australia
IF YOU COULD TAKE ONE COUNTY CRICKETER'S BEST SHOT AND ADD IT TO YOUR OWN GAME? Ben Slater's back-foot flick off his pads
WHAT WOULD YOU DO IF YOU WERE IN CHARGE OF COUNTY CRICKET? Introduce free hits for no-balls in the County Championship, make Powerplays last for 10 overs in T20 cricket, use Kookaburra balls instead of the Dukes. Can you tell I'm a batter?
WHAT WOULD YOU DO IF YOU WERE PRIME MINISTER? Work on a scheme which ensures that everyone has to vote
STRANGEST THING YOU'VE DONE DURING LOCKDOWN? Building Lego
FAVOURITE SMELL? Linseed oil
GUILTY PLEASURE? Pizza
TWITTER: @lordbudinger

MICHAEL BURGESS

RHB / WK / R0 / W0

FULL NAME: Michael Gregory Kerran Burgess
BORN: July 8, 1994, Epsom, Surrey
SQUAD NO: 61
HEIGHT: 6ft 1in
NICKNAME: Burge
EDUCATION: Cranleigh School, Surrey; Loughborough University
TEAMS: Warwickshire, Leicestershire, Sussex
ROLE: Wicketkeeper
DEBUT: First-class: 2014; List A: 2015; T20: 2016

BEST BATTING: 146 Sussex vs Nottinghamshire, Hove, 2017

BIGGEST INFLUENCE ON YOUR DEVELOPMENT AS A CRICKETER (EXCLUDING PARENTS)? Russell Cobb, head coach at Loughborough MCCU. He's a great man-manager and a very relaxed personality
FIRST CRICKET CLUB? Reigate Priory CC, Surrey
BEST INNINGS YOU'VE SEEN? Brendon McCullum's last Test innings when he scored the fastest-ever Test hundred (54 balls) against Australia at Christchurch in 2016
TOUGHEST OPPONENT IN COUNTY CRICKET? Ravichandran Ashwin
BIGGEST CRICKETING REGRET? Not learning to bowl mystery spin
WHAT WOULD YOU DO IF YOU WERE IN CHARGE OF COUNTY CRICKET? Go for a three-division Championship, ban all cricket when it's colder than 10 degrees
TWITTER: @mgkburgess

Batting	Mat	Inns	NO	Runs	HS	Ave	SR	100	50	Ct	St
First-class	38	55	4	1823	146	35.74	67.69	2	10	47	1
List A	19	17	0	363	58	21.35	99.45	0	2	10	1
T20s	38	32	8	384	56	16.00	117.07	0	1	17	6
Bowling	**Mat**	**Balls**	**Runs**	**Wkts**	**BBI**	**BBM**	**Ave**	**Econ**	**SR**	**5w**	**10**
First-class	38	36	14	0	-	-	-	2.33	-	0	0
List A	19	-	-	-	-	-	-	-	-	-	-
T20s	38	-	-	-	-	-	-	-	-	-	-

JACK BURNHAM

RHB / RM / R0 / W0

FULL NAME: Jack Tony Arthur Burnham
BORN: January 18, 1997, Durham
SQUAD NO: 8
HEIGHT: 6ft 2in
NICKNAME: Burny
EDUCATION: Deerness Valley Comprehensive School, Durham; The Durham Federation
TEAMS: Durham, England U19
ROLE: Batsman
DEBUT: First-class: 2015; List A: 2016; T20: 2016

BEST BATTING: 135 Durham vs Surrey, The Oval, 2016

MOST EXCITING DAY AS A CRICKETER? Scoring three hundreds in the 2016 U19 World Cup
CHILDHOOD SPORTING HERO? Steve Harmison
BIGGEST INFLUENCE ON YOUR DEVELOPMENT AS A CRICKETER (EXCLUDING PARENTS)? My older brother – I always wanted to be as good as him
FIRST CRICKET CLUB? Esh Winning CC, County Durham
TOUGHEST OPPONENT IN COUNTY CRICKET? Graham Onions – he always got me out
MOST ECCENTRIC TEAMMATE? Ben Raine – he loves getting in the battle on the field
WHAT WOULD YOU DO IF YOU WERE IN CHARGE OF COUNTY CRICKET? Increase the number of T20 games
WHAT WOULD YOU DO IF YOU WERE PRIME MINISTER? Increase wages for NHS staff, put more money into education, provide more homes and shelters for the homeless
STRANGEST THING YOU'VE DONE DURING LOCKDOWN? Doing puzzles – and really enjoying it!
GUILTY PLEASURE? Big Macs
TWITTER: @BurnhamMorton

Batting	Mat	Inns	NO	Runs	HS	Ave	SR	100	50	Ct	St
First-class	42	72	5	1688	135	25.19	47.79	1	10	14	0
List A	13	8	2	139	45	23.16	79.88	0	0	4	0
T20s	24	18	1	189	53*	11.11	90.43	0	1	10	0
Bowling	**Mat**	**Balls**	**Runs**	**Wkts**	**BBI**	**BBM**	**Ave**	**Econ**	**SR**	**5w**	**10**
First-class	42	61	17	0	-	-	-	1.67	-	0	0
List A	13	-	-	-	-	-	-	-	-	-	-
T20s	24	1	0	0	-	-	-	0.00	-	0	0

RORY BURNS LHB / RM / R6 / W0 / MVP98

FULL NAME: Rory Joseph Burns
BORN: August 26, 1990, Epsom, Surrey
SQUAD NO: 17
HEIGHT: 5ft 10in
NICKNAME: Fong
EDUCATION: Whitgift School, Croydon, London; City of London Freemen's; Cardiff Metropolitan University
TEAMS: England, Surrey
ROLE: Batsman
DEBUT: Test: 2018; First-class: 2011; List A: 2012; T20: 2012

BEST BATTING: 219* Surrey vs Hampshire, The Oval, 2017
BEST BOWLING: 1-18 Surrey vs Middlesex, Lord's, 2013
COUNTY CAP: 2014

FIRST CRICKET CLUB? Banstead CC, Surrey
MOST INTERESTING TEAMMATE? Kumar Sangakkara – he has a wealth of knowledge and is happy to share it with anyone at any time
SURPRISING FACT ABOUT YOU? I have a strong whisky collection at home
IF YOU WERE AN ANIMAL, WHICH WOULD IT BE? A leopard – majestic creature
TWITTER: @roryburns17

Batting	Mat	Inns	NO	Runs	HS	Ave	SR	100	50	Ct	St
Tests	23	42	0	1291	133	30.73	45.20	2	8	19	0
First-class	141	246	14	9676	219*	41.70	49.13	19	53	123	0
List A	57	55	6	1722	95	35.14	84.78	0	12	29	0
T20s	54	45	8	640	56*	17.29	123.55	0	2	21	1
Bowling	**Mat**	**Balls**	**Runs**	**Wkts**	**BBI**	**BBM**	**Ave**	**Econ**	**SR**	**5w**	**10**
Tests	23	-	-	-	-	-	-	-	-	-	-
First-class	141	186	127	2	1/18	1/18	63.50	4.09	93.0	0	0
List A	57	-	-	-	-	-	-	-	-	-	-
T20s	54	-	-	-	-	-	-	-	-	-	-

GEORGE BURROWS RHB / RMF / R0 / W0

FULL NAME: George Davidson Burrows
BORN: June 22, 1998, Wigan, Lancashire
SQUAD NO: 21
HEIGHT: 6ft 5in
EDUCATION: St John Rigby College, Wigan; Liverpool John Moores University
TEAMS: Lancashire
ROLE: Bowler
DEBUT: First-class: 2020

BEST BATTING: 1 Lancashire vs Derbyshire, Liverpool, 2020
BEST BOWLING: 2-20 Lancashire vs Derbyshire, Liverpool, 2020

MOST EXCITING DAY AS A CRICKETER? Making my first-class debut against Yorkshire in the Bob Willis Trophy last summer
CHILDHOOD SPORTING HERO? David Beckham
BIGGEST INFLUENCE ON YOUR DEVELOPMENT AS A CRICKETER (EXCLUDING PARENTS)? Graham Onions
FIRST CRICKET CLUB? Orrell Red Triangle CC, Wigan
MOST ECCENTRIC TEAMMATE? Rob Jones
GUILTY PLEASURE? A McDonald's Double Cheeseburger
NOTES: A right-arm seamer who studied Sociology at Liverpool John Moores University, Burrows was one of seven Lancashire youngsters handed new contracts towards the end of 2019. The 22-year-old made his first-class debut last summer, taking two wickets in the Roses match at Headingley and then 2-20 against Derbyshire at Liverpool

Batting	Mat	Inns	NO	Runs	HS	Ave	SR	100	50	Ct	St
First-class	2	1	0	1	1	1.00	11.11	0	0	0	0
Bowling	**Mat**	**Balls**	**Runs**	**Wkts**	**BBI**	**BBM**	**Ave**	**Econ**	**SR**	**5w**	**10**
First-class	2	240	127	4	2/20	2/38	31.75	3.17	60.0	0	0

WILL BUTTLEMAN RHB / WK / R0 / W0

FULL NAME: William Edward Lewis Buttleman
BORN: April 20, 2000, Chelmsford, Essex
SQUAD NO: 9
HEIGHT: 6ft 1in
NICKNAME: Butterz
EDUCATION: Felsted School, Essex
TEAMS: Essex
ROLE: Wicketkeeper
DEBUT: First-class: 2019

MOST EXCITING DAY AS A CRICKETER? Making my first-class debut in 2019
CHILDHOOD SPORTING HERO? Rickie Fowler
BIGGEST INFLUENCE ON YOUR DEVELOPMENT AS A CRICKETER (EXCLUDING PARENTS)? Northern District CC in Sydney (apart from Essex of course!)
FIRST CRICKET CLUB? Cloghams CC, Essex
IF YOU COULD TAKE ONE COUNTY CRICKETER'S BEST SHOT AND ADD IT TO YOUR OWN GAME? Dan Lawrence's flick
TOUGHEST OPPONENT IN COUNTY CRICKET? Duanne Olivier
WHAT WOULD YOU DO IF YOU WERE IN CHARGE OF COUNTY CRICKET? Introduce home and away kit
WHAT WOULD YOU DO IF YOU WERE PRIME MINISTER? Rent a box at the County Ground for my office in the summer
STRANGEST THING YOU'VE DONE DURING LOCKDOWN? Playing golf shots over my house
FAVOURITE SMELL? Wagamama
GUILTY PLEASURE? Jelly
TWITTER: @Will_Buttleman

Batting	Mat	Inns	NO	Runs	HS	Ave	SR	100	50	Ct	St
First-class	1	1	0	0	0	0.00	0.00	0	0	3	0
Bowling	**Mat**	**Balls**	**Runs**	**Wkts**	**BBI**	**BBM**	**Ave**	**Econ**	**SR**	**5w**	**10**
First-class	1	-	-	-	-	-	-	-	-	-	-

JOS BUTTLER

RHB / WK / R0 / W0

FULL NAME: Joseph Charles Buttler
BORN: September 8, 1990, Taunton
SQUAD NO: 6
NICKNAME: Jose
EDUCATION: King's College, Taunton
TEAMS: England, Lancashire, Comilla Victorians, Melbourne Renegades, Mumbai Indians, Rajasthan Royals, Somerset, Sydney Thunder
ROLE: Batsman/wicketkeeper
DEBUT: Test: 2014; ODI: 2012; T20I: 2011; First-class: 2009; List A: 2009; T20: 2009

BEST BATTING: 152 England vs Pakistan, Southampton, 2020

COUNTY CAP: 2013 (Somerset), 2018 (Lancashire)

TWITTER: @josbuttler

NOTES: One of English cricket's most ferocious hitters, Buttler's international and T20 duties have restricted him to just 16 Championship appearances since he left Somerset to join Lancashire in 2013. Called up for England's limited-overs squads in 2012, he made his Test debut two years later but it wasn't until his maiden hundred in 2018 that he became a regular in the Test side. Buttler was in vintage form last summer, making a match-turning 75 against Pakistan at Old Trafford before a magnificent 152 against the same opponents at the Ageas Bowl. There is no denying his extraordinary skills in the shorter forms, of which the best example was his 46-ball ODI hundred against Pakistan in Dubai in 2015 – the fastest by an England player. And, not forgetting, he is also a World Cup winner. Buttler has been retained by Rajasthan Royals for the 2021 IPL and will turn out for Manchester Originals in The Hundred this summer

Batting	Mat	Inns	NO	Runs	HS	Ave	SR	100	50	Ct	St
Tests	50	87	8	2728	152	34.53	57.01	2	18	123	1
ODIs	145	120	23	3855	150	39.74	119.05	9	20	177	32
T20Is	74	66	13	1551	77*	29.26	140.36	0	10	31	5
First-class	115	186	15	5709	152	33.38	58.77	7	33	244	3
List A	216	180	43	6021	150	43.94	119.72	11	36	229	37
T20s	270	248	45	6327	95*	31.16	144.71	0	44	149	28
Bowling	**Mat**	**Balls**	**Runs**	**Wkts**	**BBI**	**BBM**	**Ave**	**Econ**	**SR**	**5w**	**10**
Tests	50	-	-	-	-	-	-	-	-	-	-
ODIs	145	-	-	-	-	-	-	-	-	-	-
T20Is	74	-	-	-	-	-	-	-	-	-	-
First-class	115	12	11	0	-	-	-	5.50	-	0	0
List A	216	-	-	-	-	-	-	-	-	-	-
T20s	270	-	-	-	-	-	-	-	-	-	-

EDDIE BYROM

LHB / OB / R0 / W0

FULL NAME: Edward James Byrom
BORN: June 17, 1997, Harare, Zimbabwe
SQUAD NO: 97
HEIGHT: 6ft
NICKNAME: Muta
EDUCATION: King's College, Taunton
TEAMS: Somerset, Rising Stars
ROLE: Batsman
DEBUT: First-class: 2017; T20: 2019

BEST BATTING: 152 Rising Stars vs Bulawayo Metropolitan Tuskers, Kwekwe, 2017

MOST EXCITING DAY AS A CRICKETER? Making my T20 debut in 2019
CHILDHOOD SPORTING HERO? Brian Lara. Whenever West Indies were playing I would watch him bat and as soon as he got out I would change the channel
FIRST CRICKET CLUB? Taunton St Andrews CC, Somerset
IF YOU COULD TAKE ONE COUNTY CRICKETER'S BEST SHOT AND ADD IT TO YOUR OWN GAME? Ishant Sharma's defence
TOUGHEST OPPONENT IN COUNTY CRICKET? Simon Harmer
BIGGEST CRICKETING REGRET? Diving for a ball I was never going to get and dislocating my shoulder
WHAT WOULD YOU DO IF YOU WERE IN CHARGE OF COUNTY CRICKET? Ensure all pitches don't have any grass on them
GUILTY PLEASURE? Playing the guitar
TWITTER: @EddieByrom

Batting	Mat	Inns	NO	Runs	HS	Ave	SR	100	50	Ct	St
First-class	27	51	2	1379	152	28.14	45.69	3	4	15	0
T20s	14	13	1	226	54*	18.83	172.51	0	1	2	0
Bowling	**Mat**	**Balls**	**Runs**	**Wkts**	**BBI**	**BBM**	**Ave**	**Econ**	**SR**	**5w**	**10**
First-class	27	66	43	0	-	-	-	3.90	-	0	0
T20s	14	-	-	-	-	-	-	-	-	-	-

JACK CAMPBELL

RHB / LMF / R0 / W0

FULL NAME: Jack Oliver Ian Campbell
BORN: November 11, 1999, Portsmouth
SQUAD NO: 21
HEIGHT: 6ft 7in
NICKNAME: Jacko
EDUCATION: Churcher's College, Petersfield, Hampshire
TEAMS: Durham, England U19
ROLE: Bowler
DEBUT: First-class: 2019

BEST BATTING: 2 Durham MCCU vs Durham, Chester-le-Street, 2019
BEST BOWLING: 1-43 Durham vs Leicestershire, Leicester, 2019

MOST EXCITING DAY AS A CRICKETER? Making my first-class debut in 2019
CHILDHOOD SPORTING HERO? Andrew Flintoff
BIGGEST INFLUENCE ON YOUR DEVELOPMENT AS A CRICKETER (EXCLUDING PARENTS)? My old club captain who pushed me to play in the first team when I was 12 to prepare me for playing at a higher level when I was older
FIRST CRICKET CLUB? Steep CC, Hampshire
MOST ECCENTRIC TEAMMATE? Mark Wood
WHAT WOULD YOU DO IF YOU WERE IN CHARGE OF COUNTY CRICKET? Give the bowlers a chance by giving them the new ball after 40 overs
WHAT WOULD YOU DO IF YOU WERE PRIME MINISTER? Make it compulsory for all Sunderland FC's games to be on TV, lower the price of healthy foods
GUILTY PLEASURE? White chocolate
TWITTER: @jack_campbell11

Batting	Mat	Inns	NO	Runs	HS	Ave	SR	100	50	Ct	St
First-class	3	4	2	2	2	1.00	9.52	0	0	0	0
Bowling	**Mat**	**Balls**	**Runs**	**Wkts**	**BBI**	**BBM**	**Ave**	**Econ**	**SR**	**5w**	**10**
First-class	3	468	261	1	1/43	1/87	261.00	3.34	468.0	0	0

LUKAS CAREY

RHB / RFM / R0 / W0

FULL NAME: Lukas John Carey
BORN: July 17, 1997, Carmarthen, Wales
SQUAD NO: 17
EDUCATION: Pontarddulais Comprehensive School, Swansea; Gower College Swansea
TEAMS: Glamorgan
ROLE: Bowler
DEBUT: First-class: 2016; List A: 2017; T20: 2017

BEST BATTING: 62* Glamorgan vs Derbyshire, Swansea, 2019
BEST BOWLING: 4-54 Glamorgan vs Middlesex, Cardiff, 2019

TWITTER: @LukasCarey
NOTES: A graduate from Glamorgan's Academy who hails from Robert Croft's club Pontarddulais, Carey is another in the ranks of talented local products looking to reinvigorate the Welsh club. He made a promising start to his Glamorgan career in 2016, picking up seven wickets against Northants with his skiddy fast-medium seamers on his first-class debut. He had a breakthrough season in 2017, taking 35 wickets at 30.03 in 10 Championship matches as well as making his maiden first-class half-century. Carey featured regularly in all three formats in 2018 and 2019 but a side strain restricted the 23-year-old to just one appearance last summer. He signed a new two-year deal last September. "Lukas is a very talented young seamer who's shown he has got the potential to make an impact at first-class level," said Mark Wallace, Glamorgan's director of cricket

Batting	Mat	Inns	NO	Runs	HS	Ave	SR	100	50	Ct	St
First-class	30	41	6	553	62*	15.80	75.34	0	3	5	0
List A	18	10	5	124	39	24.80	91.17	0	0	3	0
T20s	9	3	2	7	5	7.00	70.00	0	0	2	0
Bowling	**Mat**	**Balls**	**Runs**	**Wkts**	**BBI**	**BBM**	**Ave**	**Econ**	**SR**	**5w**	**10**
First-class	30	4821	2830	83	4/54	7/151	34.09	3.52	58.0	0	0
List A	18	814	755	12	2/57	2/57	62.91	5.56	67.8	0	0
T20s	9	138	209	4	1/15	1/15	52.25	9.08	34.5	0	0

KIRAN CARLSON

RHB / OB / R0 / W0

FULL NAME: Kiran Shah Carlson
BORN: May 16, 1998, Cardiff
SQUAD NO: 5
HEIGHT: 5ft 11in
NICKNAME: Dink
EDUCATION: Whitchurch High School, Cardiff; Cardiff University
TEAMS: Glamorgan
ROLE: Batsman
DEBUT: First-class: 2016; List A: 2016; T20: 2017

BEST BATTING: 191 Glamorgan vs Gloucestershire, Cardiff, 2017
BEST BOWLING: 5-28 Glamorgan vs Northamptonshire, Northampton, 2016

MOST EXCITING DAY AS A CRICKETER? T20 Finals Day in 2017
CHILDHOOD SPORTING HERO? Richie McCaw
FIRST CRICKET CLUB? Cardiff CC
IF YOU COULD TAKE ONE COUNTY CRICKETER'S BEST SHOT AND ADD IT TO YOUR OWN GAME? Dan Douthwaite's straight-drive
TOUGHEST OPPONENT IN COUNTY CRICKET? Craig Overton – for his skill and pace
WHAT WOULD YOU DO IF YOU WERE IN CHARGE OF COUNTY CRICKET? Make entry free for Championship matches, play half the season with Dukes balls and the other half with Kookaburra balls
WHAT WOULD YOU DO IF YOU WERE PRIME MINISTER? Increase tax on animal products
STRANGEST THING YOU'VE DONE DURING LOCKDOWN? Faking a break-in to scare my housemate
FAVOURITE SMELL? David Lloyd's hair
SURPRISING FACT ABOUT YOU? I'm half-Indian
GUILTY PLEASURE? A cold beer
TWITTER: @kiran_carlson

Batting	Mat	Inns	NO	Runs	HS	Ave	SR	100	50	Ct	St
First-class	34	60	2	1502	191	25.89	55.58	4	4	16	0
List A	17	16	1	341	63	22.73	96.87	0	2	4	0
T20s	22	19	1	339	58	18.83	129.88	0	1	10	0
Bowling	**Mat**	**Balls**	**Runs**	**Wkts**	**BBI**	**BBM**	**Ave**	**Econ**	**SR**	**5w**	**10**
First-class	34	444	295	6	5/28	5/78	49.16	3.98	74.0	1	0
List A	17	42	47	1	1/30	1/30	47.00	6.71	42.0	0	0
T20s	22	1	1	0	-	-	-	6.00	-	0	0

BRYDON CARSE

RHB / RFM / R0 / W0

FULL NAME: Brydon Alexander Carse
BORN: July 31, 1995, Port Elizabeth, South Africa
SQUAD NO: 99
HEIGHT: 6ft 2in
NICKNAME: Cheesy
EDUCATION: Pearson High School, Port Elizabeth
TEAMS: Durham, Eastern Province, England Lions
ROLE: Bowler
DEBUT: First-class: 2016; List A: 2019; T20: 2014

BEST BATTING: 77* Durham vs Northamptonshire, Chester-le-Street, 2019
BEST BOWLING: 6-26 Durham vs Middlesex, Lord's, 2019

MOST EXCITING DAY AS A CRICKETER? Winning at Lord's with Durham
FAMILY TIES? My dad James played for Northamptonshire, Rhodesia, Eastern Province, Border and Western Province
CHILDHOOD SPORTING HERO? Mark Boucher
BIGGEST INFLUENCE ON YOUR DEVELOPMENT AS A CRICKETER (EXCLUDING PARENTS)? Geoff Cook (former Durham head coach)
FIRST CRICKET CLUB? Union CC, South Africa
IF YOU COULD TAKE ONE COUNTY CRICKETER'S BEST SHOT AND ADD IT TO YOUR OWN GAME? Alex Lees's block
TOUGHEST OPPONENT IN COUNTY CRICKET? Dane Vilas
WHAT WOULD YOU DO IF YOU WERE IN CHARGE OF COUNTY CRICKET? Allow a free hit for no-balls in four-day cricket
FAVOURITE SMELL? A leg of lamb in the slow cooker
GUILTY PLEASURE? Thai Sweet Chilli Sensations
TWITTER: @CarseBrydon

Batting	Mat	Inns	NO	Runs	HS	Ave	SR	100	50	Ct	St
First-class	25	32	8	643	77*	26.79	49.23	0	2	3	0
List A	7	1	0	2	2	2.00	28.57	0	0	2	0
T20s	23	17	4	219	35	16.84	146.00	0	0	8	0
Bowling	**Mat**	**Balls**	**Runs**	**Wkts**	**BBI**	**BBM**	**Ave**	**Econ**	**SR**	**5w**	**10**
First-class	25	3243	2090	61	6/26	7/63	34.26	3.86	53.1	3	0
List A	7	245	223	10	3/52	3/52	22.30	5.46	24.5	0	0
T20s	23	395	568	12	1/11	1/11	47.33	8.62	32.9	0	0

JACK CARSON

RHB / OB / R0 / W0

FULL NAME: Jack Joshua Carson
BORN: December 3, 2000, Craigavon, County Armagh, Northern Ireland
SQUAD NO: 16
HEIGHT: 6ft 2in
NICKNAME: Carse
EDUCATION: Bainbridge Academy, County Down, Northern Ireland; Hurstpierpoint College, West Sussex
TEAMS: Sussex
ROLE: Bowler
DEBUT: First-class: 2020

BEST BATTING: 21 Sussex vs Surrey, The Oval, 2020
BEST BOWLING: 5-93 Sussex vs Surrey, The Oval, 2020

MOST EXCITING DAY AS A CRICKETER? Making my first-class debut last summer
CHILDHOOD SPORTING HERO? Ruan Pienaar
BIGGEST INFLUENCE ON YOUR DEVELOPMENT AS A CRICKETER (EXCLUDING PARENTS)? Ian Salisbury – he has made me into a better bowler in a technical sense but also helped me to manage my emotions
IF YOU COULD TAKE ONE COUNTY CRICKETER'S BEST SHOT AND ADD IT TO YOUR OWN GAME? David Wiese's shot over long-off
TOUGHEST OPPONENT IN COUNTY CRICKET? Rory Burns – he has such a clear game plan and the skill to execute it
MOST ECCENTRIC TEAMMATE? Phil Salt – he's just plain mad
WHAT WOULD YOU DO IF YOU WERE IN CHARGE OF COUNTY CRICKET? Increase penalty points for poor pitches
STRANGEST THING YOU'VE DONE DURING LOCKDOWN? Reading a book
FAVOURITE SMELL? Petrol
GUILTY PLEASURE? Medical dramas on TV
TWITTER: @_jackcarson11

Batting	Mat	Inns	NO	Runs	HS	Ave	SR	100	50	Ct	St
First-class	4	8	0	57	21	7.12	35.62	0	0	1	0
Bowling	**Mat**	**Balls**	**Runs**	**Wkts**	**BBI**	**BBM**	**Ave**	**Econ**	**SR**	**5w**	**10**
First-class	4	649	340	15	5/93	6/139	22.66	3.14	43.2	1	0

MATT CARTER

RHB / OB / R0 / W0 / MVP72

NOTTINGHAMSHIRE

FULL NAME: Matthew Carter
BORN: May 26, 1996, Lincoln
SQUAD NO: 20
HEIGHT: 6ft 6in
NICKNAME: Long Plod
EDUCATION: Branston Community Academy, Lincolnshire
TEAMS: Nottinghamshire, England Lions
ROLE: Bowler
DEBUT: First-class: 2015; List A: 2018; T20: 2018

BEST BATTING: 33 Nottinghamshire vs Sussex, Hove, 2017
BEST BOWLING: 7-56 Nottinghamshire vs Somerset, Taunton, 2015

MOST EXCITING DAY AS A CRICKETER? Taking seven wickets in the first innings on my first-class debut
FAMILY TIES? My dad and oldest brother played at village level. My brother Andrew played for Notts, Derby and Hampshire before retiring in 2016
CHILDHOOD SPORTING HERO? Andrew Flintoff
FIRST CRICKET CLUB? Market Rasen CC, Lincolnshire
SURPRISING FACT ABOUT YOU? Any chance I get, whether for an hour or a full day, it's spent with the dog in the middle of a field shooting. I've had a lot of swimming achievements but now I'm scared of swimming
IF YOU WERE AN ANIMAL, WHICH WOULD IT BE? A gnat – so that you can bite people who are horrible to you

Batting	Mat	Inns	NO	Runs	HS	Ave	SR	100	50	Ct	St
First-class	17	27	2	241	33	9.64	48.68	0	0	16	0
List A	16	10	1	65	21*	7.22	76.47	0	0	5	0
T20s	22	4	1	34	16*	11.33	136.00	0	0	8	0
Bowling	**Mat**	**Balls**	**Runs**	**Wkts**	**BBI**	**BBM**	**Ave**	**Econ**	**SR**	**5w**	**10**
First-class	17	3546	1989	50	7/56	10/195	39.78	3.36	70.9	2	1
List A	16	701	625	23	4/40	4/40	27.17	5.34	30.4	0	0
T20s	22	420	519	23	3/14	3/14	22.56	7.41	18.2	0	0

ZAK CHAPPELL

RHB / RFM / R0 / W0

FULL NAME: Zachariah John Chappell
BORN: August 21, 1996, Grantham, Lincolnshire
SQUAD NO: 32
HEIGHT: 6ft 5in
NICKNAME: Smasher
EDUCATION: Stamford School, Lincolnshire
TEAMS: Nottinghamshire, England Lions, Gloucestershire, Leicestershire
ROLE: Allrounder
DEBUT: First-class: 2015; List A: 2015; T20: 2015

BEST BATTING: 96 Leicestershire vs Derbyshire, Derby, 2015
BEST BOWLING: 6-44 Leicestershire vs Northamptonshire, Northampton, 2018

MOST EXCITING DAY AS A CRICKETER? When a swarm of bees took over the ground in India
CHILDHOOD SPORTING HERO? Brett Lee
FIRST CRICKET CLUB? Stamford Town CC, Lincolnshire
TOUGHEST OPPONENT IN COUNTY CRICKET? Jofra Archer
WHAT WOULD YOU DO IF YOU WERE IN CHARGE OF COUNTY CRICKET? Decide that cricket cannot be played if it drops below 10 degrees
FAVOURITE SMELL? A shed
SURPRISING FACT ABOUT YOU? I can walk on my hands
GUILTY PLEASURE? Hot cross buns
TWITTER: @ZakkChappell

Batting	Mat	Inns	NO	Runs	HS	Ave	SR	100	50	Ct	St
First-class	23	34	6	598	96	21.35	56.15	0	2	5	0
List A	17	14	6	141	59*	17.62	64.38	0	1	2	0
T20s	16	10	2	67	16	8.37	131.37	0	0	6	0
Bowling	**Mat**	**Balls**	**Runs**	**Wkts**	**BBI**	**BBM**	**Ave**	**Econ**	**SR**	**5w**	**10**
First-class	23	2845	1800	53	6/44	6/53	33.96	3.79	53.6	1	0
List A	17	731	765	17	3/45	3/45	45.00	6.27	43.0	0	0
T20s	16	285	462	13	3/23	3/23	35.53	9.72	21.9	0	0

BEN CHARLESWORTH

LHB / RMF / R0 / W0

FULL NAME: Ben Geoffrey Charlesworth
BORN: November 19, 2000, Oxford
SQUAD NO: 64
HEIGHT: 6ft 3in
NICKNAME: Charlie
EDUCATION: St Edward's School, Oxford
TEAMS: Gloucestershire, England U19
ROLE: Allrounder
DEBUT: First-class: 2018; List A: 2019

BEST BATTING: 77* Gloucestershire vs Middlesex, Bristol, 2018
BEST BOWLING: 3-25 Gloucestershire vs Middlesex, Bristol, 2018
COUNTY CAP: 2018

FAMILY TIES? My brother Luke Charlesworth plays for Gloucestershire Second XI
CHILDHOOD SPORTING HERO? Kumar Sangakkara
FIRST CRICKET CLUB? Abingdon Vale CC, Oxfordshire. It was 10 minutes down the road from my house. I played and trained there from the age of five to 16
MOST INTERESTING TEAMMATE? Hamidullah Qadri (with England U19)
WHAT WOULD YOU DO IF YOU WERE IN CHARGE OF COUNTY CRICKET? Introduce free hits in red-ball cricket to bring more excitement into the longer format – and to punish bowlers for no-balls
BIGGEST CRICKETING REGRET? Not speaking to Eoin Morgan in 2018 when I played against Middlesex. I could have learned a thing or two by having a chat with him
IF YOU WERE AN ANIMAL, WHICH WOULD IT BE? A lion – I have South African genes
TWITTER: @Ben_1289

Batting	Mat	Inns	NO	Runs	HS	Ave	SR	100	50	Ct	St
First-class	15	22	2	417	77*	20.85	36.90	0	4	5	0
List A	1	1	0	14	14	14.00	63.63	0	0	0	0
Bowling	**Mat**	**Balls**	**Runs**	**Wkts**	**BBI**	**BBM**	**Ave**	**Econ**	**SR**	**5w**	**10**
First-class	15	397	234	8	3/25	3/25	29.25	3.53	49.6	0	0
List A	1	-	-	-	-	-	-	-	-	-	-

VARUN CHOPRA

RHB / LB / R3 / W0

FULL NAME: Varun Chopra
BORN: June 21, 1987, Barking, Essex
SQUAD NO: 6
HEIGHT: 6ft 1in
NICKNAME: Tiddles
EDUCATION: Ilford County High School
TEAMS: Essex, England Lions, Sussex, Tamil Union Cricket & Athletic Club, Warwickshire
ROLE: Batsman
DEBUT: First-class: 2006; List A: 2006; T20: 2006

BEST BATTING: 233* Tamil Union vs Sinhalese Sports Club, Colombo, 2012

COUNTY CAP: 2012 (Warwickshire); 2018 (Essex)

MOST EXCITING DAY AS A CRICKETER? Winning the T20 competition in 2014 off the last ball in front of a packed house at Edgbaston
FAMILY TIES? My younger brother Anuj played for Ilford CC and Essex U17s, while my older sister Anchal played for Essex Women
CHILDHOOD SPORTING HERO? Sachin Tendulkar
SURPRISING FACT ABOUT YOU? I love doing chin-ups
TWITTER: @vchops06

Batting	Mat	Inns	NO	Runs	HS	Ave	SR	100	50	Ct	St
First-class	192	317	20	10243	233*	34.48	50.80	20	50	228	0
List A	114	111	7	4789	160	46.04	77.01	12	28	41	0
T20s	115	112	13	2896	116	29.25	118.93	2	20	25	0
Bowling	**Mat**	**Balls**	**Runs**	**Wkts**	**BBI**	**BBM**	**Ave**	**Econ**	**SR**	**5w**	**10**
First-class	192	204	128	0	-	-	-	3.76	-	0	0
List A	114	18	18	0	-	-	-	6.00	-	0	0
T20s	115	-	-	-	-	-	-	-	-	-	-

DAN CHRISTIAN RHB / RM / R0 / W0 / MVP92

FULL NAME: Daniel Trevor Christian
BORN: May 4, 1983, Sydney, Australia
SQUAD NO: 54
HEIGHT: 6ft
EDUCATION: St Gregory's College, Sydney
TEAMS: Australia, Notts, Gloucestershire, Hampshire, Hobart Hurricanes, Melbourne Renegades, Middlesex, Rising Pune Supergiant, RC Bangalore, South Australia, Sydney Sixers, Victoria
ROLE: Allrounder
DEBUT: ODI: 2012; T20I: 2010; First-class: 2008; List A: 2006; T20: 2006

BEST BATTING: 129 Middlesex vs Kent, Canterbury, 2014 (T20)
BEST BOWLING: 5-14 Hobart Hurricanes vs Adelaide Strikers, Hobart, 2017 (T20)
COUNTY CAP: 2013 (Gloucestershire); 2015 (Nottinghamshire)

FIRST CRICKET CLUB? Narrandera CC, New South Wales, Australia
BEST INNINGS YOU'VE SEEN? Chris Gayle's 175 not out in the 2013 IPL (I was carrying the drinks for Royal Challengers Bangalore). He took down the Pune Warriors with the cleanest hitting I have ever seen
WHAT WOULD YOU DO IF YOU WERE IN CHARGE OF COUNTY CRICKET? Rule that balls over head height are no-balls in the T20 Blast
YOUR BIGGEST CRICKETING REGRET? Not nailing down a spot in the Australia team
TWITTER: @danchristian54

Batting	Mat	Inns	NO	Runs	HS	Ave	SR	100	50	Ct	St
ODIs	19	18	5	273	39	21.00	88.92	0	0	10	0
T20Is	16	7	3	27	9	6.75	96.42	0	0	5	0
First-class	83	141	17	3783	131*	30.50	53.77	5	16	90	0
List A	119	108	21	2844	117	32.68	101.64	2	14	43	0
T20s	347	298	82	5171	129	23.93	140.05	2	15	150	0
Bowling	**Mat**	**Balls**	**Runs**	**Wkts**	**BBI**	**BBM**	**Ave**	**Econ**	**SR**	**5w**	**10**
ODIs	19	727	595	20	5/31	5/31	29.75	4.91	36.3	1	0
T20Is	16	213	317	11	3/27	3/27	28.81	8.92	19.3	0	0
First-class	83	10301	5679	163	5/24	9/87	34.84	3.30	63.1	3	0
List A	119	3896	3585	107	6/48	6/48	33.50	5.52	36.4	3	0
T20s	347	5257	7398	259	5/14	5/14	28.56	8.44	20.2	2	0

GRAHAM CLARK

RHB / LB / R0 / W0

FULL NAME: Graham Clark
BORN: March 16, 1993, Whitehaven, Cumbria
SQUAD NO: 7
HEIGHT: 6ft 1in
NICKNAME: Schnoz
EDUCATION: St Benedict's Catholic High School, Whitehaven
TEAMS: Durham
ROLE: Batsman
DEBUT: First-class: 2015; List A: 2015; T20: 2015

BEST BATTING: 109 Durham vs Glamorgan, Chester-le-Street, 2017
BEST BOWLING: 1-10 Durham vs Sussex, Arundel, 2018

MOST EXCITING DAY AS A CRICKETER? Watching my dad win Man of the Match when Cleator won the Village Cup in 2013
CHILDHOOD SPORTING HERO? Michael Vaughan
BIGGEST INFLUENCE ON YOUR DEVELOPMENT AS A CRICKETER (EXCLUDING PARENTS)? My two older brothers Darren and Jordan. We spent countless hours playing in the backyard, in the nets, in the house even. I learnt a lot about my game through watching them play
FIRST CRICKET CLUB? Cleator CC, Cumbria
TOUGHEST OPPONENT IN COUNTY CRICKET? Sam Northeast – it's like he's batting with a barn door every time I've played against him
MOST ECCENTRIC TEAMMATE? Ben Raine – he's the most compulsive liar going around
WHAT WOULD YOU DO IF YOU WERE IN CHARGE OF COUNTY CRICKET? Increase the amount of four-day cricket in the middle of the summer
STRANGEST THING YOU'VE DONE DURING LOCKDOWN? Watching other people play Call of Duty (video game)
FAVOURITE SMELL? Roast dinner
TWITTER: @GrahamClark16

Batting	Mat	Inns	NO	Runs	HS	Ave	SR	100	50	Ct	St
First-class	34	63	1	1543	109	24.88	53.11	1	10	25	0
List A	32	32	1	665	114	21.45	81.19	1	2	11	0
T20s	58	57	4	1322	91*	24.94	142.76	0	9	28	0
Bowling	**Mat**	**Balls**	**Runs**	**Wkts**	**BBI**	**BBM**	**Ave**	**Econ**	**SR**	**5w**	**10**
First-class	34	95	58	2	1/10	1/10	29.00	3.66	47.5	0	0
List A	32	24	18	3	3/18	3/18	6.00	4.50	8.0	0	0
T20s	58	14	29	0	-	-	-	12.42	-	0	0

JORDAN CLARK RHB / RM / R0 / W0

FULL NAME: Jordan Clark
BORN: October 14, 1990, Whitehaven, Cumbria
SQUAD NO: 8
HEIGHT: 6ft 4in
EDUCATION: Sedbergh School, Cumbria
TEAMS: Surrey, Hobart Hurricanes, Lancashire
ROLE: Allrounder
DEBUT: First-class: 2015; List A: 2010; T20: 2011

BEST BATTING: 140 Lancashire vs Surrey, The Oval, 2017
BEST BOWLING: 5-58 Lancashire vs Yorkshire, Old Trafford, 2018

MOST EXCITING DAY AS A CRICKETER? Taking a hat-trick against Yorkshire in the Championship match at Old Trafford in 2018
FAMILY TIES? My younger brother Graham plays for Durham. My older brother Darren has played Minor Counties with Cumberland and together with my dad won the National Village Cup with Cleator CC in 2013
TOUGHEST OPPONENT IN COUNTY CRICKET? Darren Stevens – those nibblers...
MOST ECCENTRIC TEAMMATE? Will Jacks – he wants to hit 36 off every over
STRANGEST THING YOU'VE DONE DURING LOCKDOWN? Playing Call of Duty for three days straight
FAVOURITE SMELL? Fish
GUILTY PLEASURE? Sweet and salty popcorn
TWITTER: @Clarksy16

Batting	Mat	Inns	NO	Runs	HS	Ave	SR	100	50	Ct	St
First-class	52	76	8	1892	140	27.82	54.61	1	10	7	0
List A	51	39	8	954	79*	30.77	99.89	0	5	8	0
T20s	87	64	23	916	60	22.34	134.70	0	1	31	0
Bowling	**Mat**	**Balls**	**Runs**	**Wkts**	**BBI**	**BBM**	**Ave**	**Econ**	**SR**	**5w**	**10**
First-class	52	5690	3394	99	5/58	7/97	34.28	3.57	57.4	2	0
List A	51	1452	1536	34	4/34	4/34	45.17	6.34	42.7	0	0
T20s	87	1020	1506	53	4/22	4/22	28.41	8.85	19.2	0	0

TOM CLARK

LHB / RM / R0 / W0

FULL NAME: Thomas Geoffrey Reeves Clark
BORN: July 2, 2001, Haywards Heath, Sussex
SQUAD NO: 27
HEIGHT: 6ft 2in
EDUCATION: Ardingly College, West Sussex
TEAMS: Sussex, England U19
ROLE: Batsman
DEBUT: First-class: 2019

BEST BATTING: 65 Sussex vs Kent, Canterbury, 2020

MOST EXCITING DAY AS A CRICKETER? Representing England in our first match of the U19 World Cup in South Africa last year
CHILDHOOD SPORTING HERO? Vijay Singh
BIGGEST INFLUENCE ON YOUR DEVELOPMENT AS A CRICKETER (EXCLUDING PARENTS)? My brothers – they taught me the game
FIRST CRICKET CLUB? Horsham CC, West Sussex
IF YOU COULD TAKE ONE COUNTY CRICKETER'S BEST SHOT AND ADD IT TO YOUR OWN GAME? Jack Haynes's sweep
TOUGHEST OPPONENT IN COUNTY CRICKET? Jamie Porter – he's annoyingly consistent
MOST ECCENTRIC TEAMMATE? Mitchell Claydon – he always causes trouble
WHAT WOULD YOU DO IF YOU WERE IN CHARGE OF COUNTY CRICKET? Extend tea breaks, bring in DRS, create flatter pitches
STRANGEST THING YOU'VE DONE DURING LOCKDOWN? Going bald
FAVOURITE SMELL? Fresh laundry
IF YOU WERE AN ANIMAL, WHICH WOULD IT BE? A Labrador
GUILTY PLEASURE? Pringles
TWITTER: @tomclark2702

Batting	Mat	Inns	NO	Runs	HS	Ave	SR	100	50	Ct	St
First-class	5	9	0	123	65	13.66	40.46	0	1	2	0
Bowling	**Mat**	**Balls**	**Runs**	**Wkts**	**BBI**	**BBM**	**Ave**	**Econ**	**SR**	**5w**	**10**
First-class	5	-	-	-	-	-	-	-	-	-	-

JOE CLARKE

RHB / WK / R1 / W0 / MVP27

NOTTINGHAMSHIRE

FULL NAME: Joseph Michael Clarke
BORN: May 26, 1996, Shrewsbury, Shropshire
SQUAD NO: 33
HEIGHT: 6ft
EDUCATION: Llanfyllin High School, Powys
TEAMS: Nottinghamshire, England Lions, Karachi Kings, Worcestershire
ROLE: Batsman
DEBUT: First-class: 2015; List A: 2015; T20: 2015

BEST BATTING: 194 Worcestershire vs Derbyshire, Worcester, 2016

CHILDHOOD SPORTING HERO? Adam Gilchrist
FIRST CRICKET CLUB? Oswestry CC, Shropshire
MOST INTERESTING TEAMMATE? Ravichandran Ashwin – I could listen to him talk about life and cricket for hours
BEST INNINGS YOU'VE SEEN? Callum Ferguson's 192 for Worcestershire against Leicestershire in the 2018 One-Day Cup. Pure skill, and so good to watch from the other end
BIGGEST CRICKETING REGRET? Being not out overnight before Bank Holiday Monday
SURPRISING FACT ABOUT YOU? I can speak (some) Welsh
IF YOU WERE AN ANIMAL, WHICH WOULD IT BE? An owl – up all night
TWITTER: @joeclarke10

Batting	Mat	Inns	NO	Runs	HS	Ave	SR	100	50	Ct	St
First-class	80	138	10	4849	194	37.88	61.00	17	16	36	0
List A	62	59	5	1846	139	34.18	92.81	4	9	22	2
T20s	74	71	5	1818	124*	27.54	151.24	2	10	21	0
Bowling	**Mat**	**Balls**	**Runs**	**Wkts**	**BBI**	**BBM**	**Ave**	**Econ**	**SR**	**5w**	**10**
First-class	80	12	22	0	-	-	-	11.00	-	0	0
List A	62	-	-	-	-	-	-	-	-	-	-
T20s	74	-	-	-	-	-	-	-	-	-	-

RIKKI CLARKE

RHB / RFM / R1 / W0 / MVP90

FULL NAME: Rikki Clarke
BORN: September 29, 1981, Orsett, Essex
SQUAD NO: 81
HEIGHT: 6ft 5in
NICKNAME: Rock
EDUCATION: Broadwater Secondary, Surrey; Godalming College
TEAMS: England, Surrey, Derbyshire, Warwickshire
ROLE: Allrounder
DEBUT: Test: 2003; ODI: 2003; First-class: 2002; List A: 2001; T20: 2003

BEST BATTING: 214 Surrey vs Somerset, Guildford, 2006
BEST BOWLING: 7-55 Surrey vs Somerset, The Oval, 2017
COUNTY CAP: 2005 (Surrey); 2011 (Warwickshire); BENEFIT: 2021 (Surrey)

BIGGEST INFLUENCE ON YOUR DEVELOPMENT AS A CRICKETER (EXCLUDING PARENTS)? Graeme Welch, my former bowling coach at Warwickshire. He made me into the bowler I have become over the last few years
FIRST CRICKET CLUB? Godalming CC, Surrey
IF YOU COULD TAKE ONE COUNTY CRICKETER'S BEST SHOT AND ADD IT TO YOUR OWN GAME? Jason Roy's shot over the bowler's head for six
TOUGHEST OPPONENT IN COUNTY CRICKET? Either Darren Stevens or Tim Murtagh
MOST ECCENTRIC TEAMMATE? Jason Roy, without a doubt. He's lively to say the least
WHAT WOULD YOU DO IF YOU WERE IN CHARGE OF COUNTY CRICKET? Allow captains to shake hands on the last day at tea if both agree to a draw
STRANGEST THING YOU'VE DONE DURING LOCKDOWN? Establishing my own cricket academy business
TWITTER: @rikkiclarke81

Batting	Mat	Inns	NO	Runs	HS	Ave	SR	100	50	Ct	St
Tests	2	3	0	96	55	32.00	37.94	0	1	1	0
ODIs	20	13	0	144	39	11.07	62.06	0	0	11	0
First-class	256	390	46	11195	214	32.54		17	57	378	0
List A	232	189	27	4087	98*	25.22		0	21	106	0
T20s	169	147	40	2285	79*	21.35	122.71	0	6	87	0

Bowling	Mat	Balls	Runs	Wkts	BBI	BBM	Ave	Econ	SR	5w	10
Tests	2	174	60	4	2/7	3/11	15.00	2.06	43.5	0	0
ODIs	20	469	415	11	2/28	2/28	37.72	5.30	42.6	0	0
First-class	256	28763	15714	518	7/55		30.33	3.27	55.5	8	0
List A	232	6417	5801	154	5/26	5/26	37.66	5.42	41.6	1	0
T20s	169	2226	2799	113	4/16	4/16	24.76	7.54	19.6	0	0

MITCHELL CLAYDON

LHB / RMF / R0 / W2

FULL NAME: Mitchell Eric Claydon
BORN: November 25, 1982, Fairfield, New South Wales, Australia
SQUAD NO: 4
HEIGHT: 6ft 4in
NICKNAME: Ellen, Precious
EDUCATION: Westfield Sports High School, Sydney
TEAMS: Sussex, Canterbury, Central Districts, Durham, Kent, Yorkshire
ROLE: Bowler
DEBUT: First-class: 2005; List A: 2006; T20: 2006

BEST BATTING: 77 Kent vs Leicestershire, Leicester, 2014
BEST BOWLING: 6-104 Durham vs Somerset, Taunton, 2011
COUNTY CAP: 2016 (Kent)

CHILDHOOD SPORTING HERO? Ricky Ponting
FIRST CRICKET CLUB? St Andrews CC, New South Wales, Australia
MOST INTERESTING TEAMMATE? Heino Kuhn – he's far too clean. During the course of a game he goes around cleaning up everyone else's gear
SURPRISING FACT ABOUT YOU? I'm a magician, a keen surfer and I love to play a prank
TWITTER: @mitchellclaydon
NOTES: The 38-year-old seamer signed for Sussex in September 2019 after seven seasons at Kent. He will miss the first two games of the new season to complete the nine-match ban handed to him by the ECB last year after he was found guilty of using hand sanitiser to tamper with the ball during the Bob Willis Trophy match against Middlesex at Radlett

Batting	Mat	Inns	NO	Runs	HS	Ave	SR	100	50	Ct	St
First-class	112	145	35	1688	77	15.34	61.00	0	4	11	0
List A	110	50	17	276	19	8.36	82.88	0	0	9	0
T20s	149	50	30	191	19	9.55	89.25	0	0	27	0
Bowling	**Mat**	**Balls**	**Runs**	**Wkts**	**BBI**	**BBM**	**Ave**	**Econ**	**SR**	**5w**	**10**
First-class	112	16635	9889	310	6/104		31.90	3.56	53.6	9	0
List A	110	4799	4501	138	5/31	5/31	32.61	5.62	34.7	1	0
T20s	149	3085	4350	162	5/26	5/26	26.85	8.46	19.0	2	0

BEN COAD RHB / RFM / R0 / W1 / MVP89

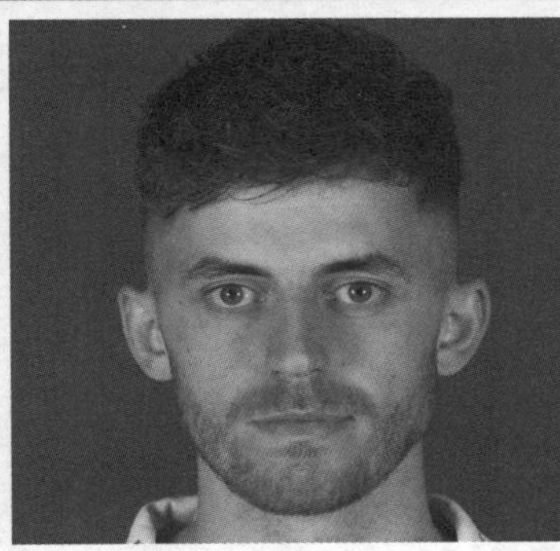

FULL NAME: Benjamin Oliver Coad
BORN: January 10, 1994, Harrogate, Yorkshire
SQUAD NO: 10
HEIGHT: 6ft 3in
NICKNAME: Hench
EDUCATION: Thirsk School & Sixth Form College, North Yorkshire
TEAMS: Yorkshire
ROLE: Bowler
DEBUT: First-class: 2016; List A: 2013; T20: 2015

BEST BATTING: 48 Yorkshire vs Surrey, Scarborough, 2019
BEST BOWLING: 6-25 Yorkshire vs Lancashire, Headingley, 2017
COUNTY CAP: 2018

MOST EXCITING DAY AS A CRICKETER? My second T20 game in 2015, playing against Warwickshire at home in front of a very good crowd and managing to take two wickets and winning the game against the defending champions
FAMILY TIES? My brothers played representative cricket at junior levels. My dad played Minor Counties for Suffolk
FIRST CRICKET CLUB? Studley Royal CC, Ripon, North Yorkshire
SURPRISING FACT ABOUT YOU? I'm a Newcastle United fan
IF YOU WERE AN ANIMAL, WHICH WOULD IT BE? A cheetah
TWITTER: @bencoad10

Batting	Mat	Inns	NO	Runs	HS	Ave	SR	100	50	Ct	St
First-class	38	50	16	519	48	15.26	65.69	0	0	2	0
List A	17	6	5	15	9	15.00	62.50	0	0	5	0
T20s	12	4	1	14	7	4.66	56.00	0	0	6	0
Bowling	**Mat**	**Balls**	**Runs**	**Wkts**	**BBI**	**BBM**	**Ave**	**Econ**	**SR**	**5w**	**10**
First-class	38	6890	3130	157	6/25	10/102	19.93	2.72	43.8	9	2
List A	17	764	748	20	4/63	4/63	37.40	5.87	38.2	0	0
T20s	12	217	323	13	3/40	3/40	24.84	8.93	16.6	0	0

JOSH COBB RHB / LB / R0 / W0

FULL NAME: Joshua James Cobb
BORN: August 17, 1990, Leicester
SQUAD NO: 4
HEIGHT: 6ft
NICKNAME: Lord
EDUCATION: Oakham School, Rutland
TEAMS: Northamptonshire, Barisal Bulls, Central Districts, Dhaka Gladiators, England U19, Leicestershire, Prime Doleshwar Sporting Club, Sylhet Superstars
ROLE: Batsman
DEBUT: First-class: 2007; List A: 2008; T20: 2008

BEST BATTING: 148* Leicestershire vs Middlesex, Lord's, 2008
BEST BOWLING: 2-11 Leicestershire vs Gloucestershire, Leicester, 2011
COUNTY CAP: 2018 (Northamptonshire)

MOST EXCITING DAY AS A CRICKETER? Winning on T20 Finals Day in 2011 with Leicestershire and in 2016 with Northamptonshire
FAMILY TIES? My dad Russell played for Leicestershire
CHILDHOOD SPORTING HERO? Shane Warne
BIGGEST INFLUENCE ON YOUR DEVELOPMENT AS A CRICKETER (EXCLUDING PARENTS)? Paul Nixon, my first captain
FIRST CRICKET CLUB? Kibworth CC, Leicestershire
IF YOU COULD TAKE ONE COUNTY CRICKETER'S BEST SHOT AND ADD IT TO YOUR OWN GAME? Wayne Madsen's sweeps (conventional and reverse)
SURPRISING FACT ABOUT YOU? At Oakham I was a member of the debating society and took an active interest in historical and modern British politics. I take a number of books and papers with me to away games which keep me busy during rain delays, much to the dismay of my teammates
GUILTY PLEASURE? KFC Krushems
TWITTER: @Cobby24

Batting	Mat	Inns	NO	Runs	HS	Ave	SR	100	50	Ct	St
First-class	126	216	22	5155	148*	26.57	50.29	4	30	53	0
List A	99	94	7	3330	146*	38.27	91.45	7	21	29	0
T20s	157	149	15	3321	103	24.78	131.52	1	19	68	0
Bowling	**Mat**	**Balls**	**Runs**	**Wkts**	**BBI**	**BBM**	**Ave**	**Econ**	**SR**	**5w**	**10**
First-class	126	2716	1607	18	2/11	2/11	89.27	3.55	150.8	0	0
List A	99	1758	1712	35	3/34	3/34	48.91	5.84	50.2	0	0
T20s	157	1479	1935	59	4/22	4/22	32.79	7.84	25.0	0	0

IAN COCKBAIN RHB / RM / R0 / W0 / MVP57

FULL NAME: Ian Andrew Cockbain
BORN: February 17, 1987, Liverpool
SQUAD NO: 28
HEIGHT: 6ft
NICKNAME: Gramps
EDUCATION: Maghull High School, Sefton, Merseyside; Liverpool John Moores University
TEAMS: Gloucestershire
ROLE: Batsman
DEBUT: First-class: 2011; List A: 2011; T20: 2011

BEST BATTING: 151* Gloucestershire vs Surrey, Bristol, 2014
BEST BOWLING: 1-23 Gloucestershire vs Durham MCCU, Bristol, 2016
COUNTY CAP: 2011; BENEFIT: 2019

FAMILY TIES? My dad Ian played for Lancashire
CHILDHOOD SPORTING HERO? Ricky Ponting
BIGGEST INFLUENCE ON YOUR DEVELOPMENT AS A CRICKETER (EXCLUDING PARENTS)? My grandad – he spent hours and hours throwing balls to me as a kid while we were watching Dad play
FIRST CRICKET CLUB? Bootle CC, Merseyside
IF YOU COULD TAKE ONE COUNTY CRICKETER'S BEST SHOT AND ADD IT TO YOUR OWN GAME? Jos Buttler's ramp
TOUGHEST OPPONENT IN COUNTY CRICKET? Darren Stevens – he's impossible to hit
WHAT WOULD YOU DO IF YOU WERE IN CHARGE OF COUNTY CRICKET? Limit the amount of travel, introduce "double play" in T20 cricket (for example, two wickets can fall when there is a catch and a run-out off the same delivery)
STRANGEST THING YOU'VE DONE DURING LOCKDOWN? Spending a couple of hours trying to make a tower of water bottles while quarantining in a hotel
FAVOURITE SMELL? A bacon butty

Batting	Mat	Inns	NO	Runs	HS	Ave	SR	100	50	Ct	St
First-class	51	86	6	2382	151*	29.77	42.81	4	13	35	0
List A	68	59	11	1633	108*	34.02	88.36	2	10	41	0
T20s	122	114	21	3064	123	32.94	131.16	1	16	58	0
Bowling	**Mat**	**Balls**	**Runs**	**Wkts**	**BBI**	**BBM**	**Ave**	**Econ**	**SR**	**5w**	**10**
First-class	51	47	44	1	1/23	1/23	44.00	5.61	47.0	0	0
List A	68	-	-	-	-	-	-	-	-	-	-
T20s	122	-	-	-	-	-	-	-	-	-	-

MICHAEL COHEN

LHB / LFM / R0 / W0

FULL NAME: Michael Alexander Robert Cohen
BORN: August 4, 1998, Cape Town, SA
SQUAD NO: 8
HEIGHT: 5ft 10in
NICKNAME: Uncoh
EDUCATION: Reddam House Constantia, Cape Town; University of South Africa
TEAMS: Derbyshire, Cape Cobras, South Africa U19, Western Province
ROLE: Bowler
DEBUT: First-class: 2017; List A: 2018; T20: 2017

BEST BATTING: 30* Derbyshire vs Nottinghamshire, Trent Bridge, 2020
BEST BOWLING: 5-40 Western Province vs South Western Districts, Rondesbosch, 2018

MOST EXCITING DAY AS A CRICKETER? Making my debut for South Africa U19 in 2017
CHILDHOOD SPORTING HERO? Wasim Akram
BIGGEST INFLUENCE ON YOUR DEVELOPMENT AS A CRICKETER (EXCLUDING PARENTS)? Two people: my sister and my Western Province coach Graham October
FIRST CRICKET CLUB? Western Province CC, Cape Town
IF YOU COULD TAKE ONE COUNTY CRICKETER'S BEST SHOT AND ADD IT TO YOUR OWN GAME? Wayne Madsen's ramp or sweep (whichever is available)
MOST ECCENTRIC TEAMMATE? Fynn Hudson-Prentice – for his energy and charisma
WHAT WOULD YOU DO IF YOU WERE IN CHARGE OF COUNTY CRICKET? Disclaimer: as a recently signed EU player with a limited experience of county cricket I can suggest only the following generic changes: 1) Can we please introduce additional tea breaks (it's cold)? 2) Pitching outside leg should be disregarded (if it's hitting in line and crashing into the stumps, it's out)
STRANGEST THING YOU'VE DONE DURING LOCKDOWN? University studies
GUILTY PLEASURE? Fluffy socks

Batting	Mat	Inns	NO	Runs	HS	Ave	SR	100	50	Ct	St
First-class	17	20	14	131	30*	21.83	32.26	0	0	1	0
List A	4	1	0	16	16	16.00	123.07	0	0	1	0
T20s	9	4	3	15	7*	15.00	93.75	0	0	0	0
Bowling	**Mat**	**Balls**	**Runs**	**Wkts**	**BBI**	**BBM**	**Ave**	**Econ**	**SR**	**5w**	**10**
First-class	17	2229	1497	57	5/40	9/70	26.26	4.02	39.1	2	0
List A	4	192	160	3	1/17	1/17	53.33	5.00	64.0	0	0
T20s	9	166	234	7	2/17	2/17	33.42	8.45	23.7	0	0

BEN COMPTON

LHB / OB / R0 / W0

FULL NAME: Benjamin Garnet Compton
BORN: March 29, 1994, Durban, South Africa
SQUAD NO: 7
HEIGHT: 6ft 1in
NICKNAME: Compo
EDUCATION: Clifton College, Durban; The Open University, Milton Keynes
TEAMS: Nottinghamshire
ROLE: Batsman
DEBUT: First-class: 2019

BEST BATTING: 16* Nottinghamshire vs Surrey, The Oval, 2019

MOST EXCITING DAY AS A CRICKETER? Making my first-class debut at Trent Bridge in 2019
CHILDHOOD SPORTING HERO? Thierry Henry
FIRST CRICKET CLUB? Wimbledon CC, London
MOST ECCENTRIC TEAMMATE? Zak Chappell – he hoovers the house 12 times a day
FAVOURITE SMELL? A bottle of Meerlust Rubicon, just opened
IF YOU WERE AN ANIMAL, WHICH WOULD IT BE? A wolf – because I would have a lot of fun howling at the moon
SURPRISING FACT ABOUT YOU? I once played with Wasim Akram – in a fundraising match. Just a pleasure and privilege to play with one of the game's all-time greats
GUILTY PLEASURE? Chocolate brownies

Batting	Mat	Inns	NO	Runs	HS	Ave	SR	100	50	Ct	St
First-class	2	3	1	43	16*	21.50	32.08	0	0	1	0
Bowling	**Mat**	**Balls**	**Runs**	**Wkts**	**BBI**	**BBM**	**Ave**	**Econ**	**SR**	**5w**	**10**
First-class	2	-	-	-	-	-	-	-	-	-	-

SAM CONNERS RHB / RFM / R0 / W0

FULL NAME: Samuel Conners
BORN: February 13, 1999, Nottingham
SQUAD NO: 59
HEIGHT: 6ft
NICKNAME: Sammy
EDUCATION: George Spencer Academy, Nottingham
TEAMS: Derbyshire, England U19
ROLE: Bowler
DEBUT: First-class: 2019; List A: 2019; T20: 2020

BEST BATTING: 21 Derbyshire vs Leicestershire, Leicester, 2020
BEST BOWLING: 3-63 Derbyshire vs Nottinghamshire, Trent Bridge, 2020

MOST EXCITING DAY AS A CRICKETER? Coming up against James Anderson at Derby in 2019
CHILDHOOD SPORTING HERO? James Anderson
BIGGEST INFLUENCE ON YOUR DEVELOPMENT AS A CRICKETER (EXCLUDING PARENTS)? Steve Kirby, our former bowling coach. He helped me to get my first contract and has developed my game hugely
FIRST CRICKET CLUB? Attenborough CC, Nottingham
TOUGHEST OPPONENT IN COUNTY CRICKET? Alex Davies – he smacks me every time
WHAT WOULD YOU DO IF YOU WERE IN CHARGE OF COUNTY CRICKET? Play a county competition in Australia every four years
WHAT WOULD YOU DO IF YOU WERE PRIME MINISTER? Make over-75s re-take their driving test, remove speed cameras
GUILTY PLEASURE? Olly Murs
TWITTER: @SamConners7

Batting	Mat	Inns	NO	Runs	HS	Ave	SR	100	50	Ct	St
First-class	7	6	3	65	21	21.66	22.49	0	0	0	0
List A	3	1	0	4	4	4.00	200.00	0	0	2	0
T20s	6	1	1	2	2*	-	100.00	0	0	0	0
Bowling	**Mat**	**Balls**	**Runs**	**Wkts**	**BBI**	**BBM**	**Ave**	**Econ**	**SR**	**5w**	**10**
First-class	7	788	441	14	3/63	4/132	31.50	3.35	56.2	0	0
List A	3	138	150	2	1/45	1/45	75.00	6.52	69.0	0	0
T20s	6	72	120	3	2/38	2/38	40.00	10.00	24.0	0	0

ALASTAIR COOK LHB / RM / R9 / W0 / MVP39

FULL NAME: Alastair Nathan Cook
BORN: December 25, 1984, Gloucester
SQUAD NO: 26
HEIGHT: 6ft 2in
NICKNAME: Chef
EDUCATION: Bedford School
TEAMS: England, Essex
ROLE: Batsman
DEBUT: Test: 2006; ODI: 2006; T20I: 2007; First-class: 2003; List A: 2003; T20: 2005

BEST BATTING: 294 England vs India, Edgbaston, 2011
BEST BOWLING: 3-13 Essex vs Northamptonshire, Chelmsford, 2005
COUNTY CAP: 2005; BENEFIT: 2014

FAMILY TIES? Dad played for the local club side and was a very good opening bat, while my mum made the teas
CHILDHOOD SPORTING HERO? Graham Gooch – I watched him playing for Essex at Chelmsford
FIRST CRICKET CLUB? Maldon CC, Essex. Both of my brothers also played for the club

Batting	Mat	Inns	NO	Runs	HS	Ave	SR	100	50	Ct	St
Tests	161	291	16	12472	294	45.35	46.95	33	57	175	0
ODIs	92	92	4	3204	137	36.40	77.13	5	19	36	0
T20Is	4	4	0	61	26	15.25	112.96	0	0	1	0
First-class	310	549	42	24230	294	47.79	50.78	67	115	333	0
List A	168	166	11	6055	137	39.06	79.97	12	35	68	0
T20s	32	30	2	892	100*	31.85	127.61	1	5	13	0
Bowling	**Mat**	**Balls**	**Runs**	**Wkts**	**BBI**	**BBM**	**Ave**	**Econ**	**SR**	**5w**	**10**
Tests	161	18	7	1	1/6	1/6	7.00	2.33	18.0	0	0
ODIs	92	-	-	-	-	-	-	-	-	-	-
T20Is	4	-	-	-	-	-	-	-	-	-	-
First-class	310	282	211	7	3/13	-	30.14	4.48	40.2	0	0
List A	168	18	10	0	-	-	-	3.33	-	0	0
T20s	32	-	-	-	-	-	-	-	-	-	-

SAM COOK RHB / RFM / R0 / W0 / MVP65

FULL NAME: Samuel James Cook
BORN: August 4, 1997, Chelmsford, Essex
SQUAD NO: 16
HEIGHT: 6ft 2in
NICKNAME: Little Chef
EDUCATION: Great Baddow High School, Chelmsford; Loughborough University
TEAMS: Essex
ROLE: Bowler
DEBUT: First-class: 2016; List A: 2018; T20: 2018

BEST BATTING: 37* Essex vs Yorkshire, Headingley, 2019
BEST BOWLING: 7-23 Essex vs Kent, Canterbury, 2019
COUNTY CAP: 2020

CHILDHOOD SPORTING HERO? Cristiano Ronaldo
BIGGEST INFLUENCE ON YOUR DEVELOPMENT AS A CRICKETER (EXCLUDING PARENTS)? Ryan ten Doeschate and Anthony McGrath
FIRST CRICKET CLUB? Writtle CC, Essex
IF YOU COULD TAKE ONE COUNTY CRICKETER'S BEST SHOT AND ADD IT TO YOUR OWN GAME? Charlie "Troy" Thurston's flick-whip
TOUGHEST OPPONENT IN COUNTY CRICKET? Hashim Amla – he seems to have more time than any other batsman I've bowled to
WHAT WOULD YOU DO IF YOU WERE IN CHARGE OF COUNTY CRICKET? Introduce pyrotechnics at Championship games
WHAT WOULD YOU DO IF YOU WERE PRIME MINISTER? Open a pub (The Downing Street Arms), appoint Jackie Weaver as foreign secretary, facetime Joe Biden
STRANGEST THING YOU'VE DONE DURING LOCKDOWN? Appearing on Kiss FM as a guest DJ
FAVOURITE SMELL? Vetiver and lavender diffuser
TWITTER: @samcook09

Batting	Mat	Inns	NO	Runs	HS	Ave	SR	100	50	Ct	St
First-class	34	35	15	140	37*	7.00	35.00	0	0	3	0
List A	12	4	2	9	6	4.50	69.23	0	0	1	0
T20s	12	3	1	0	0*	0.00	0.00	0	0	1	0
Bowling	**Mat**	**Balls**	**Runs**	**Wkts**	**BBI**	**BBM**	**Ave**	**Econ**	**SR**	**5w**	**10**
First-class	34	5095	2461	104	7/23	12/65	23.66	2.89	48.9	7	1
List A	12	582	457	11	3/37	3/37	41.54	4.71	52.9	0	0
T20s	12	204	323	8	2/25	2/25	40.37	9.50	25.5	0	0

CHRIS COOKE RHB / WK / R0 / W0 / MVP10

FULL NAME: Christopher Barry Cooke
BORN: May 30, 1986, Johannesburg, South Africa
SQUAD NO: 46
HEIGHT: 5ft 11in
NICKNAME: Jelly
EDUCATION: Bishops School, Cape Town; University of Cape Town
TEAMS: Glamorgan, Western Province
ROLE: Batsman/wicketkeeper
DEBUT: First-class: 2009; List A: 2009; T20: 2011

BEST BATTING: 171 Glamorgan vs Kent, Canterbury, 2014

COUNTY CAP: 2016

MOST EXCITING DAY AS A CRICKETER? Playing in the one-day final at Lord's in 2013
CHILDHOOD SPORTING HERO? Jonty Rhodes
FIRST CRICKET CLUB? Cape Town CC, South Africa
IF YOU COULD TAKE ONE COUNTY CRICKETER'S BEST SHOT AND ADD IT TO YOUR OWN GAME? Wayne Madsen's sweep
TOUGHEST OPPONENT IN COUNTY CRICKET? The Overton twins
WHAT WOULD YOU DO IF YOU WERE IN CHARGE OF COUNTY CRICKET? Bring back the 40-over format, trial Kookaburra balls in the Championship, push for T20 cricket to be an Olympic sport
STRANGEST THING YOU'VE DONE DURING LOCKDOWN? Cutting my own hair
GUILTY PLEASURE? A glass of Pinotage with biltong
TWITTER: @Cooky_24

Batting	Mat	Inns	NO	Runs	HS	Ave	SR	100	50	Ct	St
First-class	89	153	19	4772	171	35.61	53.69	4	32	157	6
List A	88	81	9	2607	161	36.20	98.34	3	14	54	5
T20s	113	97	20	1880	72	24.41	138.74	0	6	69	9
Bowling	**Mat**	**Balls**	**Runs**	**Wkts**	**BBI**	**BBM**	**Ave**	**Econ**	**SR**	**5w**	**10**
First-class	89	-	-	-	-	-	-	-	-	-	-
List A	88	-	-	-	-	-	-	-	-	-	-
T20s	113	-	-	-	-	-	-	-	-	-	-

JOE COOKE

LHB / RMF / R0 / W0

FULL NAME: Joe Michael Cooke
BORN: May 30, 1997, Hemel Hempstead, Hertfordshire
SQUAD NO: 57
HEIGHT: 6ft 3in
EDUCATION: Parmiter's School, Watford; Durham University
TEAMS: Glamorgan
ROLE: Batsman
DEBUT: First-class: 2017

BEST BATTING: 23 Glamorgan vs Warwickshire, Cardiff, 2020
BEST BOWLING: 1-26 Durham MCCU vs Warwickshire, Edgbaston, 2018

MOST EXCITING DAY AS A CRICKETER? Winning the MCC University final at Lord's (despite getting a golden duck)
CHILDHOOD SPORTING HERO? Jonny Wilkinson
BIGGEST INFLUENCE ON YOUR DEVELOPMENT AS A CRICKETER (EXCLUDING PARENTS)? Shane Burger – he helped me make the changes that led to me becoming a professional while I was training with KwaZulu Natal Inland in South Africa
FIRST CRICKET CLUB? Kings Langley CC, Hertfordshire
TOUGHEST OPPONENT IN COUNTY CRICKET? Jack White – he got me out twice on my Glamorgan first-class debut at Northampton last year
WHAT WOULD YOU DO IF YOU WERE IN CHARGE OF COUNTY CRICKET? Create a ball that neither swings nor seams
WHAT WOULD YOU DO IF YOU WERE PRIME MINISTER? Introduce the four-day working week
STRANGEST THING YOU'VE DONE DURING LOCKDOWN? Shaving my head (I didn't look good)
FAVOURITE SMELL? Toast
TWITTER: @cooke_joe

Batting	Mat	Inns	NO	Runs	HS	Ave	SR	100	50	Ct	St
First-class	6	6	0	76	23	12.66	31.14	0	0	7	0
Bowling	**Mat**	**Balls**	**Runs**	**Wkts**	**BBI**	**BBM**	**Ave**	**Econ**	**SR**	**5w**	**10**
First-class	6	468	308	3	1/26	1/26	102.66	3.94	156.0	0	0

PAUL COUGHLIN RHB / RFM / R0 / W0 / MVP86

FULL NAME: Paul Coughlin
BORN: October 23, 1992, Sunderland
SQUAD NO: 23
HEIGHT: 6ft 2in
NICKNAME: Coggers
EDUCATION: St Robert of Newminster Catholic School, Sunderland
TEAMS: Durham, England Lions, Nottinghamshire
ROLE: Allrounder
DEBUT: First-class: 2012; List A: 2012; T20: 2014

BEST BATTING: 90 Durham vs Derbyshire, Chester-le-Street, 2020
BEST BOWLING: 5-49 Durham vs Northamptonshire, Chester-le-Street, 2017

MOST EXCITING DAY AS A CRICKETER? Winning the One-Day Cup at Lord's in 2014
FAMILY TIES? My younger brother Josh has played for Durham. My uncle Tommy Harland played for the club when it was a Minor County. A different uncle had a homemade net in his back garden when I was a kid, and that's how I got into cricket
CHILDHOOD SPORTING HERO? Andrew Flintoff
SURPRISING FACT ABOUT YOU? I started out aiming to be a wicketkeeper. Then I tried myself as a batter. But I ended up being more of a bowler
TWITTER: @Coughlin92

Batting	Mat	Inns	NO	Runs	HS	Ave	SR	100	50	Ct	St
First-class	42	66	8	1482	90	25.55	56.39	0	8	22	0
List A	27	18	4	177	22	12.64	95.67	0	0	7	0
T20s	43	29	9	511	53	25.55	136.99	0	1	12	0
Bowling	**Mat**	**Balls**	**Runs**	**Wkts**	**BBI**	**BBM**	**Ave**	**Econ**	**SR**	**5w**	**10**
First-class	42	5291	3130	89	5/49	10/133	35.16	3.54	59.4	2	1
List A	27	977	915	18	3/36	3/36	50.83	5.61	54.2	0	0
T20s	43	613	979	47	5/42	5/42	20.82	9.58	13.0	1	0

BEN COX

RHB / WK / R0 / W0 / MVP61

WORCESTERSHIRE

FULL NAME: Oliver Benjamin Cox
BORN: February 2, 1992, Wordsley, Stourbridge, Worcestershire
SQUAD NO: 10
HEIGHT: 5ft 10in
NICKNAME: Cocko
EDUCATION: Bromsgrove School, Worcestershire
TEAMS: Worcestershire, Otago
ROLE: Wicketkeeper
DEBUT: First-class: 2009; List A: 2010; T20: 2010

BEST BATTING: 124 Worcestershire vs Gloucestershire, Cheltenham, 2017

CHILDHOOD SPORTING HERO? Jonny Wilkinson
BIGGEST INFLUENCE ON YOUR DEVELOPMENT AS A CRICKETER (EXCLUDING PARENTS)? Steve Rhodes – he taught me pretty much everything there is to know about wicketkeeping and the work that it takes to be a professional sportsman
FIRST CRICKET CLUB? Belbroughton CC, Worcestershire – a tiny village club which I had to leave because I couldn't get in the first team as a wicketkeeper
TOUGHEST OPPONENT IN COUNTY CRICKET? Justin Langer when he was at Somerset. Before playing against Langer I was told to keep quiet and not to wind him up because he plays better when he's in the battle. What a character
WHAT WOULD YOU DO IF YOU WERE IN CHARGE OF COUNTY CRICKET? Implement a "double play" – so a nick and a stumping off the same ball would mean the next batter is out too. Also: give U16s free admission to Championship matches
STRANGEST THING YOU'VE DONE DURING LOCKDOWN? Keeping a full set of gym kit in the boot of my car and training every day in my underground car park
TWITTER: @bencox10

Batting	Mat	Inns	NO	Runs	HS	Ave	SR	100	50	Ct	St
First-class	121	196	27	4764	124	28.18	60.69	4	26	330	13
List A	74	58	9	1371	122*	27.97	97.16	1	5	80	9
T20s	120	105	40	1785	59*	27.46	124.73	0	4	53	27
Bowling	**Mat**	**Balls**	**Runs**	**Wkts**	**BBI**	**BBM**	**Ave**	**Econ**	**SR**	**5w**	**10**
First-class	121	-	-	-	-	-	-	-	-	-	-
List A	74	-	-	-	-	-	-	-	-	-	-
T20s	120	-	-	-	-	-	-	-	-	-	-

JORDAN COX

RHB / WK / R0 / W0 / MVP77

FULL NAME: Jordan Matthew Cox
BORN: October 21, 2000, Portsmouth
SQUAD NO: 22
HEIGHT: 5ft 11in
EDUCATION: Felsted School, Essex
TEAMS: Kent, England U19
ROLE: Batsman/wicketkeeper
DEBUT: First-class: 2019; List A: 2019; T20: 2019

BEST BATTING: 238* Kent vs Sussex, Canterbury, 2020

MOST EXCITING DAY AS A CRICKETER? Scoring a double hundred in the Bob Willis Trophy last season
CHILDHOOD SPORTING HERO? Kevin Pietersen
FIRST CRICKET CLUB? Sandwich Town CC, Dover, Kent
TOUGHEST OPPONENT IN COUNTY CRICKET? Stuart Meaker – he tried to kill me at Canterbury
MOST ECCENTRIC TEAMMATE? Sam Billings
STRANGEST THING YOU'VE DONE DURING LOCKDOWN? Playing Call of Duty for seven hours straight
FAVOURITE SMELL? A new cricket bat
TWITTER: @jjordancox

Batting	Mat	Inns	NO	Runs	HS	Ave	SR	100	50	Ct	St
First-class	7	10	1	395	238*	43.88	48.94	1	0	7	0
List A	1	1	0	21	21	21.00	80.76	0	0	1	0
T20s	15	12	4	133	39*	16.62	111.76	0	0	6	2
Bowling	**Mat**	**Balls**	**Runs**	**Wkts**	**BBI**	**BBM**	**Ave**	**Econ**	**SR**	**5w**	**10**
First-class	7	-	-	-	-	-	-	-	-	-	-
List A	1	-	-	-	-	-	-	-	-	-	-
T20s	15	-	-	-	-	-	-	-	-	-	-

JOE CRACKNELL

RHB / RO / WO

FULL NAME: Joseph Benjamin Cracknell
BORN: March 16, 2000, Enfield, London
SQUAD NO: 48
HEIGHT: 5ft 11in
NICKNAME: Crackers
EDUCATION: London Oratory School; Durham University
TEAMS: Middlesex
ROLE: Batsman
DEBUT: T20: 2019

MOST EXCITING DAY AS A CRICKETER? Playing my first match at Lord's since signing as a professional at the beginning of last year
CHILDHOOD SPORTING HERO? Andrew Flintoff
FIRST CRICKET CLUB? North Middlesex CC, London
IF YOU COULD TAKE ONE COUNTY CRICKETER'S BEST SHOT AND ADD IT TO YOUR OWN GAME? Ian Cockbain's slap over extra cover
TOUGHEST OPPONENT IN COUNTY CRICKET? Jamie Overton – he is the fastest bowler I've ever faced
MOST ECCENTRIC TEAMMATE? Sam Robson – he's crazy
WHAT WOULD YOU DO IF YOU WERE PRIME MINISTER? Give the country a week-long holiday
STRANGEST THING YOU'VE DONE DURING LOCKDOWN? Playing darts for four hours without stopping
GUILTY PLEASURE? One Direction
TWITTER: @cracknell_joe

Batting	Mat	Inns	NO	Runs	HS	Ave	SR	100	50	Ct	St
T20s	5	5	0	129	50	25.80	141.75	0	1	0	0
Bowling	**Mat**	**Balls**	**Runs**	**Wkts**	**BBI**	**BBM**	**Ave**	**Econ**	**SR**	**5w**	**10**
T20s	5	-	-	-	-	-	-	-	-	-	-

MASON CRANE

RHB / LB / R0 / W0 / MVP74

FULL NAME: Mason Sidney Crane
BORN: February 18, 1997, Shoreham-by-Sea, Sussex
SQUAD NO: 32
HEIGHT: 5ft 10in
NICKNAME: Mase
EDUCATION: Lancing College, West Sussex
TEAMS: England, Hampshire, New South Wales
ROLE: Bowler
DEBUT: Test: 2018; T20I: 2017; First-class: 2015; List A: 2015; T20: 2015

BEST BATTING: 29 Hampshire vs Somerset, Taunton, 2017
BEST BOWLING: 5-35 Hampshire vs Warwickshire, Southampton, 2015

MOST EXCITING DAY AS A CRICKETER? My Test debut at the SCG
CHILDHOOD SPORTING HERO? Shane Warne
BIGGEST INFLUENCE ON YOUR DEVELOPMENT AS A CRICKETER (EXCLUDING PARENTS)? Two brilliant coaches: Raj Maru (director of cricket at Lancing College) and Stuart MacGill
FIRST CRICKET CLUB? Worthing CC, West Sussex
IF YOU COULD TAKE ONE COUNTY CRICKETER'S BEST SHOT AND ADD IT TO YOUR OWN GAME? James Vince's cover-drive
TOUGHEST OPPONENT IN COUNTY CRICKET? Ravi Bopara – he's such a good player of spin
IF YOU WERE AN ANIMAL, WHICH WOULD IT BE? A tortoise – because they're always at home
GUILTY PLEASURE? Singing in the car
TWITTER: @masoncrane32

Batting	Mat	Inns	NO	Runs	HS	Ave	SR	100	50	Ct	St
Tests	1	2	0	6	4	3.00	54.54	0	0	0	0
T20Is	2	-	-	-	-	-	-	-	-	0	0
First-class	42	58	19	419	29	10.74	36.15	0	0	9	0
List A	39	16	12	112	28*	28.00	82.96	0	0	14	0
T20s	37	10	8	43	12*	21.50	75.43	0	0	6	0
Bowling	**Mat**	**Balls**	**Runs**	**Wkts**	**BBI**	**BBM**	**Ave**	**Econ**	**SR**	**5w**	**10**
Tests	1	288	193	1	1/193	1/193	193.00	4.02	288.0	0	0
T20Is	2	48	62	1	1/38	1/38	62.00	7.75	48.0	0	0
First-class	42	6568	4336	96	5/35	6/69	45.16	3.96	68.4	2	0
List A	39	1982	2009	67	4/30	4/30	29.98	6.08	29.5	0	0
T20s	37	756	893	42	3/15	3/15	21.26	7.08	18.0	0	0

KENT

ZAK CRAWLEY RHB / RM / R0 / W0 / MVP46

FULL NAME: Zak Crawley
BORN: February 3, 1998, Bromley, Kent
SQUAD NO: 16
HEIGHT: 6ft 5in
EDUCATION: Tonbridge School, Kent
TEAMS: England, Kent
ROLE: Batsman
DEBUT: Test: 2019; First-class: 2017; List A: 2017; T20: 2018

BEST BATTING: 267 England vs Pakistan, Southampton, 2020

COUNTY CAP: 2019

MOST EXCITING DAY AS A CRICKETER? The final day of the Cape Town Test in January 2020
CHILDHOOD SPORTING HERO? Tiger Woods
BIGGEST INFLUENCE ON YOUR DEVELOPMENT AS A CRICKETER (EXCLUDING PARENTS)? Rob Key
FIRST CRICKET CLUB? Holmesdale CC, Sevenoaks, Kent
IF YOU COULD TAKE ONE COUNTY CRICKETER'S BEST SHOT AND ADD IT TO YOUR OWN GAME? Alastair Cook's pull or cut (take your pick)
TOUGHEST OPPONENT IN COUNTY CRICKET? Mohammad Abbas – I couldn't hit the ball
WHAT WOULD YOU DO IF YOU WERE IN CHARGE OF COUNTY CRICKET? Ban the second new ball, make compulsory the use of the heavy roller
WHAT WOULD YOU DO IF YOU WERE PRIME MINISTER? Clean the streets, allow injured veterans to live for free
STRANGEST THING YOU'VE DONE DURING LOCKDOWN? Practising my running between the wickets – extremely boring
TWITTER: @zakcrawley

Batting	Mat	Inns	NO	Runs	HS	Ave	SR	100	50	Ct	St
Tests	12	20	0	683	267	34.15	54.77	1	4	10	0
First-class	50	85	1	2724	267	32.42	58.49	5	15	43	0
List A	23	22	1	743	120	35.38	72.77	1	4	11	0
T20s	24	23	2	652	108*	31.04	150.23	1	3	8	0
Bowling	**Mat**	**Balls**	**Runs**	**Wkts**	**BBI**	**BBM**	**Ave**	**Econ**	**SR**	**5w**	**10**
Tests	12	-	-	-	-	-	-	-	-	-	-
First-class	50	66	33	0	-	-	-	3.00	-	0	0
List A	23	12	17	0	-	-	-	8.50	-	0	0
T20s	24	-	-	-	-	-	-	-	-	-	-

MATT CRITCHLEY RHB / LB / R0 / W0 / MVP21

FULL NAME: Matthew James John Critchley
BORN: August 13, 1996, Preston, Lancashire
SQUAD NO: 20
HEIGHT: 6ft 2in
NICKNAME: Critch
EDUCATION: St Michael's CE High School, Chorley; Cardinal Newman College, Preston; University of Derby
TEAMS: Derbyshire, England Lions
ROLE: Allrounder
DEBUT: First-class: 2015; List A: 2015; T20: 2016

BEST BATTING: 137* Derbyshire vs Northamptonshire, Derby, 2015
BEST BOWLING: 6-73 Derbyshire vs Leicestershire, Leicester, 2020
COUNTY CAP: 2019

CHILDHOOD SPORTING HERO? Shane Warne
BIGGEST INFLUENCE ON YOUR DEVELOPMENT AS A CRICKETER (EXCLUDING PARENTS)? Stuart MacGill – I worked with him in Australia and he has an amazing knowledge of leg-spin
FIRST CRICKET CLUB? Chorley CC, Lancashire
IF YOU COULD TAKE ONE COUNTY CRICKETER'S BEST SHOT AND ADD IT TO YOUR OWN GAME? Harvey Hosein's leave
TOUGHEST OPPONENT IN COUNTY CRICKET? James Anderson – I played against him on a green wicket at Derby and it was the stuff of nightmares
WHAT WOULD YOU DO IF YOU WERE IN CHARGE OF COUNTY CRICKET? Make tea longer
STRANGEST THING YOU'VE DONE DURING LOCKDOWN? Winning the Premier League with Aston Villa on Football Manager
GUILTY PLEASURE? McDonald's
TWITTER: @mattcritchley96

Batting	Mat	Inns	NO	Runs	HS	Ave	SR	100	50	Ct	St
First-class	53	88	10	2254	137*	28.89	59.91	3	10	34	0
List A	43	34	9	685	64*	27.40	103.47	0	2	6	0
T20s	60	45	7	678	72*	17.84	120.00	0	1	16	0
Bowling	**Mat**	**Balls**	**Runs**	**Wkts**	**BBI**	**BBM**	**Ave**	**Econ**	**SR**	**5w**	**10**
First-class	53	5281	3678	82	6/73	10/194	44.85	4.17	64.4	2	1
List A	43	1530	1674	31	4/48	4/48	54.00	6.56	49.3	0	0
T20s	60	869	1131	43	4/36	4/36	26.30	7.80	20.2	0	0

HENRY CROCOMBE

RHB / RFM / R0 / W0

SUSSEX

FULL NAME: Henry Thomas Crocombe
BORN: September 20, 2001, Eastbourne, Sussex
SQUAD NO: 14
HEIGHT: 6ft 2in
NICKNAME: Crocs
EDUCATION: Bede's Senior School, Hailsham, East Sussex
TEAMS: Sussex
ROLE: Bowler
DEBUT: First-class: 2020

BEST BATTING: 15 Sussex vs Kent, Canterbury, 2020
BEST BOWLING: 2-36 Sussex vs Surrey, The Oval, 2020

MOST EXCITING DAY AS A CRICKETER? Taking two wickets in two balls against Surrey at The Oval in last summer's Bob Willis Trophy
CHILDHOOD SPORTING HERO? Cristiano Ronaldo
BIGGEST INFLUENCE ON YOUR DEVELOPMENT AS A CRICKETER (EXCLUDING PARENTS)? James Kirtley, Sussex's former pace-bowling coach who has just become the club's T20 coach. We have worked together for five years now and he has passed on all the knowledge I have needed to be the player I am now
IF YOU COULD TAKE ONE COUNTY CRICKETER'S BEST SHOT AND ADD IT TO YOUR OWN GAME? Being a bowler, I'd rather pick another bowler's best delivery. That would be Tymal Mills's slower ball
TOUGHEST OPPONENT IN COUNTY CRICKET? Hashim Amla – because of his relentless defence in Championship cricket and his ability to build an innings
WHAT WOULD YOU DO IF YOU WERE IN CHARGE OF COUNTY CRICKET? Ensure that the long format gets as much exposure as possible, try to make the game more culturally diverse
STRANGEST THING YOU'VE DONE DURING LOCKDOWN? Bleaching my hair
FAVOURITE SMELL? Cut grass
TWITTER: @CrocombeHenry

Batting	Mat	Inns	NO	Runs	HS	Ave	SR	100	50	Ct	St
First-class	4	8	4	45	15	11.25	26.16	0	0	1	0
Bowling	**Mat**	**Balls**	**Runs**	**Wkts**	**BBI**	**BBM**	**Ave**	**Econ**	**SR**	**5w**	**10**
First-class	4	426	245	3	2/36	2/47	81.66	3.45	142.0	0	0

STEVEN CROFT RHB / RM / OB / R0 / W0 / MVP45

FULL NAME: Steven John Croft
BORN: October 11, 1984, Blackpool
SQUAD NO: 15
HEIGHT: 5ft 11in
NICKNAME: Crofty
EDUCATION: Highfield High School, Blackpool; Myerscough College, Lancashire
TEAMS: Lancashire, Auckland, Northern Districts
ROLE: Batsman
DEBUT: First-class: 2005; List A: 2003; T20: 2006

BEST BATTING: 156 Lancashire vs Northamptonshire, Old Trafford, 2014
BEST BOWLING: 6-41 Lancashire vs Worcestershire, Old Trafford, 2012
COUNTY CAP: 2010; BENEFIT: 2018

MOST EXCITING DAY AS A CRICKETER? Winning the County Championship in 2011
CHILDHOOD SPORTING HERO? Andrew Flintoff
FIRST CRICKET CLUB? Blackpool CC, Lancashire
IF YOU COULD TAKE ONE COUNTY CRICKETER'S BEST SHOT AND ADD IT TO YOUR OWN GAME? Simon Kerrigan's forward defence
TOUGHEST OPPONENT IN COUNTY CRICKET? Marcus Trescothick
WHAT WOULD YOU DO IF YOU WERE IN CHARGE OF COUNTY CRICKET? Play four-day games later in the summer
STRANGEST THING YOU'VE DONE DURING LOCKDOWN? Letting my daughter do my hair and nails
FAVOURITE SMELL? Wine by the fire
SURPRISING FACT ABOUT YOU? I grew up in Sri Lanka and learnt the game there
TWITTER: @Stevenjcroft

Batting	Mat	Inns	NO	Runs	HS	Ave	SR	100	50	Ct	St
First-class	180	275	27	8462	156	34.12	50.43	13	51	182	0
List A	157	140	24	4252	127	36.65		3	31	78	0
T20s	195	179	40	4148	94*	29.84	122.94	0	24	114	0
Bowling	**Mat**	**Balls**	**Runs**	**Wkts**	**BBI**	**BBM**	**Ave**	**Econ**	**SR**	**5w**	**10**
First-class	180	5375	2980	72	6/41	9/105	41.38	3.32	74.6	1	0
List A	157	2787	2561	62	4/24	4/24	41.30	5.51	44.9	0	0
T20s	195	1654	2049	73	3/6	3/6	28.06	7.43	22.6	0	0

MIDDLESEX

BLAKE CULLEN

RHB / RFM / R0 / W0

FULL NAME: Blake Carlton Cullen
BORN: March 31, 2002, Hounslow, London
SQUAD NO: 19
HEIGHT: 6ft 3in
NICKNAME: The Professor
EDUCATION: Hampton School, London
TEAMS: Middlesex, England U19
ROLE: Bowler
DEBUT: First-class: 2020

BEST BATTING: 34 Middlesex vs Sussex, Radlett, 2020
BEST BOWLING: 2-51 Middlesex vs Sussex, Radlett, 2020

MOST EXCITING DAY AS A CRICKETER? Making my first-class debut for Middlesex in the Bob Willis Trophy last summer
CHILDHOOD SPORTING HERO? Andrew Flintoff
FIRST CRICKET CLUB? Wycombe House CC, London
IF YOU COULD TAKE ONE COUNTY CRICKETER'S BEST SHOT AND ADD IT TO YOUR OWN GAME? Stevie Eskinazi's slap through cover
MOST ECCENTRIC TEAMMATE? Luke Hollman – he has some rare facial expressions
WHAT WOULD YOU DO IF YOU WERE IN CHARGE OF COUNTY CRICKET? Allow the second new ball after 50 overs, bring in DRS, make tea breaks longer
STRANGEST THING YOU'VE DONE DURING LOCKDOWN? Getting up for a Zoom gym session and then rolling straight back into bed
FAVOURITE SMELL? The leather on a new red Dukes
IF YOU WERE AN ANIMAL, WHICH WOULD IT BE? A dolphin – I'm enthusiastic and friendly
GUILTY PLEASURE? Bowling an unnecessary inswinger

Batting	Mat	Inns	NO	Runs	HS	Ave	SR	100	50	Ct	St
First-class	2	3	0	49	34	16.33	26.92	0	0	1	0
Bowling	**Mat**	**Balls**	**Runs**	**Wkts**	**BBI**	**BBM**	**Ave**	**Econ**	**SR**	**5w**	**10**
First-class	2	180	110	3	2/51	2/51	36.66	3.66	60.0	0	0

TOM CULLEN

RHB / WK / R0 / W0

FULL NAME: Thomas Nicholas Cullen
BORN: January 4, 1992, Perth, Australia
SQUAD NO: 54
HEIGHT: 5ft 11in
NICKNAME: TC
EDUCATION: Aquinas College, Perth; Cardiff Metropolitan University
TEAMS: Glamorgan
ROLE: Wicketkeeper
DEBUT: First-class: 2015

BEST BATTING: 63 Glamorgan vs Northamptonshire, Northampton, 2019

MOST EXCITING DAY AS A CRICKETER? Winning the University Challenge final at Lord's with Cardiff MCCU, then getting a call from Robert Croft the next morning (when I had a bit of a sore head) telling me to race back to Cardiff to travel with Glamorgan and make my debut. Two days later I was receiving my Glamorgan cap from Michael Hogan
CHILDHOOD SPORTING HERO? Growing up in Australia, I loved watching Ricky Ponting and Adam Gilchrist come to play at the WACA every year
FIRST CRICKET CLUB? South Perth CC, Western Australia
MOST INTERESTING TEAMMATE? Marnus Labuschagne – the guy has so much energy, all the time!
SURPRISING FACT ABOUT YOU? When I was younger I wanted to be a fighter pilot
IF YOU WERE AN ANIMAL, WHICH WOULD IT BE? A lion – if you're coming at me, I'm not backing down
TWITTER: @thomascullen186

Batting	Mat	Inns	NO	Runs	HS	Ave	SR	100	50	Ct	St
First-class	20	31	3	582	63	20.78	41.01	0	4	50	1
Bowling	**Mat**	**Balls**	**Runs**	**Wkts**	**BBI**	**BBM**	**Ave**	**Econ**	**SR**	**5w**	**10**
First-class	20	-	-	-	-	-	-	-	-	-	-

MIGUEL CUMMINS

LHB / RFM / R0 / W0

FULL NAME: Miguel Lamar Cummins
BORN: September 5, 1990, Barbados
SQUAD NO: 41
HEIGHT: 6ft 2in
NICKNAME: Miggy
EDUCATION: Parkinson Memorial School, Barbados; University of the West Indies
TEAMS: West Indies, Kent, Barbados, Middlesex, Trinidad & Tobago Red Steel, Worcestershire
ROLE: Bowler
DEBUT: Test: 2016; ODI: 2014; First-class: 2012; List A: 2013; T20: 2013

BEST BATTING: 29* Barbados vs Leeward Islands, Basseterre, 2016
BEST BOWLING: 7-45 Barbados vs Trinidad & Tobago, Port of Spain, 2013

WHAT WAS YOUR FIRST CRICKET CLUB? YMPC CC, Bridgetown, Barbados
BIGGEST TOPIC OF DISCUSSION IN YOUR DRESSING ROOM? Music
CRICKET STAR OF THE FUTURE? Zachary McCaskie (Barbados)
IF YOU WERE AN ANIMAL, WHICH WOULD IT BE? A killer whale – fierce but also gentle
TWITTER: @lamar_pooh
NOTES: The Bajan fast bowler has signed for Kent on a short-term deal, making him available for the first eight Championship games of the season. He had a brief stint with Middlesex at the end of last summer, taking 21 wickets at 25.47, and has previously represented Worcestershire in 2016. "He is the type of bowler who will add something different to our attack," said Paul Downton, Kent's director of cricket. "He certainly looked a handful running down the hill at the Spitfire Ground last season, and we look forward to welcoming him into our dressing room"

Batting	Mat	Inns	NO	Runs	HS	Ave	SR	100	50	Ct	St
Tests	14	22	7	114	24*	7.60	35.51	0	0	2	0
ODIs	11	3	1	10	5	5.00	37.03	0	0	1	0
First-class	82	105	42	434	29*	6.88	36.13	0	0	31	0
List A	35	14	8	62	20	10.33	68.88	0	0	10	0
T20s	14	5	4	14	10	14.00	58.33	0	0	6	0
Bowling	**Mat**	**Balls**	**Runs**	**Wkts**	**BBI**	**BBM**	**Ave**	**Econ**	**SR**	**5w**	**10**
Tests	14	1976	1084	27	6/48	9/102	40.14	3.29	73.1	1	0
ODIs	11	450	474	9	3/82	3/82	52.66	6.32	50.0	0	0
First-class	82	11291	5941	231	7/45	12/166	25.71	3.15	48.8	10	1
List A	35	1578	1256	48	4/27	4/27	26.16	4.77	32.8	0	0
T20s	14	203	303	7	3/19	3/19	43.28	8.95	29.0	0	0

BEN CURRAN

LHB / OB / R0 / W0

FULL NAME: Benjamin Jack Curran
BORN: June 7, 1996, Northampton
SQUAD NO: 57
HEIGHT: 5ft 9in
NICKNAME: Lord
EDUCATION: Wellington College, Berkshire
TEAMS: Northamptonshire, Southern Rocks
ROLE: Batsman
DEBUT: First-class: 2018; List A: 2019; T20: 2018

BEST BATTING: 83* Northamptonshire vs Sussex, Northampton, 2018

MOST EXCITING DAY AS A CRICKETER? Taking my first-ever five-wicket haul
FAMILY TIES? My dad Kevin played for Zimbabwe, Gloucestershire and Northamptonshire. My older brother Tom and younger brother Sam both play for Surrey
CHILDHOOD SPORTING HERO? My dad
FIRST CRICKET CLUB? Weybridge CC, Surrey
IF YOU COULD TAKE ONE COUNTY CRICKETER'S BEST SHOT AND ADD IT TO YOUR OWN GAME? Sam Curran's leg-side hack
TOUGHEST OPPONENT IN COUNTY CRICKET? Chris Rushworth – a county legend
WHAT WOULD YOU DO IF YOU WERE IN CHARGE OF COUNTY CRICKET? Make sure everyone plays everyone in the Championship
STRANGEST THING YOU'VE DONE DURING LOCKDOWN? Building a snowman
FAVOURITE SMELL? Strawberry
TWITTER: @curranjb_57

Batting	Mat	Inns	NO	Runs	HS	Ave	SR	100	50	Ct	St
First-class	18	32	4	927	83*	33.10	53.52	0	6	12	0
List A	3	3	0	102	69	34.00	89.47	0	1	2	0
T20s	5	5	0	54	29	10.80	103.84	0	0	2	0
Bowling	**Mat**	**Balls**	**Runs**	**Wkts**	**BBI**	**BBM**	**Ave**	**Econ**	**SR**	**5w**	**10**
First-class	18	-	-	-	-	-	-	-	-	-	-
List A	3	-	-	-	-	-	-	-	-	-	-
T20s	5	-	-	-	-	-	-	-	-	-	-

SAM CURRAN

LHB / LFM / R0 / W0

FULL NAME: Samuel Matthew Curran
BORN: June 3, 1998, Northampton
SQUAD NO: 58
HEIGHT: 5ft 11in
NICKNAME: Junior
EDUCATION: Wellington College, Berkshire
TEAMS: England, Surrey, Auckland, Chennai Super Kings, Kings XI Punjab
ROLE: Allrounder
DEBUT: Test: 2018; ODI: 2018; T20I: 2019; First-class: 2015; List A: 2015; T20: 2015

BEST BATTING: 96 Surrey vs Lancashire, The Oval, 2016
BEST BOWLING: 7-58 Surrey vs Durham, Chester-le-Street, 2016
COUNTY CAP: 2018

CHILDHOOD SPORTING HERO? Brian Lara
FAMILY TIES? My father Kevin played for Zimbabwe, and my brother Tom plays with me at Surrey. Ben, my other brother, plays for Northants. We have always been a competitive family
TWITTER: @CurranSM

Batting	Mat	Inns	NO	Runs	HS	Ave	SR	100	50	Ct	St
Tests	21	33	4	741	78	25.55	64.04	0	3	4	0
ODIs	5	4	0	25	15	6.25	48.07	0	0	0	0
T20Is	8	5	1	43	24	10.75	138.70	0	0	0	0
First-class	71	109	13	2658	96	27.68	60.34	0	18	18	0
List A	54	36	5	605	57	19.51	82.65	0	1	20	0
T20s	86	68	15	1032	55*	19.47	130.79	0	5	25	0
Bowling	**Mat**	**Balls**	**Runs**	**Wkts**	**BBI**	**BBM**	**Ave**	**Econ**	**SR**	**5w**	**10**
Tests	21	2647	1431	44	4/58	5/92	32.52	3.24	60.1	0	0
ODIs	5	168	169	5	3/35	3/35	33.80	6.03	33.6	0	0
T20Is	8	162	240	9	3/28	3/28	26.66	8.88	18.0	0	0
First-class	71	10286	5763	197	7/58	10/101	29.25	3.36	52.2	7	1
List A	54	2388	2208	71	4/32	4/32	31.09	5.54	33.6	0	0
T20s	86	1629	2339	79	4/11	4/11	29.60	8.61	20.6	0	0

TOM CURRAN

RHB / RFM / R0 / W1

FULL NAME: Thomas Kevin Curran
BORN: March 12, 1995, Cape Town, South Africa
SQUAD NO: 59
HEIGHT: 6ft
NICKNAME: TC
EDUCATION: Wellington College, Berkshire
TEAMS: England, Surrey, Delhi Capitals, Kolkata Knight Riders, Rajasthan Royals, Sydney Sixers
ROLE: Allrounder
DEBUT: Test: 2017; ODI: 2017; T20I: 2017; First-class: 2014; List A: 2013; T20: 2014

BEST BATTING: 60 Surrey vs Leicestershire, Leicester, 2015
BEST BOWLING: 7-20 Surrey vs Gloucestershire, The Oval, 2015
COUNTY CAP: 2016

CHILDHOOD SPORTING HERO? Hamilton Masakadza
FAMILY TIES? My father Kevin played for Northants and Zimbabwe, my brother Sam also plays for Surrey, and my other younger brother Ben is at Northants
SURPRISING FACT ABOUT YOU? I have a degree in Law
TWITTER: @_TC59

Batting	Mat	Inns	NO	Runs	HS	Ave	SR	100	50	Ct	St
Tests	2	3	1	66	39	33.00	55.00	0	0	0	0
ODIs	24	16	9	292	47*	41.71	95.73	0	0	5	0
T20Is	27	11	7	54	14*	13.50	114.89	0	0	8	0
First-class	59	81	11	1241	60	17.72	50.75	0	5	20	0
List A	82	55	21	728	47*	21.41	94.05	0	0	26	0
T20s	134	76	27	972	62	19.83	132.42	0	3	41	0
Bowling	**Mat**	**Balls**	**Runs**	**Wkts**	**BBI**	**BBM**	**Ave**	**Econ**	**SR**	**5w**	**10**
Tests	2	396	200	2	1/65	1/82	100.00	3.03	198.0	0	0
ODIs	24	1068	1066	28	5/35	5/35	38.07	5.98	38.1	1	0
T20Is	27	528	812	26	4/36	4/36	31.23	9.22	20.3	0	0
First-class	59	10341	5613	195	7/20	10/176	28.78	3.25	53.0	7	1
List A	82	3669	3409	120	5/16	5/16	28.40	5.57	30.5	3	0
T20s	134	2700	3979	157	4/22	4/22	25.34	8.84	17.1	0	0

SCOTT CURRIE

RHB / RMF / R0 / W0

FULL NAME: Scott William Currie
BORN: May 2, 2001, Poole, Dorset
SQUAD NO: 44
HEIGHT: 6ft 5in
EDUCATION: St Edward's RC & COFE School, Poole
TEAMS: Hampshire, England U19
ROLE: Bowler
DEBUT: First-class: 2020; T20: 2020

BEST BATTING: 38 Hampshire vs Kent, Canterbury, 2020
BEST BOWLING: 3-42 Hampshire vs Kent, Canterbury, 2020

NOTES: The tall seamer made a strong impression on his first-class debut at Canterbury last summer, dismissing Kent and England's Zak Crawley on the way to figures of 3-42 as well as making 38 in nearly two hours at the crease. Born in Poole, Currie has played Minor Counties for Dorset and is a product of the Hampshire Academy. He missed a large part of the 2019 season with a stress fracture in his back but returned to action to help the Second XI win the Championship for the first time since 2001. He signed his first rookie contract with the club in December 2019 and was called up by England for last year's U19 World Cup in South Africa, where he took seven wickets in four matches. Currie, who says he models his bowling on Glenn McGrath, is a talented footballer and was on Portsmouth's books until the age of 15

Batting	Mat	Inns	NO	Runs	HS	Ave	SR	100	50	Ct	St
First-class	1	2	0	38	38	19.00	44.18	0	0	2	0
T20s	4	2	1	2	2	2.00	50.00	0	0	0	0
Bowling	**Mat**	**Balls**	**Runs**	**Wkts**	**BBI**	**BBM**	**Ave**	**Econ**	**SR**	**5w**	**10**
First-class	1	102	58	3	3/42	3/58	19.33	3.41	34.0	0	0
T20s	4	36	58	1	1/28	1/28	58.00	9.66	36.0	0	0

ANUJ DAL

RHB / RM / R0 / W0

FULL NAME: Anuj Kailash Dal
BORN: July 8, 1996, Newcastle-under-Lyme, Staffordshire
SQUAD NO: 65
HEIGHT: 5ft 9in
NICKNAME: Nuj
EDUCATION: Nottingham High School
TEAMS: Derbyshire
ROLE: Batsman
DEBUT: First-class: 2018; List A: 2019; T20: 2018

BEST BATTING: 92 Derbyshire vs Middlesex, Derby, 2019
BEST BOWLING: 3-11 Derbyshire vs Sussex, Derby, 2019

MOST EXCITING DAY AS A CRICKETER? T20 Finals Day in 2019
CHILDHOOD SPORTING HERO? Jacques Kallis
BIGGEST INFLUENCE ON YOUR DEVELOPMENT AS A CRICKETER (EXCLUDING PARENTS)? Mal Loye, assistant coach at Derbyshire. He gave me the opportunity to move from Nottinghamshire and has believed in me ever since
FIRST CRICKET CLUB? Kimberley Institute CC, Nottinghamshire
IF YOU COULD TAKE ONE COUNTY CRICKETER'S BEST SHOT AND ADD IT TO YOUR OWN GAME? Wayne Madsen's reverse-sweep
TOUGHEST OPPONENT IN COUNTY CRICKET? Dawid Malan
MOST ECCENTRIC TEAMMATE? Matt Critchley – incredible player but he doesn't shut up
WHAT WOULD YOU DO IF YOU WERE PRIME MINISTER? Make electric cars more financially viable
STRANGEST THING YOU'VE DONE DURING LOCKDOWN? Filming cricket tutorials
FAVOURITE SMELL? A sweet shop
GUILTY PLEASURE? A bag of Haribo after a tough day in the field
TWITTER: @AnujDal

Batting	Mat	Inns	NO	Runs	HS	Ave	SR	100	50	Ct	St
First-class	19	30	5	510	92	20.40	44.15	0	3	11	0
List A	5	3	1	72	52	36.00	124.13	0	1	1	0
T20s	21	16	6	159	35	15.90	121.37	0	0	7	0
Bowling	**Mat**	**Balls**	**Runs**	**Wkts**	**BBI**	**BBM**	**Ave**	**Econ**	**SR**	**5w**	**10**
First-class	19	640	276	11	3/11	3/11	25.09	2.58	58.1	0	0
List A	5	-	-	-	-	-	-	-	-	-	-
T20s	21	6	8	0	-	-	-	8.00	-	0	0

AJEET DALE

RHB / RMF / R0 / W0

FULL NAME: Ajeet Singh Dale
BORN: July 3, 2000, Slough, Berkshire
SQUAD NO: 39
HEIGHT: 6ft 1in
NICKNAME: AJ
EDUCATION: Hall Grove School, Bagshot, Surrey; Wellington College, Berkshire
TEAMS: Hampshire
ROLE: Bowler
DEBUT: First-class: 2020

BEST BATTING: 6 Hampshire vs Sussex, Hove, 2020
BEST BOWLING: 3-20 Hampshire vs Sussex, Hove, 2020

MOST EXCITING DAY AS A CRICKETER? Making my first-class debut last year against Sussex at Hove in the Bob Willis Trophy
CHILDHOOD SPORTING HERO? Sachin Tendulkar
BIGGEST INFLUENCE ON YOUR DEVELOPMENT AS A CRICKETER (EXCLUDING PARENTS)? Nheem Amin – head coach at the Counties Cricket Academy. He taught me the game when I was very young and helped me to enjoy playing it
IF YOU COULD TAKE ONE COUNTY CRICKETER'S BEST SHOT AND ADD IT TO YOUR OWN GAME? Felix Organ's flick-off-the-pads against spin
WHAT WOULD YOU DO IF YOU WERE IN CHARGE OF COUNTY CRICKET? Create a tournament to play in the winter, improve diversity at both grassroots and elite level, have music played between overs in non-televised white-ball games
WHAT WOULD YOU DO IF YOU WERE PRIME MINISTER? Get back in the EU, improve diversity among MPs, include education on racism in the national curriculum
STRANGEST THING YOU'VE DONE DURING LOCKDOWN? TikTok videos
FAVOURITE SMELL? A pair of new trainers
GUILTY PLEASURE? Married at First Sight (TV series)

Batting	Mat	Inns	NO	Runs	HS	Ave	SR	100	50	Ct	St
First-class	2	4	1	7	6	2.33	13.46	0	0	0	0
Bowling	**Mat**	**Balls**	**Runs**	**Wkts**	**BBI**	**BBM**	**Ave**	**Econ**	**SR**	**5w**	**10**
First-class	2	126	73	4	3/20	3/35	18.25	3.47	31.5	0	0

JOSH DAVEY

RHB / RFM / R0 / W0 / MVP7

FULL NAME: Joshua Henry Davey
BORN: August 3, 1990, Aberdeen, Scotland
SQUAD NO: 38
HEIGHT: 6ft
NICKNAME: JD
EDUCATION: Culford School, Bury St Edmunds; Oxford Brookes University
TEAMS: Scotland, Somerset, Hampshire, Middlesex
ROLE: Bowler
DEBUT: ODI: 2010; T20I: 2012; First-class: 2010; List A: 2010; T20: 2010

BEST BATTING: 72 Middlesex vs Oxford MCCU, Oxford, 2010
BEST BOWLING: 5-21 Somerset vs Yorkshire, Taunton, 2019

MOST EXCITING DAY AS A CRICKETER? Beating Hampshire in the One-Day Cup final at Lord's in 2019
FIRST CRICKET CLUB? Bury St Edmunds CC, Suffolk
BEST INNINGS YOU'VE SEEN? Chris Gayle's 151 not out against Kent at Taunton in 2015
TWITTER: @JoshDavey38

Batting	Mat	Inns	NO	Runs	HS	Ave	SR	100	50	Ct	St
ODIs	31	28	6	497	64	22.59	66.98	0	2	10	0
T20Is	21	10	5	83	24	16.60	131.74	0	0	12	0
First-class	38	61	12	838	72	17.10	45.46	0	3	13	0
List A	86	68	16	1210	91	23.26	66.92	0	5	27	0
T20s	49	26	14	210	24	17.50	125.74	0	0	27	0
Bowling	**Mat**	**Balls**	**Runs**	**Wkts**	**BBI**	**BBM**	**Ave**	**Econ**	**SR**	**5w**	**10**
ODIs	31	1301	1082	49	6/28	6/28	22.08	4.99	26.5	2	0
T20Is	21	448	610	24	4/34	4/34	25.41	8.16	18.6	0	0
First-class	38	4916	2309	105	5/21	8/51	21.99	2.81	46.8	2	0
List A	86	3164	2811	105	6/28	6/28	26.77	5.33	30.1	2	0
T20s	49	784	1136	52	4/34	4/34	21.84	8.69	15.0	0	0

ALEX DAVIES

RHB / WK / R1 / W0 / MVP6

FULL NAME: Alexander Luke Davies
BORN: August 23, 1994, Darwen, Lancashire
SQUAD NO: 17
HEIGHT: 5ft 8in
NICKNAME: Davo
EDUCATION: Queen Elizabeth's Grammar School, Blackburn
TEAMS: Lancashire, England Lions
ROLE: Batsman/wicketkeeper
DEBUT: First-class: 2012; List A: 2011; T20: 2014

BEST BATTING: 147 Lancashire vs Northamptonshire, Northampton, 2019

COUNTY CAP: 2017

MOST EXCITING DAY AS A CRICKETER? T20 Finals Day in 2015
CHILDHOOD SPORTING HERO? Sachin Tendulkar
FIRST CRICKET CLUB? Darwen CC, Lancashire
IF YOU COULD TAKE ONE COUNTY CRICKETER'S BEST SHOT AND ADD IT TO YOUR OWN GAME? James Anderson's reverse-sweep
TOUGHEST OPPONENT IN COUNTY CRICKET? Ryan Sidebottom
MOST ECCENTRIC TEAMMATE? Rob Jones by a country mile – he loves birdwatching and castles
WHAT WOULD YOU DO IF YOU WERE PRIME MINISTER? Promote Blackburn Rovers to the Premier League
STRANGEST THING YOU'VE DONE DURING LOCKDOWN? Reading the memoirs of Marcus Aurelius (Roman emperor)
FAVOURITE SMELL? Lunch at Old Trafford at 12.55 when you're in the field
TWITTER: @aldavies23

Batting	Mat	Inns	NO	Runs	HS	Ave	SR	100	50	Ct	St
First-class	80	122	6	4103	147	35.37	57.15	5	27	163	15
List A	49	46	3	1380	147	32.09	90.49	1	7	48	11
T20s	64	59	9	1439	94*	28.78	127.68	0	11	36	10
Bowling	**Mat**	**Balls**	**Runs**	**Wkts**	**BBI**	**BBM**	**Ave**	**Econ**	**SR**	**5w**	**10**
First-class	80	6	6	0	-	-	-	6.00	-	0	0
List A	49	-	-	-	-	-	-	-	-	-	-
T20s	64	-	-	-	-	-	-	-	-	-	-

JACK DAVIES

LHB / WK / R0 / W0

FULL NAME: Jack Leo Benjamin Davies
BORN: March 30, 2000, Reading
SQUAD NO: 23
HEIGHT: 5ft 8in
NICKNAME: Davo
EDUCATION: Wellington College, Berkshire
TEAMS: Middlesex, England U19
ROLE: Wicketkeeper/batsman
DEBUT: First-class: 2020; T20: 2020

BEST BATTING: 13 Middlesex vs Kent, Canterbury, 2020

MOST EXCITING DAY AS A CRICKETER? Making my first-class debut last year
CHILDHOOD SPORTING HERO? Tiger Woods
FIRST CRICKET CLUB? Henley CC, Oxfordshire
IF YOU COULD TAKE ONE COUNTY CRICKETER'S BEST SHOT AND ADD IT TO YOUR OWN GAME? Tim Murtagh's blind pull
TOUGHEST OPPONENT IN COUNTY CRICKET? Darren Stevens
MOST ECCENTRIC TEAMMATE? Nick Gubbins – because of his dress sense on the golf course
BIGGEST CRICKETING REGRET? All those leaves which have blown my pads off
STRANGEST THING YOU'VE DONE DURING LOCKDOWN? Letting my Middlesex teammate Max Holden cook me a meal
FAVOURITE SMELL? Lavender
IF YOU WERE AN ANIMAL, WHICH WOULD IT BE? A shark
GUILTY PLEASURE? Mamma Mia
TWITTER: @daviesjlb

Batting	Mat	Inns	NO	Runs	HS	Ave	SR	100	50	Ct	St
First-class	1	1	0	13	13	13.00	20.31	0	0	0	0
T20s	4	4	0	48	23	12.00	106.66	0	0	0	0
Bowling	**Mat**	**Balls**	**Runs**	**Wkts**	**BBI**	**BBM**	**Ave**	**Econ**	**SR**	**5w**	**10**
First-class	1	-	-	-	-	-	-	-	-	-	-
T20s	4	-	-	-	-	-	-	-	-	-	-

STEVEN DAVIES LHB / WK / R6 / W0 / MVP56

SOMERSET

FULL NAME: Steven Michael Davies
BORN: June 17, 1986, Bromsgrove, Worcestershire
SQUAD NO: 11
HEIGHT: 6ft
NICKNAME: Davos
EDUCATION: King Charles High School, Kidderminster
TEAMS: England, Somerset, Surrey, Worcestershire
ROLE: Batsman/wicketkeeper
DEBUT: ODI: 2009; T20I: 2009; First-class: 2005; List A: 2003; T20: 2006

BEST BATTING: 200* Surrey vs Glamorgan, Cardiff, 2015

COUNTY CAP: 2011 (Surrey); 2017 (Somerset)

MOST EXCITING DAY AS A CRICKETER? Making my England debut in 2009
CHILDHOOD SPORTING HERO? Adam Gilchrist
FIRST CRICKET CLUB? Victoria Carpets CC, Kidderminster, Worcestershire
IF YOU COULD TAKE ONE COUNTY CRICKETER'S BEST SHOT AND ADD IT TO YOUR OWN GAME? Anyone who has a decent sweep shot!
TOUGHEST OPPONENT IN COUNTY CRICKET? Chris Rushworth – relentless
MOST ECCENTRIC TEAMMATE? Peter Trego – an entertainer on and off the field
SURPRISING FACT ABOUT YOU? I'm a session harp player
GUILTY PLEASURE? Pop music
TWITTER: @SteveDavies43

Batting	Mat	Inns	NO	Runs	HS	Ave	SR	100	50	Ct	St
ODIs	8	8	0	244	87	30.50	105.62	0	1	8	0
T20Is	5	5	0	102	33	20.40	124.39	0	0	2	1
First-class	231	384	37	13417	200*	38.66	60.58	25	62	551	33
List A	184	173	14	5645	127*	35.50		9	35	147	42
T20s	151	142	8	2826	99*	21.08	141.44	0	16	69	23
Bowling	**Mat**	**Balls**	**Runs**	**Wkts**	**BBI**	**BBM**	**Ave**	**Econ**	**SR**	**5w**	**10**
ODIs	8	-	-	-	-	-	-	-	-	-	-
T20Is	5	-	-	-	-	-	-	-	-	-	-
First-class	231	-	-	-	-	-	-	-	-	-	-
List A	184	-	-	-	-	-	-	-	-	-	-
T20s	151	-	-	-	-	-	-	-	-	-	-

WILL DAVIS RHB / RFM / R0 / W0

FULL NAME: William Samuel Davis
BORN: March 6, 1996, Stafford
SQUAD NO: 44
HEIGHT: 6ft 2in
NICKNAME: Spaceman
EDUCATION: Stafford Grammar School
TEAMS: Leicestershire, Derbyshire, England U19
ROLE: Bowler
DEBUT: First-class: 2015; List A: 2016; T20: 2019

BEST BATTING: 39* Leicestershire vs Glamorgan, Cardiff, 2019
BEST BOWLING: 7-146 Derbyshire vs Glamorgan, Colwyn Bay, 2016

MOST EXCITING DAY AS A CRICKETER? Taking my maiden five-wicket haul in first-class cricket against Glamorgan at Colwyn Bay in 2016
CHILDHOOD SPORTING HERO? Cristiano Ronaldo
SURPRISING FACT ABOUT YOU? I have to turn at the end of my bowling mark before running in
TWITTER: @W_Davis44
NOTES: The former Derbyshire and England U19 seamer was an important part of the bowling attack which helped the Foxes reach the quarter-finals of the T20 Blast last summer and signed a new deal with the club in November. The 24-year-old enjoyed his best season in red-ball cricket in 2019, taking 29 wickets at 32.89, but appeared in only two of Derbyshire's five matches in the Bob Willis Trophy last year

Batting	Mat	Inns	NO	Runs	HS	Ave	SR	100	50	Ct	St
First-class	26	36	12	282	39*	11.75	45.12	0	0	3	0
List A	4	2	1	17	15*	17.00	70.83	0	0	1	0
T20s	19	6	4	6	4*	3.00	40.00	0	0	7	0
Bowling	**Mat**	**Balls**	**Runs**	**Wkts**	**BBI**	**BBM**	**Ave**	**Econ**	**SR**	**5w**	**10**
First-class	26	3756	2323	72	7/146	8/204	32.26	3.71	52.1	1	0
List A	4	135	178	2	1/60	1/60	89.00	7.91	67.5	0	0
T20s	19	287	409	16	3/24	3/24	25.56	8.55	17.9	0	0

LIAM DAWSON RHB / SLA / R1 / W0

FULL NAME: Liam Andrew Dawson
BORN: March 1, 1990, Swindon
SQUAD NO: 8
HEIGHT: 5ft 8in
NICKNAME: Lemmy
EDUCATION: The John Bentley School, Wiltshire
TEAMS: England, Hampshire, Comilla Victorians, Essex, Mountaineers, Peshawar Zalmi, Rangpur Riders
ROLE: Allrounder
DEBUT: Test: 2016; ODI: 2016; T20I: 2016; First-class: 2007; List A: 2007; T20: 2008

BEST BATTING: 169 Hampshire vs Somerset, Southampton, 2011
BEST BOWLING: 7-51 Mountaineers vs Mashonaland Eagles, Mutare Sports Club, 2011
COUNTY CAP: 2013 (Hampshire)

MOST EXCITING DAY AS A CRICKETER? My England debut in 2016
FAMILY TIES? I got into the game watching my dad play for Goatacre CC in Wiltshire. My brother Brad has played Minor Counties for Wiltshire
CHILDHOOD SPORTING HERO? Shane Warne
TWITTER: @daws128

Batting	Mat	Inns	NO	Runs	HS	Ave	SR	100	50	Ct	St
Tests	3	6	2	84	66*	21.00	42.63	0	1	2	0
ODIs	3	2	0	14	10	7.00	82.35	0	0	0	0
T20Is	6	2	1	17	10	17.00	212.50	0	0	2	0
First-class	152	247	27	7363	169	33.46	49.27	9	41	147	0
List A	160	130	23	3529	113*	32.98	95.32	3	18	72	0
T20s	169	126	31	1914	82	20.14	114.06	0	5	75	0
Bowling	**Mat**	**Balls**	**Runs**	**Wkts**	**BBI**	**BBM**	**Ave**	**Econ**	**SR**	**5w**	**10**
Tests	3	526	298	7	2/34	4/101	42.57	3.39	75.1	0	0
ODIs	3	84	96	3	2/70	2/70	32.00	6.85	28.0	0	0
T20Is	6	120	152	5	3/27	3/27	30.40	7.60	24.0	0	0
First-class	152	14541	7220	205	7/51	8/129	35.21	2.97	70.9	3	0
List A	160	6206	4890	162	6/47	6/47	30.18	4.72	38.3	1	0
T20s	169	2699	3278	120	5/17	5/17	27.31	7.28	22.4	1	0

JOSH DE CAIRES

RHB / RM / R0 / W0

FULL NAME: Joshua Michael de Caires
BORN: April 25, 2002, Paddington, London
SQUAD NO: 99
HEIGHT: 6ft
EDUCATION: St Albans School, Hertfordshire; University of Leeds
TEAMS: Middlesex
ROLE: Batsman

MOST EXCITING DAY AS A CRICKETER? Signing for Middlesex last year
CHILDHOOD SPORTING HERO? Alastair Cook
IF YOU COULD TAKE ONE COUNTY CRICKETER'S BEST SHOT AND ADD IT TO YOUR OWN GAME? Joe Cracknell's slog to cow corner
TOUGHEST OPPONENT IN COUNTY CRICKET? I haven't played county cricket yet, but Sean Ervine once got me out twice in the same match – the first time bowling seam and then bowling spin
GUILTY PLEASURE? Shadow-batting
TWITTER: @josh_decaires
NOTES: A top-order batsman who turns 19 in April, de Caires is the son of Mike Atherton and great-grandson of former West Indies batsman Frank de Caires. He signed his first professional contract with Middlesex last August which lasts through his university studies until the end of the 2023 season. De Caires has come through the Middlesex Academy, scoring 90 on his club debut for the U14 side and making his first appearance for the Second XI at the age of 15. In 2019 he made his maiden Second XI hundred – 118 against Hampshire at Newport. "He is a very talented top-order batsman with good pedigree," said Stuart Law, Middlesex's head coach. "We look forward to working with him over the coming years and helping in his development as a player and a young man"

MARCHANT DE LANGE RHB / RF / R0 / W0 / MVP68

FULL NAME: Marchant de Lange
BORN: October 13, 1990, Tzaneen, Transvaal, South Africa
SQUAD NO: 90
HEIGHT: 6ft 7in
NICKNAME: Shanna
TEAMS: South Africa, Somerset, Barbados Tridents, Durban Heat, Easterns, Free State, Glamorgan, Knights, Kolkata Knight Riders, Mumbai Indians, Titans
ROLE: Bowler
DEBUT: Test: 2011; ODI: 2012; T20I: 2012; First-class: 2010; List A: 2010; T20: 2011

BEST BATTING: 113 Glamorgan vs Northamptonshire, Northampton, 2020
BEST BOWLING: 7-23 Knights vs Titans, Centurion, 2016

MOST EXCITING DAY AS A CRICKETER? Making my international debut for South Africa
CHILDHOOD SPORTING HERO? Brett Lee
FIRST CRICKET CLUB? Tzaneen CC, Limpopo, South Africa
IF YOU COULD TAKE ONE COUNTY CRICKETER'S BEST SHOT AND ADD IT TO YOUR OWN GAME? Wayne Madsen's ramp
TOUGHEST OPPONENT IN COUNTY CRICKET? James Hildreth
SURPRISING FACT ABOUT YOU? I love art
GUILTY PLEASURE? Cupcakes
TWITTER: @Marchant90

Batting	Mat	Inns	NO	Runs	HS	Ave	SR	100	50	Ct	St
Tests	2	2	0	9	9	4.50	47.36	0	0	1	0
ODIs	4	-	-	-	-	-	-	-	-	0	0
T20Is	6	-	-	-	-	-	-	-	-	1	0
First-class	85	114	17	1581	113	16.29	76.15	1	3	36	0
List A	95	66	18	750	58*	15.62	108.06	0	2	25	0
T20s	101	40	17	263	28*	11.43	130.84	0	0	24	0
Bowling	**Mat**	**Balls**	**Runs**	**Wkts**	**BBI**	**BBM**	**Ave**	**Econ**	**SR**	**5w**	**10**
Tests	2	448	277	9	7/81	8/126	30.77	3.70	49.7	1	0
ODIs	4	209	198	10	4/46	4/46	19.80	5.68	20.9	0	0
T20Is	6	140	228	7	2/26	2/26	32.57	9.77	20.0	0	0
First-class	85	15714	9386	314	7/23	11/62	29.89	3.58	50.0	11	2
List A	95	4684	4273	169	5/49	5/49	25.28	5.47	27.7	4	0
T20s	101	1978	2848	111	4/23	4/23	25.65	8.63	17.8	0	0

HARRY DEARDEN

LHB / OB / R0 / W0

FULL NAME: Harry Edward Dearden
BORN: May 7, 1997, Bury, Lancashire
SQUAD NO: 5
HEIGHT: 5ft 8in
NICKNAME: Dasher
EDUCATION: Tottington High School, Bury; Bury College
TEAMS: Leicestershire
ROLE: Batsman
DEBUT: First-class: 2016; List A: 2018; T20: 2018

BEST BATTING: 87 Leicestershire vs Glamorgan, Leicester, 2017
BEST BOWLING: 1-0 Leicestershire vs Kent, Leicester, 2017

MOST EXCITING DAY AS A CRICKETER? Making my first-class debut in 2016
CHILDHOOD SPORTING HERO? Roy Keane
BIGGEST INFLUENCE ON YOUR DEVELOPMENT AS A CRICKETER (EXCLUDING PARENTS)? My grandad
TOUGHEST OPPONENT IN COUNTY CRICKET? Liam Norwell
MOST ECCENTRIC TEAMMATE? Dieter Klein
WHAT WOULD YOU DO IF YOU WERE IN CHARGE OF COUNTY CRICKET? Introduce "double runs" for a nominated over in T20 cricket
SURPRISING FACT ABOUT YOU? I was on a Channel 4 roadshow for the 2001 Ashes series, having a split-screen with Shane Warne
TWITTER: @HarryDearden97

Batting	Mat	Inns	NO	Runs	HS	Ave	SR	100	50	Ct	St
First-class	42	72	2	1503	87	21.47	43.56	0	7	28	0
List A	10	10	0	341	91	34.10	89.97	0	3	2	0
T20s	22	21	3	348	61	19.33	104.81	0	1	8	0
Bowling	**Mat**	**Balls**	**Runs**	**Wkts**	**BBI**	**BBM**	**Ave**	**Econ**	**SR**	**5w**	**10**
First-class	42	124	108	2	1/0	1/0	54.00	5.22	62.0	0	0
List A	10	-	-	-	-	-	-	-	-	-	-
T20s	22	-	-	-	-	-	-	-	-	-	-

JOSH DELL

RHB / RM / R0 / W0

WORCESTERSHIRE

FULL NAME: Joshua Jamie Dell
BORN: September 26, 1997, Tenbury Wells, Worcestershire
SQUAD NO: 52
HEIGHT: 6ft 3in
NICKNAME: Dellboy
EDUCATION: Abberley Hall School, Worcestershire; Cheltenham College
TEAMS: Worcestershire, England U19
ROLE: Batsman
DEBUT: First-class: 2019; List A: 2018

BEST BATTING: 61 Worcestershire vs Durham, Worcester, 2019

MOST EXCITING DAY AS A CRICKETER? Making my first-class debut in 2019
CHILDHOOD SPORTING HERO? Jonny Wilkinson
FIRST CRICKET CLUB? Ombersley CC, Worcestershire. I've been playing there since I was 11
BEST INNINGS YOU'VE SEEN? AB de Villiers's 162 not out off 66 balls against West Indies at Sydney in the 2015 World Cup
IF YOU COULD TAKE ONE COUNTY CRICKETER'S BEST SHOT AND ADD IT TO YOUR OWN GAME? Dillon Pennington's clip off the legs
IF YOU WERE AN ANIMAL, WHICH WOULD IT BE? A Philippine eagle
GUILTY PLEASURE? A cup of tea and some Jammie Dodgers

Batting	Mat	Inns	NO	Runs	HS	Ave	SR	100	50	Ct	St
First-class	7	12	0	158	61	13.16	31.47	0	1	5	0
List A	1	1	0	46	46	46.00	102.22	0	0	1	0
Bowling	**Mat**	**Balls**	**Runs**	**Wkts**	**BBI**	**BBM**	**Ave**	**Econ**	**SR**	**5w**	**10**
First-class	7	-	-	-	-	-	-	-	-	-	-
List A	1	-	-	-	-	-	-	-	-	-	-

JOE DENLY RHB / LB / R4 / W0

FULL NAME: Joseph Liam Denly
BORN: March 16, 1986, Canterbury, Kent
SQUAD NO: 6
HEIGHT: 6ft
NICKNAME: Denners
EDUCATION: Chaucer Technology School, Canterbury
TEAMS: England, Kent, Barisal Burners, Brisbane Heat, Kolkata Knight Riders, Lahore Qalandars, Middlesex, Sydney Sixers
ROLE: Batsman
DEBUT: Test: 2019; ODI: 2009; T20I: 2009; First-class: 2004; List A: 2004; T20: 2004

BEST BATTING: 227 Kent vs Worcestershire, Worcester, 2017
BEST BOWLING: 4-36 Kent vs Derbyshire, Derby, 2018
COUNTY CAP: 2008 (Kent); 2012 (Middlesex); BENEFIT: 2019 (Kent)

FIRST CRICKET CLUB? Whitstable CC, Kent
WHAT WOULD YOU DO IF YOU WERE IN CHARGE OF COUNTY CRICKET? Introduce specialist fielders that just field and do nothing else
TWITTER: @joed1986

Batting	Mat	Inns	NO	Runs	HS	Ave	SR	100	50	Ct	St
Tests	15	28	0	827	94	29.53	39.64	0	6	7	0
ODIs	16	13	0	446	87	34.30	70.90	0	4	7	0
T20Is	13	12	2	125	30	12.50	105.93	0	0	4	0
First-class	212	366	25	12474	227	36.58	54.95	29	63	88	0
List A	159	150	16	4902	150*	36.58	76.83	8	26	54	0
T20s	227	220	18	5492	127	27.18	121.90	4	31	85	0
Bowling	**Mat**	**Balls**	**Runs**	**Wkts**	**BBI**	**BBM**	**Ave**	**Econ**	**SR**	**5w**	**10**
Tests	15	390	219	2	2/42	2/42	109.50	3.36	195.0	0	0
ODIs	16	102	101	1	1/24	1/24	101.00	5.94	102.0	0	0
T20Is	13	72	93	7	4/19	4/19	13.28	7.75	10.2	0	0
First-class	212	5096	2710	68	4/36	6/114	39.85	3.19	74.9	0	0
List A	159	1406	1199	47	4/35	4/35	25.51	5.11	29.9	0	0
T20s	227	631	834	34	4/19	4/19	24.52	7.93	18.5	0	0

CHRIS DENT LHB / SLA / WK / R4 / W0 / MVP34

FULL NAME: Christopher David James Dent
BORN: January 20, 1991, Bristol
SQUAD NO: 15
HEIGHT: 5ft 9in
NICKNAME: Denty
EDUCATION: Backwell School, North Somerset; SGS Filton College, Bristol
TEAMS: Gloucestershire, England U19
ROLE: Batsman
DEBUT: First-class: 2010; List A: 2009; T20: 2010

BEST BATTING: 268 Gloucestershire vs Glamorgan, Bristol, 2015
BEST BOWLING: 2-21 Gloucestershire vs Sussex, Hove, 2016
COUNTY CAP: 2010

MOST EXCITING DAY AS A CRICKETER? The 2015 Lord's one-day final
CHILDHOOD SPORTING HERO? Brian Lara
FIRST CRICKET CLUB? Cleeve CC, Somerset
IF YOU COULD TAKE ONE COUNTY CRICKETER'S BEST SHOT AND ADD IT TO YOUR OWN GAME? Wayne Madsen's upper-cut
TOUGHEST OPPONENT IN COUNTY CRICKET? Darren Stevens – he's got me out more times than any other bowler
BIGGEST CRICKETING REGRET? Every time I was out in the 90s trying to hit a six
WHAT WOULD YOU DO IF YOU WERE IN CHARGE OF COUNTY CRICKET? Introduce a new rule which says that if you hit the ball against the stumps at the other end, it's worth five runs (unless the bowler touches it)
FAVOURITE SMELL? Jean Paul Gaultier
GUILTY PLEASURE? Double cream
TWITTER: @cdent15

Batting	Mat	Inns	NO	Runs	HS	Ave	SR	100	50	Ct	St
First-class	147	263	23	9151	268	38.12	51.45	18	53	160	0
List A	70	65	5	1946	151*	32.43	93.15	3	6	24	0
T20s	60	54	7	1096	87	23.31	126.70	0	7	22	0
Bowling	**Mat**	**Balls**	**Runs**	**Wkts**	**BBI**	**BBM**	**Ave**	**Econ**	**SR**	**5w**	**10**
First-class	147	1220	813	9	2/21	2/21	90.33	3.99	135.5	0	0
List A	70	438	412	12	4/43	4/43	34.33	5.64	36.5	0	0
T20s	60	120	168	5	1/4	1/4	33.60	8.40	24.0	0	0

JADE DERNBACH RHB / RFM / R0 / W1

FULL NAME: Jade Winston Dernbach
BORN: March 3, 1986, Johannesburg, South Africa
SQUAD NO: 16
HEIGHT: 6ft 2in
NICKNAME: DJ Dooshla
EDUCATION: St John the Baptist School, Woking
TEAMS: England, Surrey, Melbourne Stars, Wellington
ROLE: Bowler
DEBUT: ODI: 2011; T20I: 2011; First-class: 2003; List A: 2005; T20: 2005

BEST BATTING: 56* Surrey vs Northamptonshire, Northampton, 2011
BEST BOWLING: 6-47 Surrey vs Leicestershire, Leicester, 2010
COUNTY CAP: 2011; BENEFIT: 2019

MOST EXCITING DAY AS A CRICKETER? Making my England debut in 2011
CHILDHOOD SPORTING HERO? Percy Montgomery
FIRST CRICKET CLUB? Old Woking Remnants CC, Surrey
IF YOU COULD TAKE ONE COUNTY CRICKETER'S BEST SHOT AND ADD IT TO YOUR OWN GAME? Alastair Cook's pull
TOUGHEST OPPONENT IN COUNTY CRICKET? Will Jefferson – he was just too tall
MOST ECCENTRIC TEAMMATE? Tom Curran – he's got loads of flair
WHAT WOULD YOU DO IF YOU WERE IN CHARGE OF COUNTY CRICKET? Reduce the number of teams and games
WHAT WOULD YOU DO IF YOU WERE PRIME MINISTER? Increase the number of cycle lanes in London
STRANGEST THING YOU'VE DONE DURING LOCKDOWN? Raising a child
TWITTER: @jwd_16

Batting	Mat	Inns	NO	Runs	HS	Ave	SR	100	50	Ct	St
ODIs	24	8	1	19	5	2.71	48.71	0	0	5	0
T20Is	34	7	2	24	12	4.80	114.28	0	0	8	0
First-class	113	139	47	871	56*	9.46	-	0	1	17	0
List A	144	51	19	242	31	7.56	82.59	0	0	31	0
T20s	160	42	18	178	24*	7.41	102.29	0	0	37	0
Bowling	**Mat**	**Balls**	**Runs**	**Wkts**	**BBI**	**BBM**	**Ave**	**Econ**	**SR**	**5w**	**10**
ODIs	24	1234	1308	31	4/45	4/45	42.19	6.35	39.8	0	0
T20Is	34	702	1020	39	4/22	4/22	26.15	8.71	18.0	0	0
First-class	113	18222	10139	311	6/47	-	32.60	3.33	58.5	10	0
List A	144	6283	6181	228	6/35	6/35	27.10	5.90	27.5	3	0
T20s	160	3242	4610	173	4/22	4/22	26.64	8.53	18.7	0	0

SEAN DICKSON

RHB / RM / R0 / W0

FULL NAME: Sean Robert Dickson
BORN: September 2, 1991, Johannesburg, South Africa
SQUAD NO: 58
HEIGHT: 5ft 11in
NICKNAME: Dicko
EDUCATION: King Edward VII School, Johannesburg; University of Pretoria
TEAMS: Durham, Kent, Northerns
ROLE: Batsman
DEBUT: First-class: 2013; List A: 2013; T20: 2014

BEST BATTING: 318 Kent vs Northamptonshire, Beckenham, 2017
BEST BOWLING: 1-15 Northerns vs Griqualand West, Centurion, 2015

MOST EXCITING DAY AS A CRICKETER? Achieving my highest score of 318 against Northants at Beckenham in 2017
CHILDHOOD SPORTING HERO? Jonty Rhodes
BIGGEST INFLUENCE ON YOUR DEVELOPMENT AS A CRICKETER (EXCLUDING PARENTS)? Jimmy Cook (former South Africa and Somerset batsman). He coached me as a junior
FIRST CRICKET CLUB? Old Park Sports Club, Johannesburg
TOUGHEST OPPONENT IN COUNTY CRICKET? Graham Onions – never had any idea which way it was going
MOST ECCENTRIC TEAMMATE? Brydon Carse – he does not have an off switch
WHAT WOULD YOU DO IF YOU WERE IN CHARGE OF COUNTY CRICKET? Allow thicker bats
WHAT WOULD YOU DO IF YOU WERE PRIME MINISTER? Make public transport free, invest in hover cars, ban telemarketing
STRANGEST THING YOU'VE DONE DURING LOCKDOWN? No Pants Sunday
FAVOURITE SMELL? A Nando's half-chicken with peri-peri chips
GUILTY PLEASURE? Cheese
TWITTER: @Seano_146

Batting	Mat	Inns	NO	Runs	HS	Ave	SR	100	50	Ct	St
First-class	74	125	9	3833	318	33.04	50.00	10	15	63	0
List A	42	38	2	992	99	27.55	75.84	0	8	13	0
T20s	21	15	4	250	53	22.72	120.19	0	1	12	0
Bowling	**Mat**	**Balls**	**Runs**	**Wkts**	**BBI**	**BBM**	**Ave**	**Econ**	**SR**	**5w**	**10**
First-class	74	96	53	2	1/15	2/40	26.50	3.31	48.0	0	0
List A	42	12	20	0	-	-	-	10.00	-	0	0
T20s	21	6	9	1	1/9	1/9	9.00	9.00	6.0	0	0

ANEURIN DONALD

RHB / OB / R1 / W0

FULL NAME: Aneurin Henry Thomas Donald
BORN: December 20, 1996, Swansea
SQUAD NO: 12
HEIGHT: 6ft 3in
NICKNAME: Don
EDUCATION: Pontarddulais Comprehensive School, Swansea; Gower College Swansea
TEAMS: Hampshire, Glamorgan, England U19
ROLE: Batsman
DEBUT: First-class: 2014; List A: 2015; T20: 2015

BEST BATTING: 234 Glamorgan vs Derbyshire, Colwyn Bay, 2016

MOST EXCITING DAY AS A CRICKETER? Hard to choose between the last Lord's one-day final in 2019 and making a first-class double hundred at Colwyn Bay in 2016
FAMILY TIES? My grand-uncle Bernard Hedges scored Glamorgan's first one-day century
CHILDHOOD SPORTING HERO? Gavin Henson
BIGGEST INFLUENCE ON YOUR DEVELOPMENT AS A CRICKETER (EXCLUDING PARENTS)? Jacques Rudolph – he passed on a lot of wisdom about batting and life while I was at Glamorgan
IF YOU COULD TAKE ONE COUNTY CRICKETER'S BEST SHOT AND ADD IT TO YOUR OWN GAME? James Vince's lofted extra-cover drive
TOUGHEST OPPONENT IN COUNTY CRICKET? Darren Stevens
WHAT WOULD YOU DO IF YOU WERE PRIME MINISTER? Nothing – but as first minister of Wales I may have some ideas...
FAVOURITE SMELL? Welsh salt-marsh lamb
GUILTY PLEASURE? Slogging a red Dukes
TWITTER: @AneurinDonald12

Batting	Mat	Inns	NO	Runs	HS	Ave	SR	100	50	Ct	St
First-class	48	86	5	2610	234	32.22	73.31	3	15	35	0
List A	30	27	1	424	57	16.30	82.65	0	2	13	0
T20s	54	49	3	927	76	20.15	136.52	0	5	33	0
Bowling	**Mat**	**Balls**	**Runs**	**Wkts**	**BBI**	**BBM**	**Ave**	**Econ**	**SR**	**5w**	**10**
First-class	48	-	-	-	-	-	-	-	-	-	-
List A	30	-	-	-	-	-	-	-	-	-	-
T20s	54	-	-	-	-	-	-	-	-	-	-

DAN DOUTHWAITE RHB / RMF / R0 / W0 / MVP76

FULL NAME: Daniel Alexander Douthwaite
BORN: February 8, 1997, Kingston-upon-Thames, Surrey
SQUAD NO: 88
HEIGHT: 6ft 1in
NICKNAME: Jugs
EDUCATION: Reed's School, Cobham, Surrey; Cardiff Metropolitan University
TEAMS: Glamorgan, Warwickshire
ROLE: Allrounder
DEBUT: First-class: 2019; List A: 2018; T20: 2018

BEST BATTING: 100* Cardiff MCCU vs Sussex, Hove, 2019
BEST BOWLING: 4-48 Glamorgan vs Derbyshire, Derby, 2019

MOST EXCITING DAY AS A CRICKETER? Making 52 not out to chase down 348 in a One-Day Cup match against Sussex at Hove in 2019
CHILDHOOD SPORTING HERO? Andrew Flintoff
BIGGEST INFLUENCE ON YOUR DEVELOPMENT AS A CRICKETER (EXCLUDING PARENTS)? Keith Medlycott at Surrey
FIRST CRICKET CLUB? Stoke d'Abernon CC, Cobham, Surrey
IF YOU COULD TAKE ONE COUNTY CRICKETER'S BEST SHOT AND ADD IT TO YOUR OWN GAME? Nat Sciver's "Natmeg"
TOUGHEST OPPONENT IN COUNTY CRICKET? Phil Salt – he always whacks me
WHAT WOULD YOU DO IF YOU WERE IN CHARGE OF COUNTY CRICKET? Push for a Champions League tournament for the winners of each country's T20 competition
WHAT WOULD YOU DO IF YOU WERE PRIME MINISTER? Introduce 99p coins
STRANGEST THING YOU'VE DONE DURING LOCKDOWN? Getting throw-downs from my mum
GUILTY PLEASURE? Kebabs
TWITTER: @DanDouthwaite

Batting	Mat	Inns	NO	Runs	HS	Ave	SR	100	50	Ct	St
First-class	14	25	2	603	100*	26.21	59.76	1	2	4	0
List A	4	4	2	99	52*	49.50	147.76	0	1	2	0
T20s	16	14	4	139	24	13.90	116.80	0	0	3	0
Bowling	**Mat**	**Balls**	**Runs**	**Wkts**	**BBI**	**BBM**	**Ave**	**Econ**	**SR**	**5w**	**10**
First-class	14	1868	1375	35	4/48	6/137	39.28	4.41	53.3	0	0
List A	4	138	126	5	3/43	3/43	25.20	5.47	27.6	0	0
T20s	16	156	242	5	1/7	1/7	48.40	9.30	31.2	0	0

LEUS DU PLOOY LHB / SLA / R0 / W0 / MVP66

FULL NAME: Jacobus Leus du Plooy
BORN: January 12, 1995, Pretoria, South Africa
SQUAD NO: 76
HEIGHT: 5ft 11in
EDUCATION: Afrikaanse Hoër Seunskool (Affies), Pretoria; University of South Africa
TEAMS: Derbyshire, Free State, Knights, Northerns, Titans
ROLE: Batsman
DEBUT: First-class: 2015; List A: 2014; T20: 2014

BEST BATTING: 181 Free State vs Namibia, Windhoek, 2015
BEST BOWLING: 3-76 Northerns vs Western Province, Pretoria, 2019

CHILDHOOD SPORTING HERO? AB de Villiers
BIGGEST INFLUENCE ON YOUR DEVELOPMENT AS A CRICKETER (EXCLUDING PARENTS)? My brothers – because of the time we spent playing in the backyard
FIRST CRICKET CLUB? Tenterden CC, Ashford, Kent
IF YOU COULD TAKE ONE COUNTY CRICKETER'S BEST SHOT AND ADD IT TO YOUR OWN GAME? Anuj Dal's block
MOST ECCENTRIC TEAMMATE? Fynn Hudson-Prentice – because of his Brighton ways
WHAT WOULD YOU DO IF YOU WERE IN CHARGE OF COUNTY CRICKET? Allow another overseas player per county to keep the standard as strong as possible, stricter monitoring of pitches
FAVOURITE SMELL? Linseed oil
GUILTY PLEASURE? Häagen-Dazs Salted Caramel ice cream

Batting	Mat	Inns	NO	Runs	HS	Ave	SR	100	50	Ct	St
First-class	58	91	12	3666	181	46.40	49.18	12	19	51	0
List A	45	42	10	1865	155	58.28	87.51	5	10	23	0
T20s	49	43	13	918	70	30.60	118.14	0	5	17	0
Bowling	**Mat**	**Balls**	**Runs**	**Wkts**	**BBI**	**BBM**	**Ave**	**Econ**	**SR**	**5w**	**10**
First-class	58	1697	1218	25	3/76	3/76	48.72	4.30	67.8	0	0
List A	45	399	389	11	3/19	3/19	35.36	5.84	36.2	0	0
T20s	49	164	203	13	4/15	4/15	15.61	7.42	12.6	0	0

BEN DUCKETT LHB / OB / WK / R2 / W0 / MVP9

FULL NAME: Ben Matthew Duckett
BORN: October 17, 1994, Farnborough, Kent
SQUAD NO: 17
HEIGHT: 5ft 9in
NICKNAME: Ducky
EDUCATION: Millfield School, Somerset; Winchester House School; Stowe School
TEAMS: England, Nottinghamshire, Hobart Hurricanes, Northamptonshire, Islamabad United
ROLE: Batsman
DEBUT: Test: 2016; ODI: 2016; T20I: 2019; First-class: 2013; List A: 2013; T20: 2012

BEST BATTING: 282* Northamptonshire vs Sussex, Northampton, 2016
BEST BOWLING: 1-21 Northamptonshire vs Kent, Beckenham, 2017
COUNTY CAP: 2016 (Northamptonshire)

CHILDHOOD SPORTING HERO? Brian Lara
FIRST CRICKET CLUB? Glastonbury CC, Somerset
IF YOU COULD TAKE ONE COUNTY CRICKETER'S BEST SHOT AND ADD IT TO YOUR OWN GAME? Joe Clarke's cover-drive
TOUGHEST OPPONENT IN COUNTY CRICKET? Joe Leach
WHAT WOULD YOU DO IF YOU WERE IN CHARGE OF COUNTY CRICKET? Bring back day/night Championship matches
STRANGEST THING YOU'VE DONE DURING LOCKDOWN? Bleaching my hair blonde
SURPRISING FACT ABOUT YOU? I have a tattoo of a duck with the number 17 and a cricket bat on one side of my bottom
TWITTER: @benduckett11

Batting	Mat	Inns	NO	Runs	HS	Ave	SR	100	50	Ct	St
Tests	4	7	0	110	56	15.71	57.89	0	1	1	0
ODIs	3	3	0	123	63	41.00	80.92	0	2	0	0
T20Is	1	1	0	9	9	9.00	128.57	0	0	0	0
First-class	95	164	8	6140	282*	39.35	71.74	18	26	71	3
List A	73	68	7	2341	220*	38.37	99.49	3	16	38	3
T20s	108	102	20	2442	96	29.78	132.42	0	14	45	2
Bowling	**Mat**	**Balls**	**Runs**	**Wkts**	**BBI**	**BBM**	**Ave**	**Econ**	**SR**	**5w**	**10**
Tests	4	-	-	-	-	-	-	-	-	-	-
ODIs	3	-	-	-	-	-	-	-	-	-	-
T20Is	1	-	-	-	-	-	-	-	-	-	-
First-class	95	89	67	1	1/21	1/32	67.00	4.51	89.0	0	0
List A	73	-	-	-	-	-	-	-	-	-	-
T20s	108	-	-	-	-	-	-	-	-	-	-

MATT DUNN

LHB / RFM / R0 / W0

FULL NAME: Matthew Peter Dunn
BORN: May 5, 1992, Egham, Surrey
SQUAD NO: 4
HEIGHT: 6ft 1in
NICKNAME: Dunny
EDUCATION: Bishopsgate School; Bearwood College, Wokingham
TEAMS: Surrey, England U19
ROLE: Bowler
DEBUT: First-class: 2010; List A: 2011; T20: 2013

BEST BATTING: 31* Surrey vs Kent, Guildford, 2014
BEST BOWLING: 5-43 Surrey vs Somerset, Guildford, 2019

MOST EXCITING DAY AS A CRICKETER? Taking five wickets on debut for Surrey in 2011
CHILDHOOD SPORTING HERO? Brett Lee
FIRST CRICKET CLUB? Egham CC, Surrey
BEST INNINGS YOU'VE SEEN? Aaron Finch's hundred against Middlesex at The Oval in the 2018 T20 Blast
TOUGHEST OPPONENT IN COUNTY CRICKET? Fidel Edwards – he broke my rib once
YOUR BIGGEST CRICKETING REGRET? Not working on my batting from a younger age
SURPRISING FACT ABOUT YOU? I lived in Norway when I was younger, and I can breakdance. And I absolutely love coffee
TWITTER: @MatthewDunn05

Batting	Mat	Inns	NO	Runs	HS	Ave	SR	100	50	Ct	St
First-class	42	49	22	174	31*	6.44	19.52	0	0	9	0
List A	1	-	-	-	-	-	-	-	-	1	0
T20s	20	3	1	3	2	1.50	60.00	0	0	4	0
Bowling	**Mat**	**Balls**	**Runs**	**Wkts**	**BBI**	**BBM**	**Ave**	**Econ**	**SR**	**5w**	**10**
First-class	42	6295	4092	117	5/43	8/128	34.97	3.90	53.8	4	0
List A	1	36	32	2	2/32	2/32	16.00	5.33	18.0	0	0
T20s	20	375	550	26	3/8	3/8	21.15	8.80	14.4	0	0

BEN DWARSHUIS LHB / LFM

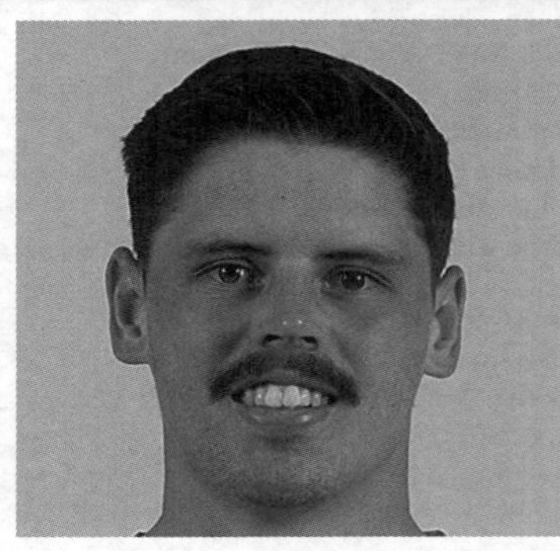

FULL NAME: Benjamin James Dwarshuis
BORN: June 23, 1994, Kareela, New South Wales, Australia
SQUAD NO: TBC
TEAMS: Worcestershire, New South Wales, Sydney Sixers
ROLE: Bowler
DEBUT: List A: 2016; T20: 2014

BEST BATTING: 42* Sydney Sixers vs Melbourne Stars, Melbourne, 2020 (T20)
BEST BOWLING: 4-13 Sydney Sixers vs Melbourne Renegades, Hobart, 2020 (T20)

TWITTER: @bendwarshuis
NOTES: Worcestershire have signed the Australian left-arm seamer for their T20 Blast campaign this summer. Dwarshuis is part of the Sydney Sixers side which has won back-to-back Big Bash titles over the last two years, with the 26-year-old finishing as the team's leading wicket-taker in the 2020/21 edition. His overall economy rate of 8.05 in 69 matches for the Sixers may appear a little high but does not reveal that he is often charged with bowling during the "Power Surge" overs or at the death. Worcestershire are hoping that Dwarshuis will fill the T20 role recently vacated by left-armer Wayne Parnell. "The left-arm option gives a variety to the attack and a bit more balance," said Paul Pridgeon, chairman of the club's steering group. "He is also quite a capable batter down the order. He likes to give it a hit with the bat and has been relatively successful in doing that in white-ball cricket." Dwarshuis was a surprise pick for Australia's T20I tour to New Zealand in 2018 and was bought by Kings XI Punjab in the same year, although he is yet to play international cricket and sat on the bench for his Indian franchise. Injuries have restricted his appearances for New South Wales and he is still to make his first-class debut for his state side

Batting	Mat	Inns	NO	Runs	HS	Ave	SR	100	50	Ct	St
List A	5	3	1	13	9	6.50	65.00	0	0	1	0
T20s	69	33	17	272	42*	17.00	124.77	0	0	16	0
Bowling	**Mat**	**Balls**	**Runs**	**Wkts**	**BBI**	**BBM**	**Ave**	**Econ**	**SR**	**5w**	**10**
List A	5	234	230	8	2/37	2/37	28.75	5.89	29.2	0	0
T20s	69	1456	1954	85	4/13	4/13	22.98	8.05	17.1	0	0

BRETT D'OLIVEIRA RHB / LB / R0 / W0 / MVP40

FULL NAME: Brett Louis D'Oliveira
BORN: February 28, 1992, Worcester
SQUAD NO: 15
HEIGHT: 5ft 9in
NICKNAME: Dolly
EDUCATION: Blessed Edward Oldcorne Catholic College, Worcester; Worcester Sixth Form College
TEAMS: Worcestershire, England Lions
ROLE: Allrounder
DEBUT: First-class: 2012; List A: 2011; T20: 2012

BEST BATTING: 202* Worcestershire vs Glamorgan, Cardiff, 2016
BEST BOWLING: 7-92 Worcestershire vs Glamorgan, Cardiff, 2019
COUNTY CAP: 2012

MOST EXCITING DAY AS A CRICKETER? Helping Worcestershire win the T20 Blast for the first time in 2018
FAMILY TIES? My grandad Basil played for England and Worcestershire and also went on to coach Worcestershire. My dad Damian played for Worcestershire and went on to be assistant coach and Academy director
CHILDHOOD SPORTING HERO? Michael Jordan
FIRST CRICKET CLUB? Worcester Dominies & Guild CC
IF YOU COULD TAKE ONE COUNTY CRICKETER'S BEST SHOT AND ADD IT TO YOUR OWN GAME? Charlie Morris's block
TOUGHEST OPPONENT IN COUNTY CRICKET? Marnus Labuschagne – he's very tough mentally
WHAT WOULD YOU DO IF YOU WERE IN CHARGE OF COUNTY CRICKET? Allow spinners to throw
STRANGEST THING YOU'VE DONE DURING LOCKDOWN? Building a fort for my son
SURPRISING FACT ABOUT YOU? I've got a coaching qualification in basketball
GUILTY PLEASURE? A cup of tea with biscuits
TWITTER: @Bdolly09

Batting	Mat	Inns	NO	Runs	HS	Ave	SR	100	50	Ct	St
First-class	64	109	4	3160	202*	30.09	55.09	8	8	30	0
List A	66	56	11	1032	79	22.93	85.57	0	6	29	0
T20s	92	67	20	1098	64	23.36	125.48	0	5	20	0
Bowling	**Mat**	**Balls**	**Runs**	**Wkts**	**BBI**	**BBM**	**Ave**	**Econ**	**SR**	**5w**	**10**
First-class	64	4942	2849	57	7/92	9/182	49.98	3.45	86.7	2	0
List A	66	2462	2166	50	3/35	3/35	43.32	5.27	49.2	0	0
T20s	92	1248	1628	45	4/26	4/26	36.17	7.82	27.7	0	0

NED ECKERSLEY RHB / WK / R1 / W0

FULL NAME: Edmund James Holden Eckersley
BORN: August 9, 1989, Oxford
SQUAD NO: 66
HEIGHT: 6ft
NICKNAME: Steady
EDUCATION: St Benedict's School, Ealing, London
TEAMS: Durham, Leicestershire, Mountaineers
ROLE: Batsman/wicketkeeper
DEBUT: First-class: 2011; List A: 2008; T20: 2011

BEST BATTING: 158 Leicestershire vs Derbyshire, Derby, 2017
BEST BOWLING: 2-29 Leicestershire vs Lancashire, Old Trafford, 2013
COUNTY CAP: 2013 (Leicestershire)

CHILDHOOD SPORTING HERO? Tiger Woods
BIGGEST INFLUENCE ON YOUR DEVELOPMENT AS A CRICKETER (EXCLUDING PARENTS)? My former coach, the late Bob Jones. He grew my love of cricket
FIRST CRICKET CLUB? Ealing CC, London
TOUGHEST OPPONENT IN COUNTY CRICKET? Darren Stevens
MOST ECCENTRIC TEAMMATE? Liam Trevaskis – he passed the time during lockdown doing paint by numbers
WHAT WOULD YOU DO IF YOU WERE IN CHARGE OF COUNTY CRICKET? Make each side play 10 Championship matches in the season, find a way to encourage better pitches, change the minimum salary for young players
WHAT WOULD YOU DO IF YOU WERE PRIME MINISTER? Find a fix for capitalism
GUILTY PLEASURE? The odd negroni
TWITTER: @nedeckersley

Batting	Mat	Inns	NO	Runs	HS	Ave	SR	100	50	Ct	St
First-class	126	223	18	6651	158	32.44	49.77	15	24	220	3
List A	44	41	5	1041	108	28.91	86.24	1	5	27	1
T20s	66	56	11	702	43	15.60	108.33	0	0	20	7
Bowling	**Mat**	**Balls**	**Runs**	**Wkts**	**BBI**	**BBM**	**Ave**	**Econ**	**SR**	**5w**	**10**
First-class	126	88	67	2	2/29	2/29	33.50	4.56	44.0	0	0
List A	44	-	-	-	-	-	-	-	-	-	-
T20s	66	-	-	-	-	-	-	-	-	-	-

STEVIE ESKINAZI RHB / WK / R0 / W0 / MVP36

FULL NAME: Stephen Sean Eskinazi
BORN: March 28, 1994, Johannesburg, South Africa
SQUAD NO: 28
HEIGHT: 6ft 2in
NICKNAME: Eski
EDUCATION: Christ Church Grammar School, Perth; University of Western Australia; University of Hertfordshire
TEAMS: Middlesex
ROLE: Batsman
DEBUT: First-class: 2015; List A: 2018; T20: 2016

BEST BATTING: 179 Middlesex vs Warwickshire, Edgbaston, 2017

COUNTY CAP: 2018

CHILDHOOD SPORTING HERO? Jacques Kallis
FIRST CRICKET CLUB? Fair Oak CC, Hampshire
IF YOU COULD TAKE ONE COUNTY CRICKETER'S BEST SHOT AND ADD IT TO YOUR OWN GAME? Tim Murtagh's "no-look" hook
TOUGHEST OPPONENT IN COUNTY CRICKET? Ollie Robinson (Sussex) – he cleans me up for fun
WHAT WOULD YOU DO IF YOU WERE IN CHARGE OF COUNTY CRICKET? Introduce a rest day for Championship matches
WHAT WOULD YOU DO IF YOU WERE PRIME MINISTER? Remove those width-restriction bollards in London
STRANGEST THING YOU'VE DONE DURING LOCKDOWN? Going back and forward to Australia
GUILTY PLEASURE? Whole bags of sweets
TWITTER: @seskinazi

Batting	Mat	Inns	NO	Runs	HS	Ave	SR	100	50	Ct	St
First-class	56	99	5	3025	179	32.18	55.28	6	12	52	0
List A	17	16	2	496	107*	35.42	90.51	1	1	6	0
T20s	40	37	3	1148	84	33.76	136.99	0	9	19	0
Bowling	**Mat**	**Balls**	**Runs**	**Wkts**	**BBI**	**BBM**	**Ave**	**Econ**	**SR**	**5w**	**10**
First-class	56	12	4	0	-	-	-	2.00	-	0	0
List A	17	-	-	-	-	-	-	-	-	-	-
T20s	40	-	-	-	-	-	-	-	-	-	-

ALEX EVANS

LHB / RFM / R0 / W0

LEICESTERSHIRE

FULL NAME: Huw Alexander Evans
BORN: August 9, 2000, Bedford
SQUAD NO: 72
HEIGHT: 6ft 2in
NICKNAME: Evo
EDUCATION: Bedford Modern School; Loughborough University
TEAMS: Leicestershire
ROLE: Bowler
DEBUT: First-class: 2019

BEST BATTING: 15 Leicestershire vs Yorkshire, Headingley, 2020
BEST BOWLING: 3-49 Loughborough MCCU vs Kent, Canterbury, 2019

CHILDHOOD SPORTING HERO? Stuart Broad
BIGGEST INFLUENCE ON YOUR DEVELOPMENT AS A CRICKETER (EXCLUDING PARENTS)? Tom Smith, former Lancashire cricketer and now Second XI coach at Leicestershire
FIRST CRICKET CLUB? Ampthill Town CC, Bedfordshire
TOUGHEST OPPONENT IN COUNTY CRICKET? Ben Coad – he can nip it around on glass
MOST ECCENTRIC TEAMMATE? Harry Swindells – he's mad as a box of frogs
FAVOURITE SMELL? Lavender
IF YOU WERE AN ANIMAL, WHICH WOULD IT BE? A crafty fox of course
GUILTY PLEASURE? A Guinness
TWITTER: @HuwAlexEvans

Batting	Mat	Inns	NO	Runs	HS	Ave	SR	100	50	Ct	St
First-class	5	8	3	32	15	6.40	61.53	0	0	1	0
Bowling	**Mat**	**Balls**	**Runs**	**Wkts**	**BBI**	**BBM**	**Ave**	**Econ**	**SR**	**5w**	**10**
First-class	5	704	369	10	3/49	4/79	36.90	3.14	70.4	0	0

LAURIE EVANS RHB / RM / R0 / W0 / MVP32

FULL NAME: Laurie John Evans
BORN: October 12, 1987, Lambeth, London
SQUAD NO: 10
HEIGHT: 6ft
NICKNAME: Loz
EDUCATION: Whitgift School; The John Fisher School, Purley; Durham University
TEAMS: Surrey, Colombo Kings, England Lions, Multan Sultans, Northamptonshire, Rajshahi Kings, Sussex, Warwickshire
ROLE: Batsman
DEBUT: First-class: 2007; List A: 2009; T20: 2009

BEST BATTING: 213* Warwickshire vs Sussex, Edgbaston, 2015
BEST BOWLING: 1-29 Warwickshire vs Sussex, Edgbaston, 2015

MOST EXCITING DAY AS A CRICKETER? Winning the T20 Blast with Warwickshire in 2014
CHILDHOOD SPORTING HERO? Jonny Wilkinson
IF YOU COULD TAKE ONE COUNTY CRICKETER'S BEST SHOT AND ADD IT TO YOUR OWN GAME? Joe Root's forward-defence
TOUGHEST OPPONENT IN COUNTY CRICKET? Sam Curran
MOST ECCENTRIC TEAMMATE? Reece Topley – for that moustache
WHAT WOULD YOU DO IF YOU WERE IN CHARGE OF COUNTY CRICKET? Reduce the amount of games, use DRS for TV games, offer free entry for kids
STRANGEST THING YOU'VE DONE DURING LOCKDOWN? Not seeing anyone
FAVOURITE SMELL? Petrol
GUILTY PLEASURE? Wine
TWITTER: @laurieevans32

Batting	Mat	Inns	NO	Runs	HS	Ave	SR	100	50	Ct	St
First-class	71	122	6	3474	213*	29.94	46.41	6	18	56	0
List A	63	57	11	1735	134*	37.71	96.98	3	5	25	0
T20s	164	150	37	3913	108*	34.62	133.91	2	27	67	0
Bowling	**Mat**	**Balls**	**Runs**	**Wkts**	**BBI**	**BBM**	**Ave**	**Econ**	**SR**	**5w**	**10**
First-class	71	366	270	2	1/29	1/29	135.00	4.42	183.0	0	0
List A	63	54	82	1	1/29	1/29	82.00	9.11	54.0	0	0
T20s	164	22	35	1	1/5	1/5	35.00	9.54	22.0	0	0

SAM EVANS

RHB / OB / R0 / W0

FULL NAME: Samuel Thomes Evans
BORN: December 20, 1997, Leicester
SQUAD NO: 21
HEIGHT: 5ft 8in
NICKNAME: Smevs
EDUCATION: Lancaster Boys School, Leicester; Wyggeston & Queen Elizabeth I College; Loughborough University
TEAMS: Leicestershire
ROLE: Batsman
DEBUT: First-class: 2017; List A: 2018

BEST BATTING: 114 Loughborough MCCU vs Northamptonshire, Northampton, 2017

CHILDHOOD SPORTING HERO? Andrew Flintoff
BIGGEST INFLUENCE ON YOUR DEVELOPMENT AS A CRICKETER (EXCLUDING PARENTS)? Trevor Ward – he helped me a lot at Leicester Ivanhoe CC
IF YOU COULD TAKE ONE COUNTY CRICKETER'S BEST SHOT AND ADD IT TO YOUR OWN GAME? Zak Crawley's pull
TOUGHEST OPPONENT IN COUNTY CRICKET? Ben Coad
WHAT WOULD YOU DO IF YOU WERE IN CHARGE OF COUNTY CRICKET? Insist on cable-knit jumpers, add leg byes to the batsman's score, play more games at outgrounds
WHAT WOULD YOU DO IF YOU WERE PRIME MINISTER? Make the football World Cup a national holiday
STRANGEST THING YOU'VE DONE DURING LOCKDOWN? Learning to juggle
FAVOURITE SMELL? Nature – the smell of fresh air and being outside
GUILTY PLEASURE? A Galaxy Caramel
TWITTER: @SamEvans97

Batting	Mat	Inns	NO	Runs	HS	Ave	SR	100	50	Ct	St
First-class	12	18	1	397	114	23.35	40.63	1	1	5	0
List A	1	1	0	20	20	20.00	71.42	0	0	0	0
Bowling	**Mat**	**Balls**	**Runs**	**Wkts**	**BBI**	**BBM**	**Ave**	**Econ**	**SR**	**5w**	**10**
First-class	12	54	46	0	-	-	-	5.11	-	0	0
List A	1	-	-	-	-	-	-	-	-	-	-

JOEY EVISON

RHB / RM / R0 / W0

FULL NAME: Joseph David Michael Evison
BORN: November 14, 2001, Peterborough, Cambridgeshire
SQUAD NO: 90
HEIGHT: 6ft 2in
NICKNAME: Evo
EDUCATION: Stamford School, Lincolnshire
TEAMS: Nottinghamshire, England U19
ROLE: Allrounder
DEBUT: First-class: 2019

BEST BATTING: 45 Nottinghamshire vs Warwickshire, Trent Bridge, 2019
BEST BOWLING: 3-38 Nottinghamshire vs Derbyshire, Trent Bridge, 2020

MOST EXCITING DAY AS A CRICKETER? Equalling the world record for the fastest fifty in Youth ODIs (50 not out off 18 balls against Sri Lanka U19 in December 2019). I share the record with Rishabh Pant
CHILDHOOD SPORTING HERO? Ben Stokes
BIGGEST INFLUENCE ON YOUR DEVELOPMENT AS A CRICKETER (EXCLUDING PARENTS)? Matt Wood (Academy director at Nottinghamshire) and Dean Headley (head of cricket at Stamford School)
FIRST CRICKET CLUB? Bourne CC, Lincolnshire
IF YOU COULD TAKE ONE COUNTY CRICKETER'S BEST SHOT AND ADD IT TO YOUR OWN GAME? Jos Buttler's ramp
TOUGHEST OPPONENT IN COUNTY CRICKET? Jeetan Patel, who I faced on my first-class debut. He was so accurate and bowled no bad balls
STRANGEST THING YOU'VE DONE DURING LOCKDOWN? Painting by numbers
FAVOURITE SMELL? My mum's Sunday roast
GUILTY PLEASURE? M&S pancakes
TWITTER: @EvisonJoey

Batting	Mat	Inns	NO	Runs	HS	Ave	SR	100	50	Ct	St
First-class	2	4	0	126	45	31.50	61.16	0	0	2	0
Bowling	**Mat**	**Balls**	**Runs**	**Wkts**	**BBI**	**BBM**	**Ave**	**Econ**	**SR**	**5w**	**10**
First-class	2	191	107	4	3/38	4/74	26.75	3.36	47.7	0	0

TOM FELL

RHB / OB / R1 / W0

FULL NAME: Thomas Charles Fell
BORN: October 17, 1993, Hillingdon, Middlesex
SQUAD NO: 29
HEIGHT: 6ft 1in
NICKNAME: Lord
EDUCATION: Tettenhall College, Wolverhampton; Oakham School, Rutland; Oxford Brookes University
TEAMS: Worcestershire
ROLE: Batsman
DEBUT: First-class: 2013; List A: 2013; T20: 2018

BEST BATTING: 171 Worcestershire vs Middlesex, Worcester, 2015

COUNTY CAP: 2013

CHILDHOOD SPORTING HERO? Tiger Woods
BIGGEST INFLUENCE ON YOUR DEVELOPMENT AS A CRICKETER (EXCLUDING PARENTS)? Steve Rhodes, former Worcestershire coach. He gave me my first contract and the opportunity to play first-team cricket so early in my career
FIRST CRICKET CLUB? Wolverhampton CC, West Midlands
IF YOU COULD TAKE ONE COUNTY CRICKETER'S BEST SHOT AND ADD IT TO YOUR OWN GAME? Kane Williamson's forward defence
TOUGHEST OPPONENT IN COUNTY CRICKET? Ben Sanderson – I think he's got me out every time I've played against him, usually without scoring a run off him
WHAT WOULD YOU DO IF YOU WERE IN CHARGE OF COUNTY CRICKET? Play more Championship cricket in June, July and August, turn the 50-over competition into a knockout which includes Minor Counties
FAVOURITE SMELL? Garlic and onion in the frying pan
GUILTY PLEASURE? Red wine with chocolate
TWITTER: @TomFell_29

Batting	Mat	Inns	NO	Runs	HS	Ave	SR	100	50	Ct	St
First-class	84	143	7	4144	171	30.47	49.75	6	17	64	0
List A	45	44	5	1369	116*	35.10	80.01	1	11	16	0
T20s	7	5	0	62	28	12.40	101.63	0	0	2	0
Bowling	**Mat**	**Balls**	**Runs**	**Wkts**	**BBI**	**BBM**	**Ave**	**Econ**	**SR**	**5w**	**10**
First-class	84	20	17	0	-	-	-	5.10	-	0	0
List A	45	-	-	-	-	-	-	-	-	-	-
T20s	7	-	-	-	-	-	-	-	-	-	-

LOCKIE FERGUSON RHB / RF

FULL NAME: Lachlan Hammond Ferguson
BORN: June 13, 1991, Auckland, New Zealand
SQUAD NO: 69
NICKNAME: Lockie
TEAMS: New Zealand, Yorkshire, Auckland, Derbyshire, Kolkata Knight Riders, Rising Pune Supergiant
ROLE: Bowler
DEBUT: Test: 2019; ODI: 2016; T20I: 2017; First-class: 2013; List A: 2015; T20: 2014

BEST BATTING: 24* Kolkata Knight Riders vs Kings XI Punjab, Sharjah, 2020 (T20)
BEST BOWLING: 5-21 New Zealand vs West Indies, Auckland, 2020 (T20)

TWITTER: @lockieferguson
NOTES: Yorkshire have secured the services of one of the premier white-ball bowlers in the world. The Kiwi quick is expected to be available for the entirety of the Vikings' T20 Blast campaign, subject to any international commitments. This will be Ferguson's second spell in county cricket after taking 16 wickets in 13 matches for Derbyshire Falcons in 2018. His T20I record for the Black Caps is outstanding and includes a spell of 5-21 against West Indies last November – the second-best figures by a New Zealand bowler in the format. He also impressed at the 2020 IPL, taking a match-turning spell of 3-15 on debut for Kolkata Knight Riders. "Lockie has got x-factor pace," said Andrew Gale, Yorkshire's first XI coach. "Pace in T20 cricket is always a good thing, but also his death bowling in particular will be hugely beneficial. We haven't had somebody who is reliable and consistent at the death for a number of years"

Batting	Mat	Inns	NO	Runs	HS	Ave	SR	100	50	Ct	St
Tests	1	2	2	1	1*	-	11.11	0	0	0	0
ODIs	37	16	7	63	19	7.00	47.72	0	0	10	0
T20Is	11	1	0	1	1	1.00	33.33	0	0	4	0
First-class	45	60	23	505	41	13.64	46.24	0	0	16	0
List A	69	37	14	177	24	7.69	63.66	0	0	20	0
T20s	59	13	9	66	24*	16.50	104.76	0	0	12	0
Bowling	**Mat**	**Balls**	**Runs**	**Wkts**	**BBI**	**BBM**	**Ave**	**Econ**	**SR**	**5w**	**10**
Tests	1	66	47	0	-	-	-	4.27	-	0	0
ODIs	37	1956	1779	69	5/45	5/45	25.78	5.45	28.3	1	0
T20Is	11	240	278	21	5/21	5/21	13.23	6.95	11.4	1	0
First-class	45	7123	3975	161	7/34	12/78	24.68	3.34	44.2	11	1
List A	69	3580	3214	126	6/27	6/27	25.50	5.38	28.4	3	0
T20s	59	1211	1535	60	5/21	5/21	25.58	7.60	20.1	1	0

ADAM FINCH

RHB / RFM / R0 / W0

FULL NAME: Adam William Finch
BORN: May 28, 2000, Wordsley, Stourbridge, Worcestershire
SQUAD NO: 61
HEIGHT: 6ft 4in
EDUCATION: Kingswinford School, West Midlands; Oldswinford Hospital Sixth Form College, Stourbridge
TEAMS: Worcestershire, England U19, Surrey
ROLE: Bowler
DEBUT: First-class: 2019; T20: 2020

BEST BATTING: 18* Worcestershire vs Australians, Worcester, 2019
BEST BOWLING: 4-38 Surrey vs Essex, Chelmsford, 2020

MOST EXCITING DAY AS A CRICKETER? My first-class debut in 2019
CHILDHOOD SPORTING HERO? David Beckham
BIGGEST INFLUENCE ON YOUR DEVELOPMENT AS A CRICKETER (EXCLUDING PARENTS)? Paul Pridgeon, former Worcestershire seamer who worked with the Academy to help bring through young players
FIRST CRICKET CLUB? Himley CC, Staffordshire
IF YOU COULD TAKE ONE COUNTY CRICKETER'S BEST SHOT AND ADD IT TO YOUR OWN GAME? Tom Westley's clip off the legs
TOUGHEST OPPONENT IN COUNTY CRICKET? Alastair Cook
WHAT WOULD YOU DO IF YOU WERE IN CHARGE OF COUNTY CRICKET? Make sure that overthrows are not marked down against the bowler
FAVOURITE SMELL? Biscuits baking
TWITTER: @Adamfinch00

Batting	Mat	Inns	NO	Runs	HS	Ave	SR	100	50	Ct	St
First-class	11	15	6	90	18*	10.00	25.06	0	0	1	0
T20s	5	1	1	3	3*	-	60.00	0	0	0	0
Bowling	**Mat**	**Balls**	**Runs**	**Wkts**	**BBI**	**BBM**	**Ave**	**Econ**	**SR**	**5w**	**10**
First-class	11	1509	897	20	4/38	4/80	44.85	3.56	75.4	0	0
T20s	5	96	147	4	1/22	1/22	36.75	9.18	24.0	0	0

STEVEN FINN

RHB / RFM / R0 / W2

FULL NAME: Steven Thomas Finn
BORN: April 4, 1989, Watford, Hertfordshire
SQUAD NO: 9
HEIGHT: 6ft 8in
NICKNAME: Cyril
EDUCATION: Parmiter's School, Watford
TEAMS: England, Middlesex, Islamabad United, Otago
ROLE: Bowler
DEBUT: Test: 2010; ODI: 2011; T20I: 2011; First-class: 2005; List A: 2007; T20: 2008

BEST BATTING: 56 England vs New Zealand, Dunedin, 2013
BEST BOWLING: 9-37 Middlesex vs Worcestershire, Worcester, 2010
COUNTY CAP: 2009

MOST EXCITING DAY AS A CRICKETER? The 2015 Ashes Test at Edgbaston
CHILDHOOD SPORTING HERO? Glenn McGrath
BIGGEST INFLUENCE ON YOUR DEVELOPMENT AS A CRICKETER (EXCLUDING PARENTS)? Angus Fraser – we had lots of chats about bowling in my early years
FIRST CRICKET CLUB? Langleybury CC, Hertfordshire
IF YOU COULD TAKE ONE COUNTY CRICKETER'S BEST SHOT AND ADD IT TO YOUR OWN GAME? Tim Murtagh's off-side flay
TOUGHEST OPPONENT IN COUNTY CRICKET? Mark Ramprakash – I think he scored a hundred every time I played against him
WHAT WOULD YOU DO IF YOU WERE IN CHARGE OF COUNTY CRICKET? Change the rule about a bouncer being a wide – it should be a no-ball!
TWITTER: @finnysteve

Batting	Mat	Inns	NO	Runs	HS	Ave	SR	100	50	Ct	St
Tests	36	47	22	279	56	11.16	30.96	0	1	8	0
ODIs	69	30	13	136	35	8.00	60.98	0	0	15	0
T20Is	21	3	3	14	8*	-	73.68	0	0	6	0
First-class	157	191	62	1266	56	9.81	40.35	0	2	49	0
List A	144	59	25	411	42*	12.08	67.48	0	0	33	0
T20s	113	24	17	62	8*	8.85	79.48	0	0	30	0
Bowling	**Mat**	**Balls**	**Runs**	**Wkts**	**BBI**	**BBM**	**Ave**	**Econ**	**SR**	**5w**	**10**
Tests	36	6412	3800	125	6/79	9/187	30.40	3.55	51.2	5	0
ODIs	69	3550	2996	102	5/33	5/33	29.37	5.06	34.8	2	0
T20Is	21	480	583	27	3/16	3/16	21.59	7.28	17.7	0	0
First-class	157	27676	15981	551	9/37	-	29.00	3.46	50.2	14	1
List A	144	6821	5847	201	5/33	5/33	29.08	5.14	33.9	3	0
T20s	113	2336	3081	139	5/16	5/16	22.16	7.91	16.8	1	0

MATTHEW FISHER RHB / RFM / R0 / W0

FULL NAME: Matthew David Fisher
BORN: November 9, 1997, York
SQUAD NO: 7
HEIGHT: 6ft 2in
NICKNAME: Nemo
EDUCATION: Easingwold School, North Yorkshire
TEAMS: Yorkshire, England Lions
ROLE: Bowler
DEBUT: First-class: 2015; List A: 2013; T20: 2015

BEST BATTING: 47* Yorkshire vs Kent, Headingley, 2019
BEST BOWLING: 5-54 Yorkshire vs Warwickshire, Headingley, 2017

BIGGEST INFLUENCE ON YOUR DEVELOPMENT AS A CRICKETER (EXCLUDING PARENTS)? Tony Pickersgill, the former age-group bowling coach at Yorkshire. He helped make my bowling technically sound and adapted to a high level at a young age
IF YOU COULD TAKE ONE COUNTY CRICKETER'S BEST SHOT AND ADD IT TO YOUR OWN GAME? Adam Lyth's cover-drive
TOUGHEST OPPONENT IN COUNTY CRICKET? Sam Billings – he made twin centuries against us at Headingley in 2019
MOST ECCENTRIC TEAMMATE? Not many eccentric individuals at Yorkshire, as you would expect
WHAT WOULD YOU DO IF YOU WERE IN CHARGE OF COUNTY CRICKET? Make boundaries bigger, have six stumps in T20 cricket, blindfold the batsmen (batters' game)
STRANGEST THING YOU'VE DONE DURING LOCKDOWN? Building a wall
SURPRISING FACT ABOUT YOU? I'm deaf in one ear
GUILTY PLEASURE? Gogglebox on TV
TWITTER: @9M_Fisher

Batting	Mat	Inns	NO	Runs	HS	Ave	SR	100	50	Ct	St
First-class	15	19	3	248	47*	15.50	30.28	0	0	6	0
List A	34	18	10	228	36*	28.50	98.70	0	0	10	0
T20s	27	8	4	33	17*	8.25	126.92	0	0	9	0
Bowling	**Mat**	**Balls**	**Runs**	**Wkts**	**BBI**	**BBM**	**Ave**	**Econ**	**SR**	**5w**	**10**
First-class	15	2324	1257	41	5/54	6/97	30.65	3.24	56.6	1	0
List A	34	1384	1366	32	3/32	3/32	42.68	5.92	43.2	0	0
T20s	27	509	781	31	5/22	5/22	25.19	9.20	16.4	1	0

LUKE FLETCHER RHB / RFM / R0 / W0

FULL NAME: Luke Jack Fletcher
BORN: September 18, 1988, Nottingham
SQUAD NO: 19
HEIGHT: 6ft 6in
NICKNAME: Fletch
EDUCATION: Henry Mellish Comprehensive School, Nottingham
TEAMS: Nottinghamshire, Derbyshire, England U19, Surrey, Wellington
ROLE: Bowler
DEBUT: First-class: 2008; List A: 2008; T20: 2009

BEST BATTING: 92 Nottinghamshire vs Hampshire, Southampton, 2009
BEST BOWLING: 5-27 Nottinghamshire vs Worcestershire, Worcester, 2018
COUNTY CAP: 2014 (Nottinghamshire)

MOST EXCITING DAY AS A CRICKETER? Winning the Lord's one-day final in 2017
CHILDHOOD SPORTING HERO? Andrew Flintoff
FIRST CRICKET CLUB? Bulwell CC, Nottinghamshire
IF YOU COULD TAKE ONE COUNTY CRICKETER'S BEST SHOT AND ADD IT TO YOUR OWN GAME? Alex Hales's lofted straight-drive
TOUGHEST OPPONENT IN COUNTY CRICKET? Ed Joyce
BIGGEST CRICKETING REGRET? Getting out on 92 – twice
WHAT WOULD YOU DO IF YOU WERE IN CHARGE OF COUNTY CRICKET? Play less games – that's it, I'm happy with how everything else is
FAVOURITE SMELL? Bacon in the morning
GUILTY PLEASURE? Toblerone
TWITTER: @fletcherluke

Batting	Mat	Inns	NO	Runs	HS	Ave	SR	100	50	Ct	St
First-class	117	174	28	2029	92	13.89	46.80	0	4	28	0
List A	75	40	16	495	53*	20.62	113.01	0	1	13	0
T20s	76	26	10	113	27	7.06	111.88	0	0	9	0
Bowling	**Mat**	**Balls**	**Runs**	**Wkts**	**BBI**	**BBM**	**Ave**	**Econ**	**SR**	**5w**	**10**
First-class	117	19720	9654	343	5/27	9/108	28.14	2.93	57.4	6	0
List A	75	3112	2936	81	5/56	5/56	36.24	5.66	38.4	1	0
T20s	76	1554	2117	87	5/43	5/43	24.33	8.17	17.8	1	0

SURREY

BEN FOAKES

RHB / WK / R0 / W0 / MVP48

FULL NAME: Benjamin Thomas Foakes
BORN: February 15, 1993, Colchester, Essex
SQUAD NO: 7
HEIGHT: 6ft 2in
EDUCATION: Tendring Technology College, Essex
TEAMS: England, Surrey, Essex
ROLE: Wicketkeeper/batsman
DEBUT: Test: 2018; ODI: 2019; T20I: 2019; First-class: 2011; List A: 2013; T20: 2014

BEST BATTING: 141* Surrey vs Hampshire, Southampton, 2016

COUNTY CAP: 2016 (Surrey)

CHILDHOOD SPORTING HERO? James Foster – he made me want to become a keeper when I first started watching Essex play as a kid
FAMILY TIES? My brother plays in the East Anglian Premier League for Frinton-on-Sea
SURPRISING FACT ABOUT YOU? I once had a tooth glued back together after being involved in a car crash. Later, while I was batting, it came unstuck and was dangling, so I tore it out at lunch and batted with no front teeth

Batting	Mat	Inns	NO	Runs	HS	Ave	SR	100	50	Ct	St
Tests	8	16	3	410	107	31.53	46.75	1	1	14	5
ODIs	1	1	1	61	61*	-	80.26	0	1	2	1
T20Is	1	-	-	-	-	-	-	-	-	1	0
First-class	114	182	30	5779	141*	38.01	51.73	10	31	233	27
List A	73	63	11	1941	92	37.32	86.49	0	18	86	11
T20s	78	53	12	905	75*	22.07	122.62	0	4	39	11
Bowling	**Mat**	**Balls**	**Runs**	**Wkts**	**BBI**	**BBM**	**Ave**	**Econ**	**SR**	**5w**	**10**
Tests	8	-	-	-	-	-	-	-	-	-	-
ODIs	1	-	-	-	-	-	-	-	-	-	-
T20Is	1	-	-	-	-	-	-	-	-	-	-
First-class	114	6	6	0	-	-	-	6.00	-	0	0
List A	73	-	-	-	-	-	-	-	-	-	-
T20s	78	-	-	-	-	-	-	-	-	-	-

WILL FRAINE

RHB / RM / R0 / W0

FULL NAME: William Alan Richard Fraine
BORN: June 13, 1996, Huddersfield
SQUAD NO: 31
EDUCATION: Silcoates School, Wakefield, West Yorkshire; Bromsgrove Sixth Form College, Worcestershire; Durham University
TEAMS: Yorkshire, Nottinghamshire
ROLE: Batsman
DEBUT: First-class: 2017; List A: 2018; T20: 2018

BEST BATTING: 106 Yorkshire vs Surrey, Scarborough, 2019

NOTES: The top-order batsman turned down an offer from Nottinghamshire to sign for his home county Yorkshire in October 2018. "There's always that pull of being a Yorkie lad," he said upon joining the White Rose. Fraine was born in Huddersfield and played for Yorkshire's age-group sides up to U19 level. After moving to a boarding school in Bromsgrove, Fraine played Second XI cricket for Worcestershire and Nottinghamshire. He made his first-class debut for Durham MCCU in 2016 but had to wait another three years to score his maiden hundred – 106 against Surrey at Scarborough. He underwent knee surgery before the start of last season but still managed to feature for Yorkshire in three Bob Willis Trophy matches and eight T20s

Batting	Mat	Inns	NO	Runs	HS	Ave	SR	100	50	Ct	St
First-class	16	24	1	522	106	22.69	47.71	1	0	9	0
List A	4	3	1	27	13	13.50	122.72	0	0	1	0
T20s	19	18	4	242	44*	17.28	154.14	0	0	14	0
Bowling	**Mat**	**Balls**	**Runs**	**Wkts**	**BBI**	**BBM**	**Ave**	**Econ**	**SR**	**5w**	**10**
First-class	16	-	-	-	-	-	-	-	-	-	-
List A	4	-	-	-	-	-	-	-	-	-	-
T20s	19	-	-	-	-	-	-	-	-	-	-

JAMES FULLER

RHB / RFM / R0 / W0 / MVP79

FULL NAME: James Kerr Fuller
BORN: January 24, 1990, Cape Town, South Africa
SQUAD NO: 26
HEIGHT: 6ft 2in
NICKNAME: Foz
EDUCATION: Westlake Boys High School, Auckland; University of Otago
TEAMS: Hampshire, Auckland, England Lions, Gloucestershire, Middlesex, Otago
ROLE: Bowler
DEBUT: First-class: 2010; List A: 2011; T20: 2011

BEST BATTING: 93 Middlesex vs Somerset, Taunton, 2016
BEST BOWLING: 6-24 Otago vs Wellington, Dunedin, 2013
COUNTY CAP: 2011 (Gloucestershire)

MOST EXCITING DAY AS A CRICKETER? The glorious Glosters winning the 2015 one-day trophy
CHILDHOOD SPORTING HERO? Shane Bond
FIRST CRICKET CLUB? North Shore CC, Auckland, New Zealand
MOST INTERESTING TEAMMATE? Tom Alsop – he's always got a science book on the go, so we have some good discussions on how the natural world works. Ryan Stevenson has some good stories of growing up in a farm in the south west
SURPRISING FACT ABOUT YOU? I have held my breath for over three minutes and 30 seconds
IF YOU WERE AN ANIMAL, WHICH WOULD IT BE? A polar bear – very good sense of smell, strong paws, big appetite
TWITTER: @James_Fuller246

Batting	Mat	Inns	NO	Runs	HS	Ave	SR	100	50	Ct	St
First-class	57	74	10	1300	93	20.31	64.70	0	6	23	0
List A	62	49	16	759	55*	23.00	102.15	0	1	21	0
T20s	99	63	23	844	53*	21.10	142.56	0	2	39	0
Bowling	**Mat**	**Balls**	**Runs**	**Wkts**	**BBI**	**BBM**	**Ave**	**Econ**	**SR**	**5w**	**10**
First-class	57	8762	5257	159	6/24	10/79	33.06	3.59	55.1	5	1
List A	62	2449	2422	75	6/35	6/35	32.29	5.93	32.6	1	0
T20s	99	1634	2423	97	6/28	6/28	24.97	8.89	16.8	1	0

GEORGE FURRER RHB / LFM / R0 / W0

FULL NAME: George William Furrer
BORN: October 10, 1998, London
SQUAD NO: 13
HEIGHT: 6ft 7in
NICKNAME: Fuzz
EDUCATION: Barker College, Sydney; University of New South Wales
TEAMS: Warwickshire
ROLE: Bowler

MOST EXCITING DAY AS A CRICKETER? The day I signed as a Bear in 2019
CHILDHOOD SPORTING HERO? Glenn McGrath
IF YOU COULD TAKE ONE COUNTY CRICKETER'S BEST SHOT AND ADD IT TO YOUR OWN GAME? Ed Pollock's slog-sweep off one knee to a fast bowler
TOUGHEST OPPONENT IN COUNTY CRICKET? Matt Parkinson on a turning day-four wicket – he rags them square
MOST ECCENTRIC TEAMMATE? Michael Burgess – he loves an impersonation
WHAT WOULD YOU DO IF YOU WERE IN CHARGE OF COUNTY CRICKET? Have finals for red-ball cricket, reduce the amount of bonus points and increase points for wins, allow more overseas players
STRANGEST THING YOU'VE DONE DURING LOCKDOWN? Building a gym in my garage
FAVOURITE SMELL? My mum's home-cooked meal
GUILTY PLEASURE? A glass of red
NOTES: The 22-year-old fast bowler signed a two-year contract at Edgbaston in September 2019 following a trial with Warwickshire's Second XI. Furrer was born in London and has a British passport but grew up in Australia, representing Eastern Suburbs in Sydney grade cricket. He was also part of the New South Wales Academy and played for their U19 side. A tall and pacy left-armer, he nevertheless describes himself as "not an out-and-out fast bowler... I pride myself on my skills, my ability to swing the ball and deliver it from a good height". He plays club cricket for Birmingham Premier League side Moseley CC

WARWICKSHIRE

GEORGE GARRETT

RHB / RMF / R0 / W0

FULL NAME: George Anthony Garrett
BORN: March 4, 2000, Harpenden, Hertfordshire
SQUAD NO: 44
HEIGHT: 6ft 4in
NICKNAME: Gazza
EDUCATION: Shrewsbury School; University of Birmingham
TEAMS: Warwickshire
ROLE: Bowler
DEBUT: First-class: 2019; T20: 2019

BEST BATTING: 24 Warwickshire vs Essex, Edgbaston, 2019
BEST BOWLING: 2-53 Warwickshire vs Nottinghamshire, Trent Bridge, 2019

CHILDHOOD SPORTING HERO? Lionel Messi
BIGGEST INFLUENCE ON YOUR DEVELOPMENT AS A CRICKETER (EXCLUDING PARENTS)? Paul Greetham (Academy director at Warwickshire) – he has never let me take my foot off the gas
FIRST CRICKET CLUB? Harpenden CC, Hertfordshire
IF YOU COULD TAKE ONE COUNTY CRICKETER'S BEST SHOT AND ADD IT TO YOUR OWN GAME? Jason Roy's on-drive
TOUGHEST OPPONENT IN COUNTY CRICKET? Joe Clarke – it went for four wherever I bowled
MOST ECCENTRIC TEAMMATE? Oliver Hannon-Dalby – for his northern wit
WHAT WOULD YOU DO IF YOU WERE IN CHARGE OF COUNTY CRICKET? Set up an FA-Cup-style one-day competition which includes Minor Counties, start an U19 County Championship
STRANGEST THING YOU'VE DONE DURING LOCKDOWN? Growing sideburns
IF YOU WERE AN ANIMAL, WHICH WOULD IT BE? A robin – Bristol City till I die
GUILTY PLEASURE? Friday night Red Stripe
TWITTER: @Georgegarrett14

Batting	Mat	Inns	NO	Runs	HS	Ave	SR	100	50	Ct	St
First-class	3	4	2	32	24	16.00	35.16	0	0	0	0
T20s	2	-	-	-	-	-	-	-	-	0	0
Bowling	**Mat**	**Balls**	**Runs**	**Wkts**	**BBI**	**BBM**	**Ave**	**Econ**	**SR**	**5w**	**10**
First-class	3	509	302	8	2/53	4/125	37.75	3.55	63.6	0	0
T20s	2	24	39	1	1/19	1/19	39.00	9.75	24.0	0	0

GEORGE GARTON

LHB / LF / R0 / W0 / MVP20

FULL NAME: George Henry Simmons Garton
BORN: April 15, 1997, Brighton
SQUAD NO: 15
HEIGHT: 6ft 1in
NICKNAME: Garts
EDUCATION: Hurstpierpoint College, West Sussex
TEAMS: Sussex, England Lions
ROLE: Bowler
DEBUT: First-class: 2016; List A: 2016; T20: 2016

BEST BATTING: 59* Sussex vs Worcestershire, Hove, 2019
BEST BOWLING: 5-26 Sussex vs Essex, Hove, 2020

MOST EXCITING DAY AS A CRICKETER? Playing my first game for England Lions
CHILDHOOD SPORTING HERO? I didn't have one
FIRST CRICKET CLUB? Preston Nomads CC, West Sussex
BEST INNINGS YOU'VE SEEN? Phil Salt's Championship hundred against Derbyshire at Hove in 2018 – that was some serious ball-striking
IF YOU COULD TAKE ONE COUNTY CRICKETER'S BEST SHOT AND ADD IT TO YOUR OWN GAME? Wayne Madsen's ramp
TOUGHEST OPPONENT IN COUNTY CRICKET? Kumar Sangakkara
WHAT WOULD YOU DO IF YOU WERE IN CHARGE OF COUNTY CRICKET? Remove the limit on bouncers
STRANGEST THING YOU'VE DONE DURING LOCKDOWN? Trying to learn another language
FAVOURITE SMELL? A bonfire
GUILTY PLEASURE? Cadbury Dairy Milk
TWITTER: @george_garton

Batting	Mat	Inns	NO	Runs	HS	Ave	SR	100	50	Ct	St
First-class	17	23	6	322	59*	18.94	56.00	0	3	10	0
List A	24	11	2	103	38	11.44	86.55	0	0	11	0
T20s	23	9	5	103	34*	25.75	115.73	0	0	8	0
Bowling	**Mat**	**Balls**	**Runs**	**Wkts**	**BBI**	**BBM**	**Ave**	**Econ**	**SR**	**5w**	**10**
First-class	17	1995	1331	40	5/26	9/76	33.27	4.00	49.8	1	0
List A	24	942	993	29	4/43	4/43	34.24	6.32	32.4	0	0
T20s	23	366	503	25	4/16	4/16	20.12	8.24	14.6	0	0

EMILIO GAY

LHB / RM / R0 / W0

FULL NAME: Emilio Nico Gay
BORN: April 14, 2000, Bedford
SQUAD NO: 19
HEIGHT: 6ft 2in
NICKNAME: Nico
EDUCATION: Rushmoor School, Bedford; Bedford School
TEAMS: Northamptonshire
ROLE: Batsman
DEBUT: First-class: 2019

BEST BATTING: 77* Northamptonshire vs Glamorgan, Northampton, 2020

MOST EXCITING DAY AS A CRICKETER? Signing my first professional contract with Northamptonshire in 2019
CHILDHOOD SPORTING HERO? Floyd Mayweather
BIGGEST INFLUENCE ON YOUR DEVELOPMENT AS A CRICKETER (EXCLUDING PARENTS)? Jack Mousley – my coach at Bedfordshire
MOST ECCENTRIC TEAMMATE? Luke Procter
WHAT WOULD YOU DO IF YOU WERE IN CHARGE OF COUNTY CRICKET? Play more day/night games in the Championship to help make it more appealing to the public, make sure that runs and wickets are rewarded by international selection, increase the amount of white-ball games in Second XI cricket
STRANGEST THING YOU'VE DONE DURING LOCKDOWN? Not training for months
GUILTY PLEASURE? Reality TV shows
TWITTER: @emilio_nico1

Batting	Mat	Inns	NO	Runs	HS	Ave	SR	100	50	Ct	St
First-class	5	6	1	121	77*	24.20	44.98	0	1	5	0
Bowling	**Mat**	**Balls**	**Runs**	**Wkts**	**BBI**	**BBM**	**Ave**	**Econ**	**SR**	**5w**	**10**
First-class	5	-	-	-	-	-	-	-	-	-	-

OLIVER GIBSON

RHB / RFM / R0 / W0

FULL NAME: Oliver James Gibson
BORN: July 7, 2000, Northallerton, Yorkshire
SQUAD NO: 73
HEIGHT: 5ft 11in
NICKNAME: Gibbo
EDUCATION: Queen Elizabeth Grammar School, Hexham, Northumberland; Derwentside Sixth Form College, Consett, County Durham
TEAMS: Durham
ROLE: Bowler

NOTES: A seamer who has come through the Durham Academy, Gibson featured in matchday squads in the 2019 County Championship and last season's T20 Blast but is still awaiting his first-team debut. He signed a youth contract with the county in November 2019 after making three appearances in the previous year's Second XI Championship. He also played a handful of Second XI Trophy matches in a Durham side which reached the final, where they lost to Kent, and took seven wickets at 16.57 in four second-team T20 games. The 20-year-old signed a new deal with the club last October. Gibson plays his club cricket for Shotley Bridge CC in the north-west of County Durham, home of his boyhood hero Paul Collingwood

NATHAN GILCHRIST

RHB / RFM / R0 / W0

FULL NAME: Nathan Nicholas Gilchrist
BORN: June 11, 2000, Harare, Zimbabwe
SQUAD NO: 17
HEIGHT: 6ft 5in
NICKNAME: Gilly
EDUCATION: St Stithians School, Johannesburg; King's College, Taunton
TEAMS: Kent, Somerset
ROLE: Bowler
DEBUT: First-class: 2020

BEST BATTING: 25 Kent vs Surrey, The Oval, 2020

MOST EXCITING DAY AS A CRICKETER? Making my first-class debut last summer
CHILDHOOD SPORTING HERO? Dale Steyn
FIRST CRICKET CLUB? Staplegrove CC, Somerset. The cricket field was right next to a herd of cows
IF YOU COULD TAKE ONE COUNTY CRICKETER'S BEST SHOT AND ADD IT TO YOUR OWN GAME? George Bartlett's cover-drive
TOUGHEST OPPONENT IN COUNTY CRICKET? Ravi Bopara – very experienced and he once smacked me to all parts in a Second XI T20 game
MOST ECCENTRIC TEAMMATE? Ollie Robinson – he loves a dive!
WHAT WOULD YOU DO IF YOU WERE IN CHARGE OF COUNTY CRICKET? Get more games on TV, introduce a transfer window, allow more bumpers per over
STRANGEST THING YOU'VE DONE DURING LOCKDOWN? Dressing up in drag for a Zoom quiz
FAVOURITE SMELL? A BBQ
IF YOU WERE AN ANIMAL, WHICH WOULD IT BE? A leopard
GUILTY PLEASURE? Sweets
TWITTER: @nathgilchrist

Batting	Mat	Inns	NO	Runs	HS	Ave	SR	100	50	Ct	St
First-class	1	2	0	38	25	19.00	48.10	0	0	0	0
Bowling	**Mat**	**Balls**	**Runs**	**Wkts**	**BBI**	**BBM**	**Ave**	**Econ**	**SR**	**5w**	**10**
First-class	1	54	52	0	-	-	-	5.77	-	0	0

RICHARD GLEESON

RHB / RFM / R0 / W0

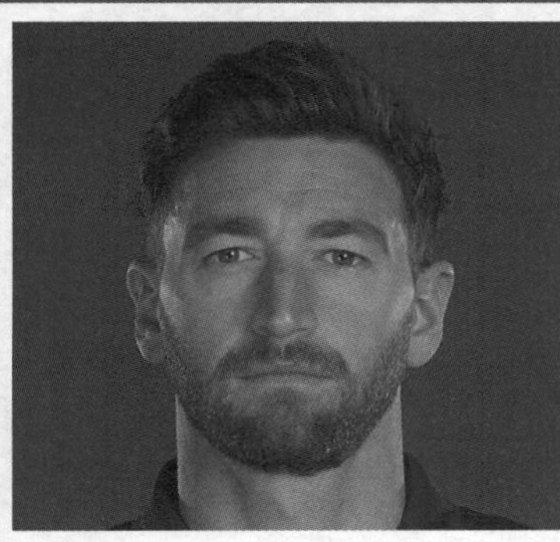

FULL NAME: Richard James Gleeson
BORN: December 2, 1987, Blackpool
SQUAD NO: 11
HEIGHT: 6ft 4in
NICKNAME: Granddaddy
EDUCATION: Baines High School, Lancashire; University of Cumbria
TEAMS: Lancashire, England Lions, Melbourne Renegades, Northamptonshire, Rangpur Riders
ROLE: Bowler
DEBUT: First-class: 2015; List A: 2016; T20: 2016

BEST BATTING: 31 Northamptonshire vs Gloucestershire, Bristol, 2016
BEST BOWLING: 6-43 Lancashire vs Leicestershire, Leicester, 2019

MOST EXCITING DAY AS A CRICKETER? Becoming a pro at the age of 28
FAMILY TIES? My father ran the bar at our local cricket club, my sister ran the kitchen, and my brother-in-law was the first XI captain
CHILDHOOD SPORTING HERO? Steven Gerrard
FIRST CRICKET CLUB? Blackpool CC, Lancashire
MOST INTERESTING TEAMMATE? Steven Crook
SURPRISING FACT ABOUT YOU? I am a published poet
TWITTER: @RicGleeson

Batting	Mat	Inns	NO	Runs	HS	Ave	SR	100	50	Ct	St
First-class	34	39	16	259	31	11.26	34.07	0	0	8	0
List A	21	13	5	53	13	6.62	42.06	0	0	3	0
T20s	50	11	6	24	7*	4.80	85.71	0	0	10	0
Bowling	**Mat**	**Balls**	**Runs**	**Wkts**	**BBI**	**BBM**	**Ave**	**Econ**	**SR**	**5w**	**10**
First-class	34	5526	3053	143	6/43	10/113	21.34	3.31	38.6	10	1
List A	21	841	816	28	5/47	5/47	29.14	5.82	30.0	1	0
T20s	50	984	1288	50	3/12	3/12	25.76	7.85	19.6	0	0

BRANDON GLOVER RHB / RFM / R0 / W0

FULL NAME: Brandon Dale Glover
BORN: April 3, 1997, Johannesburg, SA
SQUAD NO: 20
HEIGHT: 6ft 2in
NICKNAME: The Camel
EDUCATION: St Stithians College, Johannesburg; Stellenbosch University, Western Province
TEAMS: Netherlands, Northamptonshire, Boland, South Africa U19
ROLE: Bowler
DEBUT: ODI: 2019; T20I: 2019; First-class: 2016; List A: 2017; T20: 2019

BEST BATTING: 12* Boland vs Gauteng, Paarl, 2019
BEST BOWLING: 4-83 Boland vs Free State, Bloemfontein, 2017

MOST EXCITING DAY AS A CRICKETER? Winning the ICC World T20 Qualifier with Netherlands in 2019 and being named Player of the Match in the final game
CHILDHOOD SPORTING HERO? Dale Steyn
BIGGEST INFLUENCE ON YOUR DEVELOPMENT AS A CRICKETER (EXCLUDING PARENTS)? Along with my school coaches, simply watching Brett Lee and Dale Steyn made me want to break down their bowling actions and try to copy them myself
FIRST CRICKET CLUB? Old Parks Sports Club, Johannesburg
IF YOU COULD TAKE ONE COUNTY CRICKETER'S BEST SHOT AND ADD IT TO YOUR OWN GAME? Adam Rossington's pull
TOUGHEST OPPONENT IN COUNTY CRICKET? Craig Overton
FAVOURITE SMELL? Popcorn

Batting	Mat	Inns	NO	Runs	HS	Ave	SR	100	50	Ct	St
ODIs	1	-	-	-	-	-	-	-	-	1	0
T20Is	19	4	3	2	1*	2.00	25.00	0	0	3	0
First-class	10	15	6	38	12*	4.22	30.64	0	0	1	0
List A	6	5	2	55	27	18.33	67.90	0	0	1	0
T20s	25	5	4	2	1*	2.00	22.22	0	0	6	0
Bowling	**Mat**	**Balls**	**Runs**	**Wkts**	**BBI**	**BBM**	**Ave**	**Econ**	**SR**	**5w**	**10**
ODIs	1	60	37	1	1/37	1/37	37.00	3.70	60.0	0	0
T20Is	19	390	448	28	4/12	4/12	16.00	6.89	13.9	0	0
First-class	10	1320	827	24	4/83	5/104	34.45	3.75	55.0	0	0
List A	6	236	198	4	2/60	2/60	49.50	5.03	59.0	0	0
T20s	25	492	603	35	4/12	4/12	17.22	7.35	14.0	0	0

BILLY GODLEMAN LHB / LB / R2 / W0

FULL NAME: Billy Ashley Godleman
BORN: February 11, 1989, Camden, London
SQUAD NO: 1
HEIGHT: 6ft 2in
NICKNAME: Chief
EDUCATION: Islington Green School, London
TEAMS: Derbyshire, Essex, Middlesex
ROLE: Batsman
DEBUT: First-class: 2005; List A: 2007; T20: 2006

BEST BATTING: 227 Derbyshire vs Glamorgan, Swansea, 2019

COUNTY CAP: 2015 (Derbyshire)

MOST EXCITING DAY AS A CRICKETER? T20 Finals Day in 2008
BIGGEST INFLUENCE ON YOUR DEVELOPMENT AS A CRICKETER (EXCLUDING PARENTS)? David Houghton (Derbyshire head coach). I've had the great fortune of crossing paths with Houghts at different stages of my career. At every point, both as a cricketer and a person, he has helped me to learn and improve more than anyone. The wisest cricket brain. The rare skill of keeping things simple. Always keeps cricket in perspective and a great sense of humour
FIRST CRICKET CLUB? Brondesbury CC, London
IF YOU COULD TAKE ONE COUNTY CRICKETER'S BEST SHOT AND ADD IT TO YOUR OWN GAME? Wayne Madsen – all sweeps!
TOUGHEST OPPONENT IN COUNTY CRICKET? Steve Kirby – he was a top bowler and hard competitor
WHAT WOULD YOU DO IF YOU WERE IN CHARGE OF COUNTY CRICKET? Play more Championship cricket in June, July and August
STRANGEST THING YOU'VE DONE DURING LOCKDOWN? Self-isolation!
GUILTY PLEASURE? Fry-ups

Batting	Mat	Inns	NO	Runs	HS	Ave	SR	100	50	Ct	St
First-class	163	293	13	9029	227	32.24	47.06	21	41	100	0
List A	69	67	8	2559	137	43.37	78.47	6	12	23	0
T20s	88	82	7	1820	92	24.26	116.14	0	12	38	0
Bowling	**Mat**	**Balls**	**Runs**	**Wkts**	**BBI**	**BBM**	**Ave**	**Econ**	**SR**	**5w**	**10**
First-class	163	30	35	0	-	-	-	7.00	-	0	0
List A	69	-	-	-	-	-	-	-	-	-	-
T20s	88	-	-	-	-	-	-	-	-	-	-

LEWIS GOLDSWORTHY RHB / SLA / R0 / W0

FULL NAME: Lewis Peter Goldsworthy
BORN: January 8, 2001, Cornwall
SQUAD NO: 44
HEIGHT: 5ft 7in
NICKNAME: Golders
EDUCATION: Cambourne Science & International Academy, Cornwall; Millfield School, Street, Somerset
TEAMS: Somerset, England U19
ROLE: Allrounder
DEBUT: T20: 2020

MOST EXCITING DAY AS A CRICKETER? Making my debut for Somerset during last summer's T20 Blast
CHILDHOOD SPORTING HERO? Wayne Rooney
FIRST CRICKET CLUB? Troon CC, Cornwall
TWITTER: @lewisgoldsworthy
NOTES: The left-arm spinner and middle-order batsman signed his first professional contract with Somerset in September 2019 and looked at ease on his T20 debut last summer, scoring a breezy 38 not out in a stand of 110 with Babar Azam and taking 2-24 from four overs in the victory over Glamorgan at Cardiff. Born and raised in Cornwall, Goldsworthy has been playing Minor Counties since 2017 and scored 178 for Somerset U17 against Surrey U17 three years ago. Impressive performances for the club's Second XI led to a call-up to the England U19 squad last year and he was the team's joint-leading wicket-taker in South Africa during last year's World Cup, taking 12 wickets at 9.58 with an economy rate of just 2.34

Batting	Mat	Inns	NO	Runs	HS	Ave	SR	100	50	Ct	St
T20s	3	1	1	38	38*	-	131.03	0	0	1	0
Bowling	**Mat**	**Balls**	**Runs**	**Wkts**	**BBI**	**BBM**	**Ave**	**Econ**	**SR**	**5w**	**10**
T20s	3	66	86	5	2/21	2/21	17.20	7.81	13.2	0	0

DOMINIC GOODMAN RHB / RFM / R0 / W0

FULL NAME: Dominic Charles Goodman
BORN: October 23, 2000, Ashford, Kent
SQUAD NO: TBC
HEIGHT: 6ft 5in
NICKNAME: Len
EDUCATION: Dr Challenor's Grammar School, Amersham, Buckinghamshire; University of Exeter
TEAMS: Gloucestershire
ROLE: Allrounder

MOST EXCITING DAY AS A CRICKETER? Being 12th man when Gloucestershire pulled off a fourth-day victory at Derby
CHILDHOOD SPORTING HERO? Andrew Flintoff
BIGGEST INFLUENCE ON YOUR DEVELOPMENT AS A CRICKETER (EXCLUDING PARENTS)? Tim Hancock – he brought me through the Gloucestershire Academy
IF YOU COULD TAKE ONE COUNTY CRICKETER'S BEST SHOT AND ADD IT TO YOUR OWN GAME? Miles Hammond's switch-hit
TOUGHEST OPPONENT IN COUNTY CRICKET? Jofra Archer in a Second XI game – I hadn't faced a bowler of that pace until then
MOST ECCENTRIC TEAMMATE? Tom Price – he's always shadow-batting or practising his golf swing
WHAT WOULD YOU DO IF YOU WERE IN CHARGE OF COUNTY CRICKET? Introduce day/night Championship fixtures at the beginning and end of the season, free entry for children to T20 Blast games
WHAT WOULD YOU DO IF YOU WERE PRIME MINISTER? Get more lanes on the M25, subsidise independent cafes across the UK
STRANGEST THING YOU'VE DONE DURING LOCKDOWN? Mixing pesto with scrambled eggs
FAVOURITE SMELL? A flat white early in the morning
GUILTY PLEASURE? Pringles
TWITTER: @dominic_goodman

BEN GREEN — RHB / RFM / R0 / W0

FULL NAME: Benjamin George Frederick Green
BORN: September 28, 1997, Exeter, Devon
SQUAD NO: 54
HEIGHT: 6ft 2in
NICKNAME: Neil
EDUCATION: St Peter's Preparatory School, Lympstone, Devon; Exeter School
TEAMS: Somerset, England U19
ROLE: Allrounder
DEBUT: First-class: 2018; List A: 2018; T20: 2016

BEST BATTING: 54 Somerset vs Glamorgan, Taunton, 2020
BEST BOWLING: 1-8 Somerset vs Hampshire, Southampton, 2018

MOST EXCITING DAY AS A CRICKETER? Playing in the Bob Willis Trophy final at Lord's last summer
CHILDHOOD SPORTING HERO? Jonny Wilkinson
FIRST CRICKET CLUB? Clyst St George CC, East Devon
IF YOU COULD TAKE ONE COUNTY CRICKETER'S BEST SHOT AND ADD IT TO YOUR OWN GAME? Tom Abell's cover-drive
TOUGHEST OPPONENT IN COUNTY CRICKET? The combination of Kyle Abbott and Dale Steyn on a green pitch at the Ageas Bowl. It was only my second game!
WHAT WOULD YOU DO IF YOU WERE IN CHARGE OF COUNTY CRICKET? Start up mental-health sessions for current players who may have struggled through the pandemic
FAVOURITE SMELL? A bonfire
TWITTER: @Ben_Green28

Batting	Mat	Inns	NO	Runs	HS	Ave	SR	100	50	Ct	St
First-class	5	9	0	170	54	18.88	38.20	0	1	3	0
List A	3	3	2	35	26*	35.00	79.54	0	0	0	0
T20s	4	3	1	36	14	18.00	120.00	0	0	2	0
Bowling	**Mat**	**Balls**	**Runs**	**Wkts**	**BBI**	**BBM**	**Ave**	**Econ**	**SR**	**5w**	**10**
First-class	5	42	17	1	1/8	1/17	17.00	2.42	42.0	0	0
List A	3	66	70	1	1/52	1/52	70.00	6.36	66.0	0	0
T20s	4	54	89	4	4/26	4/26	22.25	9.88	13.5	0	0

LEWIS GREGORY RHB / RFM / R0 / W1 / MVP11

FULL NAME: Lewis Gregory
BORN: May 24, 1992, Plymouth, Devon
SQUAD NO: 24
HEIGHT: 6ft
NICKNAME: Mowgli
EDUCATION: Hele's School, Plymouth
TEAMS: England, Somerset, Brisbane Heat, Islamabad United, Peshawar Zalmi, Rangpur Rangers
ROLE: Allrounder
DEBUT: T20I: 2019; First-class: 2011; List A: 2010; T20: 2011

BEST BATTING: 137 Somerset vs Middlesex, Lord's, 2017
BEST BOWLING: 6-32 Somerset vs Kent, Canterbury, 2019
COUNTY CAP: 2015

MOST EXCITING DAY AS A CRICKETER? Taking my maiden first-class five-wicket haul at Lord's and scoring my maiden first-class hundred at the same ground
CHILDHOOD SPORTING HERO? Tiger Woods
TOUGHEST OPPONENT IN COUNTY CRICKET? Jeetan Patel
SURPRISING FACT ABOUT YOU? I'm a black belt in taekwondo
TWITTER: @Lewisgregory23

Batting	Mat	Inns	NO	Runs	HS	Ave	SR	100	50	Ct	St
T20Is	8	6	1	35	15	7.00	116.66	0	0	0	0
First-class	89	132	13	2569	137	21.58	57.88	2	8	49	0
List A	76	57	6	1206	105*	23.64	100.83	1	7	27	0
T20s	129	101	25	1690	76*	22.23	145.43	0	5	57	0
Bowling	**Mat**	**Balls**	**Runs**	**Wkts**	**BBI**	**BBM**	**Ave**	**Econ**	**SR**	**5w**	**10**
T20Is	8	66	92	1	1/10	1/10	92.00	8.36	66.0	0	0
First-class	89	13028	7100	282	6/32	11/53	25.17	3.26	46.1	14	2
List A	76	2948	2941	106	4/23	4/23	27.74	5.98	27.8	0	0
T20s	129	2131	3170	118	4/15	4/15	26.86	8.92	18.0	0	0

GAVIN GRIFFITHS RHB / RFM / R0 / W0

FULL NAME: Gavin Timothy Griffiths
BORN: November 19, 1993, Ormskirk, Lancashire
SQUAD NO: 93
HEIGHT: 6ft 2in
NICKNAME: Gavlar
EDUCATION: St Michael's CE High School, Chorley; St Mary's College, Crosby
TEAMS: Leicestershire, England U19, Hampshire, Lancashire
ROLE: Bowler
DEBUT: First-class: 2017; List A: 2014; T20: 2015

BEST BATTING: 40 Leicestershire vs Middlesex, Leicester, 2018
BEST BOWLING: 6-49 Leicestershire vs Durham, Chester-le-Street, 2018

MOST EXCITING DAY AS A CRICKETER? T20 Finals Day in 2015 when I was at Lancashire
CHILDHOOD SPORTING HERO? Wayne Rooney
BIGGEST INFLUENCE ON YOUR DEVELOPMENT AS A CRICKETER (EXCLUDING PARENTS)? John Stanworth, Lancashire Academy director
FIRST CRICKET CLUB? Ormskirk CC, Lancashire
IF YOU COULD TAKE ONE COUNTY CRICKETER'S BEST SHOT AND ADD IT TO YOUR OWN GAME? Colin Ackermann's sweep
TOUGHEST OPPONENT IN COUNTY CRICKET? James Pattinson – great presence
WHAT WOULD YOU DO IF YOU WERE IN CHARGE OF COUNTY CRICKET? Introduce a 10-day break in the middle of the season
SURPRISING FACT ABOUT YOU? I have played chess for England
GUILTY PLEASURE? Singing in the car
TWITTER: @Gavvlar

Batting	Mat	Inns	NO	Runs	HS	Ave	SR	100	50	Ct	St
First-class	26	36	13	326	40	14.17	34.13	0	0	4	0
List A	22	10	8	29	15*	14.50	37.66	0	0	11	0
T20s	47	15	14	41	11	41.00	78.84	0	0	9	0
Bowling	**Mat**	**Balls**	**Runs**	**Wkts**	**BBI**	**BBM**	**Ave**	**Econ**	**SR**	**5w**	**10**
First-class	26	3589	1936	60	6/49	10/83	32.26	3.23	59.8	1	1
List A	22	976	978	29	4/30	4/30	33.72	6.01	33.6	0	0
T20s	47	760	1051	39	4/35	4/35	26.94	8.29	19.4	0	0

TIM GROENEWALD RHB / RFM / R0 / W0

FULL NAME: Timothy Duncan Groenewald
BORN: January 10, 1984, Pietermaritzburg, South Africa
SQUAD NO: 12
HEIGHT: 6ft
NICKNAME: Timmy G
EDUCATION: Maritzburg College; University of South Africa
TEAMS: Kent, Derbyshire, Somerset, Warwickshire
ROLE: Bowler
DEBUT: First-class: 2006; List A: 2006; T20: 2006

KENT

BEST BATTING: 78 Warwickshire vs Bangladesh A, Edgbaston, 2008
BEST BOWLING: 6-50 Derbyshire vs Surrey, Whitgift School, 2009
COUNTY CAP: 2011 (Derbyshire); 2016 (Somerset)

CHILDHOOD SPORTING HERO? Hansie Cronje
BIGGEST INFLUENCE ON YOUR DEVELOPMENT AS A CRICKETER (EXCLUDING PARENTS)? Chris Rogers – he was my captain at Derbyshire and then at Somerset and he helped me understand how to get the best out of myself
FIRST CRICKET CLUB? Sutton Coldfield CC, Birmingham
IF YOU COULD TAKE ONE COUNTY CRICKETER'S BEST SHOT AND ADD IT TO YOUR OWN GAME? Zak Crawley's hook
TOUGHEST OPPONENT IN COUNTY CRICKET? Mark Ramprakash – saw him get a few hundreds early in my career. Just so mentally tough
WHAT WOULD YOU DO IF YOU WERE IN CHARGE OF COUNTY CRICKET? Bring back a two-division Championship, bring back the 40-over format, move T20 Finals Day to Lord's or The Oval
STRANGEST THING YOU'VE DONE DURING LOCKDOWN? Surviving without coffee shops
GUILTY PLEASURE? Chocolate and bread, though not together
TWITTER: @timmyg12

Batting	Mat	Inns	NO	Runs	HS	Ave	SR	100	50	Ct	St
First-class	139	200	66	2375	78	17.72	50.52	0	6	45	0
List A	109	64	24	793	57	19.82	111.37	0	2	26	0
T20s	114	48	20	401	41	14.32	124.53	0	0	29	0
Bowling	**Mat**	**Balls**	**Runs**	**Wkts**	**BBI**	**BBM**	**Ave**	**Econ**	**SR**	**5w**	**10**
First-class	139	23179	11904	403	6/50	9/136	29.53	3.08	57.5	16	0
List A	109	4321	4051	123	4/22	4/22	32.93	5.62	35.1	0	0
T20s	114	2065	2829	99	4/21	4/21	28.57	8.21	20.8	0	0

NICK GUBBINS

LHB / LB / R1 / W0

MIDDLESEX

FULL NAME: Nicholas Richard Trail Gubbins
BORN: December 31, 1993, Richmond, Surrey
SQUAD NO: 18
HEIGHT: 6ft
NICKNAME: Cathy
EDUCATION: Radley College, Oxfordshire; University of Leeds
TEAMS: Middlesex, England Lions
ROLE: Batsman
DEBUT: First-class: 2013; List A: 2014; T20: 2015

BEST BATTING: 201* Middlesex vs Lancashire, Lord's, 2016

COUNTY CAP: 2016

MOST EXCITING DAY AS A CRICKETER? Winning the Championship on the last day of the 2016 season
FAMILY TIES? My dad played one ODI for Singapore
CHILDHOOD SPORTING HERO? Marcus Trescothick
BIGGEST INFLUENCE ON YOUR DEVELOPMENT AS A CRICKETER (EXCLUDING PARENTS)? Andy Wagner, my coach when I was at school
FIRST CRICKET CLUB? Stirlands CC, Chichester, West Sussex
IF YOU COULD TAKE ONE COUNTY CRICKETER'S BEST SHOT AND ADD IT TO YOUR OWN GAME? Jos Buttler's ramp
TOUGHEST OPPONENT IN COUNTY CRICKET? Fidel Edwards – he had me on toast for breakfast
WHAT WOULD YOU DO IF YOU WERE IN CHARGE OF COUNTY CRICKET? Encourage better pitches, fewer teams and more time between games
GUILTY PLEASURE? Oreo ice cream
TWITTER: @ngubbins18

Batting	Mat	Inns	NO	Runs	HS	Ave	SR	100	50	Ct	St
First-class	77	137	2	4534	201*	33.58	48.93	8	27	29	0
List A	56	55	2	2067	141	39.00	94.12	5	12	11	0
T20s	37	34	0	566	75	16.64	123.31	0	2	15	0
Bowling	**Mat**	**Balls**	**Runs**	**Wkts**	**BBI**	**BBM**	**Ave**	**Econ**	**SR**	**5w**	**10**
First-class	77	75	54	0	-	-	-	4.32	-	0	0
List A	56	-	-	-	-	-	-	-	-	-	-
T20s	37	6	8	0	-	-	-	8.00	-	0	0

BROOKE GUEST

RHB / WK / R0 / W0

FULL NAME: Brooke David Guest
BORN: May 14, 1997, Whitworth Park, Manchester
SQUAD NO: 29
HEIGHT: 5ft 11in
NICKNAME: Guesty
EDUCATION: Kent Street Senior High School, Perth; Murdoch University, Perth
TEAMS: Derbyshire, Australia U19, Lancashire
ROLE: Wicketkeeper
DEBUT: First-class: 2018; List A: 2019; T20: 2020

BEST BATTING: 17 Lancashire vs Middlesex, Lord's, 2019

MOST EXCITING DAY AS A CRICKETER? Playing at Lord's
CHILDHOOD SPORTING HERO? Adam Gilchrist
BIGGEST INFLUENCE ON YOUR DEVELOPMENT AS A CRICKETER (EXCLUDING PARENTS)? Wayne Andrews was my first batting coach and he helped through junior cricket at Western Australia
FIRST CRICKET CLUB? South Perth CC, Australia
IF YOU COULD TAKE ONE COUNTY CRICKETER'S BEST SHOT AND ADD IT TO YOUR OWN GAME? Jos Buttler's ramp
STRANGEST THING YOU'VE DONE DURING LOCKDOWN? Cutting my own hair
GUILTY PLEASURE? Chocolate

Batting	Mat	Inns	NO	Runs	HS	Ave	SR	100	50	Ct	St
First-class	3	4	0	36	17	9.00	33.64	0	0	5	0
List A	2	2	0	41	36	20.50	78.84	0	0	0	1
T20s	4	3	3	36	22*	-	133.33	0	0	3	0
Bowling	**Mat**	**Balls**	**Runs**	**Wkts**	**BBI**	**BBM**	**Ave**	**Econ**	**SR**	**5w**	**10**
First-class	3	-	-	-	-	-	-	-	-	-	-
List A	2	-	-	-	-	-	-	-	-	-	-
T20s	4	-	-	-	-	-	-	-	-	-	-

HARRY GURNEY

RHB / LFM

FULL NAME: Harry Frederick Gurney
BORN: October 20, 1986, Nottingham
SQUAD NO: 11
HEIGHT: 6ft 2in
NICKNAME: Gramps
EDUCATION: Loughborough Grammar School; University of Leeds
TEAMS: England, Nottinghamshire, Kolkata Knight Riders, Leicestershire, Melbourne Renegades
ROLE: Bowler
DEBUT: ODI: 2014; T20I: 2014; First-class: 2007; List A: 2009; T20: 2009

BEST BATTING: 6 Nottinghamshire vs Somerset, Taunton, 2018 (T20)
BEST BOWLING: 5-30 Nottinghamshire vs Derbyshire, Derby, 2019 (T20)
COUNTY CAP: 2014 (Nottinghamshire)

MOST EXCITING DAY AS A CRICKETER? The T20I between England and India at Edgbaston in 2014
BIGGEST INFLUENCE ON YOUR DEVELOPMENT AS A CRICKETER (EXCLUDING PARENTS)? Mick Newell (former Notts coach and now director of cricket) – he backed me after signing me from Leicestershire as an unknown
FIRST CRICKET CLUB? Loughborough Town CC, Leicestershire
TOUGHEST OPPONENT IN COUNTY CRICKET? Mark Ramprakash
WHAT WOULD YOU DO IF YOU WERE IN CHARGE OF COUNTY CRICKET? Abolish the toss – away captains choose to bat or bowl
FAVOURITE SMELL? A new book
TWITTER: @gurneyhf
NOTES: Last November Gurney signed a one-year contract with Nottinghamshire to play white-ball cricket

Batting	Mat	Inns	NO	Runs	HS	Ave	SR	100	50	Ct	St
ODIs	10	6	4	15	6*	7.50	45.45	0	0	1	0
T20Is	2	-	-	-	-	-	-	-	-	0	0
First-class	103	131	63	424	42*	6.23	40.57	0	0	12	0
List A	93	29	18	61	13*	5.54	50.00	0	0	7	0
T20s	156	25	18	27	6	3.85	79.41	0	0	18	0
Bowling	**Mat**	**Balls**	**Runs**	**Wkts**	**BBI**	**BBM**	**Ave**	**Econ**	**SR**	**5w**	**10**
ODIs	10	455	432	11	4/55	4/55	39.27	5.69	41.3	0	0
T20Is	2	48	55	3	2/26	2/26	18.33	6.87	16.0	0	0
First-class	103	16909	9472	310	6/25	9/136	30.55	3.36	54.5	8	0
List A	93	3934	3870	114	5/24	5/24	33.94	5.90	34.5	3	0
T20s	156	3281	4291	190	5/30	5/30	22.58	7.84	17.2	1	0

SAM HAIN RHB / RM / R0 / W0 / MVP62

FULL NAME: Samuel Robert Hain
BORN: July 16, 1995, Hong Kong
SQUAD NO: 16
HEIGHT: 6ft
NICKNAME: Ched
EDUCATION: The Southport School, Queensland, Australia
TEAMS: Warwickshire, Australia U19, England Lions
ROLE: Batsman
DEBUT: First-class: 2014; List A: 2013; T20: 2016

BEST BATTING: 208 Warwickshire vs Northamptonshire, Edgbaston, 2014

COUNTY CAP: 2018

MOST EXCITING DAY AS A CRICKETER? Winning the One-Day Cup in 2016
CHILDHOOD SPORTING HERO? Bryson DeChambeau
IF YOU COULD TAKE ONE COUNTY CRICKETER'S BEST SHOT AND ADD IT TO YOUR OWN GAME? Oliver Hannon-Dalby's shots out of the bunker – unmatched
MOST ECCENTRIC TEAMMATE? Adam Hose
STRANGEST THING YOU'VE DONE DURING LOCKDOWN? Getting a dog
TWITTER: @Sammiehain

Batting	Mat	Inns	NO	Runs	HS	Ave	SR	100	50	Ct	St
First-class	80	125	12	4043	208	35.77	46.31	10	21	69	0
List A	58	56	9	2810	161*	59.78	86.46	10	15	22	0
T20s	66	64	10	1976	95	36.59	126.34	0	13	38	0
Bowling	**Mat**	**Balls**	**Runs**	**Wkts**	**BBI**	**BBM**	**Ave**	**Econ**	**SR**	**5w**	**10**
First-class	80	42	31	0	-	-	-	4.42	-	0	0
List A	58	-	-	-	-	-	-	-	-	-	-
T20s	66	-	-	-	-	-	-	-	-	-	-

TOM HAINES

LHB / RM / R0 / W0

SUSSEX

FULL NAME: Thomas Jacob Haines
BORN: October 28, 1998, Crawley, West Sussex
SQUAD NO: 20
HEIGHT: 5ft 11in
NICKNAME: Hainus
EDUCATION: Tanbridge House School, Horsham; Hurstpierpoint College, West Sussex
TEAMS: Sussex
ROLE: Batsman
DEBUT: First-class: 2016

BEST BATTING: 124 Sussex vs Durham, Arundel, 2018
BEST BOWLING: 1-9 Sussex vs Durham, Chester-le-Street, 2019

CHILDHOOD SPORTING HERO? Marcus Trescothick
BIGGEST INFLUENCE ON YOUR DEVELOPMENT AS A CRICKETER (EXCLUDING PARENTS)? Former Sussex batsman Jeremy Heath. He coached me from the age of 10 and I still speak to him now
FIRST CRICKET CLUB? Brockham Green CC, Surrey
IF YOU COULD TAKE ONE COUNTY CRICKETER'S BEST SHOT AND ADD IT TO YOUR OWN GAME? Marcus Trescothick's cover-drive
TOUGHEST OPPONENT IN COUNTY CRICKET? Darren Stevens – a genius
MOST ECCENTRIC TEAMMATE? Phil Salt – a nutter
BIGGEST CRICKETING REGRET? Not bowling leggies
WHAT WOULD YOU DO IF YOU WERE IN CHARGE OF COUNTY CRICKET? Push for matches on free-to-air TV
WHAT WOULD YOU DO IF YOU WERE PRIME MINISTER? Hand in my resignation
STRANGEST THING YOU'VE DONE DURING LOCKDOWN? Selling takeaway beer at a pub
FAVOURITE SMELL? Freshly cut grass
IF YOU WERE AN ANIMAL, WHICH WOULD IT BE? A sloth
GUILTY PLEASURE? Jaffa Cakes
TWITTER: @tomhaines

Batting	Mat	Inns	NO	Runs	HS	Ave	SR	100	50	Ct	St
First-class	21	35	1	832	124	24.47	48.91	2	2	6	0
Bowling	**Mat**	**Balls**	**Runs**	**Wkts**	**BBI**	**BBM**	**Ave**	**Econ**	**SR**	**5w**	**10**
First-class	21	804	366	9	1/9	2/73	40.66	2.73	89.3	0	0

ALEX HALES

RHB / RM

FULL NAME: Alexander Daniel Hales
BORN: January 3, 1989, Hillingdon, London
SQUAD NO: 10
HEIGHT: 6ft 5in
EDUCATION: Chesham High School, Buckinghamshire
TEAMS: England, Nottinghamshire, Adelaide Strikers, Hobart Hurricanes, Islamabad United, Melbourne Renegades, Sunrisers, Sydney Thunder, Worcestershire
ROLE: Batsman
DEBUT: Test: 2015; ODI: 2014; T20I: 2011; First-class: 2008; List A: 2008; T20: 2009

BEST BATTING: 116* England vs Sri Lanka, Chittagong, 2014 (T20)

COUNTY CAP: 2011 (Nottinghamshire)

FIRST CRICKET CLUB? Denham CC, Buckinghamshire. We lived in a bungalow on the cricket ground
CHILDHOOD SPORTING HERO? Dominic Cork
TWITTER: @AlexHales1
NOTES: Hales made his most recent first-class appearance back in 2017 and now plays white-ball cricket only. He was left unsold at the auction for this year's IPL but turned out for Sydney Thunder in the Big Bash over the winter

Batting	Mat	Inns	NO	Runs	HS	Ave	SR	100	50	Ct	St
Tests	11	21	0	573	94	27.28	43.84	0	5	8	0
ODIs	70	67	3	2419	171	37.79	95.72	6	14	27	0
T20Is	60	60	7	1644	116*	31.01	136.65	1	8	32	0
First-class	107	182	6	6655	236	37.81	59.06	13	38	84	0
List A	175	169	6	6260	187*	38.40	99.09	17	32	66	0
T20s	290	287	20	8066	116*	30.20	144.70	4	51	144	0
Bowling	**Mat**	**Balls**	**Runs**	**Wkts**	**BBI**	**BBM**	**Ave**	**Econ**	**SR**	**5w**	**10**
Tests	11	18	2	0	-	-	-	0.66	-	0	0
ODIs	70	-	-	-	-	-	-	-	-	-	-
T20Is	60	-	-	-	-	-	-	-	-	-	-
First-class	107	311	173	3	2/63	2/63	57.66	3.33	103.6	0	0
List A	175	4	10	0	-	-	-	15.00	-	0	0
T20s	290	3	7	0	-	-	-	14.00	-	0	0

HASEEB HAMEED RHB / LB / R1 / W0

FULL NAME: Haseeb Hameed
BORN: January 17, 1997, Bolton, Lancashire
SQUAD NO: 99
HEIGHT: 6ft
NICKNAME: Has
EDUCATION: Bolton School
TEAMS: England, Nottinghamshire, Lancashire
ROLE: Batsman
DEBUT: Test: 2016; First-class: 2015; List A: 2017

BEST BATTING: 122 Lancashire vs Nottinghamshire, Trent Bridge, 2015

COUNTY CAP: 2016 (Lancashire)

MOST EXCITING DAY AS A CRICKETER? Making my Test debut in 2016
CHILDHOOD SPORTING HERO? Sachin Tendulkar
BIGGEST INFLUENCE ON YOUR DEVELOPMENT AS A CRICKETER (EXCLUDING PARENTS)? John Stanworth at Lancashire
FIRST CRICKET CLUB? Tonge CC, Bolton, Greater Manchester
IF YOU COULD TAKE ONE COUNTY CRICKETER'S BEST SHOT AND ADD IT TO YOUR OWN GAME? Jos Buttler's ramp
TOUGHEST OPPONENT IN COUNTY CRICKET? Graham Onions
MOST ECCENTRIC TEAMMATE? Luke Fletcher – because he worked in Hooters
WHAT WOULD YOU DO IF YOU WERE PRIME MINISTER? Put an end to all road works
STRANGEST THING YOU'VE DONE DURING LOCKDOWN? Cooking a meal
GUILTY PLEASURE? Dandelion and Burdock (drink)
TWITTER: @HaseebHameed97

Batting	Mat	Inns	NO	Runs	HS	Ave	SR	100	50	Ct	St
Tests	3	6	1	219	82	43.80	34.21	0	2	4	0
First-class	68	113	11	3179	122	31.16	37.37	5	18	43	0
List A	19	19	3	556	88	34.75	78.08	0	4	3	0
Bowling	**Mat**	**Balls**	**Runs**	**Wkts**	**BBI**	**BBM**	**Ave**	**Econ**	**SR**	**5w**	**10**
Tests	3	-	-	-	-	-	-	-	-	-	-
First-class	68	42	21	0	-	-	-	3.00	-	0	0
List A	19	-	-	-	-	-	-	-	-	-	-

MILES HAMMOND

LHB / OB / R0 / W0

FULL NAME: Miles Arthur Halhead Hammond
BORN: January 11, 1996, Cheltenham, Gloucestershire
SQUAD NO: 88
HEIGHT: 6ft 1in
NICKNAME: Hammer
EDUCATION: St Edward's School, Oxford; University of the Arts London
TEAMS: Gloucestershire, England U19
ROLE: Batsman
DEBUT: First-class: 2013; List A: 2013; T20: 2013

BEST BATTING: 123* Gloucestershire vs Middlesex, Bristol, 2018
BEST BOWLING: 1-29 MCC vs Nepal, Kirtipur, 2019
COUNTY CAP: 2013

MOST EXCITING DAY AS A CRICKETER? Beating Yorkshire at Headingley on my Gloucestershire debut
FIRST CRICKET CLUB? Cumnor CC, Oxford
CHILDHOOD SPORTING HERO? Marcus Trescothick
WHAT WOULD YOU DO IF YOU WERE IN CHARGE OF COUNTY CRICKET? Change the lbw law: you can be out even if the ball pitches outside leg stump
BIGGEST CRICKETING REGRET? Choosing initially to bowl off-spin
SURPRISING FACT ABOUT YOU? I wear my house key around my neck
IF YOU WERE AN ANIMAL, WHICH WOULD IT BE? A poison dart frog
TWITTER: @hammo125

Batting	Mat	Inns	NO	Runs	HS	Ave	SR	100	50	Ct	St
First-class	27	46	3	1014	123*	23.58	42.25	2	5	23	0
List A	8	6	0	185	95	30.83	73.12	0	1	1	0
T20s	39	35	0	845	63	24.14	138.52	0	3	17	0
Bowling	**Mat**	**Balls**	**Runs**	**Wkts**	**BBI**	**BBM**	**Ave**	**Econ**	**SR**	**5w**	**10**
First-class	27	472	368	2	1/29	1/37	184.00	4.67	236.0	0	0
List A	8	114	97	5	2/18	2/18	19.40	5.10	22.8	0	0
T20s	39	12	17	0	-	-	-	8.50	-	0	0

PETER HANDSCOMB RHB / WK / R0 / W0

FULL NAME: Peter Stephen Patrick Handscomb
BORN: April 26, 1991, Melbourne, Australia
SQUAD NO: 29
HEIGHT: 6ft 4in
EDUCATION: Deakin University, Melbourne
TEAMS: Australia, Middlesex, Durham, Gloucestershire, Hobart Hurricanes, Melbourne Stars, Rising Pune Supergiant, Victoria, Yorkshire
ROLE: Batsman/wicketkeeper
DEBUT: Test: 2016; ODI: 2017; T20I: 2019; First-class: 2011; List A: 2011; T20: 2012

BEST BATTING: 215 Victoria vs New South Wales, Sydney, 2016

COUNTY CAP: 2015 (Gloucestershire)

TWITTER: @phandscomb54
NOTES: The Australian batsman-wicketkeeper signed for Middlesex on a two-year deal in November 2019 but could not join up with the club last year on account of the pandemic. He is due to captain the side in the County Championship and One-Day Cup this summer. Born to British parents but raised in Australia, Handscomb passed 50 in each of his first four Test matches, including two centuries, but hasn't played for Australia in any format since 2019. The Victorian captains his state side in the Sheffield Shield and played his first season with Hobart Hurricanes during the 2020/21 Big Bash after nine years at Melbourne Stars. He has had previous county stints with Gloucestershire (2015), Yorkshire (2017) and Durham (2018)

Batting	Mat	Inns	NO	Runs	HS	Ave	SR	100	50	Ct	St
Tests	16	29	5	934	110	38.91	49.83	2	4	28	0
ODIs	22	20	1	632	117	33.26	97.38	1	4	14	0
T20Is	2	2	1	33	20*	33.00	100.00	0	0	0	0
First-class	116	194	14	6924	215	38.46	53.72	15	41	188	4
List A	110	100	15	3306	140	38.89	89.91	3	21	101	5
T20s	97	86	21	1526	103*	23.47	119.12	1	5	49	13
Bowling	**Mat**	**Balls**	**Runs**	**Wkts**	**BBI**	**BBM**	**Ave**	**Econ**	**SR**	**5w**	**10**
Tests	16	-	-	-	-	-	-	-	-	-	-
ODIs	22	-	-	-	-	-	-	-	-	-	-
T20Is	2	-	-	-	-	-	-	-	-	-	-
First-class	116	66	79	0	-	-	-	7.18	-	0	0
List A	110	-	-	-	-	-	-	-	-	-	-
T20s	97	-	-	-	-	-	-	-	-	-	-

GEORGE HANKINS RHB / OB / R0 / W0

FULL NAME: George Thomas Hankins
BORN: January 4, 1997, Bath
SQUAD NO: 21
HEIGHT: 6ft 1in
NICKNAME: Hanks
EDUCATION: Kingswood School, Bath; Millfield School, Somerset
TEAMS: Gloucestershire, England U19
ROLE: Batsman
DEBUT: First-class: 2016; List A: 2017; T20: 2017

BEST BATTING: 116 Gloucestershire vs Northamptonshire, Northampton, 2016

COUNTY CAP: 2016

FAMILY TIES? I got into the game watching my uncle play club cricket on Saturdays. My younger brother Harry also plays for Gloucestershire
MOST EXCITING DAY AS A CRICKETER? Taking 7-9 against Clifton School in Year 8
FIRST CRICKET CLUB? Bath CC, Somerset
BEST INNINGS YOU'VE SEEN? Liam Norwell scoring a century as a nightwatchman in 2016 – amazing quality from a No.11
SURPRISING FACT ABOUT YOU? I have no earlobes
TWITTER: @hankins1997

Batting	Mat	Inns	NO	Runs	HS	Ave	SR	100	50	Ct	St
First-class	33	53	2	1091	116	21.39	48.83	1	7	36	0
List A	15	15	1	535	92	38.21	73.28	0	5	11	0
T20s	8	4	0	24	14	6.00	61.53	0	0	1	0
Bowling	**Mat**	**Balls**	**Runs**	**Wkts**	**BBI**	**BBM**	**Ave**	**Econ**	**SR**	**5w**	**10**
First-class	33	13	13	0	-	-	-	6.00	-	0	0
List A	15	-	-	-	-	-	-	-	-	-	-
T20s	8	-	-	-	-	-	-	-	-	-	-

HARRY HANKINS

RHB / RMF / R0 / W0

FULL NAME: Harry John Hankins
BORN: April 24, 1999, Bath, Somerset
SQUAD NO: TBC
EDUCATION: Beechen Cliff School, Bath
TEAMS: Gloucestershire
ROLE: Bowler
DEBUT: First-class: 2019

BEST BATTING: 9 Gloucestershire vs Derbyshire, Bristol, 2019

TWITTER: @hanks_99
NOTES: A right-arm seamer who has come through the Gloucestershire Academy, Hankins is the young brother of county teammate George. He made his first appearance for Gloucestershire in the club's U17 side in 2016 and quickly moved up the ranks, making his Second XI debut the following season, when he was also Bath CC's Young Player of the Year. Hankins was handed his senior county debut at the beginning of the 2019 season in the Championship match against Derbyshire at Bristol. He has not appeared in the first team since then, although he did play in a warm-up match against Somerset at Taunton last season and dismissed Roelof van der Merwe, caught by his brother George. Hankins, who turns 22 in April, was also able to get some cricket for Bath despite the ongoing pandemic, playing in the renamed West of England Covid League

Batting	Mat	Inns	NO	Runs	HS	Ave	SR	100	50	Ct	St
First-class	1	1	0	9	9	9.00	52.94	0	0	0	0
Bowling	**Mat**	**Balls**	**Runs**	**Wkts**	**BBI**	**BBM**	**Ave**	**Econ**	**SR**	**5w**	**10**
First-class	1	198	101	0	-	-	-	3.06	-	0	0

OLIVER HANNON-DALBY LHB / RFM / R0 / W0 / MVP58

FULL NAME: Oliver James Hannon-Dalby
BORN: June 20, 1989, Halifax, Yorkshire
SQUAD NO: 20
HEIGHT: 6ft 8in
NICKNAME: Owl Face
EDUCATION: Brooksbank School, West Yorkshire; Leeds Metropolitan University
TEAMS: Warwickshire, Yorkshire
ROLE: Bowler
DEBUT: First-class: 2008; List A: 2011; T20: 2012

BEST BATTING: 40 Warwickshire vs Somerset, Taunton, 2014
BEST BOWLING: 6-33 Warwickshire vs Gloucestershire, Bristol, 2020

MOST EXCITING DAY AS A CRICKETER? T20 Finals Day in 2014
CHILDHOOD SPORTING HERO? Alan Shearer
BIGGEST INFLUENCE ON YOUR DEVELOPMENT AS A CRICKETER (EXCLUDING PARENTS)? Fred Hemmingway, my first coach at Copley CC
FIRST CRICKET CLUB? Copley CC, West Yorkshire
TOUGHEST OPPONENT IN COUNTY CRICKET? Kumar Sangakkara – he toyed with me like a cat with a mouse
WHAT WOULD YOU DO IF YOU WERE IN CHARGE OF COUNTY CRICKET? All grounds to have Lord's-standard teas, compulsory pre-season tours to Barbados, do something to help the bowlers in white-ball cricket
WHAT WOULD YOU DO IF YOU WERE PRIME MINISTER? Arrest anyone who drove 200 miles to "test their eyes" during a lockdown, ban all trophy hunting, appoint my dog Toby as foreign secretary
STRANGEST THING YOU'VE DONE DURING LOCKDOWN? Building a rocking horse
FAVOURITE SMELL? The top of my dog's head
TWITTER: @OHD_20

Batting	Mat	Inns	NO	Runs	HS	Ave	SR	100	50	Ct	St
First-class	75	91	31	449	40	7.48	26.88	0	0	8	0
List A	43	15	9	91	21*	15.16	95.78	0	0	14	0
T20s	60	12	7	53	14*	10.60	96.36	0	0	12	0
Bowling	**Mat**	**Balls**	**Runs**	**Wkts**	**BBI**	**BBM**	**Ave**	**Econ**	**SR**	**5w**	**10**
First-class	75	11594	6107	200	6/33	12/110	30.53	3.16	57.9	7	1
List A	43	1978	2075	65	5/27	5/27	31.92	6.29	30.4	1	0
T20s	60	1252	1829	75	4/20	4/20	24.38	8.76	16.6	0	0

SIMON HARMER RHB / OB / R0 / W3 / MVP1

FULL NAME: Simon Ross Harmer
BORN: February 10, 1989, Pretoria, SA
SQUAD NO: 11
HEIGHT: 6ft 2in
NICKNAME: Big Red
EDUCATION: Pretoria Boys High School; Nelson Mandela Metropolitan University, Port Elizabeth
TEAMS: South Africa, Essex, Border, Eastern Province, Jozi Stars, Titans, Warriors
ROLE: Bowler
DEBUT: Test: 2015; First-class: 2009; List A: 2010; T20: 2011

BEST BATTING: 102* Essex vs Surrey, The Oval, 2018
BEST BOWLING: 9-95 Essex vs Middlesex, Chelmsford, 2017
COUNTY CAP: 2018

MOST EXCITING DAY AS A CRICKETER? Making my international debut for South Africa at Newlands
CHILDHOOD SPORTING HERO? Jacques Kallis
FIRST CRICKET CLUB? Pretoria High School Old Boys CC, South Africa
IF YOU COULD TAKE ONE COUNTY CRICKETER'S BEST SHOT AND ADD IT TO YOUR OWN GAME? Ryan ten Doeschate's pull
WHAT WOULD YOU DO IF YOU WERE IN CHARGE OF COUNTY CRICKET? Create a revenue-share model, like the one Cricket Australia implements, to commercialise the image rights of county players; make it mandatory that every county has a director of cricket to bridge the gap between the changeroom and the boardroom; allow overseas players who sign multi-year deals the choice of a tier-two or tier-five visa so they can have similar rights to their colleagues
TWITTER: @Simon_Harmer_

Batting	Mat	Inns	NO	Runs	HS	Ave	SR	100	50	Ct	St
Tests	5	6	1	58	13	11.60	33.33	0	0	1	0
First-class	151	227	44	4403	102*	24.06	49.25	2	22	150	0
List A	83	70	21	1002	44*	20.44	97.85	0	0	55	0
T20s	109	63	21	765	43	18.21	126.86	0	0	56	0
Bowling	**Mat**	**Balls**	**Runs**	**Wkts**	**BBI**	**BBM**	**Ave**	**Econ**	**SR**	**5w**	**10**
Tests	5	1148	588	20	4/61	7/153	29.40	3.07	57.4	0	0
First-class	151	36145	17508	646	9/95	14/128	27.10	2.90	55.9	37	7
List A	83	3858	3299	78	4/42	4/42	42.29	5.13	49.4	0	0
T20s	109	2011	2550	84	4/19	4/19	30.35	7.60	23.9	0	0

JAMES HARRIS

RHB / RMF / R0 / W3

FULL NAME: James Alexander Russell Harris
BORN: May 16, 1990, Morriston, Swansea
SQUAD NO: 5
HEIGHT: 6ft 1in
NICKNAME: Bones
EDUCATION: Pontarddulais Comprehensive School, Swansea; Gorseinon College, Swansea
TEAMS: Middlesex, England Lions, Glamorgan, Kent
ROLE: Bowler
DEBUT: First-class: 2007; List A: 2007; T20: 2008

BEST BATTING: 87* Glamorgan vs Nottinghamshire, Swansea, 2007
BEST BOWLING: 9-34 Middlesex vs Durham, Lord's, 2015
COUNTY CAP: 2010 (Glamorgan); 2015 (Middlesex)

MOST EXCITING DAY AS A CRICKETER? Toby Roland-Jones taking a hat-trick to win the 2016 County Championship
CHILDHOOD SPORTING HERO? Jacques Kallis
BIGGEST INFLUENCE ON YOUR DEVELOPMENT AS A CRICKETER (EXCLUDING PARENTS)? Glamorgan legend Alan Jones – he taught me the values of the game that have shaped me into the cricketer I am today
FIRST CRICKET CLUB? Pontarddulais CC, South Wales
IF YOU COULD TAKE ONE COUNTY CRICKETER'S BEST SHOT AND ADD IT TO YOUR OWN GAME? It's a toss-up between James Vince's cover-drive and Jos Buttler's ramp
TOUGHEST OPPONENT IN COUNTY CRICKET? Ravi Bopara
STRANGEST THING YOU'VE DONE DURING LOCKDOWN? Baking bread and making almond milk
GUILTY PLEASURE? An almond croissant
TWITTER: @James_Harris9

Batting	Mat	Inns	NO	Runs	HS	Ave	SR	100	50	Ct	St
First-class	148	216	51	3862	87*	23.40	-	0	18	42	0
List A	64	37	8	417	117	14.37	73.80	1	0	14	0
T20s	58	28	13	164	18	10.93	104.45	0	0	8	0
Bowling	**Mat**	**Balls**	**Runs**	**Wkts**	**BBI**	**BBM**	**Ave**	**Econ**	**SR**	**5w**	**10**
First-class	148	25613	14197	494	9/34	13/103	28.73	3.32	51.8	15	2
List A	64	2726	2648	88	4/38	4/38	30.09	5.82	30.9	0	0
T20s	58	1030	1594	48	4/23	4/23	33.20	9.28	21.4	0	0

MARCUS HARRIS

LHB / OB / R0 / W0

FULL NAME: Marcus Sinclair Harris
BORN: July 21, 1992, Perth, Australia
SQUAD NO: 4
TEAMS: Australia, Leicestershire, Melbourne Renegades, Perth Scorchers, Victoria, Western Australia
ROLE: Batsman
DEBUT: Test: 2018; First-class: 2011; List A: 2011; T20: 2014

BEST BATTING: 240* Victoria vs New South Wales, Melbourne, 2018

TWITTER: @MarcusHarris14

NOTES: Leicestershire have signed the Australian Test opener to play in the County Championship and the One-Day Cup this summer. The left-hander was a late overseas replacement for South African allrounder Wiaan Mulder, whose increasing international commitments led to the cancellation of his contract. Harris made waves in March 2011 when aged 18 he scored 157 for Western Australia in his third first-class match, but it was only after his move to Victoria five years later that he began to fulfil his talent. He made 1,515 runs at 56.11 in the 2018/19 Sheffield Shield, including a career-best 250 not out against New South Wales, and made his Test debut that season. Harris hasn't been able to nail down a spot in the Test team but was recalled for the 2020/21 series against India on the back of another strong domestic season in which he scored the second double hundred of his career. "Marcus is a high-class opening batsman and will add both quality and experience to the top of our batting order," said Paul Nixon, Leicestershire's head coach. "He will also add a high-class option to our 50-over side, which fits the bill with [club captain] Colin Ackermann winning selection for Manchester Originals in The Hundred"

Batting	Mat	Inns	NO	Runs	HS	Ave	SR	100	50	Ct	St
Tests	10	19	1	428	79	23.77	50.83	0	2	7	0
First-class	103	187	12	6733	250*	38.47	55.10	14	30	50	0
List A	45	44	2	1231	84	29.30	86.69	0	7	11	0
T20s	48	47	1	970	85	21.08	122.47	0	4	17	0
Bowling	**Mat**	**Balls**	**Runs**	**Wkts**	**BBI**	**BBM**	**Ave**	**Econ**	**SR**	**5w**	**10**
Tests	10	-	-	-	-	-	-	-	-	-	-
First-class	103	78	64	0	-	-	-	4.92	-	0	0
List A	45	-	-	-	-	-	-	-	-	-	-
T20s	48	-	-	-	-	-	-	-	-	-	-

TOM HARTLEY

RHB / SLA / R0 / W0

FULL NAME: Tom William Hartley
BORN: May 3, 1998, Ormskirk, Lancashire
SQUAD NO: 2
HEIGHT: 6ft 4in
NICKNAME: TDF
EDUCATION: Merchant Taylors' School, Crosby, Merseyside
TEAMS: Lancashire
ROLE: Bowler
DEBUT: First-class: 2020; T20: 2020

BEST BATTING: 13* Lancashire vs Nottinghamshire, Trent Bridge, 2020
BEST BOWLING: 3-79 Lancashire vs Derbyshire, Liverpool, 2020

MOST EXCITING DAY AS A CRICKETER? Last summer's T20 Finals Day
CHILDHOOD SPORTING HERO? Graeme Swann
BIGGEST INFLUENCE ON YOUR DEVELOPMENT AS A CRICKETER (EXCLUDING PARENTS)? My captain at Ormskirk CC – for giving me plenty of overs in my younger years
FIRST CRICKET CLUB? Ormskirk CC, Lancashire
IF YOU COULD TAKE ONE COUNTY CRICKETER'S BEST SHOT AND ADD IT TO YOUR OWN GAME? Keaton Jennings's reverse-sweep
TOUGHEST OPPONENT IN COUNTY CRICKET? Ben Slater
MOST ECCENTRIC TEAMMATE? George Balderson – he's from Stockport but puts on a posh-boy accent
WHAT WOULD YOU DO IF YOU WERE IN CHARGE OF COUNTY CRICKET? Bring in five-day matches, play more games at outgrounds, play more games against southern counties
STRANGEST THING YOU'VE DONE DURING LOCKDOWN? Allowing my sister to cut my hair
GUILTY PLEASURE? Chocolate Digestives
TWITTER: @tomhartley100

Batting	Mat	Inns	NO	Runs	HS	Ave	SR	100	50	Ct	St
First-class	4	4	3	35	13*	35.00	21.21	0	0	2	0
T20s	11	2	1	4	4	4.00	57.14	0	0	1	0
Bowling	**Mat**	**Balls**	**Runs**	**Wkts**	**BBI**	**BBM**	**Ave**	**Econ**	**SR**	**5w**	**10**
First-class	4	666	324	6	3/79	3/117	54.00	2.91	111.0	0	0
T20s	11	216	256	6	2/21	2/21	42.66	7.11	36.0	0	0

JACK HAYNES

RHB / OB / R0 / W0

WORCESTERSHIRE

FULL NAME: Jack Alexander Haynes
BORN: January 30, 2001, Worcester
SQUAD NO: 17
HEIGHT: 6ft 1in
NICKNAME: Clunesy
EDUCATION: Malvern College
TEAMS: Worcestershire, England U19
ROLE: Batsman
DEBUT: First-class: 2019; List A: 2018; T20: 2020

BEST BATTING: 51 Worcestershire vs Warwickshire, Worcester, 2020

MOST EXCITING DAY AS A CRICKETER? Making my first-class debut in 2019
FAMILY TIES? My father Gavin played more than 200 matches for Worcestershire in the 1990s and my older brother Josh plays for Leeds/Bradford MCCU
CHILDHOOD SPORTING HERO? Alastair Cook
FIRST CRICKET CLUB? Ombersley CC, Worcestershire
IF YOU COULD TAKE ONE COUNTY CRICKETER'S BEST SHOT AND ADD IT TO YOUR OWN GAME? Daryl Mitchell's shot off the hip
STRANGEST THING YOU'VE DONE DURING LOCKDOWN? Lots of shadow-batting
IF YOU WERE AN ANIMAL, WHICH WOULD IT BE? A racehorse
TWITTER: @jack_haynes1

Batting	Mat	Inns	NO	Runs	HS	Ave	SR	100	50	Ct	St
First-class	10	16	2	404	51	28.85	51.07	0	2	2	0
List A	1	1	0	33	33	33.00	86.84	0	0	1	0
T20s	7	7	0	149	41	21.28	137.96	0	0	2	0
Bowling	**Mat**	**Balls**	**Runs**	**Wkts**	**BBI**	**BBM**	**Ave**	**Econ**	**SR**	**5w**	**10**
First-class	10	-	-	-	-	-	-	-	-	-	-
List A	1	-	-	-	-	-	-	-	-	-	-
T20s	7	-	-	-	-	-	-	-	-	-	-

TRAVIS HEAD

LHB / OB / R0 / W0

FULL NAME: Travis Michael Head
BORN: December 29, 1993, Adelaide, Australia
SQUAD NO: 62
TEAMS: Australia, Sussex, Adelaide Strikers, Delhi Daredevils, Royal Challengers Bangalore, South Australia, Worcestershire, Yorkshire
ROLE: Batsman
DEBUT: Test: 2018; ODI: 2016; T20I: 2016; First-class: 2012; List A: 2013; T20: 2013

BEST BATTING: 233 South Australia vs Western Australia, Perth, 2021
BEST BOWLING: 3-42 South Australia vs New South Wales, Adelaide, 2015

TWITTER: @travishead34
NOTES: The Australian batsman initially signed for Sussex ahead of the 2020 season but had his contract deferred to this summer in the wake of the pandemic. He will be available across all formats throughout the season, subject to his international commitments. Head was named South Australia's youngest-ever captain in 2015 at the age of 21 and made his international limited-overs debuts in 2016, followed by his Test bow two years later. He has been in and out of the side since the 2019 Ashes but reconfirmed his long-format credentials by scoring a career-best 223 off 245 balls for his state side against Western Australia earlier this year. The 27-year-old had a previous stint with Worcestershire in 2018 and his part-time off-spin should come in handy for the Sharks in their T20 Blast campaign

Batting	Mat	Inns	NO	Runs	HS	Ave	SR	100	50	Ct	St
Tests	19	31	2	1153	161	39.75	49.65	2	7	12	0
ODIs	42	39	2	1273	128	34.40	90.02	1	10	12	0
T20Is	16	15	3	319	48*	26.58	130.20	0	0	4	0
First-class	114	206	12	7908	223	40.76	59.15	15	48	53	0
List A	96	92	4	3373	202	38.32	95.06	8	17	30	0
T20s	84	81	12	2106	101*	30.52	134.39	1	9	25	0
Bowling	**Mat**	**Balls**	**Runs**	**Wkts**	**BBI**	**BBM**	**Ave**	**Econ**	**SR**	**5w**	**10**
Tests	19	126	76	0	-	-	-	3.61	-	0	0
ODIs	42	765	737	12	2/22	2/22	61.41	5.78	63.7	0	0
T20Is	16	24	39	1	1/16	1/16	39.00	9.75	24.0	0	0
First-class	114	4960	3199	47	3/42	4/64	68.06	3.86	105.5	0	0
List A	96	1320	1315	22	2/9	2/9	59.77	5.97	60.0	0	0
T20s	84	415	589	22	3/16	3/16	26.77	8.51	18.8	0	0

TOM HELM

RHB / RFM / R0 / W0

FULL NAME: Thomas George Helm
BORN: May 7, 1994, Aylesbury, Buckinghamshire
SQUAD NO: 7
HEIGHT: 6ft 4in
NICKNAME: Cheddy
EDUCATION: The Misbourne School, Buckinghamshire
TEAMS: Middlesex, England Lions, Glamorgan
ROLE: Bowler
DEBUT: First-class: 2013; List A: 2013; T20: 2016

BEST BATTING: 52 Middlesex vs Derbyshire, Lord's, 2018
BEST BOWLING: 5-36 Middlesex vs Worcestershire, Worcester, 2019

MOST EXCITING DAY AS A CRICKETER? Signing my first professional contract
FAMILY TIES? My brother Sam played Minor Counties for Buckinghamshire
CHILDHOOD SPORTING HERO? Frank Lampard
FIRST CRICKET CLUB? Chesham CC, Buckinghamshire
IF YOU COULD TAKE ONE COUNTY CRICKETER'S BEST SHOT AND ADD IT TO YOUR OWN GAME? Tim Murtagh's pull
TOUGHEST OPPONENT IN COUNTY CRICKET? Kumar Sangakkara
MOST ECCENTRIC TEAMMATE? Sam Robson – he loves his goats
STRANGEST THING YOU'VE DONE DURING LOCKDOWN? University work
FAVOURITE SMELL? McDonald's
TWITTER: @tomhelm7

Batting	Mat	Inns	NO	Runs	HS	Ave	SR	100	50	Ct	St
First-class	30	41	8	559	52	16.93	47.05	0	1	9	0
List A	40	24	8	206	30	12.87	71.28	0	0	15	0
T20s	43	19	12	93	28*	13.28	106.89	0	0	4	0
Bowling	**Mat**	**Balls**	**Runs**	**Wkts**	**BBI**	**BBM**	**Ave**	**Econ**	**SR**	**5w**	**10**
First-class	30	4437	2359	79	5/36	7/140	29.86	3.18	56.1	3	0
List A	40	1816	1742	56	5/33	5/33	31.10	5.75	32.4	2	0
T20s	43	864	1239	54	5/11	5/11	22.94	8.60	16.0	1	0

CHARLIE HEMPHREY

RHB / OB / R0 / W0

FULL NAME: Charlie Richard Hemphrey
BORN: August 31, 1989, Doncaster, Yorkshire
SQUAD NO: 22
HEIGHT: 6ft 2in
NICKNAME: Bronson
EDUCATION: Harvey Grammar School, Folkestone, Kent
TEAMS: Glamorgan, Queensland
ROLE: Batsman
DEBUT: First-class: 2015; List A: 2015

BEST BATTING: 118 Queensland vs South Australia, Brisbane, 2015
BEST BOWLING: 2-56 Queensland vs South Australia, Adelaide, 2016

FAMILY TIES? My sister Phillipa played for Kent U13
FIRST CRICKET CLUB? Hythe CC, Kent. It used to be under the English Channel
BEST INNINGS YOU'VE SEEN? Alastair Cook's 244 at the MCG during the 2017/18 Ashes. Grit and determination
MOST INTERESTING TEAMMATE? Lukas Carey aka 'The Bont'
IF YOU WERE AN ANIMAL, WHICH WOULD IT BE? A leopard – shrewd, smart, enjoys the sun, determined when needed and loves a feed
TWITTER: @chemp1989

Batting	Mat	Inns	NO	Runs	HS	Ave	SR	100	50	Ct	St
First-class	51	95	6	2575	118	28.93	41.26	4	16	38	0
List A	22	20	0	430	87	21.50	77.47	0	2	9	0
Bowling	**Mat**	**Balls**	**Runs**	**Wkts**	**BBI**	**BBM**	**Ave**	**Econ**	**SR**	**5w**	**10**
First-class	51	915	640	8	2/56	3/91	80.00	4.19	114.3	0	0
List A	22	156	151	2	1/18	1/18	75.50	5.80	78.0	0	0

RYAN HIGGINS

RHB / OB / R0 / W1 / MVP4

FULL NAME: Ryan Francis Higgins
BORN: January 6, 1995, Harare, Zimbabwe
SQUAD NO: 29
HEIGHT: 5ft 11in
NICKNAME: Fizzer
EDUCATION: Peterhouse School, Marondera, Zimbabwe; Bradfield College, Reading
TEAMS: Gloucestershire, Middlesex, England U19
ROLE: Allrounder
DEBUT: First-class: 2017; List A: 2014; T20: 2014

BEST BATTING: 199 Gloucestershire vs Leicestershire, Leicester, 2019
BEST BOWLING: 7-42 Gloucestershire vs Warwickshire, Bristol, 2020
COUNTY CAP: 2018 (Gloucestershire)

MOST EXCITING DAY AS A CRICKETER? T20 Finals Day last year
CHILDHOOD SPORTING HERO? Michael Hussey
FIRST CRICKET CLUB? Falkland CC, Berkshire
TOUGHEST OPPONENT IN COUNTY CRICKET? Hassan Azad – he simply does not get out against us
MOST ECCENTRIC TEAMMATE? AJ Tye – socks, socks and more socks
BIGGEST CRICKETING REGRET? My time in Sydney – I did not take the game seriously out there
WHAT WOULD YOU DO IF YOU WERE IN CHARGE OF COUNTY CRICKET? Make four-day cricket free to watch, introduce music in Championship cricket, encourage the private ownership of counties (like in football's Premier League)
STRANGEST THING YOU'VE DONE DURING LOCKDOWN? Batting in my living room
GUILTY PLEASURE? Popcorn
TWITTER: @ryanhiggins21

Batting	Mat	Inns	NO	Runs	HS	Ave	SR	100	50	Ct	St
First-class	38	61	9	1786	199	34.34	65.25	5	6	12	0
List A	33	29	5	680	81*	28.33	97.00	0	3	5	0
T20s	75	67	18	1221	77*	24.91	132.42	0	4	19	0
Bowling	**Mat**	**Balls**	**Runs**	**Wkts**	**BBI**	**BBM**	**Ave**	**Econ**	**SR**	**5w**	**10**
First-class	38	6361	2746	127	7/42	11/96	21.62	2.59	50.0	5	1
List A	33	915	845	24	4/50	4/50	35.20	5.54	38.1	0	0
T20s	75	808	1193	47	5/13	5/13	25.38	8.85	17.1	1	0

JAMES HILDRETH

RHB / RM / R7 / W0

FULL NAME: James Charles Hildreth
BORN: September 9, 1984, Milton Keynes, Buckinghamshire
SQUAD NO: 25
HEIGHT: 5ft 10in
NICKNAME: Hildy
EDUCATION: Millfield School, Somerset
TEAMS: Somerset, England Lions
ROLE: Batsman
DEBUT: First-class: 2003; List A: 2003; T20: 2004

BEST BATTING: 303* Somerset vs Warwickshire, Taunton, 2009
BEST BOWLING: 2-39 Somerset vs Hampshire, Taunton, 2009
COUNTY CAP: 2007; BENEFIT: 2017

MOST EXCITING DAY AS A CRICKETER? Winning the T20 Cup in 2005, captaining England Lions and captaining Somerset
CHILDHOOD SPORTING HERO? Ricky Ponting
IF YOU COULD TAKE ONE COUNTY CRICKETER'S BEST SHOT AND ADD IT TO YOUR OWN GAME? Jos Buttler's scoop
TOUGHEST OPPONENT IN COUNTY CRICKET? Shane Warne
MOST ECCENTRIC TEAMMATE? Peter Trego
SURPRISING FACT ABOUT YOU? I'm a big MK Dons fan
TWITTER: @dreth25

Batting	Mat	Inns	NO	Runs	HS	Ave	SR	100	50	Ct	St
First-class	267	440	31	17282	303*	42.25	-	46	77	233	0
List A	212	199	36	5781	159	35.46	-	7	27	79	0
T20s	196	183	32	3694	107*	24.46	124.25	1	16	72	0
Bowling	**Mat**	**Balls**	**Runs**	**Wkts**	**BBI**	**BBM**	**Ave**	**Econ**	**SR**	**5w**	**10**
First-class	267	576	492	6	2/39		82.00	5.12	96.0	0	0
List A	212	150	185	6	2/26	2/26	30.83	7.40	25.0	0	0
T20s	196	169	247	10	3/24	3/24	24.70	8.76	16.9	0	0

LEWIS HILL

RHB / WK / R0 / W0

FULL NAME: Lewis John Hill
BORN: October 5, 1990, Leicester
SQUAD NO: 23
HEIGHT: 5ft 8in
NICKNAME: Hilly
EDUCATION: Hastings High School, Hinckley; John Cleveland College, Hinckley
TEAMS: Leicestershire
ROLE: Wicketkeeper
DEBUT: First-class: 2015; List A: 2012; T20: 2015

BEST BATTING: 126 Leicestershire vs Surrey, The Oval, 2015

MOST EXCITING DAY AS A CRICKETER? Making my maiden first-class hundred for Leicestershire at The Oval in 2015 and having Kevin Pietersen and Kumar Sangakkara shake my hand at the end of the day
FAMILY TIES? My dad and brother both play for Lutterworth CC
FIRST CRICKET CLUB? Lutterworth CC, Leicestershire
SURPRISING FACT ABOUT YOU? I was targeted by armed robbers twice while working at my local newsagents
TWITTER: @ljhill23

Batting	Mat	Inns	NO	Runs	HS	Ave	SR	100	50	Ct	St
First-class	41	71	9	1459	126	23.53	49.02	1	5	96	3
List A	41	37	2	846	118	24.17	94.41	1	3	24	2
T20s	51	40	8	585	58	18.28	122.12	0	1	18	2
Bowling	**Mat**	**Balls**	**Runs**	**Wkts**	**BBI**	**BBM**	**Ave**	**Econ**	**SR**	**5w**	**10**
First-class	41	12	6	0	-	-	-	3.00	-	0	0
List A	41	-	-	-	-	-	-	-	-	-	-
T20s	51	-	-	-	-	-	-	-	-	-	-

MICHAEL HOGAN

RHB / RFM / R0 / W3

FULL NAME: Michael Garry Hogan
BORN: May 31, 1981, Newcastle, Australia
SQUAD NO: 31
HEIGHT: 6ft 5in
NICKNAME: Hulk
TEAMS: Glamorgan, Hobart Hurricanes, Western Australia
ROLE: Bowler
DEBUT: First-class: 2009; List A: 2009; T20: 2010

BEST BATTING: 57 Glamorgan vs Lancashire, Colwyn Bay, 2015
BEST BOWLING: 7-92 Glamorgan vs Gloucestershire, Bristol, 2013
COUNTY CAP: 2013

MOST EXCITING DAY AS A CRICKETER? Defending three when I was bowling the final over in a T20 game against Kent a few years ago
CHILDHOOD SPORTING HERO? Glenn McGrath
SURPRISING FACT ABOUT YOU? I'm very boring
TWITTER: @hoges31
NOTES: The Western Australian seamer signed a new one-year deal last November that will see him go past his 40th birthday. Hogan took his 600th first-class wicket last year and has been at Glamorgan since 2013. "Michael Hogan has arguably been one of Glamorgan's greatest-ever bowlers – he'd be in the conversation for an all-time Glamorgan XI," said Mark Wallace, the club's director of cricket. "He's been a fantastic servant for Glamorgan and it's great news him signing on for another year. It's invaluable to have Michael doing his stuff on the field and his experience in the dressing room for the younger players"

Batting	Mat	Inns	NO	Runs	HS	Ave	SR	100	50	Ct	St
First-class	159	225	89	2248	57	16.52	85.28	0	3	79	0
List A	69	28	18	171	27	17.10	82.60	0	0	25	0
T20s	97	21	13	78	17*	9.75	102.63	0	0	41	0
Bowling	**Mat**	**Balls**	**Runs**	**Wkts**	**BBI**	**BBM**	**Ave**	**Econ**	**SR**	**5w**	**10**
First-class	159	32753	14749	602	7/92	10/87	24.50	2.70	54.4	23	2
List A	69	3556	3017	102	5/44	5/44	29.57	5.09	34.8	1	0
T20s	97	1966	2565	105	5/17	5/17	24.42	7.82	18.7	1	0

MAX HOLDEN

LHB / OB / R0 / W0 / MVP49

FULL NAME: Max David Edward Holden
BORN: December 18, 1997, Cambridge
SQUAD NO: 4
HEIGHT: 6ft 1in
NICKNAME: Pepsi
EDUCATION: Sawston Village College, Cambridge; Hills Road Sixth Form College, Cambridge
TEAMS: Middlesex, England Lions, Northamptonshire
ROLE: Batsman
DEBUT: First-class: 2017; List A: 2017; T20: 2018

BEST BATTING: 153 Northamptonshire vs Kent, Beckenham, 2017
BEST BOWLING: 2-59 Northamptonshire vs Kent, Beckenham, 2017

MOST EXCITING DAY AS A CRICKETER? My first T20 at Lord's
CHILDHOOD SPORTING HERO? Thierry Henry
FIRST CRICKET CLUB? Cambridge St Giles CC, Cambridgeshire. It had a 20-metre leg-side boundary
IF YOU COULD TAKE ONE COUNTY CRICKETER'S BEST SHOT AND ADD IT TO YOUR OWN GAME? Sam Robson's cut
WHAT WOULD YOU DO IF YOU WERE IN CHARGE OF COUNTY CRICKET? Ban slips and lbws
STRANGEST THING YOU'VE DONE DURING LOCKDOWN? Baking a birthday cake for my teammate Jack Davies
FAVOURITE SMELL? My mum's cooking
GUILTY PLEASURE? Harry Potter
TWITTER: @maxholden_4

Batting	Mat	Inns	NO	Runs	HS	Ave	SR	100	50	Ct	St
First-class	43	78	4	2031	153	27.44	46.29	3	8	15	0
List A	11	10	1	412	166	45.77	90.74	1	2	2	0
T20s	16	16	2	419	102*	29.92	135.16	1	1	7	0
Bowling	**Mat**	**Balls**	**Runs**	**Wkts**	**BBI**	**BBM**	**Ave**	**Econ**	**SR**	**5w**	**10**
First-class	43	636	452	5	2/59	3/94	90.40	4.26	127.2	0	0
List A	11	120	93	1	1/29	1/29	93.00	4.65	120.0	0	0
T20s	16	6	12	0	-	-	-	12.00	-	0	0

IAN HOLLAND

RHB / RMF / R0 / W0

FULL NAME: Ian Gabriel Holland
BORN: October 3, 1990, Wisconsin, USA
SQUAD NO: 22
HEIGHT: 6ft
NICKNAME: Dutchy
EDUCATION: Ringwood Secondary College, Melbourne
TEAMS: USA, Hampshire, Northamptonshire, Victoria
ROLE: Allrounder
DEBUT: ODI: 2019; First-class: 2016; List A: 2017; T20: 2017

BEST BATTING: 143 Hampshire vs Warwickshire, Southampton, 2019
BEST BOWLING: 6-20 Hampshire vs Surrey, Arundel, 2020

CHILDHOOD SPORTING HERO? James Hird (Aussie rules)
FIRST CRICKET CLUB? Ringwood CC, Melbourne, Australia
IF YOU COULD TAKE ONE COUNTY CRICKETER'S BEST SHOT AND ADD IT TO YOUR OWN GAME? Mason Crane's cut (it's a gun!)
TOUGHEST OPPONENT IN COUNTY CRICKET? Darren Stevens – he's a wizard
WHAT WOULD YOU DO IF YOU WERE IN CHARGE OF COUNTY CRICKET? Reduce the schedule by about 20 per cent so that players have more time between games, no more than 90 overs in a day of red-ball cricket, no limit on the number of bouncers per over
STRANGEST THING YOU'VE DONE DURING LOCKDOWN? Growing multiple styles of facial hair
GUILTY PLEASURE? Doughnuts
TWITTER: @IanHolland22

Batting	Mat	Inns	NO	Runs	HS	Ave	SR	100	50	Ct	St
ODIs	8	8	0	244	75	30.50	76.48	0	2	3	0
First-class	31	48	6	986	143	23.47	43.95	1	5	13	0
List A	21	20	4	400	75	25.00	83.33	0	3	8	0
T20s	14	12	7	173	65	34.60	131.06	0	1	2	0
Bowling	**Mat**	**Balls**	**Runs**	**Wkts**	**BBI**	**BBM**	**Ave**	**Econ**	**SR**	**5w**	**10**
ODIs	8	275	209	7	3/11	3/11	29.85	4.56	39.2	0	0
First-class	31	3559	1493	57	6/60	7/77	26.19	2.51	62.4	1	0
List A	21	729	703	17	3/11	3/11	41.35	5.78	42.8	0	0
T20s	14	169	212	4	1/25	1/25	53.00	7.52	42.2	0	0

LUKE HOLLMAN

LHB / LB / R0 / W0

MIDDLESEX

FULL NAME: Luke Barnaby Kurt Hollman
BORN: September 16, 2000, Islington, London
SQUAD NO: 56
HEIGHT: 6ft 3in
NICKNAME: Donny
EDUCATION: Acland Burghley School, Camden, London
TEAMS: Middlesex, England U19
ROLE: Allrounder
DEBUT: T20: 2020

MOST EXCITING DAY AS A CRICKETER? Making my T20 debut for Middlesex at Lord's
CHILDHOOD SPORTING HERO? Brian Lara
FIRST CRICKET CLUB? North Middlesex CC, London
IF YOU COULD TAKE ONE COUNTY CRICKETER'S BEST SHOT AND ADD IT TO YOUR OWN GAME? Ravi Bopara's shot over extra cover
TOUGHEST OPPONENT IN COUNTY CRICKET? David Wiese
WHAT WOULD YOU DO IF YOU WERE IN CHARGE OF COUNTY CRICKET? Increase the amount of Championship cricket in the middle of the summer, allow three overseas players in the T20 Blast
FAVOURITE SMELL? Linseed oil

Batting	Mat	Inns	NO	Runs	HS	Ave	SR	100	50	Ct	St
T20s	7	7	3	139	46	34.75	139.00	0	0	2	0
Bowling	**Mat**	**Balls**	**Runs**	**Wkts**	**BBI**	**BBM**	**Ave**	**Econ**	**SR**	**5w**	**10**
T20s	7	144	163	9	3/18	3/18	18.11	6.79	16.0	0	0

ALEX HORTON

RHB / WK / R0 / W0

FULL NAME: Alex Jack Horton
BORN: January 7, 2004, Newport, Monmouthshire, Wales
SQUAD NO: 12
TEAMS: Glamorgan
ROLE: Wicketkeeper/batsman

TWITTER: @AlexQuidge12
NOTES: Horton only turned 17 this year but is already attracting rave reviews as a keeper-batsman of outstanding talent. A product of the Welsh state-school system, he moved to St Edward's Oxford on a scholarship at the age of 13. "The first time I did a keeping session with Alex he was 12 and I genuinely couldn't believe how good he was," recalled Mark Wallace, Glamorgan's director of cricket. "I can remember hitting balls to him and thinking, 'This is ridiculous'." With a five-year contract duly signed last summer, Horton will combine his cricket with his A-Level studies. "Alex coming through could represent something quite important for us," added Wallace. "He made his second-team debut for Glamorgan in 2019, got a fifty and kept like an old head. It was a seamless step up for a then 15-year-old. He's very much the all-round package"

ADAM HOSE

RHB / RM / R0 / W0

WARWICKSHIRE

FULL NAME: Adam John Hose
BORN: October 25, 1992, Newport, Isle of Wight
SQUAD NO: 21
HEIGHT: 6ft 5in
NICKNAME: Pipe
EDUCATION: Carisbrooke School, Newport
TEAMS: Warwickshire, Somerset, Wellington
ROLE: Batsman
DEBUT: First-class: 2016; List A: 2015; T20: 2015

BEST BATTING: 111 Warwickshire vs Nottinghamshire, Edgbaston, 2019

MOST EXCITING DAY AS A CRICKETER? T20 Finals Day with Birmingham Bears in 2017
CHILDHOOD SPORTING HERO? Kevin Pietersen
FIRST CRICKET CLUB? Ventnor CC, Isle of Wight
BEST INNINGS YOU'VE SEEN? Roelof van der Merwe's 165 not out to beat Surrey in the 2017 One-Day Cup. We were chasing 291 and it wasn't looking good at 22-5…
IF YOU COULD TAKE ONE COUNTY CRICKETER'S BEST SHOT AND ADD IT TO YOUR OWN GAME? Jos Buttler's scoop
TOUGHEST OPPONENT IN COUNTY CRICKET? Darren Stevens on an early-season greentop
FAVOURITE SMELL? A Sunday roast
GUILTY PLEASURE? Caramel Digestives
TWITTER: @adamhose21

Batting	Mat	Inns	NO	Runs	HS	Ave	SR	100	50	Ct	St
First-class	19	35	1	746	111	21.94	44.99	1	4	5	0
List A	29	24	1	761	101*	33.08	90.27	1	4	16	0
T20s	54	53	5	1457	119	30.35	145.70	1	9	23	0
Bowling	**Mat**	**Balls**	**Runs**	**Wkts**	**BBI**	**BBM**	**Ave**	**Econ**	**SR**	**5w**	**10**
First-class	19	-	-	-	-	-	-	-	-	-	-
List A	29	-	-	-	-	-	-	-	-	-	-
T20s	54	-	-	-	-	-	-	-	-	-	-

HARVEY HOSEIN

RHB / WK / R0 / W0

FULL NAME: Harvey Richard Hosein
BORN: August 12, 1996, Chesterfield, Derbyshire
SQUAD NO: 16
HEIGHT: 6ft
NICKNAME: General
EDUCATION: Denstone College, Staffordshire
TEAMS: Derbyshire
ROLE: Wicketkeeper
DEBUT: First-class: 2014; List A: 2016; T20: 2016

BEST BATTING: 138* Derbyshire vs Durham, Derby, 2019

MOST EXCITING DAY AS A CRICKETER? Equalling a world record by taking seven catches on my first-class debut in 2014
CHILDHOOD SPORTING HERO? David Beckham
FIRST CRICKET CLUB? Matlock CC, Peak District, Derbyshire
IF YOU COULD TAKE ONE COUNTY CRICKETER'S BEST SHOT AND ADD IT TO YOUR OWN GAME? Wayne Madsen's upper-cut over the keeper
TOUGHEST OPPONENT IN COUNTY CRICKET? James Anderson
WHAT WOULD YOU DO IF YOU WERE IN CHARGE OF COUNTY CRICKET? Introduce an overseas county competition during the winter, bring back the 16-game Championship season, ban green wickets
STRANGEST THING YOU'VE DONE DURING LOCKDOWN? Drawing pictures
TWITTER: @HarveyHosein16

Batting	Mat	Inns	NO	Runs	HS	Ave	SR	100	50	Ct	St
First-class	51	86	15	2209	138*	31.11	45.22	2	16	121	5
List A	13	9	3	139	41*	23.16	106.92	0	0	8	3
T20s	10	4	4	11	10*	-	100.00	0	0	8	0
Bowling	**Mat**	**Balls**	**Runs**	**Wkts**	**BBI**	**BBM**	**Ave**	**Econ**	**SR**	**5w**	**10**
First-class	51	-	-	-	-	-	-	-	-	-	-
List A	13	-	-	-	-	-	-	-	-	-	-
T20s	10	-	-	-	-	-	-	-	-	-	-

GLOUCESTERSHIRE

BENNY HOWELL RHB / RM / R0 / W0

FULL NAME: Benny Alexander Cameron Howell
BORN: October 5, 1988, Bordeaux, France
SQUAD NO: 13
HEIGHT: 5ft 11in
NICKNAME: Novak
EDUCATION: The Oratory School, Reading
TEAMS: Gloucestershire, Hampshire, Khulna Titans, Melbourne Renegades, Rangpur Riders
ROLE: Allrounder
DEBUT: First-class: 2011; List A: 2010; T20: 2011

BEST BATTING: 163 Gloucestershire vs Glamorgan, Cardiff, 2017
BEST BOWLING: 5-57 Gloucestershire vs Leicestershire, Leicester, 2013
COUNTY CAP: 2012 (Gloucestershire)

MOST EXCITING DAY AS A CRICKETER? The 2015 one-day final at Lord's
CHILDHOOD SPORTING HERO? Steve Waugh
BIGGEST INFLUENCE ON YOUR DEVELOPMENT AS A CRICKETER (EXCLUDING PARENTS)? In a general sense, all baseball pitchers – they have incredible skills that are honed over thousands of hours of practice
FIRST CRICKET CLUB? Stoke Row CC, Oxfordshire
TOUGHEST OPPONENT IN COUNTY CRICKET? Michael Hogan – he's a very skilful bowler with an awkward action and he never stops running in
WHAT WOULD YOU DO IF YOU WERE IN CHARGE OF COUNTY CRICKET? Organise a winter competition, encourage an objective review of umpire performances
STRANGEST THING YOU'VE DONE DURING LOCKDOWN? Setting my alarm for 3.22am so I would have exactly two hours to meditate before sunrise – that was during my two-week quarantine in Australia
GUILTY PLEASURE? A nightly ritual serving of natural yoghurt, peanut butter, hazelnut butter, banana and berries
TWITTER: @bennyhowell510

Batting	Mat	Inns	NO	Runs	HS	Ave	SR	100	50	Ct	St
First-class	86	136	13	3378	163	27.46	54.35	2	18	52	0
List A	86	72	14	2050	122	35.34	90.70	1	13	27	0
T20s	123	100	29	1605	57	22.60	124.90	0	4	52	0
Bowling	**Mat**	**Balls**	**Runs**	**Wkts**	**BBI**	**BBM**	**Ave**	**Econ**	**SR**	**5w**	**10**
First-class	86	6455	3222	96	5/57	8/96	33.56	2.99	67.2	1	0
List A	86	3043	2640	76	3/37	3/37	34.73	5.20	40.0	0	0
T20s	123	2225	2582	132	5/18	5/18	19.56	6.96	16.8	1	0

FYNN HUDSON-PRENTICE RHB / RMF / R0 / W0

FULL NAME: Fynn Jake Hudson-Prentice
BORN: January 12, 1996, Haywards Heath, Sussex
SQUAD NO: 33
HEIGHT: 6ft
NICKNAME: Jack Sparrow
EDUCATION: Warden Park School, Cuckfield, West Sussex; Bede's Senior School, Hailsham, East Sussex
TEAMS: Derbyshire, Sussex
ROLE: Allrounder
DEBUT: First-class: 2015; List A: 2014; T20: 2019

BEST BATTING: 99 Derbyshire vs Middlesex, Derby, 2019
BEST BOWLING: 3-27 Derbyshire vs Worcestershire, Kidderminster, 2019

MOST EXCITING DAY AS A CRICKETER? Finishing 91 not out when we chased down 265 to beat Nottinghamshire in the Bob Willis Trophy last year
BIGGEST INFLUENCE ON YOUR DEVELOPMENT AS A CRICKETER (EXCLUDING PARENTS)? Steve Kirby – he has been a great friend, mentor and coach over the last four years of my career, helping me to where I am now
FIRST CRICKET CLUB? St Andrews CC, Burgess Hill, West Sussex
IF YOU COULD TAKE ONE COUNTY CRICKETER'S BEST SHOT AND ADD IT TO YOUR OWN GAME? Wayne Madsen's upper-cut
TOUGHEST OPPONENT IN COUNTY CRICKET? Dawid Malan – he always makes a hundred against us
WHAT WOULD YOU DO IF YOU WERE IN CHARGE OF COUNTY CRICKET? Make red-ball cricket regional rather than using divisions, complete all white-ball cricket in set blocks (no Championship cricket in between)
STRANGEST THING YOU'VE DONE DURING LOCKDOWN? Bleaching my hair blond
FAVOURITE SMELL? Fresh rosemary
TWITTER: @fynnhudson33

Batting	Mat	Inns	NO	Runs	HS	Ave	SR	100	50	Ct	St
First-class	15	25	4	571	99	27.19	63.51	0	3	2	0
List A	3	2	0	67	48	33.50	95.71	0	0	0	0
T20s	15	8	2	110	31*	18.33	111.11	0	0	4	0
Bowling	**Mat**	**Balls**	**Runs**	**Wkts**	**BBI**	**BBM**	**Ave**	**Econ**	**SR**	**5w**	**10**
First-class	15	1140	621	21	3/27	6/69	29.57	3.26	54.2	0	0
List A	3	84	112	0	-	-	-	8.00	-	0	0
T20s	15	246	372	12	2/2	2/2	31.00	9.07	20.5	0	0

ALEX HUGHES

RHB / RM / R0 / W0

FULL NAME: Alex Lloyd Hughes
BORN: September 29, 1991, Wordsley, Staffordshire
SQUAD NO: 18
HEIGHT: 6ft
NICKNAME: Yozza
EDUCATION: Ounsdale High School, Wolverhampton; University of Worcester
TEAMS: Derbyshire
ROLE: Allrounder
DEBUT: First-class: 2013; List A: 2012; T20: 2011

BEST BATTING: 142 Derbyshire vs Gloucestershire, Bristol, 2017
BEST BOWLING: 4-46 Derbyshire vs Glamorgan, Derby, 2014
COUNTY CAP: 2017

MOST EXCITING DAY AS A CRICKETER? T20 Finals Day in 2019
CHILDHOOD SPORTING HERO? My brother
FIRST CRICKET CLUB? Wombourne CC, Staffordshire
IF YOU COULD TAKE ONE COUNTY CRICKETER'S BEST SHOT AND ADD IT TO YOUR OWN GAME? Wayne Madsen's sweep
TOUGHEST OPPONENT IN COUNTY CRICKET? Myself
WHAT WOULD YOU DO IF YOU WERE IN CHARGE OF COUNTY CRICKET? Appoint Matt Critchley to do all the decision-making for me while I watch the cricket
WHAT WOULD YOU DO IF YOU WERE PRIME MINISTER? Have tea with the Queen and her dogs
IF YOU WERE AN ANIMAL, WHICH WOULD IT BE? A pterodactyl
GUILTY PLEASURE? Watching Call of Duty streamers
TWITTER: @Yozza18

Batting	Mat	Inns	NO	Runs	HS	Ave	SR	100	50	Ct	St
First-class	73	127	11	3317	142	28.59	46.17	6	13	53	0
List A	65	44	8	852	96*	23.66	92.70	0	3	27	0
T20s	87	66	17	803	43*	16.38	119.31	0	0	35	0
Bowling	**Mat**	**Balls**	**Runs**	**Wkts**	**BBI**	**BBM**	**Ave**	**Econ**	**SR**	**5w**	**10**
First-class	73	3501	1814	36	4/46	4/75	50.38	3.10	97.2	0	0
List A	65	2027	1898	43	4/44	4/44	44.13	5.61	47.1	0	0
T20s	87	1373	1833	53	4/42	4/42	34.58	8.01	25.9	0	0

SEAN HUNT RHB / LFM / R0 / W0

FULL NAME: Sean Frank Hunt
BORN: December 7, 2001, Guildford, Surrey
SQUAD NO: 21
HEIGHT: 6ft 5in
NICKNAME: Hunty
EDUCATION: Howard of Effingham School, Surrey
TEAMS: Sussex
ROLE: Bowler

MOST EXCITING DAY AS A CRICKETER? Playing grade cricket in Adelaide for West Torrens CC last winter
CHILDHOOD SPORTING HERO? Mitchell Johnson
BIGGEST INFLUENCE ON YOUR DEVELOPMENT AS A CRICKETER (EXCLUDING PARENTS)? Geoff Arnold, my former bowling coach at Surrey
IF YOU COULD TAKE ONE COUNTY CRICKETER'S BEST SHOT AND ADD IT TO YOUR OWN GAME? Laurie Evans's aerial cover-drive
WHAT WOULD YOU DO IF YOU WERE IN CHARGE OF COUNTY CRICKET? Increase the amount of day/night Championship matches, allow more overseas players, reduce the number of counties
FAVOURITE SMELL? Freshy baked chocolate brownies
TWITTER: @seanhunt139
NOTES: The left-arm pace bowler was Surrey Academy Player of the Year in 2019 but signed his first professional contract with Sussex in January. "The approach from Sussex came completely out of the blue – but when the offer came to play for a such prestigious county, I had no hesitation in accepting such a fantastic opportunity," said Hunt. The 19-year-old from Guildford trained with the England Young Lions squad last summer and impressed with a five-wicket haul in a North vs South youth match. He spent last winter at the Darren Lehmann Cricket Academy in Adelaide, turning out for West Torrens CC in grade cricket. "He has been one of the most successful bowlers at Academy level in the south-east and has bowled a significant number of overs," said Sussex T20 coach James Kirtley. "He has a bowling engine; he is left arm and he swings it. He knows the areas he needs to improve on, and I can see some outstanding potential"

LIAM HURT

RHB / RFM / R0 / W0

FULL NAME: Liam Jack Hurt
BORN: March 15, 1994, Preston, Lancashire
SQUAD NO: 22
HEIGHT: 6ft 3in
NICKNAME: Tyrone
EDUCATION: Balshaw's CE High School, Leyland, Lancashire
TEAMS: Lancashire, Leicestershire
ROLE: Bowler
DEBUT: First-class: 2019; List A: 2015; T20: 2019

BEST BATTING: 38 Lancashire vs Leicestershire, Leicester, 2019
BEST BOWLING: 4-27 Lancashire vs Durham, Chester-le-Street, 2020

MOST EXCITING DAY AS A CRICKETER? Making my first-class debut in 2019
CHILDHOOD SPORTING HERO? Andrew Flintoff
FIRST CRICKET CLUB? Leyland CC, Lancashire
MOST ECCENTRIC TEAMMATE? Tom Bailey
WHAT WOULD YOU DO IF YOU WERE IN CHARGE OF COUNTY CRICKET? Make tea longer, introduce DRS, incentivise bigger crowds
WHAT WOULD YOU DO IF YOU WERE PRIME MINISTER? Get compensation from whoever started Covid
STRANGEST THING YOU'VE DONE DURING LOCKDOWN? Running for fun
FAVOURITE SMELL? Garlic bread
GUILTY PLEASURE? Watching Friends
TWITTER: @LiamHurt

Batting	Mat	Inns	NO	Runs	HS	Ave	SR	100	50	Ct	St
First-class	3	3	0	41	38	13.66	42.70	0	0	0	0
List A	5	3	2	34	15*	34.00	79.06	0	0	1	0
T20s	4	1	0	0	0	0.00	0.00	0	0	3	0
Bowling	**Mat**	**Balls**	**Runs**	**Wkts**	**BBI**	**BBM**	**Ave**	**Econ**	**SR**	**5w**	**10**
First-class	3	438	248	7	4/27	5/71	35.42	3.39	62.5	0	0
List A	5	198	193	7	2/24	2/24	27.57	5.84	28.2	0	0
T20s	4	60	110	2	2/29	2/29	55.00	11.00	30.0	0	0

BRETT HUTTON

RHB / RMF / R0 / W0

FULL NAME: Brett Alan Hutton
BORN: February 6, 1993, Doncaster, Yorkshire
SQUAD NO: 16
HEIGHT: 6ft 3in
NICKNAME: Bert
EDUCATION: Worksop College, Nottinghamshire
TEAMS: Nottinghamshire, England U19, Northamptonshire
ROLE: Bowler
DEBUT: First-class: 2011; List A: 2011; T20: 2016

BEST BATTING: 74 Nottinghamshire vs Durham, Trent Bridge, 2016
BEST BOWLING: 8-57 Northamptonshire vs Gloucestershire, Northampton, 2018

CHILDHOOD SPORTING HERO? Tiger Woods
BIGGEST INFLUENCE ON YOUR DEVELOPMENT AS A CRICKETER (EXCLUDING PARENTS)? Paul Franks, Nottinghamshire's assistant coach – I played cricket with him from a young age, watching him and learning
FIRST CRICKET CLUB? Worksop CC, Nottinghamshire
IF YOU COULD TAKE ONE COUNTY CRICKETER'S BEST SHOT AND ADD IT TO YOUR OWN GAME? Adam Rossington's sweep against the spinners
TOUGHEST OPPONENT IN COUNTY CRICKET? James Hildreth
WHAT WOULD YOU DO IF YOU WERE IN CHARGE OF COUNTY CRICKET? Bring back a 50-over knockout competition including Minor Counties
SURPRISING FACT ABOUT YOU? I have a stamp collection
GUILTY PLEASURE? Cutting the grass
TWITTER: @BrettAH26

Batting	Mat	Inns	NO	Runs	HS	Ave	SR	100	50	Ct	St
First-class	58	89	12	1380	74	17.92	43.11	0	4	35	0
List A	15	11	5	173	34*	28.83	93.01	0	0	5	0
T20s	9	7	4	50	18*	16.66	106.38	0	0	3	0
Bowling	**Mat**	**Balls**	**Runs**	**Wkts**	**BBI**	**BBM**	**Ave**	**Econ**	**SR**	**5w**	**10**
First-class	58	9377	5181	193	8/57	10/106	26.84	3.31	48.5	9	2
List A	15	728	776	16	3/72	3/72	48.50	6.39	45.5	0	0
T20s	9	172	255	5	2/28	2/28	51.00	8.89	34.4	0	0

COLIN INGRAM

LHB / LB / R0 / W0

GLAMORGAN

FULL NAME: Colin Alexander Ingram
BORN: July 3, 1985, Port Elizabeth, SA
SQUAD NO: 41
HEIGHT: 5ft 10in
NICKNAME: Stingray
EDUCATION: Woodbridge College, Eastern Cape, South Africa
TEAMS: South Africa, Glamorgan, Adelaide Strikers, Delhi Daredevils, Eastern Province, Hobart Hurricanes, Somerset, Warriors
ROLE: Allrounder
DEBUT: ODI: 2010; T20I: 2010; First-class: 2004; List A: 2005; T20: 2007

BEST BATTING: 190 Eastern Province vs KwaZulu-Natal, Port Elizabeth, 2009
BEST BOWLING: 4-16 Eastern Province vs Boland, Port Elizabeth, 2006
COUNTY CAP: 2017 (Glamorgan)

MOST EXCITING DAY AS A CRICKETER? Scoring a hundred on my ODI debut
CHILDHOOD SPORTING HERO? Gary Kirsten
BIGGEST INFLUENCE ON YOUR DEVELOPMENT AS A CRICKETER (EXCLUDING PARENTS)? Too many to mention – I feel like I've got so many people with me when I step onto the field
FIRST CRICKET CLUB? Old Grey CC, Port Elizabeth, South Africa
IF YOU COULD TAKE ONE COUNTY CRICKETER'S BEST SHOT AND ADD IT TO YOUR OWN GAME? Liam Livingstone's ramp-flick
TOUGHEST OPPONENT IN COUNTY CRICKET? David Masters
WHAT WOULD YOU DO IF YOU WERE IN CHARGE OF COUNTY CRICKET? Start Championship games at 10am, hand out free tickets for the T20 Blast at schools
GUILTY PLEASURE? Chocolate milk
TWITTER: @CAIngram41

Batting	Mat	Inns	NO	Runs	HS	Ave	SR	100	50	Ct	St
ODIs	31	29	3	843	124	32.42	82.32	3	3	12	0
T20Is	9	9	1	210	78	26.25	129.62	0	1	2	0
First-class	111	195	17	6641	190	37.30		14	30	75	0
List A	186	178	18	7584	142	47.40	90.13	18	48	65	0
T20s	280	273	39	6942	127*	29.66	138.97	4	41	86	0
Bowling	**Mat**	**Balls**	**Runs**	**Wkts**	**BBI**	**BBM**	**Ave**	**Econ**	**SR**	**5w**	**10**
ODIs	31	6	17	0	-	-	-	17.00	-	0	0
T20Is	9	-	-	-	-	-	-	-	-	-	-
First-class	111	3516	2132	50	4/16	5/50	42.64	3.63	70.3	0	0
List A	186	1482	1345	40	4/39	4/39	33.62	5.44	37.0	0	0
T20s	280	949	1247	38	4/32	4/32	32.81	7.88	24.9	0	0

WILL JACKS

RHB / RM / R0 / W0 / MVP3

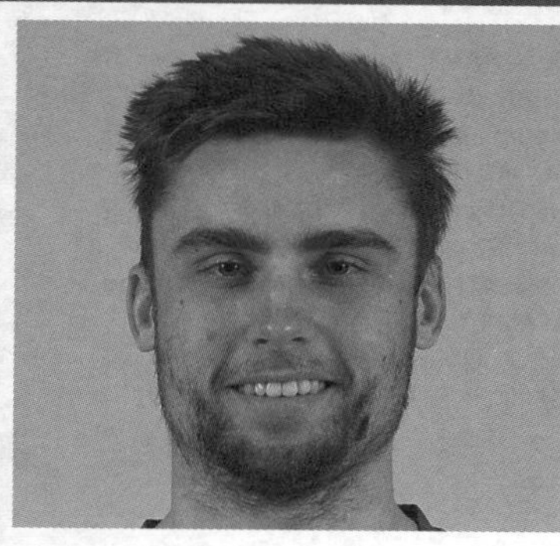

FULL NAME: William George Jacks
BORN: November 21, 1998, Chertsey, Surrey
SQUAD NO: 9
HEIGHT: 6ft 2in
NICKNAME: Jacko
EDUCATION: St George's College, Weybridge
TEAMS: Surrey, England Lions, Hobart Hurricanes
ROLE: Batsman
DEBUT: First-class: 2018; List A: 2018; T20: 2018

BEST BATTING: 120 Surrey vs Kent, Beckenham, 2019

MOST EXCITING DAY AS A CRICKETER? Winning the County Championship in 2018
CHILDHOOD SPORTING HERO? Kevin Pietersen
FIRST CRICKET CLUB? Valley End CC, Surrey
IF YOU COULD TAKE ONE COUNTY CRICKETER'S BEST SHOT AND ADD IT TO YOUR OWN GAME? Joe Root's back-foot punch
TOUGHEST OPPONENT IN COUNTY CRICKET? Rashid Khan – I can't pick him
MOST ECCENTRIC TEAMMATE? Jason Roy – he's a mad man
WHAT WOULD YOU DO IF YOU WERE IN CHARGE OF COUNTY CRICKET? Play more T20 games on the weekend
IF YOU WERE AN ANIMAL, WHICH WOULD IT BE? The great Altior (racehorse)
TWITTER: @Wjacks9

Batting	Mat	Inns	NO	Runs	HS	Ave	SR	100	50	Ct	St
First-class	24	39	4	996	120	28.45	50.68	1	7	28	0
List A	22	21	0	506	121	24.09	95.65	1	2	13	0
T20s	44	38	3	760	65	21.71	144.76	0	5	19	0
Bowling	**Mat**	**Balls**	**Runs**	**Wkts**	**BBI**	**BBM**	**Ave**	**Econ**	**SR**	**5w**	**10**
First-class	24	168	104	0	-	-	-	3.71	-	0	0
List A	22	482	423	11	2/32	2/32	38.45	5.26	43.8	0	0
T20s	44	236	284	14	4/15	4/15	20.28	7.22	16.8	0	0

LYNDON JAMES

RHB / RMF / R0 / W0

FULL NAME: Lyndon Wallace James
BORN: December 27, 1998, Worksop, Nottinghamshire
SQUAD NO: 45
HEIGHT: 6ft 3in
NICKNAME: LJ
EDUCATION: Oakham School, Rutland
TEAMS: Nottinghamshire
ROLE: Allrounder
DEBUT: First-class: 2018; List A: 2019

BEST BATTING: 36* Nottinghamshire vs Leicestershire, Leicester, 2020
BEST BOWLING: 3-54 Nottinghamshire vs Essex, Trent Bridge, 2018

CHILDHOOD SPORTING HERO? Andrew Flintoff
BIGGEST INFLUENCE ON YOUR DEVELOPMENT AS A CRICKETER (EXCLUDING PARENTS)? My brother – because of all the back-yard cricket we played together
FIRST CRICKET CLUB? Ordsall Bridon CC, Nottinghamshire
IF YOU COULD TAKE ONE COUNTY CRICKETER'S BEST SHOT AND ADD IT TO YOUR OWN GAME? Sol Budinger's hack
TOUGHEST OPPONENT IN COUNTY CRICKET? Simon Harmer – I faced him on debut
MOST ECCENTRIC TEAMMATE? Ben Compton – he has a passion for grapes
WHAT WOULD YOU DO IF YOU WERE IN CHARGE OF COUNTY CRICKET? Allow gloves for fielders in April
WHAT WOULD YOU DO IF YOU WERE PRIME MINISTER? Organise trade agreements with Australia and New Zealand to facilitate free movement of people
STRANGEST THING YOU'VE DONE DURING LOCKDOWN? Building a squat rack out of stools and drawers
FAVOURITE SMELL? The ocean
GUILTY PLEASURE? Call of Duty (video game)
TWITTER: @LyndonJames27

Batting	Mat	Inns	NO	Runs	HS	Ave	SR	100	50	Ct	St
First-class	2	3	1	50	36*	25.00	84.74	0	0	1	0
List A	1	1	0	0	0	0.00	0.00	0	0	1	0
Bowling	**Mat**	**Balls**	**Runs**	**Wkts**	**BBI**	**BBM**	**Ave**	**Econ**	**SR**	**5w**	**10**
First-class	2	186	123	4	3/54	3/68	30.75	3.96	46.5	0	0
List A	1	-	-	-	-	-	-	-	-	-	-

KEATON JENNINGS

LHB / RM / R1 / W0 / MVP53

FULL NAME: Keaton Kent Jennings
BORN: June 19, 1992, Johannesburg, South Africa
SQUAD NO: 1
HEIGHT: 6ft 4in
NICKNAME: Jet
EDUCATION: King Edward VII School; University of South Africa
TEAMS: England, Lancashire, Durham, Gauteng, South Africa U19
ROLE: Batsman
DEBUT: Test: 2016; First-class: 2011; List A: 2012; T20: 2014

BEST BATTING: 221* Durham vs Yorkshire, Chester-le-Street, 2016
BEST BOWLING: 3-37 Durham vs Sussex, Chester-le-Street, 2017
COUNTY CAP: 2018 (Lancashire)

MOST EXCITING DAY AS A CRICKETER? Making my Test debut in 2016
FAMILY TIES? My brother Dylan, uncle Kenneth and father Ray have all played first-class cricket in South Africa
CHILDHOOD SPORTING HERO? Michael Hussey
BIGGEST INFLUENCE ON YOUR DEVELOPMENT AS A CRICKETER (EXCLUDING PARENTS)? Andy Flower
FIRST CRICKET CLUB? Pirates CC, Johannesburg, South Africa
MOST ECCENTRIC TEAMMATE? Mark Wood – you've really got to keep your wits about you with him around
GUILTY PLEASURE? I eat a lot of chocolate
TWITTER: @JetJennings

Batting	Mat	Inns	NO	Runs	HS	Ave	SR	100	50	Ct	St
Tests	17	32	1	781	146*	25.19	42.49	2	1	17	0
First-class	138	241	16	7501	221*	33.33	45.28	18	28	113	0
List A	68	67	12	2271	139	41.29	83.27	4	17	31	0
T20s	62	43	16	954	108	35.33	120.45	1	3	11	0
Bowling	**Mat**	**Balls**	**Runs**	**Wkts**	**BBI**	**BBM**	**Ave**	**Econ**	**SR**	**5w**	**10**
Tests	17	73	55	0	-	-	-	4.52	-	0	0
First-class	138	1761	988	30	3/37	4/48	32.93	3.36	58.7	0	0
List A	68	594	614	11	2/19	2/19	55.81	6.20	54.0	0	0
T20s	62	510	628	22	4/37	4/37	28.54	7.38	23.1	0	0

MANRAJ JOHAL RHB / RFM / R0 / W0

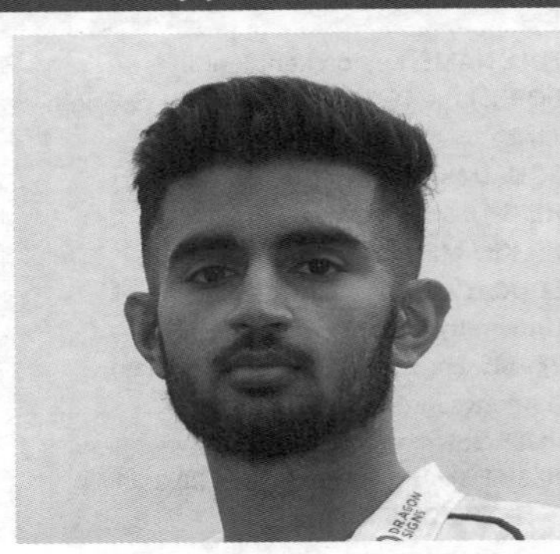

FULL NAME: Manraj Singh Johal
BORN: October 12, 2001, Birmingham
SQUAD NO: 5
HEIGHT: 6ft 1in
NICKNAME: Manny
EDUCATION: Oldbury Academy; Sandwell College, West Midlands
TEAMS: Warwickshire
ROLE: Bowler

MOST EXCITING DAY AS A CRICKETER? The day I heard that I was signing my first contract as a professional with Warwickshire
CHILDHOOD SPORTING HERO? Brett Lee
BIGGEST INFLUENCE ON YOUR DEVELOPMENT AS A CRICKETER (EXCLUDING PARENTS)? Kadeer Ali, the former Worcestershire batsman and now their Second XI coach. He helped me to join a premier-league club which was so important for my development. I also played with him in a couple of Minor Counties games for Staffordshire
FIRST CRICKET CLUB? Olton & West Warwickshire CC
NOTES: The Staffordshire seamer became a professional in October after signing his first contract with Warwickshire. Johal, who plays his club cricket for West Bromwich Dartmouth CC in the Birmingham & District Premier League, has worked his way through the ranks since first representing Warwickshire at U11 level. "Manraj has a nice repeatable action with a good heavy ball and he has impressed us at every opportunity when he has been around the professional ranks," said Ian Westwood, Warwickshire's Second XI coach. "He bowled a lot of overs [in 2019] and showed real promise in his performances in the Second XI and for Staffordshire"

MICHAEL JONES

RHB / OB / R0 / W0

FULL NAME: Michael Alexander Jones
BORN: January 5, 1998, Ormskirk, Lancashire
SQUAD NO: 10
HEIGHT: 6ft 3in
NICKNAME: Conqs
EDUCATION: Ormskirk School; Myerscough College, Preston; Edge Hill University, Ormskirk
TEAMS: Scotland, Durham
ROLE: Batsman
DEBUT: ODI: 2018; First-class: 2018; List A: 2018

BEST BATTING: 82 Durham vs Nottinghamshire, Trent Bridge, 2020

MOST EXCITING DAY AS A CRICKETER? The World Cup Qualifier between Scotland and West Indies at Harare in 2018. We fell five runs short of a win which would have meant qualification for the 2019 World Cup
CHILDHOOD SPORTING HERO? Steven Gerrard
IF YOU COULD TAKE ONE COUNTY CRICKETER'S BEST SHOT AND ADD IT TO YOUR OWN GAME? Stuart Poynter's sweep
TOUGHEST OPPONENT IN COUNTY CRICKET? Duanne Olivier – he's sharp
MOST ECCENTRIC TEAMMATE? Brydon Carse – he's got a lot of energy!
WHAT WOULD YOU DO IF YOU WERE IN CHARGE OF COUNTY CRICKET? Introduce free hits for no-balls in first-class cricket
WHAT WOULD YOU DO IF YOU WERE PRIME MINISTER? I would have taken a Swedish approach to Covid
STRANGEST THING YOU'VE DONE DURING LOCKDOWN? Growing a beard
FAVOURITE SMELL? Sauvage by Christian Dior
GUILTY PLEASURE? Sugar doughnuts
TWITTER: @mikejones04

Batting	Mat	Inns	NO	Runs	HS	Ave	SR	100	50	Ct	St
ODIs	8	8	0	281	87	35.12	70.07	0	3	3	0
First-class	5	8	0	106	82	13.25	30.72	0	1	2	0
List A	8	8	0	281	87	35.12	70.07	0	3	3	0
Bowling	**Mat**	**Balls**	**Runs**	**Wkts**	**BBI**	**BBM**	**Ave**	**Econ**	**SR**	**5w**	**10**
ODIs	8	-	-	-	-	-	-	-	-	-	-
First-class	5	-	-	-	-	-	-	-	-	-	-
List A	8	-	-	-	-	-	-	-	-	-	-

ROB JONES

RHB / LB / R0 / W0

LANCASHIRE

FULL NAME: Robert Peter Jones
BORN: November 3, 1995, Warrington, Cheshire
SQUAD NO: 12
HEIGHT: 5ft 11in
NICKNAME: Jonah
EDUCATION: Bridgewater High School, Warrington; Priestley College
TEAMS: Lancashire, England U19
ROLE: Batsman
DEBUT: First-class: 2016; List A: 2018; T20: 2017

BEST BATTING: 122 Lancashire vs Middlesex, Lord's, 2019
BEST BOWLING: 1-18 Lancashire vs Worcestershire, Worcester, 2018

MOST EXCITING DAY AS A CRICKETER? Scoring a first-class hundred at Lord's
CHILDHOOD SPORTING HERO? Ole Gunnar Solskjaer
BIGGEST INFLUENCE ON YOUR DEVELOPMENT AS A CRICKETER (EXCLUDING PARENTS)? Bob Milne – he gave me a chance at the Cheshire Academy
FIRST CRICKET CLUB? Stretton CC, Warrington, Cheshire
TOUGHEST OPPONENT IN COUNTY CRICKET? Rikki Clarke – he challenges everything about your batting technique
WHAT WOULD YOU DO IF YOU WERE IN CHARGE OF COUNTY CRICKET? Schedule more four-day cricket
WHAT WOULD YOU DO IF YOU WERE PRIME MINISTER? Make hiking compulsory, get rid of various subjects at school (maths, science, English), fix a limit on the time people are allowed to spend on their phones
STRANGEST THING YOU'VE DONE DURING LOCKDOWN? Running 11km with 10kg on my back
FAVOURITE SMELL? McDonald's
GUILTY PLEASURE? Birdwatching
TWITTER: @robpeterjones

Batting	Mat	Inns	NO	Runs	HS	Ave	SR	100	50	Ct	St
First-class	30	45	5	1175	122	29.37	37.81	2	5	27	0
List A	13	10	2	205	65	25.62	79.76	0	1	8	0
T20s	12	7	4	77	38*	25.66	105.47	0	0	7	0
Bowling	**Mat**	**Balls**	**Runs**	**Wkts**	**BBI**	**BBM**	**Ave**	**Econ**	**SR**	**5w**	**10**
First-class	30	90	42	1	1/18	1/18	42.00	2.80	90.0	0	0
List A	13	122	122	2	1/3	1/3	61.00	6.00	61.0	0	0
T20s	12	-	-	-	-	-	-	-	-	-	-

CHRIS JORDAN

RHB / RFM / R0 / W1

FULL NAME: Christopher James Jordan
BORN: October 4, 1988, Christ Church, Barbados
SQUAD NO: 8
HEIGHT: 6ft
EDUCATION: Combermere School, Barbados; Dulwich College, London
TEAMS: England, Sussex, Barbados, Kings XI Punjab, Perth Scorchers, RC Bangalore, Sunrisers Hyderabad, Surrey, Sydney Thunder
ROLE: Allrounder
DEBUT: Test: 2014; ODI: 2013; T20I: 2013; First-class: 2007; List A: 2007; T20: 2008

BEST BATTING: 166 Sussex vs Northamptonshire, Northampton, 2019
BEST BOWLING: 7-43 Barbados vs Combined Campuses & Colleges, Bridgetown, 2013
COUNTY CAP: 2014 (Sussex)

FIRST CRICKET CLUB? Spartan Juniors CC, Barbados
MOST INTERESTING TEAMMATE? Jofra Archer – no matter what is going on in his life, whenever he gets on that 22 yards of pitch he turns it on
TWITTER: @ChrisJordan94
NOTES: Jordan was retained by Kings XI Punjab for the 2021 IPL after impressing in his debut season for the franchise during last year's delayed tournament. The fast-bowling allrounder recently became England's leading T20 wicket-taker and last year played his first ODI since 2016. He hasn't played Test cricket since 2015

Batting	Mat	Inns	NO	Runs	HS	Ave	SR	100	50	Ct	St
Tests	8	11	1	180	35	18.00	56.25	0	0	14	0
ODIs	34	23	9	170	38*	12.14	88.08	0	0	19	0
T20Is	55	32	15	247	36	14.52	129.31	0	0	29	0
First-class	114	159	23	3443	166	25.31		3	15	137	0
List A	84	56	15	634	55	15.46		0	1	45	0
T20s	212	126	51	1052	45*	14.02	117.80	0	0	121	0
Bowling	**Mat**	**Balls**	**Runs**	**Wkts**	**BBI**	**BBM**	**Ave**	**Econ**	**SR**	**5w**	**10**
Tests	8	1530	752	21	4/18	7/50	35.80	2.94	72.8	0	0
ODIs	34	1618	1611	45	5/29	5/29	35.80	5.97	35.9	1	0
T20Is	55	1152	1671	66	4/6	4/6	25.31	8.70	17.4	0	0
First-class	114	18986	10730	335	7/43	9/58	32.02	3.39	56.6	10	0
List A	84	3798	3633	121	5/28	5/28	30.02	5.73	31.3	2	0
T20s	212	4219	6012	225	4/6	4/6	26.72	8.54	18.7	0	0

ROB KEOGH

RHB / OB / R0 / W0

FULL NAME: Robert Ian Keogh
BORN: October 21, 1991, Dunstable, Bedfordshire
SQUAD NO: 14
HEIGHT: 6ft 2in
NICKNAME: Keezy
EDUCATION: Queensbury Upper School, Dunstable; Dunstable College
TEAMS: Northamptonshire
ROLE: Allrounder
DEBUT: First-class: 2012; List A: 2010; T20: 2011

BEST BATTING: 221 Northamptonshire vs Hampshire, Southampton, 2013
BEST BOWLING: 9-52 Northamptonshire vs Glamorgan, Northampton, 2016
COUNTY CAP: 2019

MOST EXCITING DAY AS A CRICKETER? Winning the domestic T20 competition in 2013
FIRST CRICKET CLUB? Dunstable Town CC, Bedfordshire. I got into cricket watching my dad play for the club. I owe a lot to DTCC – especially Brian Chapman
IF YOU COULD TAKE ONE COUNTY CRICKETER'S BEST SHOT AND ADD IT TO YOUR OWN GAME? Ben Duckett's reverse-sweep
TOUGHEST OPPONENT IN COUNTY CRICKET? Joe Leach – he's a skilful bowler who I've had a lot of good battles with over the years
MOST ECCENTRIC TEAMMATE? Nathan Buck – a man of terrible gags and pranks
WHAT WOULD YOU DO IF YOU WERE IN CHARGE OF COUNTY CRICKET? Give an hour for lunch and an hour for tea, make pitches flatter, ban slip fielders
STRANGEST THING YOU'VE DONE DURING LOCKDOWN? Going for runs and downloading the Strava app to track my distance
GUILTY PLEASURE? Peanut M&Ms
TWITTER: @RobKeogh91

Batting	Mat	Inns	NO	Runs	HS	Ave	SR	100	50	Ct	St
First-class	83	135	8	3687	221	29.03	49.93	9	10	24	0
List A	46	42	3	1272	134	32.61	87.42	2	11	9	0
T20s	59	36	10	574	59*	22.07	113.43	0	1	26	0
Bowling	**Mat**	**Balls**	**Runs**	**Wkts**	**BBI**	**BBM**	**Ave**	**Econ**	**SR**	**5w**	**10**
First-class	83	6598	3871	89	9/52	13/125	43.49	3.52	74.1	1	1
List A	46	1002	925	8	2/26	2/26	115.62	5.53	125.2	0	0
T20s	59	300	397	16	3/30	3/30	24.81	7.94	18.7	0	0

SIMON KERRIGAN

RHB / SLA / R0 / W2

FULL NAME: Simon Christopher Kerrigan
BORN: May 10, 1989, Preston, Lancashire
SQUAD NO: 10
HEIGHT: 5ft 9in
NICKNAME: Kegs
EDUCATION: Corpus Christi High School, Lancashire; Preston College; Edge Hill University, Ormskirk
TEAMS: England, Northamptonshire, Lancashire
ROLE: Bowler
DEBUT: Test: 2013; First-class: 2010; List A: 2011; T20: 2010

BEST BATTING: 62* Lancashire vs Hampshire, Southport, 2013
BEST BOWLING: 9-51 Lancashire vs Hampshire, Liverpool, 2011
COUNTY CAP: 2013 (Lancashire)

MOST EXCITING DAY AS A CRICKETER? Winning the County Championship with Lancashire at Taunton in 2011
CHILDHOOD SPORTING HERO? Andrew Flintoff – he used to live two minutes away from me
BIGGEST INFLUENCE ON YOUR DEVELOPMENT AS A CRICKETER (EXCLUDING PARENTS)? John Stanworth (Lancashire Academy) and Peter Moores – both are brilliant coaches and man-managers. They know what to say and what not to say at just the right times
IF YOU COULD TAKE ONE COUNTY CRICKETER'S BEST SHOT AND ADD IT TO YOUR OWN GAME? Any shot by Nathan Buck
TOUGHEST OPPONENT IN COUNTY CRICKET? Marcus Trescothick
WHAT WOULD YOU DO IF YOU WERE IN CHARGE OF COUNTY CRICKET? Introduce a rake option as an alternative to the heavy roller between innings
FAVOURITE SMELL? Cheese
TWITTER: @Kegs10

Batting	Mat	Inns	NO	Runs	HS	Ave	SR	100	50	Ct	St
Tests	1	1	1	1	1*	-	8.33	0	0	0	0
First-class	106	123	42	1059	62*	13.07	37.70	0	3	37	0
List A	35	15	6	30	10	3.33	50.84	0	0	11	0
T20s	24	4	4	9	4*	-	180.00	0	0	11	0
Bowling	**Mat**	**Balls**	**Runs**	**Wkts**	**BBI**	**BBM**	**Ave**	**Econ**	**SR**	**5w**	**10**
Tests	1	48	53	0	-	-	-	6.62	-	0	0
First-class	106	20785	9933	325	9/51	12/192	30.56	2.86	63.9	13	3
List A	35	1456	1302	28	3/21	3/21	46.50	5.36	52.0	0	0
T20s	24	516	595	20	3/17	3/17	29.75	6.91	25.8	0	0

RASHID KHAN RHB / LB

FULL NAME: Rashid Khan Arman
BORN: September 20, 1998, Nangarhar, Afghanistan
SQUAD NO: 1
TEAMS: Afghanistan, Sussex, Adelaide Strikers, Durban Heat, Guyana Amazon Warriors, Kabul Zwanan, Lahore Qalandars, Quetta Gladiators, Sunrisers Hyderabad
ROLE: Bowler
DEBUT: Test: 2018; ODI: 2015; T20I: 2015; First-class: 2016; List A: 2015; T20: 2015

BEST BATTING: 56* Kabul Zwanan vs Balkh Legends, Sharjah, 2018 (T20)
BEST BOWLING: 5-3 Afghanistan vs Ireland, Greater Noida, 2017 (T20)

TWITTER: @rashidkhan_19
NOTES: Sussex have re-signed the 22-year-old leg-spinner for a third T20 Blast campaign. Rashid was the first Afghan to sign for an English county when he joined Sussex ahead of the 2018 season and he played a huge part in taking the club to the final of that year's competition. He impressed again in 2019 and in all has taken 24 wickets in 20 matches at an economy rate of 6.97. Possessing a lethal googly, Rashid is the biggest talent to emerge from Afghanistan and has played in the major T20 leagues all over the world. As of March 2021, he was the No.1 bowler in the ICC T20I rankings. He is also due to play for Trent Rockets in this year's Hundred competition

Batting	Mat	Inns	NO	Runs	HS	Ave	SR	100	50	Ct	St
Tests	4	7	0	106	51	15.14	79.69	0	1	0	0
ODIs	74	58	9	1008	60*	20.57	103.27	0	5	25	0
T20Is	48	23	12	163	33	14.81	125.38	0	0	20	0
First-class	8	11	1	231	52	23.10	77.00	0	2	0	0
List A	76	59	9	1029	60*	20.58	103.93	0	5	26	0
T20s	249	132	45	1062	56*	12.20	145.28	0	1	77	0
Bowling	**Mat**	**Balls**	**Runs**	**Wkts**	**BBI**	**BBM**	**Ave**	**Econ**	**SR**	**5w**	**10**
Tests	4	938	485	23	6/49	11/104	21.08	3.10	40.7	3	1
ODIs	74	3732	2601	140	7/18	7/18	18.57	4.18	26.6	4	0
T20Is	48	1098	1124	89	5/3	5/3	12.62	6.14	12.3	2	0
First-class	8	2117	1012	58	8/74	12/122	17.44	2.86	36.5	7	2
List A	76	3839	2689	144	7/18	7/18	18.67	4.20	26.6	4	0
T20s	249	5737	6005	344	5/3	5/3	17.45	6.28	16.6	2	0

FEROZE KHUSHI

RHB / OB / R0 / W0

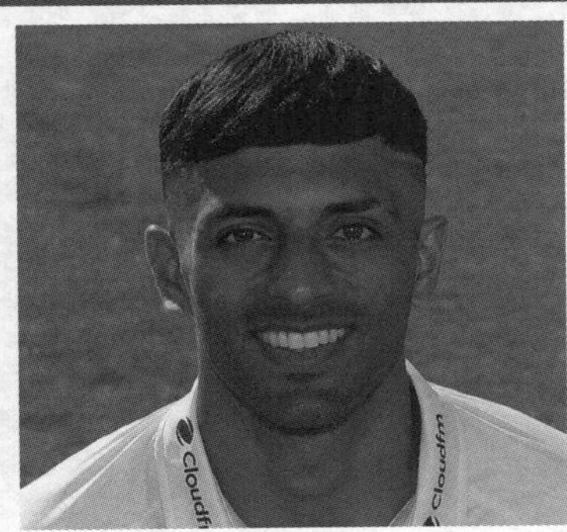

FULL NAME: Feroze Isa Nazir Khushi
BORN: June 23, 1999, Whipps Cross, Essex
SQUAD NO: 23
HEIGHT: 6ft 1in
NICKNAME: Fink
EDUCATION: Kelmscott School, Walthamstow, London
TEAMS: Essex
ROLE: Batsman
DEBUT: First-class: 2020; T20: 2020

BEST BATTING: 66 Essex vs Surrey, Chelmsford, 2020

MOST EXCITING DAY AS A CRICKETER? When I hit six sixes in the last over of a school match when we needed 30 runs to win
CHILDHOOD SPORTING HERO? Shahid Afridi
SURPRISING FACT ABOUT YOU? I went to the same school as Fabrice Muamba
NOTES: The 21-year-old batsman broke into the senior team last year, playing in four matches of Essex's triumphant campaign in the Bob Willis Trophy. Khushi made 45 on his first-class debut against Kent at Chelmsford and followed it up with 66 versus Surrey at the same ground. He also played in one T20 Blast fixture and was handed a new one-year contract last September. Khushi first signed for Essex in October 2017 after a number of impressive performances for the club's Second XI. He played regularly for the seconds in 2019, scoring 567 runs at 47.25, as well as compiling an unbeaten 120 for Suffolk in the Minor Counties Championship

Batting	Mat	Inns	NO	Runs	HS	Ave	SR	100	50	Ct	St
First-class	4	5	0	125	66	25.00	54.34	0	1	5	0
T20s	1	1	0	0	0	0.00	0.00	0	0	0	0
Bowling	**Mat**	**Balls**	**Runs**	**Wkts**	**BBI**	**BBM**	**Ave**	**Econ**	**SR**	**5w**	**10**
First-class	4	-	-	-	-	-	-	-	-	-	-
T20s	1	-	-	-	-	-	-	-	-	-	-

NICK KIMBER

RHB / RMF / R0 / W0

FULL NAME: Nicholas John Henry Kimber
BORN: January 16, 2001, Lincoln
SQUAD NO: 12
HEIGHT: 6ft 2in
NICKNAME: Kimbo
EDUCATION: William Farr Church of England School, Lincoln; Oakham School, Rutland
TEAMS: Surrey, England U19
ROLE: Bowler

MOST EXCITING DAY AS A CRICKETER? An U19 match between England and India at Chelmsford in 2019 – we lost by one wicket
CHILDHOOD SPORTING HERO? Stuart Broad
BIGGEST INFLUENCE ON YOUR DEVELOPMENT AS A CRICKETER (EXCLUDING PARENTS)? Neil Johnson, the former Zimbabwe allrounder and now director of cricket at Oakham School. He taught me a lot about the game and how to play it properly
FIRST CRICKET CLUB? Lindum CC, Lincolnshire
IF YOU COULD TAKE ONE COUNTY CRICKETER'S BEST SHOT AND ADD IT TO YOUR OWN GAME? James Taylor's pull
WHAT WOULD YOU DO IF YOU WERE IN CHARGE OF COUNTY CRICKET? Play more pink-ball cricket, set up a franchise system
WHAT WOULD YOU DO IF YOU WERE PRIME MINISTER? Invest in a space programme which rivals Elon Musk
STRANGEST THING YOU'VE DONE DURING LOCKDOWN? Yoga on Zoom
IF YOU WERE AN ANIMAL, WHICH WOULD IT BE? A koala
GUILTY PLEASURE? Doughnuts
TWITTER: @NKimber11

FRED KLAASSEN RHB / LMF / R0 / W0

FULL NAME: Frederick Jack Klaassen
BORN: November 13, 1992, Haywards Heath, Sussex
SQUAD NO: 18
HEIGHT: 6ft 5in
NICKNAME: TFD
EDUCATION: University of Otago, Dunedin, New Zealand
TEAMS: Netherlands, Kent
ROLE: Bowler
DEBUT: ODI: 2018; T20I: 2018; First-class: 2019; List A: 2017; T20: 2018

BEST BATTING: 14* Kent vs Loughborough MCCU, Canterbury, 2019
BEST BOWLING: 4-44 Kent vs Middlesex, Canterbury, 2020

CHILDHOOD SPORTING HERO? Steven Gerrard
BIGGEST INFLUENCE ON YOUR DEVELOPMENT AS A CRICKETER (EXCLUDING PARENTS)? Ryan Campbell, Netherlands head coach
FIRST CRICKET CLUB? Cornwall CC, Auckland, New Zealand
IF YOU COULD TAKE ONE COUNTY CRICKETER'S BEST SHOT AND ADD IT TO YOUR OWN GAME? Zak Crawley's pull
TOUGHEST OPPONENT IN COUNTY CRICKET? Hashim Amla
WHAT WOULD YOU DO IF YOU WERE IN CHARGE OF COUNTY CRICKET? Create a transfer window; include Scotland, Netherlands and Ireland in the 50-over competition; add the Big Bash bonus-point rule to the T20 Blast
STRANGEST THING YOU'VE DONE DURING LOCKDOWN? Taking part in bowling masterclasses at 11pm
TWITTER: @freddieklaassen

Batting	Mat	Inns	NO	Runs	HS	Ave	SR	100	50	Ct	St
ODIs	4	3	1	30	13	15.00	57.69	0	0	2	0
T20Is	21	7	1	33	13	5.50	97.05	0	0	10	0
First-class	3	4	2	37	14*	18.50	18.87	0	0	3	0
List A	21	15	8	87	16*	12.42	63.97	0	0	11	0
T20s	47	10	3	41	13	5.85	102.50	0	0	19	0
Bowling	**Mat**	**Balls**	**Runs**	**Wkts**	**BBI**	**BBM**	**Ave**	**Econ**	**SR**	**5w**	**10**
ODIs	4	240	150	10	3/30	3/30	15.00	3.75	24.0	0	0
T20Is	21	415	581	20	3/31	3/31	29.05	8.40	20.7	0	0
First-class	3	432	250	6	4/44	4/80	41.66	3.47	72.0	0	0
List A	21	1006	865	31	3/30	3/30	27.90	5.15	32.4	0	0
T20s	47	966	1415	47	3/31	3/31	30.10	8.78	20.5	0	0

DIETER KLEIN

RHB / LMF / R0 / W0

FULL NAME: Dieter Klein
BORN: October 31, 1988, Lichtenburg, North West Province, South Africa
SQUAD NO: 77
HEIGHT: 5ft 9in
NICKNAME: Diets
EDUCATION: Hoërskool Lichtenburg, South Africa
TEAMS: Germany, Leicestershire, Lions, North West
ROLE: Bowler
DEBUT: T20I: 2020; First-class: 2008; List A: 2008; T20: 2013

BEST BATTING: 94 Leicestershire vs Glamorgan, Cardiff, 2018
BEST BOWLING: 8-72 North West vs Northerns, Potchefstroom, 2014

MOST EXCITING DAY AS A CRICKETER? Sharing a partnership of almost 300 with my brother in a 40-over club match. More recently, the epic win over Lancashire in the Bob Willis Trophy last summer
CHILDHOOD SPORTING HERO? Jonty Rhodes
BIGGEST INFLUENCE ON YOUR DEVELOPMENT AS A CRICKETER (EXCLUDING PARENTS)? I am grateful to a lot of people and coaches, but Gordon Parsons (ex-Leicestershire cricketer) was a big influence as coach of Highveld Lions
TOUGHEST OPPONENT IN COUNTY CRICKET? Wayne Madsen – he somehow survives those unplayable balls that would normally get you a wicket
MOST ECCENTRIC TEAMMATE? Chris Wright – he has an obsession with good coffee and has coffee dates in the physio room with Will Garvey (Leicestershire physio)
STRANGEST THING YOU'VE DONE DURING LOCKDOWN? Putting my girlfriend on my back as a weight while doing my squat exercises

Batting	Mat	Inns	NO	Runs	HS	Ave	SR	100	50	Ct	St
T20Is	2	2	2	48	31*	-	218.18	0	0	0	0
First-class	68	96	19	1443	94	18.74	75.86	0	6	19	0
List A	33	19	4	206	46	13.73	79.53	0	0	1	0
T20s	33	21	10	128	31*	11.63	113.27	0	0	9	0
Bowling	**Mat**	**Balls**	**Runs**	**Wkts**	**BBI**	**BBM**	**Ave**	**Econ**	**SR**	**5w**	**10**
T20Is	2	48	41	2	1/12	1/12	20.50	5.12	24.0	0	0
First-class	68	9821	6371	221	8/72	10/125	28.82	3.89	44.4	10	1
List A	33	1577	1368	49	5/35	5/35	27.91	5.20	32.1	1	0
T20s	33	568	744	26	3/27	3/27	28.61	7.85	21.8	0	0

TOM KOHLER-CADMORE

RHB / OB / R1 / W0

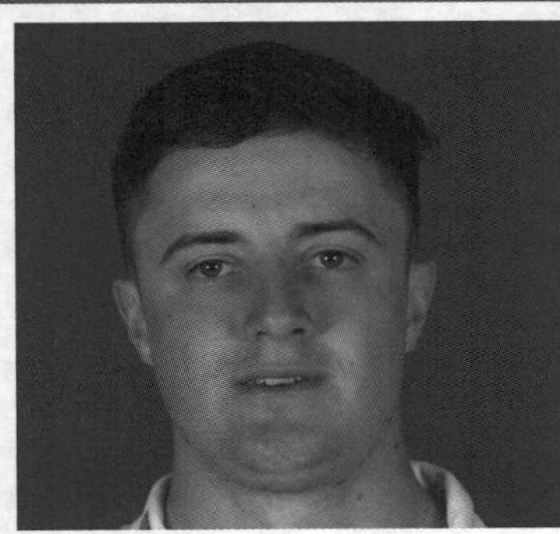

FULL NAME: Tom Kohler-Cadmore
BORN: August 19, 1994, Chatham, Kent
SQUAD NO: 32
HEIGHT: 6ft 2in
NICKNAME: Pepsi
EDUCATION: Malvern College, Worcestershire
TEAMS: Yorkshire, England Lions, Peshawar Zalmi, Quetta Gladiators, Worcestershire
ROLE: Batsman
DEBUT: First-class: 2014; List A: 2013; T20: 2014

BEST BATTING: 176 Yorkshire vs Leeds/Bradford MCCU, Weetwood, 2019

COUNTY CAP: 2019 (Yorkshire)

MOST EXCITING DAY AS A CRICKETER? My first Roses derby
BIGGEST INFLUENCE ON YOUR DEVELOPMENT AS A CRICKETER (EXCLUDING PARENTS)? My school coaches Noel Brett and Mark Hardinges – they put in so many hours of training with me, as did my Worcester coaches
IF YOU COULD TAKE ONE COUNTY CRICKETER'S BEST SHOT AND ADD IT TO YOUR OWN GAME? Jos Buttler's ramp
WHAT WOULD YOU DO IF YOU WERE IN CHARGE OF COUNTY CRICKET? Go back to 40-over cricket, play the first month of the season somewhere warm
SURPRISING FACT ABOUT YOU? I've been called the songbird of my generation by people who have heard me sing
TWITTER: @tomkcadmore

Batting	Mat	Inns	NO	Runs	HS	Ave	SR	100	50	Ct	St
First-class	66	108	8	3459	176	34.59	55.47	9	15	87	0
List A	56	54	1	1808	164	34.11	86.79	3	10	29	0
T20s	85	85	7	2310	127	29.61	140.08	1	17	50	0
Bowling	**Mat**	**Balls**	**Runs**	**Wkts**	**BBI**	**BBM**	**Ave**	**Econ**	**SR**	**5w**	**10**
First-class	66	-	-	-	-	-	-	-	-	-	-
List A	56	-	-	-	-	-	-	-	-	-	-
T20s	85	-	-	-	-	-	-	-	-	-	-

KENT

HEINO KUHN

RHB / WK / R0 / W0

FULL NAME: Heino Gunther Kuhn
BORN: April 1, 1984, Piet Retief, South Africa
SQUAD NO: 4
HEIGHT: 5ft 10in
NICKNAME: H
TEAMS: South Africa, Kent, Dhaka Dynamites, Nelson Mandela Bay Giants, Northerns, Titans
ROLE: Batsman
DEBUT: Test: 2017; T20I: 2009; First-class: 2005; List A: 2005; T20: 2007

BEST BATTING: 244* Titans vs Lions, Benoni, 2015

COUNTY CAP: 2018

MOST EXCITING DAY AS A CRICKETER? Making my Test debut for South Africa against England at Lord's
CHILDHOOD SPORTING HERO? Roger Federer
BIGGEST INFLUENCE ON YOUR DEVELOPMENT AS A CRICKETER (EXCLUDING PARENTS)? Richard Pybus, my first professional coach at Titans in South Africa
TOUGHEST OPPONENT IN COUNTY CRICKET? Tymal Mills – he's a great T20 bowler
MOST ECCENTRIC TEAMMATE? Zak Crawley – he is aged 22 going on 55!
STRANGEST THING YOU'VE DONE DURING LOCKDOWN? Raising a baby
FAVOURITE SMELL? Rosemary
GUILTY PLEASURE? A pecan-and-maple Danish pastry
TWITTER: @HeinoKuhn

Batting	Mat	Inns	NO	Runs	HS	Ave	SR	100	50	Ct	St
Tests	4	8	0	113	34	14.12	38.04	0	0	1	0
T20Is	7	6	2	49	29	12.25	116.66	0	0	5	0
First-class	175	307	28	11442	244*	41.01	-	24	58	374	18
List A	174	159	18	4859	141*	34.46	89.69	13	22	179	22
T20s	133	113	19	2425	83*	25.79	126.56	0	13	80	6
Bowling	**Mat**	**Balls**	**Runs**	**Wkts**	**BBI**	**BBM**	**Ave**	**Econ**	**SR**	**5w**	**10**
Tests	4	-	-	-	-	-	-	-	-	-	-
T20Is	7	-	-	-	-	-	-	-	-	-	-
First-class	175	6	12	0	-	-	-	12.00	-	0	0
List A	174	-	-	-	-	-	-	-	-	-	-
T20s	133	-	-	-	-	-	-	-	-	-	-

MARNUS LABUSCHAGNE

RHB / LB / R0 / W0

FULL NAME: Marnus Labuschagne
BORN: June 22, 1994, Klerksdorp, North West Province, South Africa
SQUAD NO: 99
TEAMS: Australia, Glamorgan, Brisbane Heat, Queensland
ROLE: Batsman
DEBUT: Test: 2018; ODI: 2020; First-class: 2014; List A: 2015; T20: 2017

BEST BATTING: 215 Australia vs New Zealand, Sydney, 2020
BEST BOWLING: 3-45 Australia vs Pakistan, Abu Dhabi, 2018

TWITTER: @marnus3cricket
NOTES: Labuschagne initially signed a two-year contract for Glamorgan in November 2019 but has extended his deal to run until the end of 2022 after not being able to join up with the Welsh county last summer. The Australian batsman will be available across all formats, subject to international commitments. Labuschagne made a huge impact in his first season at Cardiff in 2019, scoring five centuries and five fifties in 10 Championship matches before playing a starring role for Australia in the Ashes. He scored 897 runs in five Tests during the 2019/20 season down under; only Ricky Ponting, Matthew Hayden and Wally Hammond have scored more in an Australian Test summer. The 26-year-old was ranked No.3 in the ICC's Test batting rankings as of March 2021

Batting	Mat	Inns	NO	Runs	HS	Ave	SR	100	50	Ct	St
Tests	18	31	0	1885	215	60.80	54.94	5	10	15	0
ODIs	13	12	0	473	108	39.41	91.13	1	3	4	0
First-class	85	153	9	6467	215	44.90	54.07	16	36	82	0
List A	48	47	2	1683	135	37.40	88.16	2	14	17	0
T20s	16	15	1	273	49	19.50	113.75	0	0	7	0
Bowling	**Mat**	**Balls**	**Runs**	**Wkts**	**BBI**	**BBM**	**Ave**	**Econ**	**SR**	**5w**	**10**
Tests	18	822	500	12	3/45	5/119	41.66	3.64	68.5	0	0
ODIs	13	24	36	0	-	-	-	9.00	-	0	0
First-class	85	4137	2645	59	3/45	5/77	44.83	3.83	70.1	0	0
List A	48	492	512	8	3/46	3/46	64.00	6.24	61.5	0	0
T20s	16	144	227	11	3/13	3/13	20.63	9.45	13.0	0	0

TOM LACE

RHB / WK / R0 / W0

FULL NAME: Thomas Cresswell Lace
BORN: May 27, 1998, Hammersmith
SQUAD NO: 8
HEIGHT: 5ft 9in
NICKNAME: Lacey
EDUCATION: Millfield School, Somerset; Royal Holloway, University of London
TEAMS: Gloucestershire, Derbyshire, Middlesex
ROLE: Batsman
DEBUT: First-class: 2018; List A: 2019

BEST BATTING: 143 Derbyshire vs Glamorgan, Swansea, 2019

MOST EXCITING DAY AS A CRICKETER? Making my first-class debut for Derbyshire in 2019
CHILDHOOD SPORTING HERO? Frank Lampard
FIRST CRICKET CLUB? Sheen Park Colts, Wycombe, Buckinghamshire
IF YOU COULD TAKE ONE COUNTY CRICKETER'S BEST SHOT AND ADD IT TO YOUR OWN GAME? Wayne Madsen's upper-cut
TOUGHEST OPPONENT IN COUNTY CRICKET? Graham Wagg
WHAT WOULD YOU DO IF YOU WERE IN CHARGE OF COUNTY CRICKET? Make the morning football warm-up compulsory
STRANGEST THING YOU'VE DONE DURING LOCKDOWN? Walking through golf courses in the dark trying to find Pro V1 golf balls. Josh Shaw is also guilty of this
FAVOURITE SMELL? When you walk past a Subway
GUILTY PLEASURE? The Greatest Showman (musical)
TWITTER: @tom_lace

Batting	Mat	Inns	NO	Runs	HS	Ave	SR	100	50	Ct	St
First-class	19	35	1	1157	143	34.02	45.76	3	4	13	0
List A	9	7	0	115	48	16.42	78.76	0	0	2	0
Bowling	**Mat**	**Balls**	**Runs**	**Wkts**	**BBI**	**BBM**	**Ave**	**Econ**	**SR**	**5w**	**10**
First-class	19	-	-	-	-	-	-	-	-	-	-
List A	9	12	20	2	2/20	2/20	10.00	10.00	6.0	0	0

DANNY LAMB RHB / RFM / R0 / W0 / MVP55

FULL NAME: Daniel John Lamb
BORN: September 7, 1995, Preston, Lancashire
SQUAD NO: 26
HEIGHT: 6ft
NICKNAME: Sherman
EDUCATION: St Michael's CE High School, Chorley; Cardinal Newman College, Preston; Edge Hill University, Ormskirk
TEAMS: Lancashire
ROLE: Allrounder
DEBUT: First-class: 2018; List A: 2017; T20: 2017

BEST BATTING: 50* Lancashire vs Derbyshire, Liverpool, 2020
BEST BOWLING: 4-55 Lancashire vs Yorkshire, Headingley, 2020

MOST EXCITING DAY AS A CRICKETER? The T20 Roses match at Headingley in 2019 – we won by nine runs
FAMILY TIES? My younger sister Emma plays for Lancashire and we have played together regularly for Bramhall in the Cheshire Premier League
CHILDHOOD SPORTING HERO? Brad Friedel
FIRST CRICKET CLUB? Hoghton CC, Lancashire
TOUGHEST OPPONENT IN COUNTY CRICKET? James Vince
WHAT WOULD YOU DO IF YOU WERE IN CHARGE OF COUNTY CRICKET? Have two new balls in T20 (one for each end), introduce the "Power Surge" innovation from the Big Bash
SURPRISING FACT ABOUT YOU? I was Blackburn Rovers Academy goalkeeper from U9 to U16 level
TWITTER: @lamby236

Batting	Mat	Inns	NO	Runs	HS	Ave	SR	100	50	Ct	St
First-class	8	11	3	210	50*	26.25	46.77	0	1	2	0
List A	2	2	2	5	4*	-	83.33	0	0	0	0
T20s	22	10	6	123	29*	30.75	99.19	0	0	1	0
Bowling	**Mat**	**Balls**	**Runs**	**Wkts**	**BBI**	**BBM**	**Ave**	**Econ**	**SR**	**5w**	**10**
First-class	8	733	438	18	4/55	7/72	24.33	3.58	40.7	0	0
List A	2	120	108	4	2/51	2/51	27.00	5.40	30.0	0	0
T20s	22	324	436	17	3/30	3/30	25.64	8.07	19.0	0	0

MATT LAMB

RHB / RM / R0 / W0

WARWICKSHIRE

FULL NAME: Matthew James Lamb
BORN: July 19, 1996, Wolverhampton, Staffordshire
SQUAD NO: 7
HEIGHT: 6ft 4in
NICKNAME: Jon
EDUCATION: North Bromsgrove High School, Worcestershire
TEAMS: Warwickshire
ROLE: Batsman
DEBUT: First-class: 2016; List A: 2017; T20: 2019

BEST BATTING: 173 Warwickshire vs Essex, Edgbaston, 2019
BEST BOWLING: 1-15 Warwickshire vs Essex, Edgbaston, 2019

MOST EXCITING DAY AS A CRICKETER? Beating Middlesex at Lord's in 2017 inside three days after we were bowled out for 126 on the first day
CHILDHOOD SPORTING HERO? Paul Gascoigne
BIGGEST INFLUENCE ON YOUR DEVELOPMENT AS A CRICKETER (EXCLUDING PARENTS)? Former wicketkeeper/batsman Tony Frost, now Warwickshire's batting coach. He has supported me on and off the field
FIRST CRICKET CLUB? Barnt Green CC, Worcestershire
TOUGHEST OPPONENT IN COUNTY CRICKET? Simon Harmer
WHAT WOULD YOU DO IF YOU WERE IN CHARGE OF COUNTY CRICKET? Return to a two-division Championship, no run-outs for backing up, and 12 runs if you hit it out the ground
SURPRISING FACT ABOUT YOU? I was about to quit cricket until I was luckily selected for a Second XI game against Worcestershire in September 2015 and managed to score 142
GUILTY PLEASURE? Homemade cheesecake
TWITTER: @Lamb_Matt

Batting	Mat	Inns	NO	Runs	HS	Ave	SR	100	50	Ct	St
First-class	19	32	2	791	173	26.36	40.98	1	4	6	0
List A	3	3	0	61	47	20.33	89.70	0	0	1	0
T20s	5	5	2	102	35	34.00	130.76	0	0	0	0
Bowling	**Mat**	**Balls**	**Runs**	**Wkts**	**BBI**	**BBM**	**Ave**	**Econ**	**SR**	**5w**	**10**
First-class	19	362	254	6	1/15	1/15	42.33	4.20	60.3	0	0
List A	3	6	9	0	-	-	-	9.00	-	0	0
T20s	5	-	-	-	-	-	-	-	-	-	-

TOM LAMMONBY LHB / LMF / R0 / W0 / MVP24

FULL NAME: Thomas Alexander Lammonby
BORN: June 2, 2000, Exeter, Devon
SQUAD NO: 15
HEIGHT: 6ft
NICKNAME: Lammers
EDUCATION: Exeter School
TEAMS: Somerset, England U19
ROLE: Allrounder
DEBUT: First-class: 2020; T20: 2019

BEST BATTING: 116 Somerset vs Essex, Lord's, 2020
BEST BOWLING: 1-4 Somerset vs Gloucestershire, Taunton

MOST EXCITING DAY AS A CRICKETER? Scoring a hundred in the Bob Willis Trophy final at Lord's last summer
CHILDHOOD SPORTING HERO? Ricky Ponting
FIRST CRICKET CLUB? Exeter CC, Devon
IF YOU COULD TAKE ONE COUNTY CRICKETER'S BEST SHOT AND ADD IT TO YOUR OWN GAME? Either Tom Abell's back-foot punch or Steven Davies's cover-drive
TOUGHEST OPPONENT IN COUNTY CRICKET? Alastair Cook
BIGGEST CRICKETING REGRET? Not playing at the 2018 U19 World Cup because of injury
FAVOURITE SMELL? The beach
IF YOU WERE AN ANIMAL, WHICH WOULD IT BE? I'd like to be a tiger but I'm actually more of a goldfish – forgetful, a bit boring, but everyone has wanted one at some stage
GUILTY PLEASURE? Chocolate eclairs
TWITTER: @TomLammonby

Batting	Mat	Inns	NO	Runs	HS	Ave	SR	100	50	Ct	St
First-class	6	11	2	459	116	51.00	51.68	3	0	4	0
T20s	18	14	5	209	43*	23.22	159.54	0	0	5	0
Bowling	**Mat**	**Balls**	**Runs**	**Wkts**	**BBI**	**BBM**	**Ave**	**Econ**	**SR**	**5w**	**10**
First-class	6	72	38	2	1/4	1/4	19.00	3.16	36.0	0	0
T20s	18	150	263	9	2/32	2/32	29.22	10.52	16.6	0	0

GEORGE LAVELLE

LHB / WK / R0 / W0

FULL NAME: George Isaac Davies Lavelle
BORN: March 24, 2000, Ormskirk, Lancashire
SQUAD NO: 24
HEIGHT: 5ft 8in
NICKNAME: Spizza
EDUCATION: Merchant Taylors' School, Crosby, Merseyside
TEAMS: Lancashire, England U19
ROLE: Wicketkeeper/batsman
DEBUT: First-class: 2020; T20: 2020

BEST BATTING: 13 Lancashire vs Derbyshire, Liverpool, 2020

MOST EXCITING DAY AS A CRICKETER? Playing against Yorkshire at Old Trafford on my T20 debut last summer
CHILDHOOD SPORTING HERO? Steven Gerrard
FIRST CRICKET CLUB? Ormskirk CC, Lancashire
IF YOU COULD TAKE ONE COUNTY CRICKETER'S BEST SHOT AND ADD IT TO YOUR OWN GAME? Tom Hartley's reverse-sweep
TOUGHEST OPPONENT IN COUNTY CRICKET? Joe Root
WHAT WOULD YOU DO IF YOU WERE IN CHARGE OF COUNTY CRICKET? Ensure that there is always a cheesecake option at lunch
WHAT WOULD YOU DO IF YOU WERE PRIME MINISTER? Scrap university fees
STRANGEST THING YOU'VE DONE DURING LOCKDOWN? Chipping golf balls down the stairs
FAVOURITE SMELL? Italian food
GUILTY PLEASURE? Ice cream
TWITTER: @Glavelle_181

Batting	Mat	Inns	NO	Runs	HS	Ave	SR	100	50	Ct	St
First-class	1	2	0	20	13	10.00	34.48	0	0	2	0
T20s	2	2	0	18	12	9.00	90.00	0	0	0	0
Bowling	**Mat**	**Balls**	**Runs**	**Wkts**	**BBI**	**BBM**	**Ave**	**Econ**	**SR**	**5w**	**10**
First-class	1	-	-	-	-	-	-	-	-	-	-
T20s	2	-	-	-	-	-	-	-	-	-	-

DAN LAWRENCE RHB / LB / R1 / W0 / MVP95

FULL NAME: Daniel William Lawrence
BORN: July 12, 1997, Whipps Cross, Essex
SQUAD NO: 28
EDUCATION: Trinity Catholic High School, Woodford Green, London
TEAMS: England, Essex, Brisbane Heat
ROLE: Batsman
DEBUT: Test: 2021; First-class: 2015; List A: 2016; T20: 2015

BEST BATTING: 161 Essex vs Surrey, The Oval, 2015
BEST BOWLING: 2-63 Essex vs MCC, Barbados, 2018
COUNTY CAP: 2017

FAMILY TIES? My dad is the groundsman at Chingford CC and played at the club for many years. My great uncle played for England
CHILDHOOD SPORTING HERO? David Beckham
TWITTER: @DanLawrence288
NOTES: Lawrence has been on England's radar ever since he made 161 as a 17-year-old in 2015 in his second Championship appearance. The following year he passed 1,000 first-class runs in his first full season at Chelmsford and was the Cricket Writers' Young Player of the Year in 2017 after contributing three hundreds to Essex's title-winning campaign. He made his England Lions debut that year. Lawrence was a key contributor when Essex won the Championship-T20 double in 2019 and impressed hugely during the England Lions tour to Australia the following winter. He played for Brisbane Heat in the 2020/21 edition of the Big Bash before making his Test debut in Sri Lanka earlier this year

Batting	Mat	Inns	NO	Runs	HS	Ave	SR	100	50	Ct	St
Tests	5	10	1	248	73	27.55	44.44	0	2	1	0
First-class	79	127	14	4196	161	37.13	51.56	10	20	56	0
List A	28	25	0	670	115	26.80	89.09	1	4	9	0
T20s	64	58	7	1317	86	25.82	139.21	0	6	20	0
Bowling	**Mat**	**Balls**	**Runs**	**Wkts**	**BBI**	**BBM**	**Ave**	**Econ**	**SR**	**5w**	**10**
Tests	5	18	17	0	-	-	-	5.66	-	0	0
First-class	79	672	396	9	2/63	2/8	44.00	3.53	74.6	0	0
List A	28	573	597	11	3/35	3/35	54.27	6.25	52.0	0	0
T20s	64	372	463	21	3/21	3/21	22.04	7.46	17.7	0	0

JACK LEACH

LHB / SLA / R0 / W3

SOMERSET

FULL NAME: Matthew Jack Leach
BORN: June 22, 1991, Taunton, Somerset
SQUAD NO: 17
HEIGHT: 6ft
NICKNAME: Nut
EDUCATION: Bishop Fox's Community School; Richard Huish College; Cardiff Metropolitan University
TEAMS: England, Somerset
ROLE: Bowler
DEBUT: Test: 2018; First-class: 2012; List A: 2012

BEST BATTING: 92 England vs Ireland, Lord's, 2019
BEST BOWLING: 8-85 Somerset vs Essex, Taunton, 2018
COUNTY CAP: 2017

FIRST CRICKET CLUB? Taunton Deane CC, Somerset
BEST INNINGS YOU'VE SEEN? Marcus Trescothick's 13-ball fifty in a T20 in 2010
WHAT WOULD YOU DO IF YOU WERE IN CHARGE OF COUNTY CRICKET? Change the lbw law so that you can be given out even if you are hit outside the line
SURPRISING FACT ABOUT YOU? I wrote a letter to Marcus Trescothick asking for advice when I was about 10 years old. He sent me a long reply and I still have the letter. What a man
TWITTER: @jackleach1991

Batting	Mat	Inns	NO	Runs	HS	Ave	SR	100	50	Ct	St
Tests	16	28	8	273	92	13.65	34.77	0	1	9	0
First-class	96	134	33	1191	92	11.79	35.01	0	3	42	0
List A	16	5	2	22	18	7.33	44.00	0	0	9	0
Bowling	**Mat**	**Balls**	**Runs**	**Wkts**	**BBI**	**BBM**	**Ave**	**Econ**	**SR**	**5w**	**10**
Tests	16	3703	1859	62	5/83	8/153	29.98	3.01	59.7	2	0
First-class	96	18454	8414	321	8/85	12/102	26.21	2.73	57.4	21	3
List A	16	824	641	21	3/7	3/7	30.52	4.66	39.2	0	0

JOE LEACH

RHB / RFM / R0 / W3 / MVP96

FULL NAME: Joseph Leach
BORN: October 30, 1990, Stafford
SQUAD NO: 23
HEIGHT: 6ft
NICKNAME: SSB
EDUCATION: Shrewsbury School; University of Leeds
TEAMS: Worcestershire
ROLE: Allrounder
DEBUT: First-class: 2012; List A: 2012; T20: 2013

BEST BATTING: 114 Worcestershire vs Gloucestershire, Cheltenham, 2013
BEST BOWLING: 6-73 Worcestershire vs Warwickshire, Edgbaston, 2015
COUNTY CAP: 2012

MOST EXCITING DAY AS A CRICKETER? Winning Championship promotion in 2014
BIGGEST INFLUENCE ON YOUR DEVELOPMENT AS A CRICKETER (EXCLUDING PARENTS)? Grandpa – for endlessly throwing me balls in the nets
FIRST CRICKET CLUB? Stone CC, Staffordshire. Never play on the back foot at Stone!
IF YOU COULD TAKE ONE COUNTY CRICKETER'S BEST SHOT AND ADD IT TO YOUR OWN GAME? Charlie Morris's back-foot drive
TOUGHEST OPPONENT IN COUNTY CRICKET? Wayne Madsen
MOST INTERESTING TEAMMATE? Thilan Samaraweera – because of the stories he told about the attack on the Sri Lanka bus in Lahore
BIGGEST CRICKETING REGRET? Being injured for T20 Finals Day in 2018
GUILTY PLEASURE? Escape to the Country on TV
TWITTER: @joeleach230

Batting	Mat	Inns	NO	Runs	HS	Ave	SR	100	50	Ct	St
First-class	93	138	17	2919	114	24.12	63.60	2	18	23	0
List A	38	28	8	539	63	26.95	100.00	0	1	13	0
T20s	54	33	8	261	24	10.44	113.47	0	0	10	0

Bowling	Mat	Balls	Runs	Wkts	BBI	BBM	Ave	Econ	SR	5w	10
First-class	93	15174	8615	330	6/73	10/122	26.10	3.40	45.9	13	1
List A	38	1707	1719	43	4/30	4/30	39.97	6.04	39.6	0	0
T20s	54	849	1355	52	5/33	5/33	26.05	9.57	16.3	1	0

JACK LEANING

RHB / RM / R0 / W0 / MVP60

FULL NAME: Jack Andrew Leaning
BORN: October 18, 1993, Bristol
SQUAD NO: 34
HEIGHT: 6ft
EDUCATION: Archbishop Holgate's School, York; York College
TEAMS: Kent, England U19, Yorkshire
ROLE: Batsman
DEBUT: First-class: 2013; List A: 2012; T20: 2013

BEST BATTING: 220* Kent vs Sussex, Canterbury, 2020
BEST BOWLING: 2-20 Yorkshire vs Hampshire, Southampton, 2019
COUNTY CAP: 2016 (Yorkshire)

TWITTER: @JackLeaning1
NOTES: The former Yorkshire batsman signed for Kent in August 2019 in a bid to revive a career which started so promisingly, and it appears to have had the desired effect. Leaning scored a career-best 220 not out against Sussex at Canterbury, sharing a stand of 423 with fellow double-centurion Jordan Cox – the biggest partnership in Kent's first-class history. But the fact that Leaning managed only 59 runs from his other seven red-ball innings last summer showed that he is yet to rediscover the consistency that marked his early days at Yorkshire. Son of former York City goalkeeper Andy, Leaning wrote himself into the Yorkshire record books when he hit an unbeaten 164 for the county's U14 side against Cheshire. He made his first-class debut in 2013 and scored his maiden Championship century two years later. His season-haul of 922 runs in 2015 earned him the Cricket Writers' Club Young Player of the Year award. But the runs dried up thereafter, with last year's double century representing his first hundred since 2017

Batting	Mat	Inns	NO	Runs	HS	Ave	SR	100	50	Ct	St
First-class	73	116	12	3234	220*	31.09	42.65	5	16	61	0
List A	50	43	7	1061	131*	29.47	79.29	2	5	24	0
T20s	63	54	14	1153	64	28.82	133.91	0	3	26	0
Bowling	**Mat**	**Balls**	**Runs**	**Wkts**	**BBI**	**BBM**	**Ave**	**Econ**	**SR**	**5w**	**10**
First-class	73	712	457	8	2/20	2/25	57.12	3.85	89.0	0	0
List A	50	303	286	9	5/22	5/22	31.77	5.66	33.6	1	0
T20s	63	60	88	1	1/15	1/15	88.00	8.80	60.0	0	0

ALEX LEES

LHB / LB / R2 / W0 / MVP17

FULL NAME: Alexander Zak Lees
BORN: April 14, 1993, Halifax, Yorkshire
SQUAD NO: 19
HEIGHT: 6ft 3in
NICKNAME: Leesy
EDUCATION: Holy Trinity Senior School, Halifax
TEAMS: Durham, England Lions, Yorkshire
ROLE: Batsman
DEBUT: First-class: 2010; List A: 2011; T20: 2013

BEST BATTING: 275* Yorkshire vs Derbyshire, Chesterfield, 2013
BEST BOWLING: 2-51 Yorkshire vs Middlesex, Lord's, 2016
COUNTY CAP: 2014 (Yorkshire)

CHILDHOOD SPORTING HERO? Brian Lara
FIRST CRICKET CLUB? Bradshaw & Illingworth CC, Halifax
MOST INTERESTING TEAMMATE? Mark Wood
SURPRISING FACT ABOUT YOU? I do a bit of magic on the side
IF YOU WERE AN ANIMAL, WHICH WOULD IT BE? A dog
TWITTER: @aleesy14
NOTES: Lees joined Durham on a three-year permanent deal in August 2018 following a tough couple of seasons at Yorkshire. The left-handed opener has since recovered the form of his early career, falling narrowly short of 1,000 first-class runs in 2019 and also impressing in 50-over cricket. He was outstanding for Durham last season, finishing as the club's top run-scorer in both the Bob Willis Trophy (386 at 48.25) and the T20 Blast (365 at 52.14). Another strong season this summer could draw the attention of the England selectors

Batting	Mat	Inns	NO	Runs	HS	Ave	SR	100	50	Ct	St
First-class	115	198	13	6450	275*	34.86	47.50	16	30	81	0
List A	54	49	5	1533	115	34.84	75.48	2	12	18	0
T20s	55	52	6	1350	77*	29.34	121.40	0	8	19	0
Bowling	**Mat**	**Balls**	**Runs**	**Wkts**	**BBI**	**BBM**	**Ave**	**Econ**	**SR**	**5w**	**10**
First-class	115	67	96	3	2/51	2/51	32.00	8.59	22.3	0	0
List A	54	-	-	-	-	-	-	-	-	-	-
T20s	55	-	-	-	-	-	-	-	-	-	-

NED LEONARD RHB / RFM / R0 / W0

FULL NAME: Edward Owen Leonard
BORN: August 15, 2002, Hammersmith, London
SQUAD NO: 19
HEIGHT: 6ft 2in
NICKNAME: Deadly
EDUCATION: Millfield School, Somerset
TEAMS: Somerset, England U19
ROLE: Bowler

MOST EXCITING DAY AS A CRICKETER? Signing my first professional contract at Somerset
CHILDHOOD SPORTING HERO? Jonny Wilkinson
BIGGEST INFLUENCE ON YOUR DEVELOPMENT AS A CRICKETER (EXCLUDING PARENTS)? Mark Garaway – director of cricket at Millfield School
IF YOU COULD TAKE ONE COUNTY CRICKETER'S BEST SHOT AND ADD IT TO YOUR OWN GAME? James Hildreth's pull
TOUGHEST OPPONENT IN COUNTY CRICKET? Delray Rawlins – it felt like he knew where the ball was going to land even before I bowled it
WHAT WOULD YOU DO IF YOU WERE IN CHARGE OF COUNTY CRICKET? Remove the free-hit rule from T20 and one-day formats, allow three bouncers per over
STRANGEST THING YOU'VE DONE DURING LOCKDOWN? Shaving my head
FAVOURITE SMELL? A wood fire in the pub
TWITTER: @n_leoand
NOTES: The England U19 fast bowler signed his first professional contract with Somerset last September having worked his way up the ranks since joining the Academy in 2017. "Ned possesses genuine pace and has the ability to pose a strong wicket-taking threat with the new and old ball," said Academy director Steve Snell. "We have a number of high-quality pace bowlers at the club and Ned has a great opportunity to learn from, practise with and compete in the company of top-level practitioners"

RICHARD LEVI RHB / RM / R0 / W0

FULL NAME: Richard Ernst Levi
BORN: January 14, 1988, Johannesburg
SQUAD NO: 88
HEIGHT: 6ft
NICKNAME: Bear
EDUCATION: Wynberg Boys' High School, Cape Town; University of South Africa
TEAMS: South Africa, Northamptonshire, Cape Cobras, Mumbai Indians, Somerset, Western Province
ROLE: Batsman
DEBUT: T20I: 2012; First-class: 2006; List A: 2005; T20: 2008

BEST BATTING: 168 Northamptonshire vs Essex, Northampton, 2015

COUNTY CAP: 2017 (Northamptonshire)

CHILDHOOD SPORTING HERO? Gary Kirsten
BIGGEST INFLUENCE ON YOUR DEVELOPMENT AS A CRICKETER (EXCLUDING PARENTS)? Richard Pybus, my coach at Cape Cobras
FIRST CRICKET CLUB? Claremont CC, Cape Town, South Africa
IF YOU COULD TAKE ONE COUNTY CRICKETER'S BEST SHOT AND ADD IT TO YOUR OWN GAME? Josh Cobb's nurdle
WHAT WOULD YOU DO IF YOU WERE IN CHARGE OF COUNTY CRICKET? Never ask a cricketer what they want...
STRANGEST THING YOU'VE DONE DURING LOCKDOWN? Being productive
FAVOURITE SMELL? Champagne over steel
IF YOU WERE AN ANIMAL, WHICH WOULD IT BE? A bear. It's pretty self-explanatory, right?
TWITTER: @RichardLevi88

Batting	Mat	Inns	NO	Runs	HS	Ave	SR	100	50	Ct	St
T20Is	13	13	2	236	117*	21.45	141.31	1	1	4	0
First-class	106	176	18	5722	168	36.21	68.10	10	32	89	0
List A	140	132	6	4614	166	36.61	104.53	8	29	44	0
T20s	215	206	13	5422	117*	28.09	144.24	3	34	59	0
Bowling	**Mat**	**Balls**	**Runs**	**Wkts**	**BBI**	**BBM**	**Ave**	**Econ**	**SR**	**5w**	**10**
T20Is	13	-	-	-	-	-	-	-	-	-	-
First-class	106	-	-	-	-	-	-	-	-	-	-
List A	140	-	-	-	-	-	-	-	-	-	-
T20s	215	-	-	-	-	-	-	-	-	-	-

JAKE LIBBY

RHB / OB / R0 / W0 / MVP19

WORCESTERSHIRE

FULL NAME: Jacob Daniel Libby
BORN: January 3, 1993, Plymouth, Devon
SQUAD NO: 2
HEIGHT: 5ft 8in
NICKNAME: Libs
EDUCATION: Plymouth College; Truro College, Cornwall; Cardiff Metropolitan University
TEAMS: Worcestershire, Northamptonshire, Nottinghamshire
ROLE: Batsman
DEBUT: First-class: 2014; List A: 2019; T20: 2018

BEST BATTING: 184 Worcestershire vs Glamorgan, Worcester, 2020
BEST BOWLING: 2-45 Worcestershire vs Glamorgan, Worcester, 2020

CHILDHOOD SPORTING HERO? Tiger Woods
BIGGEST INFLUENCE ON YOUR DEVELOPMENT AS A CRICKETER (EXCLUDING PARENTS)? Sean Hooper – my old coach from Cornwall who I still seek advice from to this day
FIRST CRICKET CLUB? Menheniot & Looe CC, Cornwall
IF YOU COULD TAKE ONE COUNTY CRICKETER'S BEST SHOT AND ADD IT TO YOUR OWN GAME? Luke Fletcher's forward defence
TOUGHEST OPPONENT IN COUNTY CRICKET? Chris Rushworth
WHAT WOULD YOU DO IF YOU WERE IN CHARGE OF COUNTY CRICKET? Allow baseball mitts for fielding in T20, ban the Dukes ball!
WHAT WOULD YOU DO IF YOU WERE PRIME MINISTER? Resign. I wouldn't want all that pressure and public negativity – cricket is bad enough!
STRANGEST THING YOU'VE DONE DURING LOCKDOWN? Yoga
FAVOURITE SMELL? My Labrador
GUILTY PLEASURE? Chocolate Buttons
TWITTER: @JakeLibby1

Batting	Mat	Inns	NO	Runs	HS	Ave	SR	100	50	Ct	St
First-class	60	105	6	3072	184	31.03	43.02	6	14	21	0
List A	7	5	0	117	66	23.40	101.73	0	1	1	0
T20s	29	23	4	687	75*	36.15	135.50	0	3	10	0
Bowling	**Mat**	**Balls**	**Runs**	**Wkts**	**BBI**	**BBM**	**Ave**	**Econ**	**SR**	**5w**	**10**
First-class	60	548	342	6	2/45	2/45	57.00	3.74	91.3	0	0
List A	7	-	-	-	-	-	-	-	-	-	-
T20s	29	42	54	1	1/11	1/11	54.00	7.71	42.0	0	0

ARRON LILLEY

RHB / OB / R0 / W0

FULL NAME: Arron Mark Lilley
BORN: April 1, 1991, Tameside, Lancashire
SQUAD NO: 7
HEIGHT: 6ft 2in
NICKNAME: Bigshow
EDUCATION: Mossley Hollins High School, Tameside; Ashton Sixth Form
TEAMS: Leicestershire, Lancashire
ROLE: Allrounder
DEBUT: First-class: 2013; List A: 2012; T20: 2013

BEST BATTING: 63 Lancashire vs Derbyshire, Southport, 2015
BEST BOWLING: 5-23 Lancashire vs Derbyshire, Southport, 2015

MOST EXCITING DAY AS A CRICKETER? Winning the T20 Blast with Lancashire in 2015
CHILDHOOD SPORTING HERO? Shane Warne
FIRST CRICKET CLUB? Micklehurst CC, Greater Manchester. My grandad and dad played there before me
IF YOU COULD TAKE ONE COUNTY CRICKETER'S BEST SHOT AND ADD IT TO YOUR OWN GAME? Alex Hales's flat-bat shot
TOUGHEST OPPONENT IN COUNTY CRICKET? Kumar Sangakkara
MOST ECCENTRIC TEAMMATE? Dieter Klein – he's got so much energy
WHAT WOULD YOU DO IF YOU WERE IN CHARGE OF COUNTY CRICKET? Ban the bouncer!
FAVOURITE SMELL? Freshly baked cookies
TWITTER: @Arronlilley20

Batting	Mat	Inns	NO	Runs	HS	Ave	SR	100	50	Ct	St
First-class	16	20	5	444	63	29.60	88.27	0	2	5	0
List A	19	11	1	100	25	10.00	113.63	0	0	10	0
T20s	94	65	9	1064	69	19.00	150.70	0	2	46	0
Bowling	**Mat**	**Balls**	**Runs**	**Wkts**	**BBI**	**BBM**	**Ave**	**Econ**	**SR**	**5w**	**10**
First-class	16	2721	1428	43	5/23	6/151	33.20	3.14	63.2	2	0
List A	19	570	530	15	4/30	4/30	35.33	5.57	38.0	0	0
T20s	94	1106	1366	43	3/31	3/31	31.76	7.41	25.7	0	0

JAKE LINTOTT

RHB / SLW / R0 / W0

WARWICKSHIRE

FULL NAME: Jacob Benedict Lintott
BORN: April 22, 1993, Taunton, Somerset
SQUAD NO: 23
HEIGHT: 5ft 11in
NICKNAME: Linsanity
EDUCATION: Queen's College, Taunton
TEAMS: Warwickshire, Gloucestershire, Hampshire
ROLE: Bowler
DEBUT: T20: 2017

MOST EXCITING DAY AS A CRICKETER? Signing my first professional contract with Warwickshire earlier this year
CHILDHOOD SPORTING HERO? Kevin Pietersen
BIGGEST INFLUENCE ON YOUR DEVELOPMENT AS A CRICKETER (EXCLUDING PARENTS)? Piers McBride, my county age-group coach at Somerset. He was very supportive and still works with me now at my club Clevedon CC
IF YOU COULD TAKE ONE COUNTY CRICKETER'S BEST SHOT AND ADD IT TO YOUR OWN GAME? Jos Buttler's ramp
TOUGHEST OPPONENT IN COUNTY CRICKET? James Vince
MOST ECCENTRIC TEAMMATE? We're not a particularly eccentric squad, but I would go for Henry Brookes – top lad, good banter, dressing-room DJ
WHAT WOULD YOU DO IF YOU WERE IN CHARGE OF COUNTY CRICKET? Group together all T20 cricket in one block to stop transferring from red- to white-ball format, introduce an FA-Cup-type competition instead of the current 50-over tournament (with all clubs in the country taking part), make it compulsory for counties to have a spin-bowling coach as well as a fast-bowling coach
GUILTY PLEASURE? Exeter City FC
TWITTER: @lintott23

Batting	Mat	Inns	NO	Runs	HS	Ave	SR	100	50	Ct	St
T20s	13	8	3	36	12	7.20	75.00	0	0	7	0
Bowling	**Mat**	**Balls**	**Runs**	**Wkts**	**BBI**	**BBM**	**Ave**	**Econ**	**SR**	**5w**	**10**
T20s	13	269	296	14	3/11	3/11	21.14	6.60	19.2	0	0

LIAM LIVINGSTONE RHB / LB / R0 / W0 / MVP75

FULL NAME: Liam Stephen Livingstone
BORN: August 4, 1993, Barrow-in-Furness, Cumbria
SQUAD NO: 7
HEIGHT: 6ft 2in
EDUCATION: Chetwynde School, Barrow-in-Furness
TEAMS: England, Lancashire, Karachi Kings, Perth Scorchers, Peshawar Zalmi, Rajasthan Royals
ROLE: Batsman
DEBUT: T20I: 2018; First-class: 2016; List A: 2015; T20: 2015

BEST BATTING: 224 Lancashire vs Warwickshire, Old Trafford, 2017
BEST BOWLING: 6-52 Lancashire vs Surrey, Old Trafford, 2017
COUNTY CAP: 2017

MOST EXCITING DAY AS A CRICKETER? Winning the T20 Blast in 2015
FAMILY TIES? My father and brother played low-level club cricket
CHILDHOOD SPORTING HERO? Andrew Flintoff – he was so good to watch as a young kid. Shane Warne – I was a leg-spinner growing up
FIRST CRICKET CLUB? Barrow CC, Cumbria
SURPRISING FACT ABOUT YOU? I once scored 350 in a club game
TWITTER: @liaml4893
NOTES: Livingstone was re-signed by Rajasthan Royals for the 2021 IPL having opted out of last year's tournament to focus on red-ball cricket

Batting	Mat	Inns	NO	Runs	HS	Ave	SR	100	50	Ct	St
T20Is	2	2	0	16	16	8.00	84.21	0	0	0	0
First-class	56	87	14	2992	224	40.98	59.48	7	15	69	0
List A	55	46	3	1552	129	36.09	99.48	1	10	25	0
T20s	128	123	9	3133	100	27.48	140.36	1	18	53	0
Bowling	**Mat**	**Balls**	**Runs**	**Wkts**	**BBI**	**BBM**	**Ave**	**Econ**	**SR**	**5w**	**10**
T20Is	2	-	-	-	-	-	-	-	-	-	-
First-class	56	2829	1306	39	6/52	6/52	33.48	2.76	72.5	1	0
List A	55	1305	1134	23	3/51	3/51	49.30	5.21	56.7	0	0
T20s	128	642	849	47	4/17	4/17	18.06	7.93	13.6	0	0

DAVID LLOYD

RHB / OB / R0 / W0

GLAMORGAN

FULL NAME: David Liam Lloyd
BORN: June 15, 1992, St Asaph, Denbighshire, Wales
SQUAD NO: 73
HEIGHT: 5ft 9in
NICKNAME: Dai
EDUCATION: Darland High School, Wrexham; Shrewsbury School
TEAMS: Glamorgan
ROLE: Batsman
DEBUT: First-class: 2012; List A: 2014; T20: 2014

BEST BATTING: 119 Glamorgan vs Gloucestershire, Bristol, 2018
BEST BOWLING: 3-36 Glamorgan vs Northamptonshire, Swansea, 2016

MOST EXCITING DAY AS A CRICKETER? Scoring my maiden first-class hundred for Glamorgan in 2016
CHILDHOOD SPORTING HERO? Lee Trundle
BIGGEST INFLUENCE ON YOUR DEVELOPMENT AS A CRICKETER (EXCLUDING PARENTS)? Paul Pridgeon, the former Worcestershire seamer
FIRST CRICKET CLUB? Brymbo CC, Clwyd, Wales
IF YOU COULD TAKE ONE COUNTY CRICKETER'S BEST SHOT AND ADD IT TO YOUR OWN GAME? An Ian Bell drive
TOUGHEST OPPONENT IN COUNTY CRICKET? Rashid Khan – it's always a huge challenge to face all his variations
BIGGEST CRICKETING REGRET? Getting 97 not out in a T20 against Kent in 2016
STRANGEST THING YOU'VE DONE DURING LOCKDOWN? Running a half-marathon in my garden
FAVOURITE SMELL? Peshwari naan
SURPRISING FACT ABOUT YOU? I have a degree in Economics
GUILTY PLEASURE? Wrexham AFC
TWITTER: @lloyddl2010

Batting	Mat	Inns	NO	Runs	HS	Ave	SR	100	50	Ct	St
First-class	69	116	12	2939	119	28.25	59.55	4	11	34	0
List A	46	40	2	942	92	24.78	85.24	0	5	12	0
T20s	53	47	2	1099	97*	24.42	127.79	0	6	16	0
Bowling	**Mat**	**Balls**	**Runs**	**Wkts**	**BBI**	**BBM**	**Ave**	**Econ**	**SR**	**5w**	**10**
First-class	69	4345	2812	61	3/36	3/53	46.09	3.88	71.2	0	0
List A	46	745	741	17	5/53	5/53	43.58	5.96	43.8	1	0
T20s	53	54	81	5	2/13	2/13	16.20	9.00	10.8	0	0

ADAM LYTH

LHB / OB / R3 / W0 / MVP22

FULL NAME: Adam Lyth
BORN: September 25, 1987, Whitby, Yorkshire
SQUAD NO: 9
HEIGHT: 5ft 9in
NICKNAME: Budge
EDUCATION: Caedmon School; Whitby Community School
TEAMS: England, Yorkshire, Multan Sultans, Rangpur Riders
ROLE: Batsman
DEBUT: Test: 2015; First-class: 2007; List A: 2006; T20: 2008

BEST BATTING: 251 Yorkshire vs Lancashire, Old Trafford, 2014
BEST BOWLING: 2-9 Yorkshire vs Middlesex, Scarborough, 2016
COUNTY CAP: 2010

MOST EXCITING DAY AS A CRICKETER? My Test debut for England in 2015
FAMILY TIES? My brother and dad played for Scarborough and my grandad played for Whitby CC
CHILDHOOD SPORTING HERO? Brian Lara
BIGGEST INFLUENCE ON YOUR DEVELOPMENT AS A CRICKETER (EXCLUDING PARENTS)? Phil Hart, my former coach at Scarborough
TOUGHEST OPPONENT IN COUNTY CRICKET? Graham Onions – I'd say he's got me out more than any other bowler
STRANGEST THING YOU'VE DONE DURING LOCKDOWN? Starting to cook
SURPRISING FACT ABOUT YOU? I had trials with Manchester City before choosing cricket
GUILTY PLEASURE? Whisky
TWITTER: @lythy09

Batting	Mat	Inns	NO	Runs	HS	Ave	SR	100	50	Ct	St
Tests	7	13	0	265	107	20.38	50.09	1	0	8	0
First-class	181	304	15	10894	251	37.69	-	24	58	236	0
List A	122	115	8	3765	144	35.18	93.84	5	18	55	0
T20s	124	115	3	2993	161	26.72	144.51	1	18	64	0
Bowling	**Mat**	**Balls**	**Runs**	**Wkts**	**BBI**	**BBM**	**Ave**	**Econ**	**SR**	**5w**	**10**
Tests	7	6	0	0	-	-	-	0.00	-	0	0
First-class	181	2827	1699	36	2/9	2/9	47.19	3.60	78.5	0	0
List A	122	360	373	6	2/27	2/27	62.16	6.21	60.0	0	0
T20s	124	408	493	22	5/31	5/31	22.40	7.25	18.5	1	0

WAYNE MADSEN RHB / OB / R5 / W0 / MVP88

DERBYSHIRE

FULL NAME: Wayne Lee Madsen
BORN: January 2, 1984, Durban, South Africa
SQUAD NO: 77
HEIGHT: 5ft 11in
NICKNAME: Psycho
EDUCATION: Highbury Preparatory School; Kearsney College; University of South Africa
TEAMS: Derbyshire, Dolphins, KwaZulu-Natal, Multan Sultans, Peshawar Zalmi
ROLE: Batsman
DEBUT: First-class: 2004; List A: 2004; T20: 2010

BEST BATTING: 231* Derbyshire vs Northamptonshire, Northampton, 2012
BEST BOWLING: 3-45 KwaZulu-Natal vs Eastern Province, Port Elizabeth, 2008
COUNTY CAP: 2011; BENEFIT: 2017

CHILDHOOD SPORTING HERO? Jonty Rhodes
BIGGEST INFLUENCE ON YOUR DEVELOPMENT AS A CRICKETER (EXCLUDING PARENTS)? My uncle Trevor – he coached me when I was a kid and watching him play for South Africa inspired me to play the game
FIRST CRICKET CLUB? Crusaders CC, Durban, South Africa. I got a golden duck in my first game
IF YOU COULD TAKE ONE COUNTY CRICKETER'S BEST SHOT AND ADD IT TO YOUR OWN GAME? James Vince – the one that goes over extra-cover
TOUGHEST OPPONENT IN COUNTY CRICKET? Graham Onions – he had it on a string
MOST ECCENTRIC TEAMMATE? Fynn Hudson-Prentice – for his hair-dos
WHAT WOULD YOU DO IF YOU WERE IN CHARGE OF COUNTY CRICKET? Modify the 50-over competition so that it involves those playing in The Hundred and get the Minor Counties involved too
FAVOURITE SMELL? A braai
GUILTY PLEASURE? Amarula (South African liqueur)
TWITTER: @waynemadsen2017

Batting	Mat	Inns	NO	Runs	HS	Ave	SR	100	50	Ct	St
First-class	189	337	24	12177	231*	38.90	51.42	31	62	199	0
List A	105	97	17	3323	138	41.53	89.93	6	19	69	0
T20s	124	121	20	3006	86*	29.76	133.12	0	20	43	0
Bowling	**Mat**	**Balls**	**Runs**	**Wkts**	**BBI**	**BBM**	**Ave**	**Econ**	**SR**	**5w**	**10**
First-class	189	3085	1712	33	3/45	-	51.87	3.32	93.4	0	0
List A	105	668	573	16	3/27	3/27	35.81	5.14	41.7	0	0
T20s	124	492	645	19	2/20	2/20	33.94	7.86	25.8	0	0

SAQIB MAHMOOD

RHB / RFM / R0 / W0

FULL NAME: Saqib Mahmood
BORN: February 25, 1997, Birmingham
SQUAD NO: 25
HEIGHT: 6ft 3in
NICKNAME: Saq
EDUCATION: Matthew Moss High School, Rochdale
TEAMS: England, Lancashire, Peshawar Zalmi
ROLE: Bowler
DEBUT: ODI: 2020; T20I: 2019; First-class: 2016; List A: 2016; T20: 2015

BEST BATTING: 34 Lancashire vs Middlesex, Old Trafford, 2019
BEST BOWLING: 4-48 Lancashire vs Bristol, Cheltenham, 2019

TWITTER: @SaqMahmood25
NOTES: Mahmood made his full Lancashire debut in 2015 before having a big impact at the 2016 U19 World Cup, becoming a regular for England Lions. Injuries and tough competition for places initially limited his opportunities for his county, but the 24-year-old was exceptional in 2019 – particularly in the One-Day Cup in which he took 28 wickets at 18.50 to be named Player of the Tournament. Mahmood made his T20 international debut for England later that year, followed by his ODI debut in February 2020. He was part of England's Test "bubble" squad last year without making an appearance, and was also on the reserve list for last winter's tours to Sri Lanka and India. Earlier this year he appeared for Peshawar Zalmi in the Pakistan Super League and is due to play for Manchester Originals in The Hundred

Batting	Mat	Inns	NO	Runs	HS	Ave	SR	100	50	Ct	St
ODIs	4	1	0	12	12	12.00	80.00	0	0	1	0
T20Is	6	2	1	7	4	7.00	100.00	0	0	1	0
First-class	16	18	7	154	34	14.00	30.67	0	0	1	0
List A	31	13	6	129	45	18.42	88.35	0	0	8	0
T20s	34	7	4	19	6	6.33	73.07	0	0	3	0

Bowling	Mat	Balls	Runs	Wkts	BBI	BBM	Ave	Econ	SR	5w	10
ODIs	4	197	156	5	2/36	2/36	31.20	4.75	39.4	0	0
T20Is	6	108	190	3	1/20	1/20	63.33	10.55	36.0	0	0
First-class	16	2136	1214	42	4/48	5/120	28.90	3.41	50.8	0	0
List A	31	1499	1422	55	6/37	6/37	25.85	5.69	27.2	3	0
T20s	34	621	868	42	4/14	4/14	20.66	8.38	14.7	0	0

DAWID MALAN LHB / LB / R3 / W0 / MVP99

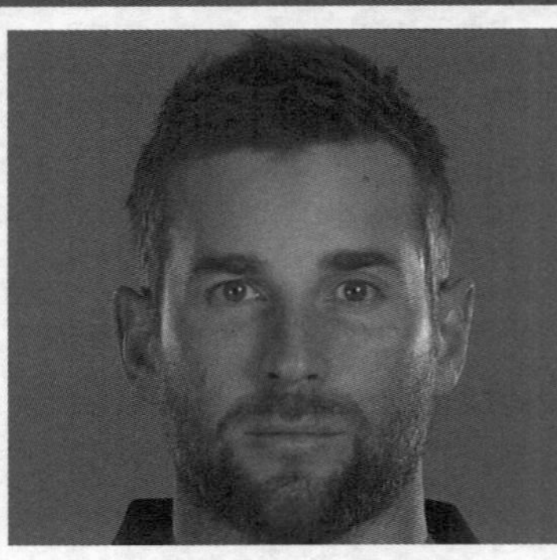

FULL NAME: Dawid Johannes Malan
BORN: September 3, 1987, Roehampton
SQUAD NO: 29
HEIGHT: 6ft
EDUCATION: Paarl Boys' High School; University of South Africa
TEAMS: England, Yorkshire, Comilla Warriors, Boland, Hobart Hurricanes, Khulna Titans, Middlesex, Islamabad United, Peshawar Zalmi, Punjab Kings
ROLE: Batsman
DEBUT: Test: 2017; ODI: 2019; T20I: 2017; First-class: 2006; List A: 2006; T20: 2006

BEST BATTING: 219 Yorkshire vs Derbyshire, Headingley, 2020
BEST BOWLING: 5-61 Middlesex vs Lancashire, Liverpool, 2012
COUNTY CAP: 2010 (Middlesex); BENEFIT: 2019 (Middlesex)

FAMILY TIES? My dad Dawid played for Transvaal B and Western Province B and my brother Charl played for MCC Young Cricketers and Loughborough MCCU
CHILDHOOD SPORTING HERO? Gary Kirsten
SURPRISING FACT ABOUT YOU? I love to go to the cinema by myself
TWITTER: @DJMalan29
NOTES: Malan is set to make his IPL debut this year after being signed by Punjab Kings. He was the ICC's No.1-ranked T20I batsman as of March

Batting	Mat	Inns	NO	Runs	HS	Ave	SR	100	50	Ct	St
Tests	15	26	0	724	140	27.84	41.08	1	6	11	0
ODIs	1	1	0	24	24	24.00	80.00	0	0	0	0
T20Is	19	19	3	855	103*	53.43	149.47	1	9	4	0
First-class	191	326	21	11561	219	37.90	52.80	26	60	200	0
List A	149	145	21	5135	185*	41.41	83.76	10	25	51	0
T20s	223	218	34	6117	117	33.24	128.61	5	35	77	0
Bowling	**Mat**	**Balls**	**Runs**	**Wkts**	**BBI**	**BBM**	**Ave**	**Econ**	**SR**	**5w**	**10**
Tests	15	156	70	0	-	-	-	2.69	-	0	0
ODIs	1	-	-	-	-	-	-	-	-	-	-
T20Is	19	12	27	1	1/27	1/27	27.00	13.50	12.0	0	0
First-class	191	4093	2455	61	5/61	5/61	40.24	3.59	67.0	1	0
List A	149	1347	1310	40	4/25	4/25	32.75	5.83	33.6	0	0
T20s	223	567	722	23	2/10	2/10	31.39	7.64	24.6	0	0

PIETER MALAN

RHB / RM / WK / R0 / W0

FULL NAME: Pieter Jacobus Malan
BORN: August 13, 1989, Nelspruit, Transvaal, South Africa
SQUAD NO: 31
TEAMS: South Africa, Warwickshire, Boland, Cape Cobras, Northerns, Titans, Western Province
ROLE: Batsman
DEBUT: Test: 2020; First-class: 2007; List A: 2007; T20: 2010

BEST BATTING: 211* Western Province vs Namibia, Walvis Bay, 2016
BEST BOWLING: 5-35 Western Province vs Eastern Province, 2017, Port Elizabeth

TWITTER: @pieterm87
NOTES: Warwickshire have added experience and solidity to their top order with the signing of Malan for the entire County Championship campaign. The right-handed opener has been a consistent run-scorer in South African domestic cricket for the last 15 years, registering 17 centuries across the last six seasons alone. His performances earned him international recognition in January 2020, when he made his Test debut against England at Cape Town. He scored 84 in the second innings, holding the tourists at bay for more than six hours before South Africa eventually succumbed. Two matches later he was discarded and hasn't featured for his country since. "We have got some very talented young batsmen in our top order and for them to work with, and bat out in the middle with, someone of Pieter's experience and quality will be brilliant for them," said Paul Farbrace, Warwickshire's director of cricket. "Pieter is also a very impressive man, friendly, likeable and polite, but with real inner steel and with a point to prove. I know how much he wants to come to the Bears and score some serious runs"

Batting	Mat	Inns	NO	Runs	HS	Ave	SR	100	50	Ct	St
Tests	3	6	0	156	84	26.00	29.43	0	1	3	0
First-class	157	262	20	10691	211*	44.17	48.57	33	45	108	0
List A	112	111	14	4382	169*	45.17	75.43	12	21	52	1
T20s	36	36	10	1091	140*	41.96	114.72	1	5	17	0
Bowling	**Mat**	**Balls**	**Runs**	**Wkts**	**BBI**	**BBM**	**Ave**	**Econ**	**SR**	**5w**	**10**
Tests	3	12	5	0	-	-	-	2.50	-	0	0
First-class	157	895	479	20	5/35	6/36	23.95	3.21	44.7	1	0
List A	112	143	164	0	-	-	-	6.88	-	0	0
T20s	36	24	30	2	2/30	2/30	15.00	7.50	12.0	0	0

MITCHELL MARSH RHB / RMF

FULL NAME: Mitchell Ross Marsh
BORN: October 20, 1991, Perth, Australia
SQUAD NO: 8
TEAMS: Australia, Middlesex, Deccan Chargers, Perth Scorchers, Pune Warriors, Rising Pune Supergiants, Sunrisers Hyderabad, Western Australia
ROLE: Allrounder
DEBUT: Test: 2014; ODI: 2011; T20I: 2011; First-class: 2009; List A: 2009; T20: 2009

BEST BATTING: 93* Perth Scorchers vs Brisbane Heat, Perth, 2020 (T20)
BEST BOWLING: 4-6 Western Australia vs New South Wales, Perth, 2010 (T20)

TWITTER: @mitchmarsh235
NOTES: The Australian allrounder has been signed by Middlesex for this summer's T20 Blast campaign and will be available for at least the group stage. The 29-year-old had been due to join up with the club last summer only for the deal to be cancelled due to the pandemic. The son of former Test opener Geoff, and brother to fellow international batsman Shaun, Mitchell has racked up more than 100 appearances across all formats for Australia, the highlight of which was his 181 on his home ground at Perth in the third Test against England in 2017, sharing a 301-run partnership with his captain Steve Smith. He hasn't played Test cricket since the 2019 Ashes. Marsh is a three-time winner of the Big Bash League with Perth Scorchers and is playing in this year's IPL for Sunrisers Hyderabad, his fourth franchise in the competition

Batting	Mat	Inns	NO	Runs	HS	Ave	SR	100	50	Ct	St
Tests	32	55	5	1260	181	25.20	50.68	2	3	16	0
ODIs	60	56	9	1615	102*	34.36	90.37	1	12	28	0
T20Is	20	20	5	325	45	21.66	116.07	0	0	7	0
First-class	102	176	14	5210	211	32.16	55.54	11	21	53	0
List A	116	109	22	3232	124	37.14	90.68	3	22	57	0
T20s	113	105	29	2334	93*	30.71	126.91	0	12	45	0
Bowling	**Mat**	**Balls**	**Runs**	**Wkts**	**BBI**	**BBM**	**Ave**	**Econ**	**SR**	**5w**	**10**
Tests	32	2853	1623	42	5/46	7/86	38.64	3.41	67.9	1	0
ODIs	60	1949	1803	49	5/33	5/33	36.79	5.55	39.7	1	0
T20Is	20	120	159	7	2/6	2/6	22.71	7.95	17.1	0	0
First-class	102	8579	4838	158	6/84	9/156	30.62	3.38	54.2	2	0
List A	116	3335	3014	94	5/33	5/33	32.06	5.42	35.4	2	0
T20s	113	1044	1459	53	4/6	4/6	27.52	8.38	19.6	0	0

BEN MCDERMOTT

RHB / WK

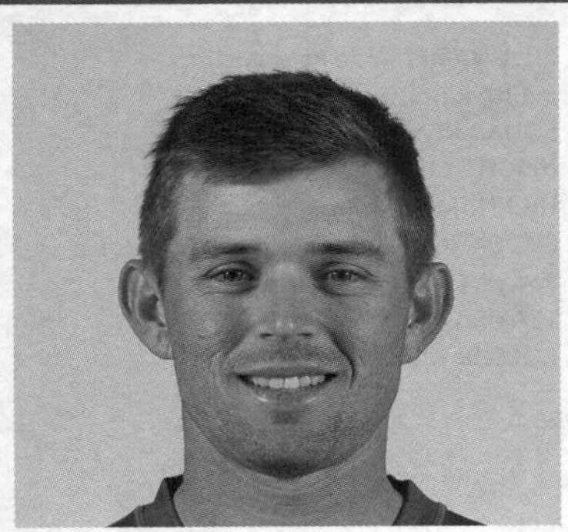

FULL NAME: Benjamin Reginald McDermott
BORN: December 12, 1994, Brisbane, Australia
SQUAD NO: 47
HEIGHT: 6ft
TEAMS: Australia, Derbyshire, Brisbane Heat, Hobart Hurricanes, Melbourne Renegades, Queensland, Tasmania
ROLE: Wicketkeeper/batsman
DEBUT: T20I: 2018; First-class: 2014; List A: 2014; T20: 2014

BEST BATTING: 114 Hobart Hurricanes vs Melbourne Renegades, Melbourne, 2017 (T20)

TWITTER: @benmcdermott100

NOTES: A hard-hitting keeper-batsman, McDermott is the son of former Australian fast bowler Craig. He made his Big Bash debut for Brisbane Heat in 2014 at the age of 19 before switching to Hobart Hurricanes ahead of the 2016/17 campaign, hitting 114 from 52 balls in his second innings for the franchise to inspire a record chase of 223. McDermott's strokeplay caught the attention of the Australian selectors, who handed him his T20I debut in October 2018. He was recalled to squad for the 2020/21 tour of New Zealand following strong performances in the Big Bash. McDermott was initially signed by Derbyshire on a white-ball contract for the 2020 season, later deferred in the wake of the pandemic. He will be available in both the One-Day Cup and the T20 Blast

Batting	Mat	Inns	NO	Runs	HS	Ave	SR	100	50	Ct	St
T20Is	12	10	3	98	32*	14.00	93.33	0	0	8	0
First-class	38	67	8	2011	107*	34.08	43.26	2	15	26	0
List A	21	21	2	936	117	49.26	78.39	3	5	20	0
T20s	73	68	15	1660	114	31.32	130.70	1	7	35	2
Bowling	**Mat**	**Balls**	**Runs**	**Wkts**	**BBI**	**BBM**	**Ave**	**Econ**	**SR**	**5w**	**10**
T20Is	12	-	-	-	-	-	-	-	-	-	-
First-class	38	102	75	0	-	-	-	4.41	-	0	0
List A	21	-	-	-	-	-	-	-	-	-	-
T20s	73	-	-	-	-	-	-	-	-	-	-

GLAMORGAN

JAMIE MCILROY RHB / LFM / R0 / W0

FULL NAME: Jamie Peter McIlroy
BORN: June 19, 1994, Hereford
SQUAD NO: 35
HEIGHT: 6ft 3in
NICKNAME: Macca
EDUCATION: Builth Wells High School, Powys; Coleg Powys, Newtown
TEAMS: Glamorgan
ROLE: Bowler

MOST EXCITING DAY AS A CRICKETER? Hard to choose between winning the Minor Counties National Knockout Cup with Herefordshire and signing my first professional contract at Glamorgan
CHILDHOOD SPORTING HERO? Ryan Giggs
BIGGEST INFLUENCE ON YOUR DEVELOPMENT AS A CRICKETER (EXCLUDING PARENTS)? Ed Price, my former Herefordshire U17 coach. He was the first person to teach me how to correctly swing a ball and control it with the wrist position
FIRST CRICKET CLUB? Builth Wells CC, Powys
IF YOU COULD TAKE ONE COUNTY CRICKETER'S BEST SHOT AND ADD IT TO YOUR OWN GAME? James Vince's cover-drive
TOUGHEST OPPONENT IN COUNTY CRICKET? I'd have to say this was Jimmy Adams during a Second XI game
MOST ECCENTRIC TEAMMATE? Tom Cullen
WHAT WOULD YOU DO IF YOU WERE IN CHARGE OF COUNTY CRICKET? Come up with more incentives to entice spectators, push to get more games on the television
WHAT WOULD YOU DO IF YOU WERE PRIME MINISTER? Change to four-day working weeks during the summer months
STRANGEST THING YOU'VE DONE DURING LOCKDOWN? Making banana bread
GUILTY PLEASURE? A Greggs sausage roll
TWITTER: @Jamiemcilroy94

CONOR MCKERR

RHB / RFM / R0 / W0

FULL NAME: Conor McKerr
BORN: January 19, 1998, Johannesburg, South Africa
SQUAD NO: 83
HEIGHT: 6ft 6in
NICKNAME: Tree
EDUCATION: St John's College, Johannesburg
TEAMS: Surrey, Derbyshire, South Africa U19
ROLE: Bowler
DEBUT: First-class: 2017; List A: 2019

BEST BATTING: 29 Surrey vs Yorkshire, The Oval, 2018
BEST BOWLING: 5-54 Derbyshire vs Northamptonshire, Northampton, 2017

CHILDHOOD SPORTING HERO? Graeme Smith
BIGGEST INFLUENCE ON YOUR DEVELOPMENT AS A CRICKETER (EXCLUDING PARENTS)? Alec Stewart – he gave me the opportunity to be a professional cricketer
FIRST CRICKET CLUB? Randburg CC, Johannesburg
IF YOU COULD TAKE ONE COUNTY CRICKETER'S BEST SHOT AND ADD IT TO YOUR OWN GAME? Rory Burns' block
TOUGHEST OPPONENT IN COUNTY CRICKET? Jonny Bairstow
STRANGEST THING YOU'VE DONE DURING LOCKDOWN? Road-running
IF YOU WERE AN ANIMAL, WHICH WOULD IT BE? A rhino – I'm from Africa and I'm relatively fast
GUILTY PLEASURE? Muffins
TWITTER: @cemckerr83

Batting	Mat	Inns	NO	Runs	HS	Ave	SR	100	50	Ct	St
First-class	14	15	4	133	29	12.09	41.43	0	0	2	0
List A	6	6	2	56	26*	14.00	88.88	0	0	3	0
Bowling	**Mat**	**Balls**	**Runs**	**Wkts**	**BBI**	**BBM**	**Ave**	**Econ**	**SR**	**5w**	**10**
First-class	14	1705	1054	38	5/54	10/141	27.73	3.70	44.8	2	1
List A	6	311	334	8	3/56	3/56	41.75	6.44	38.8	0	0

MATTIE MCKIERNAN RHB / LB / R0 / W0

FULL NAME: Matthew Henry McKiernan
BORN: June 14, 1994, Orrell, Lancashire
SQUAD NO: 21
HEIGHT: 6ft 1in
NICKNAME: Macca
EDUCATION: Lowton High School, Leigh, Greater Manchester; St John Rigby College, Wigan; Edge Hill University, Ormskirk
TEAMS: Derbyshire
ROLE: Bowler
DEBUT: First-class: 2019; T20: 2018

BEST BATTING: 52 Derbyshire vs Lancashire, Liverpool, 2020
BEST BOWLING: 2-3 Derbyshire vs Nottinghamshire, Trent Bridge, 2020

MOST EXCITING DAY AS A CRICKETER? My Derbyshire T20 debut in 2018
CHILDHOOD SPORTING HERO? Shane Warne
BIGGEST INFLUENCE ON YOUR DEVELOPMENT AS A CRICKETER (EXCLUDING PARENTS)? Karl Brown, the former Lancashire batsman. I've played club cricket with him for many years and have always looked up to him
FIRST CRICKET CLUB? Leigh CC, Wigan
IF YOU COULD TAKE ONE COUNTY CRICKETER'S BEST SHOT AND ADD IT TO YOUR OWN GAME? Kane Williamson's third-man dab
TOUGHEST OPPONENT IN COUNTY CRICKET? David Wiese – he ruined my first-class debut
STRANGEST THING YOU'VE DONE DURING LOCKDOWN? Borrowing part of the gym at Derby and moving it into the back room at home
FAVOURITE SMELL? Hand sanitiser
TWITTER: @MattieMcKiernan

Batting	Mat	Inns	NO	Runs	HS	Ave	SR	100	50	Ct	St
First-class	3	6	0	110	52	18.33	28.49	0	1	6	0
T20s	9	8	2	72	25	12.00	126.31	0	0	2	0
Bowling	**Mat**	**Balls**	**Runs**	**Wkts**	**BBI**	**BBM**	**Ave**	**Econ**	**SR**	**5w**	**10**
First-class	3	62	48	2	2/3	2/16	24.00	4.64	31.0	0	0
T20s	9	132	158	2	2/22	2/22	79.00	7.18	66.0	0	0

LEWIS MCMANUS RHB / WK / R0 / W0

FULL NAME: Lewis David McManus
BORN: October 9, 1994, Poole, Dorset
SQUAD NO: 18
HEIGHT: 5ft 8in
NICKNAME: Lewy
EDUCATION: Clayesmore School, Bournemouth; University of Exeter
TEAMS: Hampshire, England U19
ROLE: Wicketkeeper/batsman
DEBUT: First-class: 2015; List A: 2016; T20: 2016

BEST BATTING: 132* Hampshire vs Surrey, Southampton, 2016

MOST EXCITING DAY AS A CRICKETER? My maiden first-class century in 2016
CHILDHOOD SPORTING HERO? Floyd Mayweather
SURPRISING FACT ABOUT YOU? I once saw James Tomlinson (former Hampshire seamer) take a one-handed catch at fine-leg while holding a banana in the other hand during a first-class game
TWITTER: @lewis_mcmanus

Batting	Mat	Inns	NO	Runs	HS	Ave	SR	100	50	Ct	St
First-class	44	63	6	1556	132*	27.29	49.02	1	7	94	12
List A	32	25	5	430	47	21.50	88.47	0	0	24	8
T20s	48	38	8	475	59	15.83	126.66	0	1	15	9
Bowling	**Mat**	**Balls**	**Runs**	**Wkts**	**BBI**	**BBM**	**Ave**	**Econ**	**SR**	**5w**	**10**
First-class	44	-	-	-	-	-	-	-	-	-	-
List A	32	-	-	-	-	-	-	-	-	-	-
T20s	48	-	-	-	-	-	-	-	-	-	-

STUART MEAKER RHB / RFM / R0 / W1

FULL NAME: Stuart Christopher Meaker
BORN: January 21, 1989, Pietermaritzburg, South Africa
SQUAD NO: 12
HEIGHT: 5ft 11in
NICKNAME: Ten Bears
EDUCATION: Cranleigh Senior School, Surrey
TEAMS: England, Sussex, Auckland, Surrey
ROLE: Bowler
DEBUT: ODI: 2011; T20I: 2012; First-class: 2008; List A: 2008; T20: 2010

BEST BATTING: 94 Surrey vs Bangladeshis, The Oval, 2010
BEST BOWLING: 8-52 Surrey vs Somerset, The Oval, 2012
COUNTY CAP: 2012 (Surrey)

MOST EXCITING DAY AS A CRICKETER? Making my England debut in India
CHILDHOOD SPORTING HERO? Allan Donald
BIGGEST INFLUENCE ON YOUR DEVELOPMENT AS A CRICKETER (EXCLUDING PARENTS)? Former England bowling coach Kevin Shine – he got me on the ECB set-up at a young age
FIRST CRICKET CLUB? Normandy CC, Guildford, Surrey
WHAT WOULD YOU DO IF YOU WERE IN CHARGE OF COUNTY CRICKET? Disallow added time, eradicate Powerplays, bring back uncovered wickets
WHAT WOULD YOU DO IF YOU WERE PRIME MINISTER? Make university free, subsidise childcare, create a National Cricket Day
FAVOURITE SMELL? Smoked bacon
GUILTY PLEASURE? Shania Twain
TWITTER: @SMeaker18

Batting	Mat	Inns	NO	Runs	HS	Ave	SR	100	50	Ct	St
ODIs	2	2	0	2	1	1.00	12.50	0	0	0	0
T20Is	2	-	-	-	-	-	-	-	-	1	0
First-class	92	123	25	1551	94	15.82	38.53	0	6	20	0
List A	73	38	18	198	50	9.90	63.46	0	1	21	0
T20s	32	11	6	46	17	9.20	121.05	0	0	13	0
Bowling	**Mat**	**Balls**	**Runs**	**Wkts**	**BBI**	**BBM**	**Ave**	**Econ**	**SR**	**5w**	**10**
ODIs	2	114	110	2	1/45	1/45	55.00	5.78	57.0	0	0
T20Is	2	47	70	2	1/28	1/28	35.00	8.93	23.5	0	0
First-class	92	14043	8926	281	8/52	11/167	31.76	3.81	49.9	11	2
List A	73	2762	2842	80	4/37	4/37	35.52	6.17	34.5	0	0
T20s	32	519	774	26	4/30	4/30	29.76	8.94	19.9	0	0

DUSTIN MELTON

RHB / RFM / R0 / W0

FULL NAME: Dustin Renton Melton
BORN: April 11, 1995, Harare, Zimbabwe
SQUAD NO: 13
HEIGHT: 6ft 4in
NICKNAME: Dusty
EDUCATION: Pretoria Boys High School; University of Pretoria
TEAMS: Derbyshire
ROLE: Bowler
DEBUT: First-class: 2019; T20: 2020

BEST BATTING: 11 Derbyshire vs Lancashire, Liverpool, 2020
BEST BOWLING: 4-22 Derbyshire vs Leicestershire, Leicester, 2020

MOST EXCITING DAY AS A CRICKETER? Making my first-class debut against the Australians at Derby in 2019
CHILDHOOD SPORTING HERO? Dale Steyn
FIRST CRICKET CLUB? Tuks CC, Pretoria, South Africa
IF YOU COULD TAKE ONE COUNTY CRICKETER'S BEST SHOT AND ADD IT TO YOUR OWN GAME? Anyone who can play the pull shot!
TOUGHEST OPPONENT IN COUNTY CRICKET? Alex Hales – on one occasion he took me for 17 in an over and it felt like there was nowhere I could bowl at him
MOST ECCENTRIC TEAMMATE? Alex Hughes – I once bought a drink out for him while he was batting and saw him eat a bug that was sat in his glove. He said it was for protein
WHAT WOULD YOU DO IF YOU WERE IN CHARGE OF COUNTY CRICKET? Boost investment in women's cricket
STRANGEST THING YOU'VE DONE DURING LOCKDOWN? Practising my golf chips into a paddling pool
FAVOURITE SMELL? Crispy bacon
GUILTY PLEASURE? Video games
TWITTER: @Dusty_Melts

Batting	Mat	Inns	NO	Runs	HS	Ave	SR	100	50	Ct	St
First-class	6	7	3	12	11	3.00	23.07	0	0	1	0
T20s	4	-	-	-	-	-	-	-	-	4	0
Bowling	**Mat**	**Balls**	**Runs**	**Wkts**	**BBI**	**BBM**	**Ave**	**Econ**	**SR**	**5w**	**10**
First-class	6	611	382	10	4/22	5/47	38.20	3.75	61.1	0	0
T20s	4	78	124	4	2/37	2/37	31.00	9.53	19.5	0	0

BEN MIKE

RHB / RFM / R0 / W0

FULL NAME: Benjamin Wentworth Munro Mike
BORN: August 24, 1998, Nottingham
SQUAD NO: 8
HEIGHT: 6ft 1in
NICKNAME: Benny
EDUCATION: Loughborough Grammar School
TEAMS: Leicestershire, Warwickshire
ROLE: Bowler
DEBUT: First-class: 2018; List A: 2018; T20: 2019

BEST BATTING: 72 Warwickshire vs Hampshire, Southampton, 2019
BEST BOWLING: 5-37 Leicestershire vs Sussex, Hove, 2018

CHILDHOOD SPORTING HERO? Ronaldinho
BIGGEST INFLUENCE ON YOUR DEVELOPMENT AS A CRICKETER (EXCLUDING PARENTS)? Dips Patel at Leicestershire and Brad Spencer in Perth
FIRST CRICKET CLUB? Radcliffe-On-Trent CC, Nottingham
IF YOU COULD TAKE ONE COUNTY CRICKETER'S BEST SHOT AND ADD IT TO YOUR OWN GAME? Ian Bell's cover-drive
TOUGHEST OPPONENT IN COUNTY CRICKET? Kyle Abbott
BIGGEST CRICKETING REGRET? Trying to be perfect
WHAT WOULD YOU DO IF YOU WERE IN CHARGE OF COUNTY CRICKET? Bring back classic jumpers, schedule one pink-ball Championship match a year
GUILTY PLEASURE? Tesco cookies after a day's play
TWITTER: @benmike_

Batting	Mat	Inns	NO	Runs	HS	Ave	SR	100	50	Ct	St
First-class	15	24	3	392	72	18.66	42.19	0	2	4	0
List A	4	4	0	80	41	20.00	79.20	0	0	0	0
T20s	14	11	3	140	37	17.50	138.61	0	0	4	0
Bowling	**Mat**	**Balls**	**Runs**	**Wkts**	**BBI**	**BBM**	**Ave**	**Econ**	**SR**	**5w**	**10**
First-class	15	1896	1313	40	5/37	9/94	32.82	4.15	47.4	1	0
List A	4	90	145	1	1/47	1/47	145.00	9.66	90.0	0	0
T20s	14	143	238	8	3/38	3/38	29.75	9.98	17.8	0	0

CRAIG MILES RHB / RFM / R0 / W3

FULL NAME: Craig Neil Miles
BORN: July 20, 1994, Swindon, Wiltshire
SQUAD NO: 18
HEIGHT: 6ft 4in
NICKNAME: Milo
EDUCATION: Bradon Forest School, Purton, Wiltshire; SGS Filton College, Bristol
TEAMS: Warwickshire, Gloucestershire
ROLE: Bowler
DEBUT: First-class: 2011; List A: 2011; T20: 2013

BEST BATTING: 62* Gloucestershire vs Worcestershire, Cheltenham, 2014
BEST BOWLING: 6-63 Gloucestershire vs Northamptonshire, Northampton, 2015
COUNTY CAP: 2011 (Gloucestershire)

MOST EXCITING DAY AS A CRICKETER? Beating Surrey in the 2015 One-Day Cup final at Lord's when I was with Gloucestershire
FAMILY TIES? My older brother Adam has played for Cardiff MCCU and for New Zealand side Otago in first-class cricket
CHILDHOOD SPORTING HERO? Wayne Rooney
FIRST CRICKET CLUB? Purton CC, Swindon
IF YOU COULD TAKE ONE COUNTY CRICKETER'S BEST SHOT AND ADD IT TO YOUR OWN GAME? Oliver Hannon-Dalby's pick-up off the hip
TOUGHEST OPPONENT IN COUNTY CRICKET? Kyle Abbott
WHAT WOULD YOU DO IF YOU WERE IN CHARGE OF COUNTY CRICKET? Allow the second new ball after 60 overs, bring back the 40-over format
SURPRISING FACT ABOUT YOU? I played football for Swindon Town Academy until I was 13
TWITTER: @cmiles34

Batting	Mat	Inns	NO	Runs	HS	Ave	SR	100	50	Ct	St
First-class	76	107	17	1447	62*	16.07	45.98	0	5	19	0
List A	37	15	3	115	31	9.58	76.15	0	0	5	0
T20s	13	5	2	13	8	4.33	92.85	0	0	4	0
Bowling	**Mat**	**Balls**	**Runs**	**Wkts**	**BBI**	**BBM**	**Ave**	**Econ**	**SR**	**5w**	**10**
First-class	76	12161	7612	276	6/63	10/121	27.57	3.75	44.0	14	1
List A	37	1553	1632	44	4/29	4/29	37.09	6.30	35.2	0	0
T20s	13	265	351	15	3/25	3/25	23.40	7.94	17.6	0	0

TYMAL MILLS RHB / LF

SUSSEX

FULL NAME: Tymal Solomon Mills
BORN: August 12, 1992, Dewsbury, Yorkshire
SQUAD NO: 7
HEIGHT: 6ft 1in
EDUCATION: Mildenhall College of Technology, Suffolk; University of East London
TEAMS: England, Sussex, Brisbane Heat, Essex, Hobart Hurricanes, Peshawar Zalmi, Royal Challengers Bangalore
ROLE: Bowler
DEBUT: T20I: 2016; First-class: 2011; List A: 2011; T20: 2012

BEST BATTING: 10 Sussex vs Lancashire, Hove, 2020 (T20)
BEST BOWLING: 4-22 Sussex vs Middlesex, Lord's, 2015 (T20)

MOST EXCITING DAY AS A CRICKETER? Bowling the opening delivery in the 2017 IPL
CHILDHOOD SPORTING HERO? Dion Dublin
FIRST CRICKET CLUB? Tuddenham CC, Suffolk
IF YOU COULD TAKE ONE COUNTY CRICKETER'S BEST SHOT AND ADD IT TO YOUR OWN GAME? Luke Wright's back-away, eyes-closed swipe for six
TOUGHEST OPPONENT IN COUNTY CRICKET? Paul Stirling – he always whacks me
MOST ECCENTRIC TEAMMATE? Phil Salt – he's nuts
WHAT WOULD YOU DO IF YOU WERE IN CHARGE OF COUNTY CRICKET? Allow an extra bouncer per over in T20 cricket
STRANGEST THING YOU'VE DONE DURING LOCKDOWN? Becoming a dad
FAVOURITE SMELL? A new pair of trainers
GUILTY PLEASURE? Watching horrendous TV shows with my wife
TWITTER: @tmills15
NOTES: Mills signed a T20-only contract with Sussex in 2019

Batting	Mat	Inns	NO	Runs	HS	Ave	SR	100	50	Ct	St
T20Is	5	1	0	0	0	0.00	0.00	0	0	1	0
First-class	32	38	15	260	31*	11.30	57.77	0	0	9	0
List A	23	9	5	7	3*	1.75	31.81	0	0	3	0
T20s	123	24	11	65	10	5.00	89.04	0	0	20	0
Bowling	**Mat**	**Balls**	**Runs**	**Wkts**	**BBI**	**BBM**	**Ave**	**Econ**	**SR**	**5w**	**10**
T20Is	5	114	129	3	1/27	1/27	43.00	6.78	38.0	0	0
First-class	32	3531	2008	55	4/25	5/79	36.50	3.41	64.2	0	0
List A	23	790	787	22	3/23	3/23	35.77	5.97	35.9	0	0
T20s	123	2549	3333	131	4/22	4/22	25.44	7.84	19.4	0	0

MATT MILNES RHB / RFM / R0 / W1 / MVP78

FULL NAME: Matthew Edward Milnes
BORN: July 29, 1994, Nottingham
SQUAD NO: 8
HEIGHT: 6ft 1in
NICKNAME: Mad Dog
EDUCATION: West Bridgford School, Nottinghamshire; Durham University
TEAMS: Kent, England Lions, Nottinghamshire
ROLE: Bowler
DEBUT: First-class: 2014; List A: 2019; T20: 2019

BEST BATTING: 43 Nottinghamshire vs Yorkshire, Trent Bridge, 2018
BEST BOWLING: 5-68 Kent vs Nottinghamshire, Tunbridge Wells, 2019

MOST EXCITING DAY AS A CRICKETER? Making my England Lions debut in February 2020 in Australia
BIGGEST INFLUENCE ON YOUR DEVELOPMENT AS A CRICKETER (EXCLUDING PARENTS)? My brother – I spent days on end bowling to him in the garden while he blocked half-volleys. Never got a bat either
FIRST CRICKET CLUB? Plumtree CC, Nottinghamshire
IF YOU COULD TAKE ONE COUNTY CRICKETER'S BEST SHOT AND ADD IT TO YOUR OWN GAME? Fred Klaassen's on-drive
TOUGHEST OPPONENT IN COUNTY CRICKET? Dom Sibley – when he's batting we tend to field for about four million overs
WHAT WOULD YOU DO IF YOU WERE IN CHARGE OF COUNTY CRICKET? No toss – the away team gets to choose (will encourage better pitches)
STRANGEST THING YOU'VE DONE DURING LOCKDOWN? Doing midnight bowling cartoon clinics with Fred Klaassen
GUILTY PLEASURE? Making a cup of tea just so that I can dunk about 30 biscuits
TWITTER: @mmilnes84

Batting	Mat	Inns	NO	Runs	HS	Ave	SR	100	50	Ct	St
First-class	27	38	11	388	43	14.37	39.63	0	0	13	0
List A	8	5	0	77	26	15.40	140.00	0	0	4	0
T20s	11	3	2	6	3	6.00	85.71	0	0	2	0
Bowling	**Mat**	**Balls**	**Runs**	**Wkts**	**BBI**	**BBM**	**Ave**	**Econ**	**SR**	**5w**	**10**
First-class	27	4325	2468	87	5/68	7/111	28.36	3.42	49.7	2	0
List A	8	431	494	16	5/79	5/79	30.87	6.87	26.9	1	0
T20s	11	234	363	7	3/19	3/19	51.85	9.30	33.4	0	0

ALEX MILTON

RHB / WK / R0 / W0

FULL NAME: Alexander Geoffrey Milton
BORN: May 19, 1996, Redhill, Surrey
SQUAD NO: 12
HEIGHT: 5ft 7in
NICKNAME: Milts
EDUCATION: Malvern College; Cardiff Metropolitan University
TEAMS: Worcestershire
ROLE: Wicketkeeper/batsman
DEBUT: First-class: 2016; List A: 2018

BEST BATTING: 104* Worcestershire vs Somerset, Worcester, 2018

CHILDHOOD SPORTING HERO? Sachin Tendulkar
FIRST CRICKET CLUB? Dormansland CC, Sussex
IF YOU COULD TAKE ONE COUNTY CRICKETER'S BEST SHOT AND ADD IT TO YOUR OWN GAME? Jos Buttler's scoop
TOUGHEST OPPONENT IN COUNTY CRICKET? Morné Morkel
BIGGEST CRICKETING REGRET? Getting to 60 at Lord's in the MCCU final and not going on to score a hundred
WHAT WOULD YOU DO IF YOU WERE IN CHARGE OF COUNTY CRICKET? Make the seam extremely small on the Dukes ball
STRANGEST THING YOU'VE DONE DURING LOCKDOWN? TikTok balancing acts with my girlfriend
FAVOURITE SMELL? Garlic
IF YOU WERE AN ANIMAL, WHICH WOULD IT BE? An owl – I've been told I look wise
SURPRISING FACT ABOUT YOU? I played a drum solo blindfolded in my school unplugged concert
GUILTY PLEASURE? A melt-in-the-middle chocolate dessert
TWITTER: @alex_milton12

Batting	Mat	Inns	NO	Runs	HS	Ave	SR	100	50	Ct	St
First-class	14	22	2	358	104*	17.90	46.92	1	1	12	1
List A	1	1	0	0	0	0.00	-	0	0	0	0
Bowling	**Mat**	**Balls**	**Runs**	**Wkts**	**BBI**	**BBM**	**Ave**	**Econ**	**SR**	**5w**	**10**
First-class	14	-	-	-	-	-	-	-	-	-	-
List A	1	-	-	-	-	-	-	-	-	-	-

DARYL MITCHELL RHB / RM / R6 / W0 / MVP52

FULL NAME: Daryl Keith Henry Mitchell
BORN: November 25, 1983, Badsey, Worcestershire
SQUAD NO: 27
HEIGHT: 6ft
NICKNAME: Mitch
EDUCATION: Prince Henry's High School, Evesham; University of Worcester
TEAMS: Worcestershire, Mountaineers
ROLE: Allrounder
DEBUT: First-class: 2005; List A: 2005; T20: 2005

BEST BATTING: 298 Worcestershire vs Somerset, Taunton, 2009
BEST BOWLING: 4-49 Worcestershire vs Yorkshire, Headingley, 2009
BENEFIT: 2016

CHILDHOOD SPORTING HERO? Ian Botham
BIGGEST INFLUENCE ON YOUR DEVELOPMENT AS A CRICKETER (EXCLUDING PARENTS)? Damian D'Oliveira
FIRST CRICKET CLUB? Bretforton CC, Worcestershire
IF YOU COULD TAKE ONE COUNTY CRICKETER'S BEST SHOT AND ADD IT TO YOUR OWN GAME? Ross Whiteley's smack over long-on
TOUGHEST OPPONENT IN COUNTY CRICKET? Mushtaq Ahmed – a little genius
MOST ECCENTRIC TEAMMATE? Jack Shantry – for his bowling action
BIGGEST CRICKETING REGRET? Getting bowled slogging on 298
WHAT WOULD YOU DO IF YOU WERE IN CHARGE OF COUNTY CRICKET? Ban Chris Rushworth from bowling with a new ball, make proper wool cricket jumpers compulsory
STRANGEST THING YOU'VE DONE DURING LOCKDOWN? Played "princesses" with a five-year-old, complete with crown and dress
GUILTY PLEASURE? Gin and tonic
TWITTER: @mitchwccc

Batting	Mat	Inns	NO	Runs	HS	Ave	SR	100	50	Ct	St
First-class	211	380	39	13450	298	39.44	46.09	38	52	288	0
List A	135	120	17	3466	107	33.65	81.95	4	22	56	0
T20s	170	130	32	2260	68*	23.06	118.69	0	7	70	0
Bowling	**Mat**	**Balls**	**Runs**	**Wkts**	**BBI**	**BBM**	**Ave**	**Econ**	**SR**	**5w**	**10**
First-class	211	2726	1358	29	4/49		46.82	2.98	94.0	0	0
List A	135	3181	2925	81	4/19	4/19	36.11	5.51	39.2	0	0
T20s	170	2263	2892	98	5/28	5/28	29.51	7.66	23.0	1	0

TOM MOORES LHB / WK / R0 / W0 / MVP54

FULL NAME: Thomas James Moores
BORN: September 4, 1996, Brighton, Sussex
SQUAD NO: 23
HEIGHT: 5ft 9in
EDUCATION: Loughborough Grammar School; Millfield School, Somerset
TEAMS: Nottinghamshire, England Lions, Jaffna Stallions, Lancashire, Multan Sultans
ROLE: Wicketkeeper/batsman
DEBUT: First-class: 2016; List A: 2016; T20: 2016

BEST BATTING: 106 Nottinghamshire vs Yorkshire, Trent Bridge, 2020

FAMILY TIES? My father Peter played for Sussex and was England head coach. He's now my coach at Nottinghamshire
CHILDHOOD SPORTING HERO? Adam Gilchrist
FIRST CRICKET CLUB? Barrow Town CC, Leicestershire. The club gave me my first opportunity to play men's cricket
TOUGHEST OPPONENT IN COUNTY CRICKET? Jimmy Anderson
TWITTER: @tommoores23

Batting	Mat	Inns	NO	Runs	HS	Ave	SR	100	50	Ct	St
First-class	39	66	1	1372	106	21.10	48.54	2	2	91	2
List A	21	19	3	566	76	35.37	113.65	0	5	18	5
T20s	68	60	14	1175	80*	25.54	136.94	0	6	39	7
Bowling	**Mat**	**Balls**	**Runs**	**Wkts**	**BBI**	**BBM**	**Ave**	**Econ**	**SR**	**5w**	**10**
First-class	39	-	-	-	-	-	-	-	-	-	-
List A	21	-	-	-	-	-	-	-	-	-	-
T20s	68	-	-	-	-	-	-	-	-	-	-

EOIN MORGAN

LHB / RM / R1 / W0

FULL NAME: Eoin Joseph Gerard Morgan
BORN: September 10, 1986, Dublin, Ireland
SQUAD NO: 16
HEIGHT: 5ft 9in
NICKNAME: Moggie
EDUCATION: Catholic University School, Dublin; Dulwich College, London
TEAMS: England, Ireland, Middlesex, Karachi Kings, Kolkata Knight Riders, RC Bangalore, Sunrisers, Sydney Thunder
ROLE: Batsman
DEBUT: Test: 2010; ODI: 2006; T20I: 2009; First-class: 2004; List A: 2003; T20: 2006

BEST BATTING: 209* Ireland vs UAE, Abu Dhabi, 2007
BEST BOWLING: 2-24 Middlesex vs Nottinghamshire, Lord's, 2007
COUNTY CAP: 2008

TWITTER: @Eoin16
NOTES: An Irishman by birth, Morgan switched his allegiance to England after he was named in England's provisional squad for the 2009 World T20. He made his Test debut in 2010 and scored two hundreds, but ultimately his unorthodox technique was exposed in the longer form of the game and he played the last of his 16 Tests in 2012. He was handed the ODI captaincy in 2014 and has transformed England's limited-overs cricket, leading the side to a euphoric victory in the 2019 World Cup. Morgan also leads the T20I side and captains Middlesex in the T20 Blast (when available). He is very rarely seen in four-day cricket and was re-signed by Kolkata Knight Riders for this year's IPL. He is due to play for London Spirit in The Hundred this summer

Batting	Mat	Inns	NO	Runs	HS	Ave	SR	100	50	Ct	St
Tests	16	24	1	700	130	30.43	54.77	2	3	11	0
ODIs	242	225	33	7598	148	39.57	91.44	14	46	86	0
T20Is	97	94	19	2278	91	30.37	138.98	0	14	41	0
First-class	102	169	18	5042	209*	33.39	51.02	11	24	76	1
List A	373	344	48	11551	161	39.02	91.15	22	67	126	0
T20s	307	292	43	6879	91	27.62	132.95	0	37	136	0
Bowling	**Mat**	**Balls**	**Runs**	**Wkts**	**BBI**	**BBM**	**Ave**	**Econ**	**SR**	**5w**	**10**
Tests	16	-	-	-	-	-	-	-	-	-	-
ODIs	242	-	-	-	-	-	-	-	-	-	-
T20Is	97	-	-	-	-	-	-	-	-	-	-
First-class	102	120	94	2	2/24	2/24	47.00	4.70	60.0	0	0
List A	373	42	49	0	-	-	-	7.00	-	0	0
T20s	307	-	-	-	-	-	-	-	-	-	-

DANIEL MORIARTY LHB / SLA / R0 / W0 / MVP8

FULL NAME: Daniel Thornhill Moriarty
BORN: December 2, 1999, Reigate, Surrey
SQUAD NO: 21
HEIGHT: 6ft 2in
NICKNAME: Mozza
EDUCATION: Rondesbosch Boys' High School, Cape Town
TEAMS: Surrey, South Africa U19
ROLE: Bowler
DEBUT: First-class: 2020; List A: 2020

BEST BATTING: 1 Surrey vs Sussex, The Oval, 2020
BEST BOWLING: 6-70 Surrey vs Sussex, The Oval, 2020

CHILDHOOD SPORTING HERO? Graeme Smith
BIGGEST INFLUENCE ON YOUR DEVELOPMENT AS A CRICKETER (EXCLUDING PARENTS)? Gareth Batty – he has helped me understand my game in more depth
FIRST CRICKET CLUB? Western Province CC, Cape Town
IF YOU COULD TAKE ONE COUNTY CRICKETER'S BEST SHOT AND ADD IT TO YOUR OWN GAME? Rory Burns' sweep
FAVOURITE SMELL? Fresh linen
IF YOU WERE AN ANIMAL, WHICH WOULD IT BE? Psychrolutes marcidus (blobfish) – to explore the unknowns of the deep sea
GUILTY PLEASURE? Strawberry whey

Batting	Mat	Inns	NO	Runs	HS	Ave	SR	100	50	Ct	St
First-class	2	3	0	1	1	0.33	4.34	0	0	0	0
T20s	13	-	-	-	-	-	-	-	-	1	0
Bowling	**Mat**	**Balls**	**Runs**	**Wkts**	**BBI**	**BBM**	**Ave**	**Econ**	**SR**	**5w**	**10**
First-class	2	590	342	17	6/70	11/224	20.11	3.47	34.7	3	1
T20s	13	270	311	17	3/25	3/25	18.29	6.91	15.8	0	0

JACK MORLEY

LHB / SLA / R0 / W0

FULL NAME: Jack Peter Morley
BORN: June 25, 2001, Rochdale, Lancashire
SQUAD NO: 18
HEIGHT: 5ft 11in
NICKNAME: Morles
EDUCATION: Siddal Moor Sports College, Heywood, Greater Manchester; Myerscough College, Preston, Lancashire
TEAMS: Lancashire, England U19
ROLE: Bowler
DEBUT: First-class: 2020

BEST BATTING: 3 Lancashire vs Derbyshire, Liverpool, 2020
BEST BOWLING: 4-62 Lancashire vs Derbyshire, Liverpool, 2020

MOST EXCITING DAY AS A CRICKETER? Day four of my first-class debut against Derbyshire at Liverpool last season, when I took four wickets to help us win the game
BIGGEST INFLUENCE ON YOUR DEVELOPMENT AS A CRICKETER (EXCLUDING PARENTS)? My cousin Tom Hardman – he got me into playing cricket from a young age
FIRST CRICKET CLUB? Heywood CC, Rochdale
IF YOU COULD TAKE ONE COUNTY CRICKETER'S BEST SHOT AND ADD IT TO YOUR OWN GAME? Ben Stokes's on-drive
TOUGHEST OPPONENT IN COUNTY CRICKET? Luis Reece
MOST ECCENTRIC TEAMMATE? Rob Jones
WHAT WOULD YOU DO IF YOU WERE PRIME MINISTER? Put more money into the NHS
STRANGEST THING YOU'VE DONE DURING LOCKDOWN? Taking part in a toilet-roll kick-up challenge
FAVOURITE SMELL? A barbecue
TWITTER: @jackmorley196

Batting	Mat	Inns	NO	Runs	HS	Ave	SR	100	50	Ct	St
First-class	1	1	0	3	3	3.00	6.52	0	0	0	0
Bowling	**Mat**	**Balls**	**Runs**	**Wkts**	**BBI**	**BBM**	**Ave**	**Econ**	**SR**	**5w**	**10**
First-class	1	240	71	5	4/62	5/71	14.20	1.77	48.0	0	0

CHARLIE MORRIS

RHB / RMF / R0 / W2

WORCESTERSHIRE

FULL NAME: Charles Andrew John Morris
BORN: July 6, 1992, Hereford
SQUAD NO: 31
HEIGHT: 6ft
NICKNAME: Bishop
EDUCATION: Kingswood School, Bath; King's College, Taunton; Oxford Brookes University
TEAMS: Worcestershire
ROLE: Bowler
DEBUT: First-class: 2012; List A: 2013; T20: 2013

BEST BATTING: 53* Worcestershire vs Australians, Worcester, 2019
BEST BOWLING: 7-45 Worcestershire vs Leicestershire, Leicester, 2019

MOST EXCITING DAY AS A CRICKETER? Playing in T20 Finals Day in 2019
FIRST CRICKET CLUB? Yelverton CC, Devon
IF YOU COULD TAKE ONE COUNTY CRICKETER'S BEST SHOT AND ADD IT TO YOUR OWN GAME? Joe Denly's pull
WHAT WOULD YOU DO IF YOU WERE IN CHARGE OF COUNTY CRICKET? Encourage counties to play more Second XI fixtures at county grounds, use a Dukes ball for all Second XI matches, continue to fund the MCC Universities scheme (I owe so much to the MCCU system for giving me my break in the professional game and I'd like to see others continue to have that opportunity)
WHAT WOULD YOU DO IF YOU WERE PRIME MINISTER? Bring back national service (lots of life skills can be learnt from doing this)
STRANGEST THING YOU'VE DONE DURING LOCKDOWN? Starting to drink white port and tonic
GUILTY PLEASURE? Whisky
TWITTER: @morris_9

Batting	Mat	Inns	NO	Runs	HS	Ave	SR	100	50	Ct	St
First-class	63	83	47	454	53*	12.61	29.92	0	1	12	0
List A	34	18	12	58	16*	9.66	59.18	0	0	6	0
T20s	13	4	3	6	3	6.00	75.00	0	0	3	0
Bowling	**Mat**	**Balls**	**Runs**	**Wkts**	**BBI**	**BBM**	**Ave**	**Econ**	**SR**	**5w**	**10**
First-class	63	11093	5779	197	7/45	9/109	29.33	3.12	56.3	6	0
List A	34	1403	1379	40	4/33	4/33	34.47	5.89	35.0	0	0
T20s	13	248	392	11	2/30	2/30	35.63	9.48	22.5	0	0

ED MOULTON RHB / RMF / R0 / W0

FULL NAME: Edwin Henry Taylor Moulton
BORN: April 18, 1999, Preston, Lancashire
SQUAD NO: 27
EDUCATION: Bishop Rawstone CE Academy; Myerscough College, Preston
TEAMS: Lancashire
ROLE: Bowler
DEBUT: First-class: 2020

TWITTER: @EdwinMoulton
NOTES: The seam bowler, who turns 22 in April, signed his first professional contract with Lancashire in November 2019 and made his first-class debut in the Bob Willis Trophy last summer. Moulton featured regularly for the Second XI in 2019, claiming 18 wickets across both the Championship and one-day competitions at an average of 25. He is one of three of the club's Academy graduates who are former pupils at Myerscough College, alongside Jack Morley and Owais Shah. The Preston-based college has a history of producing professional cricketers, including current Lancashire players Tom Bailey and Steven Croft. Moulton, who has also represented Leicestershire Second XI, plays in the Northern Premier League for Chorley CC, for whom he took 39 wickets at 16.00 in 2019

Batting	Mat	Inns	NO	Runs	HS	Ave	SR	100	50	Ct	St
First-class	1	2	0	0	0	0.00	0.00	0	0	0	0
Bowling	**Mat**	**Balls**	**Runs**	**Wkts**	**BBI**	**BBM**	**Ave**	**Econ**	**SR**	**5w**	**10**
First-class	1	162	110	0	-	-	-	4.07	-	0	0

DAN MOUSLEY

LHB / OB / R0 / W0

WARWICKSHIRE

FULL NAME: Daniel Richard Mousley
BORN: July 8, 2001, Birmingham
SQUAD NO: 80
HEIGHT: 6ft 2in
NICKNAME: Mouse
EDUCATION: Bablake School, Coventry
TEAMS: Warwickshire, England U19
ROLE: Batsman
DEBUT: First-class: 2019; T20: 2020

BEST BATTING: 71 Warwickshire vs Glamorgan, Cardiff, 2020

MOST EXCITING DAY AS A CRICKETER? The group match against Australia during the 2020 U19 World Cup in South Africa. It went down to the last ball of the match, just a shame we didn't come out on top
CHILDHOOD SPORTING HERO? Andrew Flintoff
BIGGEST INFLUENCE ON YOUR DEVELOPMENT AS A CRICKETER (EXCLUDING PARENTS)? My uncles who threw balls at me in the garden and in the nets every weekend and every training session – that made me very competitive
FIRST CRICKET CLUB? Nether Whitacre CC, Coleshill, Warwickshire
IF YOU COULD TAKE ONE COUNTY CRICKETER'S BEST SHOT AND ADD IT TO YOUR OWN GAME? Ben Stokes's straight-drive
TOUGHEST OPPONENT IN COUNTY CRICKET? Simon Harmer – facing him at Chelmsford on my first-class debut was a learning experience
WHAT WOULD YOU DO IF YOU WERE IN CHARGE OF COUNTY CRICKET? Have more first-class cricket, more evening games, and more TV games
FAVOURITE SMELL? Petrol
TWITTER: @danmousley80

Batting	Mat	Inns	NO	Runs	HS	Ave	SR	100	50	Ct	St
First-class	3	5	0	152	71	30.40	49.19	0	1	1	0
T20s	3	3	1	101	58*	50.50	126.25	0	1	1	0
Bowling	**Mat**	**Balls**	**Runs**	**Wkts**	**BBI**	**BBM**	**Ave**	**Econ**	**SR**	**5w**	**10**
First-class	3	54	37	0	-	-	-	4.11	-	0	0
T20s	3	12	22	1	1/9	1/9	22.00	11.00	12.0	0	0

STEVEN MULLANEY RHB / RM / R1 / W0 / MVP41

FULL NAME: Steven John Mullaney
BORN: November 19, 1986, Warrington, Cheshire
SQUAD NO: 5
HEIGHT: 5ft 8in
NICKNAME: Mull
EDUCATION: St Mary's Catholic High School, Greater Manchester
TEAMS: Nottinghamshire, England Lions, Lancashire
ROLE: Allrounder
DEBUT: First-class: 2006; List A: 2006; T20: 2006

BEST BATTING: 179 Nottinghamshire vs Warwickshire, Trent Bridge, 2019
BEST BOWLING: 5-32 Nottinghamshire vs Gloucestershire, Trent Bridge, 2017
COUNTY CAP: 2013 (Nottinghamshire)

BIGGEST INFLUENCE ON YOUR DEVELOPMENT AS A CRICKETER (EXCLUDING PARENTS)? Peter Moores – he makes it fun and makes you better as a player and a person
FIRST CRICKET CLUB? Golborne CC, Cheshire
IF YOU COULD TAKE ONE COUNTY CRICKETER'S BEST SHOT AND ADD IT TO YOUR OWN GAME? Ben Duckett's reverse-sweep
TOUGHEST OPPONENT IN COUNTY CRICKET? Graham Onions
MOST ECCENTRIC TEAMMATE? Luke Fletcher – the life and soul of the dressing room
WHAT WOULD YOU DO IF YOU WERE IN CHARGE OF COUNTY CRICKET? Give extra points for first-innings leads in the Championship, allow the top team of each of the T20 Blast groups to progress directly to Finals Day
GUILTY PLEASURE? Singing karaoke
TWITTER: @mull05

Batting	Mat	Inns	NO	Runs	HS	Ave	SR	100	50	Ct	St
First-class	143	241	9	7727	179	33.30	58.23	15	42	142	0
List A	123	91	17	2611	124	35.28	103.32	2	19	57	0
T20s	137	94	25	1203	55	17.43	141.86	0	2	62	0
Bowling	**Mat**	**Balls**	**Runs**	**Wkts**	**BBI**	**BBM**	**Ave**	**Econ**	**SR**	**5w**	**10**
First-class	143	7977	4084	113	5/32	7/46	36.14	3.07	70.5	1	0
List A	123	3981	3458	100	4/29	4/29	34.58	5.21	39.8	0	0
T20s	137	2222	2927	101	4/19	4/19	28.98	7.90	22.0	0	0

TIM MURTAGH

LHB / RFM / R0 / W8 / MVP25

FULL NAME: Timothy James Murtagh
BORN: August 2, 1981, Lambeth, London
SQUAD NO: 34
HEIGHT: 6ft
NICKNAME: Murts
EDUCATION: The John Fisher School, London; St Mary's College, Twickenham
TEAMS: Ireland, Middlesex, England U19, Surrey
ROLE: Bowler
DEBUT: Test: 2018; ODI: 2012; T20I: 2012; First-class: 2000; List A: 2000; T20: 2003

BEST BATTING: 74* Surrey vs Middlesex, The Oval, 2004
BEST BOWLING: 7-82 Middlesex vs Derbyshire, Derby, 2009
COUNTY CAP: 2008 (Middlesex); BENEFIT: 2015 (Middlesex)

MOST EXCITING DAY AS A CRICKETER? Playing a Test match at Lord's and winning the County Championship
CHILDHOOD SPORTING HERO? Robbie Fowler
BIGGEST INFLUENCE ON YOUR DEVELOPMENT AS A CRICKETER (EXCLUDING PARENTS)? Alan Butcher – my first coach at Surrey
FIRST CRICKET CLUB? Purley CC, London
TOUGHEST OPPONENT IN COUNTY CRICKET? Jack Leach – it's impossible to get him out
BIGGEST CRICKETING REGRET? Missing the 2015 World Cup through injury
FAVOURITE SMELL? Rabbit pie
GUILTY PLEASURE? Bubble baths
TWITTER: @tjmurtagh

Batting	Mat	Inns	NO	Runs	HS	Ave	SR	100	50	Ct	St
Tests	3	6	2	109	54*	27.25	82.57	0	1	0	0
ODIs	58	36	12	188	23*	7.83	63.08	0	0	16	0
T20Is	14	5	3	26	12*	13.00	104.00	0	0	3	0
First-class	236	313	90	4197	74*	18.82		0	11	65	0
List A	211	127	45	820	35*	10.00		0	0	55	0
T20s	107	39	14	227	40*	9.08	106.07	0	0	23	0
Bowling	**Mat**	**Balls**	**Runs**	**Wkts**	**BBI**	**BBM**	**Ave**	**Econ**	**SR**	**5w**	**10**
Tests	3	570	213	13	5/13	6/65	16.38	2.24	43.8	1	0
ODIs	58	3020	2290	74	5/21	5/21	30.94	4.54	40.8	1	0
T20Is	14	268	324	13	3/23	3/23	24.92	7.25	20.6	0	0
First-class	236	41436	20836	841	7/82		24.77	3.01	49.2	37	4
List A	211	9772	8133	275	5/21	5/21	29.57	4.99	35.5	1	0
T20s	107	2092	2846	113	6/24	6/24	25.18	8.16	18.5	1	0

MOHAMMAD NABI

RHB / OB

FULL NAME: Mohammad Nabi
BORN: January 1, 1985, Loger, Afghanistan
SQUAD NO: TBC
NICKNAME: Mr President
TEAMS: Afghanistan, Northamptonshire, Balkh Legends, Kent, Leicestershire, Melbourne Renegades, Rangpur Riders, St Lucia Zouks, Sunrisers
ROLE: Allrounder
DEBUT: Test: 2018; ODI: 2009; T20I: 2010; First-class: 2007; List A: 2008; T20: 2010

BEST BATTING: 89 Afghanistan vs Ireland, Greater Noida, 2017 (T20)
BEST BOWLING: 5-15 St Lucia Zouks vs St Kitts & Nevis Patriots, Port of Spain, 2020 (T20)

TWITTER: @MohammadNabi007
NOTES: The veteran off-spinning allrounder has signed up to play for Northants in the T20 Blast up until the quarter-final stage. At the time of writing, the 36-year-old was the No.1 T20I allrounder in the ICC rankings. "He has a wealth of experience from so many global tournaments," said David Ripley, head coach of Northants. "He can turn a game completely with bat and ball." Nabi was among the first wave of Afghan cricketers to play county cricket in 2018, scoring 246 runs and taking nine wickets in 13 T20s for Leicestershire. He fared less well with Kent in 2019, scoring 147 runs in nine innings, although he was the most parsimonious of the county's frontline bowlers with an economy rate of 7.23. A leading member of the Afghanistan side which has shot to prominence over the last decade, Nabi has played in the IPL and the Big Bash League. He is also due to line up for London Spirit in The Hundred this summer

Batting	Mat	Inns	NO	Runs	HS	Ave	SR	100	50	Ct	St
Tests	3	6	0	33	24	5.50	48.52	0	0	2	0
ODIs	127	114	12	2817	116	27.61	85.02	1	15	56	0
T20Is	78	72	11	1347	89	22.08	145.30	0	4	44	0
First-class	35	57	4	1284	117	24.22	51.71	2	5	20	0
List A	162	147	15	3821	146	28.94	87.98	3	18	72	0
T20s	283	239	48	4441	89	23.25	141.93	0	14	131	0
Bowling	**Mat**	**Balls**	**Runs**	**Wkts**	**BBI**	**BBM**	**Ave**	**Econ**	**SR**	**5w**	**10**
Tests	3	546	254	8	3/36	4/95	31.75	2.79	68.2	0	0
ODIs	127	6099	4372	132	4/30	4/30	33.12	4.30	46.2	0	0
T20Is	78	1564	1871	69	4/10	4/10	27.11	7.17	22.6	0	0
First-class	35	4848	2178	94	6/33	8/85	23.17	2.69	51.5	3	0
List A	162	7900	5612	180	5/12	5/12	31.17	4.26	43.8	1	0
T20s	283	5577	6458	272	5/15	5/15	23.74	6.94	20.5	1	0

NAVEEN-UL-HAQ RHB / RFM

FULL NAME: Naveen-ul-Haq Murid
BORN: September 23, 1999, Kabul, Afghanistan
SQUAD NO: 78
TEAMS: Afghanistan, Leicestershire, Guyana Amazon Warriors, Kabul Region, Kandy Tuskers, Mis Ainak Knights, Nangarhar Leopards, Sylhet Thunder
ROLE: Bowler
DEBUT: ODI: 2016; T20I: 2019; First-class: 2018; List A: 2016; T20: 2017

BEST BATTING: 20* Guyana Amazon Warriors vs Jamaica Tallawahs, Port of Spain, 2020 (T20)
BEST BOWLING: 4-14 Guyana Amazon Warriors vs Barbados Tridents, Tarouba, 2020 (T20)

TWITTER: @imnaveenulhaq
NOTES: Naveen is set to become the second Afghan to represent Leicestershire in the T20 Blast, following in the footsteps of his international teammate Mohammad Nabi. The 21-year-old has made only a handful of appearances for his country but has already built a reputation as a highly-skilled death bowler after impressing in T20 leagues around the world, most notably for Guyana Amazon Warriors in the 2020 Caribbean Premier League, when he took 11 wickets and boasted an economy rate of 6.42. The Foxes will hope Naveen can help them build on a promising T20 Blast campaign last summer, when they were pipped to a place at Finals Day by Notts Outlaws. "Naveen is an extremely consistent T20 performer in all global competitions," said Paul Nixon, Leicestershire's head coach. "His clever changes of pace mixed with quicker balls delivered with his unique bowling action make it very tough for opposing batsmen"

Batting	Mat	Inns	NO	Runs	HS	Ave	SR	100	50	Ct	St
ODIs	7	5	4	21	10*	21.00	72.41	0	0	2	0
T20Is	5	2	1	7	5	7.00	100.00	0	0	0	0
First-class	10	13	1	93	34	7.75	50.27	0	0	5	0
List A	23	14	5	92	30	10.22	70.22	0	0	5	0
T20s	50	18	9	103	20*	11.44	85.12	0	0	16	0
Bowling	**Mat**	**Balls**	**Runs**	**Wkts**	**BBI**	**BBM**	**Ave**	**Econ**	**SR**	**5w**	**10**
ODIs	7	369	356	14	4/42	4/42	25.42	5.78	26.3	0	0
T20Is	5	114	123	10	3/21	3/21	12.30	6.47	11.4	0	0
First-class	10	1304	782	31	8/35	8/61	25.22	3.59	42.0	1	0
List A	23	1183	1172	34	5/40	5/40	34.47	5.94	34.7	1	0
T20s	50	1043	1291	55	4/14	4/14	23.47	7.42	18.9	0	0

MICHAEL NESER

RHB / RFM / R0 / W0

FULL NAME: Michael Gertges Neser
BORN: March 29, 1990, Pretoria, South Africa
SQUAD NO: 30
TEAMS: Australia, Glamorgan, Adelaide Strikers, Brisbane Heat, Kings XI Punjab, Queensland
ROLE: Allrounder
DEBUT: ODI: 2018; First-class: 2010; List A: 2010; T20: 2011

BEST BATTING: 121 Queensland vs Tasmania, Adelaide, 2020
BEST BOWLING: 6-57 Queensland vs Tasmania, Hobart, 2017

NOTES: Glamorgan have signed the Australian seam-bowling allrounder as an overseas player. Neser is expected to feature mainly in Championship and 50-over cricket, with Marnus Labuschagne and Colin Ingram taking up the overseas spots in the T20 Blast. He had been due to play for Surrey last season but the deal was cancelled in the wake of the pandemic. The 31-year-old made his two ODI appearances against England in 2018 and has been on the fringes of the Australian squad for a number of years. Born in South Africa but relocated to Australia's Gold Coast aged 10, Neser has been a prolific wicket-taker in the Sheffield Shield for Queensland and scored his maiden first-class hundred against Tasmania last December. "We see him as one of the best bowling allrounders in the domestic game anywhere in the world, and he brings a great balance to our side," said Mark Wallace, Glamorgan's director of cricket

Batting	Mat	Inns	NO	Runs	HS	Ave	SR	100	50	Ct	St
ODIs	2	2	0	8	6	4.00	50.00	0	0	0	0
First-class	59	87	11	1936	121	25.47	53.11	1	11	24	0
List A	55	41	12	654	122	22.55	85.26	1	1	18	0
T20s	75	47	17	420	40*	14.00	115.06	0	0	35	0
Bowling	**Mat**	**Balls**	**Runs**	**Wkts**	**BBI**	**BBM**	**Ave**	**Econ**	**SR**	**5w**	**10**
ODIs	2	100	120	2	2/46	2/46	60.00	7.20	50.0	0	0
First-class	59	10457	5020	195	6/57	8/76	25.74	2.88	53.6	4	0
List A	55	2551	2227	64	4/41	4/41	34.79	5.23	39.8	0	0
T20s	75	1454	2046	75	3/24	3/24	27.28	8.44	19.3	0	0

ARON NIJJAR

LHB / SLA / R0 / W0

FULL NAME: Aron Stuart Singh Nijjar
BORN: September 24, 1994, Goodmayes, Essex
SQUAD NO: 24
EDUCATION: Ilford County High School
TEAMS: Essex
ROLE: Bowler
DEBUT: First-class: 2015; List A: 2015; T20: 2018

BEST BATTING: 53 Essex vs Northamptonshire, Chelmsford, 2015
BEST BOWLING: 2-28 Essex vs Cambridge MCCU, Cambridge, 2019

TWITTER: @aronnijjar
NOTES: The left-arm orthodox spinner was a regular fixture in Essex's T20 side for the first time last year, doing a steady job in nine of the club's 10 matches after Australian leggie Adam Zampa was forced to cancel his Blast contract because of travel restrictions. Nijjar had already done a fine job of replacing Zampa on T20 Finals Day the previous year to help Essex lift the trophy. The 26-year-old is yet to establish himself in the first-class game, having played only once in the Championship since making a handful of appearances in 2015, and he did not feature in last year's Bob Willis Trophy. Nijjar plays his club cricket for the hugely successful Wanstead & Snaresbrook

Batting	Mat	Inns	NO	Runs	HS	Ave	SR	100	50	Ct	St
First-class	13	15	5	237	53	23.70	45.22	0	1	3	0
List A	3	1	0	21	21	21.00	70.00	0	0	4	0
T20s	12	4	2	9	5	4.50	75.00	0	0	5	0
Bowling	**Mat**	**Balls**	**Runs**	**Wkts**	**BBI**	**BBM**	**Ave**	**Econ**	**SR**	**5w**	**10**
First-class	13	1175	785	19	2/28	3/48	41.31	4.00	61.8	0	0
List A	3	126	107	1	1/39	1/39	107.00	5.09	126.0	0	0
T20s	12	258	338	12	3/22	3/22	28.16	7.86	21.5	0	0

SAM NORTHEAST RHB / OB / R4 / W0

FULL NAME: Sam Alexander Northeast
BORN: October 16, 1989, Ashford, Kent
SQUAD NO: 17
HEIGHT: 5ft 11in
NICKNAME: Nick Knight
EDUCATION: Harrow School, London
TEAMS: Hampshire, England Lions, Kent
ROLE: Batsman
DEBUT: First-class: 2007; List A: 2007; T20: 2010

BEST BATTING: 191 Kent vs Derbyshire, Canterbury, 2016
BEST BOWLING: 1-60 Kent vs Gloucestershire, Cheltenham, 2013
COUNTY CAP: 2012 (Kent)

TWITTER: @sanortheast
NOTES:Tipped for England since his early teens, Northeast scored his maiden first-class hundred for Kent in 2009 and went on to score more than 13,000 runs for the club. After a much publicised move to Hampshire in February 2018, Northeast struggled with injury and form in his first season on the south coast, although he did make an unbeaten 75 in Hampshire's victory over his old club in the Lord's one-day final, an innings which began with Kent fans booing him to the crease. The 31-year-old hit his stride in 2019, passing 1,000 first-class runs for the fourth time in five seasons, but fell below his usual high standards in red-ball and T20 cricket last summer

Batting	Mat	Inns	NO	Runs	HS	Ave	SR	100	50	Ct	St
First-class	170	288	21	10365	191	38.82	55.80	24	53	85	0
List A	106	98	10	2986	132	33.93	77.13	4	17	38	0
T20s	125	115	12	2960	114	28.73	128.19	1	20	33	0
Bowling	**Mat**	**Balls**	**Runs**	**Wkts**	**BBI**	**BBM**	**Ave**	**Econ**	**SR**	**5w**	**10**
First-class	170	178	147	1	1/60	1/60	147.00	4.95	178.0	0	0
List A	106	-	-	-	-	-	-	-	-	-	-
T20s	125	-	-	-	-	-	-	-	-	-	-

LIAM NORWELL

RHB / RFM / R0 / W2

FULL NAME: Liam Connor Norwell
BORN: December 27, 1991, Bournemouth
SQUAD NO: 24
HEIGHT: 6ft 3in
NICKNAME: Pasty
EDUCATION: Redruth School, Cornwall
TEAMS: Warwickshire, Gloucestershire
ROLE: Bowler
DEBUT: First-class: 2011; List A: 2012; T20: 2012

BEST BATTING: 102 Gloucestershire vs Derbyshire, Bristol, 2016
BEST BOWLING: 8-43 Gloucestershire vs Leicestershire, Leicester, 2017
COUNTY CAP: 2011 (Gloucestershire)

MOST EXCITING DAY AS A CRICKETER? The first time I played at Lord's, which was for Gloucestershire in 2017. Previously I had either been unavailable or left out for matches when we played there
CHILDHOOD SPORTING HERO? Andrew Flintoff
FIRST CRICKET CLUB? Redruth CC, Cornwall
IF YOU COULD TAKE ONE COUNTY CRICKETER'S BEST SHOT AND ADD IT TO YOUR OWN GAME? Oliver Hannon-Dalby's cover-drive
BIGGEST CRICKETING REGRET? Not learning enough from the senior players in the first years of my career
WHAT WOULD YOU DO IF YOU WERE IN CHARGE OF COUNTY CRICKET? Bring back a white-ball knockout competition with a Lord's final
STRANGEST THING YOU'VE DONE DURING LOCKDOWN? Wearing a Deadpool costume while doing a TikTok dance with my wife
GUILTY PLEASURE? Angel Delight
TWITTER: @LCNorwell

Batting	Mat	Inns	NO	Runs	HS	Ave	SR	100	50	Ct	St
First-class	73	94	37	842	102	14.77	45.24	1	2	16	0
List A	17	10	2	47	16	5.87	69.11	0	0	2	0
T20s	25	5	5	5	2*	-	71.42	0	0	10	0
Bowling	**Mat**	**Balls**	**Runs**	**Wkts**	**BBI**	**BBM**	**Ave**	**Econ**	**SR**	**5w**	**10**
First-class	73	12851	7145	266	8/43	10/65	26.86	3.33	48.3	11	3
List A	17	780	716	23	6/52	6/52	31.13	5.50	33.9	2	0
T20s	25	446	706	13	3/27	3/27	54.30	9.49	34.3	0	0

MARCUS O'RIORDAN

RHB / OB / R0 / W0

FULL NAME: Marcus Kevin O'Riordan
BORN: January 25, 1998, Pembury, Kent
SQUAD NO: 55
HEIGHT: 5ft 10in
NICKNAME: Ray
EDUCATION: Holmewood House School, Tunbridge Wells; Tonbridge School
TEAMS: Kent
ROLE: Allrounder
DEBUT: First-class: 2019; T20: 2019

BEST BATTING: 52* Kent vs Hampshire, Canterbury, 2020
BEST BOWLING: 3-50 Kent vs Sussex, Canterbury, 2020

MOST EXCITING DAY AS A CRICKETER? My T20 debut for Kent against Surrey at Canterbury in 2019
CHILDHOOD SPORTING HERO? Roger Federer
BIGGEST INFLUENCE ON YOUR DEVELOPMENT AS A CRICKETER (EXCLUDING PARENTS)? Andy Whittall, my housemaster at Tonbridge School. He suggested I start bowling off-spin instead of medium pace
FIRST CRICKET CLUB? Tunbridge Wells CC, Kent
IF YOU COULD TAKE ONE COUNTY CRICKETER'S BEST SHOT AND ADD IT TO YOUR OWN GAME? Alex Blake's lofted drive over cover for six
TOUGHEST OPPONENT IN COUNTY CRICKET? Alastair Cook – it felt like he could score off pretty much any ball in the few overs that I have bowled at him
WHAT WOULD YOU DO IF YOU WERE IN CHARGE OF COUNTY CRICKET? Introduce a 32-team FA Cup-style knockout competition (50 overs or T20) consisting of first-class counties, Minor Counties and qualifying club sides
WHAT WOULD YOU DO IF YOU WERE PRIME MINISTER? Increase educational funding for sport and the arts, push for affordable and environment-friendly housing solutions, set up mandatory regular lie-detector tests for politicians

Batting	Mat	Inns	NO	Runs	HS	Ave	SR	100	50	Ct	St
First-class	6	10	3	237	52*	33.85	42.39	0	1	1	0
T20s	1	-	-	-	-	-	-	-	-	0	0
Bowling	**Mat**	**Balls**	**Runs**	**Wkts**	**BBI**	**BBM**	**Ave**	**Econ**	**SR**	**5w**	**10**
First-class	6	415	288	8	3/50	4/72	36.00	4.16	51.8	0	0
T20s	1	12	13	0	-	-	-	6.50	-	0	0

DUANNE OLIVIER

RHB / RFM / R0 / W0

FULL NAME: Duanne Olivier
BORN: May 9, 1992, Groblersdal, Limpopo, South Africa
SQUAD NO: 74
HEIGHT: 6ft 3in
TEAMS: South Africa, Yorkshire, Derbyshire, Free State, Jaffna Stallions, Jozi Stars, Knights
ROLE: Bowler
DEBUT: Test: 2017; ODI: 2019; First-class: 2011; List A: 2011; T20: 2011

BEST BATTING: 72 Free State vs Namibia, Bloemfontein, 2014
BEST BOWLING: 6-37 South Africa vs Pakistan, Centurion, 2018

MOST EXCITING DAY AS A CRICKETER? Making my Test debut against Sri Lanka at Johannesburg in 2017
CHILDHOOD SPORTING HERO? Allan Donald
BIGGEST INFLUENCE ON YOUR DEVELOPMENT AS A CRICKETER (EXCLUDING PARENTS)? My wife – she always pushes me to be better and inspires me every day
IF YOU COULD TAKE ONE COUNTY CRICKETER'S BEST SHOT AND ADD IT TO YOUR OWN GAME? Wayne Madsen's ramp over the keeper
WHAT WOULD YOU DO IF YOU WERE IN CHARGE OF COUNTY CRICKET? Offer free entrance for everybody for the first game of the season, create more events which involve the local community, have a day in which the local cricket, football and rugby-league sides play against one another in each of those three sports
STRANGEST THING YOU'VE DONE DURING LOCKDOWN? Painting a whole room
TWITTER: @Duanne992

Batting	Mat	Inns	NO	Runs	HS	Ave	SR	100	50	Ct	St
Tests	10	12	5	26	10*	3.71	27.95	0	0	2	0
ODIs	2	-	-	-	-	-	-	-	-	0	0
First-class	114	147	48	1263	72	12.75	43.06	0	3	33	0
List A	49	25	10	201	25*	13.40	65.68	0	0	7	0
T20s	56	17	11	85	15*	14.16	87.62	0	0	8	0
Bowling	**Mat**	**Balls**	**Runs**	**Wkts**	**BBI**	**BBM**	**Ave**	**Econ**	**SR**	**5w**	**10**
Tests	10	1440	924	48	6/37	11/96	19.25	3.85	30.0	3	1
ODIs	2	114	124	3	2/73	2/73	41.33	6.52	38.0	0	0
First-class	114	19634	10544	456	6/37	11/96	23.12	3.22	43.0	24	4
List A	49	2013	1777	63	4/34	4/34	28.20	5.29	31.9	0	0
T20s	56	1092	1569	66	4/28	4/28	23.77	8.62	16.5	0	0

FELIX ORGAN

RHB / OB / R0 / W0

FULL NAME: Felix Spencer Organ
BORN: June 2, 1999, Sydney, Australia
SQUAD NO: 3
HEIGHT: 5ft 10in
EDUCATION: Canford School, Dorset
TEAMS: Hampshire, England U19
ROLE: Allrounder
DEBUT: First-class: 2017; List A: 2018; T20: 2020

BEST BATTING: 100 Hampshire vs Kent, Southampton, 2019
BEST BOWLING: 5-25 Hampshire vs Surrey, Southampton, 2019

NOTES: The 21-year-old batting allrounder signed his first professional contract with Hampshire in early 2018 and made a strong impression that summer, scoring his maiden first-class hundred against Kent. He also took his first five-wicket haul, proving that he is a more than handy off-spinner. Organ struggled with the bat in last summer's Bob Willis Trophy, though his seven wickets at 12.85 were a boon for a depleted Hampshire bowling attack. He also made his debut in the T20 Blast, conceding a miserly 54 runs from eight overs across two matches. Born in Sydney, Organ has come through the Hampshire youth system and was vice-captain of the side which won the U17 County Championship in 2015

Batting	Mat	Inns	NO	Runs	HS	Ave	SR	100	50	Ct	St
First-class	12	19	0	376	100	19.78	44.33	1	2	5	0
List A	4	2	0	0	0	0.00	0.00	0	0	2	0
T20s	3	3	0	21	9	7.00	91.30	0	0	0	0
Bowling	**Mat**	**Balls**	**Runs**	**Wkts**	**BBI**	**BBM**	**Ave**	**Econ**	**SR**	**5w**	**10**
First-class	12	437	215	15	5/25	5/25	14.33	2.95	29.1	1	0
List A	4	63	33	2	1/6	1/6	16.50	3.14	31.5	0	0
T20s	3	48	54	3	2/21	2/21	18.00	6.75	16.0	0	0

SOMERSET

CRAIG OVERTON RHB / RFM / R0 / W0 / MVP2

FULL NAME: Craig Overton
BORN: April 10, 1994, Barnstaple, Devon
SQUAD NO: 12
HEIGHT: 6ft 5in
NICKNAME: Goober
EDUCATION: West Buckland School, Devon
TEAMS: England, Somerset
ROLE: Allrounder
DEBUT: Test: 2017; ODI: 2018; First-class: 2012; List A: 2012; T20: 2014

BEST BATTING: 138 Somerset vs Hampshire, Taunton, 2016
BEST BOWLING: 6-24 Somerset vs Cardiff MCCU, Taunton, 2019
COUNTY CAP: 2016

MOST EXCITING DAY AS A CRICKETER? Making my England Test debut in 2017
FAMILY TIES? My father played Minor Counties and my twin Jamie now plays for Surrey
FIRST CRICKET CLUB? North Devon CC, Bideford
TOUGHEST OPPONENT IN COUNTY CRICKET? Kumar Sangakkara
BIGGEST CRICKETING REGRET? Not winning the Championship
WHAT WOULD YOU DO IF YOU WERE IN CHARGE OF COUNTY CRICKET? Get rid of the Mankad rule, ensure more Championship matches are played at the height of summer
WHAT WOULD YOU DO IF YOU WERE PRIME MINISTER? Improve budgets for police
STRANGEST THING YOU'VE DONE DURING LOCKDOWN? Gardening
TWITTER: @craigoverton12

Batting	Mat	Inns	NO	Runs	HS	Ave	SR	100	50	Ct	St
Tests	4	8	2	124	41*	20.66	40.78	0	0	1	0
ODIs	1	-	-	-	-	-	-	-	-	2	0
First-class	95	140	18	2640	138	21.63	64.15	1	11	67	0
List A	69	50	16	756	66*	22.23	116.84	0	2	31	0
T20s	49	26	10	267	35*	16.68	118.14	0	0	22	0
Bowling	**Mat**	**Balls**	**Runs**	**Wkts**	**BBI**	**BBM**	**Ave**	**Econ**	**SR**	**5w**	**10**
Tests	4	707	403	9	3/105	4/116	44.77	3.42	78.5	0	0
ODIs	1	42	55	0	-	-	-	7.85	-	0	0
First-class	95	15659	7862	322	6/24	9/51	24.41	3.01	48.6	9	0
List A	69	3178	2820	90	5/18	5/18	31.33	5.32	35.3	1	0
T20s	49	906	1426	42	3/17	3/17	33.95	9.44	21.5	0	0

JAMIE OVERTON

RHB / RF / R0 / W0 / MVP12

FULL NAME: Jamie Overton
BORN: April 10, 1994, Barnstaple, Devon
SQUAD NO: 88
HEIGHT: 6ft 5in
NICKNAME: J
EDUCATION: West Buckland School, Devon
TEAMS: Surrey, England Lions, Northamptonshire, Somerset
ROLE: Bowler
DEBUT: First-class: 2012; List A: 2012; T20: 2015

BEST BATTING: 120 Somerset vs Warwickshire, Edgbaston, 2020
BEST BOWLING: 6-95 Somerset vs Middlesex, Taunton, 2013

MOST EXCITING DAY AS A CRICKETER? Being included in the 30-man Test "bubble" squad last summer
FAMILY TIES? My dad played for Devon and my twin brother Craig plays for Somerset
CHILDHOOD SPORTING HERO? Cristiano Ronaldo
BIGGEST INFLUENCE ON YOUR DEVELOPMENT AS A CRICKETER (EXCLUDING PARENTS)? Clifford Dark, my club coach at North Devon CC. He offered me the opportunity to play at a higher age-group level and gave me lots of confidence
IF YOU COULD TAKE ONE COUNTY CRICKETER'S BEST SHOT AND ADD IT TO YOUR OWN GAME? Jos Buttler's ramp shot
WHAT WOULD YOU DO IF YOU WERE PRIME MINISTER? Lower taxes
STRANGEST THING YOU'VE DONE DURING LOCKDOWN? Attempting to cut my own hair
FAVOURITE SMELL? A cooked dinner
IF YOU WERE AN ANIMAL, WHICH WOULD IT BE? A horse
TWITTER: @JamieOverton

Batting	Mat	Inns	NO	Runs	HS	Ave	SR	100	50	Ct	St
First-class	69	99	21	1506	120	19.30	83.66	1	8	38	0
List A	42	31	8	399	40*	17.34	114.65	0	0	19	0
T20s	59	29	13	268	40*	16.75	167.50	0	0	34	0
Bowling	**Mat**	**Balls**	**Runs**	**Wkts**	**BBI**	**BBM**	**Ave**	**Econ**	**SR**	**5w**	**10**
First-class	69	8974	5319	179	6/95	8/143	29.71	3.55	50.1	4	0
List A	42	1662	1742	57	4/42	4/42	30.56	6.28	29.1	0	0
T20s	59	1057	1684	57	5/47	5/47	29.54	9.55	18.5	1	0

CALLUM PARKINSON RHB / SLA / R0 / W0 / MVP71

FULL NAME: Callum Francis Parkinson
BORN: October 24, 1996, Bolton, Lancashire
SQUAD NO: 10
HEIGHT: 5ft 8in
NICKNAME: Parky
EDUCATION: Bolton School; Canon Slade, Bolton
TEAMS: Leicestershire, Derbyshire
ROLE: Bowler
DEBUT: First-class: 2016; List A: 2017; T20: 2017

BEST BATTING: 75 Leicestershire vs Kent, Canterbury, 2017
BEST BOWLING: 8-148 Leicestershire vs Worcestershire, Worcester, 2017

FAMILY TIES? My twin brother Matt plays for England and Lancashire
CHILDHOOD SPORTING HERO? Kevin Nolan
FIRST CRICKET CLUB? Heaton CC, Bolton
IF YOU COULD TAKE ONE COUNTY CRICKETER'S BEST SHOT AND ADD IT TO YOUR OWN GAME? Colin Ackermann's sweep – he never seems to miss when he plays it against my bowling
TOUGHEST OPPONENT IN COUNTY CRICKET? That's a close one between Ben Duckett and Wayne Madsen – both 360-degree batsmen and very good players of spin
WHAT WOULD YOU DO IF YOU WERE IN CHARGE OF COUNTY CRICKET? Start a T10 competition and allow five men out of the ring in the middle overs of 50-over cricket
WHAT WOULD YOU DO IF YOU WERE PRIME MINISTER? Take Saturdays off to watch Bolton Wanderers home and away, invest in Bolton Wanderers, appoint myself manager of Bolton Wanderers
STRANGEST THING YOU'VE DONE DURING LOCKDOWN? Watching all 20 seasons of Made in Chelsea
GUILTY PLEASURE? The Notebook (rom-com film)
TWITTER: @cal_parky

Batting	Mat	Inns	NO	Runs	HS	Ave	SR	100	50	Ct	St
First-class	28	42	8	635	75	18.67	40.91	0	1	4	0
List A	13	11	3	222	52*	27.75	87.40	0	1	2	0
T20s	52	28	15	192	27*	14.76	100.00	0	0	9	0
Bowling	**Mat**	**Balls**	**Runs**	**Wkts**	**BBI**	**BBM**	**Ave**	**Econ**	**SR**	**5w**	**10**
First-class	28	4207	2340	54	8/148	10/185	43.33	3.33	77.9	1	1
List A	13	552	589	4	1/34	1/34	147.25	6.40	138.0	0	0
T20s	52	996	1258	52	4/20	4/20	24.19	7.57	19.1	0	0

MATT PARKINSON RHB / LB / R0 / W0

FULL NAME: Matthew William Parkinson
BORN: October 24, 1996, Bolton, Lancashire
SQUAD NO: 28
HEIGHT: 5ft 9in
NICKNAME: Daddy
EDUCATION: Canon Slade School, Bolton
TEAMS: England, Lancashire
ROLE: Bowler
DEBUT: ODI: 2020; T20I: 2019; First-class: 2016; List A: 2018; T20: 2017

BEST BATTING: 14 Lancashire vs Middlesex, Lord's, 2017
BEST BOWLING: 6-23 Lancashire vs Sussex, Old Trafford, 2019
COUNTY CAP: 2019

MOST EXCITING DAY AS A CRICKETER? Making my T20I debut for England
CHILDHOOD SPORTING HERO? Kevin Nolan
BIGGEST INFLUENCE ON YOUR DEVELOPMENT AS A CRICKETER (EXCLUDING PARENTS)? Stuart MacGill and Jeetan Patel
FIRST CRICKET CLUB? Heaton CC, Bolton
TOUGHEST OPPONENT IN COUNTY CRICKET? Wayne Madsen – best player of spin in the country, sweeps really well and never lets you settle
MOST ECCENTRIC TEAMMATE? Rob Jones – he loves birds and walking
WHAT WOULD YOU DO IF YOU WERE IN CHARGE OF COUNTY CRICKET? Play Championship matches on used pitches, scrap draws, play more T20
TWITTER: @mattypark96

Batting	Mat	Inns	NO	Runs	HS	Ave	SR	100	50	Ct	St
ODIs	2	-	-	-	-	-	-	-	-	0	0
T20Is	2	-	-	-	-	-	-	-	-	0	0
First-class	20	26	9	90	14	5.29	26.47	0	0	6	0
List A	27	11	8	43	15*	14.33	52.43	0	0	4	0
T20s	49	8	4	17	7*	4.25	73.91	0	0	5	0
Bowling	**Mat**	**Balls**	**Runs**	**Wkts**	**BBI**	**BBM**	**Ave**	**Econ**	**SR**	**5w**	**10**
ODIs	2	64	63	0	-	-	-	5.90	-	0	0
T20Is	2	36	61	5	4/47	4/47	12.20	10.16	7.2	0	0
First-class	20	3029	1564	62	6/23	10/165	25.22	3.09	48.8	3	1
List A	27	1366	1178	42	5/51	5/51	28.04	5.17	32.5	2	0
T20s	49	1056	1287	80	4/23	4/23	16.08	7.31	13.2	0	0

WAYNE PARNELL

LHB / LFM / R0 / W0

FULL NAME: Wayne Dillon Parnell
BORN: July 30, 1989, Port Elizabeth, SA
SQUAD NO: 15
HEIGHT: 6ft 2in
NICKNAME: Parnygram
EDUCATION: Nelson Mandela University
TEAMS: South Africa, Northamptonshire, Delhi Daredevils, Eastern Province, Glamorgan, Karachi Kings, Kent, Sussex, Warriors, Western Province, Worcestershire
ROLE: Allrounder
DEBUT: Test: 2010; ODI: 2009; T20I: 2009; First-class: 2006; List A: 2007; T20: 2008

BEST BATTING: 111* Cape Cobras vs Warriors, Paarl, 2016
BEST BOWLING: 7-51 Cape Cobras vs Dolphins, Cape Town, 2016

MOST EXCITING DAY AS A CRICKETER? Winning the T20 Blast with Worcestershire in 2018
CHILDHOOD SPORTING HERO? Raúl
BIGGEST INFLUENCE ON YOUR DEVELOPMENT AS A CRICKETER (EXCLUDING PARENTS)? Russell Domingo – he was my first coach as a pro and also coached South Africa. He's probably underrated because he wasn't a pro cricketer, but he's a great man-manager
FIRST CRICKET CLUB? Northville CC, Port Elizabeth
TOUGHEST OPPONENT IN COUNTY CRICKET? Liam Livingstone – I love his positive and attacking mindset when he bats
STRANGEST THING YOU'VE DONE DURING LOCKDOWN? Starting to read books which aren't about sport
TWITTER: @WayneParnell

Batting	Mat	Inns	NO	Runs	HS	Ave	SR	100	50	Ct	St
Tests	6	4	0	67	23	16.75	37.22	0	0	3	0
ODIs	65	38	14	508	56	21.16	78.39	0	1	12	0
T20Is	40	13	9	114	29*	28.50	118.75	0	0	5	0
First-class	75	101	11	2502	111*	27.80	52.68	2	15	23	0
List A	165	115	32	2087	129	25.14	87.72	2	6	31	0
T20s	207	121	46	1461	99	19.48	123.70	0	4	36	0
Bowling	**Mat**	**Balls**	**Runs**	**Wkts**	**BBI**	**BBM**	**Ave**	**Econ**	**SR**	**5w**	**10**
Tests	6	556	414	15	4/51	6/89	27.60	4.46	37.0	0	0
ODIs	65	2911	2738	94	5/48	5/48	29.12	5.64	30.9	2	0
T20Is	40	749	1038	41	4/13	4/13	25.31	8.31	18.2	0	0
First-class	75	11431	6542	220	7/51	12/105	29.73	3.43	51.9	7	1
List A	165	7431	6750	233	6/51	6/51	28.96	5.45	31.8	5	0
T20s	207	4072	5317	209	4/13	4/13	25.44	7.83	19.4	0	0

RISHI PATEL

RHB / LB / R0 / W0

FULL NAME: Rishi Ketan Patel
BORN: July 26, 1998, Chigwell, Essex
SQUAD NO: 26
HEIGHT: 6ft 2in
NICKNAME: The Chancellor
EDUCATION: Brentwood School, Essex
TEAMS: Leicestershire, Essex
ROLE: Batsman
DEBUT: First-class: 2019; List A: 2019

BEST BATTING: 35 Essex vs Yorkshire, Chelmsford, 2019

MOST EXCITING DAY AS A CRICKETER? Winning the County Championship with Essex at Taunton in 2019
CHILDHOOD SPORTING HERO? Sachin Tendulkar
FIRST CRICKET CLUB? Ilford CC, London
IF YOU COULD TAKE ONE COUNTY CRICKETER'S BEST SHOT AND ADD IT TO YOUR OWN GAME? Dan Lawrence's flick shot over mid-wicket
TOUGHEST OPPONENT IN COUNTY CRICKET? Ben Coad – he's got great skills and does not offer any bad balls
MOST ECCENTRIC TEAMMATE? Harry Swindells – a joker with loads of energy and just does not shut up
WHAT WOULD YOU DO IF YOU WERE IN CHARGE OF COUNTY CRICKET? Make sure every T20 Blast game is shown on TV, go back to a two-division Championship
STRANGEST THING YOU'VE DONE DURING LOCKDOWN? Grinding coffee beans
FAVOURITE SMELL? Freshly cut grass
IF YOU WERE AN ANIMAL, WHICH WOULD IT BE? A dolphin – they're so relaxed
TWITTER: @Rishikpatel26

Batting	Mat	Inns	NO	Runs	HS	Ave	SR	100	50	Ct	St
First-class	7	10	0	170	35	17.00	45.09	0	0	6	0
List A	3	3	0	65	35	21.66	91.54	0	0	0	0
Bowling	**Mat**	**Balls**	**Runs**	**Wkts**	**BBI**	**BBM**	**Ave**	**Econ**	**SR**	**5w**	**10**
First-class	7	-	-	-	-	-	-	-	-	-	-
List A	3	-	-	-	-	-	-	-	-	-	-

RYAN PATEL

LHB / RMF / R0 / W0

FULL NAME: Ryan Patel
BORN: October 26, 1997, Sutton, Surrey
SQUAD NO: 26
HEIGHT: 5ft 10in
NICKNAME: FP
EDUCATION: Whitgift School, Croydon
TEAMS: Surrey, England U19
ROLE: Allrounder
DEBUT: First-class: 2017; List A: 2019; T20: 2019

BEST BATTING: 100* Surrey vs Essex, The Oval, 2019
BEST BOWLING: 6-5 Surrey vs Somerset, Guildford, 2018

MOST EXCITING DAY AS A CRICKETER? Winning the County Championship in 2018
CHILDHOOD SPORTING HERO? Thierry Henry
BIGGEST INFLUENCE ON YOUR DEVELOPMENT AS A CRICKETER (EXCLUDING PARENTS)? Sid Lahiri, director of the Rajasthan Royals Academy in Cobham who has also worked with Surrey age-group sides
FIRST CRICKET CLUB? Old Rutlishians CC, London
BEST INNINGS YOU'VE SEEN? Kumar Sangakkara's double hundred against Essex at Chelmsford in 2017
IF YOU COULD TAKE ONE COUNTY CRICKETER'S BEST SHOT AND ADD IT TO YOUR OWN GAME? Ian Bell's cover-drive
GUILTY PLEASURE? Beer

Batting	Mat	Inns	NO	Runs	HS	Ave	SR	100	50	Ct	St
First-class	26	42	4	926	100*	24.36	39.30	1	2	14	0
List A	3	3	1	57	41*	28.50	95.00	0	0	1	0
T20s	7	3	1	7	5*	3.50	70.00	0	0	1	0
Bowling	**Mat**	**Balls**	**Runs**	**Wkts**	**BBI**	**BBM**	**Ave**	**Econ**	**SR**	**5w**	**10**
First-class	26	1347	773	15	6/5	6/12	51.53	3.44	89.8	1	0
List A	3	72	82	2	2/65	2/65	41.00	6.83	36.0	0	0
T20s	7	21	36	0	-	-	-	10.28	-	0	0

SAMIT PATEL RHB / SLA / R4 / W0 / MVP23

FULL NAME: Samit Rohit Patel
BORN: November 30, 1984, Leicester
SQUAD NO: 21
HEIGHT: 5ft 8in
NICKNAME: Sarnie
EDUCATION: Worksop College
TEAMS: England, Nottinghamshire, Dambulla Viiking, Glamorgan, Islamabad United, Lahore Qalandars, Melbourne Renegades, Rajshahi Kings, Wellington
ROLE: Allrounder
DEBUT: Test: 2012; ODI: 2008; T20I: 2011; First-class: 2002; List A: 2002; T20: 2003

BEST BATTING: 257* Nottinghamshire vs Gloucestershire, Bristol, 2017
BEST BOWLING: 7-68 Nottinghamshire vs Hampshire, Southampton, 2011
COUNTY CAP: 2008 (Nottinghamshire); BENEFIT: 2017 (Nottinghamshire)

FAMILY TIES? My brother Akhil played for Nottinghamshire for two years
CHILDHOOD SPORTING HERO? Stephen Fleming
FIRST CRICKET CLUB? Kimberley Institute CC, Nottinghamshire
BEST INNINGS YOU'VE SEEN? Sachin Tendulkar's double century in the 2004 Sydney Test – for the mental strength he showed in not playing a cover-drive
WHAT WOULD YOU DO IF YOU WERE IN CHARGE OF COUNTY CRICKET? Change the rules so that you can't be run out backing up
TWITTER: @Samitpatel21

Batting	Mat	Inns	NO	Runs	HS	Ave	SR	100	50	Ct	St
Tests	6	9	0	151	42	16.77	44.67	0	0	3	0
ODIs	36	22	7	482	70*	32.13	93.23	0	1	7	0
T20Is	18	14	2	189	67	15.75	109.24	0	1	3	0
First-class	231	376	20	12692	257*	35.65	62.71	26	64	140	0
List A	245	212	34	6270	136*	35.22	85.38	8	33	70	0
T20s	305	256	54	5239	90*	25.93	125.81	0	30	90	0
Bowling	**Mat**	**Balls**	**Runs**	**Wkts**	**BBI**	**BBM**	**Ave**	**Econ**	**SR**	**5w**	**10**
Tests	6	858	421	7	2/27	3/164	60.14	2.94	122.5	0	0
ODIs	36	1187	1091	24	5/41	5/41	45.45	5.51	49.4	1	0
T20Is	18	252	321	7	2/6	2/6	45.85	7.64	36.0	0	0
First-class	231	26909	13650	357	7/68		38.23	3.04	75.3	5	1
List A	245	8319	7491	225	6/13	6/13	33.29	5.40	36.9	2	0
T20s	305	5509	6713	247	4/5	4/5	27.17	7.31	22.3	0	0

STEVEN PATTERSON

RHB / RMF / R0 / W2

FULL NAME: Steven Andrew Patterson
BORN: October 3, 1983, Beverley, Yorkshire
SQUAD NO: 17
HEIGHT: 6ft 4in
NICKNAME: Dead Man
EDUCATION: Malet Lambert School, Hull; St Mary's Sixth Form College, Hull; University of Leeds
TEAMS: Yorkshire
ROLE: Bowler
DEBUT: First-class: 2005; List A: 2003; T20: 2009

BEST BATTING: 63* Yorkshire vs Warwickshire, Edgbaston, 2016
BEST BOWLING: 6-40 Yorkshire vs Essex, Chelmsford, 2018
COUNTY CAP: 2012; BENEFIT: 2017

MOST EXCITING DAY AS A CRICKETER? It's very hard to choose between making my Championship debut at Scarborough, receiving my first XI cap, and winning the County Championship in 2014 and 2015
FAMILY TIES? My grandad played for Durham before World War II
CHILDHOOD SPORTING HERO? Shaun Pollock

Batting	Mat	Inns	NO	Runs	HS	Ave	SR	100	50	Ct	St
First-class	159	190	43	2377	63*	16.17	39.46	0	4	31	0
List A	96	40	21	249	25*	13.10		0	0	17	0
T20s	63	9	4	9	3*	1.80	42.85	0	0	10	0
Bowling	**Mat**	**Balls**	**Runs**	**Wkts**	**BBI**	**BBM**	**Ave**	**Econ**	**SR**	**5w**	**10**
First-class	159	25686	11651	420	6/40	8/94	27.74	2.72	61.1	8	0
List A	96	4116	3524	122	6/32	6/32	28.88	5.13	33.7	2	0
T20s	63	1290	1811	61	4/30	4/30	29.68	8.42	21.1	0	0

LIAM PATTERSON-WHITE LHB / SLA / R0 / W0

FULL NAME: Liam Anthony Patterson-White
BORN: November 8, 1998, Sunderland, County Durham
SQUAD NO: 87
HEIGHT: 6ft
NICKNAME: Patto
EDUCATION: Worksop College, Nottinghamshire
TEAMS: Nottinghamshire, England U19
ROLE: Allrounder
DEBUT: First-class: 2019

BEST BATTING: 58* Nottinghamshire vs Yorkshire, Scarborough, 2019
BEST BOWLING: 5-73 Nottinghamshire vs Somerset, Taunton, 2019

MOST EXCITING DAY AS A CRICKETER? Making my professional debut in 2019
CHILDHOOD SPORTING HERO? James Taylor
BIGGEST INFLUENCE ON YOUR DEVELOPMENT AS A CRICKETER (EXCLUDING PARENTS)? Ant Botha – assistant coach at Nottinghamshire. He helped me when working with the Academy and Second XI teams and continues to back me, showing why I deserve to represent Nottinghamshire
FIRST CRICKET CLUB? Bashford Mill CC, Nottingham
IF YOU COULD TAKE ONE COUNTY CRICKETER'S BEST SHOT AND ADD IT TO YOUR OWN GAME? Joe Root's back-foot punch
TOUGHEST OPPONENT IN COUNTY CRICKET? Zak Crawley – it always feels like he's one step ahead of me when I'm bowling at him
STRANGEST THING YOU'VE DONE DURING LOCKDOWN? Learning to make different types of coffee
FAVOURITE SMELL? A scented candle
TWITTER: @LiamPattersonW2

Batting	Mat	Inns	NO	Runs	HS	Ave	SR	100	50	Ct	St
First-class	5	8	2	91	58*	15.16	29.35	0	1	3	0
Bowling	**Mat**	**Balls**	**Runs**	**Wkts**	**BBI**	**BBM**	**Ave**	**Econ**	**SR**	**5w**	**10**
First-class	5	809	420	20	5/73	6/107	21.00	3.11	40.4	1	0

DAVID PAYNE

RHB / LFM / R0 / W0 / MVP37

FULL NAME: David Alan Payne
BORN: February 15, 1991, Poole, Dorset
SQUAD NO: 14
HEIGHT: 6ft 3in
NICKNAME: Sid
EDUCATION: Lytchett Minster Secondary & Sixth Form, Poole, Dorset
TEAMS: Gloucestershire, England U19
ROLE: Bowler
DEBUT: First-class: 2011; List A: 2009; T20: 2010

BEST BATTING: 67* Gloucestershire vs Glamorgan, Cardiff, 2016
BEST BOWLING: 6-26 Gloucestershire vs Leicestershire, Bristol, 2011
COUNTY CAP: 2011

MOST EXCITING DAY AS A CRICKETER? Michael Klinger and Jack Taylor scoring hundreds to chase down 320 in 50-odd overs in a Championship match at New Road in 2016
CHILDHOOD SPORTING HERO? David Beckham
FIRST CRICKET CLUB? Parley CC, Dorset
WHAT WOULD YOU DO IF YOU WERE IN CHARGE OF COUNTY CRICKET? Set a maximum of 75 overs per day for four-day cricket
SURPRISING FACT ABOUT YOU? I was cutting my own hair even in pre-Covid times
TWITTER: @sidpayne7

Batting	Mat	Inns	NO	Runs	HS	Ave	SR	100	50	Ct	St
First-class	99	122	39	1652	67*	19.90	47.14	0	6	31	0
List A	66	27	17	171	36*	17.10	76.68	0	0	19	0
T20s	93	23	14	49	10	5.44	87.50	0	0	17	0
Bowling	**Mat**	**Balls**	**Runs**	**Wkts**	**BBI**	**BBM**	**Ave**	**Econ**	**SR**	**5w**	**10**
First-class	99	16163	8413	277	6/26	9/96	30.37	3.12	58.3	4	0
List A	66	2867	2746	110	7/29	7/29	24.96	5.74	26.0	3	0
T20s	93	1837	2551	115	5/24	5/24	22.18	8.33	15.9	1	0

DILLON PENNINGTON

RHB / RFM / R0 / W0

FULL NAME: Dillon Young Pennington
BORN: February 26, 1999, Shrewsbury, Shropshire
SQUAD NO: 22
HEIGHT: 6ft 4in
NICKNAME: Dill
EDUCATION: Wrekin College, Shropshire; University of Worcester
TEAMS: Worcestershire, England U19
ROLE: Bowler
DEBUT: First-class: 2018; List A: 2018; T20: 2018

BEST BATTING: 37 Worcestershire vs Somerset, Worcester, 2018
BEST BOWLING: 4-53 Worcestershire vs Yorkshire, Scarborough, 2018

MOST EXCITING DAY AS A CRICKETER? Winning on T20 Finals Day in 2018
CHILDHOOD SPORTING HERO? Andrew Flintoff
FIRST CRICKET CLUB? Shrewsbury CC, Shropshire
TOUGHEST OPPONENT IN COUNTY CRICKET? Kane Williamson
BIGGEST CRICKETING REGRET? Being injured a lot of the time and causing hell for the Worcestershire backroom staff
STRANGEST THING YOU'VE DONE DURING LOCKDOWN? Making my own pasta – it was a very messy experience
FAVOURITE SMELL? Strawberry
IF YOU WERE AN ANIMAL, WHICH WOULD IT BE? A dog – because they don't have to think about a lot
TWITTER: @DillonPenning14

Batting	Mat	Inns	NO	Runs	HS	Ave	SR	100	50	Ct	St
First-class	15	26	5	153	37	7.28	37.87	0	0	5	0
List A	3	2	1	7	4*	7.00	28.00	0	0	2	0
T20s	22	8	5	27	10*	9.00	103.84	0	0	5	0
Bowling	**Mat**	**Balls**	**Runs**	**Wkts**	**BBI**	**BBM**	**Ave**	**Econ**	**SR**	**5w**	**10**
First-class	15	2353	1327	41	4/53	6/80	32.36	3.38	57.3	0	0
List A	3	156	178	8	5/67	5/67	22.25	6.84	19.5	1	0
T20s	22	390	594	21	4/9	4/9	28.28	9.13	18.5	0	0

MICHAEL PEPPER

RHB / WK / R0 / W0

FULL NAME: Michael-Kyle Steven Pepper
BORN: June 25, 1998, Harlow, Essex
SQUAD NO: 19
HEIGHT: 6ft 2in
NICKNAME: Peps
EDUCATION: The Perse School, Cambridge
TEAMS: Essex
ROLE: Wicketkeeper/batsman
DEBUT: First-class: 2018; T20: 2018

BEST BATTING: 22 Essex vs Somerset, Chelmsford, 2018

FIRST CRICKET CLUB? Wendens Ambo CC, Saffron Walden
MOST INTERESTING TEAMMATE? Feroze Khushi – he watches from inside the downstairs changing room
NOTES: The 22-year-old wicketkeeper/batsman signed his first contract with the club in September 2018 after making his Championship and T20 debuts earlier that summer. Essex's understudy to Adam Wheater, he was sidelined after appendix surgery in the early part of the 2019 season and made just one Championship appearance that summer. He didn't get a go in red-ball cricket last year but played in five matches at the end of the Eagles' T20 Blast campaign, making a career-best 34 not out against Sussex at Hove. The former Cambridgeshire keeper signed a new one-year deal last November. "Michael has always performed well when called upon and he has a great role model in Adam Wheater to learn from," said Anthony McGrath, Essex's head coach. "Hopefully he can crack on in 2021 and really stake his claim for a place in the first team"

Batting	Mat	Inns	NO	Runs	HS	Ave	SR	100	50	Ct	St
First-class	3	6	0	61	22	10.16	39.35	0	0	6	0
T20s	9	8	3	102	34*	20.40	98.07	0	0	4	0
Bowling	**Mat**	**Balls**	**Runs**	**Wkts**	**BBI**	**BBM**	**Ave**	**Econ**	**SR**	**5w**	**10**
First-class	3	-	-	-	-	-	-	-	-	-	-
T20s	9	-	-	-	-	-	-	-	-	-	-

TOBY PETTMAN

RHB / RFM / R0 / W0

FULL NAME: Toby Henry Somerville Pettman
BORN: May 11, 1998, Kingston-upon-Thames, Surrey
SQUAD NO: 15
HEIGHT: 6ft 7in
NICKNAME: Tobe
EDUCATION: Tonbridge School, Kent; Jesus College, Oxford
TEAMS: Nottinghamshire
ROLE: Bowler
DEBUT: First-class: 2017

BEST BATTING: 54* Oxford University vs Cambridge University, Oxford, 2018
BEST BOWLING: 5-19 Oxford University vs Cambridge University, Cambridge, 2019

MOST EXCITING DAY AS A CRICKETER? Winning the Cuppers final (the inter-collegiate competition at Oxford) in a super over which was followed by a pitch invasion
CHILDHOOD SPORTING HERO? Darren Stevens – he's an inspiration to all of us who don't bowl 90mph
BIGGEST INFLUENCE ON YOUR DEVELOPMENT AS A CRICKETER (EXCLUDING PARENTS)? Graham Charlesworth – my coach at Oxford
IF YOU COULD TAKE ONE COUNTY CRICKETER'S BEST SHOT AND ADD IT TO YOUR OWN GAME? Why don't you ask us about which bowler's action we'd most like to have? Clearly a batsman's game!
TOUGHEST OPPONENT IN COUNTY CRICKET? I'm about to find out...
MOST ECCENTRIC TEAMMATE? Zak Chappell – he asks the questions nobody had thought of but which we're now really glad we know the answers to
WHAT WOULD YOU DO IF YOU WERE PRIME MINISTER? Make Cadbury Freddos cost 10p (like they used to), get rid of parking tickets
STRANGEST THING YOU'VE DONE DURING LOCKDOWN? My finals exam
FAVOURITE SMELL? Food
GUILTY PLEASURE? Chess

Batting	Mat	Inns	NO	Runs	HS	Ave	SR	100	50	Ct	St
First-class	7	8	1	122	54*	17.42	31.36	0	1	3	0
Bowling	**Mat**	**Balls**	**Runs**	**Wkts**	**BBI**	**BBM**	**Ave**	**Econ**	**SR**	**5w**	**10**
First-class	7	1494	698	33	5/19	8/80	21.15	2.80	45.2	2	0

MATHEW PILLANS

RHB / RFM / R0 / W0

FULL NAME: Mathew William Pillans
BORN: July 4, 1991, Pretoria, South Africa
SQUAD NO: 13
HEIGHT: 6ft 4in
NICKNAME: Tarzan
EDUCATION: Pretoria Boys High School
TEAMS: Yorkshire, Dolphins, KwaZulu-Natal, Leicestershire, Northerns, Surrey
ROLE: Bowler
DEBUT: First-class: 2012; List A: 2013; T20: 2014

BEST BATTING: 56 Leicestershire vs Northamptonshire, Northampton, 2017
BEST BOWLING: 6-67 Dolphins vs Knights, Durban, 2015

MOST EXCITING DAY AS A CRICKETER? Taking my first 10-wicket haul in a first-class match, for the Dolphins against the Knights at Kingsmead in 2015
FAMILY TIES? My mum played for the Springbok hockey team for 13 years and my dad played rugby in Zimbabwe and represented the World XV
CHILDHOOD SPORTING HERO? Brett Lee
IF YOU COULD TAKE ONE COUNTY CRICKETER'S BEST SHOT AND ADD IT TO YOUR OWN GAME? Jason Roy's pull in front of square
MOST ECCENTRIC TEAMMATE? Harry Brook – he plays some crazy shots in the nets and has the talent to pull them off
WHAT WOULD YOU DO IF YOU WERE IN CHARGE OF COUNTY CRICKET? Put cameras into the nets so that players can work on their game
WHAT WOULD YOU DO IF YOU WERE PRIME MINISTER? Increase salaries for public workers – police, nurses etc
SURPRISING FACT ABOUT YOU? I had open-heart surgery when I was 12
TWITTER: @matwilpil

Batting	Mat	Inns	NO	Runs	HS	Ave	SR	100	50	Ct	St
First-class	42	59	5	730	56	13.51	64.71	0	1	20	0
List A	19	13	5	133	31	16.62	91.09	0	0	5	0
T20s	43	20	9	184	34*	16.72	108.23	0	0	9	0
Bowling	**Mat**	**Balls**	**Runs**	**Wkts**	**BBI**	**BBM**	**Ave**	**Econ**	**SR**	**5w**	**10**
First-class	42	6505	3710	131	6/67	10/129	28.32	3.42	49.6	3	1
List A	19	734	688	32	5/29	5/29	21.50	5.62	22.9	1	0
T20s	43	782	1150	40	3/15	3/15	28.75	8.82	19.5	0	0

JACK PLOM

LHB / RFM / R0 / W0

FULL NAME: Jack Henry Plom
BORN: August 27, 1999, Basildon, Essex
SQUAD NO: 77
HEIGHT: 6ft 3in
NICKNAME: Plommy
EDUCATION: Gable Hall School, Corringham; South Essex College, Southend-on-Sea
TEAMS: Essex, England U19
ROLE: Bowler
DEBUT: First-class: 2018; T20: 2020

MOST EXCITING DAY AS A CRICKETER? My T20 debut in 2020
CHILDHOOD SPORTING HERO? Andrew Flintoff
BIGGEST INFLUENCE ON YOUR DEVELOPMENT AS A CRICKETER (EXCLUDING PARENTS)? Club cricket – first growing up with it and then learning my trade between the ages of 14 and 18
FIRST CRICKET CLUB? Shenfield CC, Brentwood, Essex
WHAT WOULD YOU DO IF YOU WERE IN CHARGE OF COUNTY CRICKET? Introduce a "last-man-stands" rule in T20 cricket so that the not-out batsman can bat on his own
WHAT WOULD YOU DO IF YOU WERE PRIME MINISTER? Make Friday part of the weekend
STRANGEST THING YOU'VE DONE DURING LOCKDOWN? Going to Tesco to pass the time
IF YOU WERE AN ANIMAL, WHICH WOULD IT BE? A giraffe – I've got a long neck
GUILTY PLEASURE? Chocolate

Batting	Mat	Inns	NO	Runs	HS	Ave	SR	100	50	Ct	St
First-class	1	-	-	-	-	-	-	-	-	-	-
T20s	5	3	1	7	5	3.50	77.77	0	0	2	0

Bowling	Mat	Balls	Runs	Wkts	BBI	BBM	Ave	Econ	SR	5w	10
First-class	1	-	-	-	-	-	-	-	-	-	-
T20s	5	100	129	7	3/32	3/32	18.42	7.74	14.2	0	0

LIAM PLUNKETT

RHB / RFM / R0 / W3

FULL NAME: Liam Edward Plunkett
BORN: April 6, 1985, Middlesbrough
SQUAD NO: 28
HEIGHT: 6ft 4in
NICKNAME: Pudsy
EDUCATION: Nunthorpe Comprehensive School; Teesside Tertiary College
TEAMS: England, Surrey, Chattogram Challengers, Delhi Daredevils, Durham, Melbourne Stars, Sylhet Sixers, Yorkshire
ROLE: Bowler
DEBUT: Test: 2005; ODI: 2005; T20I: 2006; First-class: 2003; List A: 2003; T20: 2003

BEST BATTING: 126 Yorkshire vs Hampshire, Headingley, 2016
BEST BOWLING: 6-33 Durham vs Leeds/Bradford MCCU, Headingley, 2013
COUNTY CAP: 2013 (Yorkshire)

FIRST CRICKET CLUB? Marske CC, North Yorkshire
MOST INTERESTING TEAMMATE? Mark Wood – he's funny and annoying at the same time
IF YOU WERE AN ANIMAL, WHICH WOULD IT BE? A bear – it links in with my nickname
TWITTER: @Liam628

Batting	Mat	Inns	NO	Runs	HS	Ave	SR	100	50	Ct	St
Tests	13	20	5	238	55*	15.86	46.75	0	1	3	0
ODIs	89	50	19	646	56	20.83	102.70	0	1	26	0
T20Is	22	11	4	42	18	6.00	123.52	0	0	7	0
First-class	158	216	39	4378	126	24.73		3	22	86	0
List A	215	133	50	1677	72	20.20	100.78	0	3	64	0
T20s	158	93	36	825	41	14.47	130.95	0	0	43	0
Bowling	**Mat**	**Balls**	**Runs**	**Wkts**	**BBI**	**BBM**	**Ave**	**Econ**	**SR**	**5w**	**10**
Tests	13	2659	1536	41	5/64	9/176	37.46	3.46	64.8	1	0
ODIs	89	4137	4010	135	5/52	5/52	29.70	5.81	30.6	1	0
T20Is	22	476	627	25	3/21	3/21	25.08	7.90	19.0	0	0
First-class	158	23909	14433	453	6/33		31.86	3.62	52.7	11	1
List A	215	9275	8592	283	5/52	5/52	30.36	5.55	32.7	1	0
T20s	158	2992	4019	146	5/31	5/31	27.52	8.05	20.4	1	0

HARRY PODMORE RHB / RFM / R0 / W1 / MVP70

FULL NAME: Harry William Podmore
BORN: July 23, 1994, Hammersmith, London
SQUAD NO: 1
HEIGHT: 6ft 3in
NICKNAME: Nu-Nu
EDUCATION: Twyford CE High School, London
TEAMS: Kent, Derbyshire, Glamorgan, Middlesex
ROLE: Bowler
DEBUT: First-class: 2016; List A: 2014; T20: 2014

BEST BATTING: 66* Derbyshire vs Sussex, Hove, 2017
BEST BOWLING: 6-36 Kent vs Middlesex, Canterbury, 2018
COUNTY CAP: 2019 (Kent)

MOST EXCITING DAY AS A CRICKETER? Receiving my Kent cap in 2019
CHILDHOOD SPORTING HERO? David Beckham
FIRST CRICKET CLUB? Ealing CC, Middlesex
IF YOU COULD TAKE ONE COUNTY CRICKETER'S BEST SHOT AND ADD IT TO YOUR OWN GAME? Joe Denly's cover-drive
TOUGHEST OPPONENT IN COUNTY CRICKET? Alastair Cook
MOST ECCENTRIC TEAMMATE? Daniel Bell-Drummond – you can't stop him talking
WHAT WOULD YOU DO IF YOU WERE IN CHARGE OF COUNTY CRICKET? Build more stadiums, bump up the wages!
STRANGEST THING YOU'VE DONE DURING LOCKDOWN? Cycling from Whitstable to London and back (it took me just over 10 hours)
FAVOURITE SMELL? My WoodWick candle
SURPRISING FACT ABOUT YOU? I have my family crest tattooed on my chest
GUILTY PLEASURE? Call of Duty (video game)
TWITTER: @harrypod16

Batting	Mat	Inns	NO	Runs	HS	Ave	SR	100	50	Ct	St
First-class	45	65	18	852	66*	18.12	49.10	0	3	12	0
List A	18	8	2	111	40	18.50	94.87	0	0	6	0
T20s	21	8	3	32	9	6.40	57.14	0	0	9	0
Bowling	**Mat**	**Balls**	**Runs**	**Wkts**	**BBI**	**BBM**	**Ave**	**Econ**	**SR**	**5w**	**10**
First-class	45	7517	3756	149	6/36	8/110	25.20	2.99	50.4	4	0
List A	18	866	910	18	4/57	4/57	50.55	6.30	48.1	0	0
T20s	21	367	572	18	3/13	3/13	31.77	9.35	20.3	0	0

ED POLLOCK

LHB / OB / R0 / W0

FULL NAME: Edward John Pollock
BORN: July 10, 1995, High Wycombe, Buckinghamshire
SQUAD NO: 28
HEIGHT: 5ft 10in
EDUCATION: Royal Grammar School, Worcester; Shrewsbury School; Durham University
TEAMS: Warwickshire
ROLE: Batsman
DEBUT: First-class: 2015; List A: 2018; T20: 2017

BEST BATTING: 52 Durham MCCU vs Gloucestershire, Bristol, 2017

MOST EXCITING DAY AS A CRICKETER? Finals Day of the 2017 T20 Blast, even though my team (Birmingham Bears) didn't win it
FAMILY TIES? My dad and brother have both captained Cambridge University
CHILDHOOD SPORTING HERO? Marcus Trescothick
FIRST CRICKET CLUB? Barnt Green CC, Worcestershire. Andy and Grant Flower have both played for the club
IF YOU COULD TAKE ONE COUNTY CRICKETER'S BEST SHOT AND ADD IT TO YOUR OWN GAME? Dom Sibley's leave
TOUGHEST OPPONENT IN COUNTY CRICKET? James Anderson – he never misses the spot
MOST ECCENTRIC TEAMMATE? Michael Burgess – he owns a black cab
FAVOURITE SMELL? Linseed oil
IF YOU WERE AN ANIMAL, WHICH WOULD IT BE? A mayfly – they have a lifespan of 24 hours, so it's over almost before it's begun, much like most of my innings
SURPRISING FACT ABOUT YOU? I am a published poet
TWITTER: @EdPollock10

Batting	Mat	Inns	NO	Runs	HS	Ave	SR	100	50	Ct	St
First-class	5	7	1	184	52	30.66	50.13	0	1	1	0
List A	17	15	0	362	57	24.13	128.36	0	2	4	0
T20s	34	34	0	724	77	21.29	167.59	0	4	8	0
Bowling	**Mat**	**Balls**	**Runs**	**Wkts**	**BBI**	**BBM**	**Ave**	**Econ**	**SR**	**5w**	**10**
First-class	5	-	-	-	-	-	-	-	-	-	-
List A	17	-	-	-	-	-	-	-	-	-	-
T20s	34	-	-	-	-	-	-	-	-	-	-

OLLIE POPE

RHB / WK / R1 / W0

FULL NAME: Oliver John Douglas Pope
BORN: January 2, 1998, Chelsea, London
SQUAD NO: 32
HEIGHT: 5ft 10in
NICKNAME: Pope-dog
EDUCATION: Cranleigh School, Surrey
TEAMS: England, Surrey
ROLE: Batsman
DEBUT: Test: 2018; First-class: 2017; List A: 2016; T20: 2017

BEST BATTING: 251 Surrey vs MCC, Dubai, 2019

COUNTY CAP: 2018

FIRST CRICKET CLUB? Grayshott CC, Hampshire
BEST INNINGS YOU'VE SEEN? Aaron Finch's hundred against Middlesex in the 2018 T20 Blast – he made the boundary look 30 yards away
MOST INTERESTING TEAMMATE? Kumar Sangakkara – he just didn't stop scoring runs for Surrey and was amazing to watch
TWITTER: @opope32

Batting	Mat	Inns	NO	Runs	HS	Ave	SR	100	50	Ct	St
Tests	17	28	3	798	135*	31.92	50.92	1	5	19	0
First-class	47	72	10	3125	251	50.40	60.25	9	12	55	0
List A	28	25	5	751	93*	37.55	80.40	0	5	8	0
T20s	36	34	8	736	48	28.30	134.06	0	0	15	0
Bowling	**Mat**	**Balls**	**Runs**	**Wkts**	**BBI**	**BBM**	**Ave**	**Econ**	**SR**	**5w**	**10**
Tests	17	-	-	-	-	-	-	-	-	-	-
First-class	47	-	-	-	-	-	-	-	-	-	-
List A	28	-	-	-	-	-	-	-	-	-	-
T20s	36	-	-	-	-	-	-	-	-	-	-

JAMIE PORTER RHB / RMF / R0 / W5 / MVP42

ESSEX

FULL NAME: James Alexander Porter
BORN: May 25, 1993, Leytonstone, Essex
SQUAD NO: 44
HEIGHT: 6ft 1in
NICKNAME: Ports
EDUCATION: Oaks Park High School, Ilford; Epping Forest College, Essex
TEAMS: Essex, England Lions
ROLE: Bowler
DEBUT: First-class: 2014; List A: 2015; T20: 2017

BEST BATTING: 34 Essex vs Glamorgan, Cardiff, 2015
BEST BOWLING: 7-41 Essex vs Worcestershire, Chelmsford, 2018
COUNTY CAP: 2015

MOST EXCITING DAY AS A CRICKETER? Fielding at point as a sub fielder for England at Lord's
FIRST CRICKET CLUB? Chingford CC, London
IF YOU COULD TAKE ONE COUNTY CRICKETER'S BEST SHOT AND ADD IT TO YOUR OWN GAME? Alastair Cook's pull
TOUGHEST OPPONENT IN COUNTY CRICKET? Kumar Sangakkara – when he got set then you were in for a tough day
MOST ECCENTRIC TEAMMATE? Feroze Khushi – it's often hard to know if he is being serious
WHAT WOULD YOU DO IF YOU WERE IN CHARGE OF COUNTY CRICKET? Make the Championship two divisions of nine teams each, two up and two down. Simple
WHAT WOULD YOU DO IF YOU WERE PRIME MINISTER? Have tea with the Queen, appoint Dan Lawrence as my deputy, bring back free school lunches
STRANGEST THING YOU'VE DONE DURING LOCKDOWN? Hitting a golf ball from my garden over the house (no cars were damaged)
FAVOURITE SMELL? Pie and mash
TWITTER: @jamieporter93

Batting	Mat	Inns	NO	Runs	HS	Ave	SR	100	50	Ct	St
First-class	90	105	38	387	34	5.77	24.15	0	0	27	0
List A	31	12	8	35	7*	8.75	52.23	0	0	7	0
T20s	19	5	4	5	1*	5.00	71.42	0	0	5	0
Bowling	**Mat**	**Balls**	**Runs**	**Wkts**	**BBI**	**BBM**	**Ave**	**Econ**	**SR**	**5w**	**10**
First-class	90	15533	8554	356	7/41	12/95	24.02	3.30	43.6	13	2
List A	31	1378	1193	33	4/29	4/29	36.15	5.19	41.7	0	0
T20s	19	325	476	17	4/20	4/20	28.00	8.78	19.1	0	0

MATTY POTTS RHB / RFM / R0 / W0 / MVP97

FULL NAME: Matthew James Potts
BORN: October 29, 1998, Sunderland, County Durham
SQUAD NO: 35
HEIGHT: 6ft 2in
NICKNAME: Harry
EDUCATION: St Robert of Newminster Catholic School, Sunderland
TEAMS: Durham, England U19
ROLE: Bowler
DEBUT: First-class: 2017; List A: 2018; T20: 2019

BEST BATTING: 53* Durham vs Derbyshire, Chester-le-Street, 2017
BEST BOWLING: 3-48 Durham vs Glamorgan, Chester-le-Street, 2017

CHILDHOOD SPORTING HERO? Kevin Pietersen
BIGGEST INFLUENCE ON YOUR DEVELOPMENT AS A CRICKETER (EXCLUDING PARENTS)? Paul Collingwood
FIRST CRICKET CLUB? Philadelphia CC, Tyne & Wear
IF YOU COULD TAKE ONE COUNTY CRICKETER'S BEST SHOT AND ADD IT TO YOUR OWN GAME? Scott Steel's switch-hit
TOUGHEST OPPONENT IN COUNTY CRICKET? Darren Stevens – you shouldn't be allowed to move the ball that much
MOST ECCENTRIC TEAMMATE? Cameron Bancroft
WHAT WOULD YOU DO IF YOU WERE IN CHARGE OF COUNTY CRICKET? Establish a conference league system, set up a charity fund for disabled cricket
WHAT WOULD YOU DO IF YOU WERE PRIME MINISTER? I'd say "Brexit means Brexit"
STRANGEST THING YOU'VE DONE DURING LOCKDOWN? Shaving my head
GUILTY PLEASURE? Coffee and biscuits
TWITTER: @mattyjpotts

Batting	Mat	Inns	NO	Runs	HS	Ave	SR	100	50	Ct	St
First-class	11	16	4	176	53*	14.66	45.01	0	1	2	0
List A	9	3	0	53	30	17.66	72.60	0	0	2	0
T20s	22	9	5	28	12	7.00	96.55	0	0	5	0
Bowling	**Mat**	**Balls**	**Runs**	**Wkts**	**BBI**	**BBM**	**Ave**	**Econ**	**SR**	**5w**	**10**
First-class	11	1632	809	19	3/48	5/106	42.57	2.97	85.8	0	0
List A	9	324	319	13	4/62	4/62	24.53	5.90	24.9	0	0
T20s	22	431	567	30	3/8	3/8	18.90	7.89	14.3	0	0

NICK POTTS

RHB / RFM / R0 / W0

FULL NAME: Nicholas James Potts
BORN: July 17, 2002, Burton-on-Trent, Staffordshire
SQUAD NO: 26
HEIGHT: 6ft 1in
EDUCATION: De Ferrers Academy, Burton-on-Trent
TEAMS: Derbyshire
ROLE: Bowler

MOST EXCITING DAY AS A CRICKETER? Taking three wickets in an England Young Lions trial match last summer
CHILDHOOD SPORTING HERO? James Anderson
BIGGEST INFLUENCE ON YOUR DEVELOPMENT AS A CRICKETER (EXCLUDING PARENTS)? Steve Kirby, my former bowling coach at Derbyshire. He helped me to understand my bowling action and showed me what I need to do to be successful at a high level
IF YOU COULD TAKE ONE COUNTY CRICKETER'S BEST SHOT AND ADD IT TO YOUR OWN GAME? Ben Stokes' slog-sweep
TOUGHEST OPPONENT IN COUNTY CRICKET? Wayne Madsen – he hit the ball back at me so hard when I bowled to him in a practice game
MOST ECCENTRIC TEAMMATE? Fynn Hudson-Prentice – because of his Instagram stories and his hair
WHAT WOULD YOU DO IF YOU WERE IN CHARGE OF COUNTY CRICKET? Get the County Championship on TV, offer free tickets to under-16s for county matches, introduce DRS to domestic cricket
WHAT WOULD YOU DO IF YOU WERE PRIME MINISTER? Encourage more sport in schools, introduce a day of voluntary work, change the working week to four days
STRANGEST THING YOU'VE DONE DURING LOCKDOWN? Watching all 11 seasons of Modern Family, multiple times
FAVOURITE SMELL? Vanilla
GUILTY PLEASURE? Solving a Rubik's Cube

STUART POYNTER

RHB / WK / R0 / W0

FULL NAME: Stuart William Poynter
BORN: October 18, 1990, Hammersmith, London
SQUAD NO: 90
HEIGHT: 5ft 7in
NICKNAME: Stuey
EDUCATION: Teddington School, London
TEAMS: Ireland, Durham, Middlesex, Warwickshire
ROLE: Wicketkeeper/batsman
DEBUT: Test: 2019; ODI: 2014; T20I: 2015; First-class: 2010; List A: 2012; T20: 2015

BEST BATTING: 170 Durham vs Derbyshire, Derby, 2018

MOST EXCITING DAY AS A CRICKETER? Making my Test debut for Ireland in 2019
FAMILY TIES? My uncle Deryck and my brother Andrew both played for Ireland
CHILDHOOD SPORTING HERO? Jack Russell
FIRST CRICKET CLUB? Sunbury CC, Surrey
IF YOU COULD TAKE ONE COUNTY CRICKETER'S BEST SHOT AND ADD IT TO YOUR OWN GAME? The Keaton Jennings leave
STRANGEST THING YOU'VE DONE DURING LOCKDOWN? Home-schooling – possibly the hardest thing ever
GUILTY PLEASURE? Westlife
TWITTER: @spoynter_90

Batting	Mat	Inns	NO	Runs	HS	Ave	SR	100	50	Ct	St
Tests	1	2	0	1	1	0.50	9.09	0	0	2	1
ODIs	21	19	5	185	36	13.21	66.54	0	0	22	1
T20Is	25	21	6	240	39	16.00	112.67	0	0	13	2
First-class	41	65	2	1437	170	22.80	64.23	2	5	117	4
List A	47	40	9	581	109	18.74	85.94	1	0	42	3
T20s	67	51	20	725	61*	23.38	124.57	0	1	36	10
Bowling	**Mat**	**Balls**	**Runs**	**Wkts**	**BBI**	**BBM**	**Ave**	**Econ**	**SR**	**5w**	**10**
Tests	1	-	-	-	-	-	-	-	-	-	-
ODIs	21	-	-	-	-	-	-	-	-	-	-
T20Is	25	-	-	-	-	-	-	-	-	-	-
First-class	41	24	21	0	-	-	-	5.25	-	0	0
List A	47	-	-	-	-	-	-	-	-	-	-
T20s	67	-	-	-	-	-	-	-	-	-	-

JOSH POYSDEN

LHB / LB / R0 / W0

FULL NAME: Joshua Edward Poysden
BORN: August 8, 1991, Shoreham-by-Sea, Sussex
SQUAD NO: 14
HEIGHT: 5ft 10in
NICKNAME: Dobby
EDUCATION: Cardinal Newman School, Hove; Anglia Ruskin University
TEAMS: Yorkshire, England Lions, Warwickshire
ROLE: Bowler
DEBUT: First-class: 2011; List A: 2013; T20: 2014

BEST BATTING: 47 Cambridge MCCU vs Surrey, Cambridge, 2011
BEST BOWLING: 5-29 Warwickshire vs Glamorgan, Edgbaston, 2018

MOST EXCITING DAY AS A CRICKETER? Any day that I've seen Sam Hain bowl
CHILDHOOD SPORTING HERO? Mushtaq Ahmed
BIGGEST INFLUENCE ON YOUR DEVELOPMENT AS A CRICKETER (EXCLUDING PARENTS)? Dick Roberts – a great man who was in charge of the colts section at Brighton & Hove CC
IF YOU COULD TAKE ONE COUNTY CRICKETER'S BEST SHOT AND ADD IT TO YOUR OWN GAME? Gary Ballance's forward defence
TOUGHEST OPPONENT IN COUNTY CRICKET? Marcus Trescothick
WHAT WOULD YOU DO IF YOU WERE IN CHARGE OF COUNTY CRICKET? Make a rule that play stops when the temperature drops below 15 degrees
STRANGEST THING YOU'VE DONE DURING LOCKDOWN? That's a close one between starting a podcast (Spin Badger) and building a golf course in my garden
FAVOURITE SMELL? Bacon cooking in the morning
SURPRISING FACT ABOUT YOU? I have a mild obsession with sausage dogs
GUILTY PLEASURE? Playing Call of Duty until the early hours
TWITTER: @JoshPoysden14

Batting	Mat	Inns	NO	Runs	HS	Ave	SR	100	50	Ct	St
First-class	14	14	4	96	47	9.60	36.22	0	0	2	0
List A	32	16	6	35	10*	3.50	52.23	0	0	7	0
T20s	32	11	9	13	9*	6.50	118.18	0	0	8	0
Bowling	**Mat**	**Balls**	**Runs**	**Wkts**	**BBI**	**BBM**	**Ave**	**Econ**	**SR**	**5w**	**10**
First-class	14	1549	1084	33	5/29	8/133	32.84	4.19	46.9	2	0
List A	32	1281	1248	30	3/33	3/33	41.60	5.84	42.7	0	0
T20s	32	594	751	26	4/51	4/51	28.88	7.58	22.8	0	0

OLLIE PRICE

RHB / OB / R0 / W0

FULL NAME: Oliver Joseph Price
BORN: June 12, 2001, Oxford
SQUAD NO: TBC
EDUCATION: Magdalen College School, Oxford
TEAMS: Gloucestershire
ROLE: Allrounder

TWITTER: @ollieprice67
NOTES: The 19-year-old allrounder joined his elder brother Tom in signing a first professional contract at Gloucestershire in January 2020. An off-spinner and and right-handed batsman, Price was educated at Magdalen College School in Oxford and joined the Gloucestershire Academy in December 2016. He and brother Tom played for their local side Great & Little Tew, a club which also produced Gloucestershire siblings Jack and Matt Taylor. In 2019 he joined Oxford CC where he opened the batting in the Home Counties Premier League and helped the club gain promotion. Price has captained in all the Oxfordshire age-groups and made his Minor Counties debut aged 17, as well as being a regular for Gloucestershire at U17 and U19 level. He featured strongly in the club's Second XI in 2019, making a half-century against a Sussex attack which included Jofra Archer. Price is yet to make his first-team debut for the club

TOM PRICE

RHB / RMF / R0 / W0

FULL NAME: Thomas James Price
BORN: January 2, 2000, Oxford
SQUAD NO: TBC
EDUCATION: Magdalen College School, Oxford
TEAMS: Gloucestershire
ROLE: Allrounder
DEBUT: First-class: 2020; List A: 2019

BEST BOWLING: 1-69 Gloucestershire vs Worcestershire, Bristol, 2020

TWITTER: @_tomprice_
NOTES: An emerging seam-bowling allrounder, Price was handed his first professional contract by Gloucestershire in January 2020, putting pen to paper on a two-year deal. He was given his first-class debut in last summer's Bob Willis Trophy match against Worcestershire at Bristol, claiming the wicket of Daryl Mitchell as the first of his career. The 21-year-old made his List-A debut against Australia A at Bristol in August 2019 and received the Academy Player of the Year award at the end of that year after finishing as Gloucestershire's second-highest wicket-taker in the Second XI Championship, with a haul of 14 at 30.57. His brother is Ollie Price, who also signed for the club last year

Batting	Mat	Inns	NO	Runs	HS	Ave	SR	100	50	Ct	St
First-class	1	2	0	0	0	0.00	0.00	0	0	0	0
List A	1	1	0	0	0	0.00	-	0	0	0	0
Bowling	**Mat**	**Balls**	**Runs**	**Wkts**	**BBI**	**BBM**	**Ave**	**Econ**	**SR**	**5w**	**10**
First-class	1	108	80	1	1/69	1/80	80.00	4.44	108.0	0	0
List A	1	36	52	0	-	-	-	8.66	-	0	0

NILS PRIESTLEY

LHB / SLA / R0 / W0

FULL NAME: Nils Oscar Priestley
BORN: September 18, 2000, Sutton Coldfield, Warwickshire
SQUAD NO: 53
HEIGHT: 6ft 3in
NICKNAME: Nee-Lo-Green
EDUCATION: Blessed Robert Sutton School, Burton-upon-Trent, Staffordshire; Loughborough University
TEAMS: Derbyshire
ROLE: Batsman

MOST EXCITING DAY AS A CRICKETER? Signing my first professional contract before the start of last season
CHILDHOOD SPORTING HERO? Sebastian Larsson
BIGGEST INFLUENCE ON YOUR DEVELOPMENT AS A CRICKETER (EXCLUDING PARENTS)? My old school and club coach Clive Jacobs – he got me into the first team and exposed me to a good standard of cricket
FIRST CRICKET CLUB? Lullington Park CC, Derbyshire
TOUGHEST OPPONENT IN COUNTY CRICKET? Coming up against Liam Plunkett in Second XI cricket when I was 15 was a bit of an experience: men around the bat with him slinging the ball down at my head. I'd seen him on TV just a couple of weeks earlier
MOST ECCENTRIC TEAMMATE? Fynn Hudson-Prentice – he's from the south so sounds a bit posher and then wears some urban garms
WHAT WOULD YOU DO IF YOU WERE IN CHARGE OF COUNTY CRICKET? Have a shorter season, introduce T20 franchise leagues, make rules to allow Academy graduates more opportunities
STRANGEST THING YOU'VE DONE DURING LOCKDOWN? Trying to ride the horse belonging to my girlfriend's little sister. Didn't last long
FAVOURITE SMELL? Burning wood
GUILTY PLEASURE? Cadbury Dairy Milk
TWITTER: @nilspriestly

LUKE PROCTER

LHB / RMF / R0 / W0

FULL NAME: Luke Anthony Procter
BORN: June 24, 1988, Oldham, Lancashire
SQUAD NO: 2
HEIGHT: 5ft 11in
NICKNAME: Dicky
EDUCATION: Counthill School, Oldham
TEAMS: Northamptonshire, Lancashire
ROLE: Allrounder
DEBUT: First-class: 2010; List A: 2009; T20: 2011

BEST BATTING: 137 Lancashire vs Hampshire, Old Trafford, 2016
BEST BOWLING: 7-71 Lancashire vs Surrey, Liverpool, 2012

MOST EXCITING DAY AS A CRICKETER? Winning the County Championship with Lancashire in 2011
CHILDHOOD SPORTING HERO? Jonah Lomu
FIRST CRICKET CLUB? Oldham CC, Lancashire
TOUGHEST OPPONENT IN COUNTY CRICKET? David Masters – he got me out every time
WHAT WOULD YOU DO IF YOU WERE IN CHARGE OF COUNTY CRICKET? Change the Championship back to how it was (two divisions, each county plays 16 games), allow only one overseas player per county
STRANGEST THING YOU'VE DONE DURING LOCKDOWN? Making a bird box
FAVOURITE SMELL? I can't smell anything!
IF YOU WERE AN ANIMAL, WHICH WOULD IT BE? A bird
SURPRISING FACT ABOUT YOU? I'm a level-two umpire
TWITTER: @vvsprocter

Batting	Mat	Inns	NO	Runs	HS	Ave	SR	100	50	Ct	St
First-class	98	155	17	4308	137	31.21	44.58	4	22	24	0
List A	45	35	12	710	97	30.86	88.75	0	5	7	0
T20s	37	24	7	240	25*	14.11	102.12	0	0	10	0
Bowling	**Mat**	**Balls**	**Runs**	**Wkts**	**BBI**	**BBM**	**Ave**	**Econ**	**SR**	**5w**	**10**
First-class	98	6842	3949	108	7/71	8/79	36.56	3.46	63.3	3	0
List A	45	1090	1042	23	3/29	3/29	45.30	5.73	47.3	0	0
T20s	37	296	438	14	3/22	3/22	31.28	8.87	21.1	0	0

HAMIDULLAH QADRI

RHB / OB / R0 / W0

FULL NAME: Hamidullah Qadri
BORN: December 5, 2000, Kandahar, Afghanistan
SQUAD NO: 75
HEIGHT: 5ft 7in
NICKNAME: Hammy
EDUCATION: Chellaston Academy, Derby; Derby Moor Academy
TEAMS: Kent, Derbyshire, England U19
ROLE: Bowler
DEBUT: First-class: 2017; List A: 2017; T20: 2017

BEST BATTING: 17* Derbyshire vs Lancashire, Old Trafford, 2019
BEST BOWLING: 5-60 Derbyshire vs Glamorgan, Cardiff, 2017

MOST EXCITING DAY AS A CRICKETER? Taking a five-wicket haul on my first-class debut for Derbyshire at Cardiff in 2017
CHILDHOOD SPORTING HERO? Saqlain Mushtaq
BIGGEST INFLUENCE ON YOUR DEVELOPMENT AS A CRICKETER (EXCLUDING PARENTS)? Steve Stubbings at Derbyshire – he was my first-ever coach. After seeing me in the nets for the first time, he took me under his wing and helped me a lot
FIRST CRICKET CLUB? Alvaston & Boulton CC, Derbyshire
TOUGHEST OPPONENT IN COUNTY CRICKET? Dane Vilas – he's a 360-degree player
WHAT WOULD YOU DO IF YOU WERE IN CHARGE OF COUNTY CRICKET? Make sure that T20 isn't squeezed between Championship fixtures and is played in an entirely separate block
SURPRISING FACT ABOUT YOU? I learnt the art of off-spin by watching YouTube clips
TWITTER: @Hamid_Qadri2000

Batting	Mat	Inns	NO	Runs	HS	Ave	SR	100	50	Ct	St
First-class	14	25	10	92	17*	6.13	31.72	0	0	6	0
List A	3	1	0	4	4	4.00	50.00	0	0	1	0
T20s	1	-	-	-	-	-	-	-	-	0	0
Bowling	**Mat**	**Balls**	**Runs**	**Wkts**	**BBI**	**BBM**	**Ave**	**Econ**	**SR**	**5w**	**10**
First-class	14	1631	930	24	5/60	6/76	38.75	3.42	67.9	1	0
List A	3	61	61	1	1/31	1/31	61.00	6.00	61.0	0	0
T20s	1	6	12	0	-	-	-	12.00	-	0	0

IMRAN QAYYUM

RHB / SLA / R0 / W0

KENT

FULL NAME: Imran Qayyum
BORN: May 23, 1993, Ealing, Middlesex
SQUAD NO: 11
HEIGHT: 5ft 11in
NICKNAME: Imy
EDUCATION: Villiers High School, Ealing; Greenford High School, Ealing; City University of London
TEAMS: Kent
ROLE: Bowler
DEBUT: First-class: 2016; List A: 2017; T20: 2017

BEST BATTING: 39 Kent vs Leicestershire, Canterbury, 2017
BEST BOWLING: 3-158 Kent vs Northamptonshire, Northampton, 2016

MOST EXCITING DAY AS A CRICKETER? Playing alongside Geraint Jones
FAMILY TIES? Dad played in Pakistan, my brother plays club cricket in Hertfordshire
FIRST CRICKET CLUB? Perivale Phoenicians CC, Ealing, London
SURPRISING FACT ABOUT YOU? I hate sleeping because it makes me feel that I am missing out on life. I also talk in my sleep
IF YOU WERE AN ANIMAL, WHICH WOULD IT BE? A cheetah
TWITTER: @ImranQC

Batting	Mat	Inns	NO	Runs	HS	Ave	SR	100	50	Ct	St
First-class	6	9	4	55	39	11.00	36.42	0	0	3	0
List A	29	19	6	99	26*	7.61	64.70	0	0	5	0
T20s	45	9	6	51	21*	17.00	130.76	0	0	8	0
Bowling	**Mat**	**Balls**	**Runs**	**Wkts**	**BBI**	**BBM**	**Ave**	**Econ**	**SR**	**5w**	**10**
First-class	6	823	524	12	3/158	3/46	43.66	3.82	68.5	0	0
List A	29	1368	1178	29	4/33	4/33	40.62	5.16	47.1	0	0
T20s	45	860	1158	45	5/21	5/21	25.73	8.07	19.1	1	0

MATT QUINN

RHB / RMF / R0 / W0

FULL NAME: Matthew Richard Quinn
BORN: February 28, 1993, Auckland, New Zealand
SQUAD NO: 94
HEIGHT: 6ft 4in
NICKNAME: Quinny
EDUCATION: Sacred Heart College, Auckland; Auckland University of Technology
TEAMS: Essex, Auckland, New Zealand U19
ROLE: Bowler
DEBUT: First-class: 2013; List A: 2013; T20: 2012

BEST BATTING: 50 Auckland vs Canterbury, Auckland, 2013
BEST BOWLING: 7-76 Essex vs Gloucestershire, Cheltenham, 2016

FAMILY TIES? My great grandad played social cricket in Yorkshire
CHILDHOOD SPORTING HERO? Shane Bond
BIGGEST INFLUENCE ON YOUR DEVELOPMENT AS A CRICKETER (EXCLUDING PARENTS)? Rex Smith, PJ Thomas, Tim Wilson and Paresh Vallabh – all from my local club Cornwall CC in Auckland. They taught me a lot to help me move from schoolboy to men's cricket
IF YOU COULD TAKE ONE COUNTY CRICKETER'S BEST SHOT AND ADD IT TO YOUR OWN GAME? Varun Chopra's pull
WHAT WOULD YOU DO IF YOU WERE IN CHARGE OF COUNTY CRICKET? Push for more televised cricket, reduce the number of Powerplay overs from six to four at the beginning of a T20 innings, ban Will Buttleman from playing football
STRANGEST THING YOU'VE DONE DURING LOCKDOWN? Adopting a pigeon as a pet
SURPRISING FACT ABOUT YOU? I was once attacked by a goose
GUILTY PLEASURE? An early afternoon nap
TWITTER: @quinny_cricket

Batting	Mat	Inns	NO	Runs	HS	Ave	SR	100	50	Ct	St
First-class	36	46	11	360	50	10.28	47.36	0	1	7	0
List A	34	19	11	128	36	16.00	73.14	0	0	4	0
T20s	65	12	10	28	8*	14.00	100.00	0	0	13	0
Bowling	**Mat**	**Balls**	**Runs**	**Wkts**	**BBI**	**BBM**	**Ave**	**Econ**	**SR**	**5w**	**10**
First-class	36	6771	3715	123	7/76	11/163	30.20	3.29	55.0	1	1
List A	34	1714	1682	46	4/71	4/71	36.56	5.88	37.2	0	0
T20s	65	1276	1879	70	4/20	4/20	26.84	8.83	18.2	0	0

BEN RAINE

LHB / RMF / R0 / W3 / MVP82

FULL NAME: Benjamin Alexander Raine
BORN: September 14, 1991, Sunderland
SQUAD NO: 44
HEIGHT: 6ft
NICKNAME: Ranger
EDUCATION: St Aidan's Catholic Academy, Sunderland
TEAMS: Durham, Leicestershire, Otago
ROLE: Bowler
DEBUT: First-class: 2011; List A: 2011; T20: 2014

BEST BATTING: 82 Durham vs Northamptonshire, Chester-le-Street, 2019
BEST BOWLING: 6-27 Durham vs Sussex, Hove, 2019
COUNTY CAP: 2018 (Leicestershire)

MOST EXCITING DAY AS A CRICKETER? Winning in three days at Lord's in 2019
BIGGEST INFLUENCE ON YOUR DEVELOPMENT AS A CRICKETER (EXCLUDING PARENTS)? Lloyd Tennant at Leicestershire – he encouraged me to take bowling seriously, which shaped my career
FIRST CRICKET CLUB? Murton CC, County Durham
BIGGEST CRICKETING REGRET? Taking far too long to realise that it doesn't really matter if I have a bad game
WHAT WOULD YOU DO IF YOU WERE IN CHARGE OF COUNTY CRICKET? Go back to a 40-over competition and play it in March and April
WHAT WOULD YOU DO IF YOU WERE PRIME MINISTER? Make parking in a disabled space when you aren't disabled punishable by life in prison, introduce incentives to help local pubs
FAVOURITE SMELL? Fear
GUILTY PLEASURE? Call of Duty
TWITTER: @BenRaine88

Batting	Mat	Inns	NO	Runs	HS	Ave	SR	100	50	Ct	St
First-class	83	136	15	2589	82	21.39	48.42	0	10	16	0
List A	28	20	2	392	83	21.77	107.10	0	1	9	0
T20s	67	52	11	876	113	21.36	134.76	1	3	16	0
Bowling	**Mat**	**Balls**	**Runs**	**Wkts**	**BBI**	**BBM**	**Ave**	**Econ**	**SR**	**5w**	**10**
First-class	83	14494	7279	276	6/27	9/96	26.37	3.01	52.5	8	0
List A	28	1226	1161	27	3/31	3/31	43.00	5.68	45.4	0	0
T20s	67	1029	1561	55	3/7	3/7	28.38	9.10	18.7	0	0

ADIL RASHID

RHB / LB

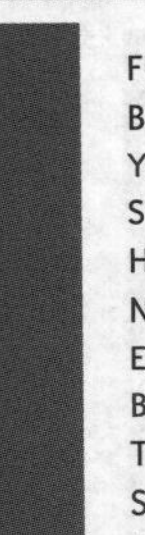

FULL NAME: Adil Usman Rashid
BORN: February 17, 1988, Bradford, Yorkshire
SQUAD NO: 3
HEIGHT: 5ft 8in
NICKNAME: Rash
EDUCATION: Heaton School, Bradford; Bellevue Sixth Form College, Bradford
TEAMS: England, Yorkshire, Adelaide Strikers, Dhaka Dynamites, South Australia
ROLE: Bowler
DEBUT: Test: 2015; ODI: 2009; T20I: 2009; First-class: 2006; List A: 2006; T20: 2008

BEST BATTING: 36* Yorkshire vs Uva Next, Johannesburg, 2012 (T20)
BEST BOWLING: 4-19 Yorkshire vs Durham, Headingley, 2017 (T20)
COUNTY CAP: 2008; BENEFIT: 2018

CHILDHOOD SPORTING HERO? Shane Warne
SURPRISING FACT ABOUT YOU? I have a big FIFA (video game) rivalry with Moeen Ali
TWITTER: @AdilRashid03
NOTES: Rashid has signed a new deal to play white-ball cricket for Yorkshire this summer and is due to turn out for Northern Superchargers in The Hundred

Batting	Mat	Inns	NO	Runs	HS	Ave	SR	100	50	Ct	St
Tests	19	33	5	540	61	19.28	42.51	0	2	4	0
ODIs	106	48	14	644	69	18.94	102.71	0	1	31	0
T20Is	52	18	10	56	9*	7.00	81.15	0	0	12	0
First-class	175	251	41	6822	180	32.48		10	37	79	0
List A	224	131	39	1765	71	19.18	91.83	0	2	70	0
T20s	179	89	34	691	36*	12.56	104.38	0	0	49	0

Bowling	Mat	Balls	Runs	Wkts	BBI	BBM	Ave	Econ	SR	5w	10
Tests	19	3816	2390	60	5/49	7/178	39.83	3.75	63.6	2	0
ODIs	106	5255	4909	155	5/27	5/27	31.67	5.60	33.9	2	0
T20Is	52	1050	1316	51	3/11	3/11	25.80	7.52	20.5	0	0
First-class	175	29901	17949	512	7/107	11/114	35.05	3.60	58.4	20	1
List A	224	10372	9402	301	5/27	5/27	31.23	5.43	34.4	3	0
T20s	179	3663	4539	201	4/19	4/19	22.58	7.43	18.2	0	0

DELRAY RAWLINS LHB / SLA / R0 / W0 / MVP28

FULL NAME: Delray Millard Wendell Rawlins
BORN: September 14, 1997, Bermuda
SQUAD NO: 9
HEIGHT: 6ft 2in
NICKNAME: Del
EDUCATION: St Bede's School, East Sussex
TEAMS: Bermuda, Sussex, England U19
ROLE: Allrounder
DEBUT: T20I: 2019; First-class: 2017; List A: 2017; T20: 2018

BEST BATTING: 100 Sussex vs Lancashire, Old Trafford, 2019
BEST BOWLING: 3-21 Sussex vs Durham, Hove, 2019

MOST EXCITING DAY AS A CRICKETER? T20 Finals Day in 2018
CHILDHOOD SPORTING HERO? Brian Lara
BIGGEST INFLUENCE ON YOUR DEVELOPMENT AS A CRICKETER (EXCLUDING PARENTS)? David Moore (former Australian first-class cricketer and Bermuda coach) – he was one of the first coaches to give me a chance as a young cricketer
FIRST CRICKET CLUB? Warwick Workmen's Club, Bermuda – playing there helped me grow a love for the sport
IF YOU COULD TAKE ONE COUNTY CRICKETER'S BEST SHOT AND ADD IT TO YOUR OWN GAME? Jos Buttler's ramp
IF YOU WERE AN ANIMAL, WHICH WOULD IT BE? A cheetah
SURPRISING FACT ABOUT YOU? I eat pineapple slices out of the tin
TWITTER: @Delraw90

Batting	Mat	Inns	NO	Runs	HS	Ave	SR	100	50	Ct	St
T20Is	11	11	0	261	63	23.72	129.85	0	1	9	0
First-class	19	34	1	894	100	27.09	57.71	1	6	5	0
List A	11	11	0	285	53	25.90	109.61	0	2	7	0
T20s	43	40	4	827	69	22.97	139.22	0	3	26	0
Bowling	**Mat**	**Balls**	**Runs**	**Wkts**	**BBI**	**BBM**	**Ave**	**Econ**	**SR**	**5w**	**10**
T20Is	11	222	285	5	2/22	2/22	57.00	7.70	44.4	0	0
First-class	19	1313	818	14	3/19	3/52	58.42	3.73	93.7	0	0
List A	11	300	269	3	1/27	1/27	89.66	5.38	100.0	0	0
T20s	43	342	418	15	3/21	3/21	27.86	7.33	22.8	0	0

LUIS REECE LHB / LMF / R0 / W1 / MVP35

FULL NAME: Luis Michael Reece
BORN: August 4, 1990, Taunton, Somerset
SQUAD NO: 10
HEIGHT: 6ft 2in
NICKNAME: Rexy
EDUCATION: St Michael's School; Myerscough College; Leeds Metropolitan University
TEAMS: Derbyshire, Chittagong Vikings, Dhaka Platoon, Lancashire
ROLE: Allrounder
DEBUT: First-class: 2012; List A: 2011; T20: 2016

BEST BATTING: 184 Derbyshire vs Sussex, Derby, 2019
BEST BOWLING: 7-20 Derbyshire vs Gloucestershire, Derby, 2018
COUNTY CAP: 2019 (Derbyshire)

CHILDHOOD SPORTING HERO? Brian Lara
FIRST CRICKET CLUB? Vernon Carus CC, Lancashire
IF YOU COULD TAKE ONE COUNTY CRICKETER'S BEST SHOT AND ADD IT TO YOUR OWN GAME? Chris Gayle's ability to hit spinners straight down the ground for six
TOUGHEST OPPONENT IN COUNTY CRICKET? Marcus Trescothick
WHAT WOULD YOU DO IF YOU WERE IN CHARGE OF COUNTY CRICKET? Bring back the MCC Universities scheme
STRANGEST THING YOU'VE DONE DURING LOCKDOWN? Home-schooling
FAVOURITE SMELL? Christmas dinner
SURPRISING FACT ABOUT YOU? As a kid I played chess at national level
GUILTY PLEASURE? An afternoon nap
TWITTER: @lreece17

Batting	Mat	Inns	NO	Runs	HS	Ave	SR	100	50	Ct	St
First-class	67	120	8	3805	184	33.97	50.20	7	22	33	0
List A	40	36	5	908	128	29.29	87.98	1	5	11	0
T20s	51	48	5	1066	97*	24.79	125.11	0	8	18	0
Bowling	**Mat**	**Balls**	**Runs**	**Wkts**	**BBI**	**BBM**	**Ave**	**Econ**	**SR**	**5w**	**10**
First-class	67	5149	2612	101	7/20	7/38	25.86	3.04	50.9	4	0
List A	40	938	964	19	4/35	4/35	50.73	6.16	49.3	0	0
T20s	51	510	697	24	3/33	3/33	29.04	8.20	21.2	0	0

NICO REIFER

RHB / RM / R0 / W0

FULL NAME: Nico Reifer
BORN: November 11, 2000, Bridgetown, Barbados
SQUAD NO: 27
HEIGHT: 6ft 4in
NICKNAME: Reif
EDUCATION: Queen's College, Bridgetown; Whitgift School, Croydon
TEAMS: Surrey
ROLE: Allrounder

MOST EXCITING DAY AS A CRICKETER? Singing the Surrey song for the first time after a win
CHILDHOOD SPORTING HERO? Ricky Ponting
BIGGEST INFLUENCE ON YOUR DEVELOPMENT AS A CRICKETER (EXCLUDING PARENTS)? Dexter Toppin, former South African cricketer and current Barbados coach – he was the first coach I ever had and still helps me out today
FIRST CRICKET CLUB? Wanderers CC, Christ Church, Barbados
IF YOU COULD TAKE ONE COUNTY CRICKETER'S BEST SHOT AND ADD IT TO YOUR OWN GAME? Hashim Amla's cover-drive
TOUGHEST OPPONENT IN COUNTY CRICKET? Kyle Abbott – he's pacy and consistent. It's very hard to get on top of him
STRANGEST THING YOU'VE DONE DURING LOCKDOWN? Spending a whole day playing the PlayStation4
FAVOURITE SMELL? Coconut
IF YOU WERE AN ANIMAL, WHICH WOULD IT BE? A wolf
GUILTY PLEASURE? Ice cream
TWITTER: @reifzzzz

GEORGE RHODES

RHB / OB / R0 / W0

FULL NAME: George Harry Rhodes
BORN: October 26, 1993, Birmingham
SQUAD NO: 34
HEIGHT: 6ft
NICKNAME: Sherlock
EDUCATION: The Chase School, Malvern; University of Worcester
TEAMS: Leicestershire, Worcestershire
ROLE: Allrounder
DEBUT: First-class: 2016; List A: 2016; T20: 2016

BEST BATTING: 61* Leicestershire vs Northamptonshire, Leicester, 2019
BEST BOWLING: 2-83 Worcestershire vs Kent, Canterbury, 2016

FAMILY TIES? My father Steve played for England and Worcestershire, and my grandfather William played first-class cricket for Nottinghamshire
CHILDHOOD SPORTING HERO? Tiger Woods
BIGGEST INFLUENCE ON YOUR DEVELOPMENT AS A CRICKETER (EXCLUDING PARENTS)? Damian D'Oliveira, the former Academy director at Worcestershire
FIRST CRICKET CLUB? Rushwick CC, Worcestershire
TOUGHEST OPPONENT IN COUNTY CRICKET? Darren Stevens – he bowls swinging nippers and shin-hunters
WHAT WOULD YOU DO IF YOU WERE IN CHARGE OF COUNTY CRICKET? Divide the Championship into groups leading to a knockout
STRANGEST THING YOU'VE DONE DURING LOCKDOWN? Building furniture
FAVOURITE SMELL? A pint of Guinness
TWITTER: @Ghrhodes

Batting	Mat	Inns	NO	Runs	HS	Ave	SR	100	50	Ct	St
First-class	28	52	8	956	61*	21.72	38.64	0	5	14	0
List A	10	7	1	228	106	38.00	89.41	1	1	6	0
T20s	20	15	6	103	30*	11.44	100.00	0	0	8	0
Bowling	**Mat**	**Balls**	**Runs**	**Wkts**	**BBI**	**BBM**	**Ave**	**Econ**	**SR**	**5w**	**10**
First-class	28	869	631	6	2/83	2/83	105.16	4.35	144.8	0	0
List A	10	240	252	5	2/34	2/34	50.40	6.30	48.0	0	0
T20s	20	114	164	10	4/13	4/13	16.40	8.63	11.4	0	0

WILL RHODES

LHB / RMF / R0 / W0 / MVP16

WARWICKSHIRE

FULL NAME: William Michael Harry Rhodes
BORN: March 2, 1995, Nottingham
SQUAD NO: 35
HEIGHT: 6ft 1in
NICKNAME: Codhead
EDUCATION: Cottingham High School, Hull
TEAMS: Warwickshire, England U19, Essex, Yorkshire
ROLE: Allrounder
DEBUT: First-class: 2015; List A: 2013; T20: 2013

BEST BATTING: 207 Warwickshire vs Worcestershire, Worcester, 2020
BEST BOWLING: 5-17 Warwickshire vs Essex, Chelmsford, 2019

MOST EXCITING DAY AS A CRICKETER? Winning the 2015 County Championship with Yorkshire
CHILDHOOD SPORTING HERO? Nick Barmby
BIGGEST INFLUENCE ON YOUR DEVELOPMENT AS A CRICKETER (EXCLUDING PARENTS)? Richard Damms – my coach when I was in the Yorkshire Academy
FIRST CRICKET CLUB? Cottingham CC, East Riding of Yorkshire
IF YOU COULD TAKE ONE COUNTY CRICKETER'S BEST SHOT AND ADD IT TO YOUR OWN GAME? Oliver Hannon-Dalby's leave
MOST ECCENTRIC TEAMMATE? Jonathan Trott – he did some strange things
WHAT WOULD YOU DO IF YOU WERE IN CHARGE OF COUNTY CRICKET? Forbid play on weekends and bank holidays
STRANGEST THING YOU'VE DONE DURING LOCKDOWN? Deciding to study again
FAVOURITE SMELL? An ice-cold beer after a day in the field
GUILTY PLEASURE? Chocolate Hobnobs
TWITTER: @willrhodes_152

Batting	Mat	Inns	NO	Runs	HS	Ave	SR	100	50	Ct	St
First-class	55	88	4	3097	207	36.86	50.47	6	14	33	0
List A	32	28	2	569	69	21.88	77.83	0	2	12	0
T20s	42	38	6	401	46	12.53	115.22	0	0	6	0
Bowling	**Mat**	**Balls**	**Runs**	**Wkts**	**BBI**	**BBM**	**Ave**	**Econ**	**SR**	**5w**	**10**
First-class	55	3382	1753	53	5/17	9/55	33.07	3.10	63.8	1	0
List A	32	629	612	13	2/22	2/22	47.07	5.83	48.3	0	0
T20s	42	385	577	22	3/27	3/27	26.22	8.99	17.5	0	0

KEMAR ROACH

RHB / RFM / R0 / W0

FULL NAME: Kemar Andre Jamal Roach
BORN: June 30, 1988, St Lucy, Barbados
SQUAD NO: 66
TEAMS: West Indies, Surrey, Antigua Hawksbills, Barbados, Brisbane Heat, Deccan Chargers, Jamaica Tallawahs, St Lucia Zouks, Worcestershire
ROLE: Bowler
DEBUT: Test: 2009; ODI: 2008; T20I: 2008; First-class: 2008; List A: 2007; T20: 2008

BEST BATTING: 53 Barbados vs Leeward Islands, Basseterre, 2016
BEST BOWLING: 7-23 Barbados vs Combined Campuses & Colleges, Charlestown, 2010

NOTES: Surrey have signed the West Indies fast bowler for the first seven Championship games, subject to travel restrictions. "I am absolutely thrilled to be joining Surrey for the early part of the summer," said Roach. "Two grounds I wanted to play at as a kid were the two Ovals, Kensington and The Oval, home of Surrey." The 32-year-old is one of only nine West Indies bowlers to have taken more than 200 Test wickets and continues to be a mainstay of their bowling attack. His only previous experience of county cricket was a brief spell at Worcestershire in 2011. With Sam Curran and Tom Curran on IPL duty, Roach should be a valuable asset in April and May. "He's a highly skilled bowler who we feel will suit the conditions of the early part of the English domestic season," said Alec Stewart, Surrey's director of cricket. "He is vastly experienced at international and domestic level and bowled very well in last summer's Test series in England without amassing the wicket haul he really deserved"

Batting	Mat	Inns	NO	Runs	HS	Ave	SR	100	50	Ct	St
Tests	61	99	20	907	41	11.48	38.38	0	0	15	0
ODIs	92	57	34	308	34	13.39	53.47	0	0	21	0
T20Is	11	1	1	3	3*	-	150.00	0	0	1	0
First-class	121	170	34	1803	53	13.25		0	3	36	0
List A	116	71	42	400	34	13.79		0	0	26	0
T20s	46	13	5	59	12	7.37	113.46	0	0	18	0
Bowling	**Mat**	**Balls**	**Runs**	**Wkts**	**BBI**	**BBM**	**Ave**	**Econ**	**SR**	**5w**	**10**
Tests	61	11062	5721	205	6/48	10/146	27.90	3.10	53.9	9	1
ODIs	92	4459	3763	124	6/27	6/27	30.34	5.06	35.9	3	0
T20Is	11	234	284	10	2/25	2/25	28.40	7.28	23.4	0	0
First-class	121	18923	10111	384	7/23	10/146	26.33	3.20	49.2	15	1
List A	116	5423	4511	155	6/27	6/27	29.10	4.99	34.9	3	0
T20s	46	912	1229	28	3/18	3/18	43.89	8.08	32.5	0	0

OLLIE ROBINSON RHB / WK / R0 / W0

FULL NAME: Oliver Graham Robinson
BORN: December 1, 1998, Sidcup, Kent
SQUAD NO: 21
HEIGHT: 5ft 8in
NICKNAME: Bob
EDUCATION: Hurstmere School, London; Chislehurst & Sidcup Grammar, London
TEAMS: Kent, England Lions
ROLE: Wicketkeeper/batsman
DEBUT: First-class: 2018; List A: 2017; T20: 2019

BEST BATTING: 143 Kent vs Warwickshire, Edgbaston, 2019

MOST EXCITING DAY AS A CRICKETER? Making my England Lions debut in March 2020 in Australia
CHILDHOOD SPORTING HERO? Thierry Henry
BIGGEST INFLUENCE ON YOUR DEVELOPMENT AS A CRICKETER (EXCLUDING PARENTS)? Matt Walker, head coach at Kent
FIRST CRICKET CLUB? Sidcup CC, London
IF YOU COULD TAKE ONE COUNTY CRICKETER'S BEST SHOT AND ADD IT TO YOUR OWN GAME? Zak Crawley's pull
TOUGHEST OPPONENT IN COUNTY CRICKET? Dom Sibley – we can never get him out for less than 100
MOST ECCENTRIC TEAMMATE? Heino Kuhn – everything has to be perfectly arranged in his spot in the dressing room
WHAT WOULD YOU DO IF YOU WERE IN CHARGE OF COUNTY CRICKET? Play each competition in blocks (no T20s between four-day matches)
STRANGEST THING YOU'VE DONE DURING LOCKDOWN? Hitting toilet roll with a bat for a video
TWITTER: @ollierobinson7

Batting	Mat	Inns	NO	Runs	HS	Ave	SR	100	50	Ct	St
First-class	23	36	2	983	143	28.91	58.54	2	4	77	0
List A	8	5	0	132	49	26.40	75.00	0	0	4	0
T20s	14	11	1	140	53	14.00	102.94	0	1	8	2
Bowling	**Mat**	**Balls**	**Runs**	**Wkts**	**BBI**	**BBM**	**Ave**	**Econ**	**SR**	**5w**	**10**
First-class	23	-	-	-	-	-	-	-	-	-	-
List A	8	-	-	-	-	-	-	-	-	-	-
T20s	14	-	-	-	-	-	-	-	-	-	-

OLLIE ROBINSON RHB / RFM / R0 / W2 / MVP51

FULL NAME: Oliver Edward Robinson
BORN: December 1, 1993, Margate, Kent
SQUAD NO: 25
HEIGHT: 6ft 5in
NICKNAME: The Rig
EDUCATION: King's School, Canterbury
TEAMS: Sussex, England Lions, Hampshire, Yorkshire
ROLE: Bowler
DEBUT: First-class: 2015; List A: 2013; T20: 2014

BEST BATTING: 110 Sussex vs Durham, Chester-le-Street, 2015
BEST BOWLING: 8-34 Sussex vs Middlesex, Hove, 2019
COUNTY CAP: 2019 (Sussex)

MOST EXCITING DAY AS A CRICKETER? Playing for England Lions at the MCG
CHILDHOOD SPORTING HERO? Andrew Flintoff
BIGGEST INFLUENCE ON YOUR DEVELOPMENT AS A CRICKETER (EXCLUDING PARENTS)? Myself – no one else can do it for you
FIRST CRICKET CLUB? Margate CC, Kent
IF YOU COULD TAKE ONE COUNTY CRICKETER'S BEST SHOT AND ADD IT TO YOUR OWN GAME? Ian Bell's cover-drive
TOUGHEST OPPONENT IN COUNTY CRICKET? Jonathan Trott – I found it hard to bowl to him early in my career
MOST ECCENTRIC TEAMMATE? Phil Salt – he's a loose character
WHAT WOULD YOU DO IF YOU WERE IN CHARGE OF COUNTY CRICKET? Play five-day matches in the County Championship
IF YOU WERE AN ANIMAL, WHICH WOULD IT BE? A sloth
GUILTY PLEASURE? My stamp collection
TWITTER: @ollierobinson25

Batting	Mat	Inns	NO	Runs	HS	Ave	SR	100	50	Ct	St
First-class	58	85	16	1438	110	20.84	62.35	1	5	19	0
List A	14	10	3	122	30	17.42	89.70	0	0	6	0
T20s	44	22	10	61	18*	5.08	80.26	0	0	17	0
Bowling	**Mat**	**Balls**	**Runs**	**Wkts**	**BBI**	**BBM**	**Ave**	**Econ**	**SR**	**5w**	**10**
First-class	58	10783	5445	250	8/34	14/135	21.78	3.02	43.1	14	4
List A	14	576	568	14	3/31	3/31	40.57	5.91	41.1	0	0
T20s	44	786	1154	40	4/15	4/15	28.85	8.80	19.6	0	0

SAM ROBSON

RHB / LB / R2 / W0

FULL NAME: Samuel David Robson
BORN: July 1, 1989, Sydney, Australia
SQUAD NO: 12
HEIGHT: 6ft
NICKNAME: Bronco
EDUCATION: Marcellin College, Sydney
TEAMS: England, Middlesex, Australia U19
ROLE: Batsman
DEBUT: Test: 2014; First-class: 2009; List A: 2008; T20: 2011

BEST BATTING: 231 Middlesex vs Warwickshire, Lord's, 2016
BEST BOWLING: 2-0 Middlesex vs Surrey, The Oval, 2020
COUNTY CAP: 2013

MOST EXCITING DAY AS A CRICKETER? Scoring a Test hundred at Headingley in 2014
CHILDHOOD SPORTING HERO? Michael Slater
BIGGEST INFLUENCE ON YOUR DEVELOPMENT AS A CRICKETER (EXCLUDING PARENTS)? In terms of coaches: Mark O'Neill, Mark Ramprakash, Richard Scott, and my brother Angus. The players that stand out are Andrew Strauss and Chris Rogers
FIRST CRICKET CLUB? Randwick Junior CC, New South Wales, Australia
TOUGHEST OPPONENT IN COUNTY CRICKET? James Anderson
WHAT WOULD YOU DO IF YOU WERE IN CHARGE OF COUNTY CRICKET? Continue to look after and embrace the County Championship – there is no other domestic competition in the world that has such a rich history; make the T20 Blast a shorter competition so that each game is a big event
STRANGEST THING YOU'VE DONE DURING LOCKDOWN? Cycling a 50km round trip to the only McDonald's in London that was open for takeaway

Batting	Mat	Inns	NO	Runs	HS	Ave	SR	100	50	Ct	St
Tests	7	11	0	336	127	30.54	44.50	1	1	5	0
First-class	162	286	19	9965	231	37.32	51.31	23	40	152	0
List A	20	18	0	603	106	33.50	73.35	1	3	8	0
T20s	5	5	2	75	28*	25.00	115.38	0	0	3	0
Bowling	**Mat**	**Balls**	**Runs**	**Wkts**	**BBI**	**BBM**	**Ave**	**Econ**	**SR**	**5w**	**10**
Tests	7	-	-	-	-	-	-	-	-	-	-
First-class	162	277	205	6	2/0	2/0	34.16	4.44	46.1	0	0
List A	20	36	43	1	1/27	1/27	43.00	7.16	36.0	0	0
T20s	5	24	31	3	3/31	3/31	10.33	7.75	8.0	0	0

GARETH RODERICK

RHB / WK / R0 / W0

FULL NAME: Gareth Hugh Roderick
BORN: August 29, 1991, Durban, South Africa
SQUAD NO: 9
HEIGHT: 6ft
NICKNAME: Roders
EDUCATION: Maritzburg College, South Africa
TEAMS: Worcestershire, Gloucestershire, KwaZulu-Natal
ROLE: Batsman/wicketkeeper
DEBUT: First-class: 2011; List A: 2011; T20: 2011

BEST BATTING: 171 Gloucestershire vs Leicestershire, Bristol, 2014

COUNTY CAP: 2013 (Gloucestershire)

MOST EXCITING DAY AS A CRICKETER? Winning the Lord's one-day final with Gloucestershire in 2015
CHILDHOOD SPORTING HERO? Steve Waugh
FIRST CRICKET CLUB? Northwood Crusaders CC, Durban
IF YOU COULD TAKE ONE COUNTY CRICKETER'S BEST SHOT AND ADD IT TO YOUR OWN GAME? Jos Buttler's ramp
TOUGHEST OPPONENT IN COUNTY CRICKET? Ryan Harris. I faced him once playing for Gloucestershire against Australia A and it was the best spell of bowling I have ever faced – but I got through it!
WHAT WOULD YOU DO IF YOU WERE IN CHARGE OF COUNTY CRICKET? Go back to each county playing 16 first-class games, make the season run until later in the year
STRANGEST THING YOU'VE DONE DURING LOCKDOWN? Baking (never again)
FAVOURITE SMELL? My newborn's hair after a bath
TWITTER: @Roders369

Batting	Mat	Inns	NO	Runs	HS	Ave	SR	100	50	Ct	St
First-class	100	163	21	4902	171	34.52	50.67	6	32	277	5
List A	51	41	6	1184	104	33.82	83.08	2	8	50	4
T20s	41	24	8	213	32	13.31	119.66	0	0	20	1
Bowling	**Mat**	**Balls**	**Runs**	**Wkts**	**BBI**	**BBM**	**Ave**	**Econ**	**SR**	**5w**	**10**
First-class	100	-	-	-	-	-	-	-	-	-	-
List A	51	-	-	-	-	-	-	-	-	-	-
T20s	41	-	-	-	-	-	-	-	-	-	-

TOBY ROLAND-JONES

RHB / RFM / R0 / W2

FULL NAME: Tobias Skelton Roland-Jones
BORN: January 29, 1988, Ashford, Surrey
SQUAD NO: 21
HEIGHT: 6ft 3in
NICKNAME: Rojo
EDUCATION: Hampton School, Greater London; University of Leeds
TEAMS: England, Middlesex
ROLE: Bowler
DEBUT: Test: 2017; ODI: 2017; First-class: 2010; List A: 2010; T20: 2011

BEST BATTING: 103* Middlesex vs Yorkshire, Lord's, 2015
BEST BOWLING: 7-52 Middlesex vs Gloucestershire, Northwood, 2019
COUNTY CAP: 2012

MOST EXCITING DAY AS A CRICKETER? The final day of the 2016 County Championship
CHILDHOOD SPORTING HERO? Ryan Giggs
BIGGEST INFLUENCE ON YOUR DEVELOPMENT AS A CRICKETER (EXCLUDING PARENTS)? Richard Johnson, my former bowling coach at Middlesex. When I entered the game aged 21, he understood what my game needed and where it could go
IF YOU COULD TAKE ONE COUNTY CRICKETER'S BEST SHOT AND ADD IT TO YOUR OWN GAME? Steven Finn's on-drive – if the ball doesn't cannon into his shin, it's a thing of beauty
TOUGHEST OPPONENT IN COUNTY CRICKET? Nick Compton – he was so determined to not just score runs but to wear teams down
FAVOURITE SMELL? Fear
TWITTER: @tobyrj21

Batting	Mat	Inns	NO	Runs	HS	Ave	SR	100	50	Ct	St
Tests	4	6	2	82	25	20.50	69.49	0	0	0	0
ODIs	1	1	1	37	37*	-	100.00	0	0	0	0
First-class	114	159	30	2824	103*	21.89	58.14	1	11	33	0
List A	79	47	15	684	65	21.37	95.13	0	1	13	0
T20s	54	31	12	317	40	16.68	128.34	0	0	15	0
Bowling	**Mat**	**Balls**	**Runs**	**Wkts**	**BBI**	**BBM**	**Ave**	**Econ**	**SR**	**5w**	**10**
Tests	4	536	334	17	5/57	8/129	19.64	3.73	31.5	1	0
ODIs	1	42	34	1	1/34	1/34	34.00	4.85	42.0	0	0
First-class	114	19597	10387	403	7/52	12/105	25.77	3.18	48.6	19	4
List A	79	3671	3181	126	4/10	4/10	25.24	5.19	29.1	0	0
T20s	54	1065	1549	64	5/21	5/21	24.20	8.72	16.6	1	0

BILLY ROOT

LHB / OB / R0 / W0

FULL NAME: William Thomas Root
BORN: August 5, 1992, Sheffield
SQUAD NO: 7
HEIGHT: 5ft 11in
NICKNAME: Ferret
EDUCATION: Worksop College, Nottinghamshire; Leeds Metropolitan University
TEAMS: Glamorgan, Nottinghamshire
ROLE: Batsman
DEBUT: First-class: 2015; List A: 2017; T20: 2017

BEST BATTING: 229 Glamorgan vs Northamptonshire, Northampton, 2019
BEST BOWLING: 3-29 Nottinghamshire vs Sussex, Hove, 2017

MOST EXCITING DAY AS A CRICKETER? T20 Finals Day in 2017 when I was at Notts
FAMILY TIES? My dad was a good cricketer and my brother plays the occasional game
CHILDHOOD SPORTING HERO? Graham Thorpe
BIGGEST INFLUENCE ON YOUR DEVELOPMENT AS A CRICKETER (EXCLUDING PARENTS)? My brother
FIRST CRICKET CLUB? Sheffield Collegiate CC
IF YOU COULD TAKE ONE COUNTY CRICKETER'S BEST SHOT AND ADD IT TO YOUR OWN GAME? Stuart Poynter's upper-cut
TOUGHEST OPPONENT IN COUNTY CRICKET? Jofra Archer
MOST ECCENTRIC TEAMMATE? Marnus Labuschagne – do I need to explain why?
WHAT WOULD YOU DO IF YOU WERE IN CHARGE OF COUNTY CRICKET? Introduce play-offs and a final for the Championship, bring in Super Overs in the T20 Blast
WHAT WOULD YOU DO IF YOU WERE PRIME MINISTER? Probably have a pint with Rishi Sunak
STRANGEST THING YOU'VE DONE DURING LOCKDOWN? Zoom meetings in fancy-dress
TWITTER: @Rootdog22

Batting	Mat	Inns	NO	Runs	HS	Ave	SR	100	50	Ct	St
First-class	33	56	3	1751	229	33.03	55.39	5	4	8	0
List A	24	20	4	773	113*	48.31	92.57	2	3	7	0
T20s	32	24	6	372	40	20.66	105.68	0	0	12	0
Bowling	**Mat**	**Balls**	**Runs**	**Wkts**	**BBI**	**BBM**	**Ave**	**Econ**	**SR**	**5w**	**10**
First-class	33	269	176	8	3/29	3/29	22.00	3.92	33.6	0	0
List A	24	292	310	6	2/36	2/36	51.66	6.36	48.6	0	0
T20s	32	18	37	0	-	-	-	12.33	-	0	0

JOE ROOT

RHB / OB / R3 / W0

FULL NAME: Joseph Edward Root
BORN: December 30, 1990, Sheffield
SQUAD NO: 66
HEIGHT: 6ft
NICKNAME: Rootfish
EDUCATION: King Ecgbert School, Sheffield; Worksop College, Nottinghamshire
TEAMS: England, Yorkshire, Sydney Thunder
ROLE: Batsman
DEBUT: Test: 2012; ODI: 2013; T20I: 2012; First-class: 2010; List A: 2009; T20: 2011

BEST BATTING: 254 England vs Pakistan, Old Trafford, 2016
BEST BOWLING: 5-8 England vs India, Ahmedabad, 2021
COUNTY CAP: 2012

FAMILY TIES? My dad played club cricket and represented Nottinghamshire Second XI and colts. My brother Billy has played for Notts and is currently at Glamorgan
CHILDHOOD SPORTING HERO? Michael Vaughan
FIRST CRICKET CLUB? Sheffield Collegiate CC
TWITTER: @root66

Batting	Mat	Inns	NO	Runs	HS	Ave	SR	100	50	Ct	St
Tests	103	189	14	8617	254	49.24	54.95	20	49	134	0
ODIs	149	140	21	5962	133*	50.10	86.90	16	33	74	0
T20Is	32	30	5	893	90*	35.72	126.30	0	5	18	0
First-class	163	285	25	12705	254	48.86	55.81	30	66	173	0
List A	188	178	27	7246	133*	47.98	85.63	17	42	86	0
T20s	77	71	14	1897	92*	33.28	128.17	0	13	34	0
Bowling	**Mat**	**Balls**	**Runs**	**Wkts**	**BBI**	**BBM**	**Ave**	**Econ**	**SR**	**5w**	**10**
Tests	103	3079	1604	37	5/8	5/33	43.35	3.12	83.2	1	0
ODIs	149	1552	1491	26	3/52	3/52	57.34	5.76	59.6	0	0
T20Is	32	84	139	6	2/9	2/9	23.16	9.92	14.0	0	0
First-class	163	5012	2621	57	5/8	5/33	45.98	3.13	87.9	1	0
List A	188	2139	1990	40	3/52	3/52	49.75	5.58	53.4	0	0
T20s	77	366	527	17	2/7	2/7	31.00	8.63	21.5	0	0

ADAM ROSSINGTON

RHB / WK / R0 / W0

FULL NAME: Adam Matthew Rossington
BORN: May 5, 1993, Edgware, London
SQUAD NO: 7
HEIGHT: 6ft
NICKNAME: Rosso
EDUCATION: Belmont Preparatory School, Surrey; Mill Hill School, London
TEAMS: Northamptonshire, England U19, Middlesex
ROLE: Batsman/wicketkeeper
DEBUT: First-class: 2010; List A: 2012; T20: 2011

BEST BATTING: 138* Northamptonshire vs Sussex, Arundel, 2016

CHILDHOOD SPORTING HERO? Alec Stewart
FIRST CRICKET CLUB? Barnet CC, London
TOUGHEST OPPONENT IN COUNTY CRICKET? Jeetan Patel
BIGGEST CRICKETING REGRET? That I've never played in the Hong Kong Sixes
WHAT WOULD YOU DO IF YOU WERE IN CHARGE OF COUNTY CRICKET? Introduce free hits for front-foot no-balls in Championship cricket
FAVOURITE SMELL? A roast dinner
IF YOU WERE AN ANIMAL, WHICH WOULD IT BE? A horse – so that I could go up the Cheltenham Hill
SURPRISING FACT ABOUT YOU? I can't ride a bicycle
GUILTY PLEASURE? Music of the 1980s and 90s
TWITTER: @rossington17

Batting	Mat	Inns	NO	Runs	HS	Ave	SR	100	50	Ct	St
First-class	80	129	13	4099	138*	35.33	66.30	7	28	175	11
List A	49	44	7	1381	97	37.32	99.42	0	11	34	5
T20s	84	79	6	1548	85	21.20	139.20	0	9	38	14
Bowling	**Mat**	**Balls**	**Runs**	**Wkts**	**BBI**	**BBM**	**Ave**	**Econ**	**SR**	**5w**	**10**
First-class	80	120	86	0	-	-	-	4.30	-	0	0
List A	49	-	-	-	-	-	-	-	-	-	-
T20s	84	-	-	-	-	-	-	-	-	-	-

JASON ROY

RHB / RM / R1 / W0

FULL NAME: Jason Jonathan Roy
BORN: July 21, 1990, Durban, South Africa
SQUAD NO: 20
HEIGHT: 6ft
NICKNAME: Roy the Boy
EDUCATION: Whitgift School, Croydon
TEAMS: England, Surrey, Delhi Capitals, Gujarat Lions, Lahore Qalandars, Perth Scorchers, Quetta Gladiators, Sydney Sixers, Sylhet Sixers
ROLE: Batsman
DEBUT: Test: 2019; ODI: 2015; T20I: 2014; First-class: 2010; List A: 2008; T20: 2008

BEST BATTING: 143 Surrey vs Lancashire, The Oval, 2015
BEST BOWLING: 3-9 Surrey vs Gloucestershire, Bristol, 2014
COUNTY CAP: 2014

MOST EXCITING DAY AS A CRICKETER? There's been quite a few of them – winning the Championship with Surrey, making my England T20, ODI and Test debuts, scoring my first century for England in ODI cricket and winning the World Cup in 2019
CHILDHOOD SPORTING HERO? Jacques Kallis
TWITTER: @JasonRoy20

Batting	Mat	Inns	NO	Runs	HS	Ave	SR	100	50	Ct	St
Tests	5	10	0	187	72	18.70	58.80	0	1	1	0
ODIs	93	89	2	3483	180	40.03	106.67	9	18	32	0
T20Is	38	38	0	890	78	23.42	144.01	0	5	5	0
First-class	87	144	11	4850	143	36.46	80.75	9	23	75	0
List A	189	180	8	6543	180	38.04	106.94	16	34	70	0
T20s	230	225	11	5941	122*	27.76	142.74	4	40	104	0
Bowling	**Mat**	**Balls**	**Runs**	**Wkts**	**BBI**	**BBM**	**Ave**	**Econ**	**SR**	**5w**	**10**
Tests	5	-	-	-	-	-	-	-	-	-	-
ODIs	93	-	-	-	-	-	-	-	-	-	-
T20Is	38	-	-	-	-	-	-	-	-	-	-
First-class	87	712	495	14	3/9	4/47	35.35	4.17	50.8	0	0
List A	189	6	12	0	-	-	-	12.00	-	0	0
T20s	230	18	39	1	1/23	1/23	39.00	13.00	18.0	0	0

CHRIS RUSHWORTH RHB / RFM / R0 / W5

FULL NAME: Christopher Rushworth
BORN: July 11, 1986, Sunderland
SQUAD NO: 22
HEIGHT: 6ft 2in
NICKNAME: Russian
EDUCATION: Castle View Comprehensive School, Sunderland
TEAMS: Durham
ROLE: Bowler
DEBUT: First-class: 2010; List A: 2004; T20: 2011

BEST BATTING: 57 Durham vs Kent, Canterbury, 2017
BEST BOWLING: 9-52 Durham vs Northamptonshire, Chester-le-Street, 2014
BENEFIT: 2019

MOST EXCITING DAY AS A CRICKETER? The Lord's one-day final in 2014
FAMILY TIES? My brother Lee represented England U19 and my cousin Phil Mustard played for England, Durham and Gloucestershire
CHILDHOOD SPORTING HERO? Shaun Pollock
BIGGEST INFLUENCE ON YOUR DEVELOPMENT AS A CRICKETER (EXCLUDING PARENTS)? Geoff Cook (former Durham coach) – he coached me when I was a young lad and then was there to hand me a second opportunity to play professional cricket
FIRST CRICKET CLUB? Hylton Colliery CC, Sunderland
IF YOU COULD TAKE ONE COUNTY CRICKETER'S BEST SHOT AND ADD IT TO YOUR OWN GAME? Dom Sibley's forward defence
TOUGHEST OPPONENT IN COUNTY CRICKET? Riki Wessels – he always scores runs against Durham. He hits the ball to unusual places and frustrates the hell out of me
BIGGEST CRICKETING REGRET? Trying to sweep Liam Dawson while my partner was on 99 at the other end. I was the last man. Oops
TWITTER: @ChrisRush22

Batting	Mat	Inns	NO	Runs	HS	Ave	SR	100	50	Ct	St
First-class	131	186	59	1514	57	11.92	61.44	0	1	28	0
List A	72	30	15	188	38*	12.53	87.85	0	0	18	0
T20s	85	15	9	20	5	3.33	50.00	0	0	18	0
Bowling	**Mat**	**Balls**	**Runs**	**Wkts**	**BBI**	**BBM**	**Ave**	**Econ**	**SR**	**5w**	**10**
First-class	131	23321	11634	510	9/52	15/95	22.81	2.99	45.7	26	4
List A	72	3139	2765	111	5/31	5/31	24.90	5.28	28.2	2	0
T20s	85	1623	2121	78	3/14	3/14	27.19	7.84	20.8	0	0

JOSH RYMELL

RHB / RO / WO

FULL NAME: Joshua Sean Rymell
BORN: April 4, 2001, Ipswich, Suffolk
SQUAD NO: 49
EDUCATION: Ipswich School; Colchester Sixth Form College
TEAMS: Essex
ROLE: Batsman

TWITTER: @josh_rymell
NOTES: Rymell has come through the player pathway system at Essex and agreed a new one-year deal last November, having first signed for the club earlier last year. The next step will be pushing his case for selection in the senior side. "Josh has been in and around the first team for a year or so now and is a great prospect for the future," said Anthony McGrath, Essex's head coach. "He's come through the Essex Academy and is a talented batsman, and everybody at the club is excited to see how he develops." Rymell served notice of his talent in May 2017 when he scored 114 off 107 balls on his debut for Colchester and East Essex in the Essex League Cup. He made 19 appearances for Essex Second XI in 2019, with a high score of 87 against Durham in a 50-over match at Chelmsford. The 20-year-old suffered an injury to his cruciate ligament later that year but is now back to full fitness

OLLIE SALE

RHB / RFM / R0 / W0

FULL NAME: Oliver Richard Trethowan Sale
BORN: September 30, 1995, Newcastle-under-Lyme, Staffordshire
SQUAD NO: 82
HEIGHT: 6ft 2in
NICKNAME: Snail
EDUCATION: Sherborne School, Dorset; Newcastle University
TEAMS: Somerset
ROLE: Bowler
DEBUT: T20: 2016

MOST EXCITING DAY AS A CRICKETER? Playing a T20 at Edgbaston last year. I can't wait to play in front of a crowd
BIGGEST INFLUENCE ON YOUR DEVELOPMENT AS A CRICKETER (EXCLUDING PARENTS)? My school coach Alan Willows – he not only developed me as a cricketer but also drove me to Somerset Academy sessions
FIRST CRICKET CLUB? Tavistock CC, Devon
IF YOU COULD TAKE ONE COUNTY CRICKETER'S BEST SHOT AND ADD IT TO YOUR OWN GAME? Tom Abell's ramp
MOST ECCENTRIC TEAMMATE? Jack Brooks – senior headband warrior and chief mischief-maker
WHAT WOULD YOU DO IF YOU WERE IN CHARGE OF COUNTY CRICKET? Replace Second XI cricket with an U23 competition
STRANGEST THING YOU'VE DONE DURING LOCKDOWN? Playing the PlayStation 4 for about 10 hours a day
GUILTY PLEASURE? Fantasy Premier League
TWITTER: @olliesale1

Batting	Mat	Inns	NO	Runs	HS	Ave	SR	100	50	Ct	St
T20s	10	5	3	20	14*	10.00	105.26	0	0	3	0
Bowling	**Mat**	**Balls**	**Runs**	**Wkts**	**BBI**	**BBM**	**Ave**	**Econ**	**SR**	**5w**	**10**
T20s	10	196	341	13	3/32	3/32	26.23	10.43	15.0	0	0

MATT SALISBURY

RHB / RMF / R0 / W0

FULL NAME: Matthew Edward Thomas Salisbury
BORN: April 18, 1993, Chelmsford, Essex
SQUAD NO: 32
HEIGHT: 6ft 2in
NICKNAME: Great Wall
EDUCATION: Shenfield High School, Essex; Anglia Ruskin University, Cambridge
TEAMS: Durham, Essex, Hampshire
ROLE: Bowler
DEBUT: First-class: 2012; List A: 2014; T20: 2014

BEST BATTING: 37 Durham vs Warwickshire, Edgbaston, 2018
BEST BOWLING: 6-37 Durham vs Middlesex, Chester-le-Street, 2018

FIRST CRICKET CLUB? Shenfield CC, Essex
TWITTER: @mattsalisbury10
NOTES: The right-arm seamer has had a stop-start career staggered between three counties but appears to have found his feet at Durham. Salisbury was first given a chance at Essex and got a run in their first team in 2014, only to be released the following year. He made his Hampshire debut in 2017 but could not nail down a place in the side, before enjoying a breakthrough season in 2018 after being signed by Durham, taking 44 first-class wickets at 24.77 in his first season at the Riverside. He hasn't played T20 cricket since 2014

Batting	Mat	Inns	NO	Runs	HS	Ave	SR	100	50	Ct	St
First-class	34	56	11	379	37	8.42	31.01	0	0	4	0
List A	13	3	2	8	5*	8.00	32.00	0	0	2	0
T20s	8	2	2	2	1*	-	100.00	0	0	2	0
Bowling	**Mat**	**Balls**	**Runs**	**Wkts**	**BBI**	**BBM**	**Ave**	**Econ**	**SR**	**5w**	**10**
First-class	34	4914	2952	95	6/37	7/107	31.07	3.60	51.7	1	0
List A	13	510	492	14	4/55	4/55	35.14	5.78	36.4	0	0
T20s	8	172	256	10	2/19	2/19	25.60	8.93	17.2	0	0

PHIL SALT RHB / OB / WK / R0 / W0 / MVP44

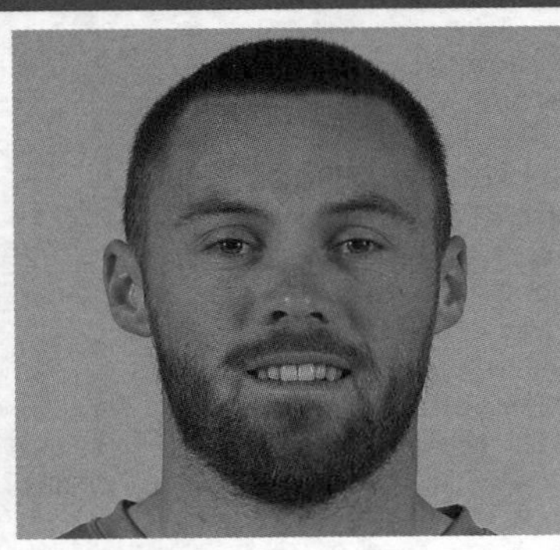

FULL NAME: Philip Dean Salt
BORN: August 28, 1996, Bodelwyddan, Denbighshire, Wales
SQUAD NO: 28
HEIGHT: 6ft
NICKNAME: Hotdog
EDUCATION: Harrison College, Barbados; Reed's School, Surrey
TEAMS: Sussex, Adelaide Strikers, Barbados Tridents, England Lions, Islamabad United
ROLE: Batsman
DEBUT: First-class: 2016; List A: 2015; T20: 2016

BEST BATTING: 148 Sussex vs Derbyshire, Hove, 2018
BEST BOWLING: 1-32 Sussex vs Warwickshire, Hove, 2018

MOST EXCITING DAY AS A CRICKETER? Winning the Caribbean Premier League with Barbados Tridents in 2019 – I had been flow in as an emergency replacement for the final
CHILDHOOD SPORTING HERO? Brian Lara
BIGGEST INFLUENCE ON YOUR DEVELOPMENT AS A CRICKETER (EXCLUDING PARENTS)? Three people in particular: Mike Yardy, Keith Medlycott and Jason Gillespie
FIRST CRICKET CLUB? St Asaph CC, North Wales
TOUGHEST OPPONENT IN COUNTY CRICKET? Either Chris Rushworth or Tim Murtagh with a new ball in their hand
FAVOURITE SMELL? Freshly turned soil
SURPRISING FACT ABOUT YOU? I once picked up Sir Garry Sobers' Indian takeaway by accident
TWITTER: @PhilSalt1

Batting	Mat	Inns	NO	Runs	HS	Ave	SR	100	50	Ct	St
First-class	38	66	2	1967	148	30.73	72.50	4	10	33	0
List A	16	16	1	494	137*	32.93	104.66	1	2	5	0
T20s	92	89	6	2041	78*	24.59	151.29	0	15	41	1
Bowling	**Mat**	**Balls**	**Runs**	**Wkts**	**BBI**	**BBM**	**Ave**	**Econ**	**SR**	**5w**	**10**
First-class	38	54	32	1	1/32	1/32	32.00	3.55	54.0	0	0
List A	16	-	-	-	-	-	-	-	-	-	-
T20s	92	-	-	-	-	-	-	-	-	-	-

ANDREW SALTER RHB / OB / R0 / W0

FULL NAME: Andrew Graham Salter
BORN: June 1, 1993, Haverfordwest, Pembrokeshire, Wales
SQUAD NO: 21
HEIGHT: 5ft 9in
NICKNAME: Salts
EDUCATION: Milford Haven School, Pembrokeshire; Cardiff Metropolitan University
TEAMS: Glamorgan, England U19
ROLE: Bowler
DEBUT: First-class: 2012; List A: 2012; T20: 2014

BEST BATTING: 88 Glamorgan vs Gloucestershire, Cardiff, 2017
BEST BOWLING: 4-80 Glamorgan vs Warwickshire, Edgbaston, 2018

MOST EXCITING DAY AS A CRICKETER? The Lord's one-day final in 2013
CHILDHOOD SPORTING HERO? Tiger Woods
BIGGEST INFLUENCE ON YOUR DEVELOPMENT AS A CRICKETER (EXCLUDING PARENTS)? Glamorgan legend Alan Jones
FIRST CRICKET CLUB? St Ishmaels CC, Pembrokeshire
TOUGHEST OPPONENT IN COUNTY CRICKET? Wayne Madsen – he's a brilliant sweeper
MOST ECCENTRIC TEAMMATE? Nick Selman – for his celebrations after taking a catch in the slip cordon
STRANGEST THING YOU'VE DONE DURING LOCKDOWN? Wearing my Glamorgan kit at home
FAVOURITE SMELL? Petrol
SURPRISING FACT ABOUT YOU? I co-manage a motorcycle initiative called Baffle Culture which aims at "seizing the opportunity to bring like-minded riders together"
GUILTY PLEASURE? Toasted banana bread with butter
TWITTER: @AndySalts

Batting	Mat	Inns	NO	Runs	HS	Ave	SR	100	50	Ct	St
First-class	56	87	17	1629	88	23.27	42.64	0	8	28	0
List A	36	28	10	371	51	20.61	88.12	0	1	9	0
T20s	77	44	22	337	39*	15.31	116.20	0	0	21	0
Bowling	**Mat**	**Balls**	**Runs**	**Wkts**	**BBI**	**BBM**	**Ave**	**Econ**	**SR**	**5w**	**10**
First-class	56	7177	4130	86	4/80	6/69	48.02	3.45	83.4	0	0
List A	36	1288	1155	17	2/41	2/41	67.94	5.38	75.7	0	0
T20s	77	1122	1518	53	4/12	4/12	28.64	8.11	21.1	0	0

BEN SANDERSON RHB / RMF / R0 / W3 / MVP69

FULL NAME: Ben William Sanderson
BORN: January 3, 1989, Sheffield
SQUAD NO: 26
HEIGHT: 6ft
NICKNAME: Sandoooo
EDUCATION: Ecclesfield School, Sheffield; Sheffield College
TEAMS: Northamptonshire, England U19, Yorkshire
ROLE: Bowler
DEBUT: First-class: 2008; List A: 2010; T20: 2010

BEST BATTING: 42 Northamptonshire vs Kent, Canterbury, 2015
BEST BOWLING: 8-73 Northamptonshire vs Gloucestershire, Northampton, 2016
COUNTY CAP: 2018 (Northamptonshire)

MOST EXCITING DAY AS A CRICKETER? T20 Finals Day in 2016
CHILDHOOD SPORTING HERO? Darren Gough
BIGGEST INFLUENCE ON YOUR DEVELOPMENT AS A CRICKETER (EXCLUDING PARENTS)? Steve Oldham – my first bowling coach. And then Kevin Sharp – he played a big part in getting me back into the professional game
FIRST CRICKET CLUB? Whitley Hall CC, Sheffield
IF YOU COULD TAKE ONE COUNTY CRICKETER'S BEST SHOT AND ADD IT TO YOUR OWN GAME? Adam Rossington's pull
TOUGHEST OPPONENT IN COUNTY CRICKET? Daryl Mitchell
BIGGEST CRICKETING REGRET? Being a bowler
GUILTY PLEASURE? A cup of tea with a pack of chocolate Hobnobs
TWITTER: @sando567

Batting	Mat	Inns	NO	Runs	HS	Ave	SR	100	50	Ct	St
First-class	62	80	30	444	42	8.88	44.84	0	0	9	0
List A	33	15	6	99	31	11.00	69.71	0	0	9	0
T20s	45	15	11	36	12*	9.00	94.73	0	0	6	0
Bowling	**Mat**	**Balls**	**Runs**	**Wkts**	**BBI**	**BBM**	**Ave**	**Econ**	**SR**	**5w**	**10**
First-class	62	10953	4842	244	8/73	10/55	19.84	2.65	44.8	13	2
List A	33	1317	1306	37	3/36	3/36	35.29	5.94	35.5	0	0
T20s	45	850	1240	51	4/21	4/21	24.31	8.75	16.6	0	0

DANE SCHADENDORF

RHB / WK / R0 / W0

FULL NAME: Dane Schadendorf
BORN: July 31, 2002, Harare, Zimbabwe
SQUAD NO: 89
HEIGHT: 5ft 9in
NICKNAME: Shado
EDUCATION: Ruzawi School, Mashonaland East, Zimbabwe; St John's College, Harare
TEAMS: Nottinghamshire, Zimbabwe U19
ROLE: Wicketkeeper/batsman

MOST EXCITING DAY AS A CRICKETER? Signing for Nottinghamshire last December
CHILDHOOD SPORTING HERO? AB de Villiers
BIGGEST INFLUENCE ON YOUR DEVELOPMENT AS A CRICKETER (EXCLUDING PARENTS)? My brother – I used to watch him play growing up and I always wanted to be up there playing with him. I've always remembered that and it pushes me to keep getting better
IF YOU COULD TAKE ONE COUNTY CRICKETER'S BEST SHOT AND ADD IT TO YOUR OWN GAME? Joe Root's back-foot drive
WHAT WOULD YOU DO IF YOU WERE PRIME MINISTER? Stop using fossil fuels, make public transport free of charge, subsidise electric cars
STRANGEST THING YOU'VE DONE DURING LOCKDOWN? Cleaning my room
FAVOURITE SMELL? Petrol
GUILTY PLEASURE? Golf
TWITTER: @DaneSchadendorf
NOTES: Nottinghamshire signed the 18-year-old wicketkeeper/batsman on a two-year deal last December. Schadendorf has made 10 appearances for Zimbabwe U19 but holds a British passport and has chosen to commit his future to English domestic cricket. He played in the U19 World Cup last year before representing Caythorpe CC in the Nottinghamshire Premier League. "As soon as I walked into Trent Bridge for the first time, I could imagine how special it must be to play with a full house in here," Schadendorf said shortly after joining Notts. "That first day in training with the lads was just an unreal experience. My game is probably more suited to white-ball cricket at the moment, but I'm working really hard on my red-ball game"

GEORGE SCOTT RHB / RM / R0 / W0

FULL NAME: George Frederick Buchan Scott
BORN: November 6, 1995, Hemel Hempstead, Hertfordshire
SQUAD NO: 17
HEIGHT: 6ft 2in
NICKNAME: Scotty
EDUCATION: Beechwood Park School, St Albans; St Albans School; University of Leeds
TEAMS: Gloucestershire, Middlesex
ROLE: Allrounder
DEBUT: First-class: 2015; List A: 2015; T20: 2015

BEST BATTING: 55 Middlesex vs Leicestershire, Lord's, 2019
BEST BOWLING: 2-34 Gloucestershire vs Warwickshire, Bristol, 2020

MOST EXCITING DAY AS A CRICKETER? Making my T20 debut in 2015
FAMILY TIES? I have three brothers who have all played Minor Counties for Hertfordshire
CHILDHOOD SPORTING HERO? Danny Cipriani
BIGGEST INFLUENCE ON YOUR DEVELOPMENT AS A CRICKETER (EXCLUDING PARENTS)? Lenny Cooper, my coach at primary school
FIRST CRICKET CLUB? Potters Bar CC, Hertfordshire
IF YOU COULD TAKE ONE COUNTY CRICKETER'S BEST SHOT AND ADD IT TO YOUR OWN GAME? Chris Dent's pull
FAVOURITE SMELL? Freshly baked brownies
SURPRISING FACT ABOUT YOU? I was a music scholar at St Albans School, playing the piano and the bassoon
TWITTER: @georgefbscott

Batting	Mat	Inns	NO	Runs	HS	Ave	SR	100	50	Ct	St
First-class	16	24	5	344	55	18.10	40.61	0	1	5	0
List A	11	10	3	194	63	27.71	123.56	0	1	5	0
T20s	31	24	9	341	38*	22.73	105.24	0	0	15	0
Bowling	**Mat**	**Balls**	**Runs**	**Wkts**	**BBI**	**BBM**	**Ave**	**Econ**	**SR**	**5w**	**10**
First-class	16	696	396	8	2/34	2/49	49.50	3.41	87.0	0	0
List A	11	216	239	1	1/65	1/65	239.00	6.63	216.0	0	0
T20s	31	72	119	3	1/14	1/14	39.66	9.91	24.0	0	0

GEORGE SCRIMSHAW RHB / RMF / R0 / W0

FULL NAME: George Louis Sheridan Scrimshaw
BORN: February 10, 1998, Burton-on-Trent, Staffordshire
SQUAD NO: 9
HEIGHT: 6ft 7in
NICKNAME: Scrim, Scrimmy, Tank
EDUCATION: Thomas Russel Junior School; John Taylor High School, Burton-on-Trent
TEAMS: Derbyshire, Worcestershire
ROLE: Bowler
DEBUT: T20: 2017

CHILDHOOD SPORTING HERO? Dale Steyn – I love his aggression. For a fast bowler like myself, he's a role model
FAMILY TIES? My dad and grandad both played county age-group cricket
FIRST CRICKET CLUB? Dunstall CC, Burton-upon-Trent, Staffordshire – aka Deer Park, home of the Stags
MOST INTERESTING TEAMMATE? My ex-Worcestershire teammate Dillon Pennington – he's a very funny and clueless individual
SURPRISING FACT ABOUT YOU? I once hit 16 sixes in a row in Kwik Cricket
TWITTER: @Gscrimshaw98
NOTES: The tall fast bowler was released by Worcestershire last year following a succession of injuries but signed a one-season deal with Derbyshire in March. "George's potential is clear to see," said Dave Houghton, Derbyshire's head of cricket. "He's tall, quick and skilful with the ball. There will be a lot of rotation with the bowlers this season. Everybody will get the chance to develop and impress [and] George gives us another option in that regard"

Batting	Mat	Inns	NO	Runs	HS	Ave	SR	100	50	Ct	St
T20s	4	1	1	1	1*	-	50.00	0	0	0	0
Bowling	**Mat**	**Balls**	**Runs**	**Wkts**	**BBI**	**BBM**	**Ave**	**Econ**	**SR**	**5w**	**10**
T20s	4	60	90	3	1/20	1/20	30.00	9.00	20.0	0	0

TOM SCRIVEN

RHB / RMF / R0 / W0

FULL NAME: Thomas Antony Rhys Scriven
BORN: November 18, 1998, Oxford
SQUAD NO: 33
EDUCATION: Magdalen College School, Oxford
TEAMS: Hampshire, England U19
ROLE: Allrounder
DEBUT: First-class: 2020; T20: 2018

BEST BATTING: 68 Hampshire vs Kent, Canterbury, 2020
BEST BOWLING: 2-24 Hampshire vs Kent, Canterbury, 2020

MOST EXCITING DAY AS A CRICKETER? Making my Hampshire debut in the T20 Blast in 2018
CHILDHOOD SPORTING HERO? Andrew Flintoff
BIGGEST INFLUENCE ON YOUR DEVELOPMENT AS A CRICKETER (EXCLUDING PARENTS)? A combination of school and player pathways at Berkshire
IF YOU COULD TAKE ONE COUNTY CRICKETER'S BEST SHOT AND ADD IT TO YOUR OWN GAME? Ian Bell's cover-drive
TOUGHEST OPPONENT IN COUNTY CRICKET? I haven't played enough Championship cricket to know yet...
MOST ECCENTRIC TEAMMATE? Chris Wood – he's a very funny guy
STRANGEST THING YOU'VE DONE DURING LOCKDOWN? Playing way too much Wii golf
FAVOURITE SMELL? Petrol
GUILTY PLEASURE? Ben and Jerry's ice cream

Batting	Mat	Inns	NO	Runs	HS	Ave	SR	100	50	Ct	St
First-class	2	3	0	84	68	28.00	45.40	0	1	1	0
T20s	2	1	0	2	2	2.00	28.57	0	0	0	0
Bowling	**Mat**	**Balls**	**Runs**	**Wkts**	**BBI**	**BBM**	**Ave**	**Econ**	**SR**	**5w**	**10**
First-class	2	126	79	3	2/24	2/59	26.33	3.76	42.0	0	0
T20s	2	6	8	0	-	-	-	8.00	-	0	0

GLAMORGAN

NICK SELMAN RHB / RM / R0 / W0

FULL NAME: Nicholas James Selman
BORN: October 18, 1995, Brisbane, Australia
SQUAD NO: 9
HEIGHT: 6ft 2in
NICKNAME: Sellers
EDUCATION: Matthew Flinders Anglican College, Queensland, Australia
TEAMS: Glamorgan
ROLE: Batsman
DEBUT: First-class: 2016; List A: 2016; T20: 2016

BEST BATTING: 150 Glamorgan vs Gloucestershire, Newport, 2019
BEST BOWLING: 1-22 Glamorgan vs Northamptonshire, Cardiff, 2019

CHILDHOOD SPORTING HERO? Jonathan Brown (Aussie rules footballer)
BIGGEST INFLUENCE ON YOUR DEVELOPMENT AS A CRICKETER (EXCLUDING PARENTS)? Brad Murphy, my coach in Queensland who threw me thousands of balls
FIRST CRICKET CLUB? Maleny CC, Queensland, Australia
IF YOU COULD TAKE ONE COUNTY CRICKETER'S BEST SHOT AND ADD IT TO YOUR OWN GAME? Alex Hales's square-drive
TOUGHEST OPPONENT IN COUNTY CRICKET? Steve Magoffin – he's the most skilful bowler I've come up against and always took my front pad off
WHAT WOULD YOU DO IF YOU WERE IN CHARGE OF COUNTY CRICKET? Use Kookaburra balls in the Championship, play 10 red-ball games a season, allow the batting side a maximum of 120 overs
STRANGEST THING YOU'VE DONE DURING LOCKDOWN? Shaving my head
FAVOURITE SMELL? A freshly oiled bat
GUILTY PLEASURE? A schooner of XXXX Gold and a chicken parmigiana
TWITTER: @nickselman22

Batting	Mat	Inns	NO	Runs	HS	Ave	SR	100	50	Ct	St
First-class	56	103	6	2742	150	28.26	45.47	7	13	64	0
List A	9	9	0	242	92	26.88	67.78	0	1	3	0
T20s	18	15	1	396	78	28.28	130.69	0	2	4	0
Bowling	**Mat**	**Balls**	**Runs**	**Wkts**	**BBI**	**BBM**	**Ave**	**Econ**	**SR**	**5w**	**10**
First-class	56	45	36	1	1/22	1/22	36.00	4.80	45.0	0	0
List A	9	-	-	-	-	-	-	-	-	-	-
T20s	18	-	-	-	-	-	-	-	-	-	-

OWAIS SHAH

LHB / LB / R0 / W0

FULL NAME: Syed Mohammed Owais Shah
BORN: October 1, 1998, Glasgow, Scotland
SQUAD NO: 19
HEIGHT: 5ft 10in
NICKNAME: Ace
EDUCATION: Bellahouston Academy, Glasgow; Myerscough College, Preston, Lancashire
TEAMS: Lancashire, Scotland U19
ROLE: Batsman

CHILDHOOD SPORTING HERO? Brian Lara
BIGGEST INFLUENCE ON YOUR DEVELOPMENT AS A CRICKETER (EXCLUDING PARENTS)? Con de Lange, the former Scotland captain who sadly passed away in 2019 at the age of 38. He coached me at Western Warriors in Scotland and always believed in me, pushing me to the limits and making me achieve things that I hadn't thought I could achieve
IF YOU COULD TAKE ONE COUNTY CRICKETER'S BEST SHOT AND ADD IT TO YOUR OWN GAME? Kumar Sangakkara's cover-drive
TOUGHEST OPPONENT IN COUNTY CRICKET? Mark Wood – he's quick
WHAT WOULD YOU DO IF YOU WERE IN CHARGE OF COUNTY CRICKET? Allow for more rest days between Championship matches, make the T20 Blast longer
STRANGEST THING YOU'VE DONE DURING LOCKDOWN? Becoming a Call of Duty freak
TWITTER: @OwaisShah
NOTES: Not to be confused with the former England batsman, Shah is a 22-year-old left-handed opener who signed his first professional contract ahead of the 2020 season. The former Scotland U19 international has come through the Lancashire Academy and impressed for the county in the 2019 Second XI Championship, scoring a hundred and averaging 50.60 from six innings. Born in Glasgow, Shah moved to Lancashire in 2017 to further his career and has played club cricket for Highfield CC in the Liverpool and District Competition

JOSH SHAW

RHB / RMF / R0 / W0

FULL NAME: Joshua Shaw
BORN: January 3, 1996, Wakefield, Yorkshire
SQUAD NO: 5
HEIGHT: 6ft 1in
EDUCATION: Crofton Academy, West Yorkshire; Skills Exchange College, Wakefield
TEAMS: Gloucestershire, England U19, Yorkshire
ROLE: Bowler
DEBUT: First-class: 2016; List A: 2019; T20: 2015

BEST BATTING: 42 Yorkshire vs Somerset, Headingley, 2018
BEST BOWLING: 5-79 Gloucestershire vs Sussex, Bristol, 2016
COUNTY CAP: 2016 (Gloucestershire)

MOST EXCITING DAY AS A CRICKETER? Taking a hat-trick for Yorkshire Academy in the Yorkshire League Cup final in 2014
FAMILY TIES? My father Chris played for Yorkshire. We lived on the back of Streethouse CC so I was always around cricket from a young age
CHILDHOOD SPORTING HERO? Andrew Flintoff
FIRST CRICKET CLUB? Wakefield Thornes CC, West Yorkshire
MOST INTERESTING TEAMMATE? Ryan Higgins – he's always got an opinion on something
SURPRISING FACT ABOUT YOU? I passed my driving test with no minors
IF YOU WERE AN ANIMAL, WHICH WOULD IT BE? A dog – you are loved no matter what
TWITTER: @joshuashaw1

Batting	Mat	Inns	NO	Runs	HS	Ave	SR	100	50	Ct	St
First-class	39	52	9	461	42	10.72	38.48	0	0	8	0
List A	1	-	-	-	-	-	-	-	-	0	0
T20s	9	2	1	1	1	1.00	50.00	0	0	2	0

Bowling	Mat	Balls	Runs	Wkts	BBI	BBM	Ave	Econ	SR	5w	10
First-class	39	5668	3485	97	5/79	6/102	35.92	3.68	58.4	2	0
List A	1	42	52	0	-	-	-	7.42	-	0	0
T20s	9	132	213	4	2/39	2/39	53.25	9.68	33.0	0	0

JACK SHUTT

RHB / OB / R0 / W0

FULL NAME: Jack William Shutt
BORN: June 24, 1997, Barnsley
SQUAD NO: 24
HEIGHT: 6ft 1in
NICKNAME: Sushi
EDUCATION: Kirk Balk School, Barnsley; Thomas Rotherham College, South Yorkshire
TEAMS: Yorkshire
ROLE: Bowler
DEBUT: First-class: 2020; T20: 2019

BEST BATTING: 7* Yorkshire vs Durham, Chester-le-Street, 2020
BEST BOWLING: 2-14 Yorkshire vs Nottinghamshire, Trent Bridge, 2020

MOST EXCITING DAY AS A CRICKETER? Playing in the Roses T20 Blast match at Headingley in 2019 – my first-team debut for Yorkshire
CHILDHOOD SPORTING HERO? Cristiano Ronaldo
BIGGEST INFLUENCE ON YOUR DEVELOPMENT AS A CRICKETER (EXCLUDING PARENTS)? Ian Swallow (ex-Yorkshire off-spinner) – he taught me how to play the game at Elsecar CC and was the man who got me bowling off-spin
IF YOU COULD TAKE ONE COUNTY CRICKETER'S BEST SHOT AND ADD IT TO YOUR OWN GAME? Ian Bell's cover-drive
TOUGHEST OPPONENT IN COUNTY CRICKET? Glenn Maxwell – he's very destructive and has a lot of scoring areas
WHAT WOULD YOU DO IF YOU WERE IN CHARGE OF COUNTY CRICKET? Play more Championship games in the summer months when the pitches take turn, try to make the game more accessible to fans who work full-time
STRANGEST THING YOU'VE DONE DURING LOCKDOWN? Learning magic tricks
GUILTY PLEASURE? A BBQ chicken pizza
TWITTER: @jackshutt_24

Batting	Mat	Inns	NO	Runs	HS	Ave	SR	100	50	Ct	St
First-class	3	4	3	7	7*	7.00	11.86	0	0	2	0
T20s	11	4	3	0	0*	0.00	0.00	0	0	3	0
Bowling	**Mat**	**Balls**	**Runs**	**Wkts**	**BBI**	**BBM**	**Ave**	**Econ**	**SR**	**5w**	**10**
First-class	3	116	104	2	2/14	2/63	52.00	5.37	58.0	0	0
T20s	11	216	271	12	5/11	5/11	22.58	7.52	18.0	1	0

DOM SIBLEY

RHB / OB / R1 / W0

FULL NAME: Dominic Peter Sibley
BORN: September 5, 1995, Epsom, Surrey
SQUAD NO: 45
HEIGHT: 6ft 3in
NICKNAME: Frocko
EDUCATION: Whitgift School, Croydon
TEAMS: England, Warwickshire, Surrey
ROLE: Batsman
DEBUT: Test: 2019; First-class: 2013; List A: 2013; T20: 2016

BEST BATTING: 244 Warwickshire vs Kent, Canterbury, 2019
BEST BOWLING: 2-103 Surrey vs Hampshire, Southampton, 2016

FIRST CRICKET CLUB? Ashtead CC, Surrey
BEST INNINGS YOU'VE SEEN? Kevin Pietersen's hundred against South Africa in the 2012 Headingley Test
WHAT WOULD YOU DO IF YOU WERE IN CHARGE OF COUNTY CRICKET? Introduce free hits for no-balls in four-day cricket
BIGGEST CRICKETING REGRET? Playing while I did my A-Levels
SURPRISING FACT ABOUT YOU? I am half-French
TWITTER: @DomSibley

Batting	Mat	Inns	NO	Runs	HS	Ave	SR	100	50	Ct	St
Tests	18	31	2	882	133*	30.41	35.53	2	4	10	0
First-class	86	146	13	5212	244	39.18	40.65	15	24	65	0
List A	22	20	2	416	115	23.11	78.19	1	0	10	0
T20s	35	32	3	859	74*	29.62	121.49	0	7	17	0
Bowling	**Mat**	**Balls**	**Runs**	**Wkts**	**BBI**	**BBM**	**Ave**	**Econ**	**SR**	**5w**	**10**
Tests	18	6	7	0	-	-	-	7.00	-	0	0
First-class	86	380	271	4	2/103	2/117	67.75	4.27	95.0	0	0
List A	22	54	62	1	1/20	1/20	62.00	6.88	54.0	0	0
T20s	35	228	338	5	2/33	2/33	67.60	8.89	45.6	0	0

PETER SIDDLE

RHB / RFM / R0 / W0

FULL NAME: Peter Matthew Siddle
BORN: November 25, 1984, Traralgon, Victoria, Australia
SQUAD NO: 64
HEIGHT: 6ft 2in
NICKNAME: Sid Vicious
TEAMS: Australia, Essex, Adelaide Strikers, Lancashire, Melbourne Renegades, Nottinghamshire, Tasmania, Victoria
ROLE: Bowler
DEBUT: Test: 2008; ODI: 2009; T20I: 2009; First-class: 2005; List A: 2005; T20: 2006

BEST BATTING: 103* Australia A vs Scotland, Edinburgh, 2013
BEST BOWLING: 8-54 Victoria vs South Australia, Adelaide, 2015
COUNTY CAP: 2014 (Nottinghamshire)

TWITTER: @petersiddle403
NOTES: The combatlve Australian seamer did not make it to the UK in 2020 because of travel restrictions but is due to return this summer to complete his two-year contract. Siddle will be available to play across all formats. The 36-year-old had a devastating impact in his first season at Chelmsford in 2018 (37 wickets at 16.41) and was superb again the following summer (34 at 20.09) to help Essex win the County Championship. After 221 wickets in 67 Tests, he retired from international cricket at the end of 2019. Last May Siddle joined Tasmania after 15 years at Victoria, and he continues to be a star performer for Adelaide Strikers in the Big Bash

Batting	Mat	Inns	NO	Runs	HS	Ave	SR	100	50	Ct	St
Tests	67	94	15	1164	51	14.73	47.16	0	2	19	0
ODIs	20	6	3	31	10*	10.33	103.33	0	0	1	0
T20Is	2	1	1	1	1*	-	100.00	0	0	0	0
First-class	184	247	47	3474	103*	17.37	50.56	1	6	58	0
List A	64	33	11	251	62	11.40	97.28	0	1	6	0
T20s	73	20	11	48	11	5.33	73.84	0	0	14	0
Bowling	**Mat**	**Balls**	**Runs**	**Wkts**	**BBI**	**BBM**	**Ave**	**Econ**	**SR**	**5w**	**10**
Tests	67	13907	6777	221	6/54	9/104	30.66	2.92	62.9	8	0
ODIs	20	901	743	17	3/55	3/55	43.70	4.94	53.0	0	0
T20Is	2	48	58	3	2/24	2/24	19.33	7.25	16.0	0	0
First-class	184	35630	17035	631	8/54	9/77	26.99	2.86	56.4	24	0
List A	64	3222	2553	76	4/27	4/27	33.59	4.75	42.3	0	0
T20s	73	1485	1812	78	5/16	5/16	23.23	7.32	19.0	1	0

RYAN SIDEBOTTOM RHB / RMF / R0 / W0

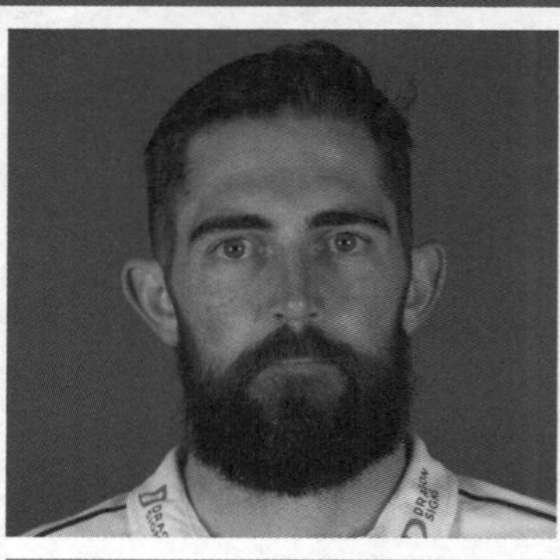

FULL NAME: Ryan Nathan Sidebottom
BORN: August 14, 1989, Shepparton, Victoria, Australia
SQUAD NO: 22
HEIGHT: 6ft 2in
NICKNAME: Siddy
EDUCATION: Wanganui Park Secondary College, Victoria, Australia
TEAMS: Warwickshire, Victoria
ROLE: Bowler
DEBUT: First-class: 2013

BEST BATTING: 27* Warwickshire vs Kent, Edgbaston, 2019
BEST BOWLING: 6-35 Warwickshire vs Northamptonshire, Northampton, 2018

CHILDHOOD SPORTING HERO? Glenn McGrath
BIGGEST INFLUENCE ON YOUR DEVELOPMENT AS A CRICKETER (EXCLUDING PARENTS)? My brothers
FIRST CRICKET CLUB? Northerners CC, Victoria, Australia. The club was formed after a merger between Tallygaroopna CC and Congupna CC in the early 2000s
MOST ECCENTRIC TEAMMATE? Henry Brookes – for his wardrobe
WHAT WOULD YOU DO IF YOU WERE PRIME MINISTER? Cut taxes, increase funding to the NHS, make physical education compulsory at school
STRANGEST THING YOU'VE DONE DURING LOCKDOWN? Shaving my head
SURPRISING FACT ABOUT YOU? I've got four brothers, one of whom plays Aussie rules for Collingwood. We grew up in Tallygaroopna near Melbourne, but I have a British passport because my mum moved to Devon
TWITTER: @ryansidebottom2

Batting	Mat	Inns	NO	Runs	HS	Ave	SR	100	50	Ct	St
First-class	21	30	16	100	27*	7.14	28.65	0	0	5	0
Bowling	**Mat**	**Balls**	**Runs**	**Wkts**	**BBI**	**BBM**	**Ave**	**Econ**	**SR**	**5w**	**10**
First-class	21	2783	1697	59	6/35	10/96	28.76	3.65	47.1	1	1

JOHN SIMPSON

LHB / WK / R0 / W0 / MVP38

FULL NAME: John Andrew Simpson
BORN: July 13, 1988, Bury, Lancashire
SQUAD NO: 20
HEIGHT: 5ft 11in
NICKNAME: Simmo
EDUCATION: St Gabriel's RC High School, Bury; Holy Cross College, Bury
TEAMS: Middlesex, England U19
ROLE: Wicketkeeper/batsman
DEBUT: First-class: 2009; List A: 2009; T20: 2009

BEST BATTING: 167* Middlesex vs Lancashire, Old Trafford, 2019

COUNTY CAP: 2011

CHILDHOOD SPORTING HERO? Tiger Woods
BIGGEST INFLUENCE ON YOUR DEVELOPMENT AS A CRICKETER (EXCLUDING PARENTS)? Grandpa – he supported me hugely in the lead-up to signing my first professional contract
FIRST CRICKET CLUB? Ramsbottom CC, Greater Manchester
IF YOU COULD TAKE ONE COUNTY CRICKETER'S BEST SHOT AND ADD IT TO YOUR OWN GAME? James Vince's clip off his legs
TOUGHEST OPPONENT IN COUNTY CRICKET? Graham Onions
WHAT WOULD YOU DO IF YOU WERE IN CHARGE OF COUNTY CRICKET? Encourage different types of pitches so that there is a variety
STRANGEST THING YOU'VE DONE DURING LOCKDOWN? Using my microwave for a shoulder press and nearly lifting it through the ceiling
FAVOURITE SMELL? Muffins out the oven
SURPRISING FACT ABOUT YOU? I don't drink tea or coffee
TWITTER: @johnsimpson_88

Batting	Mat	Inns	NO	Runs	HS	Ave	SR	100	50	Ct	St
First-class	160	254	39	6930	167*	32.23	47.49	7	39	486	25
List A	93	72	11	1587	82*	26.01	86.76	0	8	81	19
T20s	119	104	19	2063	84*	24.27	130.15	0	7	57	21
Bowling	**Mat**	**Balls**	**Runs**	**Wkts**	**BBI**	**BBM**	**Ave**	**Econ**	**SR**	**5w**	**10**
First-class	160	18	23	0	-	-	-	7.66	-	0	0
List A	93	-	-	-	-	-	-	-	-	-	-
T20s	119	-	-	-	-	-	-	-	-	-	-

PREM SISODIYA RHB / SLA / R0 / W0

FULL NAME: Prem Sisodiya
BORN: September 21, 1998, Cardiff, Wales
SQUAD NO: 32
HEIGHT: 5ft 11in
NICKNAME: Premo
EDUCATION: Clifton College, Bristol; Cardiff Metropolitan University
TEAMS: Glamorgan, England U19
ROLE: Bowler
DEBUT: First-class: 2018; T20: 2019

BEST BATTING: 38 Glamorgan vs Derbyshire, Swansea, 2018
BEST BOWLING: 4-79 Cardiff MCCU vs Somerset, Taunton, 2019

MOST EXCITING DAY AS A CRICKETER? Making my first-class debut in 2018
CHILDHOOD SPORTING HERO? Sachin Tendulkar
BIGGEST INFLUENCE ON YOUR DEVELOPMENT AS A CRICKETER (EXCLUDING PARENTS)? John Derrick, former Glamorgan allrounder and coach
FIRST CRICKET CLUB? Cardiff CC
IF YOU COULD TAKE ONE COUNTY CRICKETER'S BEST SHOT AND ADD IT TO YOUR OWN GAME? Babar Azam's run-down to third-man
TOUGHEST OPPONENT IN COUNTY CRICKET? Tony Palladino – I couldn't hit him off the square
MOST ECCENTRIC TEAMMATE? Callum Taylor – for his terrible hair colours
BIGGEST CRICKETING REGRET? Trying to switch-hit when I was on 97
WHAT WOULD YOU DO IF YOU WERE IN CHARGE OF COUNTY CRICKET? Create a new tournament based on football's FA Cup
STRANGEST THING YOU'VE DONE DURING LOCKDOWN? Trying to become a DJ
GUILTY PLEASURE? Nando's
TWITTER: @PremSisodiya

Batting	Mat	Inns	NO	Runs	HS	Ave	SR	100	50	Ct	St
First-class	4	7	1	83	38	13.83	48.82	0	0	2	0
T20s	11	2	2	4	4*	-	400.00	0	0	2	0
Bowling	**Mat**	**Balls**	**Runs**	**Wkts**	**BBI**	**BBM**	**Ave**	**Econ**	**SR**	**5w**	**10**
First-class	4	731	369	15	4/79	5/73	24.60	3.02	48.7	0	0
T20s	11	264	302	11	3/26	3/26	27.45	6.86	24.0	0	0

BEN SLATER

LHB / OB / R1 / W0

FULL NAME: Benjamin Thomas Slater
BORN: August 26, 1991, Chesterfield, Derbyshire
SQUAD NO: 26
HEIGHT: 5ft 11in
NICKNAME: Slats
EDUCATION: Netherthorpe School, Staveley; Leeds Metropolitan University
TEAMS: Nottinghamshire, Derbyshire, Leicestershire, Southern Rocks
ROLE: Batsman
DEBUT: First-class: 2012; List A: 2012; T20: 2012

BEST BATTING: 172 Leicestershire vs Lancashire, Worcester, 2020

MOST EXCITING DAY AS A CRICKETER? Chasing down 150 in 15 overs in the fourth innings against Lancashire during my loan spell at Leicestershire last summer
CHILDHOOD SPORTING HERO? Brian Lara
FIRST CRICKET CLUB? Chesterfield CC, Derbyshire
IF YOU COULD TAKE ONE COUNTY CRICKETER'S BEST SHOT AND ADD IT TO YOUR OWN GAME? Wayne Madsen's sweep
BIGGEST CRICKETING REGRET? Getting out for 99 against Middlesex in the first game of 2018
STRANGEST THING YOU'VE DONE DURING LOCKDOWN? Doing my girlfriend's make-up for her (it didn't end well)
IF YOU WERE AN ANIMAL, WHICH WOULD IT BE? An elephant
GUILTY PLEASURE? White-chocolate-chip cookies
TWITTER: @BennySlats

Batting	Mat	Inns	NO	Runs	HS	Ave	SR	100	50	Ct	St
First-class	88	161	7	5029	172	32.65	45.58	7	26	32	0
List A	36	33	4	1611	148*	55.55	86.98	5	9	3	0
T20s	11	11	0	236	57	21.45	105.82	0	1	0	0
Bowling	**Mat**	**Balls**	**Runs**	**Wkts**	**BBI**	**BBM**	**Ave**	**Econ**	**SR**	**5w**	**10**
First-class	88	105	113	0	-	-	-	6.45	-	0	0
List A	36	-	-	-	-	-	-	-	-	-	-
T20s	11	-	-	-	-	-	-	-	-	-	-

WILL SMEED RHB / OB / R0 / W0

FULL NAME: William Conrad Francis Smeed
BORN: October 26, 2001, Cambridge
SQUAD NO: 23
HEIGHT: 6ft
NICKNAME: Smeedy
EDUCATION: King's College, Taunton
TEAMS: Somerset, England U19
ROLE: Batsman
DEBUT: T20: 2020

MOST EXCITING DAY AS A CRICKETER? Making my first-team debut for Somerset in the T20 Blast last summer
CHILDHOOD SPORTING HERO? Jonny Wilkinson
IF YOU COULD TAKE ONE COUNTY CRICKETER'S BEST SHOT AND ADD IT TO YOUR OWN GAME? Tom Banton's reverse-sweep
MOST ECCENTRIC TEAMMATE? Ben Green – when he had his mullet and moustache
NOTES: The top-order batsman signed his first professional contract with Somerset last August, a two-year deal which runs until the end of the 2022 season. Smeed made his T20 debut for the club last summer and showed a glimpse of his talent with a 49-ball 82 which nearly carried Somerset to a target of 204 against Gloucestershire at Taunton. The 19-year-old, who also bowls off-spin, made his Second XI debut in 2018 but missed most of the following season because of a shoulder injury sustained while playing for England U19. In his first game back he scored a magnificent 243 from 260 balls for Somerset's U17 side. "Will has displayed the key characteristics of someone who has the ambition to get to the very top of the game," said Steve Snell, Somerset's Academy director. "He has some obvious strengths in his batting and many bowlers in the south-west will have seen the brute power and high levels of concentration which have enabled his impressive run-scoring in youth cricket to date"

Batting	Mat	Inns	NO	Runs	HS	Ave	SR	100	50	Ct	St
T20s	5	5	0	94	82	18.80	117.50	0	1	2	0
Bowling	**Mat**	**Balls**	**Runs**	**Wkts**	**BBI**	**BBM**	**Ave**	**Econ**	**SR**	**5w**	**10**
T20s	5	-	-	-	-	-	-	-	-	-	-

JAMIE SMITH

RHB / WK / R0 / W0

FULL NAME: Jamie Luke Smith
BORN: July 12, 2000, Epsom, Surrey
SQUAD NO: 11
HEIGHT: 6ft 2in
NICKNAME: Smudger
EDUCATION: Whitgift School, Croydon
TEAMS: Surrey
ROLE: Batsman/wicketkeeper
DEBUT: First-class: 2019; List A: 2019; T20: 2018

BEST BATTING: 127 Surrey vs MCC, Dubai, 2019

MOST EXCITING DAY AS A CRICKETER? The first day of a new season
CHILDHOOD SPORTING HERO? Mark Noble
FIRST CRICKET CLUB? Sutton CC, Surrey
BEST INNINGS YOU'VE SEEN? An opening partnership of nearly 200 between Aaron Finch and Jason Roy in the T20 against Middlesex at The Oval in 2018
IF YOU COULD TAKE ONE COUNTY CRICKETER'S BEST SHOT AND ADD IT TO YOUR OWN GAME? Mark Stoneman's pull
WHAT WOULD YOU DO IF YOU WERE IN CHARGE OF COUNTY CRICKET? Make lunch and tea longer
IF YOU WERE AN ANIMAL, WHICH WOULD IT BE? A dolphin
TWITTER: @jamiesm148

Batting	Mat	Inns	NO	Runs	HS	Ave	SR	100	50	Ct	St
First-class	14	25	2	739	127	32.13	48.04	1	3	13	2
List A	5	5	0	110	40	22.00	88.70	0	0	2	0
T20s	12	7	3	96	38*	24.00	95.04	0	0	6	0
Bowling	**Mat**	**Balls**	**Runs**	**Wkts**	**BBI**	**BBM**	**Ave**	**Econ**	**SR**	**5w**	**10**
First-class	14	-	-	-	-	-	-	-	-	-	-
List A	5	-	-	-	-	-	-	-	-	-	-
T20s	12	-	-	-	-	-	-	-	-	-	-

RUAIDHRI SMITH

RHB / RMF / R0 / W0

FULL NAME: Ruaidhri Alexander James Smith
BORN: August 5, 1994, Glasgow, Scotland
SQUAD NO: 20
HEIGHT: 6ft 2in
NICKNAME: Trotts
EDUCATION: The Cathedral School, Llandaff; Shrewsbury School; University of Bristol
TEAMS: Scotland, Glamorgan
ROLE: Bowler
DEBUT: ODI: 2016; T20I: 2019; First-class: 2013; List A: 2013; T20: 2014

BEST BATTING: 57* Glamorgan vs Gloucestershire, Bristol, 2014
BEST BOWLING: 5-87 Glamorgan vs Durham, Cardiff, 2018

CHILDHOOD SPORTING HERO? Jonny Wilkinson
BIGGEST INFLUENCE ON YOUR DEVELOPMENT AS A CRICKETER (EXCLUDING PARENTS)? Phil Makinson, my coach at St Fagans CC (Cardiff)
IF YOU COULD TAKE ONE COUNTY CRICKETER'S BEST SHOT AND ADD IT TO YOUR OWN GAME? David Lloyd's pull-hook
TOUGHEST OPPONENT IN COUNTY CRICKET? Babar Azam
WHAT WOULD YOU DO IF YOU WERE IN CHARGE OF COUNTY CRICKET? Bring back the 40-over competition, bring back the Lord's one-day final, increase the number of points for draws in the Championship
STRANGEST THING YOU'VE DONE DURING LOCKDOWN? Delivery driving
SURPRISING FACT ABOUT YOU? Born in Scotland, Irish mother, English father, raised in Wales
GUILTY PLEASURE? Doughnuts
TWITTER: @ruaidhrismith

Batting	Mat	Inns	NO	Runs	HS	Ave	SR	100	50	Ct	St
ODIs	2	1	0	10	10	10.00	166.66	0	0	0	0
T20Is	2	1	1	9	9*	-	128.57	0	0	0	0
First-class	30	44	6	681	57*	17.92	60.15	0	2	4	0
List A	18	11	3	71	14	8.87	92.20	0	0	4	0
T20s	25	13	7	89	22*	14.83	117.10	0	0	7	0
Bowling	**Mat**	**Balls**	**Runs**	**Wkts**	**BBI**	**BBM**	**Ave**	**Econ**	**SR**	**5w**	**10**
ODIs	2	90	97	1	1/34	1/34	97.00	6.46	90.0	0	0
T20Is	2	41	66	0	-	-	-	9.65	-	0	0
First-class	30	3576	2329	68	5/87	7/148	34.25	3.90	52.5	1	0
List A	18	572	591	18	4/7	4/7	32.83	6.19	31.7	0	0
T20s	25	429	595	20	4/6	4/6	29.75	8.32	21.4	0	0

TOM SMITH

RHB / SLA / R0 / W0 / MVP84

FULL NAME: Thomas Michael John Smith
BORN: August 29, 1987, Eastbourne, Sussex
SQUAD NO: 6
HEIGHT: 5ft 9in
NICKNAME: Smudge
EDUCATION: Seaford Head Community College, East Sussex; Sussex Downs College
TEAMS: Gloucestershire, Middlesex, Surrey, Sussex
ROLE: Bowler
DEBUT: First-class: 2007; List A: 2006; T20: 2007

BEST BATTING: 84 Gloucestershire vs Leicestershire, Cheltenham, 2019
BEST BOWLING: 4-35 Gloucestershire vs Kent, Canterbury, 2014
COUNTY CAP: 2013 (Gloucestershire)

MOST EXCITING DAY AS A CRICKETER? Beating Surrey in the One-Day Cup final at Lord's in 2015
CHILDHOOD SPORTING HERO? James Kirtley
BIGGEST INFLUENCE ON YOUR DEVELOPMENT AS A CRICKETER (EXCLUDING PARENTS)? I had some great coaches in my early years at Sussex but the most important for my career have been two Gloucestershire coaches: John Bracewell and Richard Dawson
FIRST CRICKET CLUB? Eastbourne CC, East Sussex
TOUGHEST OPPONENT IN COUNTY CRICKET? James Anderson – I had the honour of facing him on my Championship debut and he got me out in both innings
MOST ECCENTRIC TEAMMATE? Benny Howell and his 42 bowling variations
WHAT WOULD YOU DO IF YOU WERE IN CHARGE OF COUNTY CRICKET? Remove the lbw law that says it's not out if it pitches outside leg (if it's hitting, you're out); develop a water-resistant ball (bowling spin with a wet ball is rubbish); establish a more effective procedure than dragging the boundary rope around the outfield to dry it in between rain breaks
FAVOURITE SMELL? Nail-polish remover
GUILTY PLEASURE? Cookie butter

Batting	Mat	Inns	NO	Runs	HS	Ave	SR	100	50	Ct	St
First-class	50	69	13	1346	84	24.03	37.70	0	4	15	0
List A	83	42	19	513	65	22.30	74.78	0	1	36	0
T20s	138	50	35	294	36*	19.60	113.51	0	0	45	0
Bowling	**Mat**	**Balls**	**Runs**	**Wkts**	**BBI**	**BBM**	**Ave**	**Econ**	**SR**	**5w**	**10**
First-class	50	6845	3868	78	4/35	6/155	49.58	3.39	87.7	0	0
List A	83	3070	2766	68	4/26	4/26	40.67	5.40	45.1	0	0
T20s	138	2598	3167	137	5/16	5/16	23.11	7.31	18.9	3	0

SHANE SNATER RHB / RMF / R0 / W0

FULL NAME: Shane Snater
BORN: March 24, 1996, Harare, Zimbabwe
SQUAD NO: 29
EDUCATION: St John's College, Harare
TEAMS: Netherlands, Essex, Kent, Southern Rocks
ROLE: Bowler
DEBUT: ODI: 2018; T20I: 2018; First-class: 2016; List A: 2017; T20: 2018

BEST BATTING: 50* Netherlands vs Namibia, Dubai, 2017
BEST BOWLING: 5-45 Southern Rocks vs Matabeleland Tuskers, Harare, 2020

TWITTER: @ShaneSnater
NOTES: Essex signed the Netherlands seamer following a successful trial period at the club in 2018. Snater played a handful of games during the club's successful T20 campaign the following summer and appeared six times in last year's competition. The 25-year-old signed a one-year contract extension in November. "Shane is a trusted and reliable player," said Anthony McGrath, Essex's head coach. "Although he's not always found game-time easy to come by, he's always put in a shift whenever he's played." Snater grew up in Harare and represented Zimbabwe U17 but holds a Dutch passport and made his ODI and T20I debut for Netherlands in 2018. He signed for Zimbabwean side Southern Rocks last December and took eight wickets in his first red-ball game for the club, including his third five-wicket haul in just his fourth first-class match

Batting	Mat	Inns	NO	Runs	HS	Ave	SR	100	50	Ct	St
ODIs	2	2	0	12	12	6.00	85.71	0	0	3	0
T20Is	13	6	1	18	10	3.60	112.50	0	0	2	0
First-class	4	5	2	86	50*	28.66	72.88	0	1	1	0
List A	16	11	3	68	23*	8.50	76.40	0	0	10	0
T20s	25	11	5	49	16*	8.16	125.64	0	0	9	0
Bowling	**Mat**	**Balls**	**Runs**	**Wkts**	**BBI**	**BBM**	**Ave**	**Econ**	**SR**	**5w**	**10**
ODIs	2	71	63	1	1/41	1/41	63.00	5.32	71.0	0	0
T20Is	13	209	337	13	3/42	3/42	25.92	9.67	16.0	0	0
First-class	4	712	418	20	5/45	8/94	20.90	3.52	35.6	3	0
List A	16	627	561	14	5/60	5/60	40.07	5.36	44.7	1	0
T20s	25	395	664	22	3/42	3/42	30.18	10.08	17.9	0	0

NATHAN SOWTER RHB / LB / R0 / W0

FULL NAME: Nathan Adam Sowter
BORN: October 12, 1992, Penrith, New South Wales, Australia
SQUAD NO: 72
HEIGHT: 5ft 11in
NICKNAME: Racing Snake
EDUCATION: Hills Sport High School, New South Wales
TEAMS: Middlesex
ROLE: Bowler
DEBUT: First-class: 2017; List A: 2016; T20: 2015

BEST BATTING: 57* Middlesex vs Glamorgan, Cardiff, 2019
BEST BOWLING: 3-42 Middlesex vs Lancashire, Old Trafford, 2019

MOST EXCITING DAY AS A CRICKETER? Beating Sussex at Lord's in last year's T20 Blast after Tom Helm defended five runs off the last over
CHILDHOOD SPORTING HERO? Ricky Ponting
FIRST CRICKET CLUB? Rooty Hill RSL CC – a small club not far from where I grew up in western Sydney
WHAT WOULD YOU DO IF YOU WERE IN CHARGE OF COUNTY CRICKET? Ban red-ball cricket in April, make bigger boundaries in T20
STRANGEST THING YOU'VE DONE DURING LOCKDOWN? Doing squats using a bag full of beers as weights
SURPRISING FACT ABOUT YOU? I'm a glazier by trade
GUILTY PLEASURE? Coca-Cola
TWITTER: @nsowter

Batting	Mat	Inns	NO	Runs	HS	Ave	SR	100	50	Ct	St
First-class	10	17	3	246	57*	17.57	72.99	0	2	9	0
List A	19	12	3	134	31	14.88	76.13	0	0	17	0
T20s	64	21	8	85	13*	6.53	100.00	0	0	26	0
Bowling	**Mat**	**Balls**	**Runs**	**Wkts**	**BBI**	**BBM**	**Ave**	**Econ**	**SR**	**5w**	**10**
First-class	10	1462	795	18	3/42	4/100	44.16	3.26	81.2	0	0
List A	19	1008	928	36	6/62	6/62	25.77	5.52	28.0	1	0
T20s	64	1228	1655	56	4/23	4/23	29.55	8.08	21.9	0	0

BILLY STANLAKE

LHB / RFM / R0 / W0

FULL NAME: Billy Stanlake
BORN: November 4, 1994, Hervey Bay, Australia
SQUAD NO: TBC
HEIGHT: 6ft 8in
TEAMS: Australia, Derbyshire, Adelaide Strikers, Melbourne Stars, Queensland, Royal Challengers Bangalore, Sunrisers Hyderabad
ROLE: Bowler
DEBUT: ODI: 2017; T20I: 2017; First-class: 2015; List A: 2015; T20: 2015

BEST BATTING: 4* Queensland vs New South Wales, Sydney, 2019
BEST BOWLING: 3-50 Queensland vs South Australia, Brisbane, 2015

TWITTER: @BillyJS94
NOTES: Derbyshire have signed the 6ft 8in Australian fast bowler to play in all formats. Stanlake has played only seven first-class matches since making his debut in 2015, largely down to a series of back problems. In 2019 he was due to play for Derbyshire in the T20 Blast only to withdraw injured. But the 26-year-old has established himself in the shorter formats. He was called up to Australia's squad for his ODI and T20I debuts in early 2017 and made his first appearance in the IPL that same year, before helping Adelaide Strikers to their first Big Bash title in 2017/18. "There's not too many players of his quality available for all formats, so it's really pleasing to get him in," said Dave Houghton, Derbyshire's head of cricket. "He's tall and he bowls at a high pace with good bounce and variation. He's someone who has made his name with the white ball, but he's determined to show what he can do in first-class cricket as well. That hunger will be huge for us, and he's a great addition to our bowling attack"

Batting	Mat	Inns	NO	Runs	HS	Ave	SR	100	50	Ct	St
ODIs	7	5	2	4	2	1.33	14.28	0	0	1	0
T20Is	19	2	1	9	7	9.00	75.00	0	0	0	0
First-class	8	13	7	9	4*	1.50	11.11	0	0	2	0
List A	30	18	13	16	4*	3.20	19.51	0	0	5	0
T20s	76	15	12	30	7	10.00	65.21	0	0	8	0
Bowling	**Mat**	**Balls**	**Runs**	**Wkts**	**BBI**	**BBM**	**Ave**	**Econ**	**SR**	**5w**	**10**
ODIs	7	354	324	7	3/35	3/35	46.28	5.49	50.5	0	0
T20Is	19	420	544	27	4/8	4/8	20.14	7.77	15.5	0	0
First-class	8	1260	656	21	3/50	6/103	31.23	3.12	60.0	0	0
List A	30	1596	1368	35	4/24	4/24	39.08	5.14	45.6	0	0
T20s	76	1609	2149	81	4/8	4/8	26.53	8.01	19.8	0	0

MITCHELL STANLEY

RHB / RFM / R0 / W0

FULL NAME: Mitchell Terry Stanley
BORN: March 17, 2001, Telford, Shropshire
SQUAD NO: 38
HEIGHT: 6ft 4in
NICKNAME: Lurch
EDUCATION: Idsall School, Shifnal, Shropshire; Shrewsbury Sixth Form College
TEAMS: Worcestershire
ROLE: Bowler

MOST EXCITING DAY AS A CRICKETER? When I was told I was going to be offered a contract with Worcestershire in 2019
CHILDHOOD SPORTING HERO? Brett Lee
BIGGEST INFLUENCE ON YOUR DEVELOPMENT AS A CRICKETER (EXCLUDING PARENTS)? Luke Sharples – he has coached me all the way from the beginning and always seems to know what will work for me and what won't work for me
TOUGHEST OPPONENT IN COUNTY CRICKET? Hamish Rutherford
MOST ECCENTRIC TEAMMATE? Dillon Pennington – he doesn't know where his own feet are
WHAT WOULD YOU DO IF YOU WERE IN CHARGE OF COUNTY CRICKET? Implement a rule that bowlers can deliver the ball from 18 yards once a batsman gets passed 100; No.10 and 11 in the batting order score double runs
NOTES: The 20-year-old fast bowler signed his first professional contract with Worcestershire in November 2019 after overcoming a series of injuries and making his Second XI debut earlier that year. Stanley is a product of the club's Academy and has featured in age-group cricket for Shropshire. He is yet to make his senior debut but signed a new one-year deal in December. "Mitchell is raw but now part of that exciting bowling group and should, as [this] season goes on, be pushing the other guys and knocking on the door," said Alan Richardson, Worcestershire's bowling coach. "You watch him, and there are some real raw materials there. He is nice and tall, and is getting more athletic and stronger the more time he spends with us. He has got that little bit of devil in his eye where you think, 'He's got that fast bowler's mentality'"

CAMERON STEEL

RHB / LB / R0 / W0

DURHAM

FULL NAME: Cameron Tate Steel
BORN: September 13, 1995, Greenbrae, California, USA
SQUAD NO: 14
HEIGHT: 5ft 10in
NICKNAME: Moggy
EDUCATION: Millfield Prep School, Somerset; Scotch College, Perth, Australia; Durham University
TEAMS: Durham
ROLE: Batsman
DEBUT: First-class: 2014; List A: 2017; T20: 2017

BEST BATTING: 224 Durham vs Leicestershire, Leicester, 2017
BEST BOWLING: 2-7 Durham vs Glamorgan, Cardiff, 2018

BIGGEST INFLUENCE ON YOUR DEVELOPMENT AS A CRICKETER (EXCLUDING PARENTS)? David Beale, my first coach at school in Somerset. He convinced me to stop playing chess and start attending cricket practice
FIRST CRICKET CLUB? Glastonbury CC, Somerset
IF YOU COULD TAKE ONE COUNTY CRICKETER'S BEST SHOT AND ADD IT TO YOUR OWN GAME? Dawid Malan's cut shot
TOUGHEST OPPONENT IN COUNTY CRICKET? Ollie Robinson (Sussex). He seems to make a lot of front pads magnetic to leather
WHAT WOULD YOU DO IF YOU WERE IN CHARGE OF COUNTY CRICKET? Hold a round of Championship games overseas or in Ireland/Scotland, allow 12 players per side (as with Second XI cricket)
STRANGEST THING YOU'VE DONE DURING LOCKDOWN? Running a half-marathon in a hotel room during a 14-day quarantine
TWITTER: @CameronSteel2

Batting	Mat	Inns	NO	Runs	HS	Ave	SR	100	50	Ct	St
First-class	40	70	2	2007	224	29.51	40.55	3	11	18	0
List A	11	10	1	181	77	20.11	67.03	0	1	1	0
T20s	6	6	0	93	37	15.50	125.67	0	0	2	0
Bowling	**Mat**	**Balls**	**Runs**	**Wkts**	**BBI**	**BBM**	**Ave**	**Econ**	**SR**	**5w**	**10**
First-class	40	856	638	21	2/7	4/99	30.38	4.47	40.7	0	0
List A	11	30	47	0	-	-	-	9.40	-	0	0
T20s	6	48	88	2	2/60	2/60	44.00	11.00	24.0	0	0

SCOTT STEEL

RHB / OB / R0 / W0

FULL NAME: Scott Steel
BORN: April 20, 1999, Durham
SQUAD NO: 55
HEIGHT: 6ft
NICKNAME: Steely
EDUCATION: Belmont Community School, Durham, New College Durham
TEAMS: Leicestershire, Durham
ROLE: Batsman
DEBUT: First-class: 2019; List A: 2019; T20: 2019

BEST BATTING: 39 Durham vs Middlesex, Lord's, 2019

MOST EXCITING DAY AS A CRICKETER? Equalling the record for the fastest T20 fifty for Durham
CHILDHOOD SPORTING HERO? AB de Villiers
FIRST CRICKET CLUB? Durham City CC
IF YOU COULD TAKE ONE CRICKETER'S BEST SHOT AND ADD IT TO YOUR OWN GAME? AB de Villiers' sweep over fine-leg
TOUGHEST OPPONENT IN COUNTY CRICKET? Tim Murtagh at Lord's
WHAT WOULD YOU DO IF YOU WERE IN CHARGE OF COUNTY CRICKET? Set up a T10 competition, bring in Super Overs, play music for boundaries and wickets in Championship cricket
WHAT WOULD YOU DO IF YOU WERE PRIME MINISTER? Lower taxes, reduce house prices
STRANGEST THING YOU'VE DONE DURING LOCKDOWN? Baking a cake
FAVOURITE SMELL? Christmas candles
IF YOU WERE AN ANIMAL, WHICH WOULD IT BE? A seal – chubby and lazy like me
GUILTY PLEASURE? Takeaways
TWITTER: @scottsteel102

Batting	Mat	Inns	NO	Runs	HS	Ave	SR	100	50	Ct	St
First-class	2	4	0	48	39	12.00	71.64	0	0	1	0
List A	8	7	0	227	68	32.42	80.78	0	2	3	0
T20s	21	17	0	409	70	24.05	132.36	0	2	2	0
Bowling	**Mat**	**Balls**	**Runs**	**Wkts**	**BBI**	**BBM**	**Ave**	**Econ**	**SR**	**5w**	**10**
First-class	2	42	16	0	-	-	-	2.28	-	0	0
List A	8	54	53	1	1/38	1/38	53.00	5.88	54.0	0	0
T20s	21	240	274	11	3/20	3/20	24.90	6.85	21.8	0	0

KENT

DARREN STEVENS RHB / RM / R3 / W4 / MVP15

FULL NAME: Darren Ian Stevens
BORN: April 30, 1976, Leicester
SQUAD NO: 3
HEIGHT: 5ft 11in
NICKNAME: Stevo
EDUCATION: John Cleveland College, Hinckley; Charles Keene College, Leicester
TEAMS: Kent, Comilla Victorians, Derbyshire, Dhaka Gladiators, Leicestershire, Mid West Rhinos, Otago
ROLE: Allrounder
DEBUT: First-class: 1997; List A: 1997; T20: 2003

BEST BATTING: 237 Kent vs Yorkshire, Headingley, 2019
BEST BOWLING: 8-75 Kent vs Leicestershire, Canterbury, 2017
COUNTY CAP: 2002 (Leicestershire); 2005 (Kent); BENEFIT: 2016 (Kent)

MOST EXCITING DAY AS A CRICKETER? T20 Finals Day in 2007 at Edgbaston
CHILDHOOD SPORTING HERO? Michael Jordan
BIGGEST INFLUENCE ON YOUR DEVELOPMENT AS A CRICKETER (EXCLUDING PARENTS)? My former teammate turned coach Neil Burns
FIRST CRICKET CLUB? Swallows Green CC, Hinckley, Leicestershire
IF YOU COULD TAKE ONE COUNTY CRICKETER'S BEST SHOT AND ADD IT TO YOUR OWN GAME? Alastair Cook's pull
TOUGHEST OPPONENT IN COUNTY CRICKET? Glen Chapple – he never gave away any freebies
WHAT WOULD YOU DO IF YOU WERE IN CHARGE OF COUNTY CRICKET? Make the County Championship one division, bring back 40-over cricket, scrap the pink ball
FAVOURITE SMELL? A log fire
SURPRISING FACT ABOUT YOU? I am colour blind with browns, reds and greens. I struggled when I was with Otago in New Zealand because there were no sightscreens!
TWITTER: @Stevo208

Batting	Mat	Inns	NO	Runs	HS	Ave	SR	100	50	Ct	St
First-class	308	482	30	15710	237	34.75		34	79	200	0
List A	314	289	31	7612	147	29.50		7	46	127	0
T20s	212	191	40	4001	90	26.49	136.41	0	17	66	0
Bowling	**Mat**	**Balls**	**Runs**	**Wkts**	**BBI**	**BBM**	**Ave**	**Econ**	**SR**	**5w**	**10**
First-class	308	28979	13472	546	8/75		24.67	2.78	53.0	29	2
List A	314	6383	5114	160	6/25	6/25	31.96	4.80	39.8	3	0
T20s	212	2248	2968	114	4/14	4/14	26.03	7.92	19.7	0	0

RYAN STEVENSON

RHB / RFM / R0 / W0

FULL NAME: Ryan Anthony Stevenson
BORN: April 2, 1992, Torquay
SQUAD NO: 47
HEIGHT: 6ft 2in
NICKNAME: Raz
EDUCATION: King Edward VI Community College, Devon
TEAMS: Hampshire
ROLE: Bowler
DEBUT: First-class: 2015; List A: 2016; T20: 2016

BEST BATTING: 51 Hampshire vs Surrey, The Oval, 2019
BEST BOWLING: 4-70 Hampshire vs Middlesex, Radlett, 2020

MOST EXCITING DAY AS A CRICKETER? Making my first-class debut in 2015
FAMILY TIES? My dad has played for Devon over-50s
CHILDHOOD SPORTING HERO? Shaun Pollock
FIRST CRICKET CLUB? Dartington & Totnes CC, Devon
IF YOU COULD TAKE ONE COUNTY CRICKETER'S BEST SHOT AND ADD IT TO YOUR OWN GAME? The Aneurin Donald back-hand slice
WHAT WOULD YOU DO IF YOU WERE IN CHARGE OF COUNTY CRICKET? Introduce an FA Cup-style knockout competition
WHAT WOULD YOU DO IF YOU WERE PRIME MINISTER? Scrap political parties and ban mobile phones
IF YOU WERE AN ANIMAL, WHICH WOULD IT BE? A snow leopard or a cow – my two favourite animals
GUILTY PLEASURE? Chicken dippers and a Galaxy Smooth Milk
TWITTER: @ryanstevenson47

Batting	Mat	Inns	NO	Runs	HS	Ave	SR	100	50	Ct	St
First-class	7	7	1	124	51	20.66	51.23	0	1	1	0
List A	3	1	0	0	0	0.00	0.00	0	0	0	0
T20s	21	11	5	54	17	9.00	120.00	0	0	4	0
Bowling	**Mat**	**Balls**	**Runs**	**Wkts**	**BBI**	**BBM**	**Ave**	**Econ**	**SR**	**5w**	**10**
First-class	7	773	460	9	4/70	4/70	51.11	3.57	85.8	0	0
List A	3	120	142	2	1/28	1/28	71.00	7.10	60.0	0	0
T20s	21	369	586	14	2/28	2/28	41.85	9.52	26.3	0	0

GRANT STEWART

RHB / RFM / R0 / W0

FULL NAME: Grant Stewart
BORN: February 19, 1994, Kalgoorlie, Western Australia, Australia
SQUAD NO: 9
HEIGHT: 6ft 3in
NICKNAME: Stewie
EDUCATION: All Saints College, New South Wales; University of Newcastle, NSW
TEAMS: Kent
ROLE: Allrounder
DEBUT: First-class: 2017; List A: 2018; T20: 2018

BEST BATTING: 103 Kent vs Middlesex, Canterbury, 2018
BEST BOWLING: 6-22 Kent vs Middlesex, Canterbury, 2018

MOST EXCITING DAY AS A CRICKETER? My first-class debut for Kent against Glamorgan at Canterbury in 2017
CHILDHOOD SPORTING HERO? Steve Waugh
BIGGEST INFLUENCE ON YOUR DEVELOPMENT AS A CRICKETER (EXCLUDING PARENTS)? My older brothers
SURPRISING FACT ABOUT YOU? I was a wicketkeeper until I was 16
TWITTER: @GStewart195

Batting	Mat	Inns	NO	Runs	HS	Ave	SR	100	50	Ct	St
First-class	21	32	4	671	103	23.96	66.04	1	4	3	0
List A	5	4	1	69	44	23.00	62.72	0	0	1	0
T20s	15	12	5	86	21*	12.28	100.00	0	0	4	0
Bowling	**Mat**	**Balls**	**Runs**	**Wkts**	**BBI**	**BBM**	**Ave**	**Econ**	**SR**	**5w**	**10**
First-class	21	2497	1407	44	6/22	8/58	31.97	3.38	56.7	1	0
List A	5	242	152	8	3/17	3/17	19.00	3.76	30.2	0	0
T20s	15	282	420	9	2/23	2/23	46.66	8.93	31.3	0	0

BEN STOKES

LHB / RFM / R0 / W0

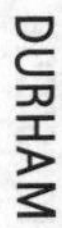

FULL NAME: Benjamin Andrew Stokes
BORN: June 4, 1991, Christchurch, New Zealand
SQUAD NO: 38
HEIGHT: 6ft 2in
NICKNAME: Stoker
EDUCATION: Cockermouth School, Cumbria
TEAMS: England, Durham, Melbourne Renegades, Rajasthan Royals, Rising Pune Supergiant
ROLE: Allrounder
DEBUT: Test: 2013; ODI: 2011; T20I: 2011; First-class: 2010; List A: 2009; T20: 2010

BEST BATTING: 258 England vs South Africa, Cape Town, 2016
BEST BOWLING: 7-67 Durham vs Sussex, Chester-le-Street, 2014

CHILDHOOD SPORTING HERO? Herschelle Gibbs
FIRST CRICKET CLUB? Cockermouth CC, Cumbria
SURPRISING FACT ABOUT YOU? My father played one Test match for New Zealand in rugby league. I was a right-handed batsman when I was younger
TWITTER: @benstokes38

Batting	Mat	Inns	NO	Runs	HS	Ave	SR	100	50	Ct	St
Tests	71	130	5	4631	258	37.04	58.12	10	24	81	0
ODIs	95	81	15	2682	102*	40.63	93.94	3	20	45	0
T20Is	29	25	6	358	47*	18.84	134.08	0	0	14	0
First-class	147	251	13	8424	258	35.39	-	18	43	122	0
List A	166	145	24	4583	164	37.87	96.56	7	27	76	0
T20s	134	123	20	2668	107*	25.90	136.12	2	9	59	0
Bowling	**Mat**	**Balls**	**Runs**	**Wkts**	**BBI**	**BBM**	**Ave**	**Econ**	**SR**	**5w**	**10**
Tests	71	9275	5115	163	6/22	8/161	31.38	3.30	56.9	4	0
ODIs	95	2912	2920	70	5/61	5/61	41.71	6.01	41.6	1	0
T20Is	29	418	611	16	3/26	3/26	38.18	8.77	26.1	0	0
First-class	147	17162	9864	335	7/67	10/121	29.44	3.44	51.2	7	1
List A	166	4587	4407	134	5/61	5/61	32.88	5.76	34.2	1	0
T20s	134	1657	2350	72	4/16	4/16	32.63	8.50	23.0	0	0

OLLY STONE

RHB / RF / R0 / W0

WARWICKSHIRE

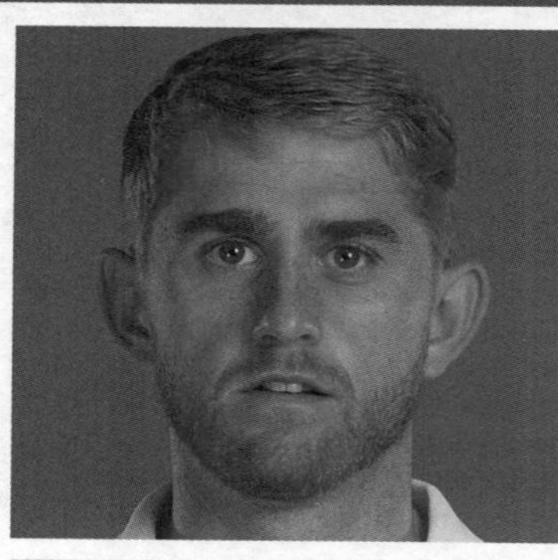

FULL NAME: Oliver Peter Stone
BORN: October 9, 1993, Norwich
SQUAD NO: 6
HEIGHT: 6ft 2in
NICKNAME: Stoney
EDUCATION: Thorpe St Andrew High School, Norwich; Moulton College, Northamptonshire
TEAMS: England, Warwickshire, Northamptonshire
ROLE: Bowler
DEBUT: Test: 2019; ODI: 2018; First-class: 2012; List A: 2012; T20: 2011

BEST BATTING: 60 Northamptonshire vs Kent, Northampton, 2016
BEST BOWLING: 8-80 Warwickshire vs Sussex, Edgbaston, 2018

FIRST CRICKET CLUB? Vauxhall Mallards CC, Norfolk. Home of the ducks
BEST INNINGS YOU'VE SEEN? David Willey's 27-ball 60 for my former county Northants in the 2013 final of the T20 Blast
WHAT WOULD YOU DO IF YOU WERE IN CHARGE OF COUNTY CRICKET? Allow bowlers to put their feet up after a spell
SURPRISING FACT ABOUT YOU? My great-grandad created the Twix chocolate bar
TWITTER: @ollystone2

Batting	Mat	Inns	NO	Runs	HS	Ave	SR	100	50	Ct	St
Tests	2	4	0	20	19	5.00	52.63	0	0	1	0
ODIs	4	1	1	9	9*	-	128.57	0	0	0	0
First-class	39	51	11	610	60	15.25	48.48	0	1	17	0
List A	30	14	9	122	24*	24.40	70.93	0	0	13	0
T20s	51	16	9	66	22*	9.42	110.00	0	0	14	0
Bowling	**Mat**	**Balls**	**Runs**	**Wkts**	**BBI**	**BBM**	**Ave**	**Econ**	**SR**	**5w**	**10**
Tests	2	208	97	7	3/29	4/68	13.85	2.79	29.7	0	0
ODIs	4	96	97	1	1/23	1/23	97.00	6.06	96.0	0	0
First-class	39	5834	3225	134	8/80	11/96	24.06	3.31	43.5	6	1
List A	30	1125	1023	24	4/71	4/71	42.62	5.45	46.8	0	0
T20s	51	948	1405	48	3/22	3/22	29.27	8.89	19.7	0	0

MARK STONEMAN

LHB / OB / R5 / W0

FULL NAME: Mark Daniel Stoneman
BORN: June 26, 1987, Newcastle
SQUAD NO: 23
HEIGHT: 5ft 10in
NICKNAME: Rocky
EDUCATION: Whickham Comprehensive School, Newcastle Upon Tyne
TEAMS: England, Surrey, Durham
ROLE: Batsman
DEBUT: Test: 2017; First-class: 2007; List A: 2008; T20: 2010

BEST BATTING: 197 Surrey vs Sussex, Guildford, 2017

COUNTY CAP: 2018 (Surrey)

MOST EXCITING DAY AS A CRICKETER? Captaining the Durham side which won the 2014 One-Day Cup at Lord's
FAMILY TIES? Grandfather played and umpired locally for many years. Dad played all over the north-east as a local pro
SURPRISING FACT ABOUT YOU? The Lion King makes me cry
TWITTER: @mark23stone

Batting	Mat	Inns	NO	Runs	HS	Ave	SR	100	50	Ct	St
Tests	11	20	1	526	60	27.68	44.27	0	5	1	0
First-class	194	339	8	11286	197	34.09	57.49	23	58	89	0
List A	82	78	5	2763	144*	37.84	92.74	6	17	23	0
T20s	73	67	4	1284	89*	20.38	118.01	0	7	28	0
Bowling	**Mat**	**Balls**	**Runs**	**Wkts**	**BBI**	**BBM**	**Ave**	**Econ**	**SR**	**5w**	**10**
Tests	11	-	-	-	-	-	-	-	-	-	-
First-class	194	216	165	0	-	-	-	4.58	-	0	0
List A	82	4	8	1	1/8	1/8	8.00	12.00	4.0	0	0
T20s	73	-	-	-	-	-	-	-	-	-	-

HARRY SWINDELLS

RHB / WK / R0 / W0

FULL NAME: Harry John Swindells
BORN: February 21, 1999, Leicester
SQUAD NO: 28
HEIGHT: 5ft 8in
NICKNAME: Dumbo
EDUCATION: Brockington College, Leicestershire; Lutterworth College; Loughborough College
TEAMS: Leicestershire, England U19
ROLE: Wicketkeeper/batsman
DEBUT: First-class: 2019; List A: 2018; T20: 2018

BEST BATTING: 52* Leicestershire vs Nottinghamshire, Leicester, 2020

CHILDHOOD SPORTING HERO? AB de Villiers
BIGGEST INFLUENCE ON YOUR DEVELOPMENT AS A CRICKETER (EXCLUDING PARENTS)? Mick Whitmore and Daz Hill – my first coaches in club cricket
FIRST CRICKET CLUB? Narborough & Littlethorpe CC, Leicestershire
IF YOU COULD TAKE ONE COUNTY CRICKETER'S BEST SHOT AND ADD IT TO YOUR OWN GAME? Adam Lyth's pull
TOUGHEST OPPONENT IN COUNTY CRICKET? Ben Coad – he doesn't bowl bad balls
WHAT WOULD YOU DO IF YOU WERE IN CHARGE OF COUNTY CRICKET? Increase the number of four-day games in the middle of the summer
STRANGEST THING YOU'VE DONE DURING LOCKDOWN? Enjoying going for a run
FAVOURITE SMELL? A roast dinner
GUILTY PLEASURE? Ben and Jerry's ice cream
TWITTER: @harryswindells1

Batting	Mat	Inns	NO	Runs	HS	Ave	SR	100	50	Ct	St
First-class	12	17	2	356	52*	23.73	41.01	0	1	23	1
List A	4	2	0	43	28	21.50	79.62	0	0	2	0
T20s	18	16	1	281	63	18.73	109.76	0	3	6	0
Bowling	**Mat**	**Balls**	**Runs**	**Wkts**	**BBI**	**BBM**	**Ave**	**Econ**	**SR**	**5w**	**10**
First-class	12	-	-	-	-	-	-	-	-	-	-
List A	4	-	-	-	-	-	-	-	-	-	-
T20s	18	-	-	-	-	-	-	-	-	-	-

JONATHAN TATTERSALL

RHB / WK / R0 / W0

FULL NAME: Jonathan Andrew Tattersall
BORN: December 15, 1994, Harrogate, Yorkshire
SQUAD NO: 12
HEIGHT: 5ft 8in
NICKNAME: Tatts
EDUCATION: King James's School, Knaresborough
TEAMS: Yorkshire, England U19
ROLE: Wicketkeeper/batsman
DEBUT: First-class: 2018; List A: 2013; T20: 2018

BEST BATTING: 135* Yorkshire vs Leeds/Bradford MCCU, Weetwood, 2019

MOST EXCITING DAY AS A CRICKETER? Beating Surrey at Scarborough in the penultimate over of the 2019 Championship match
CHILDHOOD SPORTING HERO? Michael Vaughan
BIGGEST INFLUENCE ON YOUR DEVELOPMENT AS A CRICKETER (EXCLUDING PARENTS)? Two people: Tim Boon who helped my batting while I was with England U19, and Yorkshire Academy coach Richard Damms who helped me understand the game better
IF YOU COULD TAKE ONE COUNTY CRICKETER'S BEST SHOT AND ADD IT TO YOUR OWN GAME? Jos Buttler's reverse-sweep
FAVOURITE SMELL? Freshly cut grass – then you know it's the cricket season
GUILTY PLEASURE? Sour sweets
TWITTER: @JonnyTatts

Batting	Mat	Inns	NO	Runs	HS	Ave	SR	100	50	Ct	St
First-class	27	41	4	1273	135*	34.40	40.64	1	8	64	4
List A	15	11	2	375	89	41.66	112.95	0	4	16	3
T20s	31	22	8	364	53*	26.00	126.82	0	1	22	6
Bowling	**Mat**	**Balls**	**Runs**	**Wkts**	**BBI**	**BBM**	**Ave**	**Econ**	**SR**	**5w**	**10**
First-class	27	-	-	-	-	-	-	-	-	-	-
List A	15	-	-	-	-	-	-	-	-	-	-
T20s	31	-	-	-	-	-	-	-	-	-	-

BRAD TAYLOR

RHB / OB / R0 / W0

FULL NAME: Bradley Jacob Taylor
BORN: March 14, 1997, Winchester, Hampshire
SQUAD NO: 93
HEIGHT: 6ft
NICKNAME: Techno
EDUCATION: Eggar's School, Alton, Hampshire; Alton College
TEAMS: Hampshire, England U19
ROLE: Bowler
DEBUT: First-class: 2013; List A: 2013; T20: 2014

BEST BATTING: 36 Hampshire vs Cardiff MCCU, Southampton, 2016
BEST BOWLING: 4-64 Hampshire vs Lancashire, Southport, 2013

FIRST CRICKET CLUB? Holybourne CC, Hampshire
CHILDHOOD SPORTING HERO? Daniel Vettori
SURPRISING FACT ABOUT YOU? I'm a massive Southampton fan and I go to the home games whenever I can
TWITTER: @bradtay93
NOTES: A former England U19 captain, Taylor became the youngest player to represent Hampshire since 1867 when he made his debut in 2013 aged 16 years and 154 days. But he has struggled to establish himself as a first-team regular at the Ageas Bowl since then. The 24-year-old made only three appearances in 2019 – two in the T20 Blast and a solitary outing in the One-Day Cup – and none at all during last year's truncated season

Batting	Mat	Inns	NO	Runs	HS	Ave	SR	100	50	Ct	St
First-class	6	10	3	133	36	19.00	44.63	0	0	2	0
List A	18	15	5	355	69	35.50	65.74	0	3	7	0
T20s	8	4	1	23	9*	7.66	82.14	0	0	3	0
Bowling	**Mat**	**Balls**	**Runs**	**Wkts**	**BBI**	**BBM**	**Ave**	**Econ**	**SR**	**5w**	**10**
First-class	6	798	544	13	4/64	4/106	41.84	4.09	61.3	0	0
List A	18	852	661	15	4/26	4/26	44.06	4.65	56.8	0	0
T20s	8	104	128	4	2/20	2/20	32.00	7.38	26.0	0	0

CALLUM TAYLOR

RHB / OB / R0 / W0

FULL NAME: Callum Zinzan Taylor
BORN: June 19, 1998, Newport, Monmouthshire
SQUAD NO: 4
HEIGHT: 6ft
EDUCATION: The Southport School, Queensland, Australia
TEAMS: Glamorgan
ROLE: Allrounder
DEBUT: First-class: 2020; T20: 2019

BEST BATTING: 106 Glamorgan vs Northamptonshire, Northampton, 2020
BEST BOWLING: 1-20 Glamorgan vs Northamptonshire, Northampton, 2020

MOST EXCITING DAY AS A CRICKETER? Scoring a hundred on my first-class debut at Northampton last year
CHILDHOOD SPORTING HERO? Michael Clarke
FIRST CRICKET CLUB? Surfers Paradise CC, Queensland, Australia
IF YOU COULD TAKE ONE COUNTY CRICKETER'S BEST SHOT AND ADD IT TO YOUR OWN GAME? Jason Roy's on-drive
WHAT WOULD YOU DO IF YOU WERE IN CHARGE OF COUNTY CRICKET? Create a knockout competition like the FA Cup to be played in Abu Dhabi and Dubai in the winter
WHAT WOULD YOU DO IF YOU WERE PRIME MINISTER? Attend cricket matches
STRANGEST THING YOU'VE DONE DURING LOCKDOWN? Dying my hair white
FAVOURITE SMELL? Lavender
GUILTY PLEASURE? Waffles
TWITTER: @CallumZTaylor

Batting	Mat	Inns	NO	Runs	HS	Ave	SR	100	50	Ct	St
First-class	2	4	0	153	106	38.25	67.10	1	0	0	0
T20s	11	10	3	99	23	14.14	90.82	0	0	5	0
Bowling	**Mat**	**Balls**	**Runs**	**Wkts**	**BBI**	**BBM**	**Ave**	**Econ**	**SR**	**5w**	**10**
First-class	2	156	81	2	1/20	1/20	40.50	3.11	78.0	0	0
T20s	11	42	52	3	2/9	2/9	17.33	7.42	14.0	0	0

JACK TAYLOR

RHB / OB / R0 / W0

FULL NAME: Jack Martin Robert Taylor
BORN: November 12, 1991, Banbury, Oxfordshire
SQUAD NO: 10
HEIGHT: 6ft
NICKNAME: JT
EDUCATION: Chipping Norton School, Oxfordshire
TEAMS: Gloucestershire
ROLE: Batsman
DEBUT: First-class: 2010; List A: 2011; T20: 2011

BEST BATTING: 156 Gloucestershire vs Northamptonshire, Cheltenham, 2015
BEST BOWLING: 4-16 Gloucestershire vs Glamorgan, Bristol, 2016
COUNTY CAP: 2010

MOST EXCITING DAY AS A CRICKETER? Beating Surrey in the One-Day Cup final at Lord's in 2015
BIGGEST INFLUENCE ON YOUR DEVELOPMENT AS A CRICKETER (EXCLUDING PARENTS)? John Bracewell, my former coach at Gloucestershire. He gave me an opportunity and supported me through my issues with my bowling action
FIRST CRICKET CLUB? Great & Little Tew CC, Oxfordshire
TOUGHEST OPPONENT IN COUNTY CRICKET? Brett D'Oliveira
WHAT WOULD YOU DO IF YOU WERE IN CHARGE OF COUNTY CRICKET? Organise a knockout one-day competition which includes Minor Counties
WHAT WOULD YOU DO IF YOU WERE PRIME MINISTER? Sort out government guidance on nutrition and diet, which is currently stuck in the stone age
STRANGEST THING YOU'VE DONE DURING LOCKDOWN? Shadow-batting in my bedroom while wearing my club kit
GUILTY PLEASURE? Getting into bed at 7pm
TWITTER: @jacktaylor141

Batting	Mat	Inns	NO	Runs	HS	Ave	SR	100	50	Ct	St
First-class	79	122	9	3300	156	29.20	61.86	7	9	40	0
List A	51	41	8	1100	75	33.33	118.27	0	9	22	0
T20s	91	72	21	1061	80	20.80	143.76	0	2	28	0
Bowling	**Mat**	**Balls**	**Runs**	**Wkts**	**BBI**	**BBM**	**Ave**	**Econ**	**SR**	**5w**	**10**
First-class	79	5716	3345	75	4/16	5/140	44.60	3.51	76.2	0	0
List A	51	1185	1027	29	4/38	4/38	35.41	5.20	40.8	0	0
T20s	91	634	862	26	4/16	4/16	33.15	8.15	24.3	0	0

JAMES TAYLOR

RHB / RFM / R0 / W0

FULL NAME: James Philip Arthur Taylor
BORN: January 19, 2001, Stoke-on-Trent, Staffordshire
SQUAD NO: 25
HEIGHT: 6ft 3in
NICKNAME: JT
EDUCATION: Trentham High School, Stoke-on-Trent; Newcastle-under-Lyme College, Staffordshire
TEAMS: Surrey, Derbyshire, England U19
ROLE: Bowler
DEBUT: First-class: 2017; List A: 2019; T20: 2020

BEST BATTING: 22 Surrey vs Essex, Chelmsford, 2020
BEST BOWLING: 3-26 Derbyshire vs Leeds/Bradford MCCU, Derby, 2019

MOST EXCITING DAY AS A CRICKETER? Making my first-class debut for Surrey last summer
CHILDHOOD SPORTING HERO? James Anderson
FIRST CRICKET CLUB? Barlaston CC, Staffordshire. Always stay on the front foot because the wicket is slow and low at Barlaston
BEST INNINGS YOU'VE SEEN? Wayne Madsen's Championship hundred against Northants at Chesterfield in 2018. On a turning wicket, he made it look easy
IF YOU COULD TAKE ONE COUNTY CRICKETER'S BEST SHOT AND ADD IT TO YOUR OWN GAME? Hashim Amla's drive
TOUGHEST OPPONENT IN COUNTY CRICKET? Phil Salt – he hit me for 28 in my first-ever over in T20 cricket
MOST ECCENTRIC TEAMMATE? Gareth Batty – he has lots of energy all the time
STRANGEST THING YOU'VE DONE DURING LOCKDOWN? Letting my dad cut my hair
GUILTY PLEASURE? Dairy Milk Oreo
TWITTER: @_Jamestaylor19

Batting	Mat	Inns	NO	Runs	HS	Ave	SR	100	50	Ct	St
First-class	5	7	3	45	22	11.25	34.61	0	0	1	0
List A	1	1	1	6	6*	-	100.00	0	0	0	0
T20s	2	1	0	3	3	3.00	50.00	0	0	0	0
Bowling	**Mat**	**Balls**	**Runs**	**Wkts**	**BBI**	**BBM**	**Ave**	**Econ**	**SR**	**5w**	**10**
First-class	5	516	322	11	3/26	6/74	29.27	3.74	46.9	0	0
List A	1	42	66	2	2/66	2/66	33.00	9.42	21.0	0	0
T20s	2	12	34	1	1/6	1/6	34.00	17.00	12.0	0	0

MATT TAYLOR

RHB / LMF / R0 / W1

FULL NAME: Matthew David Taylor
BORN: July 8, 1994, Banbury, Oxfordshire
SQUAD NO: 36
HEIGHT: 6ft 2in
NICKNAME: Bomber
EDUCATION: Chipping Norton Secondary School, Oxfordshire
TEAMS: Gloucestershire
ROLE: Bowler
DEBUT: First-class: 2013; List A: 2011; T20: 2015

BEST BATTING: 48 Gloucestershire vs Glamorgan, Bristol, 2018
BEST BOWLING: 5-15 Gloucestershire vs Cardiff MCCU, Bristol, 2018
COUNTY CAP: 2013

FAMILY TIES? My older brother Jack also plays for Gloucestershire. My dad and grandad both played Minor Counties for Oxfordshire
CHILDHOOD SPORTING HERO? Darren Gough
BIGGEST INFLUENCE ON YOUR DEVELOPMENT AS A CRICKETER (EXCLUDING PARENTS)? Rupert Evans – he first selected me to play Minor Counties for Oxfordshire when I was very young
FIRST CRICKET CLUB? Great & Little Tew CC, Oxfordshire
TOUGHEST OPPONENT IN COUNTY CRICKET? Martin Guptill – he once got a double hundred and hit us all round Bristol during a four-day match
STRANGEST THING YOU'VE DONE DURING LOCKDOWN? Chipping golf balls down the hallway into a bed sheet hanging off the door frame
GUILTY PLEASURE? Pizza
TWITTER: @matt_taylor94

Batting	Mat	Inns	NO	Runs	HS	Ave	SR	100	50	Ct	St
First-class	57	74	30	557	48	12.65	41.56	0	0	7	0
List A	28	9	6	41	16	13.66	87.23	0	0	5	0
T20s	38	9	5	28	9*	7.00	82.35	0	0	7	0
Bowling	**Mat**	**Balls**	**Runs**	**Wkts**	**BBI**	**BBM**	**Ave**	**Econ**	**SR**	**5w**	**10**
First-class	57	8715	5064	153	5/15	7/133	33.09	3.48	56.9	5	0
List A	28	1251	1174	20	3/39	3/39	58.70	5.63	62.5	0	0
T20s	38	689	1011	34	3/16	3/16	29.73	8.80	20.2	0	0

TOM TAYLOR RHB / RMF / R0 / W0 / MVP83

FULL NAME: Thomas Alexander Ian Taylor
BORN: December 21, 1994, Stoke-on-Trent, Staffordshire
SQUAD NO: 12
HEIGHT: 6ft 3in
NICKNAME: TT
EDUCATION: Trentham High School, Stoke-on-Trent; Newcastle-under-Lyme College; Leeds Metropolitan University
TEAMS: Northamptonshire, Derbyshire, Leicestershire
ROLE: Allrounder
DEBUT: First-class: 2014; List A 2014; T20: 2020

BEST BATTING: 80 Derbyshire vs Kent, Derby, 2016
BEST BOWLING: 6-47 Leicestershire vs Sussex, Hove, 2019

FAMILY TIES? My father, cousins and uncles all play cricket; other family members used to run my home club. My brother James used to play for Derbyshire and now plays for Surrey
CHILDHOOD SPORTING HERO? David Beckham
FIRST CRICKET CLUB? Barlaston CC, Stoke-on-Trent, Staffordshire
IF YOU COULD TAKE ONE COUNTY CRICKETER'S BEST SHOT AND ADD IT TO YOUR OWN GAME? Wayne Madsen's glide over the keeper
WHAT WOULD YOU DO IF YOU WERE IN CHARGE OF COUNTY CRICKET? Give all counties the same budget, stick with a three-division County Championship
STRANGEST THING YOU'VE DONE DURING LOCKDOWN? Road-biking
GUILTY PLEASURE? Harry Potter
TWITTER: @TomTaylor43

Batting	Mat	Inns	NO	Runs	HS	Ave	SR	100	50	Ct	St
First-class	33	49	8	821	80	20.02	45.25	0	4	8	0
List A	12	7	2	242	98*	48.40	113.61	0	2	6	0
T20s	7	7	1	120	50*	20.00	142.85	0	1	3	0
Bowling	**Mat**	**Balls**	**Runs**	**Wkts**	**BBI**	**BBM**	**Ave**	**Econ**	**SR**	**5w**	**10**
First-class	33	5242	3084	96	6/47	10/122	32.12	3.52	54.6	3	1
List A	12	602	602	13	3/48	3/48	46.30	6.00	46.3	0	0
T20s	7	96	137	4	2/38	2/38	34.25	8.56	24.0	0	0

RYAN TEN DOESCHATE RHB / RM / R1 / W0 / MVP93

FULL NAME: Ryan Neil ten Doeschate
BORN: June 30, 1980, Port Elizabeth, SA
SQUAD NO: 27
HEIGHT: 5ft 11in
EDUCATION: University of Cape Town
TEAMS: Netherlands, Essex, Adelaide Strikers, Canterbury, Comilla Victorians, Dhaka Dynamites, Kolkata Knight Riders, Lahore Qalandars, Otago, Rajshahi Kings, Western Province
ROLE: Allrounder
DEBUT: ODI: 2006; T20I: 2008; First-class: 2003; List A: 2003; T20: 2003

BEST BATTING: 259* Netherlands vs Canada, Pretoria, 2006
BEST BOWLING: 6-20 Netherlands vs Canada, Pretoria, 2006
COUNTY CAP: 2006

TWITTER: @rtendo27
NOTES: The veteran Netherlands allrounder became Essex skipper in 2016 and immediately led the club to Championship promotion and then the title in successive seasons. After winning a second Championship trophy in 2019, the 40-year-old handed over the four-day captaincy to Tom Westley and was back in the ranks to help Essex secure the Bob Willis Trophy last summer. He was also the club's leading run-scorer in the T20 Blast, scoring 255 runs in eight matches. This will be his 19th season at Chelmsford. Ten Doeschate has played T20 cricket all over the globe, including for Kolkata Knight Riders in the IPL. For Netherlands he scored four consecutive hundreds in the ICC Intercontinental Cup in 2006, including a competition-record 259 not out against Canada in Pretoria. He made a century against England at Nagpur in the 2011 World Cup, becoming the first Netherlands batsman to make a hundred in the World Cup finals, and scored a second hundred against Ireland at Kolkata

Batting	Mat	Inns	NO	Runs	HS	Ave	SR	100	50	Ct	St
ODIs	33	32	9	1541	119	67.00	87.70	5	9	13	0
T20Is	22	22	10	533	59	44.41	133.25	0	3	4	0
First-class	193	282	39	10984	259*	45.20	-	29	50	118	0
List A	225	189	55	6053	180	45.17	-	11	31	68	0
T20s	369	329	78	7524	121*	29.97	134.06	2	34	131	0
Bowling	**Mat**	**Balls**	**Runs**	**Wkts**	**BBI**	**BBM**	**Ave**	**Econ**	**SR**	**5w**	**10**
ODIs	33	1580	1327	55	4/31	4/31	24.12	5.03	28.7	0	0
T20Is	22	210	245	13	3/23	3/23	18.84	7.00	16.1	0	0
First-class	193	10988	7207	213	6/20	-	33.83	3.93	51.5	7	0
List A	225	5469	5257	174	5/50	5/50	30.21	5.76	31.4	1	0
T20s	369	2147	2922	114	4/24	4/24	25.63	8.16	18.8	0	0

AARON THOMASON RHB / RFM / R0 / W0

FULL NAME: Aaron Dean Thomason
BORN: June 26, 1997, Birmingham
SQUAD NO: 24
HEIGHT: 5ft 10in
NICKNAME: Thomo
EDUCATION: Barr Beacon School, Walsall
TEAMS: Sussex, England U19, Warwickshire
ROLE: Allrounder
DEBUT: First-class: 2019; List A: 2014; T20: 2016

BEST BATTING: 90 Sussex vs Worcestershire, Kidderminster, 2019
BEST BOWLING: 2-107 Sussex vs Australia A, Arundel, 2019

MOST EXCITING DAY AS A CRICKETER? Making my Warwickshire debut at Lord's
FAMILY TIES? We are members of Sutton Coldfield CC, where my brother plays and my whole family go to watch each Saturday. My great-grandad watched us play all the time. He left me some medals he was awarded for service in the war which I treasure
CHILDHOOD SPORTING HERO? Andrew Flintoff
SURPRISING FACT ABOUT YOU? Me and Chris Woakes went to the same school – it was a non-cricket-playing school

Batting	Mat	Inns	NO	Runs	HS	Ave	SR	100	50	Ct	St
First-class	7	14	0	240	90	17.14	42.25	0	1	2	0
List A	17	13	6	176	28	25.14	98.32	0	0	6	0
T20s	32	24	7	309	47	18.17	128.75	0	0	13	0

Bowling	Mat	Balls	Runs	Wkts	BBI	BBM	Ave	Econ	SR	5w	10
First-class	7	451	358	4	2/107	2/119	89.50	4.76	112.7	0	0
List A	17	388	460	14	4/45	4/45	32.85	7.11	27.7	0	0
T20s	32	372	670	24	3/33	3/33	27.91	10.80	15.5	0	0

JORDAN THOMPSON LHB / RMF / R0 / W0 / MVP14

FULL NAME: Jordan Aaron Thompson
BORN: October 9, 1996, Leeds
SQUAD NO: 44
HEIGHT: 6ft 1in
NICKNAME: Lizard
EDUCATION: Benton Park School, Leeds
TEAMS: Yorkshire
ROLE: Allrounder
DEBUT: First-class: 2019; List A: 2019; T20: 2018

BEST BATTING: 98 Yorkshire vs Nottinghamshire, Trent Bridge, 2020
BEST BOWLING: 5-31 Yorkshire vs Leicestershire, Headingley, 2020

MOST EXCITING DAY AS A CRICKETER? Making my Yorkshire T20 debut at Worcester in 2018
CHILDHOOD SPORTING HERO? Andrew Flintoff
BIGGEST INFLUENCE ON YOUR DEVELOPMENT AS A CRICKETER (EXCLUDING PARENTS)? All my Academy coaches at Yorkshire – over the last 10 years they've helped me develop to the level of the first-team squad
IF YOU COULD TAKE ONE COUNTY CRICKETER'S BEST SHOT AND ADD IT TO YOUR OWN GAME? Ian Bell's cover-drive
TOUGHEST OPPONENT IN COUNTY CRICKET? Morné Morkel
MOST ECCENTRIC TEAMMATE? Harry Brook – he names each of his bats
STRANGEST THING YOU'VE DONE DURING LOCKDOWN? Shaving my hair, very badly
SURPRISING FACT ABOUT YOU? I am a Type 1 diabetic
GUILTY PLEASURE? A McDonald's on the journey back after an away win
TWITTER: @Tommo455

Batting	Mat	Inns	NO	Runs	HS	Ave	SR	100	50	Ct	St
First-class	7	9	1	270	98	33.75	61.08	0	2	2	0
List A	1	-	-	-	-	-	-	-	-	0	0
T20s	26	20	8	202	50	16.83	151.87	0	1	8	0
Bowling	**Mat**	**Balls**	**Runs**	**Wkts**	**BBI**	**BBM**	**Ave**	**Econ**	**SR**	**5w**	**10**
First-class	7	864	351	20	5/31	5/51	17.55	2.43	43.2	1	0
List A	1	30	43	0	-	-	-	8.60	-	0	0
T20s	26	426	640	20	3/23	3/23	32.00	9.01	21.3	0	0

ALEX THOMSON

RHB / OB / R0 / W0

FULL NAME: Alexander Thomas Thomson
BORN: October 30, 1993, Stoke-on-Trent, Staffordshire
SQUAD NO: 29
HEIGHT: 6ft 5in
NICKNAME: Sarge
EDUCATION: Denstone College, Uttoxeter, Staffordshire; Cardiff Metropolitan University
TEAMS: Warwickshire
ROLE: Allrounder
DEBUT: First-class: 2014; List A: 2018; T20: 2018

BEST BATTING: 46 Warwickshire vs Northamptonshire, Edgbaston, 2020
BEST BOWLING: 6-138 Cardiff MCCU vs Hampshire, Southampton, 2017

MOST EXCITING DAY AS A CRICKETER? My Championship debut against Yorkshire at Headingley in 2017
CHILDHOOD SPORTING HERO? Ricky Hatton
BIGGEST INFLUENCE ON YOUR DEVELOPMENT AS A CRICKETER (EXCLUDING PARENTS)? Former wicketkeeper/batsman Tony Frost, now Warwickshire's batting coach. He gives you all the time in the world and only wants the best for you
FIRST CRICKET CLUB? Leek CC, Staffordshire
IF YOU COULD TAKE ONE COUNTY CRICKETER'S BEST SHOT AND ADD IT TO YOUR OWN GAME? Eoin Morgan's reverse-sweep
TOUGHEST OPPONENT IN COUNTY CRICKET? Moeen Ali – he's a 360-degree batsman
STRANGEST THING YOU'VE DONE DURING LOCKDOWN? Learning how to tile
FAVOURITE SMELL? Fig
SURPRISING FACT ABOUT YOU? I'm an avid angler
TWITTER: @tommo1039

Batting	Mat	Inns	NO	Runs	HS	Ave	SR	100	50	Ct	St
First-class	14	18	0	316	46	17.55	41.52	0	0	5	0
List A	9	8	2	258	68*	43.00	92.47	0	2	3	0
T20s	11	6	3	39	14	13.00	108.33	0	0	3	0
Bowling	**Mat**	**Balls**	**Runs**	**Wkts**	**BBI**	**BBM**	**Ave**	**Econ**	**SR**	**5w**	**10**
First-class	14	1261	771	20	6/138	7/176	38.55	3.66	63.0	1	0
List A	9	450	379	13	3/27	3/27	29.15	5.05	34.6	0	0
T20s	11	204	277	10	4/35	4/35	27.70	8.14	20.4	0	0

CHARLIE THURSTON RHB / RM / R0 / W0

FULL NAME: Charlie Oliver Thurston
BORN: August 17, 1996, Cambridge
SQUAD NO: 96
HEIGHT: 6ft
NICKNAME: Chazza
EDUCATION: Bedford School; Loughborough University
TEAMS: Northamptonshire
ROLE: Batsman
DEBUT: First-class: 2016; List A: 2018; T20: 2018

BEST BATTING: 126 Loughborough MCCU vs Northamptonshire, Northampton, 2017

CHILDHOOD SPORTING HERO? John Terry
FIRST CRICKET CLUB? Shenley Village CC, Hertfordshire. I can just about remember meeting Brian Lara when West Indies and Pakistan once played a warm-up there
TOUGHEST OPPONENT IN COUNTY CRICKET? The combination of Craig Overton and Josh Davey when we played Somerset last year. That was the toughest spell of bowling I've faced
WHAT WOULD YOU DO IF YOU WERE IN CHARGE OF COUNTY CRICKET? Keep with a red-ball final at Lord's, make it a three-division Championship with promotion and relegation so that more teams have something to play for
STRANGEST THING YOU'VE DONE DURING LOCKDOWN? Falling off my road bike three times in a week. The bike was a write-off after the third incident
GUILTY PLEASURE? Listening to Stephen A Smith and Skip Bayless debating US sports
TWITTER: @ThurstonCharlie

Batting	Mat	Inns	NO	Runs	HS	Ave	SR	100	50	Ct	St
First-class	13	18	0	593	126	32.94	61.51	2	2	4	0
List A	4	4	0	128	53	32.00	90.78	0	1	1	0
T20s	8	7	0	98	41	14.00	102.08	0	0	5	0
Bowling	**Mat**	**Balls**	**Runs**	**Wkts**	**BBI**	**BBM**	**Ave**	**Econ**	**SR**	**5w**	**10**
First-class	13	18	16	0	-	-	-	5.33	-	0	0
List A	4	-	-	-	-	-	-	-	-	-	-
T20s	8	-	-	-	-	-	-	-	-	-	-

JOSH TONGUE

RHB / RMF / R0 / W0

FULL NAME: Joshua Charles Tongue
BORN: November 15, 1997, Redditch, Worcestershire
SQUAD NO: 24
HEIGHT: 6ft 4in
NICKNAME: Tonguey
EDUCATION: King's School, Worcester; Christopher Whitehead Language College, Worcester
TEAMS: Worcestershire, England U19
ROLE: Bowler
DEBUT: First-class: 2016; List A: 2017; T20: 2017

BEST BATTING: 41 Worcestershire vs Glamorgan, Worcester, 2017
BEST BOWLING: 6-97 Worcestershire vs Glamorgan, Worcester, 2017

MOST EXCITING DAY AS A CRICKETER? Getting called up to the England Lions squad after my first season in professional cricket
CHILDHOOD SPORTING HERO? Andrew Flintoff
BIGGEST INFLUENCE ON YOUR DEVELOPMENT AS A CRICKETER (EXCLUDING PARENTS)? Former Worcestershire allrounder Gavin Haynes – he was my first coach at the club's Academy and he's happy to help out even now
FIRST CRICKET CLUB? Redditch CC, Worcestershire
IF YOU COULD TAKE ONE COUNTY CRICKETER'S BEST SHOT AND ADD IT TO YOUR OWN GAME? Anyone's
TOUGHEST OPPONENT IN COUNTY CRICKET? Kane Williamson
FAVOURITE SMELL? A new car
GUILTY PLEASURE? A bar of Galaxy from the freezer
TWITTER: @JoshTongue

Batting	Mat	Inns	NO	Runs	HS	Ave	SR	100	50	Ct	St
First-class	35	46	9	393	41	10.62	45.22	0	0	4	0
List A	13	7	3	76	34	19.00	95.00	0	0	2	0
T20s	5	2	2	3	2*	-	150.00	0	0	2	0
Bowling	**Mat**	**Balls**	**Runs**	**Wkts**	**BBI**	**BBM**	**Ave**	**Econ**	**SR**	**5w**	**10**
First-class	35	5508	3037	124	6/97	9/98	24.49	3.30	44.4	5	0
List A	13	529	600	14	2/35	2/35	42.85	6.80	37.7	0	0
T20s	5	84	122	3	2/32	2/32	40.66	8.71	28.0	0	0

REECE TOPLEY RHB / LFM

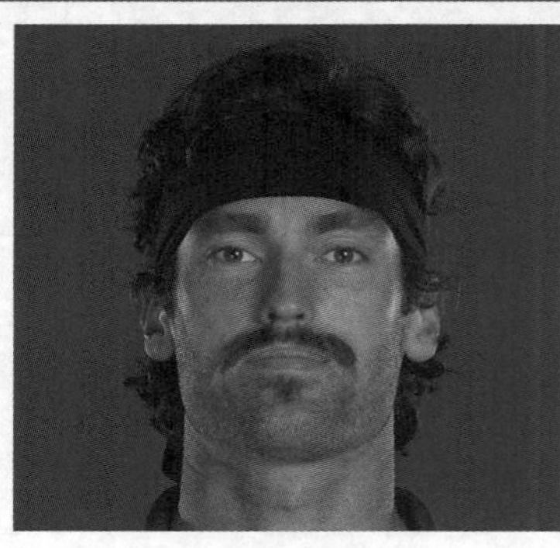

FULL NAME: Reece James William Topley
BORN: February 21, 1994, Ipswich
SQUAD NO: 24
HEIGHT: 6ft 7in
NICKNAME: Toppers
EDUCATION: Royal Hospital School, Suffolk
TEAMS: England, Surrey, Essex, Hampshire
ROLE: Bowler
DEBUT: ODI: 2015; T20I: 2015; First-class: 2011; List A: 2011; T20: 2012

BEST BATTING: 5* Essex vs Middlesex, Richmond, 2015 (T20)
BEST BOWLING: 4-20 Surrey vs Hampshire, Southampton, 2020 (T20)
COUNTY CAP: 2013 (Essex)

MOST EXCITING DAY AS A CRICKETER? Taking 4-50 for England in an ODI against South Africa in Port Elizabeth
FAMILY TIES? My father Don played for Essex and Surrey and also coached Zimbabwe. My uncle Peter played for Kent
CHILDHOOD SPORTING HERO? Kobe Bryant
BIGGEST INFLUENCE ON YOUR DEVELOPMENT AS A CRICKETER (EXCLUDING PARENTS)? Chris Silverwood, my bowling coach when I was at Essex
STRANGEST THING YOU'VE DONE DURING LOCKDOWN? Drinking a Bulgarian pale ale
SURPRISING FACT ABOUT YOU? I speak Spanish
TWITTER: @reece_topley
NOTES: Surrey signed Topley on a white-ball contract in October 2019

Batting	Mat	Inns	NO	Runs	HS	Ave	SR	100	50	Ct	St
ODIs	11	5	4	7	6	7.00	17.50	0	0	3	0
T20Is	6	1	1	1	1*	-	50.00	0	0	1	0
First-class	36	43	20	100	16	4.34	19.45	0	0	8	0
List A	56	17	11	54	19	9.00	47.78	0	0	14	0
T20s	85	15	10	22	5*	4.40	56.41	0	0	19	0
Bowling	**Mat**	**Balls**	**Runs**	**Wkts**	**BBI**	**BBM**	**Ave**	**Econ**	**SR**	**5w**	**10**
ODIs	11	517	441	17	4/50	4/50	25.94	5.11	30.4	0	0
T20Is	6	103	173	5	3/24	3/24	34.60	10.07	20.6	0	0
First-class	36	6101	3482	133	6/29	11/85	26.18	3.42	45.8	7	2
List A	56	2612	2397	94	4/16	4/16	25.50	5.50	27.7	0	0
T20s	85	1779	2423	116	4/20	4/20	20.88	8.17	15.3	0	0

PETER TREGO RHB / RM / R1 / W1 / MVP100

FULL NAME: Peter David Trego
BORN: June 12, 1981, Weston-super-Mare
SQUAD NO: 77
HEIGHT: 6ft
NICKNAME: Pirate
EDUCATION: Wyvern School, Weston-super-Mare
TEAMS: Nottinghamshire, Central Districts, England Lions, Kent, Mashonaland Eagles, Middlesex, Somerset, Sylhet Royals
ROLE: Allrounder
DEBUT: First-class: 2000; List A: 1999; T20: 2003

BEST BATTING: 154* Somerset vs Lancashire, Old Trafford, 2016
BEST BOWLING: 7-84 Somerset vs Yorkshire, Headingley, 2014
COUNTY CAP: 2007 (Somerset); BENEFIT: 2015 (Somerset)

CHILDHOOD SPORTING HERO? Robin Smith
FIRST CRICKET CLUB? Two clubs: Weston-super-Mare CC and Uphill Castle CC. I played juniors in the morning for WSM and then walked over the road in the afternoon to play men's cricket for Uphill
IF YOU COULD TAKE ONE COUNTY CRICKETER'S BEST SHOT AND ADD IT TO YOUR OWN GAME? Robin Smith's cut
TOUGHEST OPPONENT IN COUNTY CRICKET? Graeme Hick
MOST ECCENTRIC TEAMMATE? Steve Kirby – he's as mad as a box of frogs
WHAT WOULD YOU DO IF YOU WERE IN CHARGE OF COUNTY CRICKET? I wouldn't change a great deal, though I would ask Barry Hearne to market the game. He's done fantastic things with other sports, particularly darts
STRANGEST THING YOU'VE DONE DURING LOCKDOWN? Realising that the leaders of the western world are among the most incompetent and crooked of all
TWITTER: @tregs140

Batting	Mat	Inns	NO	Runs	HS	Ave	SR	100	50	Ct	St
First-class	223	332	38	9644	154*	32.80	-	15	54	90	0
List A	198	176	25	4962	147	32.86	-	10	26	55	0
T20s	202	187	22	4002	94*	24.25	125.84	0	21	54	0
Bowling	**Mat**	**Balls**	**Runs**	**Wkts**	**BBI**	**BBM**	**Ave**	**Econ**	**SR**	**5w**	**10**
First-class	223	25198	14359	395	7/84	-	36.35	3.41	63.7	5	1
List A	198	6007	5574	171	5/40	5/40	32.59	5.56	35.1	2	0
T20s	202	1728	2451	78	4/27	4/27	31.42	8.51	22.1	0	0

LIAM TREVASKIS

RHB / SLA / R0 / W0

FULL NAME: Liam Trevaskis
BORN: April 18, 1999, Carlisle, Cumberland
SQUAD NO: 80
HEIGHT: 5ft 10in
NICKNAME: T-rev
EDUCATION: Queen Elizabeth Grammar School, Penrith, Cumbria
TEAMS: Durham, England U19
ROLE: Allrounder
DEBUT: First-class: 2017; List A: 2019; T20: 2017

BEST BATTING: 64 Durham vs Leicestershire, Leicester, 2019
BEST BOWLING: 2-96 Durham vs Leicestershire, Chester-le-Street, 2019

MOST EXCITING DAY AS A CRICKETER? Playing in a T20 win against Lancashire on Sky in 2018
CHILDHOOD SPORTING HERO? Kumar Sangakkara
BIGGEST INFLUENCE ON YOUR DEVELOPMENT AS A CRICKETER (EXCLUDING PARENTS)? My brother – no one has thrown more balls at me
FIRST CRICKET CLUB? Penrith CC, Cumbria
IF YOU COULD TAKE ONE COUNTY CRICKETER'S BEST SHOT AND ADD IT TO YOUR OWN GAME? Wayne Madsen's lean-back ramp over the keeper
TOUGHEST OPPONENT IN COUNTY CRICKET? Ravichandran Ashwin – I came up against him on my first-class debut and I didn't know what ball he was going to bowl next
MOST ECCENTRIC TEAMMATE? Mark Wood – a very "out there" person, as I'm sure you've all seen
WHAT WOULD YOU DO IF YOU WERE IN CHARGE OF COUNTY CRICKET? Meet with all the county players and their backroom staff
WHAT WOULD YOU DO IF YOU WERE PRIME MINISTER? Consider the whole of the UK when making decisions
TWITTER: @LiamTrevaskis

Batting	Mat	Inns	NO	Runs	HS	Ave	SR	100	50	Ct	St
First-class	11	19	1	406	64	22.55	36.15	0	2	2	0
List A	8	3	0	16	16	5.33	84.21	0	0	0	0
T20s	31	21	7	144	31*	10.28	100.00	0	0	20	0
Bowling	**Mat**	**Balls**	**Runs**	**Wkts**	**BBI**	**BBM**	**Ave**	**Econ**	**SR**	**5w**	**10**
First-class	11	1053	536	7	2/96	3/116	76.57	3.05	150.4	0	0
List A	8	252	187	7	2/37	2/37	26.71	4.45	36.0	0	0
T20s	31	505	605	27	4/16	4/16	22.40	7.18	18.7	0	0

MUJEEB UR RAHMAN RHB / OB

FULL NAME: Mujeeb Ur Rahman
BORN: March 28, 2001, Khost, Afghanistan
SQUAD NO: 88
TEAMS: Afghanistan, Middlesex, Boost Defenders, Brisbane Heat, Comilla Victorians, Hampshire, Jamaica Tallawahs, Kings XI Punjab, Nangarhar Leopards, Peshawar Zalmi
ROLE: Bowler
DEBUT: Test: 2018; ODI: 2017; T20I: 2018; First-class: 2018; List A: 2017; T20: 2017

BEST BATTING: 27 Brisbane Heat vs Adelaide Strikers, Brisbane, 2018 (T20)
BEST BOWLING: 5-15 Brisbane Heat vs Hobart Hurricanes, 2020 (T20)

TWITTER: @MujeebR99
NOTES: The Afghan mystery spinner returns for his second T20 Blast campaign with Middlesex after taking seven wickets in 2019 at the miserly economy rate of 7.23 runs per over. The 20-year-old was due to feature for the club last summer only for the pandemic to scupper the deal. As of March 2021 Mujeeb was No.3 in the ICC T20I bowling rankings. He previously played for Hampshire in 2018 and has also impressed in the IPL and Big Bash League for Kings XI Punjab and Brisbane Heat respectively. An off-spinner with a leg-break and googly in his locker, Mujeeb burst onto the scene at the 2018 U19 World Cup and has since been a regular at senior level. In February 2018 he became the youngest player to take an ODI five-wicket haul and later that year played in Afghanistan's inaugural Test match – to date his only first-class appearance. Mujeeb will also feature as an overseas player for Northern Superchargers in The Hundred

Batting	Mat	Inns	NO	Runs	HS	Ave	SR	100	50	Ct	St
Tests	1	2	0	18	15	9.00	105.88	0	0	0	0
ODIs	43	23	12	88	18*	8.00	88.88	0	0	6	0
T20Is	19	3	3	8	8*	-	100.00	0	0	4	0
First-class	1	2	0	18	15	9.00	105.88	0	0	0	0
List A	50	25	14	92	18*	8.36	91.08	0	0	7	0
T20s	136	38	21	161	27	9.47	101.89	0	0	30	0
Bowling	**Mat**	**Balls**	**Runs**	**Wkts**	**BBI**	**BBM**	**Ave**	**Econ**	**SR**	**5w**	**10**
Tests	1	90	75	1	1/75	1/75	75.00	5.00	90.0	0	0
ODIs	43	2333	1543	70	5/50	5/50	22.04	3.96	33.3	1	0
T20Is	19	432	443	25	4/15	4/15	17.72	6.15	17.2	0	0
First-class	1	90	75	1	1/75	1/75	75.00	5.00	90.0	0	0
List A	50	2717	1790	78	5/50	5/50	22.94	3.95	34.8	1	0
T20s	136	3090	3453	147	5/15	5/15	23.48	6.70	21.0	1	0

GLOUCESTERSHIRE

GRAEME VAN BUUREN RHB / SLA / R0 / W0 / MVP43

FULL NAME: Graeme Lourens van Buuren
BORN: August 22, 1990, Pretoria, South Africa
SQUAD NO: 12
HEIGHT: 5ft 7in
NICKNAME: GV
EDUCATION: Pretoria Boys High School, South Africa
TEAMS: Gloucestershire, Northerns, Titans, South Africa U19
ROLE: Allrounder
DEBUT: First-class: 2010; List A: 2010; T20: 2011

BEST BATTING: 235 Northerns vs Eastern Province, Centurion, 2015
BEST BOWLING: 4-12 Northerns vs South Western Districts, Oudtshoorn, 2013
COUNTY CAP: 2016

MOST EXCITING DAY AS A CRICKETER? Winning promotion with Gloucestershire in 2019
CHILDHOOD SPORTING HERO? AB de Villiers
FIRST CRICKET CLUB? Tuks CC, Pretoria, South Africa
IF YOU COULD TAKE ONE COUNTY CRICKETER'S BEST SHOT AND ADD IT TO YOUR OWN GAME? Chris Dent's pull
TOUGHEST OPPONENT IN COUNTY CRICKET? Craig Overton
WHAT WOULD YOU DO IF YOU WERE IN CHARGE OF COUNTY CRICKET? Keep with this year's Championship structure, look at staging tournaments in Dubai
STRANGEST THING YOU'VE DONE DURING LOCKDOWN? Having a braai in the snow
GUILTY PLEASURE? Biltong
TWITTER: @GraemeGVB

Batting	Mat	Inns	NO	Runs	HS	Ave	SR	100	50	Ct	St
First-class	90	140	21	4955	235	41.63	61.16	10	30	49	0
List A	70	62	12	1454	119*	29.08	81.09	1	7	18	0
T20s	67	47	16	698	64	22.51	117.50	0	4	29	0
Bowling	**Mat**	**Balls**	**Runs**	**Wkts**	**BBI**	**BBM**	**Ave**	**Econ**	**SR**	**5w**	**10**
First-class	90	6011	2872	88	4/12	6/87	32.63	2.86	68.3	0	0
List A	70	2208	1754	52	5/35	5/35	33.73	4.76	42.4	1	0
T20s	67	961	1099	45	5/8	5/8	24.42	6.86	21.3	1	0

TIMM VAN DER GUGTEN RHB / RFM / R0 / W1 / MVP33

FULL NAME: Timm van der Gugten
BORN: February 25, 1991, Sydney, Australia
SQUAD NO: 64
HEIGHT: 6ft 2in
NICKNAME: Sock
EDUCATION: St Pius X College, Sydney; Swinburne University, Melbourne
TEAMS: Netherlands, Glamorgan, Hobart Hurricanes, New South Wales, Northern Districts, Tasmania
ROLE: Bowler
DEBUT: ODI: 2012; T20I: 2012; First-class: 2011; List A: 2011; T20: 2012

BEST BATTING: 60* Glamorgan vs Gloucestershire, Cardiff, 2018
BEST BOWLING: 7-42 Glamorgan vs Kent, Cardiff, 2018
COUNTY CAP: 2018

MOST EXCITING DAY AS A CRICKETER? Playing for Netherlands in the 2014 World Cup
CHILDHOOD SPORTING HERO? Pat Rafter
FIRST CRICKET CLUB? University of New South Wales CC, Australia
IF YOU COULD TAKE ONE COUNTY CRICKETER'S BEST SHOT AND ADD IT TO YOUR OWN GAME? Wayne Madsen's shot over the keeper
TOUGHEST OPPONENT IN COUNTY CRICKET? Ian Bell – he scored runs for fun against us, thank god he has retired
WHAT WOULD YOU DO IF YOU WERE IN CHARGE OF COUNTY CRICKET? Increase the number of teams to include Scotland, Netherlands and Ireland
WHAT WOULD YOU DO IF YOU WERE PRIME MINISTER? Reverse Brexit
STRANGEST THING YOU'VE DONE DURING LOCKDOWN? Running 100km in one week
GUILTY PLEASURE? Disney films

Batting	Mat	Inns	NO	Runs	HS	Ave	SR	100	50	Ct	St
ODIs	4	2	0	4	2	2.00	66.66	0	0	0	0
T20Is	39	11	4	109	40*	15.57	134.56	0	0	9	0
First-class	47	69	21	750	60*	15.62	48.82	0	3	11	0
List A	58	33	12	350	36	16.66	92.10	0	0	8	0
T20s	96	35	13	267	40*	12.13	126.54	0	0	24	0
Bowling	**Mat**	**Balls**	**Runs**	**Wkts**	**BBI**	**BBM**	**Ave**	**Econ**	**SR**	**5w**	**10**
ODIs	4	126	85	8	5/24	5/24	10.62	4.04	15.7	1	0
T20Is	39	713	847	40	3/9	3/9	21.17	7.12	17.8	0	0
First-class	47	8239	4466	165	7/42	10/121	27.06	3.25	49.9	10	1
List A	58	2566	2381	68	5/24	5/24	35.01	5.56	37.7	1	0
T20s	96	1763	2290	114	5/21	5/21	20.08	7.79	15.4	1	0

ROELOF VAN DER MERWE RHB / SLA / R0 / W0

FULL NAME: Roelof Erasmus van der Merwe
BORN: December 31, 1984, Johannesburg, SA
SQUAD NO: 52
HEIGHT: 5ft 8in
NICKNAME: Bulldog
EDUCATION: Pretoria High School, South Africa; University of Hertfordshire
TEAMS: Netherlands, South Africa, Somerset, Brisbane Heat, Delhi Daredevils, Northerns, RC Bangalore, Titans
ROLE: Allrounder
DEBUT: ODIs: 2009; T20I: 2009; First-class: 2006; List A: 2006; T20: 2008

BEST BATTING: 205* Titans vs Warriors, Benoni, 2014
BEST BOWLING: 4-22 Somerset vs Middlesex, Taunton, 2017
COUNTY CAP: 2018

BIGGEST INFLUENCE ON YOUR DEVELOPMENT AS A CRICKETER (EXCLUDING PARENTS)? Jonty Rhodes – as a kid I would watch him play for South Africa and replicate everything he did in our backyard cricket games
FIRST CRICKET CLUB? Pretoria CC, South Africa
IF YOU COULD TAKE ONE COUNTY CRICKETER'S BEST SHOT AND ADD IT TO YOUR OWN GAME? Tom Banton's reverse-sweep to seamers
TOUGHEST OPPONENT IN COUNTY CRICKET? Eoin Morgan – he hits bombs and hardly gets out!
WHAT WOULD YOU DO IF YOU WERE IN CHARGE OF COUNTY CRICKET? Have a Kookaburra ball for Championship cricket until May and then a Dukes thereafter, batting and bowling points only when a Championship match is drawn
STRANGEST THING YOU'VE DONE DURING LOCKDOWN? My wife cut me a mohawk
FAVOURITE SMELL? A freshly opened tennis-ball tube
TWITTER: @Roela52

Batting	Mat	Inns	NO	Runs	HS	Ave	SR	100	50	Ct	St
ODIs	15	8	3	96	57	19.20	101.05	0	1	4	0
T20Is	43	29	12	454	75*	26.70	131.59	0	2	19	0
First-class	71	114	16	3242	205*	33.08	69.93	6	19	57	0
List A	187	152	44	2901	165*	26.86	98.94	1	11	79	0
T20s	241	173	58	2570	89*	22.34	132.06	0	10	99	0
Bowling	**Mat**	**Balls**	**Runs**	**Wkts**	**BBI**	**BBM**	**Ave**	**Econ**	**SR**	**5w**	**10**
ODIs	15	789	658	18	3/27	3/27	36.55	5.00	43.8	0	0
T20Is	43	895	938	54	4/35	4/35	17.37	6.28	16.5	0	0
First-class	71	9175	4527	134	4/22	8/104	33.78	2.96	68.4	0	0
List A	187	8191	6654	249	5/26	5/26	26.72	4.87	32.8	4	0
T20s	241	4742	5616	226	5/32	5/32	24.84	7.10	20.9	1	0

STIAAN VAN ZYL

LHB / RM / R1 / W0

FULL NAME: Stiaan van Zyl
BORN: September 19, 1987, Cape Town, SA
SQUAD NO: 74
NICKNAME: Stigo
EDUCATION: Kenridge Primary School, Western Cape; Boland Agricultural School, Paarl
TEAMS: South Africa, Sussex, Boland, Cape Cobras, Chittagong Vikings, Comilla Warriors, Western Province
ROLE: Batsman
DEBUT: Test: 2014; First-class: 2006; List A: 2006; T20: 2008

BEST BATTING: 228 Cape Cobras vs Lions, Paarl, 2018
BEST BOWLING: 5-32 Boland vs Northerns, Paarl, 2011

MOST EXCITING DAY AS A CRICKETER? My hundred on Test debut against West Indies at Centurion in 2014
CHILDHOOD SPORTING HERO? Kumar Sangakkara
FIRST CRICKET CLUB? Wellington CC, Western Cape, South Africa
TOUGHEST OPPONENT IN COUNTY CRICKET? Darren Stevens
WHAT WOULD YOU DO IF YOU WERE IN CHARGE OF COUNTY CRICKET? Schedule the season to begin in May
STRANGEST THING YOU'VE DONE DURING LOCKDOWN? Paddling in our swimming pool
FAVOURITE SMELL? Petrol
TWITTER: @laggies74

Batting	Mat	Inns	NO	Runs	HS	Ave	SR	100	50	Ct	St
Tests	12	17	2	395	101*	26.33	50.77	1	0	6	0
First-class	175	293	42	11132	228	44.35	52.18	27	50	99	0
List A	120	110	12	3400	114*	34.69	74.39	5	18	34	0
T20s	73	66	7	1509	86*	25.57	118.63	0	9	21	0
Bowling	**Mat**	**Balls**	**Runs**	**Wkts**	**BBI**	**BBM**	**Ave**	**Econ**	**SR**	**5w**	**10**
Tests	12	403	148	6	3/20	3/22	24.66	2.20	67.1	0	0
First-class	175	5564	2535	68	5/32	7/82	37.27	2.73	81.8	1	0
List A	120	1056	927	20	4/24	4/24	46.35	5.26	52.8	0	0
T20s	73	132	191	7	2/14	2/14	27.28	8.68	18.8	0	0

RICARDO VASCONCELOS

LHB / WK / R0 / W0

FULL NAME: Ricardo Surrador Vasconcelos
BORN: October 27, 1997, Johannesburg, South Africa
SQUAD NO: 27
HEIGHT: 5ft 5in
NICKNAME: Vasco
EDUCATION: St Stithians College, Johannesburg; Stellenbosch University, Western Cape
TEAMS: Northamptonshire, Boland, South Africa U19
ROLE: Batsman/wicketkeeper
DEBUT: First-class: 2016; List A: 2016; T20: 2017

BEST BATTING: 184 Northamptonshire vs Glamorgan, Cardiff, 2019

CHILDHOOD SPORTING HERO? Kumar Sangakkara
BIGGEST INFLUENCE ON YOUR DEVELOPMENT AS A CRICKETER (EXCLUDING PARENTS)? Bongani Ndaba – my coach since I was 12
FIRST CRICKET CLUB? Old Edwardians CC, Johannesburg
IF YOU COULD TAKE ONE COUNTY CRICKETER'S BEST SHOT AND ADD IT TO YOUR OWN GAME? Ben Duckett's reverse-sweep
TOUGHEST OPPONENT IN COUNTY CRICKET? Lockie Ferguson – I ended up with two stumps out the ground and lying on the floor face down
WHAT WOULD YOU DO IF YOU WERE PRIME MINISTER? Give myself a British passport, ban plastic straws
FAVOURITE SMELL? Vanilla
GUILTY PLEASURE? One Direction
TWITTER: @RicardoVasco27

Batting	Mat	Inns	NO	Runs	HS	Ave	SR	100	50	Ct	St
First-class	38	69	6	2279	184	36.17	55.36	5	13	57	5
List A	26	25	1	713	112	29.70	80.20	1	4	19	2
T20s	13	12	3	193	45*	21.44	117.68	0	0	7	0
Bowling	**Mat**	**Balls**	**Runs**	**Wkts**	**BBI**	**BBM**	**Ave**	**Econ**	**SR**	**5w**	**10**
First-class	38	9	9	0	-	-	-	6.00	-	0	0
List A	26	-	-	-	-	-	-	-	-	-	-
T20s	13	-	-	-	-	-	-	-	-	-	-

DANE VILAS RHB / WK / R1 / W0 / MVP94

LANCASHIRE

FULL NAME: Dane James Vilas
BORN: June 10, 1985, Johannesburg, SA
SQUAD NO: 33
HEIGHT: 6ft
NICKNAME: Vili
EDUCATION: King Edward VII School, Johannesburg
TEAMS: South Africa, Lancashire, Dolphins, Gauteng, Lahore Qalandars, Lions, Western Province
ROLE: Batsman/wicketkeeper
DEBUT: Test: 2015; T20I: 2012; First-class: 2006; List A: 2006; T20: 2009

BEST BATTING: 266 Lancashire vs Glamorgan, Colwyn Bay, 2019

COUNTY CAP: 2018

TWITTER: @DaneVilas
NOTES: The former Test wicketkeeper was another South African to announce his international retirement in early 2017 and take up a Kolpak deal with Lancashire, since when he has become the club's most reliable performer as well as their captain. Vilas has scored nearly 3,000 first-class runs at an average 46.41 since arriving in Manchester, including a career-best 244 against Hampshire in 2017 which he topped two years later with 266 at Colwyn Bay. In List A cricket he has made more than 1,057 runs at 55.63 for the county, with three hundreds and five half-centuries. In February Lancashire confirmed that Vilas will captain the club as an overseas player this summer following the termination of all Kolpak contracts

Batting	Mat	Inns	NO	Runs	HS	Ave	SR	100	50	Ct	St
Tests	6	9	0	94	26	10.44	44.76	0	0	13	0
T20Is	1	-	-	-	-	-	-	-	-	0	0
First-class	161	246	29	9119	266	42.02	66.08	21	42	434	20
List A	172	157	25	4888	166	37.03	98.80	9	24	172	30
T20s	166	136	31	3012	75*	28.68	127.24	0	12	93	28

Bowling	Mat	Balls	Runs	Wkts	BBI	BBM	Ave	Econ	SR	5w	10
Tests	6	-	-	-	-	-	-	-	-	-	-
T20Is	1	-	-	-	-	-	-	-	-	-	-
First-class	161	6	3	0	-	-	-	3.00	-	0	0
List A	172	-	-	-	-	-	-	-	-	-	-
T20s	166	-	-	-	-	-	-	-	-	-	-

JAMES VINCE

RHB / RM / R2 / W0

HAMPSHIRE

FULL NAME: James Michael Vince
BORN: March 14, 1991, Cuckfield, Sussex
SQUAD NO: 14
HEIGHT: 6ft 2in
NICKNAME: JV
EDUCATION: Warminster School, Wiltshire
TEAMS: England, Hampshire, Auckland, Karachi Kings, Multan Sultans, Sydney Sixers, Sydney Thunder
ROLE: Batsman
DEBUT: Test: 2016; ODI: 2015; T20I: 2015; First-class: 2009; List A: 2009; T20: 2010

BEST BATTING: 240 Hampshire vs Essex, Southampton, 2014
BEST BOWLING: 5-41 Hampshire vs Loughborough MCCU, Southampton, 2013
COUNTY CAP: 2013

CHILDHOOD SPORTING HERO? Alan Shearer
FIRST CRICKET CLUB? Erlestoke CC, Wiltshire
IF YOU COULD TAKE ONE COUNTY CRICKETER'S BEST SHOT AND ADD IT TO YOUR OWN GAME? Kyle Abbott's straight-drive
WHAT WOULD YOU DO IF YOU WERE IN CHARGE OF COUNTY CRICKET? Play each format in a set block, don't punish clubs who prepare result pitches, reduce ticket prices
FAVOURITE SMELL? A Sunday roast
TWITTER: @vincey14

Batting	Mat	Inns	NO	Runs	HS	Ave	SR	100	50	Ct	St
Tests	13	22	0	548	83	24.90	49.81	0	3	8	0
ODIs	16	14	0	322	51	23.00	88.46	0	1	5	0
T20Is	12	12	0	340	59	28.33	123.63	0	1	5	0
First-class	162	269	20	9692	240	38.92	62.19	25	36	137	0
List A	139	130	7	4905	190	39.87	97.92	9	23	52	0
T20s	246	239	24	6544	107*	30.43	133.74	1	41	123	0
Bowling	**Mat**	**Balls**	**Runs**	**Wkts**	**BBI**	**BBM**	**Ave**	**Econ**	**SR**	**5w**	**10**
Tests	13	24	13	0	-	-	-	3.25	-	0	0
ODIs	16	42	38	1	1/18	1/18	38.00	5.42	42.0	0	0
T20Is	12	-	-	-	-	-	-	-	-	-	-
First-class	162	1669	1031	22	5/41	6/56	46.86	3.70	75.8	1	0
List A	139	174	162	3	1/18	1/18	54.00	5.58	58.0	0	0
T20s	246	78	87	3	1/5	1/5	29.00	6.69	26.0	0	0

AMAR VIRDI

RHB / OB / R0 / W0 / MVP80

FULL NAME: Guramar Singh Virdi
BORN: July 19, 1998, Chiswick, London
SQUAD NO: 19
HEIGHT: 5ft 10in
NICKNAME: Virds
EDUCATION: Guru Nanak Sikh Academy, Hayes, London
TEAMS: Surrey, England Lions
ROLE: Bowler
DEBUT: First-class: 2017

BEST BATTING: 21* Surrey vs Somerset, Taunton, 2018
BEST BOWLING: 8-61 Surrey vs Nottinghamshire, Trent Bridge, 2019

CHILDHOOD SPORTING HERO? Saqlain Mushtaq
FIRST CRICKET CLUB? Indian Gymkhana CC, London. It's the oldest South Asian cricket club in the UK
BIGGEST CRICKETING REGRET? Dropping a catch in a club cricket final
IF YOU WERE AN ANIMAL, WHICH WOULD IT BE? A lion – because that's what Sikhs are!
TWITTER: @amarsinghvirdi
NOTES: The 22-year-old is seen as the most exciting young off-spinner in the country, having taken 91 first-class wickets at an average of 28.08 in his first three seasons at The Oval. Virdi first appeared for England U19 in 2016 and made his Lions debut the following year as a late replacement for the injured Paul Coughlin, taking 4-70 against Queensland at Brisbane. He suffered a setback in 2019 when Surrey did not consider him for selection on grounds of fitness but has since addressed the problem, finishing as the club's leading wicket-taker in last summer's Bob Willis Trophy with 22 victims. Virdi was called up to England's 30-man Test squad last June and toured Sri Lanka and India earlier this year as one of three reserve spinners alongside Matt Parkinson and Mason Crane. He is yet to make his debut in either of the shorter formats

Batting	Mat	Inns	NO	Runs	HS	Ave	SR	100	50	Ct	St
First-class	28	36	18	151	21*	8.38	52.06	0	0	6	0
Bowling	**Mat**	**Balls**	**Runs**	**Wkts**	**BBI**	**BBM**	**Ave**	**Econ**	**SR**	**5w**	**10**
First-class	28	4743	2556	91	8/61	14/139	28.08	3.23	52.1	4	1

MATTHEW WAITE

RHB / RFM / R0 / W0

YORKSHIRE

FULL NAME: Matthew James Waite
BORN: December 24, 1995, Leeds
SQUAD NO: 6
NICKNAME: Pingu
EDUCATION: Brigshaw High School, West Yorkshire
TEAMS: Yorkshire
ROLE: Allrounder
DEBUT: First-class: 2017; List A: 2014; T20: 2015

BEST BATTING: 42 Yorkshire vs Nottinghamshire, Trent Bridge, 2018
BEST BOWLING: 5-16 Yorkshire vs Leeds/Bradford MCCU, Weetwood, 2019

TWITTER: @mat_waite
NOTES: A seam-bowling allrounder, Waite signed a junior professional contract with Yorkshire at the end of 2015 but is yet to have an extended run in the first team. He made his Championship debut against Somerset at Taunton in 2017 but his career has been hampered by a recurring ankle injury. He impressed in 2018 with eight wickets at an average of 27.62 in a handful of four-day matches but was rooted in the Second XI the following summer. Last year was particularly agonising for the 25-year-old after he was ruled out for the season just a day before Yorkshire's red-ball campaign got underway. But the club showed faith by offering him a two-year contract last October. "The frustration with Matthew has been his injuries, none more so than for himself, particularly [last] year when he was in the squad for Durham and had to pull out with a very freak injury before the match even started," said Martyn Moxon, Yorkshire's director of cricket. "He's someone with huge potential. He's shown his capabilities at first-team level so it's now just a matter of him hopefully having an injury-free season and he can really kick on"

Batting	Mat	Inns	NO	Runs	HS	Ave	SR	100	50	Ct	St
First-class	8	11	1	160	42	16.00	52.45	0	0	1	0
List A	13	11	3	278	71	34.75	90.55	0	1	0	0
T20s	6	3	3	34	19*	-	147.82	0	0	3	0
Bowling	**Mat**	**Balls**	**Runs**	**Wkts**	**BBI**	**BBM**	**Ave**	**Econ**	**SR**	**5w**	**10**
First-class	8	966	583	23	5/16	6/57	25.34	3.62	42.0	1	0
List A	13	486	522	16	4/65	4/65	32.62	6.44	30.3	0	0
T20s	6	60	81	2	1/6	1/6	40.50	8.10	30.0	0	0

ALEX WAKELY

RHB / RM / R0 / W0

FULL NAME: Alex George Wakely
BORN: November 3, 1988, London
SQUAD NO: 8
HEIGHT: 6ft 2in
NICKNAME: Baby Seal
EDUCATION: Bedford School
TEAMS: Northamptonshire, England U19
ROLE: Batsman
DEBUT: First-class: 2007; List A: 2005; T20: 2009

BEST BATTING: 123 Northamptonshire vs Leicestershire, Northampton, 2015
BEST BOWLING: 2-62 Northamptonshire vs Somerset, Taunton, 2007
COUNTY CAP: 2012

MOST EXCITING DAY AS A CRICKETER? My first-class debut against Somerset in 2007, playing alongside so many international players I grew up watching – Klusener, Trescothick, Langer, White, Caddick. Incredible experience
CHILDHOOD SPORTING HERO? Ricky Ponting
FIRST CRICKET CLUB? Ampthill Town CC, Bedfordshire
IF YOU COULD TAKE ONE COUNTY CRICKETER'S BEST SHOT AND ADD IT TO YOUR OWN GAME? Richard Levi's leg-side biff
TOUGHEST OPPONENT IN COUNTY CRICKET? Kumar Sangakkara – he got a hundred every time
MOST ECCENTRIC TEAMMATE? Nathan Buck – I can't explain it, you need to experience it
WHAT WOULD YOU DO IF YOU WERE IN CHARGE OF COUNTY CRICKET? Set up a three-league Championship structure with 10 fixtures for each side, four of which are played abroad
STRANGEST THING YOU'VE DONE DURING LOCKDOWN? Joining a rugby club
GUILTY PLEASURE? Indulging an obsession with trainers
TWITTER: @AlexWakely1

Batting	Mat	Inns	NO	Runs	HS	Ave	SR	100	50	Ct	St
First-class	147	235	16	6876	123	31.39	48.00	9	37	97	0
List A	90	85	8	2532	109*	32.88	86.06	2	18	32	0
T20s	133	124	25	2597	64	26.23	117.67	0	14	42	0
Bowling	**Mat**	**Balls**	**Runs**	**Wkts**	**BBI**	**BBM**	**Ave**	**Econ**	**SR**	**5w**	**10**
First-class	147	509	426	6	2/62	2/62	71.00	5.02	84.8	0	0
List A	90	136	131	5	2/14	2/14	26.20	5.77	27.2	0	0
T20s	133	12	29	0	-	-	-	14.50	-	0	0

MIDDLESEX

THILAN WALALLAWITA LHB / SLA / R0 / W0

FULL NAME: Thilan Nipuna Walallawita
BORN: June 23, 1998, Colombo, Sri Lanka
SQUAD NO: 32
HEIGHT: 5ft 11in
NICKNAME: Thils
EDUCATION: Mount Grace School, Potters Bar; Hertfordshire University
TEAMS: Middlesex
ROLE: Bowler
DEBUT: First-class: 2020; T20: 2020

BEST BATTING: 11 Middlesex vs Kent, Canterbury, 2020
BEST BOWLING: 3-28 Middlesex vs Hampshire, Radlett, 2020

MOST EXCITING DAY AS A CRICKETER? Making my Middlesex debut last summer
CHILDHOOD SPORTING HERO? Kumar Sangakkara
BIGGEST INFLUENCE ON YOUR DEVELOPMENT AS A CRICKETER (EXCLUDING PARENTS)? All my mates – they've been keeping me on my toes through thick and thin
MOST ECCENTRIC TEAMMATE? Sam Robson
WHAT WOULD YOU DO IF YOU WERE PRIME MINISTER? Bring down prices!
TWITTER: @walallawita
NOTES: Born and raised in Sri Lanka, the left-arm spinner made his first-class and T20 debuts last summer after finishing as the club's leading wicket-taker in Second XI cricket in 2019. Walallawita survived a brush with death in 2004 when the Indian Ocean tsunami hit Sri Lanka while he was having lunch with his dad in a beach-side restaurant. He came to the UK in 2012, joining Potters Bar CC in Hertfordshire and soon progressed through the Middlesex age-groups. He signed a professional contract with the club in January 2020 and qualifies as a local player

Batting	Mat	Inns	NO	Runs	HS	Ave	SR	100	50	Ct	St
First-class	5	6	2	22	11	5.50	42.30	0	0	0	0
T20s	1	1	0	0	0	0.00	0.00	0	0	0	0
Bowling	**Mat**	**Balls**	**Runs**	**Wkts**	**BBI**	**BBM**	**Ave**	**Econ**	**SR**	**5w**	**10**
First-class	5	530	245	6	3/28	4/51	40.83	2.77	88.3	0	0
T20s	1	24	19	3	3/19	3/19	6.33	4.75	8.0	0	0

ROMAN WALKER RHB / RFM / R0 / W0

FULL NAME: Roman Isaac Walker
BORN: August 6, 2000, Wrexham, Clwyd, Wales
SQUAD NO: 37
HEIGHT: 6ft 3in
NICKNAME: Stroller
EDUCATION: Ysgol Bryn Alyn, Wrexham
TEAMS: Glamorgan, England U19
ROLE: Bowler
DEBUT: List A: 2019; T20: 2019

FIRST CRICKET CLUB? Bersham CC, Wrexham
MOST INTERESTING TEAMMATE? Jacques Rudolph – for his sheer wisdom
IF YOU WERE AN ANIMAL, WHICH WOULD IT BE? An eagle – no traffic when travelling
TWITTER: @RomanWalker17
NOTES: The tall seamer signed a two-year contract with Glamorgan in December 2019 following a breakthrough season with the Welsh county which included hitting the match-sealing six on his first-team debut against Sussex at Hove in the One-Day Cup. A former England U19 cricketer, Walker did not feature for Glamorgan in last year's truncated season but will be looking to make an impression in white-ball cricket this summer, as well as eyeing up a first-class debut

Batting	Mat	Inns	NO	Runs	HS	Ave	SR	100	50	Ct	St
List A	1	1	1	7	7*	-	233.33	0	0	0	0
T20s	3	1	0	1	1	1.00	33.33	0	0	0	0
Bowling	**Mat**	**Balls**	**Runs**	**Wkts**	**BBI**	**BBM**	**Ave**	**Econ**	**SR**	**5w**	**10**
List A	1	24	21	0	-	-	-	5.25	-	0	0
T20s	3	71	119	5	3/39	3/39	23.80	10.05	14.2	0	0

MAX WALLER

RHB / LB

FULL NAME: Maximilian Thomas Charles Waller
BORN: March 3, 1988, Salisbury, Wiltshire
SQUAD NO: 10
HEIGHT: 6ft
NICKNAME: Goose
EDUCATION: Millfield School, Somerset; Bournemouth University
TEAMS: Somerset
ROLE: Bowler
DEBUT: First-class: 2009; List A: 2009; T20: 2009

BEST BATTING: 17 Somerset vs Gloucestershire, Bristol, 2017 (T20)
BEST BOWLING: 4-16 Somerset vs Warwickshire, Taunton, 2012 (T20)

MOST EXCITING DAY AS A CRICKETER? Playing in the 2009/10 T20 Champions League in India
CHILDHOOD SPORTING HERO? Shane Warne
BIGGEST INFLUENCE ON YOUR DEVELOPMENT AS A CRICKETER (EXCLUDING PARENTS)? Terry Jenner, the former Australia Test cricketer and spin-bowling coach. I loved working with him on my bowling. Also Justin Langer – he gave me an opportunity and backed me, which is just what you need as a young player
FIRST CRICKET CLUB? Bashley Rydal CC, New Forest, Hampshire
IF YOU COULD TAKE ONE COUNTY CRICKETER'S BEST SHOT AND ADD IT TO YOUR OWN GAME? The James Hildreth late-cut
BIGGEST CRICKETING REGRET? Not yet winning a T20 final for Somerset
WHAT WOULD YOU DO IF YOU WERE IN CHARGE OF COUNTY CRICKET? Create a T20 Premier League which includes all 18 counties each playing 34 games (home and away), allow three overseas players in T20, offer better rewards for clubs that do well as a business
STRANGEST THING YOU'VE DONE DURING LOCKDOWN? Throwing tea bags into a cup
TWITTER: @MaxTCWaller
NOTES: Waller signed a two-year contract to play T20 cricket last October

Batting	Mat	Inns	NO	Runs	HS	Ave	SR	100	50	Ct	St
First-class	9	10	1	91	28	10.11	42.32	0	0	5	0
List A	58	22	15	109	25*	15.57	70.77	0	0	32	0
T20s	133	32	19	96	17	7.38	78.68	0	0	79	0
Bowling	**Mat**	**Balls**	**Runs**	**Wkts**	**BBI**	**BBM**	**Ave**	**Econ**	**SR**	**5w**	**10**
First-class	9	840	493	10	3/33	3/57	49.30	3.52	84.0	0	0
List A	58	1801	1696	45	3/37	3/37	37.68	5.65	40.0	0	0
T20s	133	2588	3142	132	4/16	4/16	23.80	7.28	19.6	0	0

PAUL WALTER LHB / LMF / R0 / W0 / MVP50

FULL NAME: Paul Ian Walter
BORN: May 28, 1994, Basildon, Essex
SQUAD NO: 22
HEIGHT: 6ft 7in
EDUCATION: Billericay School, Essex
TEAMS: Essex
ROLE: Allrounder
DEBUT: First-class: 2016; List A: 2017; T20: 2016

BEST BATTING: 68* Essex vs West Indians, Chelmsford, 2017
BEST BOWLING: 3-44 Essex vs Derbyshire, Derby, 2016

TWITTER: @PWalter_22
NOTES: Walter signed a professional contract with his hometown club midway through the 2016 season and has becoming an increasingly influential contributor with bat and ball. The 6ft 7in fast-bowling allrounder played in all 10 of Essex's T20 matches last summer, impressing with seven wickets at the frugal economy rate of 6.64 and smashing a 45-ball 76 against Sussex at Chelmsford. He also lined up for five of Essex's seven matches in the Bob Willis Trophy, including the final, playing primarily as a middle-order batsman

Batting	Mat	Inns	NO	Runs	HS	Ave	SR	100	50	Ct	St
First-class	15	19	5	506	68*	36.14	49.03	0	1	2	0
List A	10	8	3	96	25	19.20	90.56	0	0	4	0
T20s	48	35	13	461	76	20.95	137.20	0	1	20	0
Bowling	**Mat**	**Balls**	**Runs**	**Wkts**	**BBI**	**BBM**	**Ave**	**Econ**	**SR**	**5w**	**10**
First-class	15	1014	593	13	3/44	4/68	45.61	3.50	78.0	0	0
List A	10	328	375	13	4/37	4/37	28.84	6.85	25.2	0	0
T20s	48	552	840	28	3/24	3/24	30.00	9.13	19.7	0	0

JARED WARNER

RHB / RFM / R0 / W0

GLOUCESTERSHIRE

FULL NAME: Jared David Warner
BORN: November 14, 1996, Wakefield, Yorkshire
SQUAD NO: 4
HEIGHT: 6ft 1in
NICKNAME: Jazz
EDUCATION: Silcoates School, West Yorkshire; Kettlethorpe High School, Wakefield
TEAMS: Gloucestershire, England U19, Sussex, Yorkshire
ROLE: Bowler
DEBUT: First-class: 2019; List A: 2019

BEST BATTING: 13* Sussex vs Middlesex, Hove, 2019
BEST BOWLING: 3-35 Sussex vs Glamorgan, Hove, 2019

MOST EXCITING DAY AS A CRICKETER? Taking 9-19 from 10.2 overs for Yorkshire Academy against Castleford in a Yorkshire Premier League North match in 2016
CHILDHOOD SPORTING HERO? Andrew Flintoff – my first memories of watching cricket are of him winning the Ashes in 2005
FIRST CRICKET CLUB? Wakefield Thornes CC, West Yorkshire
TOUGHEST OPPONENT IN COUNTY CRICKET? Jamie Porter
SURPRISING FACT ABOUT YOU? I'm a big Sheffield United fan
TWITTER: @JaredWarner96

Batting	Mat	Inns	NO	Runs	HS	Ave	SR	100	50	Ct	St
First-class	3	3	2	18	13*	18.00	32.14	0	0	0	0
List A	1	-	-	-	-	-	-	-	-	0	0
Bowling	**Mat**	**Balls**	**Runs**	**Wkts**	**BBI**	**BBM**	**Ave**	**Econ**	**SR**	**5w**	**10**
First-class	3	236	164	5	3/35	3/79	32.80	4.16	47.2	0	0
List A	1	30	32	0	-	-	-	6.40	-	0	0

JOE WEATHERLEY RHB / OB / R0 / W0 / MVP87

FULL NAME: Joe James Weatherley
BORN: January 19, 1997, Winchester, Hampshire
SQUAD NO: 5
HEIGHT: 6ft 2in
NICKNAME: Lord
EDUCATION: King Edward VI School, Southampton; The Open University, Milton Keynes
TEAMS: Hampshire, England U19, Kent
ROLE: Batsman
DEBUT: First-class: 2016; List A: 2016; T20: 2016

BEST BATTING: 126* Hampshire vs Lancashire, Old Trafford, 2018
BEST BOWLING: 1-2 Hampshire vs Nottinghamshire, Southampton, 2018

MOST EXCITING DAY AS A CRICKETER? Winning at Lord's in the 2018 One-Day Cup final
CHILDHOOD SPORTING HERO? Roger Federer
BIGGEST INFLUENCE ON YOUR DEVELOPMENT AS A CRICKETER (EXCLUDING PARENTS)? Tony Middleton, my batting coach at Hampshire
FIRST CRICKET CLUB? St Cross Symondians CC, Hampshire
TOUGHEST OPPONENT IN COUNTY CRICKET? Simon Harmer
WHAT WOULD YOU DO IF YOU WERE IN CHARGE OF COUNTY CRICKET? Introduce transfer fees, use a Kookaburra ball for Championship matches in early and late season (or just play more four-day cricket in the middle of the summer)
STRANGEST THING YOU'VE DONE DURING LOCKDOWN? Going on a road trip on the North Coast 500 in Scotland
SURPRISING FACT ABOUT YOU? My dad played at Wimbledon in the 1972 Championships
TWITTER: @Joe_Weatherley

Batting	Mat	Inns	NO	Runs	HS	Ave	SR	100	50	Ct	St
First-class	37	59	4	1421	126*	25.83	43.49	1	7	16	0
List A	20	20	4	509	105*	31.81	72.61	1	3	5	0
T20s	20	18	0	302	68	16.77	117.96	0	1	6	0
Bowling	**Mat**	**Balls**	**Runs**	**Wkts**	**BBI**	**BBM**	**Ave**	**Econ**	**SR**	**5w**	**10**
First-class	37	300	228	4	1/2	1/2	57.00	4.56	75.0	0	0
List A	20	327	221	8	4/25	4/25	27.62	4.05	40.8	0	0
T20s	20	6	9	0	-	-	-	9.00	-	0	0

NICK WELCH

RHB / LB / R0 / W0

FULL NAME: Nicholas Roy Welch
BORN: February 5, 1998, Harare, Zimbabwe
SQUAD NO: 67
HEIGHT: 5ft 11in
NICKNAME: Welchie
EDUCATION: St John's College, Harare; Whitgift School, Croydon; Loughborough University
TEAMS: Leicestershire, Mashonaland Eagles
ROLE: Batsman
DEBUT: First-class: 2014; List A: 2014; T20: 2020

BEST BATTING: 83 Mashonaland Eagles vs Southern Rocks, Harare, 2014

MOST EXCITING DAY AS A CRICKETER? Signing my first professional contract
CHILDHOOD SPORTING HERO? Ricky Ponting
IF YOU COULD TAKE ONE COUNTY CRICKETER'S BEST SHOT AND ADD IT TO YOUR OWN GAME? Joe Root's cover-drive
TOUGHEST OPPONENT IN COUNTY CRICKET? Darren Stevens – he hoops it around corners at a "nick-me" pace
WHAT WOULD YOU DO IF YOU WERE IN CHARGE OF COUNTY CRICKET? Make early-season matches begin earlier in the day so that we get a full day of cricket without going off for bad light
GUILTY PLEASURE? Country music
TWITTER: @nickwelchie

Batting	Mat	Inns	NO	Runs	HS	Ave	SR	100	50	Ct	St
First-class	5	7	0	179	83	25.57	51.43	0	1	1	0
List A	5	5	0	102	52	20.40	75.55	0	1	2	0
T20s	5	5	0	101	43	20.20	103.06	0	0	1	0
Bowling	**Mat**	**Balls**	**Runs**	**Wkts**	**BBI**	**BBM**	**Ave**	**Econ**	**SR**	**5w**	**10**
First-class	5	-	-	-	-	-	-	-	-	-	-
List A	5	-	-	-	-	-	-	-	-	-	-
T20s	5	-	-	-	-	-	-	-	-	-	-

LUKE WELLS

LHB / OB / R2 / W0

FULL NAME: Luke William Peter Wells
BORN: December 29, 1990, Eastbourne, Sussex
SQUAD NO: 3
HEIGHT: 6ft 4in
NICKNAME: Dave
EDUCATION: St Bede's, Hailsham, East Sussex; Loughborough University
TEAMS: Lancashire, Colombo, England U19, Sussex
ROLE: Batsman
DEBUT: First-class: 2010; List A: 2010; T20: 2011

BEST BATTING: 258 Sussex vs Durham, Hove, 2017
BEST BOWLING: 5-63 Sussex vs Glamorgan, Hove, 2019
COUNTY CAP: 2016 (Sussex)

MOST EXCITING DAY AS A CRICKETER? Making my first-class debut at Worcester – I scored a fifty and lifted the Division Two trophy
CHILDHOOD SPORTING HERO? Sachin Tendulkar
BIGGEST INFLUENCE ON YOUR DEVELOPMENT AS A CRICKETER (EXCLUDING PARENTS)? The legendary Les Lenham – former Sussex batsman who became a master batting coach, especially on the fundamentals of technique
FIRST CRICKET CLUB? Glynde & Beddingham CC, Sussex
IF YOU COULD TAKE ONE COUNTY CRICKETER'S BEST SHOT AND ADD IT TO YOUR OWN GAME? Joe Root's sweep
TOUGHEST OPPONENT IN COUNTY CRICKET? Glen Chapple – he swung it both ways accurately and at good pace. And he never gave up
WHAT WOULD YOU DO IF YOU WERE IN CHARGE OF COUNTY CRICKET? Allow more bend in the arm for spinners (doosras are brilliant for the game)
TWITTER: @luke_wells07

Batting	Mat	Inns	NO	Runs	HS	Ave	SR	100	50	Ct	St
First-class	141	237	16	7779	258	35.19	46.41	18	33	63	0
List A	26	20	0	232	62	11.60	63.21	0	1	5	0
T20s	5	5	0	18	11	3.60	66.66	0	0	1	0
Bowling	**Mat**	**Balls**	**Runs**	**Wkts**	**BBI**	**BBM**	**Ave**	**Econ**	**SR**	**5w**	**10**
First-class	141	5398	3172	69	5/63	5/63	45.97	3.52	78.2	1	0
List A	26	437	384	10	3/19	3/19	38.40	5.27	43.7	0	0
T20s	5	1	4	0	-	-	-	24.00	-	0	0

RIKI WESSELS

RHB / WK / R2 / W0

FULL NAME: Mattheus Hendrik Wessels
BORN: November 12, 1985, Maroochydore, Queensland, Australia
SQUAD NO: 99
HEIGHT: 5ft 11in
NICKNAME: Weaz
EDUCATION: Woodridge College, Port Elizabeth; University of Northampton
TEAMS: Worcestershire, Mid West Rhinos, Nondescripts, Northamptonshire, Nottinghamshire, Sydney Sixers
ROLE: Batsman
DEBUT: First-class: 2004; List A: 2005; T20: 2005

BEST BATTING: 202* Nottinghamshire vs Sussex, Trent Bridge, 2017
BEST BOWLING: 1-10 Mid West Rhinos vs Matabeleland Tuskers, Bulawayo, 2009
COUNTY CAP: 2014 (Nottinghamshire)

FAMILY TIES? My dad is the former South Africa captain Kepler Wessels
CHILDHOOD SPORTING HERO? Justin Langer
FIRST CRICKET CLUB? United Brothers CC, Eastern Cape, South Africa – a township-based club with some serious talent
BEST INNINGS YOU'VE SEEN? Alex Hales's 187 not out in the 2017 One-Day Cup final
WHAT WOULD YOU DO IF YOU WERE IN CHARGE OF COUNTY CRICKET? Lunch and tea should each be an hour
SURPRISING FACT ABOUT YOU? I've bungee-jumped at Victoria Falls, I lived in Colombo for six months and I love hunting
TWITTER: @rikiwessels

Batting	Mat	Inns	NO	Runs	HS	Ave	SR	100	50	Ct	St
First-class	217	359	31	11499	202*	35.05	64.32	23	59	336	16
List A	179	168	14	4765	146	30.94	101.08	5	26	121	0
T20s	226	213	27	5384	110	28.94	136.06	1	25	88	16
Bowling	**Mat**	**Balls**	**Runs**	**Wkts**	**BBI**	**BBM**	**Ave**	**Econ**	**SR**	**5w**	**10**
First-class	217	240	130	3	1/10	1/10	43.33	3.25	80.0	0	0
List A	179	49	48	1	1/0	1/0	48.00	5.87	49.0	0	0
T20s	226	-	-	-	-	-	-	-	-	-	-

TOM WESTLEY

RHB / OB / R1 / W0

FULL NAME: Thomas Westley
BORN: March 13, 1989, Cambridge
SQUAD NO: 21
HEIGHT: 6ft 2in
NICKNAME: Westie
EDUCATION: Linton Valley College, South Cambridgeshire; Hills Road College, Cambridge; Durham University
TEAMS: England, Essex, Bloomfield Cricket & Athletic Club
ROLE: Batsman
DEBUT: Test: 2017; First-class: 2007; List A: 2006; T20: 2010

BEST BATTING: 254 Essex vs Worcestershire, Chelmsford, 2016
BEST BOWLING: 4-55 Durham MCCU vs Durham, Durham University, 2010
COUNTY CAP: 2013

FAMILY TIES? My dad, uncle and brother all play for Weston Colville CC. My dad also harbours ambitions to play for England over-50s
CHILDHOOD SPORTING HERO? Jacques Kallis
SURPRISING FACT ABOUT YOU? I was one of the first students to study Harry Potter academically
TWITTER: @Westley21

Batting	Mat	Inns	NO	Runs	HS	Ave	SR	100	50	Ct	St
Tests	5	9	1	193	59	24.12	42.60	0	1	1	0
First-class	186	310	22	10218	254	35.47	51.53	21	48	118	0
List A	88	82	4	2853	134	36.57	88.68	5	22	19	0
T20s	87	80	8	2165	109*	30.06	130.34	2	7	34	0
Bowling	**Mat**	**Balls**	**Runs**	**Wkts**	**BBI**	**BBM**	**Ave**	**Econ**	**SR**	**5w**	**10**
Tests	5	24	12	0	-	-	-	3.00	-	0	0
First-class	186	5083	2693	59	4/55	5/122	45.64	3.17	86.1	0	0
List A	88	1036	861	21	4/60	4/60	41.00	4.98	49.3	0	0
T20s	87	246	311	7	2/27	2/27	44.42	7.58	35.1	0	0

BRAD WHEAL

RHB / RFM / R0 / W0

FULL NAME: Bradley Thomas James Wheal
BORN: August 28, 1996, Durban, South Africa
SQUAD NO: 58
HEIGHT: 5ft 11in
EDUCATION: Clifton School, Durban
TEAMS: Scotland, Hampshire
ROLE: Bowler
DEBUT: ODI: 2016; T20I: 2016; First-class: 2015; List A: 2016; T20: 2016

BEST BATTING: 25* Hampshire vs Somerset, Taunton, 2018
BEST BOWLING: 6-51 Hampshire vs Nottinghamshire, Trent Bridge, 2016

FIRST CRICKET CLUB? Berea Rovers CC, Durban, South Africa
MOST INTERESTING TEAMMATE? Hashim Amla – he is one of the hardest workers I've ever seen, no matter how well he is playing
IF YOU WERE AN ANIMAL, WHICH WOULD IT BE? A dolphin – who doesn't want to spend their day cruising around the ocean?
TWITTER: @Brad_wheal

Batting	Mat	Inns	NO	Runs	HS	Ave	SR	100	50	Ct	St
ODIs	13	7	3	16	14	4.00	51.61	0	0	3	0
T20Is	5	2	2	2	2*	-	100.00	0	0	1	0
First-class	28	32	10	181	25*	8.22	23.69	0	0	11	0
List A	28	16	7	63	18*	7.00	66.31	0	0	6	0
T20s	12	5	3	22	16	11.00	95.65	0	0	1	0
Bowling	**Mat**	**Balls**	**Runs**	**Wkts**	**BBI**	**BBM**	**Ave**	**Econ**	**SR**	**5w**	**10**
ODIs	13	687	508	23	3/34	3/34	22.08	4.43	29.8	0	0
T20Is	5	104	143	5	3/20	3/20	28.60	8.25	20.8	0	0
First-class	28	3718	2283	61	6/51	7/71	37.42	3.68	60.9	1	0
List A	28	1319	1154	45	4/38	4/38	25.64	5.24	29.3	0	0
T20s	12	224	317	11	3/20	3/20	28.81	8.49	20.3	0	0

ADAM WHEATER RHB / WK / R0 / W0 / MVP59

FULL NAME: Adam Jack Aubrey Wheater
BORN: February 13, 1990, Whipps Cross Hospital, London
SQUAD NO: 31
EDUCATION: Millfield School, Somerset; Anglia Ruskin University
TEAMS: Essex, Badureliya Sports Club, England U19, Hampshire, Matabeleland Tuskers
ROLE: Batsman/wicketkeeper
DEBUT: First-class: 2008; List A: 2010; T20: 2009

BEST BATTING: 204* Hampshire vs Warwickshire, Edgbaston, 2016
BEST BOWLING: 1-86 Essex vs Leicestershire, Leicester, 2012
COUNTY CAP: 2016 (Hampshire); 2020 (Essex)

NOTES: The hard-hitting wicketkeeper signed a new deal last October, keeping him at Essex until the end of next season. "Adam is an experienced campaigner and has consistently shown his quality both behind the stumps and with the bat," said Anthony McGrath, Essex's head coach. "He's a great influence in the dressing room and always wants what's best for the team, so I'm really pleased that he's extended his stay." Wheater was part of the side which won the County Championship in 2017 and again in 2019, having re-joined his old club after a spell at Hampshire. Behind Alastair Cook, the 31-year-old was Essex's most consistent run-scorer in the club's successful red-ball campaign last summer, with 291 runs at an average of 58.20

Batting	Mat	Inns	NO	Runs	HS	Ave	SR	100	50	Ct	St
First-class	144	211	28	6664	204*	36.41	64.47	12	37	254	17
List A	80	65	5	1713	135	28.55	97.38	2	9	41	12
T20s	119	96	16	1527	78	19.08	123.04	0	4	44	24
Bowling	**Mat**	**Balls**	**Runs**	**Wkts**	**BBI**	**BBM**	**Ave**	**Econ**	**SR**	**5w**	**10**
First-class	144	24	86	1	1/86	1/86	86.00	21.50	24.0	0	0
List A	80	-	-	-	-	-	-	-	-	-	-
T20s	119	-	-	-	-	-	-	-	-	-	-

GRAEME WHITE RHB / SLA

FULL NAME: Graeme Geoffrey White
BORN: April 18, 1987, Milton Keynes, Buckinghamshire
SQUAD NO: 87
HEIGHT: 5ft 11in
NICKNAME: G
EDUCATION: Royal Latin School, Buckinghamshire; Stowe School
TEAMS: Northamptonshire, England Lions, Nottinghamshire
ROLE: Bowler
DEBUT: First-class: 2006; List A: 2007; T20: 2007

BEST BATTING: 37* Northamptonshire vs Warwickshire, Edgbaston, 2020 (T20)
BEST BOWLING: 5-22 Nottinghamshire vs Lancashire, Trent Bridge, 2013 (T20)

MOST EXCITING DAY AS A CRICKETER? Winning the T20 Blast with Northamptonshire
CHILDHOOD SPORTING HERO? Phil Tufnell
BIGGEST INFLUENCE ON YOUR DEVELOPMENT AS A CRICKETER (EXCLUDING PARENTS)? David Ripley – he's coached me ever since I joined the Northants Academy
FIRST CRICKET CLUB? Milton Keynes CC, Buckinghamshire
IF YOU COULD TAKE ONE COUNTY CRICKETER'S BEST SHOT AND ADD IT TO YOUR OWN GAME? Ben Sanderson's slog over long-on
TOUGHEST OPPONENT IN COUNTY CRICKET? Kumar Sangakkara
WHAT WOULD YOU DO IF YOU WERE IN CHARGE OF COUNTY CRICKET? Make boundaries bigger, make the ball smaller
STRANGEST THING YOU'VE DONE DURING LOCKDOWN? Learning Japanese
SURPRISING FACT ABOUT YOU? I have 35 tattoos
NOTES: The Northants spinner signed a one-year contract to play white-ball cricket last October

Batting	Mat	Inns	NO	Runs	HS	Ave	SR	100	50	Ct	St
First-class	39	55	5	659	65	13.18	48.85	0	2	12	0
List A	85	52	16	543	41*	15.08	86.32	0	0	29	0
T20s	116	48	24	380	37*	15.83	141.26	0	0	41	0
Bowling	**Mat**	**Balls**	**Runs**	**Wkts**	**BBI**	**BBM**	**Ave**	**Econ**	**SR**	**5w**	**10**
First-class	39	4776	2730	65	6/44	7/89	42.00	3.42	73.4	1	0
List A	85	3216	2709	92	6/37	6/37	29.44	5.05	34.9	2	0
T20s	116	1840	2455	92	5/22	5/22	26.68	8.00	20.0	1	0

JACK WHITE

LHB / RFM / R0 / W0

FULL NAME: Curtley-Jack White
BORN: February 19, 1992, Kendal, Cumberland
SQUAD NO: 9
HEIGHT: 6ft 2in
EDUCATION: Ullswater Community College, Penrith, Cumbria; Queen Elizabeth Grammar School, Penrith
TEAMS: Northamptonshire
ROLE: Bowler
DEBUT: First-class: 2020

BEST BATTING: 7* Northampton vs Worcestershire, Northampton, 2020
BEST BOWLING: 4-35 Northampton vs Glamorgan, Northampton, 2020

MOST EXCITING DAY AS A CRICKETER? Winning the Sydney First Grade Premiership with Parramatta CC in Australia
CHILDHOOD SPORTING HERO? Hermann Maier (Austrian downhill skier)
FIRST CRICKET CLUB? Penrith CC, Cumbria
IF YOU COULD TAKE ONE COUNTY CRICKETER'S BEST SHOT AND ADD IT TO YOUR OWN GAME? Charlie Thurston's cut
STRANGEST THING YOU'VE DONE DURING LOCKDOWN? Playing a game of curling on a frozen pond near Buttermere
FAVOURITE SMELL? The Alps in the morning
GUILTY PLEASURE? Nutella
TWITTER: @CJackWhite9

Batting	Mat	Inns	NO	Runs	HS	Ave	SR	100	50	Ct	St
First-class	4	4	2	9	7*	4.50	36.00	0	0	0	0
Bowling	**Mat**	**Balls**	**Runs**	**Wkts**	**BBI**	**BBM**	**Ave**	**Econ**	**SR**	**5w**	**10**
First-class	4	528	260	13	4/35	8/83	20.00	2.95	40.6	0	0

ROBBIE WHITE RHB / WK / R0 / W0

MIDDLESEX

FULL NAME: Robert George White
BORN: September 15, 1995, Ealing, London
SQUAD NO: 14
HEIGHT: 5ft 10in
NICKNAME: Chalky
EDUCATION: Harrow School, London; Loughborough University
TEAMS: Middlesex, Essex
ROLE: Batsman/wicketkeeper
DEBUT: First-class: 2015; List A: 2018; T20: 2018

BEST BATTING: 99 Middlesex vs Kent, Canterbury, 2020

MOST EXCITING DAY AS A CRICKETER? Making my T20 debut at The Oval
CHILDHOOD SPORTING HERO? Tiger Woods
BIGGEST INFLUENCE ON YOUR DEVELOPMENT AS A CRICKETER (EXCLUDING PARENTS)? My former Middlesex teammate George Scott – I learnt a lot from our chats on the golf course
FIRST CRICKET CLUB? Ealing CC, London
TOUGHEST OPPONENT IN COUNTY CRICKET? Sam Cook
MOST ECCENTRIC TEAMMATE? Martin Andersson – he's mad, clever, unique and has plenty of theories
BIGGEST CRICKETING REGRET? Leaving my first Championship ball at Lord's…
STRANGEST THING YOU'VE DONE DURING LOCKDOWN? Living with Max Holden, Jack Davies and Tom Lace
FAVOURITE SMELL? A Lord's roast lamb
TWITTER: @rwhitey15

Batting	Mat	Inns	NO	Runs	HS	Ave	SR	100	50	Ct	St
First-class	19	28	1	450	99	16.66	42.13	0	2	25	2
List A	9	9	4	99	21*	19.80	106.45	0	0	15	2
T20s	3	2	1	11	11*	11.00	100.00	0	0	1	0
Bowling	**Mat**	**Balls**	**Runs**	**Wkts**	**BBI**	**BBM**	**Ave**	**Econ**	**SR**	**5w**	**10**
First-class	19	-	-	-	-	-	-	-	-	-	-
List A	9	-	-	-	-	-	-	-	-	-	-
T20s	3	-	-	-	-	-	-	-	-	-	-

ROSS WHITELEY

LHB / LM / R0 / W0

FULL NAME: Ross Andrew Whiteley
BORN: September 13, 1988, Sheffield
SQUAD NO: 44
HEIGHT: 6ft 2in
NICKNAME: Rossco
EDUCATION: Repton School, Derbyshire; Leeds Metropolitan University
TEAMS: Worcestershire, Derbyshire, England Lions, Multan Sultans, Sylhet Sixers
ROLE: Batsman
DEBUT: First-class: 2008; List A: 2008; T20: 2011

BEST BATTING: 130* Derbyshire vs Kent, Derby, 2011
BEST BOWLING: 2-6 Derbyshire vs Hampshire, Derby, 2012
COUNTY CAP: 2013 (Worcestershire)

FIRST CRICKET CLUB? Eckington CC, South Yorkshire
BEST INNINGS YOU'VE SEEN? Martin Guptill's 35-ball hundred for Worcestershire in a T20 match at Northampton in 2018. Some of the cleanest hitting I have ever seen
TOUGHEST OPPONENT IN COUNTY CRICKET? The Dukes ball
MOST INTERESTING TEAMMATE? Martin Guptill – because of his blow-ups after getting out
SURPRISING FACT ABOUT YOU? I once had each squad number of the 2012 Derbyshire side which won Division Two shaved onto 11 sheep
GUILTY PLEASURE? White chocolate
TWITTER: @RossWhiteley44

Batting	Mat	Inns	NO	Runs	HS	Ave	SR	100	50	Ct	St
First-class	87	142	13	3543	130*	27.46	49.63	3	19	59	0
List A	81	71	11	1660	131	27.66	99.81	1	10	23	0
T20s	131	120	31	2227	91*	25.02	143.39	0	5	51	0
Bowling	**Mat**	**Balls**	**Runs**	**Wkts**	**BBI**	**BBM**	**Ave**	**Econ**	**SR**	**5w**	**10**
First-class	87	2953	2064	40	2/6	4/43	51.60	4.19	73.8	0	0
List A	81	507	563	14	4/58	4/58	40.21	6.66	36.2	0	0
T20s	131	102	181	4	1/10	1/10	45.25	10.64	25.5	0	0

DAVID WIESE RHB / RMF

FULL NAME: David Wiese
BORN: May 18, 1985, Roodepoort, Transvaal, South Africa
SQUAD NO: 96
HEIGHT: 6ft 3in
NICKNAME: Spanish Dave
EDUCATION: University of Pretoria
TEAMS: South Africa, Sussex, Barbados Tridents, Easterns, Lahore Qalandars, Paarl Rocks, RC Bangalore, Titans
ROLE: Allrounder
DEBUT: ODI: 2015; T20I: 2013; First-class: 2005; List A: 2005; T20: 2008

BEST BATTING: 79* Sussex vs Middlesex, Lord's, 2020 (T20)
BEST BOWLING: 5-19 Titans vs Warriors, Centurion, 2010 (T20)
COUNTY CAP: 2016

MOST EXCITING DAY AS A CRICKETER? Making my ODI debut for South Africa
CHILDHOOD SPORTING HERO? Hansie Cronje – he was an amazing competitor and leader and really knew how to get the best out of his players
FIRST CRICKET CLUB? SACE CC, Mpumalanga, South Africa
TOUGHEST OPPONENT IN COUNTY CRICKET? Chris Rushworth – he always blows my shins off
WHAT WOULD YOU DO IF YOU WERE IN CHARGE OF COUNTY CRICKET? Allow Kolpaks back (ha-ha), start the season later
STRANGEST THING YOU'VE DONE DURING LOCKDOWN? Completing a 3km charity run by doing 20m shuttle runs in my garden
SURPRISING FACT ABOUT YOU? I love theatre and musicals
TWITTER: @David_Wiese
NOTES: Having previously played in all formats under the Kolpak ruling, Wiese fills one of the overseas slots this summer and will feature exclusively in the T20 Blast

Batting	Mat	Inns	NO	Runs	HS	Ave	SR	100	50	Ct	St
ODIs	6	6	1	102	41*	20.40	88.69	0	0	0	0
T20Is	20	11	4	92	28	13.14	122.66	0	0	9	0
First-class	124	194	20	5814	208	33.41	70.98	11	32	70	0
List A	148	125	27	3579	171	36.52	115.63	2	21	46	0
T20s	244	172	63	2668	79*	24.47	146.27	0	6	80	0
Bowling	**Mat**	**Balls**	**Runs**	**Wkts**	**BBI**	**BBM**	**Ave**	**Econ**	**SR**	**5w**	**10**
ODIs	6	294	316	9	3/50	3/50	35.11	6.44	32.6	0	0
T20Is	20	392	497	24	5/23	5/23	20.70	7.60	16.3	1	0
First-class	124	18071	9643	344	6/58	10/111	28.03	3.20	52.5	10	1
List A	148	5508	4937	133	5/25	5/25	37.12	5.37	41.4	1	0
T20s	244	3547	5005	183	5/19	5/19	27.34	8.46	19.3	4	0

DAVID WILLEY

LHB / LFM / R0 / W0

FULL NAME: David Jonathan Willey
BORN: February 28, 1990, Northampton
SQUAD NO: 15
HEIGHT: 6ft 1in
NICKNAME: Will Mildman
EDUCATION: Northampton School for Boys
TEAMS: England, Yorkshire, Chennai Super Kings, Northamptonshire, Perth Scorchers
ROLE: Allrounder
DEBUT: ODI: 2015; T20I: 2015; First-class: 2009; List A: 2009; T20: 2009

BEST BATTING: 104* Northamptonshire vs Gloucestershire, Northampton, 2015
BEST BOWLING: 5-29 Northamptonshire vs Gloucestershire, Northampton, 2011
COUNTY CAP: 2013 (Northamptonshire); 2016 (Yorkshire)

MOST EXCITING DAY AS A CRICKETER? Making my England debut in 2015
FAMILY TIES? My dad Peter played for England, Northamptonshire and Leicestershire
FIRST CRICKET CLUB? Old Northamptonians CC, Northampton
SURPRISING FACT ABOUT YOU? My wife Carolyn is a country singer and was a two-time X Factor contestant
IF YOU WERE AN ANIMAL, WHICH WOULD IT BE? A lion
TWITTER: @david_willey

Batting	Mat	Inns	NO	Runs	HS	Ave	SR	100	50	Ct	St
ODIs	49	29	13	377	51	23.56	88.29	0	2	22	0
T20Is	28	19	7	166	29*	13.83	131.74	0	0	12	0
First-class	71	100	12	2350	104*	26.70	64.70	2	14	17	0
List A	132	94	21	1859	167	25.46	95.62	3	7	48	0
T20s	187	140	25	2722	118	23.66	139.94	2	11	74	0
Bowling	**Mat**	**Balls**	**Runs**	**Wkts**	**BBI**	**BBM**	**Ave**	**Econ**	**SR**	**5w**	**10**
ODIs	49	2143	2037	60	5/30	5/30	33.95	5.70	35.7	1	0
T20Is	28	557	761	34	4/7	4/7	22.38	8.19	16.3	0	0
First-class	71	9854	5416	178	5/29	10/75	30.42	3.29	55.3	5	1
List A	132	4934	4679	148	5/30	5/30	31.61	5.68	33.3	2	0
T20s	187	3149	4120	180	4/7	4/7	22.88	7.85	17.4	0	0

CHRIS WOAKES

RHB / RFM / R0 / W3

WARWICKSHIRE

FULL NAME: Christopher Roger Woakes
BORN: March 2, 1989, Birmingham
SQUAD NO: 19
HEIGHT: 6ft 1in
NICKNAME: Wiz
EDUCATION: Barr Beacon Language College, Walsall
TEAMS: England, Warwickshire, Delhi Capitals, Kolkata Knight Riders, RC Bangalore, Sydney Thunder, Wellington
ROLE: Allrounder
DEBUT: Test: 2013; ODI: 2011; T20I: 2011; First-class: 2006; List A: 2007; T20: 2008

BEST BATTING: 152* Warwickshire vs Derbyshire, Derby, 2013
BEST BOWLING: 9-36 Warwickshire vs Durham, Edgbaston, 2016
COUNTY CAP: 2009

CHILDHOOD SPORTING HERO? Jacques Kallis
FAMILY TIES? My brothers played Birmingham League cricket
SURPRISING FACT ABOUT YOU? I won a keep-uppy competition when I was 10 (70 keepy-ups)
TWITTER: @chriswoakes
NOTES: The England allrounder pulled out of last year's IPL to focus on his international commitments but has been retained by Delhi Capitals for this year's tournament

Batting	Mat	Inns	NO	Runs	HS	Ave	SR	100	50	Ct	St
Tests	38	60	12	1321	137*	27.52	51.34	1	5	17	0
ODIs	104	72	21	1315	95*	25.78	90.87	0	5	45	0
T20Is	8	7	4	91	37	30.33	144.44	0	0	1	0
First-class	152	224	50	5929	152*	34.07	-	10	24	64	0
List A	186	125	37	2056	95*	23.36	90.69	0	6	62	0
T20s	111	69	36	803	57*	24.33	136.10	0	2	41	0
Bowling	**Mat**	**Balls**	**Runs**	**Wkts**	**BBI**	**BBM**	**Ave**	**Econ**	**SR**	**5w**	**10**
Tests	38	6512	3282	112	6/17	11/102	29.30	3.02	58.1	4	1
ODIs	104	4896	4521	149	6/45	6/45	30.34	5.54	32.8	3	0
T20Is	8	162	253	7	2/40	2/40	36.14	9.37	23.1	0	0
First-class	152	25563	13091	514	9/36	11/97	25.46	3.07	49.7	21	4
List A	186	8164	7497	227	6/45	6/45	33.02	5.50	35.9	3	0
T20s	111	2175	3040	121	4/21	4/21	25.12	8.38	17.9	0	0

CHRIS WOOD

RHB / LMF / R0 / W0

FULL NAME: Christopher Philip Wood
BORN: June 27, 1990, Basingstoke, Hampshire
SQUAD NO: 25
HEIGHT: 6ft 3in
NICKNAME: Nuts
EDUCATION: St Lawrence CE Primary School; Amery Hill School; Alton College, Hampshire
TEAMS: Hampshire, England U19
ROLE: Bowler
DEBUT: First-class: 2010; List A: 2010; T20: 2010

BEST BATTING: 27 Hampshire vs Surrey, The Oval, 2014 (T20)
BEST BOWLING: 5-32 Hampshire vs Somerset, Taunton, 2018 (T20)
COUNTY CAP: 2018

MOST EXCITING DAY AS A CRICKETER? Winning the 2012 One-Day Cup at Lord's
CHILDHOOD SPORTING HERO? Nathan Bracken
FIRST CRICKET CLUB? Liphook & Ripsley CC, West Sussex
SURPRISING FACT ABOUT YOU? I played football at semi-professional level
TWITTER: @CWoody27
NOTES: The left-armer announced his retirement from red-ball cricket in March 2020 and agreed a new white-ball contract with Hampshire last December

Batting	Mat	Inns	NO	Runs	HS	Ave	SR	100	50	Ct	St
First-class	43	62	6	1326	105*	23.67	64.65	1	6	14	0
List A	79	45	14	400	41	12.90	96.85	0	0	24	0
T20s	131	48	18	325	27	10.83	101.56	0	0	37	0
Bowling	**Mat**	**Balls**	**Runs**	**Wkts**	**BBI**	**BBM**	**Ave**	**Econ**	**SR**	**5w**	**10**
First-class	43	6169	3174	105	5/39	7/49	30.22	3.08	58.7	3	0
List A	79	3304	2964	105	5/22	5/22	28.22	5.38	31.4	2	0
T20s	131	2658	3671	137	5/32	5/32	26.79	8.28	19.4	1	0

LUKE WOOD

LHB / LMF / R0 / W0

FULL NAME: Luke Wood
BORN: August 2, 1995, Sheffield
SQUAD NO: 14
HEIGHT: 5ft 9in
NICKNAME: Biscuit
EDUCATION: Portland Comprehensive School, Worksop; Outwood Post 16 Centre Worksop
TEAMS: Lancashire, England U19, Nottinghamshire, Worcestershire
ROLE: Bowler
DEBUT: First-class: 2014; List A: 2016; T20: 2016

BEST BATTING: 100 Nottinghamshire vs Sussex, Trent Bridge, 2015
BEST BOWLING: 5-40 Nottinghamshire vs Cambridge MCCU, Cambridge, 2016

MOST EXCITING DAY AS A CRICKETER? Winning the T20 Blast for the second year running with Nottinghamshire in 2018
CHILDHOOD SPORTING HERO? Ryan Sidebottom
BIGGEST INFLUENCE ON YOUR DEVELOPMENT AS A CRICKETER (EXCLUDING PARENTS)? Chris Tolley, the former Notts bowler. He was my first coach at the Notts Academy and it really helped that he was also a left-arm swing bowler
FIRST CRICKET CLUB? Cuckney CC, Nottinghamshire
IF YOU COULD TAKE ONE COUNTY CRICKETER'S BEST SHOT AND ADD IT TO YOUR OWN GAME? Alastair Cook's pull
WHAT WOULD YOU DO IF YOU WERE PRIME MINISTER? Make private healthcare more affordable to relieve the pressure on the NHS
STRANGEST THING YOU'VE DONE DURING LOCKDOWN? Doing DIY (I hate DIY)
GUILTY PLEASURE? Biscuits
TWITTER: @lwood_95

Batting	Mat	Inns	NO	Runs	HS	Ave	SR	100	50	Ct	St
First-class	42	65	14	1263	100	24.76	62.58	1	5	14	0
List A	4	3	2	73	52	73.00	119.67	0	1	0	0
T20s	38	12	4	41	11	5.12	89.13	0	0	14	0
Bowling	**Mat**	**Balls**	**Runs**	**Wkts**	**BBI**	**BBM**	**Ave**	**Econ**	**SR**	**5w**	**10**
First-class	42	5561	3326	99	5/40	8/83	33.59	3.58	56.1	3	0
List A	4	126	125	5	2/36	2/36	25.00	5.95	25.2	0	0
T20s	38	613	832	31	3/16	3/16	26.83	8.14	19.7	0	0

MARK WOOD

RHB / RF / R0 / W0

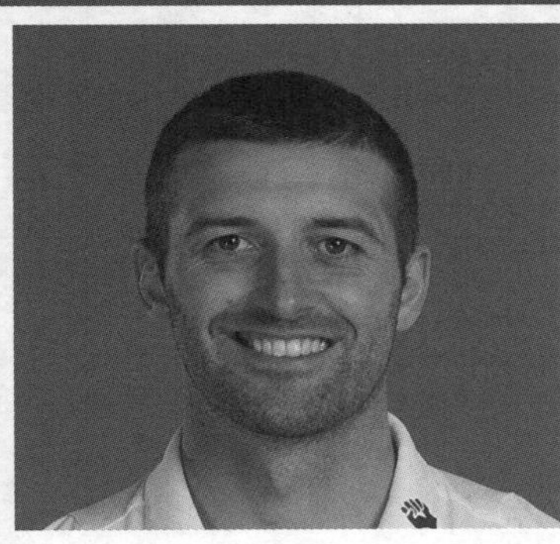

FULL NAME: Mark Andrew Wood
BORN: January 11, 1990, Ashington, Northumberland
SQUAD NO: 33
HEIGHT: 6ft
EDUCATION: Ashington High School; Newcastle College
TEAMS: England, Durham, Chennai Super Kings
ROLE: Bowler
DEBUT: Test: 2015; ODI: 2015; T20I: 2015; First-class: 2011; List A: 2011; T20: 2013

BEST BATTING: 72* Durham vs Kent, Chester-le-Street, 2017
BEST BOWLING: 6-46 Durham vs Derbyshire, Derby, 2018

FAMILY TIES? My dad Derek and uncle Neil played for Ashington CC and Minor Counties for Northumberland
CHILDHOOD SPORTING HERO? Steve Harmison
SURPRISING FACT ABOUT YOU? I was in the Newcastle United FC Academy
TWITTER: @MAWood33

Batting	Mat	Inns	NO	Runs	HS	Ave	SR	100	50	Ct	St
Tests	18	30	6	402	52	16.75	66.22	0	1	7	0
ODIs	53	17	10	56	13	8.00	88.88	0	0	12	0
T20Is	11	2	2	10	5*	-	83.33	0	0	0	0
First-class	56	91	18	1538	72*	21.06	57.23	0	5	16	0
List A	87	33	15	118	24	6.55	80.82	0	0	22	0
T20s	32	13	7	106	27*	17.66	102.91	0	0	4	0
Bowling	**Mat**	**Balls**	**Runs**	**Wkts**	**BBI**	**BBM**	**Ave**	**Econ**	**SR**	**5w**	**10**
Tests	18	3293	1772	53	5/41	9/100	33.43	3.22	62.1	2	0
ODIs	53	2699	2479	64	4/33	4/33	38.73	5.51	42.1	0	0
T20Is	11	237	360	18	3/9	3/9	20.00	9.11	13.1	0	0
First-class	56	8937	4862	179	6/46	9/100	27.16	3.26	49.9	10	0
List A	87	4078	3619	110	4/33	4/33	32.90	5.32	37.0	0	0
T20s	32	657	907	38	4/25	4/25	23.86	8.28	17.2	0	0

TOM WOOD RHB / RM / R0 / W0

FULL NAME: Thomas Anthony Wood
BORN: May 11, 1994, Derby
SQUAD NO: 24
HEIGHT: 6ft
NICKNAME: Woody
EDUCATION: Heanor Gate Science College, Derbyshire
TEAMS: Derbyshire
ROLE: Batsman
DEBUT: First-class: 2016; List A: 2016; T20: 2017

BEST BATTING: 26 Derbyshire vs Yorkshire, Headingley, 2020

MOST EXCITING DAY AS A CRICKETER? My first-class debut in 2016
CHILDHOOD SPORTING HERO? Andrew Flintoff
BIGGEST INFLUENCE ON YOUR DEVELOPMENT AS A CRICKETER (EXCLUDING PARENTS)? Tony Borrington, the former Derbyshire batsman
FIRST CRICKET CLUB? Stainsby Hall CC, Derbyshire
IF YOU COULD TAKE ONE COUNTY CRICKETER'S BEST SHOT AND ADD IT TO YOUR OWN GAME? Wayne Madsen's sweep
TOUGHEST OPPONENT IN COUNTY CRICKET? Clint McKay – he's so skilful
WHAT WOULD YOU DO IF YOU WERE IN CHARGE OF COUNTY CRICKET? Invest more in education and post-career options for players, make counties play a certain number of homegrown players
WHAT WOULD YOU DO IF YOU WERE PRIME MINISTER? Make a deal with Australia and New Zealand to ease travel arrangements
FAVOURITE SMELL? Freshly baked cookies
GUILTY PLEASURE? Reality TV
TWITTER: @tom_wood

Batting	Mat	Inns	NO	Runs	HS	Ave	SR	100	50	Ct	St
First-class	4	6	0	73	26	12.16	38.02	0	0	3	0
List A	2	1	0	44	44	44.00	107.31	0	0	0	0
T20s	4	3	0	100	67	33.33	126.58	0	1	1	0
Bowling	**Mat**	**Balls**	**Runs**	**Wkts**	**BBI**	**BBM**	**Ave**	**Econ**	**SR**	**5w**	**10**
First-class	4	-	-	-	-	-	-	-	-	-	-
List A	2	-	-	-	-	-	-	-	-	-	-
T20s	4	-	-	-	-	-	-	-	-	-	-

DAN WORRALL RHB / RFM / R0 / W0

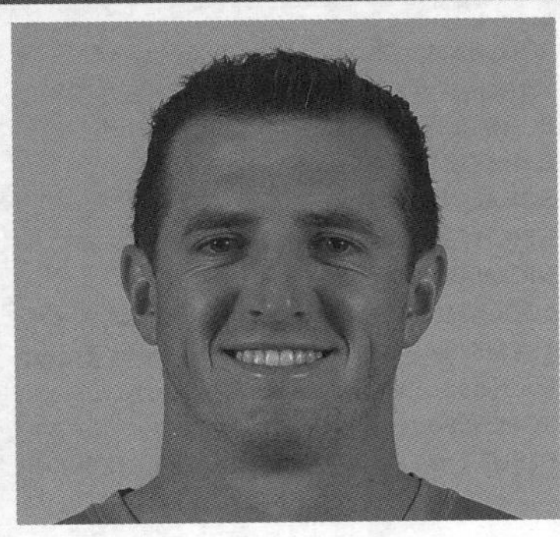

FULL NAME: Daniel James Worrall
BORN: July 10, 1991, Melbourne, Australia
SQUAD NO: 41
TEAMS: Australia, Gloucestershire, Adelaide Strikers, Melbourne Stars, South Australia
ROLE: Bowler
DEBUT: ODI: 2016; First-class: 2012; List A: 2012; T20: 2014

BEST BATTING: 50 Gloucestershire vs Glamorgan, Bristol, 2018
BEST BOWLING: 7-64 South Australia vs Western Australia, Adelaide, 2018
COUNTY CAP: 2018

NOTES: The 29-year-old Australian pace bowler returns to Gloucestershire and will be available across all formats this summer. Worrall first signed for the club ahead of the 2018 season and impressed with 16 wickets at 21.75 in his first four Championship matches before he was sidelined for the rest of the season with a foot injury. He returned to Bristol in 2019 but a stress fracture in his back restricted him to two One-Day Cup matches. Worrall made his first-class debut in 2012 and finished as the second-highest wicket-taker in the 2015/16 Sheffield Shield. He appeared in three ODIs for Australia in 2016 but hasn't played international cricket since then, largely due to persistent injury. Worrall plays for South Australia in the Sheffield Shield and for Adelaide Strikers in the Big Bash

Batting	Mat	Inns	NO	Runs	HS	Ave	SR	100	50	Ct	St
ODIs	3	1	1	6	6*	-	150.00	0	0	1	0
First-class	49	75	31	612	50	13.90	45.50	0	1	14	0
List A	31	15	10	60	16	12.00	66.66	0	0	12	0
T20s	44	16	8	127	62*	15.87	129.59	0	1	11	0
Bowling	**Mat**	**Balls**	**Runs**	**Wkts**	**BBI**	**BBM**	**Ave**	**Econ**	**SR**	**5w**	**10**
ODIs	3	158	171	1	1/43	1/43	171.00	6.49	158.0	0	0
First-class	49	10411	5362	192	7/64	10/148	27.92	3.09	54.2	7	1
List A	31	1604	1410	39	5/62	5/62	36.15	5.27	41.1	1	0
T20s	44	868	1167	37	4/23	4/23	31.54	8.06	23.4	0	0

CHRIS WRIGHT

RHB / RMF / R0 / W2

FULL NAME: Christopher Julian Clement Wright
BORN: July 14, 1985, Chipping Norton, Oxfordshire
SQUAD NO: 31
HEIGHT: 6ft 3in
NICKNAME: Dog
EDUCATION: Eggars Grammar School, Alton
TEAMS: Leicestershire, England Lions, Essex, Middlesex, Tamil Union, Warwickshire
ROLE: Bowler
DEBUT: First-class: 2004; List A: 2004; T20: 2004

BEST BATTING: 77 Essex vs Cambridge MCCU, Cambridge, 2011
BEST BOWLING: 6-22 Essex vs Leicestershire, Leicester, 2008
COUNTY CAP: 2013 (Warwickshire)

MOST EXCITING DAY AS A CRICKETER? The Lord's one-day final in 2012 when I was at Warwickshire. The scores were tied but Hampshire won on fewer wickets lost
CHILDHOOD SPORTING HERO? Mark Ramprakash
BIGGEST INFLUENCE ON YOUR DEVELOPMENT AS A CRICKETER (EXCLUDING PARENTS)? Graeme Welch, my bowling coach at Essex and then at Warwickshire
TOUGHEST OPPONENT IN COUNTY CRICKET? In my early career, Stephen Fleming. Marcus Trescothick has always been tough to bowl at in all formats
MOST ECCENTRIC TEAMMATE? Dieter Klein – he does forward-rolls all the time
WHAT WOULD YOU DO IF YOU WERE IN CHARGE OF COUNTY CRICKET? Ensure that the MCC University scheme continues and is properly funded, allow more time for training within the summer schedule
WHAT WOULD YOU DO IF YOU WERE PRIME MINISTER? Try to get people to stop complaining about everything
STRANGEST THING YOU'VE DONE DURING LOCKDOWN? Singing to my kids
TWITTER: @chriswright1985

Batting	Mat	Inns	NO	Runs	HS	Ave	SR	100	50	Ct	St
First-class	164	211	46	3031	77	18.36	48.38	0	12	29	0
List A	103	43	20	263	42	11.43	73.25	0	0	17	0
T20s	62	16	9	30	6*	4.28	90.90	0	0	13	0
Bowling	**Mat**	**Balls**	**Runs**	**Wkts**	**BBI**	**BBM**	**Ave**	**Econ**	**SR**	**5w**	**10**
First-class	164	26316	15294	464	6/22		32.96	3.48	56.7	13	0
List A	103	4025	3766	102	4/20	4/20	36.92	5.61	39.4	0	0
T20s	62	1222	1834	53	4/24	4/24	34.60	9.00	23.0	0	0

LUKE WRIGHT RHB / RM / MVP63

FULL NAME: Luke James Wright
BORN: March 7, 1985, Grantham, Lincolnshire
SQUAD NO: 10
HEIGHT: 5ft 10in
NICKNAME: Bam Bam
EDUCATION: Loughborough University; Manchester Metropolitan University
TEAMS: England, Sussex, Leicestershire, Melbourne Stars, Pune Warriors
ROLE: Batsman
DEBUT: ODI: 2007; T20I: 2007; First-class: 2003; List A 2002; T20: 2004

BEST BATTING: 153* Sussex vs Essex, Chelmsford, 2014 (T20)
BEST BOWLING: 3-17 Sussex vs Surrey, The Oval, 2006 (T20)
COUNTY CAP: 2007 (Sussex); BENEFIT: 2017 (Sussex)

BIGGEST INFLUENCE ON YOUR DEVELOPMENT AS A CRICKETER (EXCLUDING PARENTS)? My brother Ashley Wright – the best batting coach I ever had
FIRST CRICKET CLUB? Bottesford CC, Leicestershire. I played men's cricket at a really young age, which helped me develop. Lots of great memories
IF YOU COULD TAKE ONE COUNTY CRICKETER'S BEST SHOT AND ADD IT TO YOUR OWN GAME? David Wiese's huge sixes over long-on
TOUGHEST OPPONENT IN COUNTY CRICKET? Tymal Mills in training, often with no sightscreens
STRANGEST THING YOU'VE DONE DURING LOCKDOWN? Home-schooling
FAVOURITE SMELL? Mexican food
TWITTER: @lukewright204
NOTES: Sussex's white-ball captain signed a new contract last October that will see him play in the short formats until the end of 2023

Batting	Mat	Inns	NO	Runs	HS	Ave	SR	100	50	Ct	St
ODIs	50	39	4	707	52	20.20	86.21	0	2	18	0
T20Is	51	45	5	759	99*	18.97	137.00	0	4	14	0
First-class	144	223	23	7622	226*	38.11	65.54	17	38	58	0
List A	211	176	21	5126	166	33.07		11	19	66	0
T20s	325	302	27	7998	153*	29.08	142.71	7	42	97	0
Bowling	**Mat**	**Balls**	**Runs**	**Wkts**	**BBI**	**BBM**	**Ave**	**Econ**	**SR**	**5w**	**10**
ODIs	50	1038	884	15	2/34	2/34	58.93	5.10	69.2	0	0
T20Is	51	330	465	18	2/24	2/24	25.83	8.45	18.3	0	0
First-class	144	8264	4862	120	5/65		40.51	3.53	68.8	3	0
List A	211	4752	4231	111	4/12	4/12	38.11	5.34	42.8	0	0
T20s	325	1799	2563	79	3/17	3/17	32.44	8.54	22.7	0	0

ROB YATES

LHB / OB / R0 / W0

FULL NAME: Robert Michael Yates
BORN: September 19, 1999, Solihull, Warwickshire
SQUAD NO: 17
HEIGHT: 6ft 2in
NICKNAME: Robot
EDUCATION: Warwick School; University of Birmingham
TEAMS: Warwickshire
ROLE: Batsman
DEBUT: First-class: 2019; List A: 2019; T20: 2020

BEST BATTING: 141 Warwickshire vs Somerset, Edgbaston, 2019

MOST EXCITING DAY AS A CRICKETER? Scoring my maiden first-class hundred and then watching my best mate George Garrett take his maiden first-class wicket in the Championship game against Somerset in 2019
CHILDHOOD SPORTING HERO? Alastair Cook
IF YOU COULD TAKE ONE COUNTY CRICKETER'S BEST SHOT AND ADD IT TO YOUR OWN GAME? Dan Mousley's sweep
FIRST CRICKET CLUB? Moseley CC, Solihull, West Midlands
TOUGHEST OPPONENT IN COUNTY CRICKET? Kyle Abbott – for his consistency and execution
BIGGEST CRICKETING REGRET? Dropping someone on 10 who went on to make 190. The match would have been over a day earlier if I'd taken that catch
WHAT WOULD YOU DO IF YOU WERE PRIME MINISTER? Protect the environment
TWITTER: @robert_yates99

Batting	Mat	Inns	NO	Runs	HS	Ave	SR	100	50	Ct	St
First-class	17	28	1	707	141	26.18	38.21	1	3	12	0
List A	1	1	0	66	66	66.00	89.18	0	1	0	0
T20s	4	4	0	89	37	22.25	158.92	0	0	1	0
Bowling	**Mat**	**Balls**	**Runs**	**Wkts**	**BBI**	**BBM**	**Ave**	**Econ**	**SR**	**5w**	**10**
First-class	17	132	37	0	-	-	-	1.68	-	0	0
List A	1	-	-	-	-	-	-	-	-	-	-
T20s	4	-	-	-	-	-	-	-	-	-	-

SAM YOUNG RHB / OB / R0 / W0

FULL NAME: Samuel Jack Young
BORN: July 30, 2000, Plymouth, Devon
SQUAD NO: 77
HEIGHT: 6ft
EDUCATION: Millfield School, Street, Somerset
TEAMS: Somerset, England U19
ROLE: Batsman

MOST EXCITING DAY AS A CRICKETER? Receiving my England U19 cap
CHILDHOOD SPORTING HERO? Jos Buttler
BIGGEST INFLUENCE ON YOUR DEVELOPMENT AS A CRICKETER (EXCLUDING PARENTS)? Mark Garaway, the former England assistant coach and now director of cricket at Millfield School
FIRST CRICKET CLUB? Bath CC, Somerset
IF YOU COULD TAKE ONE COUNTY CRICKETER'S BEST SHOT AND ADD IT TO YOUR OWN GAME? Alastair Cook's pull
MOST ECCENTRIC TEAMMATE? Jack Brooks
FAVOURITE SMELL? Leather
IF YOU WERE AN ANIMAL, WHICH WOULD IT BE? An elephant – because I'm peaceful
GUILTY PLEASURE? Milkshakes
TWITTER: @sam_y0ung
NOTES: The top-order batsman signed a two-year deal with Somerset in September 2019 after coming up through the club's age-group system. Young has played Minor Counties for Cheshire and Devon, while also turning out for Somerset Second XI and Bath CC. The former Millfield School pupil made his England U19 debut in December 2019 and went on to make four appearances at the U19 World Cup last year, with a top score of 39 not out against Nigeria at Kimberley

SAIF ZAIB

LHB / SLA / R0 / W0

FULL NAME: Saif Ali Zaib
BORN: May 22, 1998, High Wycombe, Buckinghamshire
SQUAD NO: 5
HEIGHT: 5ft 8in
NICKNAME: Danger
EDUCATION: Royal Grammar School, High Wycombe
TEAMS: Northamptonshire
ROLE: Bowler
DEBUT: First-class: 2015; List A: 2014; T20: 2017

BEST BATTING: 65* Northamptonshire vs Glamorgan, Swansea, 2016
BEST BOWLING: 6-115 Northamptonshire vs Loughborough MCCU, Northampton, 2017

CHILDHOOD SPORTING HERO? Brian Lara
BIGGEST INFLUENCE ON YOUR DEVELOPMENT AS A CRICKETER (EXCLUDING PARENTS)? My grandad – he showed me how hard work gets rewarded
FIRST CRICKET CLUB? High Wycombe CC, Buckinghamshire
IF YOU COULD TAKE ONE COUNTY CRICKETER'S BEST SHOT AND ADD IT TO YOUR OWN GAME? Adam Rossington's pull
TOUGHEST OPPONENT IN COUNTY CRICKET? Darren Stevens
WHAT WOULD YOU DO IF YOU WERE IN CHARGE OF COUNTY CRICKET? Increase the amount of T20 cricket!
STRANGEST THING YOU'VE DONE DURING LOCKDOWN? Staying in bed the whole day (which is very unlike me)
FAVOURITE SMELL? Petrol
GUILTY PLEASURE? Cinnamon swirls
TWITTER: @zaib_05

Batting	Mat	Inns	NO	Runs	HS	Ave	SR	100	50	Ct	St
First-class	20	29	3	530	65*	20.38	46.08	0	3	5	0
List A	10	7	0	73	17	10.42	78.49	0	0	0	0
T20s	13	9	1	123	30	15.37	120.58	0	0	8	0
Bowling	**Mat**	**Balls**	**Runs**	**Wkts**	**BBI**	**BBM**	**Ave**	**Econ**	**SR**	**5w**	**10**
First-class	20	829	497	17	6/115	6/115	29.23	3.59	48.7	2	0
List A	10	174	202	3	2/22	2/22	67.33	6.96	58.0	0	0
T20s	13	96	130	2	1/20	1/20	65.00	8.12	48.0	0	0

Women's
Players

GEORGIA ADAMS

RHB / OB / MVP1

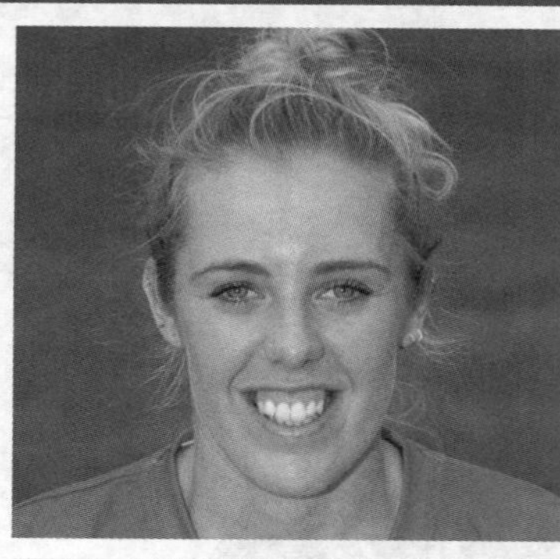

FULL NAME: Georgia Louise Adams
BORN: October 4, 1993, Chesterfield, Derbyshire
SQUAD NO: 1
HEIGHT: 5ft 9in
NICKNAME: Gadz
EDUCATION: Brighton College; Loughborough University
TEAMS: Southern Vipers, Sussex, Loughborough Lightning
ROLE: Batsman
DEBUT: List A: 2009; T20: 2009

BEST BATTING: 154* Southern Vipers vs Western Storm, Southampton, 2020
BEST BOWLING: 3-23 Southern Vipers vs Western Storm, Bristol, 2020

MOST EXCITING DAY AS A CRICKETER? Winning the Rachael Heyhoe Flint Trophy with Southern Vipers last year
CHILDHOOD SPORTING HERO? Chris Adams
BIGGEST INFLUENCE ON YOUR DEVELOPMENT AS A CRICKETER (EXCLUDING PARENTS)? Salliann Briggs – former England player and Loughborough Lightning head coach. She taught me to how to take myself out of my comfort zone
FIRST CRICKET CLUB? Henfield CC, West Sussex
WHAT WOULD YOU DO IF YOU WERE IN CHARGE OF WOMEN'S CRICKET? Have coloured clothing and a white ball for all women's cricket – including at club level
STRANGEST THING YOU'VE DONE DURING LOCKDOWN? Performing a gymnastics routine while dressed in my full Sussex kit with a tutu
GUILTY PLEASURE? Chocolate in any shape or form
TWITTER: @GeorgiaAdams01

Batting	Mat	Inns	NO	Runs	HS	Ave	SR	100	50	Ct	St
List A	62	59	6	1721	154*	32.47	68.40	3	8	34	-
T20s	87	78	13	1529	69*	23.52	98.07	0	10	37	-
Bowling	**Mat**	**Balls**	**Mdns**	**Runs**	**Wkts**	**BB**	**Ave**	**4wI**	**5wI**	**SR**	**Econ**
List A	62	919	17	586	18	3-23	32.55	0	0	51.05	3.82
T20s	87	180	0	186	8	3-9	23.25	0	0	22.50	6.20

EMILY ARLOTT RHB / RMF / MVP59

FULL NAME: Emily Louise Arlott
BORN: February 23, 1998, King's Lynn, Norfolk
SQUAD NO: 14
HEIGHT: 6ft
NICKNAME: Arlo
EDUCATION: John Masefield High School, Ledbury, Herefordshire
TEAMS: Central Sparks, Worcestershire
ROLE: Bowler
DEBUT: List A: 2013; T20: 2013

BEST BATTING: 33 Worcestershire vs Ireland, Kidderminster, 2015
BEST BOWLING: 4-25 Worcestershire vs Somerset, Kidderminster, 2019

MOST EXCITING DAY AS A CRICKETER? Playing for Central Sparks in their first-ever game in the Rachael Heyhoe Flint Trophy
CHILDHOOD SPORTING HERO? Jessica Ennis-Hill
BIGGEST INFLUENCE ON YOUR DEVELOPMENT AS A CRICKETER (EXCLUDING PARENTS)? Elliot Wilson – Academy coach at Worcestershire. He helped me progress as a cricketer from the age of 13 to where I am now. He's always been there to support me on and off the field and has been a very good friend during some tough times in my life
FIRST CRICKET CLUB? Eastnor CC, Ledbury, Herefordshire
TOUGHEST OPPONENT IN CRICKET? Katherine Brunt – such a competitor. Scoring against her is very hard because she hits such a good length almost every ball and is very aggressive and attacking
MOST ECCENTRIC TEAMMATE? Issy Wong – for the hairstyles and colours (a recent one was bright blue)
WHAT WOULD YOU DO IF YOU WERE IN CHARGE OF WOMEN'S CRICKET? Pay all regional players and make cricket more accessible to girls regardless of where they live
GUILTY PLEASURE? Nando's
TWITTER: @EmArlott

Batting	Mat	Inns	NO	Runs	HS	Ave	SR	100	50	Ct	St
List A	45	37	3	292	33	8.58	-	0	0	21	-
T20s	38	31	9	366	54	16.63	-	0	1	9	-
Bowling	**Mat**	**Balls**	**Mdns**	**Runs**	**Wkts**	**BB**	**Ave**	**4wI**	**5wI**	**SR**	**Econ**
List A	45	1577	27	1163	38	4-25	30.60	1	0	41.50	4.42
T20s	38	601	1	566	24	3-21	23.58	0	0	25.04	5.65

HOLLIE ARMITAGE

RHB / LB / MVP12

NORTHERN DIAMONDS

FULL NAME: Hollie Jade Armitage
BORN: June 14, 1997, Huddersfield
SQUAD NO: 57
HEIGHT: 5ft 9in
NICKNAME: Armo
EDUCATION: Loughborough College
TEAMS: Northern Diamonds, Yorkshire, Sydney Sixers, Tasmania, Yorkshire Diamonds
ROLE: Allrounder
DEBUT: List A: 2013; T20: 2013

BEST BATTING: 70 Yorkshire vs Staffordshire, Hanley, 2016
BEST BOWLING: 4-17 Yorkshire vs Berkshire, Finchampstead, 2016

MOST EXCITING DAY AS A CRICKETER? Getting my first professional contract with Northern Diamonds last year
CHILDHOOD SPORTING HERO? Ian Bell
FIRST CRICKET CLUB? Meltham CC, Kirklees, West Yorkshire
TOUGHEST OPPONENT IN CRICKET? Sophie Devine
WHAT WOULD YOU DO IF YOU WERE IN CHARGE OF WOMEN'S CRICKET? Offer contracts to all professional domestic players, improve the standard of women's club cricket, arrange for England-contracted players to work with the next generation
WHAT WOULD YOU DO IF YOU WERE PRIME MINISTER? No horses on the road, free public transport, import good independent coffee shops from Australia
FAVOURITE SMELL? Fresh sheets
GUILTY PLEASURE? Putting hot sauce on pretty much every meal
TWITTER: @HollieArmo

Batting	Mat	Inns	NO	Runs	HS	Ave	SR	100	50	Ct	St
List A	48	46	3	1020	70	23.72	57.49	0	8	16	-
T20s	49	46	3	608	59	14.13	94.11	0	1	17	-
Bowling	**Mat**	**Balls**	**Mdns**	**Runs**	**Wkts**	**BB**	**Ave**	**4wI**	**5wI**	**SR**	**Econ**
List A	48	844	8	670	33	4-17	20.30	1	0	25.57	4.76
T20s	49	287	1	253	10	3-15	25.30	0	0	28.70	5.28

TAMMY BEAUMONT RHB / WK / MVP92

FULL NAME: Tamsin Tilley Beaumont
BORN: March 11, 1991, Dover, Kent
SQUAD NO: 12
HEIGHT: 5ft 2in
NICKNAME: Tambo
EDUCATION: Sir Roger Manwood's School, Kent; Loughborough University
TEAMS: England, Lightning, Kent, Adelaide Strikers, Melbourne Renegades, Southern Vipers, Surrey Stars, Sydney Thunder
ROLE: Batsman
DEBUT: Test: 2013; ODI: 2009; T20I: 2009; List A: 2007; T20: 2008

BEST ODI BATTING: 168* England vs Pakistan, Taunton, 2016

MOST EXCITING DAY AS A CRICKETER? The 2017 World Cup final at Lord's
CHILDHOOD SPORTING HERO? Kelly Holmes
BIGGEST INFLUENCE ON YOUR DEVELOPMENT AS A CRICKETER (EXCLUDING PARENTS)? Carl Crowe – he was our England assistant coach on some of my first tours and has since been a close friend and mentor
FIRST CRICKET CLUB? Sandwich Town CC, Kent
TOUGHEST OPPONENT IN CRICKET? Katherine Brunt – when we play against each other we know it's a battle we both want to win, but we always leave it there on the field and are great mates off it
WHAT WOULD YOU DO IF YOU WERE IN CHARGE OF WOMEN'S CRICKET? Host an U19 Women's World Cup, invest in the development of the lower-ranked nations
WHAT WOULD YOU DO IF YOU WERE PRIME MINISTER? Increase taxes on the biggest environmental-polluting companies and incentivise green and zero-waste initiatives
STRANGEST THING YOU'VE DONE DURING LOCKDOWN? Learning to rollerblade
GUILTY PLEASURE? Listening to the Hamilton musical soundtrack on repeat
TWITTER: @Tammy_Beaumont

Batting	Mat	Inns	NO	Runs	HS	Ave	SR	100	50	Ct	St
Tests	4	6	0	132	70	22.00	40.36	0	1	3	0
ODIs	74	66	8	2618	168*	45.13	73.37	7	12	17	4
T20Is	91	75	10	1484	116	22.83	108.16	1	8	14	4
Bowling	**Mat**	**Balls**	**Runs**	**Wkts**	**BBI**	**BBM**	**Ave**	**Econ**	**SR**	**5w**	**10**
Tests	4	-	-	-	-	-	-	-	-	-	-
ODIs	74	-	-	-	-	-	-	-	-	-	-
T20Is	91	-	-	-	-	-	-	-	-	-	-

LAUREN BELL

RHB / RFM / MVP38

FULL NAME: Lauren Katie Bell
BORN: January 2, 2001, Swindon, Wiltshire
SQUAD NO: 14
HEIGHT: 6ft 1in
NICKNAME: Belly
EDUCATION: Bradfield College; Loughborough University
TEAMS: Southern Vipers, Middlesex, Berkshire
ROLE: Bowler
DEBUT: List A: 2015; T20: 2015

BEST BATTING: 36 Berkshire vs Surrey, Maidenhead, 2018
BEST BOWLING: 4-17 Berkshire vs Devon, Maidenhead, 2018

MOST EXCITING DAY AS A CRICKETER? Winning the Rachael Heyhoe Flint Trophy last year
CHILDHOOD SPORTING HERO? Cristiano Ronaldo
FIRST CRICKET CLUB? Hungerford CC, Berkshire
IF YOU COULD TAKE ONE FEMALE CRICKETER'S BEST SHOT AND ADD IT TO YOUR OWN GAME? Paige Schofield's reverse-sweep
TOUGHEST OPPONENT IN CRICKET? Heather Knight – she has played with me since I was young and knows exactly how to play me
WHAT WOULD YOU DO IF YOU WERE IN CHARGE OF WOMEN'S CRICKET? Increase the number of overseas tours
WHAT WOULD YOU DO IF YOU WERE PRIME MINISTER? Get myself a box at Manchester United, give Taylor Swift a knighthood, go to the Maldives
STRANGEST THING YOU'VE DONE DURING LOCKDOWN? Finishing coursework essays earlier than the due date
FAVOURITE SMELL? Dior Sauvage
TWITTER: @_laurenbell2

Batting	Mat	Inns	NO	Runs	HS	Ave	SR	100	50	Ct	St
List A	33	25	6	193	36	10.15	-	0	0	6	-
T20s	39	19	6	126	35	9.69	72.83	0	0	9	-
Bowling	**Mat**	**Balls**	**Mdns**	**Runs**	**Wkts**	**BB**	**Ave**	**4wI**	**5wI**	**SR**	**Econ**
List A	33	1341	17	913	48	4-17	19.02	2	0	27.93	4.08
T20s	39	604	3	634	24	2-15	26.41	0	0	25.16	6.29

MAIA BOUCHIER

RHB / RM / MVP20

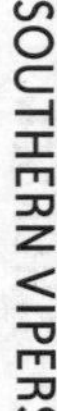

FULL NAME: Maia Emily Bouchier
BORN: December 5, 1998, Kensington, London
SQUAD NO: 16
HEIGHT: 5ft 9in
NICKNAME: The Mighty Bouch
EDUCATION: Dragon School, Oxford; Rugby School, Warwickshire; Oxford Brookes University
TEAMS: Southern Vipers, Hampshire, Auckland, Middlesex
ROLE: Allrounder
DEBUT: List A: 2014; T20: 2014

BEST BATTING: 76 Middlesex vs Somerset, Taunton, 2018
BEST BOWLING: 3-24 Middlesex vs Warwickshire, Wellesbourne, 2014

MOST EXCITING DAY AS A CRICKETER? Winning the Rachael Heyhoe Flint Trophy final with Southern Vipers last September
CHILDHOOD SPORTING HERO? Alastair Cook
BIGGEST INFLUENCE ON YOUR DEVELOPMENT AS A CRICKETER (EXCLUDING PARENTS)? Tim Roberts and Michael Powell, my old coaches at Rugby School. They helped build my confidence against quick bowlers at school, where I was playing boys' First XI cricket
FIRST CRICKET CLUB? Primrose Hill CC, London
IF YOU COULD TAKE ONE FEMALE CRICKETER'S BEST SHOT AND ADD IT TO YOUR OWN GAME? Nat Sciver's "Natmeg"
WHAT WOULD YOU DO IF YOU WERE PRIME MINISTER? Sort out the coronavirus, then buy a private jet and take my family and friends to a remote spot somewhere in New Zealand
STRANGEST THING YOU'VE DONE DURING LOCKDOWN? Taking part in a loo-roll kick-up challenge
FAVOURITE SMELL? Lavender
GUILTY PLEASURE? Marmite
TWITTER: @maiabouchier

Batting	Mat	Inns	NO	Runs	HS	Ave	SR	100	50	Ct	St
List A	40	36	6	893	76	29.76	71.15	0	5	18	-
T20s	55	51	9	655	56	15.59	-	0	1	21	-
Bowling	**Mat**	**Balls**	**Mdns**	**Runs**	**Wkts**	**BB**	**Ave**	**4wI**	**5wI**	**SR**	**Econ**
List A	40	538	4	356	15	3-24	23.73	0	0	35.86	3.97
T20s	55	210	1	197	12	3-18	16.41	0	0	17.50	5.62

GEORGIE BOYCE

RHB / RM / MVP67

FULL NAME: Georgie Eva Burton Boyce
BORN: October 4, 1998, Nottingham
SQUAD NO: 8
HEIGHT: 5ft 6in
EDUCATION: The Holgate Academy, Hucknall, Nottinghamshire; Loughborough University
TEAMS: Thunder, Lancashire, Lancashire Thunder, Nottinghamshire
ROLE: Batsman
DEBUT: List A: 2014; T20: 2013

BEST BATTING: 83 Lancashire vs Surrey, Guildford, 2019
BEST BOWLING: 2-20 Lancashire vs Yorkshire, Harrogate, 2019

MOST EXCITING DAY AS A CRICKETER? The match between Southern Vipers and Lancashire Thunder in the 2018 Kia Super League. The Vipers were coasting to their target but collapsed at the end to give us victory by nine runs
BIGGEST INFLUENCE ON YOUR DEVELOPMENT AS A CRICKETER (EXCLUDING PARENTS)? Sue Day, my primary-school PE teacher. She introduced me to cricket and took me to see some women's matches
FIRST CRICKET CLUB? Notts & Arnold CC, Nottingham
IF YOU COULD TAKE ONE FEMALE CRICKETER'S BEST SHOT AND ADD IT TO YOUR OWN GAME? Nat Sciver's back-foot punch through the leg-side
TOUGHEST OPPONENT IN CRICKET? Lizelle Lee – she smashed something like 200 runs against us in one season of the Kia Super League
WHAT WOULD YOU DO IF YOU WERE IN CHARGE OF WOMEN'S CRICKET? Make better pitches and get cricket into state schools
STRANGEST THING YOU'VE DONE DURING LOCKDOWN? Learning to shoot an air rifle
GUILTY PLEASURE? Watching Neighbours on Channel 5 daily (without fail)
TWITTER: @GeorgieBoyce

Batting	Mat	Inns	NO	Runs	HS	Ave	SR	100	50	Ct	St
List A	41	41	1	885	83	22.12	-	0	4	8	-
T20s	57	53	3	937	87	18.74	-	0	5	8	-
Bowling	**Mat**	**Balls**	**Mdns**	**Runs**	**Wkts**	**BB**	**Ave**	**4wI**	**5wI**	**SR**	**Econ**
List A	41	438	6	298	6	2-20	49.66	0	0	73.00	4.08
T20s	57	222	0	227	6	2-15	37.83	0	0	37.00	6.13

KATHERINE BRUNT

RHB / RFM / MVP43

FULL NAME: Katherine Helen Brunt
BORN: July 2, 1985, Barnsley
SQUAD NO: 26
HEIGHT: 5ft 5in
NICKNAME: Baby Rhino
EDUCATION: Penistone Grammar School, South Yorkshire
TEAMS: England, Northern Diamonds, Yorkshire, Melbourne Stars, Perth Scorchers, Yorkshire Diamonds
ROLE: Bowler
DEBUT: Test: 2004; ODI: 2005; T20I: 2005; List A: 2004; T20: 2004

BEST ODI BATTING: 72* England vs South Africa, Worcester, 2018
BEST ODI BOWLING: 5-18 England vs Australia, Wormsley, 2011

MOST EXCITING DAY AS A CRICKETER? My two Ashes Test wins in 2005 and 2014
CHILDHOOD SPORTING HERO? Darren Gough – I modelled my action on his and I saw something of his aggression in myself
BIGGEST INFLUENCE ON YOUR DEVELOPMENT AS A CRICKETER (EXCLUDING PARENTS)? My brother Daniel
FIRST CRICKET CLUB? Barnsley CC, South Yorkshire
TOUGHEST OPPONENT IN CRICKET? I've had many battles over the years but the most talented and fearless would be Australia's Alyssa Healy
BIGGEST CRICKETING REGRET? Being born in the wrong era. I would have had a safer bowling action earlier because I would have had a proper coach in this day and age. And I wouldn't have had a chronic back issue
FAVOURITE SMELL? A baby's head
SURPRISING FACT ABOUT YOU? I have dates of all my major career achievements tattooed on my ribs. The last one was "23rd July 2017" to mark the day we won the World Cup
GUILTY PLEASURE? Scampi fries
TWITTER: @KBrunt26

Batting	Mat	Inns	NO	Runs	HS	Ave	SR	100	50	Ct	St
Tests	12	15	4	171	52	15.54	29.43	0	1	3	0
ODIs	125	69	18	844	72*	16.54	77.14	0	2	37	0
T20Is	89	55	25	496	42*	16.53	113.76	0	0	25	0
Bowling	**Mat**	**Balls**	**Runs**	**Wkts**	**BBI**	**BBM**	**Ave**	**Econ**	**SR**	**5w**	**10**
Tests	12	2238	923	41	6/69	9/111	22.51	2.47	54.5	2	0
ODIs	125	6077	3540	153	5/18	5/18	23.13	3.49	39.7	5	0
T20Is	89	1931	1758	93	3/6	3/6	18.90	5.46	20.7	0	0

KATHRYN BRYCE RHB / RM / MVP2

FULL NAME: Kathryn Emma Bryce
BORN: November 17, 1997, Edinburgh, Scotland
SQUAD NO: 17
HEIGHT: 5ft 4in
EDUCATION: Loughborough University
TEAMS: Scotland, Lightning, Warwickshire, Loughborough Lightning
ROLE: Allrounder
DEBUT: T20I: 2018; List A: 2017; T20: 2017

BEST T20I BATTING: 73* Scotland vs Netherlands, Arbroath, 2019
BEST T20I BOWLING: 2-6 Scotland vs Namibia, Arbroath, 2019

MOST EXCITING DAY AS A CRICKETER? Playing in my first global qualifying tournament for Scotland in Thailand in 2015
CHILDHOOD SPORTING HERO? Andrew Flintoff
FIRST CRICKET CLUB? Watsonian CC, Edinburgh
IF YOU COULD TAKE ONE FEMALE CRICKETER'S BEST SHOT AND ADD IT TO YOUR OWN GAME? Meg Lanning's shot over cover
TOUGHEST OPPONENT IN CRICKET? Sophie Ecclestone – for the consistency of her bowling
MOST ECCENTRIC TEAMMATE? My Lightning teammate Nancy Harman – for her retro fleeces (everyone's jealous)
WHAT WOULD YOU DO IF YOU WERE IN CHARGE OF WOMEN'S CRICKET? Get girls' cricket in all schools and allow more international teams in the World Cup
WHAT WOULD YOU DO IF YOU WERE PRIME MINISTER? Take decisions to help climate change, put David Attenborough in charge, get more people active
FAVOURITE SMELL? A real Christmas tree
GUILTY PLEASURE? Grey's Anatomy
TWITTER: @Kathryn_Bryce

Batting	Mat	Inns	NO	Runs	HS	Ave	SR	100	50	Ct	St
T20Is	14	13	5	400	73*	50.00	101.26	0	3	6	0
Bowling	Mat	Balls	Runs	Wkts	BBI	BBM	Ave	Econ	SR	5w	10
T20Is	14	273	149	15	2/6	2/6	9.93	3.27	18.2	0	0

SARAH BRYCE

RHB / WK / MVP5

FULL NAME: Sarah Jennifer Bryce
BORN: January 8, 2000, Edinburgh, Scotland
SQUAD NO: 8
HEIGHT: 5ft 7in
NICKNAME: Sazzle
EDUCATION: Loughborough University
TEAMS: Scotland, Lightning, Nottinghamshire
ROLE: Wicketkeeper/batsman
DEBUT: T20I: 2018; List A: 2019; T20: 2018

BEST T20I BATTING: 65 Scotland vs Netherlands, Arbroath, 2019

MOST EXCITING DAY AS A CRICKETER? Being part of the Scotland team which beat Ireland during the T20I quadrangular series in the Netherlands in 2019
CHILDHOOD SPORTING HERO? Chris Hoy
FIRST CRICKET CLUB? Watsonian CC, Edinburgh
IF YOU COULD TAKE ONE FEMALE CRICKETER'S BEST SHOT AND ADD IT TO YOUR OWN GAME? Nat Sciver's "Natmeg"
TOUGHEST OPPONENT IN CRICKET? Sophie Ecclestone – the bounce she gets from her height can make her tricky to play
WHAT WOULD YOU DO IF YOU WERE IN CHARGE OF WOMEN'S CRICKET? Create more competitions around the world, introduce a multi-day-format league
WHAT WOULD YOU DO IF YOU WERE PRIME MINISTER? Panic, get help, try to make the country and world a better place
STRANGEST THING YOU'VE DONE DURING LOCKDOWN? Playing a kazoo for a Zoom quiz
FAVOURITE SMELL? Fresh flowers
GUILTY PLEASURE? The Vicar of Dibley
TWITTER: @Sarah_Bryce08

Batting	Mat	Inns	NO	Runs	HS	Ave	SR	100	50	Ct	St
T20Is	20	20	7	511	65	39.30	106.45	0	2	14	15
Bowling	**Mat**	**Balls**	**Runs**	**Wkts**	**BBI**	**BBM**	**Ave**	**Econ**	**SR**	**5w**	**10**
T20Is	20	-	-	-	-	-	-	-	-	-	-

AMARA CARR

RHB / WK / MVP48

FULL NAME: Amara Danielle Carr
BORN: April 17, 1994, Plymouth, Devon
SQUAD NO: 17
HEIGHT: 5ft 2in
NICKNAME: Mars
EDUCATION: University of Essex
TEAMS: Sunrisers, Devon, Middlesex, Somerset
ROLE: Wicketkeeper/batsman
DEBUT: List A: 2008; T20: 2009

BEST BATTING: 105 Devon vs Middlesex, Eastcote, 2019

CHILDHOOD SPORTING HERO? Serena Williams
BIGGEST INFLUENCE ON YOUR DEVELOPMENT AS A CRICKETER (EXCLUDING PARENTS)? My older brother. He's coached me at various times since I started playing cricket in Devon and has spent much of his free time throwing balls at me
FIRST CRICKET CLUB? Mount Wise CC, Plymouth, Devon
IF YOU COULD TAKE ONE FEMALE CRICKETER'S BEST SHOT AND ADD IT TO YOUR OWN GAME? Smriti Mandhana's shot over extra-cover. She hits the ball so cleanly
TOUGHEST OPPONENT IN CRICKET? Heather Knight – she scores runs for fun in domestic cricket
WHAT WOULD YOU DO IF YOU WERE IN CHARGE OF WOMEN'S CRICKET? Increase the amount of Test and domestic cricket (currently we don't play enough during the cricket season)
WHAT WOULD YOU DO IF YOU WERE PRIME MINISTER? Make all days of an Ashes Test a national holiday, ban single-use plastic water bottles
STRANGEST THING YOU'VE DONE DURING LOCKDOWN? Recreating a music festival in my living room. We even made a "line-up" to say who was on each "stage" and when
TWITTER: @Amara_Carr

Batting	Mat	Inns	NO	Runs	HS	Ave	SR	100	50	Ct	St
List A	91	85	6	1599	105	20.24	-	1	7	46	33
T20s	49	39	7	633	52	19.78	-	0	2	11	19
Bowling	**Mat**	**Balls**	**Mdns**	**Runs**	**Wkts**	**BB**	**Ave**	**4wI**	**5wI**	**SR**	**Econ**
List A	-	-	-	-	-	-	-	-	-	-	-
T20s	-	-	-	-	-	-	-	-	-	-	-

KELLY CASTLE

RHB / RMF / MVP72

FULL NAME: Kelly Shannon Castle
BORN: September 4, 1997, Southend-on-Sea, Essex
SQUAD NO: 7
HEIGHT: 5ft 8in
NICKNAME: KC
EDUCATION: The King Edmund School, Rochford, Essex; Anglia Ruskin University
TEAMS: Sunrisers, Essex
ROLE: Allrounder
DEBUT: List A: 2012; T20: 2011

BEST BATTING: 47 Essex vs Netherlands, Billericay, 2017
BEST BOWLING: 5-18 Essex vs Scotland, Billericay, 2015

MOST EXCITING DAY AS A CRICKETER? Getting the call to tell me I had received a full-time professional contract last year
BIGGEST INFLUENCE ON YOUR DEVELOPMENT AS A CRICKETER (EXCLUDING PARENTS)? My primary-school teacher Mr G. He's the reason I started playing and he always told me to follow my dreams
FIRST CRICKET CLUB? Rayleigh CC, Wickford, Essex
IF YOU COULD TAKE ONE FEMALE CRICKETER'S BEST SHOT AND ADD IT TO YOUR OWN GAME? Meg Lanning's flick off her pads for six
WHAT WOULD YOU DO IF YOU WERE IN CHARGE OF WOMEN'S CRICKET? Push to get women's cricket recognised as an Olympic and Paralympic sport
WHAT WOULD YOU DO IF YOU WERE PRIME MINISTER? Reduce university fees, add an extra day to the weekend called Monday Fun Day, stop cutting down trees
STRANGEST THING YOU'VE DONE DURING LOCKDOWN? Buying my brother some Nerf guns and creating an assault course in the house to shoot as many objects as possible. We kept losing the bullets so my brother decided to buy over 500 of them…
GUILTY PLEASURE? EastEnders
TWITTER: @KellyyShannon

Batting	Mat	Inns	NO	Runs	HS	Ave	SR	100	50	Ct	St
List A	47	44	4	454	47	11.35	-	0	0	7	-
T20s	44	38	11	426	48	15.77	76.61	0	0	10	-
Bowling	**Mat**	**Balls**	**Mdns**	**Runs**	**Wkts**	**BB**	**Ave**	**4wI**	**5wI**	**SR**	**Econ**
List A	47	1098	23	665	27	5-18	24.62	0	1	40.66	3.63
T20s	44	624	3	503	31	3-6	16.22	0	0	20.12	4.83

AYLISH CRANSTONE LHB / LM / MVP53

SOUTH EAST STARS

FULL NAME: Aylish Cranstone
BORN: August 28, 1994, Guildford, Surrey
SQUAD NO: 28
HEIGHT: 5ft 2in
EDUCATION: University of Exeter
TEAMS: South East Stars, Surrey, Devon, Hampshire, Surrey Stars
ROLE: Allrounder
DEBUT: List A: 2008; T20: 2010

BEST BATTING: 134* Devon vs Essex, Dunmow, 2016
BEST BOWLING: 5-5 Devon vs Leicestershire, Bolham, 2016

MOST EXCITING DAY AS A CRICKETER? Winning the deciding game against South Africa A by one run on the England U19 tour in 2013/14
CHILDHOOD SPORTING HERO? David Beckham
FIRST CRICKET CLUB? Rowledge CC, Surrey
IF YOU COULD TAKE ONE FEMALE CRICKETER'S BEST SHOT AND ADD IT TO YOUR OWN GAME? Amy Jones's straight-drive for six
TOUGHEST OPPONENT IN CRICKET? Sophie Luff – can't get her out
WHAT WOULD YOU DO IF YOU WERE PRIME MINISTER? Remove interest on student loans and introduce the four-day working week
STRANGEST THING YOU'VE DONE DURING LOCKDOWN? Taking part in a summer Olympics over Zoom in my garden with friends. It consisted of 10 events, including a gymnastic floor routine, a race to eat a packet of McCoy's Salt & Vinegar crisps and a 1km time-trial
FAVOURITE SMELL? A fish-and-chip shop as you walk past it
GUILTY PLEASURE? One Direction
TWITTER: @AylishCranstone

Batting	Mat	Inns	NO	Runs	HS	Ave	SR	100	50	Ct	St
List A	80	78	9	2001	134*	29.00	-	1	13	20	-
T20s	59	43	10	658	78*	19.93	104.77	0	3	11	-
Bowling	**Mat**	**Balls**	**Mdns**	**Runs**	**Wkts**	**BB**	**Ave**	**4wI**	**5wI**	**SR**	**Econ**
List A	80	883	16	662	23	5-5	28.78	0	1	38.39	4.49
T20s	59	153	1	120	8	3-17	15.00	0	0	19.12	4.70

KATE CROSS RHB / RFM / MVP74

FULL NAME: Kathryn Laura Cross
BORN: October 3, 1991, Manchester
SQUAD NO: 16
HEIGHT: 5ft 7in
NICKNAME: Crossy, Sunny
EDUCATION: Bury Grammar School; University of Leeds
TEAMS: England, Thunder, Lancashire, Brisbane Heat, Lancashire Thunder, Perth Scorchers, Western Australia
ROLE: Bowler
DEBUT: Test: 2014; ODI: 2013; T20I: 2013; List A: 2005; T20: 2008

BEST ODI BATTING: 8* England vs Australia, Canterbury, 2019
BEST ODI BOWLING: 5-24 England vs New Zealand, Lincoln, 2015

MOST EXCITING DAY AS A CRICKETER? The second day at the WACA in Perth during the 2013/14 Ashes – my debut Test. Taking wickets in my first spell of Test-match bowling was something I will never forget
BIGGEST INFLUENCE ON YOUR DEVELOPMENT AS A CRICKETER (EXCLUDING PARENTS)? John Stanworth – he was Academy director at Lancashire and the reason I was the first girl to be accepted onto the Academy. And he's also the main reason I began to take my cricket seriously
FIRST CRICKET CLUB? Heywood CC, Greater Manchester
TOUGHEST OPPONENT IN CRICKET? Ellyse Perry – she just loves batting, and batting…
WHAT WOULD YOU DO IF YOU WERE PRIME MINISTER? Get rid of social media, stop anyone from charging for the use of a toilet
STRANGEST THING YOU'VE DONE DURING LOCKDOWN? Going to the zoo with a mate who was dressed as an elephant
FAVOURITE SMELL? Fresh laundry
GUILTY PLEASURE? Doing online quizzes to find out what sort of potato I am
TWITTER: @katecross16

Batting	Mat	Inns	NO	Runs	HS	Ave	SR	100	50	Ct	St
Tests	3	6	3	15	4*	5.00	24.19	0	0	0	0
ODIs	28	10	6	22	8*	5.50	30.55	0	0	6	0
T20Is	13	1	1	0	0*	-	0.00	0	0	3	0
Bowling	**Mat**	**Balls**	**Runs**	**Wkts**	**BBI**	**BBM**	**Ave**	**Econ**	**SR**	**5w**	**10**
Tests	3	554	209	14	3/29	6/70	14.92	2.26	39.5	0	0
ODIs	28	1212	861	35	5/24	5/24	24.60	4.26	34.6	1	0
T20Is	13	264	296	11	2/18	2/18	26.90	6.72	24.0	0	0

NAOMI DATTANI

LHB / LMF / MVP65

FULL NAME: Naomi Dilip Dattani
BORN: April 28, 1994, Ealing, London
SQUAD NO: 23
HEIGHT: 5ft 4in
NICKNAME: Nomes
EDUCATION: Greenford High School, Ealing; Loughborough University
TEAMS: Sunrisers, Middlesex, Surrey Stars, Western Storm
ROLE: Allrounder
DEBUT: List A: 2008; T20: 2009

BEST BATTING: 71 Middlesex vs Sussex, Billingshurst, 2016
BEST BOWLING: 4-23 Middlesex vs Worcestershire, Worcester, 2010

MOST EXCITING DAY AS A CRICKETER? Winning the 2019 Kia Super League with Western Storm
CHILDHOOD SPORTING HERO? Serena Williams
BIGGEST INFLUENCE ON YOUR DEVELOPMENT AS A CRICKETER (EXCLUDING PARENTS)? Two people: a coach I worked with in Melbourne who turned my cricket around, and a fitness/mindset coach I've invested in for the last three years
FIRST CRICKET CLUB? Perivale Phonecians CC, London
IF YOU COULD TAKE ONE FEMALE CRICKETER'S BEST SHOT AND ADD IT TO YOUR OWN GAME? Smriti Mandhana's lofted drive over mid-off
TOUGHEST OPPONENT IN CRICKET? Suzie Bates – bowling to her has made me focus on my skills and find creative plans to get her out
WHAT WOULD YOU DO IF YOU WERE IN CHARGE OF WOMEN'S CRICKET? Create longer-format matches to emphasise the importance of mindset, technique and education of the game
WHAT WOULD YOU DO IF YOU WERE PRIME MINISTER? Adapt the school curriculum to teach kids earlier about life skills such as nutrition, travel, public-speaking, finances etc
STRANGEST THING YOU'VE DONE DURING LOCKDOWN? Appearing on University Challenge!
GUILTY PLEASURE? French music
TWITTER: @NaomiDattani

Batting	Mat	Inns	NO	Runs	HS	Ave	SR	100	50	Ct	St
List A	71	54	1	734	71	13.84	-	0	2	25	-
T20s	72	48	6	581	62	13.83	80.13	0	1	19	-
Bowling	**Mat**	**Balls**	**Mdns**	**Runs**	**Wkts**	**BB**	**Ave**	**4wI**	**5wI**	**SR**	**Econ**
List A	71	2021	18	1682	47	4-23	35.78	2	0	43.00	4.99
T20s	72	738	2	863	28	3-35	30.82	0	0	26.35	7.01

ALICE DAVIDSON-RICHARDS RHB / RFM / MVP69

FULL NAME: Alice Natica Davidson-Richards
BORN: May 29, 1994, Tunbridge Wells, Kent
SQUAD NO: 24
HEIGHT: 5ft 9in
NICKNAME: ADR
EDUCATION: Epsom College, Surrey; University of Leeds
TEAMS: England, South East Stars, Kent, Otago, Yorkshire Diamonds
ROLE: Allrounder
DEBUT: ODI: 2018; T20I: 2018; List A: 2010; T20: 2010

BEST ODI BATTING: 9 England vs India, Nagpur, 2018

MOST EXCITING DAY AS A CRICKETER? Being at the crease in 2016 when Kent won the double (County Championship and NatWest T20)
CHILDHOOD SPORTING HERO? Andrew Flintoff
BIGGEST INFLUENCE ON YOUR DEVELOPMENT AS A CRICKETER (EXCLUDING PARENTS)? Mark Dekker, former head coach of Kent Women. He was the person with whom I started talking about cricket, rather than just hitting or bowling balls
FIRST CRICKET CLUB? Tunbridge Wells CC, Kent
IF YOU COULD TAKE ONE FEMALE CRICKETER'S BEST SHOT AND ADD IT TO YOUR OWN GAME? Heather Knight's drive over extra-cover – glorious
TOUGHEST OPPONENT IN CRICKET? Katherine Brunt – doesn't give an inch
WHAT WOULD YOU DO IF YOU WERE PRIME MINISTER? Make tampons free, make it illegal to put milk in with the teabag, ban all skimmed milk of any kind
STRANGEST THING YOU'VE DONE DURING LOCKDOWN? Dressing up as Albert Einstein, Frida Kahlo and Muhammad Ali in one day
GUILTY PLEASURE? Loose-leaf tea
TWITTER: @alicedr24

Batting	Mat	Inns	NO	Runs	HS	Ave	SR	100	50	Ct	St
ODIs	1	1	0	9	9	9.00	28.12	0	0	0	0
T20Is	5	3	0	28	24	9.33	82.35	0	0	2	0
Bowling	**Mat**	**Balls**	**Runs**	**Wkts**	**BBI**	**BBM**	**Ave**	**Econ**	**SR**	**5w**	**10**
ODIs	1	-	-	-	-	-	-	-	-	-	-
T20Is	5	24	44	0	-	-	-	11.00	-	0	0

FREYA DAVIES RHB / RFM

FULL NAME: Freya Ruth Davies
BORN: October 27, 1995, Chichester, Sussex
SQUAD NO: 61
HEIGHT: 5ft 9in
NICKNAME: Frey-Frey
EDUCATION: Brighton College; University of Exeter
TEAMS: England, South East Stars, Sussex, Western Storm
ROLE: Bowler
DEBUT: ODI: 2019; T20I: 2019; List A: 2012; T20: 2010

BEST ODI BATTING: 2 England vs New Zealand, Dunedin, 2021
BEST ODI BOWLING: 1-30 England vs New Zealand, Christchurch, 2021

MOST EXCITING DAY AS A CRICKETER? My England debut in Sri Lanka in 2019
CHILDHOOD SPORTING HERO? Jonny Wilkinson
BIGGEST INFLUENCE ON YOUR DEVELOPMENT AS A CRICKETER (EXCLUDING PARENTS)? My older brother – I got bored watching him play so started playing myself
FIRST CRICKET CLUB? Singleton CC, West Sussex
IF YOU COULD TAKE ONE FEMALE CRICKETER'S BEST SHOT AND ADD IT TO YOUR OWN GAME? Tammy Beaumont's ramp shot
TOUGHEST OPPONENT IN CRICKET? Danni Wyatt – she's been a serious competitor for the Southern Vipers for the last few years
MOST ECCENTRIC TEAMMATE? Fran Wilson and her van-conversion retirement plan
WHAT WOULD YOU DO IF YOU WERE IN CHARGE OF WOMEN'S CRICKET? Provide kit that fits better, get women's county cricket played at better grounds, push for more domestic women's cricket on TV
GUILTY PLEASURE? Spending hours on TikTok
TWITTER: @FreyaRuth

Batting	Mat	Inns	NO	Runs	HS	Ave	SR	100	50	Ct	St
ODIs	3	1	0	2	2	2.00	33.33	0	0	0	0
T20Is	11	1	1	1	1*	-	100.00	0	0	4	0
Bowling	**Mat**	**Balls**	**Runs**	**Wkts**	**BBI**	**BBM**	**Ave**	**Econ**	**SR**	**5w**	**10**
ODIs	3	132	82	2	1/30	1/30	41.00	3.72	66.0	0	0
T20Is	11	198	191	13	4/23	4/23	14.69	5.78	15.2	0	0

GWENAN DAVIES LHB / RMF / WK / MVP27

FULL NAME: Gwenan Mai Davies
BORN: May 12, 1994, Neath, Glamorgan, Wales
SQUAD NO: 79
HEIGHT: 5ft 2in
NICKNAME: G
EDUCATION: Loughborough University
TEAMS: Central Sparks, Warwickshire, Somerset, Surrey Stars, Wales, Worcestershire, Yorkshire Diamonds
ROLE: Wicketkeeper/batsman
DEBUT: List A: 2008; T20: 2010

BEST BATTING: 96 Somerset vs Durham, Midsomer Norton, 2015
BEST BOWLING: 2-7 Wales vs Leicestershire, Wolvey, 2008

MOST EXCITING DAY AS A CRICKETER? Winning the T20 Cup with Birmingham Bears in 2019
CHILDHOOD SPORTING HERO? Brendon McCullum
BIGGEST INFLUENCE ON YOUR DEVELOPMENT AS A CRICKETER (EXCLUDING PARENTS)? John Derrick at Glamorgan helped me move up the age-groups for Wales and encouraged my aggressive nature with the bat. More recently it has been Michael Powell at Warwickshire – he took my game to the next level and is my go-to guy
FIRST CRICKET CLUB? Clydach CC, Swansea
IF YOU COULD TAKE ONE FEMALE CRICKETER'S BEST SHOT AND ADD IT TO YOUR OWN GAME? Nat Sciver's "Natmeg"
TOUGHEST OPPONENT IN CRICKET? Anya Shrubsole – whenever she gets a glimpse of a weakness in your batting, you're in trouble
MOST ECCENTRIC TEAMMATE? Issy Wong – you've got to have guts to sport those hair-dos!
WHAT WOULD YOU DO IF YOU WERE IN CHARGE OF WOMEN'S CRICKET? Create global franchises like the men have
STRANGEST THING YOU'VE DONE DURING LOCKDOWN? Reading books. It's not easy to get me to sit still, so reading has been quite out of character
GUILTY PLEASURE? An ice-cold Corona on a hot summer's day
TWITTER: @gmdavies79

Batting	Mat	Inns	NO	Runs	HS	Ave	SR	100	50	Ct	St
List A	81	79	2	1305	96	16.94	-	0	7	36	7
T20s	66	58	5	1123	66*	21.18	-	0	3	22	27
Bowling	**Mat**	**Balls**	**Mdns**	**Runs**	**Wkts**	**BB**	**Ave**	**4wI**	**5wI**	**SR**	**Econ**
List A	81	945	11	735	23	2-7	31.95	0	0	41.08	4.66
T20s	66	245	0	328	10	2-18	32.80	0	0	24.50	8.03

SOPHIA DUNKLEY RHB / LB / MVP45

FULL NAME: Sophia Ivy Dunkley
BORN: July 16, 1998, Lambeth, Surrey
SQUAD NO: 47
HEIGHT: 5ft 6in
NICKNAME: Dunks
EDUCATION: Mill Hill School, London; Loughborough University
TEAMS: England, South East Stars, Middlesex, Lancashire Thunder, Surrey Stars
ROLE: Allrounder
DEBUT: T20I: 2018; List A: 2013; T20: 2012

BEST T20I BATTING: 35 England vs West Indies, Gros Islet, 2018
BEST T20I BOWLING: 1-6 England vs Sri Lanka, Colombo, 2019

MOST EXCITING DAY AS A CRICKETER? Winning the 2018 Kia Super League with Surrey Stars
CHILDHOOD SPORTING HERO? Roger Federer
BIGGEST INFLUENCE ON YOUR DEVELOPMENT AS A CRICKETER (EXCLUDING PARENTS)? I always looked up to Beth Morgan, the former England player, when she was my coach
FIRST CRICKET CLUB? Finchley CC, London
IF YOU COULD TAKE ONE FEMALE CRICKETER'S BEST SHOT AND ADD IT TO YOUR OWN GAME? Nat Sciver's six-hit over mid-wicket
TOUGHEST OPPONENT IN CRICKET? Sophie Devine – not much margin for error when you're bowling at her
WHAT WOULD YOU DO IF YOU WERE IN CHARGE OF WOMEN'S CRICKET? Try to schedule games at the big grounds and get some adverts for women's cricket on the TV
WHAT WOULD YOU DO IF YOU WERE PRIME MINISTER? Introduce a National Baking Day, increase participation in sport at schools, set up a scheme for lonely elderly people to have some company
FAVOURITE SMELL? Freshly baked goods
GUILTY PLEASURE? Coronation Street
TWITTER: @dunkleysophia

Batting	Mat	Inns	NO	Runs	HS	Ave	SR	100	50	Ct	St
T20Is	15	7	3	78	35	19.50	93.97	0	0	7	0
Bowling	**Mat**	**Balls**	**Runs**	**Wkts**	**BBI**	**BBM**	**Ave**	**Econ**	**SR**	**5w**	**10**
T20Is	15	24	13	1	1/6	1/6	13.00	3.25	24.0	0	0

SOPHIE ECCLESTONE RHB / SLA / MVP44

FULL NAME: Sophie Ecclestone
BORN: May 6, 1999, Chester, Cheshire
SQUAD NO: 71
HEIGHT: 5ft 10in
NICKNAME: Eccles
EDUCATION: Helsby High School, Cheshire
TEAMS: England, Thunder, Lancashire, Cheshire, Lancashire Thunder
ROLE: Bowler
DEBUT: Test: 2017; ODI: 2016; T20I: 2016; List A: 2013; T20: 2014

BEST ODI BATTING: 27 England vs Australia, Leicester, 2019
BEST ODI BOWLING: 4-14 England vs India, Nagpur, 2018

MOST EXCITING DAY AS A CRICKETER? Making my Test debut in Australia
FAMILY TIES? My brother and dad played at my local club and they taught me all I know
FIRST CRICKET CLUB? Alvanley CC, Cheshire. That's my favourite ground too – great view of the surroundings
TOUGHEST OPPONENT IN COUNTY CRICKET? Anya Shrubsole – thankfully she's my England teammate but she looks horrible to face when watching her from mid-on or mid-off. And Heather Knight – because nothing seems to faze her when she's batting, no matter the situation
SURPRISING FACT ABOUT YOU? I love playing crown green bowls competitively. The other thing is that all the England girls tease me because I speak too fast and they can't understand me!
IF YOU WERE AN ANIMAL, WHICH WOULD IT BE? A koala
TWITTER: @sophecc19

Batting	Mat	Inns	NO	Runs	HS	Ave	SR	100	50	Ct	St
Tests	2	2	2	17	9*	-	44.73	0	0	0	0
ODIs	27	17	5	79	27	6.58	62.20	0	0	7	0
T20Is	42	13	7	74	17*	12.33	115.62	0	0	12	0
Bowling	**Mat**	**Balls**	**Runs**	**Wkts**	**BBI**	**BBM**	**Ave**	**Econ**	**SR**	**5w**	**10**
Tests	2	524	234	6	3/107	3/107	39.00	2.67	87.3	0	0
ODIs	27	1429	906	39	4/14	4/14	23.23	3.80	36.6	0	0
T20Is	42	945	917	61	4/18	4/18	15.03	5.82	15.4	0	0

BETHAN ELLIS RHB / RMF / MVP32

FULL NAME: Bethan Louisa Ellis
BORN: July 7, 1999, Leamington Spa, Warwickshire
SQUAD NO: 14
HEIGHT: 5ft 6in
NICKNAME: Bellis
EDUCATION: University of Birmingham; Loughborough University
TEAMS: Lightning, Warwickshire, Shropshire, Worcestershire
ROLE: Allrounder
DEBUT: List A: 2015; T20: 2016

BEST BATTING: 74 Warwickshire vs Kent, Beckenham, 2019
BEST BOWLING: 4-20 Worcestershire vs Wales, Griffithstown, 2017

MOST EXCITING DAY AS A CRICKETER? Winning the T20 Cup with the Birmingham Bears
CHILDHOOD SPORTING HERO? Ellyse Perry
BIGGEST INFLUENCE ON YOUR DEVELOPMENT AS A CRICKETER (EXCLUDING PARENTS)? Dominic Ostler at Warwickshire – he gave me confidence in my own game from a young age
FIRST CRICKET CLUB? Leamington CC, Warwickshire
TOUGHEST OPPONENT IN CRICKET? Suzie Bates – she hits the ball so cleanly and can take the game away from you very quickly
WHAT WOULD YOU DO IF YOU WERE IN CHARGE OF WOMEN'S CRICKET? Get more matches on TV or live-streamed, schedule more double-header matches with the men
WHAT WOULD YOU DO IF YOU WERE PRIME MINISTER? Lower university fees and put more sport on free-to-air TV
STRANGEST THING YOU'VE DONE DURING LOCKDOWN? Attempting to learn the guitar
FAVOURITE SMELL? Cut grass
GUILTY PLEASURE? Dark-chocolate Digestives
TWITTER: @BethanEllis7

Batting	Mat	Inns	NO	Runs	HS	Ave	SR	100	50	Ct	St
List A	28	22	4	419	74	23.27	51.47	0	4	9	-
T20s	26	19	7	168	38*	14.00	-	0	0	7	-
Bowling	**Mat**	**Balls**	**Mdns**	**Runs**	**Wkts**	**BB**	**Ave**	**4wI**	**5wI**	**SR**	**Econ**
List A	28	811	21	477	22	4-20	21.68	1	0	36.86	3.52
T20s	26	397	1	364	24	4-21	15.16	1	0	16.54	5.50

GEORGIA ELWISS RHB / RM

FULL NAME: Georgia Amanda Elwiss
BORN: May 31, 1991, Wolverhampton
SQUAD NO: 34
HEIGHT: 5ft 7in
NICKNAME: G
EDUCATION: Wolverhampton Girls' High School; Loughborough University
TEAMS: England, Southern Vipers, Sussex, Loughborough Lightning, Melbourne Stars, Staffordshire
ROLE: Allrounder
DEBUT: Test: 2015; ODI: 2011; T20I: 2011; List A: 2004; T20: 2005

BEST ODI BATTING: 77 England vs Pakistan, Taunton, 2016
BEST ODI BOWLING: 3-17 England vs India, Wormsley, 2012

MOST EXCITING DAY AS A CRICKETER? Winning the World Cup in 2017
CHILDHOOD SPORTING HERO? Allan Donald
FIRST CRICKET CLUB? Wolverhampton CC, West Midlands
IF YOU COULD TAKE ONE FEMALE CRICKETER'S BEST SHOT AND ADD IT TO YOUR OWN GAME? Nat Sciver's pull
TOUGHEST OPPONENT IN CRICKET? Ellyse Perry – unrelenting
WHAT WOULD YOU DO IF YOU WERE IN CHARGE OF WOMEN'S CRICKET? Target individual sponsorship for individual women cricketers
WHAT WOULD YOU DO IF YOU WERE PRIME MINISTER? Close all tax loopholes
STRANGEST THING YOU'VE DONE DURING LOCKDOWN? Nurturing a sourdough starter for a week
FAVOURITE SMELL? Fresh bread
GUILTY PLEASURE? Drinking good coffee
TWITTER: @gelwiss

Batting	Mat	Inns	NO	Runs	HS	Ave	SR	100	50	Ct	St
Tests	3	5	1	140	46	35.00	28.16	0	0	1	0
ODIs	36	24	5	388	77	20.42	73.20	0	2	11	0
T20Is	14	5	2	29	18	9.66	96.66	0	0	3	0
Bowling	**Mat**	**Balls**	**Runs**	**Wkts**	**BBI**	**BBM**	**Ave**	**Econ**	**SR**	**5w**	**10**
Tests	3	156	83	1	1/40	1/40	83.00	3.19	156.0	0	0
ODIs	36	1097	679	26	3/17	3/17	26.11	3.71	42.1	0	0
T20Is	14	163	161	8	2/9	2/9	20.12	5.92	20.3	0	0

TASH FARRANT LHB / LMF / MVP16

SOUTH EAST STARS

FULL NAME: Natasha Eleni Farrant
BORN: May 29, 1996, Athens, Greece
SQUAD NO: 53
HEIGHT: 5ft 5in
NICKNAME: Faz
EDUCATION: Sevenoaks School; Loughborough University
TEAMS: England, South East Stars, Kent, Southern Vipers, Western Australia
ROLE: Bowler
DEBUT: ODI: 2013; T20I: 2013; List A: 2012; T20: 2012

BEST ODI BATTING: 1* England vs West Indies, Port of Spain, 2013
BEST ODI BOWLING: 2-31 England vs New Zealand, Christchurch, 2021

CHILDHOOD SPORTING HERO? Jessica Ennis-Hill
TOUGHEST OPPONENT IN CRICKET? Nat Sciver
SURPRISING FACT ABOUT YOU? I have lived in four countries (Greece, Italy, Singapore, England)
TWITTER: @tashfarrant
NOTES: The left-arm seamer has recently broken back into the England team after a frustrating few years since making her international debut as a 17-year-old in 2013. Farrant, who was raised in Italy and Singapore before moving to Kent aged eight, was one of the first batch of female players to be awarded an ECB central contract in 2014 and was part of the England squad which went to India for the 2016 World T20. But up until the beginning of this year she had played only seven T20Is – and just one ODI – over the course of the last seven years, losing her central contract in 2019. She has fought her way back into the reckoning over the last two summers with strong domestic performances, and became one of the 41 domestic players who were handed professional contracts in 2020. Recalled to the England squad for the 2020/21 tour of New Zealand, Farrant took 2-31 at Christchurch on her return to the ODI side and also featured in the subsequent T20I series. She has represented Kent since 2012 and is a member of the South East Stars side that formed last year following the regional overhaul of the women's game. She has also been signed by Oval Invincibles for The Hundred this summer

Batting	Mat	Inns	NO	Runs	HS	Ave	SR	100	50	Ct	St
ODIs	3	1	1	1	1*	-	12.50	0	0	1	0
T20Is	15	4	3	7	3*	7.00	43.75	0	0	3	0
Bowling	**Mat**	**Balls**	**Runs**	**Wkts**	**BBI**	**BBM**	**Ave**	**Econ**	**SR**	**5w**	**10**
ODIs	3	126	78	3	2/31	2/31	26.00	3.71	42.0	0	0
T20Is	15	320	315	11	2/15	2/15	28.63	5.90	29.0	0	0

ABBEY FREEBORN

RHB / WK / MVP28

FULL NAME: Abigail Johanna Freeborn
BORN: November 12, 1996, Eastbourne, Sussex
SQUAD NO: 27
HEIGHT: 5ft 7in
NICKNAME: Freebs
EDUCATION: Loughborough University
TEAMS: Lightning, Yorkshire, Loughborough Lightning, Sussex
ROLE: Wicketkeeper/batsman
DEBUT: List A: 2013; T20: 2013

BEST BATTING: 58 Yorkshire vs Sussex, Cobham, 2019

MOST EXCITING DAY AS A CRICKETER? Finals Day of the 2019 Kia Super League
CHILDHOOD SPORTING HERO? Chris Hoy
FIRST CRICKET CLUB? Hastings & St Leonards Priory CC, East Sussex
IF YOU COULD TAKE ONE FEMALE CRICKETER'S BEST SHOT AND ADD IT TO YOUR OWN GAME? Amy Jones's drive over extra-cover
TOUGHEST OPPONENT IN CRICKET? Sophie Ecclestone – she's a very skillful bowler
WHAT WOULD YOU DO IF YOU WERE IN CHARGE OF WOMEN'S CRICKET? Schedule all women's professional games as double-headers with the men
WHAT WOULD YOU DO IF YOU WERE PRIME MINISTER? Invest in renewable energy
STRANGEST THING YOU'VE DONE DURING LOCKDOWN? Helping to dismantle a balcony
FAVOURITE SMELL? Freshly cut grass
GUILTY PLEASURE? Re-watching Grace and Frankie
TWITTER: @abbey_freeborn

Batting	Mat	Inns	NO	Runs	HS	Ave	SR	100	50	Ct	St
List A	45	35	8	627	58	23.22	60.00	0	1	31	10
T20s	41	25	8	290	37	17.05	79.23	0	0	14	20
Bowling	**Mat**	**Balls**	**Mdns**	**Runs**	**Wkts**	**BB**	**Ave**	**4wI**	**5wI**	**SR**	**Econ**
List A	-	-	-	-	-	-	-	-	-	-	-
T20s	-	-	-	-	-	-	-	-	-	-	-

JO GARDNER

RHB / OB / MVP10

FULL NAME: Jo-Anne Lynda Gardner
BORN: March 25, 1997, Newport, Isle of Wight
SQUAD NO: 14
HEIGHT: 5ft 6in
NICKNAME: Joey G
EDUCATION: Loughborough University
TEAMS: Sunrisers, Warwickshire, Loughborough Lightning, Northamptonshire
ROLE: Allrounder
DEBUT: List A: 2011; T20: 2011

BEST BATTING: 86 Northamptonshire vs Cheshire, Horton, 2016
BEST BOWLING: 6-21 Northamptonshire vs Oxfordshire, Chesterton, 2013

MOST EXCITING DAY AS A CRICKETER? Finals Day of the Kia Super League in 2019
CHILDHOOD SPORTING HERO? Steven Gerrard
FIRST CRICKET CLUB? Great Houghton CC, Northampton
TOUGHEST OPPONENT IN CRICKET? Danni Wyatt – she hits the ball hard and is always looking to attack. She's carted me around the park on a few occasions
WHAT WOULD YOU DO IF YOU WERE IN CHARGE OF WOMEN'S CRICKET? Improve sponsorship options for players' kit etc, get more women into the media, introduce a longer form of the game
WHAT WOULD YOU DO IF YOU WERE PRIME MINISTER? Increase wages for NHS and key workers, establish a pact with Australia which means that you don't require a visa for entry, reduce university fees
STRANGEST THING YOU'VE DONE DURING LOCKDOWN? Downloading a DJ app so that I could channel my inner David Guetta
FAVOURITE SMELL? A black cherry Yankee Candle
GUILTY PLEASURE? Eating Nutella from the jar
TWITTER: @JoLGardner

Batting	Mat	Inns	NO	Runs	HS	Ave	SR	100	50	Ct	St
List A	59	51	10	824	86	20.09	-	0	5	17	-
T20s	54	42	11	399	55*	12.87	-	0	2	12	-
Bowling	**Mat**	**Balls**	**Mdns**	**Runs**	**Wkts**	**BB**	**Ave**	**4wI**	**5wI**	**SR**	**Econ**
List A	59	1737	35	1071	58	6-21	18.46	0	3	29.94	3.69
T20s	54	675	6	651	20	3-25	32.55	0	0	33.75	5.78

KATIE GEORGE LHB / LFM / MVP89

FULL NAME: Katie Louise George
BORN: April 7, 1999, Haywards Heath, Sussex
SQUAD NO: 46
HEIGHT: 5ft 5in
EDUCATION: The Mountbatten School, Hampshire; Richard Taunton Sixth Form, Southampton
TEAMS: England, Western Storm, Hampshire, Southern Vipers, Yorkshire Diamonds
ROLE: Bowler
DEBUT: ODI: 2018; T20I: 2018; List A: 2013; T20: 2015

BEST ODI BATTING: 9 England vs New Zealand, Derby, 2018
BEST ODI BOWLING: 3-36 England vs New Zealand, Derby, 2018

MOST EXCITING DAY AS A CRICKETER? Making my ODI debut at Headingley in 2018
CHILDHOOD SPORTING HERO? Wasim Akram
BIGGEST INFLUENCE ON YOUR DEVELOPMENT AS A CRICKETER (EXCLUDING PARENTS)? The late Rick Kellaway, my former club coach and mentor at Old Tauntonians & Romsey CC. He was the first person who helped me slow down and think about the game
FIRST CRICKET CLUB? Poole Town CC, Dorset
IF YOU COULD TAKE ONE FEMALE CRICKETER'S BEST SHOT AND ADD IT TO YOUR OWN GAME? Danni Wyatt's effortless shot over extra-cover
TOUGHEST OPPONENT IN CRICKET? Smriti Mandhana – so strong through the off-side
WHAT WOULD YOU DO IF YOU WERE IN CHARGE OF WOMEN'S CRICKET? Keep county cricket as a key part of the summer schedule (it's the heart of the women's game), begin to decentralise Loughborough as the hub of women's cricket – as long as the standards are good enough elsewhere
FAVOURITE SMELL? The sea
GUILTY PLEASURE? Jazz
TWITTER: @KaTie_George46

Batting	Mat	Inns	NO	Runs	HS	Ave	SR	100	50	Ct	St
ODIs	2	1	0	9	9	9.00	47.36	0	0	1	0
T20Is	5	1	0	0	0	0.00	0.00	0	0	0	0
Bowling	**Mat**	**Balls**	**Runs**	**Wkts**	**BBI**	**BBM**	**Ave**	**Econ**	**SR**	**5w**	**10**
ODIs	2	75	70	4	3/36	3/36	17.50	5.60	18.7	0	0
T20Is	5	78	117	2	1/22	1/22	58.50	9.00	39.0	0	0

DANI GIBSON

RHB / RMF

FULL NAME: Danielle Rose Gibson
BORN: April 30, 2001, Cheltenham, Gloucestershire
SQUAD NO: 28
HEIGHT: 5ft 6in
NICKNAME: Gibbo
EDUCATION: Hartpury College, Gloucestershire
TEAMS: Western Storm, Wales, Gloucestershire
ROLE: Bowler
DEBUT: List A: 2015; T20: 2014

BEST BATTING: 73 Gloucestershire vs Buckinghamshire, Moreton-in-Marsh, 2015
BEST BOWLING: 5-17 Gloucestershire vs Cornwall, Falmouth, 2017

MOST EXCITING DAY AS A CRICKETER? Winning the Kia Super League for the second time with Western Storm in 2019
CHILDHOOD SPORTING HERO? Jessica Ennis-Hill
FIRST CRICKET CLUB? Dumbleton CC, Evesham, Worcestershire
IF YOU COULD TAKE ONE FEMALE CRICKETER'S BEST SHOT AND ADD IT TO YOUR OWN GAME? The "Natmeg" (Nat Sciver)
TOUGHEST OPPONENT IN CRICKET? Sophie Devine – I didn't know how I could bowl a ball at her which she couldn't hit for four
WHAT WOULD YOU DO IF YOU WERE IN CHARGE OF WOMEN'S CRICKET? Increase the number of women coaches
STRANGEST THING YOU'VE DONE DURING LOCKDOWN? Eating healthy
FAVOURITE SMELL? Yankee Candles
GUILTY PLEASURE? Having a massage
TWITTER: @Dani_Gibson01

Batting	Mat	Inns	NO	Runs	HS	Ave	SR	100	50	Ct	St
List A	26	23	3	420	73	21.00	-	0	3	10	-
T20s	39	25	5	302	36	15.10	107.09	0	0	19	-
Bowling	**Mat**	**Balls**	**Mdns**	**Runs**	**Wkts**	**BB**	**Ave**	**4wI**	**5wI**	**SR**	**Econ**
List A	26	696	8	428	34	5-17	12.58	2	1	20.47	3.68
T20s	39	508	4	451	27	3-9	16.70	0	0	18.81	5.32

SARAH GLENN RHB / LB

FULL NAME: Sarah Glenn
BORN: August 27, 1999, Derby
SQUAD NO: 3
HEIGHT: 5ft 10in
EDUCATION: Trent College, Long Eaton; The Open University, Milton Keynes
TEAMS: England, Central Sparks, Worcestershire, Derbyshire, Loughborough Lightning, Perth Scorchers
ROLE: Bowler
DEBUT: ODI: 2019; T20I: 2019; List A: 2013; T20: 2013

BEST ODI BATTING: 11 England vs New Zealand, Dunedin, 2021
BEST ODI BOWLING: 4-18 England vs Pakistan, Kuala Lumpur, 2019

MOST EXCITING DAY AS A CRICKETER? Making my England debut in 2019
CHILDHOOD SPORTING HERO? Kate Richardson-Walsh
FIRST CRICKET CLUB? Denby CC, Ripley, Derbyshire
TOUGHEST OPPONENT IN CRICKET? Meg Lanning – she has all the shots in the book
WHAT WOULD YOU DO IF YOU WERE IN CHARGE OF WOMEN'S CRICKET? Ensure that 50-over and T20 women's county cricket is continued to help the development of players who don't make the new regional teams
WHAT WOULD YOU DO IF YOU WERE PRIME MINISTER? Create more awareness of environmental issues
STRANGEST THING YOU'VE DONE DURING LOCKDOWN? Getting fully dressed in my county kit (including pads, helmet etc) while at home
FAVOURITE SMELL? A roast in the oven
GUILTY PLEASURE? Love Island
TWITTER: @Lg3Sarah

Batting	Mat	Inns	NO	Runs	HS	Ave	SR	100	50	Ct	St
ODIs	6	1	0	11	11	11.00	100.00	0	0	3	0
T20Is	18	6	2	53	26	13.25	132.50	0	0	3	0
Bowling	**Mat**	**Balls**	**Runs**	**Wkts**	**BBI**	**BBM**	**Ave**	**Econ**	**SR**	**5w**	**10**
ODIs	6	281	190	11	4/18	4/18	17.27	4.05	25.5	0	0
T20Is	18	372	337	27	3/15	3/15	12.48	5.43	13.7	0	0

KIRSTIE GORDON RHB / SLA / MVP86

FULL NAME: Kirstie Louise Gordon
BORN: October 20, 1997, Huntly, Aberdeenshire, Scotland
SQUAD NO: 48
HEIGHT: 5ft 5in
NICKNAME: Gordo
EDUCATION: Loughborough University
TEAMS: England, Lightning, Nottinghamshire, Loughborough Lightning, Scotland
ROLE: Bowler
DEBUT: Test: 2019; T20I: 2018

BEST T20I BATTING: 1* England vs Australia, North Sound, Antigua, 2018
BEST T20I BOWLING: 3-16 England vs Bangladesh, Gros Islet, St Lucia, 2018

MOST EXCITING DAY AS A CRICKETER? Making my England debut in the West Indies
CHILDHOOD SPORTING HERO? Michael Owen
BIGGEST INFLUENCE ON YOUR DEVELOPMENT AS A CRICKETER (EXCLUDING PARENTS)? Salliann Briggs – she invested a lot of time with me at Loughborough and played a huge part in helping me bridge the gap to international cricket
FIRST CRICKET CLUB? Huntly CC, Aberdeenshire
IF YOU COULD TAKE ONE FEMALE CRICKETER'S BEST SHOT AND ADD IT TO YOUR OWN GAME? Danni Wyatt's shot over extra-cover
TOUGHEST OPPONENT IN CRICKET? Ellyse Perry
WHAT WOULD YOU DO IF YOU WERE IN CHARGE OF WOMEN'S CRICKET? Play more Test matches and expand the World Cup to 14 teams
STRANGEST THING YOU'VE DONE DURING LOCKDOWN? Spending two months on my family farm, lambing sheep and feeding pet lambs
FAVOURITE SMELL? Freshly baked pastries
GUILTY PLEASURE? Cleaning the bathroom
TWITTER: @kirstiegordon97

Batting	Mat	Inns	NO	Runs	HS	Ave	SR	100	50	Ct	St
Tests	1	-	-	-	-	-	-	-	-	0	0
T20Is	5	1	1	1	1*	-	100.00	0	0	0	0
Bowling	**Mat**	**Balls**	**Runs**	**Wkts**	**BBI**	**BBM**	**Ave**	**Econ**	**SR**	**5w**	**10**
Tests	1	220	119	3	2/50	3/119	39.66	3.24	73.3	0	0
T20Is	5	114	98	8	3/16	3/16	12.25	5.15	14.2	0	0

PHOEBE GRAHAM

RHB / RMF / MVP60

FULL NAME: Phoebe Claire Graham
BORN: October 23, 1991, Steeton, Yorkshire
SQUAD NO: 17
HEIGHT: 5ft 11in
NICKNAME: PG
EDUCATION: University of Exeter
TEAMS: Northern Diamonds, Berkshire, Devon, Nottinghamshire, Yorkshire
ROLE: Bowler
DEBUT: List A: 2010; T20: 2010

BEST BATTING: 29* Northern Diamonds vs Thunder, Liverpool, 2020
BEST BOWLING: 3-14 Berkshire vs Worcestershire, Maidenhead, 2019

MOST EXCITING DAY AS A CRICKETER? Receiving my first professional contract last year
CHILDHOOD SPORTING HERO? Andrew Flintoff
BIGGEST INFLUENCE ON YOUR DEVELOPMENT AS A CRICKETER (EXCLUDING PARENTS)? Danni Warren, who last year was appointed regional director of women's cricket for the London and East region. She brought me back into the game when she was involved with Berkshire and MCC
FIRST CRICKET CLUB? Pool CC, Leeds
IF YOU COULD TAKE ONE FEMALE CRICKETER'S BEST SHOT AND ADD IT TO YOUR OWN GAME? "The Natmeg" (Nat Sciver)
TOUGHEST OPPONENT IN CRICKET? Fi Morris – she's one scary lady!
WHAT WOULD YOU DO IF YOU WERE IN CHARGE OF WOMEN'S CRICKET? Ensure that all professional cricketers are either being mentored or are mentors themselves
STRANGEST THING YOU'VE DONE DURING LOCKDOWN? Buying vibrant-coloured clothing – a fluorescent orange coat, a bright-pink smock dress…
FAVOURITE SMELL? Lavender
GUILTY PLEASURE? Painting
TWITTER: @phoebeg23

Batting	Mat	Inns	NO	Runs	HS	Ave	SR	100	50	Ct	St
List A	43	28	8	174	29*	8.70	54.71	0	0	5	-
T20s	24	9	1	81	16	10.12	91.01	0	0	2	-
Bowling	**Mat**	**Balls**	**Mdns**	**Runs**	**Wkts**	**BB**	**Ave**	**4wI**	**5wI**	**SR**	**Econ**
List A	43	1220	16	889	27	3-14	32.92	0	0	45.18	4.37
T20s	24	449	1	409	20	3-26	20.45	0	0	22.45	5.46

SUNRISERS

CORDELIA GRIFFITH RHB / RM / MVP81

FULL NAME: Cordelia Lauren Griffith
BORN: September 19, 1995, Islington, London
SQUAD NO: 6
HEIGHT: 5ft 5in
NICKNAME: Cords
EDUCATION: Chigwell School, Essex; Durham University
TEAMS: Sunrisers, Middlesex, Essex, Surrey Stars, Yorkshire Diamonds
ROLE: Batsman
DEBUT: List A: 2010; T20: 2010

BEST BATTING: 155* Essex vs Suffolk, Long Melford, 2018
BEST BOWLING: 1-6 Essex vs Berkshire, Sindlesham, 2013

MOST EXCITING DAY AS A CRICKETER? Getting my first professional contract with Sunrisers last year
CHILDHOOD SPORTING HERO? Andrew Symonds
FIRST CRICKET CLUB? Loughton CC, Essex
IF YOU COULD TAKE ONE FEMALE CRICKETER'S BEST SHOT AND ADD IT TO YOUR OWN GAME? Sophie Devine's slog-sweep
TOUGHEST OPPONENT IN CRICKET? Sarah Taylor – she was a game-changer. As a batter she could take the game away from you very quickly
MOST ECCENTRIC TEAMMATE? Jo Gardner – because of her endless puns and her array of jazzy socks
STRANGEST THING YOU'VE DONE DURING LOCKDOWN? Starting to learn Japanese
FAVOURITE SMELL? The inside of a new car
GUILTY PLEASURE? Gemma Collins: Diva Forever and Ever (reality tv show)
TWITTER: @cordeliagriff

Batting	Mat	Inns	NO	Runs	HS	Ave	SR	100	50	Ct	St
List A	40	39	3	1035	155*	28.75	-	3	4	11	-
T20s	52	43	3	591	57	14.77	80.84	0	2	9	-
Bowling	**Mat**	**Balls**	**Mdns**	**Runs**	**Wkts**	**BB**	**Ave**	**4wI**	**5wI**	**SR**	**Econ**
List A	40	271	3	192	7	1-6	27.42	0	0	38.71	4.25
T20s	52	150	0	167	2	1-12	83.50	0	0	75.00	6.68

ALEX GRIFFITHS

RHB / RMF / MVP34

FULL NAME: Alexandra Clare Griffiths
BORN: June 12, 2002, Swansea, Wales
SQUAD NO: 25
HEIGHT: 5ft 7in
NICKNAME: Ali G
EDUCATION: Cardiff Metropolitan University
TEAMS: Western Storm, Wales
ROLE: Allrounder
DEBUT: List A: 2016; T20: 2016

BEST BATTING: 80 Western Storm vs Sunrisers, Bristol, 2020
BEST BOWLING: 2-2 Wales vs Essex, Griffithstown, 2019

MOST EXCITING DAY AS A CRICKETER? Winning the Kia Super League in 2019
CHILDHOOD SPORTING HERO? My brother
BIGGEST INFLUENCE ON YOUR DEVELOPMENT AS A CRICKETER (EXCLUDING PARENTS)? My coaches in Wales: Alan Jones, John Derrick and Aimee Rees. They coached me from a young age and have stuck by me all the way
FIRST CRICKET CLUB? Port Talbot CC, Swansea
IF YOU COULD TAKE ONE FEMALE CRICKETER'S BEST SHOT AND ADD IT TO YOUR OWN GAME? Tammy Beaumont's sweep
WHAT WOULD YOU DO IF YOU WERE PRIME MINISTER? Ensure equal pay for men and women, ban all single-use plastics, free all animals in captivity
FAVOURITE SMELL? Vanilla
GUILTY PLEASURE? Chocolate
TWITTER: @alex_griff7

Batting	Mat	Inns	NO	Runs	HS	Ave	SR	100	50	Ct	St
List A	27	25	1	463	80	19.29	60.28	0	2	10	-
T20s	24	17	1	92	24	5.75	60.52	0	0	6	-
Bowling	**Mat**	**Balls**	**Mdns**	**Runs**	**Wkts**	**BB**	**Ave**	**4wI**	**5wI**	**SR**	**Econ**
List A	27	471	8	344	7	2-2	49.14	0	0	67.28	4.38
T20s	24	132	0	151	10	3-12	15.10	0	0	13.20	6.86

JENNY GUNN

RHB / RM / MVP15

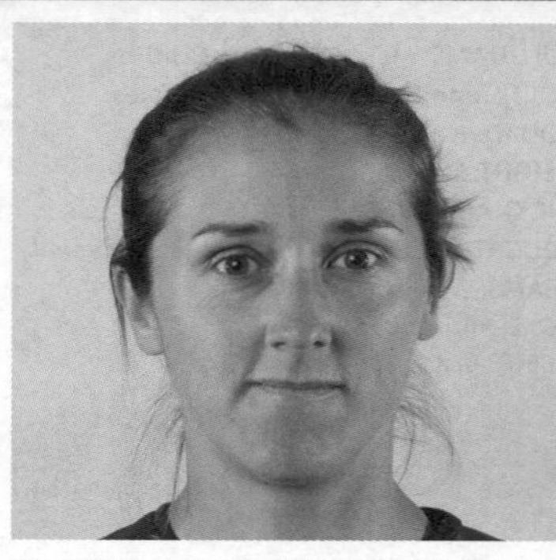

FULL NAME: Jennifer Louise Gunn
BORN: May 9, 1986, Nottingham
SQUAD NO: 24
HEIGHT: 5ft 10in
NICKNAME: Chuckie
EDUCATION: South Nottingham College
TEAMS: England, Northern Diamonds, Nottinghamshire, Loughborough Lightning, South Australia, Warwickshire, Western Australia, Yorkshire
ROLE: Allrounder
DEBUT: Test: 2004; ODI: 2004; T20I: 2004; List A: 2001; T20: 2004

BEST ODI BATTING: 73 England vs New Zealand, Taunton, 2007
BEST ODI BOWLING: 5-22 England vs Pakistan, Louth, 2013

MOST EXCITING DAY AS A CRICKETER? Winning the 2017 World Cup final at Lord's with my family all there watching
CHILDHOOD SPORTING HERO? Alan Shearer
FIRST CRICKET CLUB? Lady Bay Boots CC, Nottingham
IF YOU COULD TAKE ONE FEMALE CRICKETER'S BEST SHOT AND ADD IT TO YOUR OWN GAME? Danni Wyatt's shot over extra-cover
TOUGHEST OPPONENT IN CRICKET? Meg Lanning
MOST ECCENTRIC TEAMMATE? Hollie Armitage – just get her dancing!
WHAT WOULD YOU DO IF YOU WERE IN CHARGE OF WOMEN'S CRICKET? Do the coin toss before the warm-up, no play if the temperature is below 18 degrees
STRANGEST THING YOU'VE DONE DURING LOCKDOWN? Still getting up at 5am to walk my dog
TWITTER: @GunnJenny

Batting	Mat	Inns	NO	Runs	HS	Ave	SR	100	50	Ct	St
Tests	11	19	2	391	62*	23.00	30.38	0	1	6	0
ODIs	144	111	28	1629	73	19.62	57.19	0	5	49	0
T20Is	104	67	18	682	69	13.91	100.44	0	1	58	0
Bowling	**Mat**	**Balls**	**Runs**	**Wkts**	**BBI**	**BBM**	**Ave**	**Econ**	**SR**	**5w**	**10**
Tests	11	2189	645	29	5/19	5/59	22.24	1.76	75.4	1	0
ODIs	144	5906	3822	136	5/22	5/22	28.10	3.88	43.4	2	0
T20Is	104	1385	1487	75	5/18	5/18	19.82	6.44	18.4	1	0

ALEX HARTLEY

RHB / SLA / MVP17

FULL NAME: Alexandra Hartley
BORN: September 26, 1993, Blackburn, Lancashire
SQUAD NO: 65
HEIGHT: 5ft 4in
EDUCATION: Ribblesdale High School, Clitheroe; Loughborough College
TEAMS: England, Thunder, Lancashire, Hobart Hurricanes, Lancashire Thunder, Middlesex, Surrey Stars, Tasmania
ROLE: Bowler
DEBUT: ODI: 2016; T20I: 2016; List A: 2008; T20: 2010

BEST ODI BATTING: 3* England vs India, Nagpur, 2018
BEST ODI BOWLING: 4-24 England vs West Indies, Kingston, 2016

MOST EXCITING DAY AS A CRICKETER? Playing in the 2017 World Cup final
CHILDHOOD SPORTING HERO? Monty Panesar
FIRST CRICKET CLUB? Read CC, Burnley, Lancashire
IF YOU COULD TAKE ONE FEMALE CRICKETER'S BEST SHOT AND ADD IT TO YOUR OWN GAME? Nat Sciver's back-foot punch
TOUGHEST OPPONENT IN CRICKET? Elyse Villani – no matter where I bowl she will take me apart. Best player of spin I've come up against
WHAT WOULD YOU DO IF YOU WERE IN CHARGE OF WOMEN'S CRICKET? Anyone who trolls women's cricket online to be banned from watching men's cricket and forced to watch the women's game instead. And I'd get rid of the pitching-outside-leg lbw rule – terrible law
WHAT WOULD YOU DO IF YOU WERE PRIME MINISTER? Make Boris get a haircut
STRANGEST THING YOU'VE DONE DURING LOCKDOWN? Painted an elephant (not a real one) relentlessly for seven weeks
FAVOURITE SMELL? All candles
TWITTER: @AlexHartley93

Batting	Mat	Inns	NO	Runs	HS	Ave	SR	100	50	Ct	St
ODIs	28	12	11	10	3*	10.00	19.60	0	0	4	0
T20Is	4	1	1	2	2*	-	100.00	0	0	0	0
Bowling	**Mat**	**Balls**	**Runs**	**Wkts**	**BBI**	**BBM**	**Ave**	**Econ**	**SR**	**5w**	**10**
ODIs	28	1390	950	39	4/24	4/24	24.35	4.10	35.6	0	0
T20Is	4	70	79	3	2/19	2/19	26.33	6.77	23.3	0	0

GEORGIA HENNESSY

RHB / RFM / MVP3

FULL NAME: Georgia May Hennessy
BORN: November 4, 1996, Worcester
SQUAD NO: 64
HEIGHT: 5ft 6in
NICKNAME: Ryan Sidebottom
EDUCATION: University of Worcester
TEAMS: Western Storm, Devon, Warwickshire, Worcestershire
ROLE: Allrounder
DEBUT: List A: 2010; T20: 2013

BEST BATTING: 105 Western Storm vs Sunrisers, Bristol, 2020
BEST BOWLING: 5-38 Warwickshire vs Surrey, Cobham, 2014

MOST EXCITING DAY AS A CRICKETER? Winning the Kia Super League with Western Storm for the first time in 2017
CHILDHOOD SPORTING HERO? Andrew Flintoff
BIGGEST INFLUENCE ON YOUR DEVELOPMENT AS A CRICKETER (EXCLUDING PARENTS)? Gavin Haynes, who was my coach at Worcestershire Academy for a few years. My teammates have also been very important in helping me to fall back in love with the game after a couple of years out of it
FIRST CRICKET CLUB? Barnards Green CC, Malvern, Worcestershire
STRANGEST THING YOU'VE DONE DURING LOCKDOWN? A Disney puzzle
FAVOURITE SMELL? Garlic bread
GUILTY PLEASURE? Call of Duty
TWITTER: @GeorgiaHennessy

Batting	Mat	Inns	NO	Runs	HS	Ave	SR	100	50	Ct	St
List A	68	67	12	1523	105	27.69	-	1	7	29	-
T20s	56	51	14	1259	97*	34.02	-	0	6	15	-
Bowling	**Mat**	**Balls**	**Mdns**	**Runs**	**Wkts**	**BB**	**Ave**	**4wI**	**5wI**	**SR**	**Econ**
List A	68	1823	21	1223	55	5-38	22.23	2	2	33.14	4.02
T20s	56	616	3	592	26	3-14	22.76	0	0	23.69	5.76

LUCY HIGHAM

RHB / OB / MVP30

FULL NAME: Lucy Florence Higham
BORN: October 17, 1997, Leicester
SQUAD NO: 7
HEIGHT: 5ft 3in
EDUCATION: Leicester Grammar School; Loughborough University
TEAMS: Lightning, Nottinghamshire, Leicestershire, Loughborough Lightning
ROLE: Bowler
DEBUT: List A: 2013; T20: 2013

BEST BATTING: 74 Leicestershire vs Northamptonshire, Northampton, 2015
BEST BOWLING: 4-46 Leicestershire vs Derbyshire, Ticknall, 2014

MOST EXCITING DAY AS A CRICKETER? Playing in the Kia Super League final with Loughborough Lightning in 2018
CHILDHOOD SPORTING HERO? Ellyse Perry
BIGGEST INFLUENCE ON YOUR DEVELOPMENT AS A CRICKETER (EXCLUDING PARENTS)? Laurie Potter – he was the master in charge of cricket at my school
FIRST CRICKET CLUB? Houghton & Thurnby CC, Leicester
IF YOU COULD TAKE ONE FEMALE CRICKETER'S BEST SHOT AND ADD IT TO YOUR OWN GAME? Danni Wyatt's shot over mid-off and extra-cover
TOUGHEST OPPONENT IN CRICKET? Nat Sciver. When her team needs it most she always seems to pull it out of the bag – whether with bat, ball or in the field
MOST ECCENTRIC TEAMMATE? Sarah Bryce – because of her love for musicals and The Vicar of Dibley
WHAT WOULD YOU DO IF YOU WERE IN CHARGE OF WOMEN'S CRICKET? Try to change the perception of the female game so that it is not constantly compared to the men's
STRANGEST THING YOU'VE DONE DURING LOCKDOWN? Hitting tennis serves into a bed sheet we hung up in the back garden at our university house
TWITTER: @lucy_higham

Batting	Mat	Inns	NO	Runs	HS	Ave	SR	100	50	Ct	St
List A	57	50	5	623	74	13.84	43.35	0	2	21	-
T20s	63	43	8	550	43*	15.71	-	0	0	17	-
Bowling	**Mat**	**Balls**	**Mdns**	**Runs**	**Wkts**	**BB**	**Ave**	**4wI**	**5wI**	**SR**	**Econ**
List A	57	2375	33	1430	69	4-46	20.72	1	0	34.42	3.61
T20s	63	876	5	784	42	4-16	18.66	1	0	20.85	5.36

AMY JONES

RHB / WK / MVP100

FULL NAME: Amy Ellen Jones
BORN: June 13, 1993, Solihull, Warwickshire
SQUAD NO: 40
HEIGHT: 5ft 9in
NICKNAME: Jonesy
EDUCATION: John Willmott School; Loughborough College
TEAMS: England, Central Sparks, Warwickshire, Loughborough Lightning, Perth Scorchers, Sydney Sixers, Western Australia
ROLE: Wicketkeeper/batsman
DEBUT: Test: 2019; ODI: 2013; T20I: 2013; List A: 2008; T20: 2010

BEST ODI BATTING: 94 England vs India, Nagpur, 2018

CHILDHOOD SPORTING HERO? David Beckham
BIGGEST INFLUENCE ON YOUR DEVELOPMENT AS A CRICKETER (EXCLUDING PARENTS)? John Smart and Kelly Evenson at Warwickshire – they saw my potential and taught me the basics of batting when I was young. Then it was Salliann Briggs at Loughborough – she helped me recognise what being professional is about
FIRST CRICKET CLUB? Walmley CC, West Midlands
IF YOU COULD TAKE ONE FEMALE CRICKETER'S BEST SHOT AND ADD IT TO YOUR OWN GAME? Heather Knight's slog-sweep against the seamers
WHAT WOULD YOU DO IF YOU WERE IN CHARGE OF WOMEN'S CRICKET? Have better fitting trousers, change all ODIs to 40 overs
STRANGEST THING YOU'VE DONE DURING LOCKDOWN? Doing colouring books
FAVOURITE SMELL? A log fire
GUILTY PLEASURE? Love Island
TWITTER: @amyjones313

Batting	Mat	Inns	NO	Runs	HS	Ave	SR	100	50	Ct	St
Tests	1	1	0	64	64	64.00	45.71	0	1	1	0
ODIs	47	39	3	1017	94	28.25	83.22	0	8	31	6
T20Is	57	47	7	810	89	20.25	116.04	0	5	23	23
Bowling	**Mat**	**Balls**	**Runs**	**Wkts**	**BBI**	**BBM**	**Ave**	**Econ**	**SR**	**5w**	**10**
Tests	1	-	-	-	-	-	-	-	-	-	-
ODIs	47	-	-	-	-	-	-	-	-	-	-
T20Is	57	-	-	-	-	-	-	-	-	-	-

EVELYN JONES

LHB / SLA / MVP9

FULL NAME: Evelyn Jones
BORN: August 8, 1992, Shrewsbury, Shropshire
SQUAD NO: 11
HEIGHT: 5ft 8in
EDUCATION: Oxford Brookes University
TEAMS: Central Sparks, Lancashire, Canterbury, Lancashire Thunder, Loughborough Lightning, Shropshire, Staffordshire
ROLE: Batsman
DEBUT: List A: 2008; T20: 2010

BEST BATTING: 115* Staffordshire vs Durham, Durham, 2015
BEST BOWLING: 6-29 Shropshire vs Northumberland, Madeley, 2011

MOST EXCITING DAY AS A CRICKETER? Either winning the double for Lancashire in 2017 or getting a phone call last year telling me I was getting a professional contract
BIGGEST INFLUENCE ON YOUR DEVELOPMENT AS A CRICKETER (EXCLUDING PARENTS)? Lisa Keightley (current England Women head coach). She first selected me for the England Academy
FIRST CRICKET CLUB? Whitchurch CC, Shropshire
IF YOU COULD TAKE ONE FEMALE CRICKETER'S BEST SHOT AND ADD IT TO YOUR OWN GAME? Heather Knight's reverse-sweep (she nails it every time)
TOUGHEST OPPONENT IN CRICKET? Beth Langston – one of the best seamers in the country. She can get the new ball moving all over the place and has extra pace and bounce
WHAT WOULD YOU DO IF YOU WERE IN CHARGE OF WOMEN'S CRICKET? Strengthen the link between the grassroots and professional game (I think the new regional academies will help with this immensely)
WHAT WOULD YOU DO IF YOU WERE PRIME MINISTER? Introduce an annual National Sports Week where everyone has the week off to play or watch sport
STRANGEST THING YOU'VE DONE DURING LOCKDOWN? Buying a house!
GUILTY PLEASURE? Ozan's BBQ Pizza (my local takeaway)
TWITTER: @eve_jones11

Batting	Mat	Inns	NO	Runs	HS	Ave	SR	100	50	Ct	St
List A	82	79	11	2296	115*	33.76	-	4	12	27	-
T20s	81	75	9	1521	69	23.04	90.37	0	5	18	-
Bowling	**Mat**	**Balls**	**Mdns**	**Runs**	**Wkts**	**BB**	**Ave**	**4wI**	**5wI**	**SR**	**Econ**
List A	82	1028	25	667	22	6-29	30.31	1	1	46.72	3.89
T20s	81	264	0	274	12	3-15	22.83	0	0	22.00	6.22

HANNAH JONES — LHB / SLA / MVP62

FULL NAME: Hannah Emily Jones
BORN: February 10, 1999
SQUAD NO: 7
HEIGHT: 5ft 5in
EDUCATION: St Thomas More RC College, Manchester; Myerscough College, Lancashire
TEAMS: Thunder, Lancashire
ROLE: Bowler
DEBUT: List A: 2014; T20: 2014

BEST BATTING: 4* Thunder vs Lightning, Liverpool, 2020
BEST BOWLING: 3-17 Lancashire vs Wales, Sutton, 2014

MOST EXCITING DAY AS A CRICKETER? Getting my first professional cricket contract in 2020
CHILDHOOD SPORTING HERO? Shaun Wright-Phillips
BIGGEST INFLUENCE ON YOUR DEVELOPMENT AS A CRICKETER (EXCLUDING PARENTS)? England Women head coach Lisa Keightley – she has helped develop all aspects of my cricket and continues to support me by watching my games
FIRST CRICKET CLUB? Denton St Lawrence CC, Manchester
TOUGHEST OPPONENT IN CRICKET? Tammy Beaumont – for her all-round game
WHAT WOULD YOU DO IF YOU WERE IN CHARGE OF WOMEN'S CRICKET? Create more equality at cricket clubs by offering changing facilities for women, and more female coaches
STRANGEST THING YOU'VE DONE DURING LOCKDOWN? Training in the snow
FAVOURITE SMELL? Strawberry
GUILTY PLEASURE? Chocolate

Batting	Mat	Inns	NO	Runs	HS	Ave	SR	100	50	Ct	St
List A	26	13	7	17	4*	2.83	20.48	0	0	2	-
T20s	17	4	4	1	1*	-	25.00	0	0	2	-
Bowling	**Mat**	**Balls**	**Mdns**	**Runs**	**Wkts**	**BB**	**Ave**	**4wI**	**5wI**	**SR**	**Econ**
List A	26	1122	26	589	17	3-17	34.64	0	0	66.00	3.14
T20s	17	336	2	262	15	2-3	17.46	0	0	22.40	4.67

MARIE KELLY RHB / RM / MVP29

FULL NAME: Marie Kelly
BORN: February 9, 1996, Birmingham
SQUAD NO: 23
HEIGHT: 5ft 7in
NICKNAME: MK
EDUCATION: Loughborough University
TEAMS: Central Sparks, Warwickshire, Loughborough Lightning, Southern Vipers
ROLE: Batsman
DEBUT: List A: 2011; T20: 2012

BEST BATTING: 64 Warwickshire vs Lancashire, Newton-le-Willows, 2018
BEST BOWLING: 4-13 Warwickshire vs Surrey, Wellesbourne, 2013

MOST EXCITING DAY AS A CRICKETER? Winning the premiership flag in Australia as an overseas player for Box Hill CC
CHILDHOOD SPORTING HERO? Charlotte Edwards
FIRST CRICKET CLUB? Earlswood CC, Solihull, Warwickshire
IF YOU COULD TAKE ONE FEMALE CRICKETER'S BEST SHOT AND ADD IT TO YOUR OWN GAME? Any of Sophie Devine's huge sixes
TOUGHEST OPPONENT IN CRICKET? Suzie Bates – I've been on the end of her rampages and it is not pleasant to field against
WHAT WOULD YOU DO IF YOU WERE IN CHARGE OF WOMEN'S CRICKET? Make it compulsory for girls' cricket to be on the national curriculum in secondary schools instead of rounders, change the law so that a percentage of money bet on women's cricket goes back into a pot for developing the women's game
WHAT WOULD YOU DO IF YOU WERE PRIME MINISTER? Make transport cheaper, make all sanitary products free, reduce poverty
STRANGEST THING YOU'VE DONE DURING LOCKDOWN? Taking part in a fitness session while wearing a crayon costume
FAVOURITE SMELL? Bacon

Batting	Mat	Inns	NO	Runs	HS	Ave	SR	100	50	Ct	St
List A	64	60	6	1211	64	22.42	-	0	6	21	-
T20s	49	43	8	736	76	21.02	-	0	4	16	-
Bowling	**Mat**	**Balls**	**Mdns**	**Runs**	**Wkts**	**BB**	**Ave**	**4wI**	**5wI**	**SR**	**Econ**
List A	64	915	13	598	25	4-13	23.92	1	0	36.60	3.92
T20s	49	319	3	259	21	3-9	12.33	0	0	15.19	4.87

HEATHER KNIGHT RHB / OB / MVP36

FULL NAME: Heather Clare Knight
BORN: December 26, 1990, Plymouth
SQUAD NO: 5
HEIGHT: 5ft 7in
NICKNAME: Trev
EDUCATION: Plymstock School, Plymouth; Cardiff University
TEAMS: England, Western Storm, Berkshire, Devon, Hobart Hurricanes, Sydney Thunder, Tasmania, Western Storm
ROLE: Batsman
DEBUT: Test: 2011; ODI: 2010; T20I: 2010; List A: 2008; T20: 2009

BEST ODI BATTING: 106 England vs Pakistan, Leicester, 2017
BEST ODI BOWLING: 5-26 England vs Pakistan, Leicester, 2016

CHILDHOOD SPORTING HERO? Andy Caddick
BIGGEST INFLUENCE ON YOUR DEVELOPMENT AS A CRICKETER (EXCLUDING PARENTS)? Alastair Maiden, previously assistant coach of England Women. He bowled a lot of filthy leg-spin to me!
FIRST CRICKET CLUB? Plymstock CC, Plymouth
IF YOU COULD TAKE ONE FEMALE CRICKETER'S BEST SHOT AND ADD IT TO YOUR OWN GAME? Nat Sciver's back-foot punch
TOUGHEST OPPONENT IN CRICKET? Katherine Brunt in domestic cricket
MOST ECCENTRIC TEAMMATE? Sophie Ecclestone – she eats a burger with a knife and fork
WHAT WOULD YOU DO IF YOU WERE IN CHARGE OF WOMEN'S CRICKET? Scrap double-header matches
WHAT WOULD YOU DO IF YOU WERE PRIME MINISTER? Get more women into the cabinet, abolish stamp duty
STRANGEST THING YOU'VE DONE DURING LOCKDOWN? Making margaritas in a NutriBullet
FAVOURITE SMELL? Bacon
GUILTY PLEASURE? Also bacon
TWITTER: @heatherknight55

Batting	Mat	Inns	NO	Runs	HS	Ave	SR	100	50	Ct	St
Tests	7	13	1	386	157	32.16	41.50	1	2	7	0
ODIs	104	99	23	2935	106	38.61	71.63	1	21	33	0
T20Is	81	71	14	1295	108*	22.71	119.02	1	4	26	0
Bowling	**Mat**	**Balls**	**Runs**	**Wkts**	**BBI**	**BBM**	**Ave**	**Econ**	**SR**	**5w**	**10**
Tests	7	227	105	4	2/25	2/25	26.25	2.77	56.7	0	0
ODIs	104	1695	1247	49	5/26	5/26	25.44	4.41	34.5	1	0
T20Is	81	525	500	20	3/9	3/9	25.00	5.71	26.2	0	0

EMMA LAMB RHB / RM

FULL NAME: Emma Louise Lamb
BORN: December 16, 1997, Preston, Lancashire
SQUAD NO: 6
HEIGHT: 5ft 7in
EDUCATION: Cardinal Newman College, Preston; Edge Hill University, Ormskirk, Lancashire
TEAMS: Thunder, Lancashire, Lancashire Thunder
ROLE: Allrounder
DEBUT: List A: 2012; T20: 2012

BEST BATTING: 113* Lancashire vs Durham, Leigh, 2013
BEST BOWLING: 4-39 Lancashire vs Warwickshire, Newton-le-Willows, 2018

MOST EXCITING DAY AS A CRICKETER? Playing on TV for the first time
CHILDHOOD SPORTING HERO? Andrew Flintoff
BIGGEST INFLUENCE ON YOUR DEVELOPMENT AS A CRICKETER (EXCLUDING PARENTS)? John Stanworth, former Lancashire cricketer and head coach of England Women's Academy
FIRST CRICKET CLUB? Chorley CC, Lancashire
IF YOU COULD TAKE ONE FEMALE CRICKETER'S BEST SHOT AND ADD IT TO YOUR OWN GAME? Danni Wyatt's cover-drive for six
TOUGHEST OPPONENT IN CRICKET? Lizelle Lee – she's so hard to bowl to
WHAT WOULD YOU DO IF YOU WERE IN CHARGE OF WOMEN'S CRICKET? Create home grounds exclusively for women's cricket
WHAT WOULD YOU DO IF YOU WERE PRIME MINISTER? Make the UK green like Denmark
STRANGEST THING YOU'VE DONE DURING LOCKDOWN? Taking part in an indoor Nerf-gun tournament
FAVOURITE SMELL? Anything which contains shea butter
GUILTY PLEASURE? Banana bread
TWITTER: @EmmaLamb236

Batting	Mat	Inns	NO	Runs	HS	Ave	SR	100	50	Ct	St
List A	60	60	8	1701	113*	32.71	57.50	1	11	9	-
T20s	76	74	10	1372	72*	21.43	-	0	3	12	-
Bowling	**Mat**	**Balls**	**Mdns**	**Runs**	**Wkts**	**BB**	**Ave**	**4wI**	**5wI**	**SR**	**Econ**
List A	60	799	19	516	29	4-39	17.79	1	0	27.55	3.87
T20s	76	971	6	1061	49	4-15	21.65	2	0	19.81	6.55

BETH LANGSTON RHB / RM / MVP13

FULL NAME: Bethany Alicia Langston
BORN: September 6, 1992, Harold Wood, Essex
SQUAD NO: 42
HEIGHT: 5ft 7in
NICKNAME: Bev
EDUCATION: Loughborough University
TEAMS: England, Northern Diamonds, Yorkshire, Essex, Loughborough Lightning, Otago, Yorkshire Diamonds
ROLE: Bowler
DEBUT: ODI: 2016; T20I: 2013; List A: 2009; T20: 2009

BEST ODI BATTING: 21 England vs Sri Lanka, Colombo, 2016
BEST ODI BOWLING: 1-23 England vs Sri Lanka, Colombo, 2016

MOST EXCITING DAY AS A CRICKETER? Playing for Northern Diamonds in the final of last year's Rachael Heyhoe Flint Trophy, even though we lost to the Southern Vipers
CHILDHOOD SPORTING HERO? Daniel Vettori (he played in glasses too)
BIGGEST INFLUENCE ON YOUR DEVELOPMENT AS A CRICKETER (EXCLUDING PARENTS)? Too many coaches to name, but they all kept it fun and made me realise how much I loved the game
FIRST CRICKET CLUB? Upminster CC, London
TOUGHEST OPPONENT IN CRICKET? The toughest challenge last year was having to run your hat off the field before bowling – that was a real test of fitness levels!
MOST ECCENTRIC TEAMMATE? Helen Fenby – she sleeps on the bus with her eyes open
WHAT WOULD YOU DO IF YOU WERE IN CHARGE OF WOMEN'S CRICKET? Get more women involved in cricketing organisations and find a way to make more players full-time professionals
STRANGEST THING YOU'VE DONE DURING LOCKDOWN? Not succumbing to baking banana bread
GUILTY PLEASURE? Binge-watching Selling Sunset
TWITTER: @B_Langers92

Batting	Mat	Inns	NO	Runs	HS	Ave	SR	100	50	Ct	St
ODIs	4	2	1	21	21	21.00	100.00	0	0	2	0
T20Is	2	-	-	-	-	-	-	-	-	1	0
Bowling	**Mat**	**Balls**	**Runs**	**Wkts**	**BBI**	**BBM**	**Ave**	**Econ**	**SR**	**5w**	**10**
ODIs	4	186	94	2	1/23	1/23	47.00	3.03	93.0	0	0
T20Is	2	48	44	1	1/16	1/16	44.00	5.50	48.0	0	0

SOPHIE LUFF

RHB / RM / MVP7

FULL NAME: Sophie Natasha Luff
BORN: December 6, 1993, Taunton, Somerset
SQUAD NO: 63
HEIGHT: 5ft 2in
EDUCATION: Cardiff Metropolitan University
TEAMS: Western Storm, Somerset
ROLE: Batsman
DEBUT: List A: 2009; T20: 2010

BEST BATTING: 138* Somerset vs Wales, Taunton, 2015
BEST BOWLING: 1-27 Western Storm vs Sunrisers, Bristol, 2020

MOST EXCITING DAY AS A CRICKETER? Being out in the middle with my Western Storm teammates at the end of the 2017 Kia Super League final
CHILDHOOD SPORTING HERO? Marcus Trescothick
BIGGEST INFLUENCE ON YOUR DEVELOPMENT AS A CRICKETER (EXCLUDING PARENTS)? John Stanworth – I worked with him while I was part of the England Women's Academy
FIRST CRICKET CLUB? Weston-super-Mare CC, Somerset
TOUGHEST OPPONENT IN CRICKET? Sophie Ecclestone – a world-class bowler who loves a battle. Generates a lot of bounce with her height, and her ability to turn the ball away from the bat is always a threat
WHAT WOULD YOU DO IF YOU WERE IN CHARGE OF WOMEN'S CRICKET? Schedule more matches in the calendar year (international and domestic). And I'd love to see more women's Test cricket being played
STRANGEST THING YOU'VE DONE DURING LOCKDOWN? Using a bale of hay from my dad's farm as a gym bench for home workouts
GUILTY PLEASURE? Drumstick Squashies
TWITTER: @LuffSophie

Batting	Mat	Inns	NO	Runs	HS	Ave	SR	100	50	Ct	St
List A	87	86	23	2730	138*	43.33	-	5	16	28	-
T20s	97	81	27	1525	59*	28.24	-	0	4	28	-
Bowling	**Mat**	**Balls**	**Mdns**	**Runs**	**Wkts**	**BB**	**Ave**	**4wI**	**5wI**	**SR**	**Econ**
List A	87	284	1	245	2	1-27	122.50	0	0	142.00	5.17
T20s	97	148	0	171	5	2-12	34.20	0	0	29.60	6.93

FI MORRIS

RHB / OB / MVP8

FULL NAME: Fritha Mary Kie Morris
BORN: January 31, 1994, Reading, Berkshire
SQUAD NO: 88
HEIGHT: 5ft 6in
NICKNAME: Princess Fiona
EDUCATION: University of Exeter
TEAMS: Western Storm, Hampshire, Berkshire, Gloucestershire, Oxfordshire, Southern Vipers
ROLE: Allrounder
DEBUT: List A: 2008; T20: 2009

BEST BATTING: 127 Gloucestershire vs Oxfordshire, Charlbury, 2011
BEST BOWLING: 5-26 Western Storm vs Sunrisers, Chelmsford, 2020

CHILDHOOD SPORTING HERO? Jonny Wilkinson
BIGGEST INFLUENCE ON YOUR DEVELOPMENT AS A CRICKETER (EXCLUDING PARENTS)? My brother Digs – he bowled off-spin and I copied his action and everything he did
FIRST CRICKET CLUB? Charlbury CC, Chipping Norton, Oxfordshire
IF YOU COULD TAKE ONE FEMALE CRICKETER'S BEST SHOT AND ADD IT TO YOUR OWN GAME? Georgia Hennessy's cover-drive
TOUGHEST OPPONENT IN CRICKET? Heather Knight – she's ridiculously consistent
MOST ECCENTRIC TEAMMATE? Amanda Jade-Wellington – she's got the second-biggest Pokémon collection in the world
WHAT WOULD YOU DO IF YOU WERE IN CHARGE OF WOMEN'S CRICKET? Help to make every top-tier nation fully professional, create a women's IPL, make cricket the main sport for girls at school in the summer term
WHAT WOULD YOU DO IF YOU WERE PRIME MINISTER? Ban battery farming
STRANGEST THING YOU'VE DONE DURING LOCKDOWN? Twenty squats in a pond
FAVOURITE SMELL? Sun cream
GUILTY PLEASURE? Crumpets
TWITTER: @FiMorris8

Batting	Mat	Inns	NO	Runs	HS	Ave	SR	100	50	Ct	St
List A	66	61	9	1230	127	23.65	-	1	4	21	-
T20s	73	53	10	601	40	13.97	-	0	0	12	-
Bowling	**Mat**	**Balls**	**Mdns**	**Runs**	**Wkts**	**BB**	**Ave**	**4wI**	**5wI**	**SR**	**Econ**
List A	66	3069	67	1704	102	5-26	16.70	8	1	30.08	3.33
T20s	73	1433	12	1312	80	4-22	16.40	2	0	17.91	5.49

TARA NORRIS

LHB / LFM / MVP14

FULL NAME: Tara Gabriella Norris
BORN: June 4, 1998, Philadelphia, USA
SQUAD NO: 24
HEIGHT: 5ft 7in
NICKNAME: Tino
EDUCATION: Portslade Aldridge Community Academy, Brighton; Loughborough University
TEAMS: Southern Vipers, Sussex, Loughborough Lightning
ROLE: Bowler
DEBUT: List A: 2014; T20: 2014

BEST BATTING: 27 Sussex vs Berkshire, Horsham, 2015
BEST BOWLING: 4-45 Southern Vipers vs Western Storm, Bristol, 2020

CHILDHOOD SPORTING HERO? Serena Williams
BIGGEST INFLUENCE ON YOUR DEVELOPMENT AS A CRICKETER (EXCLUDING PARENTS)? Being part of the MCCU programme at Loughborough University
FIRST CRICKET CLUB? Horsham CC, East Sussex
IF YOU COULD TAKE ONE FEMALE CRICKETER'S BEST SHOT AND ADD IT TO YOUR OWN GAME? Suzie Bates's drive straight over the top
TOUGHEST OPPONENT IN CRICKET? Lizelle Lee
WHAT WOULD YOU DO IF YOU WERE IN CHARGE OF WOMEN'S CRICKET? Make pre-season tours compulsory, increase psychological support for professionals
WHAT WOULD YOU DO IF YOU WERE PRIME MINISTER? Change the education system so that it includes a wider variety of subjects
STRANGEST THING YOU'VE DONE DURING LOCKDOWN? A half-marathon
FAVOURITE SMELL? Roasting coffee beans
GUILTY PLEASURE? One Direction
TWITTER: @Tara_norris98

Batting	Mat	Inns	NO	Runs	HS	Ave	SR	100	50	Ct	St
List A	41	25	10	152	27	10.13	47.64	0	0	10	-
T20s	34	20	7	205	59*	15.76	97.15	0	1	8	-
Bowling	**Mat**	**Balls**	**Mdns**	**Runs**	**Wkts**	**BB**	**Ave**	**4wI**	**5wI**	**SR**	**Econ**
List A	41	1543	20	983	45	4-45	21.84	1	0	34.28	3.82
T20s	34	457	2	486	16	2-12	30.37	0	0	28.56	6.38

PAIGE SCHOLFIELD RHB / RFM / MVP11

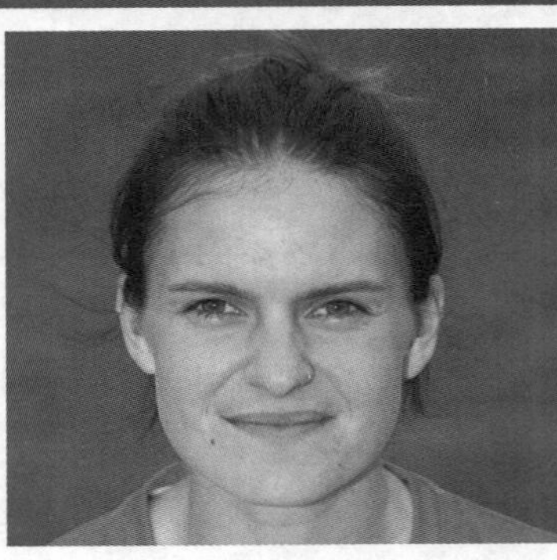

FULL NAME: Paige Jamie Scholfield
BORN: December 19, 1995, Durban, South Africa
SQUAD NO: 7
HEIGHT: 5ft 7in
EDUCATION: Beacon Academy, East Sussex; Loughborough College
TEAMS: Southern Vipers, Sussex, Loughborough Lightning
ROLE: Allrounder
DEBUT: List A: 2012; T20: 2013

BEST BATTING: 48 Sussex vs Middlesex, Ditchling, 2013
BEST BOWLING: 3-17 Sussex vs Surrey, Cobham, 2018

MOST EXCITING DAY AS A CRICKETER? Making my debut for the Southern Vipers in the 2018 Kia Super League
CHILDHOOD SPORTING HERO? Kevin Pietersen
BIGGEST INFLUENCE ON YOUR DEVELOPMENT AS A CRICKETER (EXCLUDING PARENTS)? Charlotte Edwards, the former England captain and since last year my coach at Southern Vipers
FIRST CRICKET CLUB? Bells Yew Green CC, Tunbridge Wells, Kent
TOUGHEST OPPONENT IN CRICKET? Jenny Gunn – she never bowls a bad ball
WHAT WOULD YOU DO IF YOU WERE IN CHARGE OF WOMEN'S CRICKET? Make cricket an option in PE at schools, set up competitions at club level which offer prize money
WHAT WOULD YOU DO IF YOU WERE PRIME MINISTER? Provide better housing schemes for the young and under-privileged, make all gyms free, introduce lifestyle-management classes into schools
STRANGEST THING YOU'VE DONE DURING LOCKDOWN? Building a garden bar
GUILTY PLEASURE? Taylor Swift
TWITTER: @PaigeSchol

Batting	Mat	Inns	NO	Runs	HS	Ave	SR	100	50	Ct	St
List A	53	40	8	565	48	17.65	67.50	0	0	19	-
T20s	69	60	11	663	63*	13.53	98.36	0	1	20	1
Bowling	**Mat**	**Balls**	**Mdns**	**Runs**	**Wkts**	**BB**	**Ave**	**4wI**	**5wI**	**SR**	**Econ**
List A	53	1041	9	706	26	3-17	27.15	0	0	40.03	4.06
T20s	69	452	1	476	22	3-12	21.63	0	0	20.54	6.31

NAT SCIVER RHB / RMF / MVP41

FULL NAME: Natalie Ruth Sciver
BORN: August 20, 1992, Tokyo, Japan
SQUAD NO: 39
HEIGHT: 5ft 10in
NICKNAME: Sciv
EDUCATION: Epsom College, Surrey; Loughborough University
TEAMS: England, Northern Diamonds, Surrey, Melbourne Stars, Perth Scorchers, Surrey Stars
ROLE: Allrounder
DEBUT: Test: 2014; ODI: 2013; T20I: 2013; List A: 2010; T20: 2010

BEST ODI BATTING: 137 England vs Pakistan, Leicester, 2017
BEST ODI BOWLING: 3-3 England vs West Indies, Bristol, 2017

CHILDHOOD SPORTING HERO? David Beckham
BIGGEST INFLUENCE ON YOUR DEVELOPMENT AS A CRICKETER (EXCLUDING PARENTS)? Katherine Brunt – in my first year at university she helped me realise how serious I was about getting into the England side, and also how close I was to reaching that goal
FIRST CRICKET CLUB? Stoke d'Abernon CC, Surrey
TOUGHEST OPPONENT IN CRICKET? Katherine Brunt – that's the worst thing about having a partner as a teammate: the inter-squad games are tough!
MOST ECCENTRIC TEAMMATE? Lauren Winfield-Hill – because of her dress sense. She can be a country-club member one day and a fashionable farmer (who doesn't get muddy) the next
WHAT WOULD YOU DO IF YOU WERE IN CHARGE OF WOMEN'S CRICKET? Standardise boundary sizes and make them smaller to encourage more exciting games, introduce Dukes balls in women's size for Test matches, allow bats to be slightly bigger than they are permitted to be in men's cricket
WHAT WOULD YOU DO IF YOU WERE PRIME MINISTER? Dance across the top of the stairs like Hugh Grant in Love Actually, then ban food containers that aren't recyclable
STRANGEST THING YOU'VE DONE DURING LOCKDOWN? Getting a dog
TWITTER: @natsciver

Batting	Mat	Inns	NO	Runs	HS	Ave	SR	100	50	Ct	St
Tests	5	8	0	228	88	28.50	36.07	0	1	4	0
ODIs	70	61	11	1981	137	39.62	97.34	3	14	29	0
T20Is	83	80	18	1570	82	25.32	111.90	0	9	40	0
Bowling	**Mat**	**Balls**	**Runs**	**Wkts**	**BBI**	**BBM**	**Ave**	**Econ**	**SR**	**5w**	**10**
Tests	5	351	174	2	1/30	1/30	87.00	2.97	175.5	0	0
ODIs	70	1803	1311	49	3/3	3/3	26.75	4.36	36.7	0	0
T20Is	83	1200	1275	67	4/15	4/15	19.02	6.37	17.9	0	0

ANYA SHRUBSOLE RHB / RFM

FULL NAME: Anya Shrubsole
BORN: December 7, 1991, Bath
SQUAD NO: 41
HEIGHT: 5ft 10in
NICKNAME: Hoof
EDUCATION: Hayesfield School, Bath; Loughborough University
TEAMS: England, Western Storm, Berkshire, Perth Scorchers, Somerset
ROLE: Bowler
DEBUT: Test: 2013; ODI: 2008; T20I: 2008; List A: 2004; T20: 2005

BEST ODI BATTING: 32* England vs West Indies, Worcester, 2019
BEST ODI BOWLING: 6-46 England vs India, Lord's, 2017

MOST EXCITING DAY AS A CRICKETER? The World Cup final in 2017
CHILDHOOD SPORTING HERO? Steve Redgrave
BIGGEST INFLUENCE ON YOUR DEVELOPMENT AS A CRICKETER (EXCLUDING PARENTS)? Tom Baker – my first coach at Bath CC
FIRST CRICKET CLUB? Bath CC, Somerset
TOUGHEST OPPONENT IN CRICKET? Ellyse Perry
MOST ECCENTRIC TEAMMATE? Issy Wong – the hair
WHAT WOULD YOU DO IF YOU WERE PRIME MINISTER? Reverse Brexit, pay doctors and nurses more, meet the Queen
STRANGEST THING YOU'VE DONE DURING LOCKDOWN? I couldn't do much because I'd had surgery and wore a Velcro shoe for two months
GUILTY PLEASURE? Musicals
TWITTER: @anya_shrubsole

Batting	Mat	Inns	NO	Runs	HS	Ave	SR	100	50	Ct	St
Tests	6	9	0	62	20	6.88	24.03	0	0	3	0
ODIs	70	31	10	258	32*	12.28	86.00	0	0	17	0
T20Is	79	19	10	104	29	11.55	105.05	0	0	20	0
Bowling	**Mat**	**Balls**	**Runs**	**Wkts**	**BBI**	**BBM**	**Ave**	**Econ**	**SR**	**5w**	**10**
Tests	6	1260	497	17	4/51	7/99	29.23	2.36	74.1	0	0
ODIs	70	3318	2306	90	6/46	6/46	25.62	4.16	36.8	2	0
T20Is	79	1598	1587	102	5/11	5/11	15.55	5.95	15.6	1	0

BRYONY SMITH RHB / OB / MVP75

FULL NAME: Bryony Frances Smith
BORN: December 12, 1997, Sutton, Surrey
SQUAD NO: 4
HEIGHT: 5ft 6in
NICKNAME: Bry
EDUCATION: St Andrew's High School, London; Archbishop Tenison's Sixth Form
TEAMS: England, South East Stars, Surrey, Surrey Stars
ROLE: Batsman
DEBUT: ODI: 2019; T20I: 2018; List A: 2014; T20: 2014

BEST ODI BOWLING: 1-20 England vs West Indies, Chelmsford, 2019

MOST EXCITING DAY AS A CRICKETER? Making my England ODI debut in front of my family
CHILDHOOD SPORTING HERO? Kevin Pietersen
BIGGEST INFLUENCE ON YOUR DEVELOPMENT AS A CRICKETER (EXCLUDING PARENTS)? Richard Bedbrook – as full-time women's coach at Surrey he spent lots of time working with me and planning how I would take my game to the next level
FIRST CRICKET CLUB? Wallington CC, London
IF YOU COULD TAKE ONE FEMALE CRICKETER'S BEST SHOT AND ADD IT TO YOUR OWN GAME? Sarah Taylor's reverse-sweep
TOUGHEST OPPONENT IN CRICKET? Sophie Ecclestone – she's so accurate and consistent
WHAT WOULD YOU DO IF YOU WERE IN CHARGE OF WOMEN'S CRICKET? Schedule all matches to be played at county grounds
STRANGEST THING YOU'VE DONE DURING LOCKDOWN? Trying to learn to do a handstand (it didn't go very well)
FAVOURITE SMELL? Freshly toasted bread
TWITTER: @BrySmith97

Batting	Mat	Inns	NO	Runs	HS	Ave	SR	100	50	Ct	St
ODIs	1	-	-	-	-	-	-	-	-	0	0
T20Is	3	3	0	16	15	5.33	100.00	0	0	0	0
Bowling	**Mat**	**Balls**	**Runs**	**Wkts**	**BBI**	**BBM**	**Ave**	**Econ**	**SR**	**5w**	**10**
ODIs	1	48	20	1	1/20	1/20	20.00	2.50	48.0	0	0
T20Is	3	-	-	-	-	-	-	-	-	-	-

LINSEY SMITH — LHB / SLA / MVP47

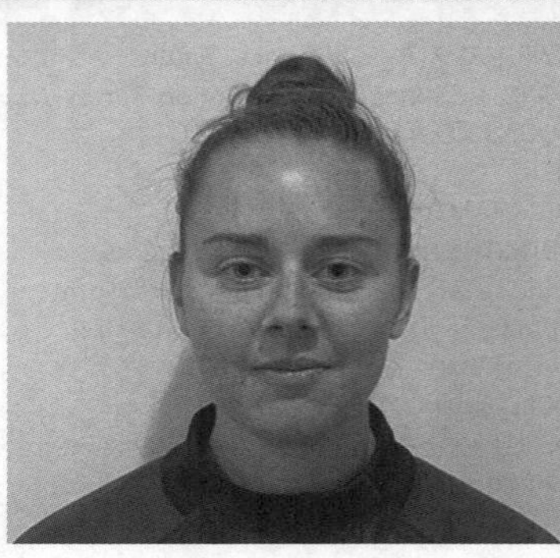

FULL NAME: Linsey Claire Neale Smith
BORN: March 10, 1995, Hillingdon, Middlesex
SQUAD NO: 50
HEIGHT: 5ft 2in
NICKNAME: Neal
EDUCATION: Loughborough University
TEAMS: England, Northern Diamonds, Sussex, Berkshire, Loughborough Lightning, Southern Vipers, Yorkshire Diamonds
ROLE: Bowler
DEBUT: T20I: 2018; List A: 2011; T20: 2011

BEST T20I BOWLING: 3-18 England vs Sri Lanka, Colombo, 2019

MOST EXCITING DAY AS A CRICKETER? Being selected in the England team for the first time at the 2018 World T20 in the West Indies
CHILDHOOD SPORTING HERO? Charlotte Edwards
BIGGEST INFLUENCE ON YOUR DEVELOPMENT AS A CRICKETER (EXCLUDING PARENTS)? John Stanworth, my coach at the England Academy. He sorted my attitude out and focused my mind on getting into the England team
FIRST CRICKET CLUB? Aston Rowant CC, Oxfordshire
IF YOU COULD TAKE ONE FEMALE CRICKETER'S BEST SHOT AND ADD IT TO YOUR OWN GAME? Amy Jones – the shot that goes over extra-cover
TOUGHEST OPPONENT IN CRICKET? Heather Knight – she has so many shots and is very hard to get out
MOST ECCENTRIC TEAMMATE? Hollie Armitage – my best pal since we were young. We're almost the same person
STRANGEST THING YOU'VE DONE DURING LOCKDOWN? Going veggie for two weeks because I was bored and wanted a challenge
FAVOURITE SMELL? Fresh rain
GUILTY PLEASURE? Elton John
TWITTER: @LinseySmith95

Batting	Mat	Inns	NO	Runs	HS	Ave	SR	100	50	Ct	St
T20Is	9	-	-	-	-	-	-	-	-	0	0
Bowling	**Mat**	**Balls**	**Runs**	**Wkts**	**BBI**	**BBM**	**Ave**	**Econ**	**SR**	**5w**	**10**
T20Is	9	186	188	13	3/18	3/18	14.46	6.06	14.3	0	0

ELLIE THRELKELD

RHB / WK / MVP25

FULL NAME: Eleanor Threlkeld
BORN: November 16, 1998, Knowsley, Lancashire
SQUAD NO: 21
HEIGHT: 5ft 6in
NICKNAME: Threlks
EDUCATION: Winstanley College, Wigan; Loughborough University
TEAMS: Thunder, Lancashire, Lancashire Thunder
ROLE: Wicketkeeper
DEBUT: List A: 2014; T20: 2013

BEST BATTING: 72 Lancashire vs Nottinghamshire, Carnforth, 2019

MOST EXCITING DAY AS A CRICKETER? Signing my first professional contract last year
CHILDHOOD SPORTING HERO? Steven Gerrard
BIGGEST INFLUENCE ON YOUR DEVELOPMENT AS A CRICKETER (EXCLUDING PARENTS)? My older brother – he got me into sport and I always wanted to be like him
FIRST CRICKET CLUB? Rainford CC, St Helens, Merseyside
IF YOU COULD TAKE ONE FEMALE CRICKETER'S BEST SHOT AND ADD IT TO YOUR OWN GAME? Fran Wilson's reverse-sweep
MOST ECCENTRIC TEAMMATE? Alex Hartley – she has no filter when she talks
WHAT WOULD YOU DO IF YOU WERE IN CHARGE OF WOMEN'S CRICKET? To be honest I think the people in charge are doing a fantastic job!
WHAT WOULD YOU DO IF YOU WERE PRIME MINISTER? Ban VAR from Premier League football, increase the minimum wage, invest more in the NHS
STRANGEST THING YOU'VE DONE DURING LOCKDOWN? A yoga training course
FAVOURITE SMELL? Coffee in the morning
GUILTY PLEASURE? Playing the ukulele
TWITTER: @EllieThrelkeld

Batting	Mat	Inns	NO	Runs	HS	Ave	SR	100	50	Ct	St
List A	48	45	3	605	72	14.40	48.36	0	2	20	22
T20s	71	61	15	715	56*	15.54	-	0	3	18	50
Bowling	**Mat**	**Balls**	**Mdns**	**Runs**	**Wkts**	**BB**	**Ave**	**4wI**	**5wI**	**SR**	**Econ**
List A	-	-	-	-	-	-	-	-	-	-	-
T20s	-	-	-	-	-	-	-	-	-	-	-

MADY VILLIERS RHB / OB / MVP77

FULL NAME: Mady Kate Villiers
BORN: August 26, 1998, Havering, Essex
SQUAD NO: 22
HEIGHT: 5ft 5in
NICKNAME: AB
EDUCATION: Shenfield High School, Brentwood, Essex
TEAMS: England, Sunrisers, Essex, Surrey Stars
ROLE: Bowler
DEBUT: T20I: 2019; List A: 2013; T20: 2013

BEST T20I BATTING: 1* England vs West Indies, Derby, 2020
BEST T20I BOWLING: 3-10 England vs New Zealand, Wellington, 2021

FIRST CRICKET CLUB? Bentley CC, Brentford, Essex
MOST INTERESTING TEAMMATE? Katherine Brunt – she has some amazing stories and is also a lunatic
IF YOU WERE AN ANIMAL, WHICH WOULD IT BE? A panda – because they eat for 16 hours every day
TWITTER: @VilliersMady
NOTES: The 22-year-old off-spinner, who is also a gun fielder and useful with the bat, was one of the Kia Super League's star performers and won the T20 title with Surrey Stars in 2018. Villiers made her international debut in 2019 and was chosen in England's squad for the T20 World Cup in Australia early last year, taking a wicket with her fourth ball in her one tournament appearance against West Indies at Sydney. She is now a regular in the T20I side, forming a potent spin trio with Sarah Glenn and Sophie Ecclestone that has helped England to clean sweeps in West Indies last autumn (5-0) and in New Zealand earlier this year (3-0). In March she took career-best figures of 3-10 against the Kiwis at Wellington. Villiers plays for Essex in county cricket and her regional side is Sunrisers, which represents the London and East region. She is also due to turn out for Trent Rockets in The Hundred this summer

Batting	Mat	Inns	NO	Runs	HS	Ave	SR	100	50	Ct	St
T20Is	12	2	1	2	1*	2.00	66.66	0	0	4	0
Bowling	**Mat**	**Balls**	**Runs**	**Wkts**	**BBI**	**BBM**	**Ave**	**Econ**	**SR**	**5w**	**10**
T20Is	12	168	184	11	3/10	3/10	16.72	6.57	15.2	0	0

FRAN WILSON RHB / OB

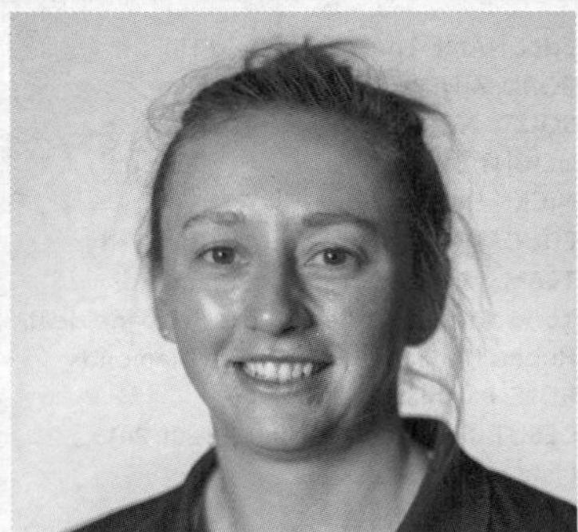

FULL NAME: Frances Claire Wilson
BORN: November 7, 1991, Farnham, Surrey
SQUAD NO: 35
HEIGHT: 5ft 4in
NICKNAME: Franki
EDUCATION: University of Bath; Loughborough University
TEAMS: England, Sunrisers, Kent, Hobart Hurricanes, Middlesex, Somerset, Sydney Thunder, Wellington, Western Storm
ROLE: Batsman
DEBUT: Test: 2017; ODI: 2010; T20I: 2010; List A: 2006; T20: 2010

BEST ODI BATTING: 85* England vs Pakistan, Kuala Lumpur, 2019

CHILDHOOD SPORTING HERO? Frank Lampard
FIRST CRICKET CLUB? Bath CC, Somerset
IF YOU COULD TAKE ONE FEMALE CRICKETER'S BEST SHOT AND ADD IT TO YOUR OWN GAME? Danni Wyatt's six over cover
MOST ECCENTRIC TEAMMATE? Katherine Brunt is one of a kind…
WHAT WOULD YOU DO IF YOU WERE IN CHARGE OF WOMEN'S CRICKET? Make sure all kit is female-specific and functional, organise a big end-of-season party for everyone involved
WHAT WOULD YOU DO IF YOU WERE PRIME MINISTER? Make the working week and holidays flexible – when you've done your work, you're done. I'd also turn elections (and politics in general) into a nationwide gameshow in which politicians are set challenges they must complete to win the votes of the public (a bit like The Apprentice)
STRANGEST THING YOU'VE DONE DURING LOCKDOWN? Developing an obsession with fantasy football
FAVOURITE SMELL? A puppy's ears
GUILTY PLEASURE? The Hills (terrible American reality TV show)
TWITTER: @fwilson07

Batting	Mat	Inns	NO	Runs	HS	Ave	SR	100	50	Ct	St
Tests	1	1	0	13	13	13.00	24.52	0	0	0	0
ODIs	33	23	2	468	85*	22.28	87.96	0	2	14	0
T20Is	30	26	10	356	43*	22.25	99.16	0	0	7	0
Bowling	**Mat**	**Balls**	**Runs**	**Wkts**	**BBI**	**BBM**	**Ave**	**Econ**	**SR**	**5w**	**10**
Tests	1	-	-	-	-	-	-	-	-	-	-
ODIs	33	-	-	-	-	-	-	-	-	-	-
T20Is	30	-	-	-	-	-	-	-	-	-	-

LAUREN WINFIELD-HILL RHB / WK / MVP63

FULL NAME: Lauren Winfield-Hill
BORN: August 16, 1990, York
SQUAD NO: 58
HEIGHT: 5ft 8in
NICKNAME: Loz
EDUCATION: Loughborough University
TEAMS: England, Northern Diamonds, Yorkshire, Adelaide Strikers, Brisbane Heat, Hobart Hurricanes, Yorkshire Diamonds
ROLE: Batsman
DEBUT: Test: 2014; ODI: 2013; T20I: 2013; List A: 2007; T20: 2010

BEST ODI BATTING: 123 England vs Pakistan, Worcester, 2016

MOST EXCITING DAY AS A CRICKETER? The 2017 World Cup final
CHILDHOOD SPORTING HERO? Alec Stewart
BIGGEST INFLUENCE ON YOUR DEVELOPMENT AS A CRICKETER (EXCLUDING PARENTS)? Graham Dilley, the former England cricketer who was head coach of the Academy at Loughborough
FIRST CRICKET CLUB? Stamford Bridge CC, Yorkshire
IF YOU COULD TAKE ONE FEMALE CRICKETER'S BEST SHOT AND ADD IT TO YOUR OWN GAME? Nat Sciver's sweep
WHAT WOULD YOU DO IF YOU WERE IN CHARGE OF WOMEN'S CRICKET? Employ more female coaches
STRANGEST THING YOU'VE DONE DURING LOCKDOWN? Starting a business…
FAVOURITE SMELL? Hugo Boss
GUILTY PLEASURE? Music of the 1970s
TWITTER: @lozwinfield

Batting	Mat	Inns	NO	Runs	HS	Ave	SR	100	50	Ct	St
Tests	3	6	0	94	35	15.66	25.06	0	0	1	0
ODIs	43	43	4	903	123	23.15	66.49	1	3	15	0
T20Is	40	31	6	552	74	22.08	111.29	0	3	16	0
Bowling	**Mat**	**Balls**	**Runs**	**Wkts**	**BBI**	**BBM**	**Ave**	**Econ**	**SR**	**5w**	**10**
Tests	3	-	-	-	-	-	-	-	-	-	-
ODIs	43	-	-	-	-	-	-	-	-	-	-
T20Is	40	-	-	-	-	-	-	-	-	-	-

ISSY WONG RHB / RF / MVP80

FULL NAME: Isabelle Eleanor Chih Ming Wong
BORN: May 15, 2002, Chelsea, London
SQUAD NO: 95
HEIGHT: 5ft 7in
NICKNAME: Wongi
EDUCATION: Shrewsbury School
TEAMS: Central Sparks, Warwickshire, Southern Vipers, Worcestershire
ROLE: Bowler
DEBUT: List A: 2018; T20: 2018

BEST BATTING: 49 Worcestershire vs Shropshire, Kidderminster, 2018
BEST BOWLING: 4-22 Worcestershire vs Cornwall, Worcester, 2018

MOST EXCITING DAY AS A CRICKETER? Becoming the first girl to play for Shrewsbury School's First XI
CHILDHOOD SPORTING HERO? Fernando Torres
BIGGEST INFLUENCE ON YOUR DEVELOPMENT AS A CRICKETER (EXCLUDING PARENTS)? Andy Barnard – the head of cricket at Shrewsbury School. He pushed me to be the best version of myself on the cricket field, in the classroom and as a person
FIRST CRICKET CLUB? Knowle & Dorridge CC, Solihull, Warwickshire
TOUGHEST OPPONENT IN CRICKET? Heather Knight. She's got such a cool head and the margin for error is tiny when bowling at her – as I found out when she kept chipping me over extra-cover for six
WHAT WOULD YOU DO IF YOU WERE PRIME MINISTER? Bring justice for the families of the 96 victims of the Hillsborough disaster, guarantee that all children in the UK are fed throughout the year
STRANGEST THING YOU'VE DONE DURING LOCKDOWN? Receiving two sets of A-Level results despite not sitting a single exam
GUILTY PLEASURE? Listening to "Life is a Highway" from the Cars soundtrack while driving
TWITTER: @Wongi95

Batting	Mat	Inns	NO	Runs	HS	Ave	SR	100	50	Ct	St
List A	15	11	3	100	49	12.50	64.93	0	0	2	-
T20s	18	12	1	60	14	5.45	95.23	0	0	3	-
Bowling	**Mat**	**Balls**	**Mdns**	**Runs**	**Wkts**	**BB**	**Ave**	**4wl**	**5wl**	**SR**	**Econ**
List A	15	525	14	362	20	4-22	18.10	3	0	26.25	4.13
T20s	18	252	0	311	12	3-21	25.91	0	0	21.00	7.40

NAT WRAITH

RHB / WK / MVP26

WESTERN STORM

FULL NAME: Natasha Agnes Jessica Wraith
BORN: October 3, 2001, Bristol
SQUAD NO: 37
HEIGHT: 5ft 6in
NICKNAME: Aggy
EDUCATION: SGS College, Gloucestershire; Cardiff Metropolitan University
TEAMS: Western Storm, Somerset, Gloucestershire
ROLE: Wicketkeeper
DEBUT: List A: 2016; T20: 2016

BEST BATTING: 68 Western Storm vs Southern Vipers, Southampton, 2020

MOST EXCITING DAY AS A CRICKETER? Playing my first match for Western Storm last summer
CHILDHOOD SPORTING HERO? Rafael Nadal
FIRST CRICKET CLUB? Frenchay CC, Bristol
IF YOU COULD TAKE ONE FEMALE CRICKETER'S BEST SHOT AND ADD IT TO YOUR OWN GAME? Smriti Mandhana's cover-drive
WHAT WOULD YOU DO IF YOU WERE IN CHARGE OF WOMEN'S CRICKET? Throw in a T10 competition
WHAT WOULD YOU DO IF YOU WERE PRIME MINISTER? Paint the door of 10 Downing Street green, make university free, keep the "Eat Out to Help Out" scheme forever
STRANGEST THING YOU'VE DONE DURING LOCKDOWN? Growing my leg hair
FAVOURITE SMELL? Petrol
GUILTY PLEASURE? The Crown
TWITTER: @NatWraith

Batting	Mat	Inns	NO	Runs	HS	Ave	SR	100	50	Ct	St
List A	26	23	3	417	68	20.85	-	0	2	15	12
T20s	26	23	7	245	42*	15.31	85.66	0	0	5	15
Bowling	**Mat**	**Balls**	**Mdns**	**Runs**	**Wkts**	**BB**	**Ave**	**4wI**	**5wI**	**SR**	**Econ**
List A	-	-	-	-	-	-	-	-	-	-	-
T20s	-	-	-	-	-	-	-	-	-	-	-

DANNI WYATT

RHB / OB / MVP54

FULL NAME: Danielle Nicole Wyatt
BORN: April 22, 1991, Stoke-on-Trent, Staffordshire
SQUAD NO: 28
HEIGHT: 5ft 4in
EDUCATION: St Peter's High School; Stoke-On-Trent Sixth Form College
TEAMS: England, Southern Vipers, Sussex, Lancashire Thunder, Melbourne Renegades, Nottinghamshire, Staffordshire, Victoria
ROLE: Batsman
DEBUT: ODI: 2010; T20I: 2010; List A: 2005; T20: 2006

BEST ODI BATTING: 110 England vs Pakistan, Kuala Lumpur, 2019
BEST ODI BOWLING: 3-7 England vs South Africa, Cuttack, 2013

CHILDHOOD SPORTING HERO? Andrew Flintoff
BIGGEST INFLUENCE ON YOUR DEVELOPMENT AS A CRICKETER (EXCLUDING PARENTS)? Andy Grice at Staffordshire – ever since I got into the U13 side he backed me when others didn't. Also Alastair Maiden when he was England Women assistant coach – he helped me turn scores of 20 or 30 into match-winning knocks
FIRST CRICKET CLUB? Whitmore CC, Staffordshire
IF YOU COULD TAKE ONE FEMALE CRICKETER'S BEST SHOT AND ADD IT TO YOUR OWN GAME? Heather Knight's leg-side shots for six
TOUGHEST OPPONENT IN CRICKET? Meg Lanning
WHAT WOULD YOU DO IF YOU WERE IN CHARGE OF WOMEN'S CRICKET? Sign a big team-sponsorship deal with Tampax
WHAT WOULD YOU DO IF YOU WERE PRIME MINISTER? Ban rounders at school (play cricket instead)
STRANGEST THING YOU'VE DONE DURING LOCKDOWN? A duet on TikTok with my mum
GUILTY PLEASURE? Dairy Milk Buttons dipped in a cup of tea
TWITTER: @Danni_wyatt

Batting	Mat	Inns	NO	Runs	HS	Ave	SR	100	50	Ct	St
ODIs	77	63	8	1046	110	19.01	80.09	1	1	17	0
T20Is	116	95	9	1675	124	19.47	122.44	2	7	27	0
Bowling	**Mat**	**Balls**	**Runs**	**Wkts**	**BBI**	**BBM**	**Ave**	**Econ**	**SR**	**5w**	**10**
ODIs	77	918	770	27	3/7	3/7	28.51	5.03	34.0	0	0
T20Is	116	759	715	46	4/11	4/11	15.54	5.65	16.5	0	0

The
Umpires

ROB BAILEY

NAME: Robert John Bailey
BORN: October 28, 1963, Biddulph, Staffordshire
HEIGHT: 6ft 3in
NICKNAME: Bailers
APPOINTED TO F-C LIST: 2006
INTERNATIONAL PANEL: 2011-2019
ELITE PANEL: 2014
TESTS UMPIRED: 1 (1 as TV)
ODIS UMPIRED: 34 (4 as TV)
T20IS UMPIRED: 36 (13 as TV)
COUNTIES AS PLAYER: Northamptonshire, Derbyshire
ROLE: Batsman; RHB OB
COUNTY DEBUT: 1982 (Northamptonshire), 2000 (Derbyshire)
TEST DEBUT: 1988
ODI DEBUT: 1985

Batting	Mat	Inns	NO	Runs	HS	Ave	SR	100	50	Ct	St
Tests	4	8	0	119	43	14.87	36.50	0	0	0	0
ODIs	4	4	2	137	43*	68.50	69.89	0	0	1	0
First-class	374	628	89	21844	224*	40.52	-	47	111	272	0
List A	396	376	65	12076	153*	38.82	-	10	79	111	0
Bowling	**Mat**	**Balls**	**Runs**	**Wkts**	**BBI**	**BBM**	**Ave**	**Econ**	**SR**	**5w**	**10**
Tests	4	-	-	-	-	-	-	-	-	-	-
ODIs	4	36	25	0	-	-	-	4.16	-	0	0
First-class	374	9713	5144	121	5/54	-	42.51	3.17	80.2	2	0
List A	396	3092	2564	72	5/45	5/45	35.61	4.97	42.9	1	0

NEIL BAINTON

NAME: Neil Laurence Bainton
BORN: October 2, 1970, Romford, Essex
HEIGHT: 5ft 8in
APPOINTED TO FIRST-CLASS LIST: 2006
ODIS UMPIRED: 8 (3 as TV)
T20IS UMPIRED: 5 (1 as TV)

CRICKETING HIGHLIGHT OF 2020? Umpiring an Essex League match in the middle of July between Wickford and Horndon on the Hill. It was my first match of the season and it was great to be on the cricket field again. I hadn't umpired a league game in Essex for many years

STRANGEST THING YOU'VE DONE DURING LOCKDOWN? Taking part in the First Class Walk with all the other first-class umpires. Each umpire had to clock up the miles individually by whatever means possible ahead of the 2020 season. Together we walked the equivalent distance from Manchester to Lahore and back again

SURPRISING FACT ABOUT YOU? I have worked for the Royal Mail as a postman during the winter months

PAUL BALDWIN

NAME: Paul Kerr Baldwin
BORN: July 18, 1973, Epsom, Surrey
APPOINTED TO FIRST-CLASS LIST: 2015
TESTS UMPIRED: 1 (1 as TV)
ODIS UMPIRED: 23 (2 as TV)
T20IS UMPIRED: 12 (1 as TV)

STRANGEST THING YOU'VE DONE DURING LOCKDOWN? Becoming an administrator on a Facebook group called The Close Call, which promotes best practice and collaboration between sports officials irrespective of the level. It grew exponentially during the first lockdown and its members range from Darrell Hair and Simon Taufel to English Premier League referees and Premiership Rugby referees, all the way down to Sunday-friendly officials
HIGHLIGHT OF YOUR PLAYING CAREER? Being selected to captain RAF Brüggen, my club side in Germany in 1996, which I skippered for the next four years

IAN BLACKWELL

NAME: Ian David Blackwell
BORN: June 10, 1978, Chesterfield, Derbyshire
HEIGHT: 6ft 2in
NICKNAME: Blackdog
APPOINTED TO FIRST-CLASS LIST: 2014
COUNTIES AS PLAYER: Derbyshire, Durham, Somerset, Warwickshire
ROLE: Allrounder; LHB SLA
COUNTY DEBUT: 1997 (Derbyshire), 2000 (Somerset), 2009 (Durham), 2012 (Warwickshire)
TEST DEBUT: 2006
ODI DEBUT: 2002

Batting	Mat	Inns	NO	Runs	HS	Ave	SR	100	50	Ct	St
Tests	1	1	0	4	4	4.00	25.00	0	0	0	0
ODIs	34	29	2	403	82	14.92	86.66	0	1	8	0
First-class	210	319	26	11595	247*	39.57	-	27	64	66	0
List A	254	233	21	5765	134*	27.19	-	3	34	64	0
T20s	77	69	9	1281	82	21.35	131.79	0	5	17	0
Bowling	**Mat**	**Balls**	**Runs**	**Wkts**	**BBI**	**BBM**	**Ave**	**Econ**	**SR**	**5w**	**10**
Tests	1	114	71	0	-	-	-	3.73	-	0	0
ODIs	34	1230	877	24	3/26	3/26	36.54	4.27	51.2	0	0
First-class	210	31618	14295	398	7/52	-	35.91	2.71	79.4	14	0
List A	254	8885	7102	207	5/26	5/26	34.30	4.79	42.9	1	0
T20s	77	1273	1508	50	4/26	4/26	30.16	7.10	25.4	0	0

MIKE BURNS

NAME: Mike Burns
BORN: February 6, 1969, Barrow-in-Furness, Lancashire
APPOINTED TO FIRST-CLASS LIST: 2016
INTERNATIONAL PANEL: 2020-
TESTS UMPIRED: 1
ODIS UMPIRED: 5 (2 as TV)
T20IS UMPIRED: 13 (4 as TV)

COUNTIES AS PLAYER: Warwickshire, Somerset
ROLE: Allrounder; RHB RM
COUNTY DEBUT: 1992 (Warwickshire), 1997 (Somerset)

Batting	Mat	Inns	NO	Runs	HS	Ave	SR	100	50	Ct	St
First-class	154	248	14	7648	221	32.68	-	8	51	142	7
List A	221	207	21	4802	115*	25.81	-	3	31	101	15
T20s	9	7	0	108	36	15.42	108.00	0	0	3	0
Bowling	**Mat**	**Balls**	**Runs**	**Wkts**	**BBI**	**BBM**	**Ave**	**Econ**	**SR**	**5w**	**10**
First-class	154	4751	2885	68	6/54	-	42.42	3.64	69.8	1	0
List A	221	1844	1769	58	4/39	4/39	30.50	5.75	31.7	0	0
T20s	9	36	55	2	1/15	1/15	27.50	9.16	18.0	0	0

NICK COOK

NAME: Nicholas Grant Billson Cook
BORN: June 17, 1956, Leicester
NICKNAME: Beast
APPOINTED TO FIRST-CLASS LIST: 2009
TESTS UMPIRED: 1
ODIS UMPIRED: 4
T20IS UMPIRED: 7

COUNTIES AS PLAYER: Leicestershire, Northamptonshire
ROLE: Bowler; RHB SLA
COUNTY DEBUT: 1978 (Leicestershire), 1986 (Northamptonshire)
TEST DEBUT: 1983
ODI DEBUT: 1984

Batting	Mat	Inns	NO	Runs	HS	Ave	SR	100	50	Ct	St
Tests	15	25	4	179	31	8.52	23.58	0	0	5	0
ODIs	3	-	-	-	-	-	-	-	-	2	0
First-class	356	365	96	3137	75	11.66	-	0	4	197	0
List A	223	89	36	491	23	9.26	-	0	0	74	0
Bowling	**Mat**	**Balls**	**Runs**	**Wkts**	**BBI**	**BBM**	**Ave**	**Econ**	**SR**	**5w**	**10**
Tests	15	4174	1689	52	6/65	11/83	32.48	2.42	80.2	4	1
ODIs	3	144	95	5	2/18	2/18	19.00	3.95	28.8	0	0
First-class	356	64460	25507	879	7/34	-	29.01	2.37	73.3	31	4
List A	223	10077	6812	200	4/22	4/22	34.06	4.05	50.3	0	0

BEN DEBENHAM

NAME: Benjamin John Debenham
BORN: October 11, 1967, Chelmsford, Essex
APPOINTED TO FIRST-CLASS LIST: 2012
ODIS UMPIRED: 1
T20IS UMPIRED: 1

CRICKETING HIGHLIGHT OF 2020? Just getting out there to play! I also enjoyed the socially distanced changing facilities, which meant an upgrade from the pavilion's smallest room to unused executive suites
STRANGEST THING YOU'VE DONE DURING LOCKDOWN? Assisting in the home birth of some puppies
STRANGEST LOCATION WHERE UMPIRED? A coffee plantation in Arusha, north Tanzania
HIGHLIGHT OF YOUR PLAYING CAREER? Captaining MCC against Melbourne CC at the MCG

MICHAEL GOUGH

NAME: Michael Andrew Gough
BORN: December 18, 1978, Hartlepool
HEIGHT: 6ft 5in
NICKNAME: Goughy
APPOINTED TO FIRST-CLASS LIST: 2009
INTERNATIONAL PANEL: 2013-2019
ELITE PANEL: 2019-

TESTS UMPIRED: 26 (8 as TV)
ODIS UMPIRED: 98 (29 as TV)
T20IS UMPIRED: 35 (10 as TV)
COUNTY AS PLAYER: Durham
ROLE: Batsman; RHB OB
COUNTY DEBUT: 1998

Batting	Mat	Inns	NO	Runs	HS	Ave	SR	100	50	Ct	St
First-class	67	119	3	2952	123	25.44	-	2	15	57	0
List A	49	45	4	974	132	23.75	-	1	3	14	0
Bowling	**Mat**	**Balls**	**Runs**	**Wkts**	**BBI**	**BBM**	**Ave**	**Econ**	**SR**	**5w**	**10**
First-class	67	2486	1350	30	5/66	-	45.00	3.25	82.8	1	0
List A	49	1136	947	21	3/26	3/26	45.09	5.00	54.0	0	0

IAN GOULD

NAME: Ian James Gould
BORN: August 19, 1957, Taplow, Buckinghamshire
HEIGHT: 5ft 7in
NICKNAME: Gunner
APPOINTED TO FIRST-CLASS LIST: 2002
INTERNATIONAL PANEL: 2006-2009
ELITE PANEL: 2009-2019
TESTS UMPIRED: 99 (25 as TV)
ODIS UMPIRED: 189 (47 as TV)
T20IS UMPIRED: 60 (19 as TV)
COUNTIES AS PLAYER: Middlesex, Sussex
ROLE: Wicketkeeper; LHB
COUNTY DEBUT: 1975 (Middlesex), 1981 (Sussex)
ODI DEBUT: 1983

Batting	Mat	Inns	NO	Runs	HS	Ave	SR	100	50	Ct	St
ODIs	18	14	2	155	42	12.91	63.78	0	0	15	3
First-class	298	399	63	8756	128	26.05	-	4	47	536	67
List A	315	270	41	4377	88	19.11	-	0	20	242	37
Bowling	**Mat**	**Balls**	**Runs**	**Wkts**	**BBI**	**BBM**	**Ave**	**Econ**	**SR**	**5w**	**10**
ODIs	18	-	-	-	-	-	-	-	-	-	-
First-class	298	478	365	7	3/10	-	52.14	4.58	68.2	0	0
List A	315	20	16	1	1/0	1/0	16.00	4.80	20.0	0	0

PETER HARTLEY

NAME: Peter John Hartley
BORN: April 18, 1960, Keighley, Yorkshire
HEIGHT: 6ft
NICKNAME: Jack
APPOINTED TO FIRST-CLASS LIST: 2003
INTERNATIONAL PANEL: 2006-2009
TESTS UMPIRED: 10 (9 as TV)
ODIS UMPIRED: 21 (10 as TV)
T20IS UMPIRED: 16 (6 as TV)
COUNTIES AS PLAYER: Warwickshire, Yorkshire, Hampshire
ROLE: Bowler; RHB RFM
COUNTY DEBUT: 1982 (Warwickshire), 1985 (Yorkshire), 1998 (Hampshire)

Batting	Mat	Inns	NO	Runs	HS	Ave	SR	100	50	Ct	St
First-class	232	283	66	4321	127*	19.91	-	2	14	68	0
List A	269	170	62	1765	83	16.34	-	0	4	46	0
Bowling	**Mat**	**Balls**	**Runs**	**Wkts**	**BBI**	**BBM**	**Ave**	**Econ**	**SR**	**5w**	**10**
First-class	232	37108	20635	683	9/41	-	30.21	3.33	54.3	23	3
List A	269	12636	9069	356	5/20	5/20	25.47	4.30	35.4	5	0

RICHARD ILLINGWORTH

NAME: Richard Keith Illingworth
BORN: August 23, 1963, Greengates, Bradford
NICKNAME: Harry, Lucy
APPOINTED TO FIRST-CLASS LIST: 2006
INTERNATIONAL PANEL: 2009-2013
ELITE PANEL: 2013-
TESTS UMPIRED: 74 (21 as TV)
ODIS UMPIRED: 132 (57 as TV)
T20IS UMPIRED: 37 (8 as TV)
COUNTIES AS PLAYER: Worcestershire, Derbyshire
ROLE: Bowler; RHB SLA
COUNTY DEBUT: 1982 (Worcs), 2001 (Derbyshire)
TEST DEBUT: 1991
ODI DEBUT: 1991

Batting	Mat	Inns	NO	Runs	HS	Ave	SR	100	50	Ct	St
Tests	9	14	7	128	28	18.28	32.08	0	0	5	0
ODIs	25	11	5	68	14	11.33	57.14	0	0	8	0
First-class	376	435	122	7027	120*	22.45	-	4	21	161	0
List A	381	185	87	1458	53*	14.87	-	0	1	93	0
Bowling	**Mat**	**Balls**	**Runs**	**Wkts**	**BBI**	**BBM**	**Ave**	**Econ**	**SR**	**5w**	**10**
Tests	9	1485	615	19	4/96	6/150	32.36	2.48	78.1	0	0
ODIs	25	1501	1059	30	3/33	3/33	35.30	4.23	50.0	0	0
First-class	376	65868	26213	831	7/50	-	31.54	2.38	79.2	27	6
List A	381	16918	11157	412	5/24	5/24	27.08	3.95	41.0	2	0

RICHARD KETTLEBOROUGH

NAME: Richard Allan Kettleborough
BORN: March 15, 1973, Sheffield
HEIGHT: 5ft 10in
NICKNAME: Ketts
APPOINTED TO FIRST-CLASS LIST: 2006
INTERNATIONAL PANEL: 2008-2011
ELITE PANEL: 2011-
TESTS UMPIRED: 93 (25 as TV)
ODIS UMPIRED: 138 (44 as TV)
T20IS UMPIRED: 34 (10 as TV)
COUNTIES AS PLAYER: Yorkshire, Middlesex
ROLE: Batsman; LHB RM
COUNTY DEBUT: 1994 (Yorkshire), 1998 (Middlesex)

Batting	Mat	Inns	NO	Runs	HS	Ave	SR	100	50	Ct	St
First-class	33	56	6	1258	108	25.16	-	1	7	20	0
List A	21	16	4	290	58	24.16	-	0	1	6	0
Bowling	**Mat**	**Balls**	**Runs**	**Wkts**	**BBI**	**BBM**	**Ave**	**Econ**	**SR**	**5w**	**10**
First-class	33	378	243	3	2/26	-	81.00	3.85	126.0	0	0
List A	21	270	230	6	2/43	2/43	38.33	5.11	45.0	0	0

NIGEL LLONG

NAME: Nigel James Llong
BORN: February 11, 1969, Ashford, Kent
HEIGHT: 6ft
NICKNAME: Nidge
APPOINTED TO FIRST-CLASS LIST: 2002
INTERNATIONAL PANEL: 2002-2012
ELITE PANEL: 2012-

TESTS UMPIRED: 91 (29 as TV)
ODIS UMPIRED: 217 (75 as TV)
T20IS UMPIRED: 65 (14 as TV)
COUNTY AS PLAYER: Kent
ROLE: Allrounder; LHB OB
COUNTY DEBUT: 1990

Batting	Mat	Inns	NO	Runs	HS	Ave	SR	100	50	Ct	St
First-class	68	108	11	3024	130	31.17	-	6	16	59	0
List A	136	115	24	2302	123	25.29	-	2	8	41	0
Bowling	**Mat**	**Balls**	**Runs**	**Wkts**	**BBI**	**BBM**	**Ave**	**Econ**	**SR**	**5w**	**10**
First-class	68	2273	1259	35	5/21	-	35.97	3.32	64.9	2	0
List A	136	1317	1210	40	4/24	4/24	30.25	5.51	32.9	0	0

GRAHAM LLOYD

NAME: Graham David Lloyd
BORN: July 1, 1969, Accrington, Lancashire
APPOINTED TO FIRST-CLASS LIST: 2014
ODIS UMPIRED: 6 (2 as TV)
T20IS UMPIRED: 2
COUNTY AS PLAYER: Lancashire
ROLE: Batsman; RHB RM

COUNTY DEBUT: 1988
ODI DEBUT: 1996

Batting	Mat	Inns	NO	Runs	HS	Ave	SR	100	50	Ct	St
ODIs	6	5	1	39	22	9.75	48.75	0	0	2	0
First-class	203	323	28	11279	241	38.23	-	24	64	140	0
List A	295	258	48	6117	134	29.12	-	4	29	67	0
Bowling	**Mat**	**Balls**	**Runs**	**Wkts**	**BBI**	**BBM**	**Ave**	**Econ**	**SR**	**5w**	**10**
ODIs	6	-	-	-	-	-	-	-	-	-	-
First-class	203	339	440	2	1/4	-	220.00	7.78	169.5	0	0
List A	295	72	103	1	1/23	1/23	103.00	8.58	72.0	0	0

NEIL MALLENDER

NAME: Neil Alan Mallender
BORN: August 13, 1961, Kirk Sandall, Yorkshire
HEIGHT: 6ft
NICKNAME: Ghostie
APPOINTED TO FIRST-CLASS LIST: 1999
INTERNATIONAL PANEL: 2002-2004
TESTS UMPIRED: 11 (5 as TV)
ODIS UMPIRED: 36 (10 as TV)
T20IS UMPIRED: 3 (1 as TV)
COUNTIES AS PLAYER: Northamptonshire, Somerset
ROLE: Bowler; RHB RFM
COUNTY DEBUT: 1980 (Northamptonshire), 1987 (Somerset)
TEST DEBUT: 1992

Batting	Mat	Inns	NO	Runs	HS	Ave	SR	100	50	Ct	St
Tests	2	3	0	8	4	2.66	36.36	0	0	0	0
First-class	345	396	122	4709	100*	17.18	-	1	10	111	0
List A	325	163	75	1146	38*	13.02	-	0	0	60	0
Bowling	**Mat**	**Balls**	**Runs**	**Wkts**	**BBI**	**BBM**	**Ave**	**Econ**	**SR**	**5w**	**10**
Tests	2	449	215	10	5/50	8/122	21.50	2.87	44.9	1	0
First-class	345	53215	24654	937	7/27	-	26.31	2.77	56.7	36	5
List A	325	15488	9849	387	7/37	7/37	25.44	3.81	40.0	3	0

DAVID MILLNS

NAME: David James Millns
BORN: February 7, 1965, Clipstone, Nottinghamshire
HEIGHT: 6ft 3in
NICKNAME: Rocket Man
APPOINTED TO FIRST-CLASS LIST: 2009
INTERNATIONAL PANEL: 2020-
TESTS UMPIRED: 1
ODIS UMPIRED: 15 (1 as TV)
T20IS UMPIRED: 17 (5 as TV)
COUNTIES AS PLAYER: Nottinghamshire, Leicestershire
ROLE: Bowler; LHB RF
COUNTY DEBUT: 1988 (Nottinghamshire), 1990 (Leicestershire)

Batting	Mat	Inns	NO	Runs	HS	Ave	SR	100	50	Ct	St
First-class	171	203	63	3082	121	22.01	-	3	8	76	0
List A	91	49	26	338	39*	14.69	-	0	0	18	0
Bowling	**Mat**	**Balls**	**Runs**	**Wkts**	**BBI**	**BBM**	**Ave**	**Econ**	**SR**	**5w**	**10**
First-class	171	26571	15129	553	9/37	-	27.35	3.41	48.0	23	4
List A	91	3931	3144	83	4/26	4/26	37.87	4.79	47.3	0	0

STEVE O'SHAUGHNESSY

NAME: Steven Joseph O'Shaughnessy
BORN: September 9, 1961, Bury, Lancashire
APPOINTED TO FIRST-CLASS LIST: 2011
ODIS UMPIRED: 9 (1 as TV)
T20IS UMPIRED: 2 (1 as TV)
COUNTIES AS PLAYER: Lancashire, Worcestershire
ROLE: Allrounder; RHB RM
COUNTY DEBUT: 1980 (Lancashire), 1988 (Worcestershire)

Batting	Mat	Inns	NO	Runs	HS	Ave	SR	100	50	Ct	St
First-class	112	181	28	3720	159*	24.31	-	5	16	57	0
List A	176	151	23	2999	101*	23.42	-	1	15	44	0
Bowling	**Mat**	**Balls**	**Runs**	**Wkts**	**BBI**	**BBM**	**Ave**	**Econ**	**SR**	**5w**	**10**
First-class	112	7179	4108	114	4/66	-	36.03	3.43	62.9	0	0
List A	176	5389	4184	115	4/17	4/17	36.38	4.65	46.8	0	0

PAUL POLLARD

NAME: Paul Raymond Pollard
BORN: September 24, 1968, Nottingham
APPOINTED TO FIRST-CLASS LIST: 2018
T20IS UMPIRED: 1 (1 as TV)
COUNTIES AS PLAYER: Nottinghamshire, Worcestershire
ROLE: Batsman; LHB RM
COUNTY DEBUT: 1987 (Nottinghamshire), 2004 (Worcestershire)

Batting	Mat	Inns	NO	Runs	HS	Ave	SR	100	50	Ct	St
First-class	192	332	24	9685	180	31.44	-	15	48	158	0
List A	187	173	17	5233	132*	33.54	-	5	33	66	0
Bowling	**Mat**	**Balls**	**Runs**	**Wkts**	**BBI**	**BBM**	**Ave**	**Econ**	**SR**	**5w**	**10**
First-class	192	275	272	4	2/79	-	68.00	5.93	68.7	0	0
List A	187	18	9	0	-	-	-	3.00	-	0	0

TIM ROBINSON

NAME: Robert Timothy Robinson
BORN: November 21, 1958, Sutton-in-Ashfield, Nottinghamshire
NICKNAME: Robbo, Chop
APPOINTED TO FIRST-CLASS LIST: 2007
INTERNATIONAL PANEL: 2013-2019
TESTS UMPIRED: 1 (1 as TV)
ODIS UMPIRED: 27 (1 as TV)
T20IS UMPIRED: 29 (12 as TV)
COUNTY AS PLAYER: Nottinghamshire
ROLE: Batsman; RHB RM
COUNTY DEBUT: 1978
TEST DEBUT: 1984
ODI DEBUT: 1984

Batting	Mat	Inns	NO	Runs	HS	Ave	SR	100	50	Ct	St
Tests	29	49	5	1601	175	36.38	41.62	4	6	8	0
ODIs	26	26	0	597	83	22.96	58.18	0	3	6	0
First-class	425	739	85	27571	220*	42.15	-	63	141	257	0
List A	397	386	40	11879	139	34.33	-	9	75	120	0
Bowling	**Mat**	**Balls**	**Runs**	**Wkts**	**BBI**	**BBM**	**Ave**	**Econ**	**SR**	**5w**	**10**
Tests	29	6	0	0	-	-	-	0.00	-	0	0
ODIs	26	-	-	-	-	-	-	-	-	-	-
First-class	425	259	289	4	1/22	-	72.25	6.69	64.7	0	0
List A	397	-	-	-	-	-	-	-	-	-	-

MARTIN SAGGERS

NAME: Martin John Saggers
BORN: May 23, 1972, King's Lynn, Norfolk
HEIGHT: 6ft 2in
NICKNAME: Saggs
APPOINTED TO FIRST-CLASS LIST: 2012
INTERNATIONAL PANEL: 2020-
TESTS UMPIRED: 2 (1 as TV)
ODIS UMPIRED: 15 (4 as TV)
T20IS UMPIRED: 11 (2 as TV)
COUNTIES AS PLAYER: Durham, Kent
ROLE: Bowler; RHB RFM
COUNTY DEBUT: 1996 (Durham), 1999 (Kent)
TEST DEBUT: 2003

Batting	Mat	Inns	NO	Runs	HS	Ave	SR	100	50	Ct	St
Tests	3	3	0	1	1	0.33	3.33	0	0	1	0
First-class	119	147	43	1165	64	11.20	-	0	2	27	0
List A	124	68	34	313	34*	9.20	-	0	0	23	0
T20s	10	1	0	5	5	5.00	62.50	0	0	2	0
Bowling	**Mat**	**Balls**	**Runs**	**Wkts**	**BBI**	**BBM**	**Ave**	**Econ**	**SR**	**5w**	**10**
Tests	3	493	247	7	2/29	3/62	35.28	3.00	70.4	0	0
First-class	119	20676	10513	415	7/79	-	25.33	3.05	49.8	18	0
List A	124	5622	4229	166	5/22	5/22	25.47	4.51	33.8	2	0
T20s	10	186	256	6	2/14	2/14	42.66	8.25	31.0	0	0

BILLY TAYLOR

NAME: Billy Victor Taylor
BORN: January 11, 1977, Southampton, Hampshire
APPOINTED TO FIRST-CLASS LIST: 2016
TESTS UMPIRED: 1
ODIS UMPIRED: 1
COUNTIES AS PLAYER: Sussex, Hampshire
ROLE: Bowler; LHB RMF
COUNTY DEBUT: 1999 (Sussex), 2004 (Hampshire)

Batting	Mat	Inns	NO	Runs	HS	Ave	SR	100	50	Ct	St
First-class	54	68	26	431	40	10.26	-	0	0	6	0
List A	142	58	28	191	21*	6.36	-	0	0	26	0
T20s	37	9	8	22	12*	22.00	84.61	0	0	3	0
Bowling	**Mat**	**Balls**	**Runs**	**Wkts**	**BBI**	**BBM**	**Ave**	**Econ**	**SR**	**5w**	**10**
First-class	54	8412	4535	136	6/32	-	33.34	3.23	61.8	4	0
List A	142	6311	4699	182	5/28	5/28	25.81	4.46	34.6	1	0
T20s	37	713	883	30	2/9	2/9	29.43	7.43	23.7	0	0

RUSSELL WARREN

NAME: Russell John Warren
BORN: September 10, 1971, Northampton
HEIGHT: 6ft 2in
NICKNAME: Rabbit
APPOINTED TO FIRST-CLASS LIST: 2014
ODIS UMPIRED: 1
T20IS UMPIRED: 3
COUNTIES AS PLAYER: Northamptonshire, Nottinghamshire
ROLE: Wicketkeeper/batsman; RHB
COUNTY DEBUT: 1992 (Northamptonshire), 2003 (Nottinghamshire)

Batting	Mat	Inns	NO	Runs	HS	Ave	SR	100	50	Ct	St
First-class	146	238	26	7776	201*	36.67	-	15	41	128	5
List A	177	162	25	3363	100*	24.54	-	1	15	135	11
T20s	2	1	0	26	26	26.00	86.66	0	0	0	0
Bowling	**Mat**	**Balls**	**Runs**	**Wkts**	**BBI**	**BBM**	**Ave**	**Econ**	**SR**	**5w**	**10**
First-class	146	6	0	0	-	-	-	0.00	-	0	0
List A	177	-	-	-	-	-	-	-	-	-	-
T20s	2	-	-	-	-	-	-	-	-	-	-

ALEX WHARF

NAME: Alexander George Wharf
BORN: June 4, 1975, Bradford, Yorkshire
HEIGHT: 6ft 4in
NICKNAME: Gangster
APPOINTED TO FIRST-CLASS LIST: 2014
INTERNATIONAL PANEL: 2018-
TESTS UMPIRED: 2
ODIS UMPIRED: 17 (5 as TV)
T20IS UMPIRED: 43 (8 as TV)
COUNTIES AS PLAYER: Yorkshire, Nottinghamshire, Glamorgan
ROLE: Allrounder; RHB RMF
COUNTY DEBUT: 1994 (Yorkshire), 1998 (Nottinghamshire), 2000 (Glamorgan)
ODI DEBUT: 2004

Batting	Mat	Inns	NO	Runs	HS	Ave	SR	100	50	Ct	St
ODIs	13	5	3	19	9	9.50	67.85	0	0	1	0
First-class	121	184	29	3570	128*	23.03	-	6	14	63	0
List A	155	109	22	1411	72	16.21	-	0	1	42	0
T20s	34	20	7	157	19	12.07	120.76	0	0	5	0
Bowling	**Mat**	**Balls**	**Runs**	**Wkts**	**BBI**	**BBM**	**Ave**	**Econ**	**SR**	**5w**	**10**
ODIs	13	584	428	18	4/24	4/24	23.77	4.39	32.4	0	0
First-class	121	16825	10941	293	6/59	-	37.34	3.90	57.4	5	1
List A	155	6497	5552	192	6/5	6/5	28.91	5.12	33.8	1	0
T20s	34	644	1028	39	4/39	4/39	26.35	9.57	16.5	0	0

Roll of
Honour

BOB WILLIS TROPHY

Central Group

Team	Mat	Won	Lost	Tied	Draw	Aban	Pts
Somerset	5	4	0	0	1	0	97
Worcestershire	5	2	1	0	2	0	74
Warwickshire	5	0	1	0	4	0	53
Northamptonshire	5	1	2	0	2	0	49
Gloucestershire	5	1	2	0	2	0	45
Glamorgan	5	0	2	0	3	0	43

North Group

Team	Mat	Won	Lost	Tied	Draw	Aban	Pts
Yorkshire	5	3	0	0	2	0	87
Derbyshire	5	2	1	0	2	0	74
Lancashire	5	2	1	0	2	0	66
Nottinghamshire	5	0	2	0	3	0	59
Leicestershire	5	1	2	0	2	0	49
Durham	5	0	2	0	3	0	41

South Group

Team	Mat	Won	Lost	Tied	Draw	Aban	Pts
Essex	5	4	0	0	1	0	90
Kent	5	3	1	0	1	0	82
Middlesex	5	2	2	0	1	0	62
Hampshire	5	2	2	0	1	0	57
Surrey	5	1	4	0	0	0	36
Sussex	5	1	4	0	0	0	12

FINAL

Somerset v Essex at Lord's
September 23-27 – Match drawn (Essex won on 1st innings)
Somerset 301 & 272-7d; Essex 337-8 (120 ov) & 179-6

Essex captain Tom Westley
photographed by Alex Davidson

Central Group							
Team	Mat	Won	Lost	Tied	N/R	Pts	Net RR
Gloucestershire	10	7	2	0	1	15	1.017
Northamptonshire	10	5	4	0	1	11	0.053
Birmingham Bears	10	5	4	0	1	11	-0.634
Somerset	10	4	5	0	1	9	0.653
Glamorgan	10	4	5	0	1	9	-0.304
Worcestershire	10	2	7	0	1	5	-0.789

North Group							
Team	Mat	Won	Lost	Tied	N/R	Pts	Net RR
Nottinghamshire	10	7	1	0	2	16	1.315
Lancashire	10	5	3	0	2	12	-0.25
Leicestershire	10	4	3	0	3	11	-0.18
Durham	10	4	5	0	1	9	0.421
Yorkshire	10	3	5	0	2	8	0.297
Derbyshire	10	1	7	0	2	4	-1.583

South Group							
Surrey	10	7	1	1	1	16	0.65
Sussex	10	6	3	0	1	13	0.377
Kent	10	5	3	1	1	12	0.108
Middlesex	10	3	5	1	1	8	-0.296
Essex	10	2	6	1	1	6	-0.003
Hampshire	10	2	7	0	1	5	-0.803

QUARTER-FINALS

Nottinghamshire v Leicestershire at Trent Bridge
October 1 – Match tied (Nottinghamshire won on higher Powerplay score)
Leicestershire 139-7 (20/20 ov); Nottinghamshire 139-7 (20/20 ov)

Surrey v Kent at The Oval
October 1 – Surrey won by 56 runs
Surrey 169-2 (20/20 ov); Kent 113-7 (20/20 ov)

Gloucestershire v Northamptonshire at Bristol
October 1 – Gloucestershire won by 7 wickets
Northamptonshire 113 (19.4/20 ov); Gloucestershire 114-3 (11.5/20 ov)

Sussex v Lancashire at Hove
October 1 – Lancashire won by 45 runs
Lancashire 140-8 (20/20 ov); Sussex 95 (17.2/20 ov)

SEMI-FINALS

Gloucestershire v Surrey at Edgbaston
October 3 – Surrey won by 6 wickets
Gloucester 73-7 (11/11 ov); Surrey 74-4 (9.4/11 ov)

Lancashire v Nottinghamshire at Edgbaston
October 4 – Nottinghamshire won by 5 wickets
Lancashire 94-4 (11/11 ov); Nottinghamshire 95-5 (8.2/11 ov)

FINAL

Surrey v Nottinghamshire at Edgbaston
October 4 – Nottinghamshire won by 6 wickets
Surrey 127-7 (16/16 ov); Nottinghamshire 129-4 (13.2/16 ov)

Ben Duckett of Notts Outlaws
photographed by Alex Davidson

RACHAEL HEYHOE FLINT TROPHY

North Group

Team	Mat	Won	Lost	Tied	N/R	Pts	Net RR
Northern Diamonds	6	5	1	0	0	23	1
Central Sparks	6	3	3	0	0	13	-0.285
Thunder	6	2	4	0	0	9	-0.515
Lightning	6	2	4	0	0	8	-0.113

South Group

Team	Mat	Won	Lost	Tied	N/R	Pts	Net RR
Southern Vipers	6	6	0	0	0	27	1.017
Western Storm	6	4	2	0	0	18	0.51
South East Stars	6	2	4	0	0	10	-0.197
Sunrisers	6	0	6	0	0	0	-1.365

FINAL

Southern Vipers v Northern Diamonds at Edgbaston
September 27 – Southern Vipers won by 38 runs
Southern Vipers 231 (49.5/50 ov); Northern Diamonds 193 (42.2/50 ov)

Ella McCaughan of Southern Vipers
photographed by Gareth Copley

Georgia Adams, who was named Player of the Tournament
photographed by Gareth Copley

BOB WILLIS TROPHY BATTING AVERAGES *Minimum of 250 runs*

Name	Mat	Inns	NO	Runs	HS	Ave	BF	SR	100	50	0	4s	6s
DJ Malan	3	5	0	332	219	66.40	421	78.85	1	1	0	45	5
JM Cox	4	6	1	324	238*	64.80	611	53.02	1	0	0	39	4
BT Slater	5	7	0	425	172	60.71	889	47.80	2	1	3	49	3
AJA Wheater	6	9	4	291	83*	58.20	614	47.39	0	2	0	34	0
AN Cook	6	11	1	563	172	56.30	1021	55.14	2	1	0	77	0
BM Duckett	5	8	1	394	150	56.28	572	68.88	2	0	0	56	0
JD Libby	5	9	0	498	184	55.33	1041	47.83	1	3	1	56	2
CN Ackermann	5	9	2	379	94	54.14	622	60.93	0	4	0	52	1
WMH Rhodes	5	9	1	423	207	52.87	816	51.83	1	0	0	51	0
BL D'Oliveira	5	8	1	367	174	52.42	538	68.21	1	1	0	48	2
TA Lammonby	6	11	2	459	116	51.00	888	51.68	3	0	2	52	5
AZ Lees	5	8	0	386	106	48.25	1010	38.21	1	3	1	39	0
AL Davies	5	8	1	337	86	48.14	548	61.49	0	4	1	54	1
TC Fell	5	9	2	336	110*	48.00	742	45.28	1	1	0	41	0
LM Reece	4	7	1	277	122	46.16	518	53.47	1	2	1	34	3
CO Thurston	5	8	0	357	115	44.62	565	63.18	1	2	0	44	3
JA Tattersall	5	7	1	265	71	44.16	733	36.15	0	3	0	32	0
JJ Weatherley	5	7	1	263	98	43.83	645	40.77	0	2	0	38	0
NRT Gubbins	4	8	0	350	192	43.75	600	58.33	1	1	1	40	1
HC Brook	5	7	1	258	66*	43.00	395	65.31	0	3	1	32	7
DKH Mitchell	5	9	0	384	110	42.66	824	46.60	1	2	1	50	0
JL du Plooy	5	7	0	296	130	42.28	524	56.48	1	1	1	40	3
GJ Harte	5	8	2	250	72	41.66	613	40.78	0	1	0	30	0
JA Haynes	5	9	2	285	51	40.71	534	53.37	0	2	0	37	0
SM Davies	6	10	2	320	123*	40.00	515	62.13	1	1	1	44	0
JA Leaning	5	8	1	279	220*	39.85	535	52.14	1	0	2	36	0
H Hameed	5	7	0	272	87	38.85	666	40.84	0	3	0	43	0
TB Abell	6	11	1	386	119	38.60	663	58.22	2	1	1	58	2
PI Walter	5	9	2	266	46	38.00	598	44.48	0	0	1	38	0
JM Clarke	5	8	1	263	133	37.57	448	58.70	1	1	0	35	0
J Overton	5	7	0	261	120	37.28	241	108.29	1	2	1	34	11
JJ Bohannon	5	7	0	257	94	36.71	632	40.66	0	2	0	23	1
PD Salt	4	8	0	290	80	36.25	447	64.87	0	3	1	38	3
JA Simpson	5	9	2	250	53	35.71	536	46.64	0	1	0	31	1
CB Cooke	5	10	1	294	82	32.66	610	48.19	0	3	2	37	0
WT Root	5	10	1	286	118	31.77	707	40.45	1	1	0	39	1
DG Bedingham	5	8	0	253	96	31.62	453	55.84	0	2	0	31	2
JL Smith	5	10	1	274	80	30.44	598	45.81	0	1	2	46	4
MDE Holden	5	10	0	299	72	29.90	617	48.46	0	1	1	42	2
BC Brown	5	10	0	270	98	27.00	558	48.38	0	2	1	35	0
HZ Finch	5	10	0	259	69	25.90	522	49.61	0	2	0	47	0
DMW Rawlins	5	10	0	252	65	25.20	305	82.62	0	1	1	33	8
EJ Byrom	6	11	0	271	117	24.63	563	48.13	1	0	1	44	0

Yorkshire's Dawid Malan
photographed by Shaun Botterill

BOB WILLIS TROPHY BOWLING AVERAGES *Minimum of 12 wickets*

Player	Mat	Overs	Mdns	Runs	Wkts	BBI	BBM	Ave	Econ	SR	5	10
BO Coad	2	69	28	87	12	5/18	8/41	7.25	1.26	34.5	1	0
OE Robinson	2	73.1	22	175	14	5/29	8/65	12.50	2.39	31.3	1	0
TJ Murtagh	4	145.5	48	318	25	5/34	7/74	12.72	2.18	35.0	2	0
C Overton	6	196.2	66	403	30	5/26	9/51	13.43	2.05	39.2	2	0
MS Crane	4	60.4	8	190	14	3/19	6/69	13.57	3.13	26.0	0	0
JH Davey	6	150.2	55	331	24	4/25	7/46	13.79	2.20	37.5	0	0
DA Payne	4	95	29	199	14	5/31	8/61	14.21	2.09	40.7	1	0
R Clarke	3	88	23	190	13	5/20	6/75	14.61	2.15	40.6	1	0
DI Stevens	5	209	64	452	29	5/37	9/72	15.58	2.16	43.2	3	0
SR Harmer	6	257.1	81	603	38	8/64	14/131	15.86	2.34	40.6	3	1
HW Podmore	3	117.3	30	307	19	5/43	7/92	16.15	2.61	37.1	1	0
JA Thompson	5	104	25	246	15	5/31	5/51	16.40	2.36	41.6	1	0
DJ Lamb	3	68.1	13	203	12	4/55	7/72	16.91	2.97	34.0	0	0
J Overton	5	89.1	27	256	15	5/48	7/64	17.06	2.87	35.6	1	0
IG Holland	5	129	41	297	17	6/60	7/77	17.47	2.30	45.5	1	0
L Gregory	3	102.3	22	318	18	6/72	8/124	17.66	3.10	34.1	1	0
MK Andersson	5	75.5	15	250	14	4/38	7/98	17.85	3.29	32.5	0	0
SJ Cook	5	140	39	318	17	5/76	7/55	18.70	2.27	49.4	1	0
JA Brooks	5	89.5	23	254	13	4/40	5/56	19.53	2.82	41.4	0	0
CJ White	4	88	20	260	13	4/35	8/83	20.00	2.95	40.6	0	0
D Moriarty	2	98.2	15	342	17	6/70	11/224	20.11	3.47	34.7	3	1
JA Porter	6	185.5	48	553	27	5/60	8/88	20.48	2.97	41.2	1	0
ML Cummins	3	92.1	28	269	13	5/62	5/74	20.69	2.91	42.5	1	0
OJ Hannon-Dalby	5	196.3	53	523	25	6/33	12/110	20.92	2.66	47.1	2	1
EG Barnard	5	148.5	40	390	18	4/25	7/78	21.66	2.62	49.6	0	0
TE Bailey	4	111.4	44	282	13	3/11	4/25	21.69	2.52	51.5	0	0
C Rushworth	4	104	14	358	16	7/108	7/137	22.37	3.44	39.0	1	0
CAJ Morris	3	99.3	21	315	14	5/80	6/104	22.50	3.16	42.6	1	0
JJ Carson	4	108.1	17	340	15	5/93	6/139	22.66	3.14	43.2	1	0
RF Higgins	5	148.4	41	391	17	7/42	11/96	23.00	2.63	52.4	1	1
GHS Garton	4	70.3	13	282	12	5/26	9/76	23.50	4.00	35.2	1	0
ME Milnes	4	119.3	29	355	15	4/46	7/112	23.66	2.97	47.8	0	0
J Leach	5	169.3	44	490	19	4/67	6/79	25.78	2.89	53.5	0	0
A Virdi	5	179	26	570	22	6/101	7/120	25.90	3.18	48.8	1	0
JC Tongue	4	117.1	26	363	14	3/38	6/80	25.92	3.09	50.2	0	0
LM Reece	4	132.3	40	340	13	3/51	5/103	26.15	2.56	61.1	0	0
MJJ Critchley	5	128.4	14	457	17	6/73	6/88	26.88	3.55	45.4	1	0
PD Trego	5	134.3	44	342	12	3/33	5/109	28.50	2.54	67.2	0	0
ZJ Chappell	4	131.2	30	431	15	4/59	6/123	28.73	3.28	52.5	0	0
SR Patel	5	156.2	36	388	13	4/80	4/114	29.84	2.48	72.1	0	0
T van der Gugten	4	119	31	362	12	3/45	5/115	30.16	3.04	59.5	0	0
DA Douthwaite	5	121.1	16	473	14	3/42	5/103	33.78	3.90	51.9	0	0

Yorkshire's Ben Coad
photographed by Ian Horrocks

BOB WILLIS TROPHY WICKETKEEPING *Minimum of 6 dismissals*

Name	Mat	Inns	Dis	Ct	St	Max Dis Inns	Dis/Inn
OB Cox	5	10	25	25	0	5 (5ct 0st)	2.50
OG Robinson	5	10	22	22	0	6 (6ct 0st)	2.20
JA Simpson	5	10	20	19	1	4 (4ct 0st)	2.00
AJA Wheater	6	10	20	17	3	5 (5ct 0st)	2.00
SM Davies	6	12	19	19	0	4 (4ct 0st)	1.58
CB Cooke	5	7	18	16	2	5 (4ct 1st)	2.57
MGK Burgess	5	8	16	15	1	3 (3ct 0st)	2.00
TJ Moores	5	10	15	14	1	3 (3ct 0st)	1.50
HR Hosein	4	7	14	13	1	4 (3ct 1st)	2.00
LD McManus	5	9	13	11	2	3 (3ct 0st)	1.44
GH Roderick	4	8	12	12	0	4 (4ct 0st)	1.50
HJ Swindells	5	8	11	11	0	3 (3ct 0st)	1.38
BC Brown	5	9	11	10	1	2 (2ct 0st)	1.22
JA Tattersall	5	5	9	9	0	3 (3ct 0st)	1.80
AM Rossington	3	5	8	8	0	4 (4ct 0st)	1.60
R Vasconcelos	5	2	7	6	1	4 (4ct 0st)	3.50
JL Smith	5	5	7	7	0	2 (2ct 0st)	1.40
AL Davies	5	6	7	7	0	3 (3ct 0st)	1.17
TN Cullen	3	2	6	6	0	4 (4ct 0st)	3.00

Worcestershire's Ben Cox
photographed by Alex Davidson

BOB WILLIS TROPHY FIELDING *Minimum of 6 catches*

Name	Mat	Inns	Ct	Max	Ct/Inn
JC Hildreth	4	8	10	2	1.25
WL Madsen	5	8	10	3	1.25
NJ Selman	5	9	10	3	1.11
AN Cook	6	10	10	4	1.00
SR Harmer	6	10	10	3	1.00
SJ Mullaney	5	10	10	4	1.00
JA Leaning	5	10	9	2	0.90
J Overton	5	10	9	3	0.90
KK Jennings	5	8	8	3	1.00
H Hameed	5	10	8	2	0.80
SD Robson	5	10	8	2	0.80
R Vasconcelos	5	6	7	2	1.17
GT Hankins	5	8	7	2	0.88
SS Eskinazi	5	10	7	2	0.70
DKH Mitchell	5	10	7	2	0.70
C Overton	6	12	7	3	0.58
SJ Croft	4	6	6	3	1.00
PD Salt	4	7	6	2	0.86
CN Ackermann	5	8	6	2	0.75

Somerset's James Hildreth
photographed by Alex Davidson

MEN'S PCA MVP TOP 50

#	Name	County	Batting	Bowling	Field	Capt.	Wins	Pld	Pts	Avg.
1	Simon Harmer	Essex	27.65	212.55	20	2	6	16	268.2	16.76
2	Craig Overton	Somerset	44.55	175.78	11	0	7	11	238.33	21.67
3	Will Jacks	Surrey	126.7	76.3	13	0	10	18	226	12.56
4	Ryan Higgins	Gloucestershire	69.14	124.24	5	0	9	16	207.38	12.96
5	Colin Ackermann	Leicestershire	128.4	54.64	12	5	5	14	205.04	14.65
6	Alex Davies	Lancashire	136.45	0	47	0	8	16	191.45	11.97
7	Josh Davey	Somerset	17.1	159.11	4	0	6	11	186.21	16.93
8	Daniel Moriarty	Surrey	0.13	168.96	2	0	10	15	181.09	12.07
9	Ben Duckett	Nottinghamshire	161.99	-0.2	10	0	9	16	180.79	11.3
10	Chris Cooke	Glamorgan	120.6	0	52	4	4	14	180.6	12.9
11	Lewis Gregory	Somerset	40.68	120.78	10	3	4	10	178.46	17.85
12	Jamie Overton	Surrey	75.67	66.18	20	0	13	16	174.85	10.93
13	Ian Holland	Hampshire	55.12	107.9	5	0	4	15	172.02	11.47
14	Jordan Thompson	Yorkshire	57.09	98.6	7	0	6	13	168.69	12.98
15	Darren Stevens	Kent	10.7	150.16	3	0	3	5	166.86	33.37
16	Will Rhodes	Warwickshire	114.52	39.09	3	5	5	14	166.61	11.9
17	Alex Lees	Durham	149.64	3.1	8	0	4	15	164.74	10.98
18	Tom Abell	Somerset	138.28	0.14	12	5	8	15	163.42	10.89
19	Jake Libby	Worcestershire	150.95	4.49	3	0	4	14	162.44	11.6
20	George Garton	Sussex	38.43	107.89	9	0	7	15	162.32	10.82
21	Matthew Critchley	Derbyshire	65.8	87.11	6	0	3	14	161.91	11.57
22	Adam Lyth	Yorkshire	110.17	33.24	9	2	6	13	160.41	12.34
23	Samit Patel	Nottinghamshire	45.26	101.79	4	0	9	16	160.05	10
24	Tom Lammonby	Somerset	141.73	7.57	4	0	6	12	159.3	13.28
25	Tim Murtagh	Middlesex	4.21	148.66	2	0	4	9	158.87	17.65
26	Tim Bresnan	Warwickshire	43.7	98.76	10	0	5	13	157.46	12.11
27	Joe Clarke	Nottinghamshire	145.68	0	2	0	9	16	156.68	9.79
28	Delray Rawlins	Sussex	94.12	50.81	4	0	7	16	155.93	9.75
29	Daniel Bell-Drummond	Kent	131.29	-0.85	11	6	8	16	155.44	9.71
30	Jake Ball	Nottinghamshire	10.44	124.76	8	0	9	13	152.2	11.71
31	Ed Barnard	Worcestershire	19.65	115.34	11	2	4	14	151.99	10.86
32	Laurie Evans	Surrey	139.05	0	3	0	8	14	150.05	10.72
33	Timm van der Gugten	Glamorgan	25.77	113.05	6	0	4	12	148.82	12.4
34	Chris Dent	Gloucestershire	127.68	0	11	1	9	15	148.68	9.91
35	Luis Reece	Derbyshire	74.79	62.91	6	0	3	13	146.7	11.28
36	Stevie Eskinazi	Middlesex	123.62	0	13	2	5	15	143.62	9.57
37	David Payne	Gloucestershire	3.54	127.03	4	0	8	15	142.57	9.5
38	John Simpson	Middlesex	100.9	0	35	0	5	15	140.9	9.39
39	Alastair Cook	Essex	125.09	0	10	0	4	6	139.09	23.18
40	Brett D'Oliveira	Worcestershire	92.1	37.41	5	0	4	13	138.51	10.65
41	Steven Mullaney	Nottinghamshire	44.98	68.38	16	0	9	16	138.36	8.65
42	Jamie Porter	Essex	4.21	126.88	3	0	4	6	138.09	23.02
43	Graeme van Buuren	Gloucestershire	62.05	61.84	5	0	9	16	137.89	8.62
44	Philip Salt	Sussex	123.69	0	8	0	5	12	136.69	11.39
45	Steven Croft	Lancashire	98.58	21.83	10	0	6	14	136.41	9.74
46	Zak Crawley	Kent	125.35	0	5	0	6	12	136.35	11.36
47	Tom Bailey	Lancashire	6.31	122.38	2	0	5	10	135.69	13.57
48	Ben Foakes	Surrey	90.09	0	35	0	9	14	134.09	9.58
49	Max Holden	Middlesex	120.89	0	7	0	5	14	132.89	9.49
50	Paul Walter	Essex	83.58	30.33	9	0	5	15	127.91	8.53

WOMEN'S PCA MVP TOP 50

#	Name	County	Batting	Bowling	Field	Capt.	Wins	Pld	Pts	Avg.
1	Georgia Adams	Southern Vipers	76.42	14.78	5	7	7	7	110.2	15.74
2	Kathryn Bryce	Lightning	21.63	57.7	5	2	2	6	88.33	14.72
3	Georgia Hennessy	Western Storm	34.39	38.11	4	0	4	6	80.5	13.42
4	Charlotte Taylor	Southern Vipers	2.87	64.31	0	0	5	5	72.18	14.44
5	Sarah Bryce	Lightning	62.73	0	6	0	2	6	70.73	11.79
6	Charlie Dean	Southern Vipers	25.75	33.64	4	0	7	7	70.39	10.06
7	Sophie Luff	Western Storm	53.13	2.33	5	4	4	6	68.46	11.41
8	Fi Morris	Western Storm	16.43	43.56	2	0	4	6	65.99	11
9	Evelyn Jones	Central Sparks	55.43	-1.85	3	3	3	6	62.58	10.43
10	Jo Gardner	Sunrisers	29.12	30.68	2	0	0	6	61.8	10.3
11	Paige Scholfield	Southern Vipers	12.61	27.06	14	0	7	7	60.67	8.67
12	Hollie Armitage	Northern Diamonds	27.8	21.83	2	3	5	7	59.63	8.52
13	Beth Langston	Northern Diamonds	13.6	38.97	1	0	5	7	58.57	8.37
14	Tara Norris	Southern Vipers	3.86	43.55	2	0	7	7	56.41	8.06
15	Jenny Gunn	Northern Diamonds	22.11	28.04	0	0	5	7	55.15	7.88
16	Tash Farrant	South East Stars	12.72	33.9	3	2	2	6	53.62	8.94
17	Alex Hartley	Thunder	3.61	42.98	3	2	2	6	53.59	8.93
18	Natalie Brown	Thunder	30.26	17.2	4	0	2	6	53.46	8.91
19	Katie Levick	Northern Diamonds	2.38	44.04	1	0	5	7	52.42	7.49
20	Maia Bouchier	Southern Vipers	26	3.31	10	0	7	7	46.31	6.62
21	Clare Boycott	Central Sparks	8.01	30.68	3	0	2	5	43.69	8.74
22	Hannah Jones	South East Stars	12.07	25.19	3	0	2	6	42.26	7.04
23	Alex MacDonald	Northern Diamonds	17.26	14.94	5	0	5	7	42.2	6.03
24	Carla Rudd	Southern Vipers	11.68	0	23	0	7	7	41.68	5.95
25	Ellie Threlkeld	Thunder	17.79	0	21	0	2	6	40.79	6.8
26	Natasha Wraith	Western Storm	15.51	0	21	0	4	6	40.51	6.75
27	Gwenan Davies	Central Sparks	25.62	0	11	0	3	6	39.62	6.6
28	Abi Freeborn	Lightning	25.46	0	12	0	2	5	39.46	7.89
29	Marie Kelly	Central Sparks	34.25	0	2	0	3	6	39.25	6.54
30	Lucy Higham	Lightning	6.46	26.4	3	0	2	6	37.86	6.31
31	Sterre Kalis	Northern Diamonds	30.38	0	2	0	5	7	37.38	5.34
32	Bethan Ellis	Lightning	17.19	14.33	3	0	2	6	36.52	6.09
33	Ella McCaughan	Southern Vipers	24.32	0	4	0	7	7	35.32	5.05
34	Alex Griffiths	Western Storm	19.22	9.92	2	0	4	6	35.14	5.86
35	Anisha Patel	Central Sparks	0.6	31.44	1	0	2	5	35.04	7.01
36	Heather Knight	Western Storm	24.05	8.64	1	0	1	2	34.69	17.34
37	Alice Capsey	South East Stars	21.57	5.86	5	0	2	6	34.43	5.74
38	Lauren Bell	Southern Vipers	0.86	27.31	1	0	4	4	33.17	8.29
39	Katie Wolfe	Sunrisers	2	30.06	1	0	0	6	33.06	5.51
40	Grace Scrivens	Sunrisers	20.15	11.69	1	0	0	6	32.84	5.47
41	Natalie Sciver	Northern Diamonds	20.68	8.38	0	0	2	2	31.06	15.53
42	Teresa Graves	Lightning	16.08	10.21	2	0	2	6	30.29	5.05
43	Katherine Brunt	Northern Diamonds	0.72	24.41	1	0	2	2	28.13	14.06
44	Sophie Ecclestone	Thunder	11.35	14.5	1	0	1	2	27.85	13.93
45	Sophia Dunkley	South East Stars	13.86	11.19	1	0	1	2	27.05	13.52
46	Alice MacLeod	Sunrisers	10.12	15.39	1	0	0	6	26.51	4.42
47	Linsey Smith	Northern Diamonds	4.38	17.68	1	0	3	4	26.06	6.52
48	Amara Carr	Sunrisers	17.06	0	9	0	0	6	26.06	4.34
49	Alicia Presland	Lightning	1.51	22.21	0	0	2	4	25.72	6.43
50	Sonali Patel	Sunrisers	3.6	20.9	1	0	0	6	25.5	4.25

NOTES